Contending Theories of International Relations

Contending Theories of International Relations

A Comprehensive Survey

THIRD EDITION

James E. Dougherty

St. Joseph's University

Robert L. Pfaltzgraff, Jr.

The Fletcher School of Law and Diplomacy,
Tufts University

1817

HARPER & ROW, PUBLISHERS, New York
Grand Rapids, Philadelphia, St. Louis, San Francisco,
London, Singapore, Sydney, Tokyo

ACKNOWLEDGMENTS

Page 13, note 42: Frederick S. Dunn, *World Politics*, I (October 1948), p. 142. Copyright © 1948 by Princeton University Press. Used by permission.

Page 181, note 79: Morton A. Kaplan, *World Politics*, XX (October 1967), p. 8. Copyright © 1967 by Princeton University Press. Used by permission.

Page 244, note 72: P. T. Bauer, *Journal of Contemporary History*, vol. 4 (1969), p. 4. Reprinted by permission.

Page 250, note 87: James Caporaso, *International Organization*, 32 (Winter 1978). Copyright © 1978 by The MIT Press. Reprinted by permission.

Page 274, note 5: Werner Levi, *Journal of Conflict Resolution*, IV (December 1960), pp. 415. Copyright © 1960 by Sage Publications. Reprinted by permission of Sage Publications, Inc.

Page 291, note 90: Arthur Gladstone, *Journal of Conflict Resolution*, III (June 1959), p. 132. Copyright © 1959 by Sage Publications. Reprinted by permission of Sage Publications, Inc.

Page 323, note 48: James C. Davies, *American Sociological Review*, XXVII (February 1962), p. 7.

Page 326, note 59: Ivo K. Feierabend and Rosalind L. Feierabend, *Journal of Conflict Resolution*, X (September 1966), p. 257. Copyright © 1966 by Sage Publications. Reprinted by permission of Sage Publications, Inc.

Page 336, note 95: Karl W. Deutsch, *Journal of Conflict Resolution*, XIV (December 1970), pp. 474–475. Copyright © 1970 by Sage Publications. Reprinted by permission of Sage Publications, Inc.

Page 358, note 194; page 359, note 195: William T. R. Fox, *The Annals (How Wars End)*, 392 (November 1970), pp. 2–3, 8.

Page 363, note 206: Oscar J. Lissitzyn, *International Conciliation*, 548 (March 1963), p. 68. Used by permission.

Page 402, note 58; pages 402–403, note 62; page 403, note 63; page 404, note 65: Robert Jervis, *World Politics*, XXXI (April 1979), pp. 296–300. Copyright © 1979 by Princeton University Press. Used by permission.

Page 407, note 100: Richard K. Betts, *World Politics*, XXXVII (January 1985), pp. 177–179. Copyright © 1986 by Princeton University Press. Used by permission.

Page 517, notes 29 and 30: R. Harrison Wagner, *World Politics*, XXXVIII (October 1985), pp. 547, 574–575. Copyright © 1986 by Princeton University Press. Used by permission.

Page 520, note 32: Kenneth A. Oye, *World Poltics*, XXXVIII (October 1985), p. 7. Copyright © 1985 by Princeton University Press. Used by permission.

Sponsoring Editor: Lauren Silverman
Project Editor: Donna DeBenedictis
Art Direction: Heather A. Ziegler
Cover Coordinator: Mary Archondes
Cover Design: Heather A. Ziegler/Ed Smith Design
Production: Willie Lane

CONTENDING THEORIES OF INTERNATIONAL RELATIONS:
A Comprehensive Survey, Third Edition

Library of Congress Cataloging-in-Publication Data

Dougherty, James E.
    Contending theories of international relations : a comprehensive survey / James E. Dougherty, Robert L. Pfaltzgraff, Jr.—3rd ed.
        p.   cm.
    Includes bibliographical references.
    ISBN 0-06-041706-4
    1. International relations. I. Pfaltzgraff, Robert L. II. Title.
JX1395.D67   1990   89-19952
327'.01—dc20   CIP

89 90 91 92   9 8 7 6 5 4 3 2 1

Contents

7   Microcosmic Theories of Violent Conflict   272

8   Macrocosmic Theories of Violent Conflict: Revolution and War   311

12 Game Theory, Gaming, Simulation, and Bargaining   507

13 International Studies: Toward the Third Millennium   535

Preface

With this new edition, *Contending Theories of International Relations* enters its third decade of university and college use. We have endeavored to preserve the basic elements of the approach that guided us in the preparation of the first two editions:

1. *An interdisciplinary method* that draws insights from traditional and behavioral-scientific fields.
2. *An effort to integrate* newer with older theories, as well as insights from different perspectives, into international phenomena.
3. *An impartial presentation* of contending theories and theorists, along with the views of their critics where appropriate.
4. *The ample citation of scholarly sources* on which our discussions and analyses are based.

Because of space constraints, we have reduced or eliminated surveys of certain theories that appeared in the earlier editions to make room for new material on the nature of theory; the paradigm for the study of international relations; the meanings of power, regime theory, neorealism, low-intensity conflict, and world-system analysis; refinements in the concepts of deterrence and arms control (both nuclear and conventional); the causes and correlates of war; and recent developments—decision-making theory especially—with regard to crisis and crisis management. The field of international theory is always changing in its substantive and methodological dimensions. Yet we remain convinced that in international relations, as in the social sciences generally, theory can be understood best when it is linked to and builds upon the enduring insights of the past. During the 1980s, no new theoretical revolutions have occurred and no radical reorganization of the field has taken place, although the paradigmatic debate has intensified. If anything, as we move toward the end of the century, changes in the international system seem to be outpacing developments in international theory, and this poses a fundamental challenge to the serious scholars and thinkers of the next generation.

It is our purpose to assist undergraduate and graduate students in their quest for an understanding of the evolving field of theory. Because a single text can do no more than point to stimulating avenues for further exploration and study, we provide extensive bibliographical footnotes. For the third edition, more than 200 new source references have been added to the more than 1200 retained from the previous edition. It is to be hoped that undergraduate students preparing term papers as well as graduate students working on more advanced research topics will benefit from this bibliographical information.

The authors embarked upon this project more than twenty years ago. While co-directing the graduate seminar in international relations theories at the University of Pennsylvania, we became aware that students felt overwhelmed by the great variety of theories that were beginning to abound in the field. It was our purpose to come to their assistance—not by propagating a single favorite theory, but by surveying the full panoply of the literature available, and trying to assess the various theories as objectively as we could, setting forth their points of intersection or overlap, of convergence or divergence. We know full well that this field is so vast and complex that the achievement of a single, unified, parsimonious yet powerful explanation of international phenomena may always prove to be elusive. Yet today more than ever, it is a fascinating and important area for study, reflection, and research.

In earlier editions we noted many persons who profoundly deserved thanks for their contributions to our intellectual development and to this work. That debt remains, for this present edition, like contemporary theory itself, builds on all that has gone before. We wish especially to acknowledge our gratitude to colleagues at St. Joseph's University, the Fletcher School of Law and Diplomacy, Tufts University, and the Institute for Foreign Policy Analysis who, over the course of decades, have contributed much to our understanding of international relations. We express thanks to the many students who have posed challenging questions about theories of international relations. Both of us have benefited immeasurably from discussions with policymakers in the United States and abroad, whose perspectives furnish an indispensable basis for assessing the relationship between theory and practice in the world as it exists, in contrast to the way we might wish it to be.

We would be remiss not to single out those who rendered valuable comments for this edition. Linda F. Brady of the Georgia Institute of Technology, Richard W. Mansbach of Iowa State University, and James Lee Ray of Florida State University took time from their demanding schedules to read the entire manuscript. Their insights and critiques enhanced the final product of our labors. We are grateful to Richard Shultz of the Fletcher School of Law and Diplomacy, Tufts University, for materials related to the discussion of low-intensity conflict in Chapter 8. We express our thanks to colleagues at the Institute for Foreign Policy Analysis, especially Jacquelyn K. Davis and Charles M. Perry, Executive Vice President and Director of Studies, respectively, for valuable insights into the linkage between theory and policy.

Marjorie Duggan of the Institute for Foreign Policy Analysis furnished indispensable help in preparing the manuscript for publication, keeping track of numerous revisions and renumbering of footnotes, as well as typing all the completed drafts. Stephanie Auer of St. Joseph's University typed some of James Dougherty's early partial drafts. David Lutkins, also of the Institute for Foreign Policy Analysis, performed outstanding service by checking the footnotes for consistency and accuracy, obtaining permissions to quotations included in the text, supervising the final proofreading, and providing other forms of research assistance. Tamah Swenson with the assistance of Kristen Miller carried out the meticulous task of preparing the index. Brian Lawler and Eric Labs also proofread the final manuscript. To all who assisted in the production of this edition, we express our gratitude. May this edition contribute to an understanding of theories of international relations for an emerging generation of scholars, students, and policymakers in the increasingly complex and heterogeneous world of the late twentieth century.

James E. Dougherty
Robert L. Pfaltzgraff, Jr.

Chapter
1

Theoretical Approaches to International Relations

*T*heory is essential in every discipline for an understanding of phenomena, for thinking about their interrelatedness, for guiding research, and—to mention a more immediately useful objective in the social sciences—for recommending sound policy action. Biological, chemical, and other scientists require adequate theories to provide purposeful direction to their work in seeking cures for diseases such as cancer. No less important are theoretical designs in the much older quest for a solution to what is generally regarded as the central problem of international relations—that of preventing war while at the same time enabling societies to preserve their finest and most cherished values. The international relations theorist rejects the tendency to substitute for careful analysis such superficial bumper-sticker slogans as "Make love, not war." A doctrine of universal love, if practiced universally, would indeed probably usher in an era of peace on earth, but such a doctrine does not seem about to be embraced by the bulk of humankind. Those who feel obliged—whether as political executives, legislators, economic decision-makers, advisers, diplomats, scholars, teachers, journalists, or voters—to take a responsible approach to international affairs must go beyond ephemeral opinions and shibboleths to a systematic study of the global system. Anyone who tries to make some sense out of the apparent incoherence of the world scene, so that discrete events, instead of being purely random, can be explained within an orderly, intelligible pattern, is a theorist at heart.

1

EARLY APPROACHES TO INTERNATIONAL RELATIONS THEORY

Efforts at theorizing about the nature of interstate relations are quite old; some in fact go back to ancient times in India, China, and Greece. Although Plato's and Aristotle's reflections on the subject are quite sketchy, the ancient Greek historian Thucydides' *History of the Peloponnesian War* is a classic treatise that any student of international relations can still read profitably.[1] Machiavelli's *The Prince*, a harbinger of modern analysis of power and the state system, emphasized a "value-free" science of foreign policymaking and statecraft.[2] Dante's *De Monarchia* became one of the first and most powerful appeals in Western political literature for an international organization capable of enforcing the peace.[3] Other early proponents of a confederation or league of nation-states were Pierre Dubois (French lawyer and political pamphleteer of the late fourteenth and early fifteenth centuries), Emeric Crucé (French monk of the late sixteenth and early seventeenth centuries), the Duc de Sully (minister of France's Henry IV), William Penn, Abbé de Saint Pierre (French publicist and theoretical reformer of the late seventeenth and early eighteenth centuries), Jean-Jacques Rousseau, Jeremy Bentham, and Immanuel Kant.[4]

Despite these classical writings, no systematic development comparable to that in internal political theories of the state occurred in international theory before World War I. Martin Wight has noted that if by "international theory" we mean a "tradition of speculation about relations between states, a tradition imagined as the twin of speculation about the State to which the name 'political theory' is appropriated," such a tradition does not exist.[5] Wight suggests that one explanation for this absence is that since Grotius (1583–1645), the Dutch jurist and statesman, and Pufendorf (1632–1694), the German jurist and historian, nearly all speculation about the international community fell under the heading of international law. He notes that most writing on interstate relations before this century was contained in the political literature of the peace writers cited above, buried in the works of historians, cloistered in the peripheral reflections of philosophers, or harbored in speeches, dispatches, and memoirs of statesmen and diplomats. Wight concludes that in the classical political tradition, "international theory, or what there is of it, is scattered, unsystematic, and mostly inaccessible to the layman," as well as being "largely repellent and intractable in form."[6] The only theory that infused the thinking of the period—and it was a theory somewhat dearer to practicing diplomats than to academicians—was that of the balance of power. Indeed, it was a collection of what seemed to be commonsense axioms rather than a rigorous theory.

The period of European history from 1648 to 1914 constituted the golden age of diplomacy, the balance of power, alliances, and international law. Nearly all political thought focused on the sovereign nation-state—

the origins, functions, and limitations of governmental powers, the rights of individuals within the state, the requirements of order, and the imperatives of national self-determination and independence. The economic order was presumed simplistically to be separate from the political and domestic politics derived from the statecraft of diplomacy. Governments were expected to promote and protect trade, but not to regulate it. Various branches of socialist thinking sought to strike out in new directions, but socialists, despite their professed internationalism, did not really produce a coherent international theory. They advanced a theory of imperialism borrowed largely from John A. Hobson (1858–1940), the British economist, and thus derivative from an economic theory indigenous to the capitalist states.[7] Until 1914, international theorists almost uniformly assumed that the structure of international society was unalterable, and that the division of the world into sovereign states was necessary and natural.[8] The study of international relations consisted almost entirely of diplomatic history and international law, rather than of investigation into the processes of the international system.

MODERN APPROACHES TO INTERNATIONAL RELATIONS THEORY

Some impetus to the serious study of international relations in this country came when the United States emerged as a world power, but ambiguities in American foreign policy, combined with the trend toward isolationism during the 1920s and 1930s, hindered the development of international relations as an intellectual discipline. A dichotomy developed between intellectual idealists who shared Woodrow Wilson's vision of the League of Nations and politicians who, feeling pressures for a "return to normalcy," blocked United States entry into the world organization. Americans demanded a moral and peaceful world order, but they were unwilling to pay the price. This dichotomy between noble impulses and tendencies toward isolationism was clearly reflected in the Kellogg-Briand Treaty of 1928, which "outlawed" war by moralistic declaration but provided no adequate means of enforcement.[9]

For a decade or more after Versailles, the two most popular approaches to teaching world affairs in American universities included courses in current events and courses in international law and organization. Current events courses were designed more to promote international understanding than to apply social science methodologies to good advantage.[10] Courses in international law emphasized discrepancies between the formal obligations of states (especially League members) and their actual conduct in an era of struggle between powers anxious to preserve the international status quo and those determined to overturn it.[11]

Whereas some English and American scholars in the period between the two world wars focused on the study of international law and organization, others looked for more dynamic, comprehensive evaluations of forces and events in interstate relations. Leading diplomatic historians searched for the "causes" or "origins" of the Great War of 1914–1918.[12] Other historians explored the phenomenon of nationalism, long regarded (up to today) as the most potent political force in the modern world despite the advent of universalist ideologies.[13] Specialized writings appeared in several areas—problems of security, war, and disarmament;[14] imperialism;[15] diplomacy and negotiation;[16] the balance of power;[17] the geographical aspects of world power (which built on the work of Alfred Thayer Mahan and Sir Halford Mackinder, treated in Chapter 2);[18] the history of international relations theory;[19] and economic factors in international relations.[20] For example, Sir Norman Angell, one of the most prolific British writers of his time and the recipient of the 1933 Nobel Peace Prize, suggested that war between highly industrialized states was a futile exercise because free trade had given rise to unprecedented interdependence, which in turn made international cooperation essential to their individual and collective well-being. A number of partial theories were in the process of being developed. Several of these later became elements of more comprehensive efforts toward synthesis after World War II.

✳ E. H. Carr and the Crisis of World Politics

By the 1930s there was a growing recognition among international relations teachers of the gap between the "utopians" and the "realists." The academic climate after World War I made it conducive for utopians to concern themselves with the means of preventing another war. Consequently, this task spurred the serious study of international relations. No scholars in that period more trenchantly analyzed the philosophical differences between utopians and realists than did Edward Hallett Carr in his celebrated work,[21] which, although published in 1939, did not have its impact in America until after World War II. Most of the following comparative analysis draws heavily from that work.

Carr saw the utopians, for the most part, as intellectual descendants of eighteenth-century Enlightenment optimism, nineteenth-century liberalism, and twentieth-century Wilsonian idealism. Utopianism is closely associated with a distinctly Anglo-American tendency to assume that statesmen enjoy broad freedom of choice in the making of foreign policy.[22] Marred by a certain self-righteousness, the utopians clung to the belief that the United States had entered World War I as a disinterested, even reluctant, champion of international morality. Emphasizing how people ought to behave in their international relationships rather than how they actually behave, the American utopians disdained balance-of-power politics (historically identified with Europe), national armaments, the use of force in international affairs, and the secret treaties of alliance that preceded World War I. Instead, they stressed international legal rights and obligations, the natural harmony of national interests—reminiscent of Adam Smith's "invisible hand"[23]—as a regulator for the preservation of international peace, a heavy reliance upon reason in human affairs, and confidence in the peace-building function of the "world court of public opinion." (The utopians, of course, might argue that the balance of power itself corresponded to the "unseen hand" that had been discredited in their view.)

Utopianism in international relations theory is based on the assumption, drawn from the eighteenth-century Enlightenment, that environing circumstances shape human conduct and that such factors can be altered as a basis for transforming human behavior. In sharp contrast to realist theory, to be discussed in Chapter 3, utopianism holds that humankind is perfectible, or at least capable of improvement. At the international level, the political environment can be transformed by the development of new institutions such as the League of Nations and the United Nations. By the establishment of norms of conduct, political behavior can be changed. Once such standards are set forth, it will be possible to create educated electorates and leadership capable of accepting them. It is assumed that enlightened public opinion can be expected to make rational decisions. Central to utopian theory, moreover, was the assumption of a harmony of interest in peace at the level of the collectivity, or nation-state, based on the interest of the individual in a peaceful world. The highest interest of the individual coincides with that of the larger community. If states have not embraced peace, it is because the leadership has not been responsive to the will of the people. An international system based on representative governments (a world made safe for democracy, in the words of Woodrow Wilson) would necessarily be a peaceful world. It is for this reason that a principal tenet of utopian theory was national self-determination. If peoples are free to select the form of government under which they want to live, they will choose representative forms of rule. The result will be to create the necessary framework for the realization of the harmony of interest in a peaceful world.

Utopianism arose at an initial stage in the development of international relations theory. In E. H. Carr's words, international relations "took its rise from a great and disastrous war; and the overwhelming purpose which dominated and inspired the pioneers of the new science was to obviate a recurrence of this disease of the international body politic."[24] It was the destructiveness of World War I that had led not only to the quest for international norms and institutions in the form of the League of Nations Covenant and the collective security framework established by its founders. In Carr's perspective, the wish is said to be the father of thought in the sense that an abiding desire to abolish war or to reduce its destructiveness shaped the approach to international relations theory. In this initial stage, purpose, or teleology, "precedes and conditions thought." Therefore, Carr contends, at the beginning of the establishment of a new field of inquiry, "the element of wish or purpose is overwhelmingly strong, and the inclination to analyze facts and means weak or nonexistent."[25] Such is the perspective that guided the development of international relations in the decades between the two world wars, especially in the United States but also in Britain. The dominant approach was to embrace what was international and to condemn what was national, and to evaluate events of the day by reference to the extent to which they conformed to the standards established by international legal norms and the League of Nations. There arose a substantial literature, highly normative in content, whose purpose was, as stated in the foreword to one such volume by G. Lowes Dickinson, "to disseminate knowledge of the facts of international relations, and to inculcate the international rather than the nationalistic way of regarding them . . . for the world cannot be saved by governments and governing classes. It can be saved only by the creation, among the peoples of the world, of such a public opinion as cannot be duped by misrepresentation nor misled by passion."[26] In addition to Dickinson, the list of contributors to this utopian literature included Nicholas Murray Butler, James T. Shotwell, Alfred Zimmern, Norman Angell, and Gilbert Murray.

As World War II approached, the gap between utopian theory and the events of the day widened. The failures of the League of Nations in the 1930s cast doubt upon the harmony of interest in peace, which appeared to accord more with the interests of satisfied, status quo powers than with the perceived needs of revisionist states seeking boundary changes, enhanced status and greater power, and, especially in the case of Nazi Germany, revenge for the humiliation of the post–World War I settlement imposed by the Versailles Treaty. Contrary to the utopian assumption, national self-determination did not always produce representative governments. Instead, the overthrow of the old monarchical order gave rise in many places, including Russia, to a more pervasive totalitarian state. The world consisted not principally of peace-loving states based upon the realization of an international harmony of interest in peace. Instead, increasingly the major actors embraced ideologies such as fascism and communism—joined, for example, in the infamous Molotov-Ribbentrop Pact of August 1939 between the Soviet Union and Nazi Germany, which set the stage for the Nazi invasion of Poland, the outbreak of World War II, the partition of Poland, and the absorption of the Baltic states into the Soviet Union, all in contravention of the standards of international conduct set forth in utopian theory. Those states that most strongly embodied and were the intellectual centers of utopian theory themselves fell far short of its precepts. The United States had rejected the Wilsonian call for internationalism and had refused to join the League of Nations, reverting instead to isolationism. In Britain the carnage of World War I that had resulted in the loss of much of a generation of manhood spawned a pacifism whose effect was to restrict greatly any ability to bring necessary force to bear within or outside the League of Nations against expansionist states such as Nazi Germany and Fascist Italy, as well as Imperial Japan, until the onset of World War II. Such was the international setting that marked the decline of the utopian phase and provided fertile intellectual ground for the reassertion and reformulation of a realist theory of international relations, discussed in Chapter 3.

Realists, in contrast to utopians, stressed power and interest, rather than ideals in international relations. Realism is basically conservative, empirical, prudent, suspicious of idealistic principles, and respectful of the lessons of history. It is more likely to produce a pessimistic than an optimistic view of international politics. Realists regard power as the fundamental concept in the social sciences (such as energy is in physics), although they admit that power relationships are often cloaked in moral and legal terms. Moreover, they criticize the utopian for preferring visionary goals to scientific analysis.

To the realist, appeals to reason and to public opinion had proved woefully weak supports for keeping the peace in the 1930s; for example, they did not save Manchuria and Ethiopia from aggression. Thus, although the idealist hoped for change that might permit disarmament, the realist emphasized national security and the need for military force to support diplomacy.

The argument pitting utopianism against realism is classic. Carr's analysis of this dialectic remains timely: "The inner meaning of the modern international crisis," he contended, "is the collapse of the whole structure of utopianism based on the concept of the harmony of interests."[27] In his view, the international morality of the interwar years merely justified the interests of the dominant English-speaking status quo powers, of the satisfied versus the unsatisfied, of the "haves" versus the "have-nots." Carr, a pragmatist, took utopians *and* realists to task. He saw that whereas the utopians ignore the lessons of history, the realists often read history too pessimistically. Whereas the idealist exaggerates freedom of choice, the realist exaggerates fixed causality and slips into determinism. While the idealist may confuse national self-interest with universal moral principles, the realist runs the risk of cynicism and "fails to provide any ground for purposive and meaningful action"[28]—that is, the realist denies that human thought modifies human action. Purpose precedes observation; the vision of a Plato comes before the analysis of an Aristotle. The vision may even seem totally unrealistic. Carr cites the alchemists who tried to turn lead into gold, noting that when their visionary project failed they began examining "facts" more carefully, thus giving birth to modern science.[29] He concludes that sound political theories contain elements of utopianism and realism, of power as well as moral values.[30]

Post–World War II Realism

Not surprisingly, World War II and its immediate aftermath shifted Western thinking on international relations further away from the idealism of the early League of Nations period toward an older and resurgent realism, from law and organization to the elements of power. Even idealistically inclined analysts—and there were many who had supported the war effort for reasons of the highest moral idealism—became skeptical of utopian programs and called instead for a merger of international law and organization, with effective power to ensure international peace, the security of nations, and the equitable settlement of disputes.

Throughout the post–World War II period, the onset of the Cold War and the emergence of the United States as a power with global interests and commitments generated within American universities a heightened interest in the study of international relations. War veterans in college showed a keen concern over "foreign affairs." Under the impact of critical international developments, the United States government greatly expanded its operations in the areas of national military security, alliances and other international organizations, and economic development assistance to foreign countries. All of these operations, of course, increased the need for trained personnel. For the first time, many American businesses became aware of international trade and investment possibilities. Scientists, alarmed at the implications of the new nuclear technology that they had just produced, entered politics as crusading novices, warning of dangers confronting humanity. Civic-minded persons zealously organized councils and associations to educate and exhort in order to make citizens aware of international problems.

Academic scholars in Britain and the United States, the two countries in which the universities had shown most progress in the interwar development of international relations, produced analyses suitable to the postwar reality. Several works published in the late 1940s emphasized the power approach to the study of international relations. One of the more frequently quoted English authors was Martin Wight, who noted that

> what distinguishes modern history from medieval history is the predominance of the idea of power over the idea of right; the very term "Power" to describe a state in its international aspect is significant; and the view of the man in the street, who is perhaps inclined to take it for granted that foreign politics are inevitably "power politics," is not without a shrewd insight.[31]

Another English scholar, Georg Schwarzenberger, analyzed power as a prime factor in international politics. In the absence of genuine international community, he asserted, groups within the international system can be expected to do what they are physically able to do rather than what they are morally exhorted to do. Power, in Schwarzenberger's view, is by no means a wanton, destructive thing. It is a combination of persuasive influence and coercive force, but those who wield power, while maintaining and exhibiting an ability to impose their wills on the noncompliant, normally prefer to achieve their ends merely by posing the threat of effective sanctions, without actually resorting to physical force. The textbooks in international relations published during the first two decades after World World II generally recognized "power" as a central concept in the field. The text that had the greatest impact on the university teaching of international relations, that of Hans J. Morgenthau, explained nation-state behavior on the basis of national interest (defined in terms of power) as the normal objective pursued by governments when possible.[32] The other important textbooks of that period all devoted on the average at least three chapters to the nature of power and the elements or factors of national power. Most contemporary political scientists and students of international relations continue to distinguish between power and influence, and to regard power as a variable of major importance.[33]

THE DEVELOPMENT OF INTERNATIONAL RELATIONS THEORY

The earlier textbooks contained some theoretical observations on such topics as nationalism, imperialism, colonialism, the emergence of the Third World, ideology, and propaganda, and the impact of economic and technological factors upon international relations. Some contained chapters on alliances, regional or functional integration, disarmament or arms control, and such specific techniques of foreign policy as intervention, nonalignment, and isolation. Seldom was there an effort to draw precise linkages between the theories, or to find out whether partial theories could be fitted together into a larger, coherent whole.[34] This is not to suggest that the authors necessarily lacked their own informing theory. But they did not present generalized theory in a systematic manner. Indeed, several of them were probably suspicious of single, overarching theories.

Throughout the period since the late 1940s, there has been a steady development of methodologies and techniques for research, analysis, and teaching in international relations, which have contributed to the growth of theory.[35] The effort toward comprehensive theory-building began with the "Great Debate" between realists and idealists (treated in Chapter 3). Originally, most of the members of both of these schools were what we now call *traditionalists*. Those who were interested in rejecting the premises of traditional international politics led the way in the development of behavioral/quantitative methodologies, but were soon joined by some realists who wished to show that the basic assessment of power could not be easily set aside.

The 1960s witnessed a considerable expansion of interest in theoretical analysis,[36] and its validation by means of such methodologies as content analysis and bivariate and multivariate correlations. Insights from the biological, psychological, anthropological, sociological, economic, and other behavioral sciences were borrowed in the effort to explain international politics. There was an emphasis on abstract model-building, as well as a variety of new approaches to the understanding of ecological factors and the individual relationships between humans and their milieu, regional integration, interaction in the international system, the causes of war, the conditions for deterrence, arms races and arms control, decision-making, games theory, and related subjects in foreign policy and international relations.

"Grand" and "Middle-Range" Theories

International relations theorists have been preoccupied with several basic questions in recent decades. Not all theorists have worked on or shown interest in all of the questions. Indeed, most of the better-known theoretical writers have devoted their attention principally to one favorite approach (usually a comprehensive or "grand" theory) or else to one or a few partial, "middle-range" theories. Under the heading of "grand" theory, which purports to explain in a generalized way a wide range of phenomena, we would include such overarching perspectives as the following:

1. the field theories of Quincy Wright and Rudolf Rummel
2. the realist (or power) theories of Hans Morgenthau, Raymond Aron, and Henry Kissinger and neorealism (Kenneth Waltz, and Karl Gottfried Kindermann)
3. the systems theories of Morton Kaplan and Richard Rosecrance. Examples of partial, middle-range theories designed to explain a limited range of phenomena with a few variables include those pertaining to
   a. the influence of the geographical environment (Alfred Thayer Mahan, Halford Mackinder, Nicholas Spykman, Harold and Margaret Sprout)
   b. communications patterns and community-building (Karl Deutsch)
   c. functionalism and sector integration (David Mitrany, Ernst Haas, Leon Lindberg, and Joseph S. Nye)
   d. deterrence (Bernard Brodie, Herman Kahn, Glenn Snyder, and Paul Diesing)
   e. international development and conflict (Nazli Choucri and Robert North)
   f. the correlates of war (J. David Singer and Melvin Small)
   g. alliance behavior (William Riker and Stephen Walt)
   h. bargaining behavior (Thomas Schelling and Anatol Rapaport)
   i. decision-making (Richard Snyder, Graham Allison, and Glenn Paige)

Even the effort to classify theories as "grand" or "middle-range" can provoke debate. They are not completely disjunctive categories; some theories might fall in between, and others might not fit well into either. The decision-making theory of Richard Snyder and his colleagues, for example, is not so much an explanatory theory with predictive power as it is a precise taxonomy or classificatory scheme, a conceptual framework that provides a researcher doing a single or comparative case study in decision-making with an orderly framework for collecting and analyzing data. Other theories of decision-making such as the "cybernetic" (John Steinbruner), "satisficing behavior" (Herbert Simon), "bureaucratic" (Morton Halperin) and "rational actor" or "organizational process" (Graham Allison) come closer to being explanatory. All of the theories mentioned above, plus others, will be treated in subsequent chapters. The purpose of mentioning them here is not so much to overwhelm, much less discourage, the student, as to indicate that there are not only many different theories, but also different types of and approaches to theorizing about international relations. Authorities in the field are not at all agreed on which would be better—to build grand theory first and let the formulation of middle-range theories flow from it, or to test out and solidify a number of middle-range theories before proceeding to a higher, more abstract level. Stanley Hoffmann, for example, prefers to start with grand theory whereas J. David Singer would lean toward laying the foundation with middle-range, empirically based theories. The situation has changed little since Glenn Snyder and Paul Diesing wrote, over a decade ago,

> In our teaching and research, we are like travelers in a houseboat, shuttling back and forth between separate "islands" of theory, whose relatedness consists only in their being commonly in the great "ocean" of "international behavior." Some theorists take up permanent residence on one island or other, others continue to shuttle, but few attempt to build bridges, perhaps because the islands seem too far apart.[37]

At the risk of oversimplifying, we can say that those who adopt a careful "counting" approach prefer the more modest hypotheses that become embodied in middle-range or even "small-scale" theories, whereas those of a more philosophizing bent favor the larger, more sweeping vision. (This is not exactly the same as the dichotomy between the quantifying behaviorists and the traditionalists, to be explained later, but it is related to that dichotomy.) Modern academicians who are often unjustly accused of knowing and writing more and more about less and less significant things often exhibit impatience or contempt toward the products of generalizing minds such as Toynbee, Parsons, or Morgenthau. Kenneth Boulding, on the other hand, shuns scholarly research on a narrow scale and urges those who would understand the international system to abandon the microscope and the infinitesimally trivial and take up the telescope to encompass the whole universe as it evolves through space and time.[38] Only then, he says, can we begin to see how the international human society on this tiny planet fits into the increasingly complex, interactive scheme of the larger universe. Since inevitable change is the fundamental law, he argues, we must throw off the apparently unchanging concepts of power politics inherited from Thucydides, Machiavelli, and Hobbes and recognize that threat and conflict will sooner or later give way to mutually beneficial cooperation and integration. Boulding strikes a novel and refreshing note that probably sounds more comforting to the philosopher than to the responsible policymaker, who thinks not in terms of aeons or centuries but of next year, next week, or tomorrow. The main point at the moment is that much depends upon one's general philosophical outlook, including one's view of history and human nature, as well as whether human nature remains pretty much the same or undergoes genuine progressive development from egoism to altruism during the course of history. Obviously society changes outwardly as a result of accumulated knowledge and the impact of education, science, technology, production, economics, religion, and culture. But whether human beings experience equally profound internal change in their psychological and moral qualities is a different question.

Logically Prior Questions

Before we examine in detail the writings of modern international theorists, certain issues ought to be considered first because they are logically prior:

1. What do we mean by "international relations"? What is the scope of the field?
2. What do we mean by "theory"? What are its functions?
3. What is the relation between theory and practice?
4. Which method is better—the inductive or the deductive?
5. What is the "level of analysis problem"?
6. On which units (or actors) should we focus our attention?
7. Which predominates—politics or economics? Or, to put it differently, is "power" being replaced by "interdependence"?
8. To what extent can or should theory be value-free?
9. What is the appropriate place of normative theory?

THE DEFINITION AND SCOPE OF INTERNATIONAL RELATIONS

Definition is only the beginning, not the end, of systematic inquiry. Modern science began, as Alfred North Whitehead noted in a 1925 lecture, when emphasis was shifted from the Aristotelian method of classification to the Pythagorean-Platonist method of measurement, yet he hastened to add that classification is necessary for orderly, logical thought.[39] Every disciplinary field should be able to define itself clearly, just as every scientific thinker should undertake a research project with a precise notion of the phenomenon to be investigated. When the subject of international relations was just emerging as a field of study within British and American universities, academicians on both sides of the Atlantic had difficulty coming to grips with its nature and scope. In 1935, Sir Alfred Zimmern suggested that "the study of international relations extends from the natural sciences at one end to moral philosophy . . . at the other." He defined the field not as a single subject or discipline but as a "bundle of subjects . . . viewed from a common angle."[40] Many teachers since his time have wryly noted with Zimmern that students who "major" in international relations wish that they knew more about history, politics, economics, geography, demography, diplomacy, international law, ethics, religion, and nearly every branch of contemporary science and technology. Certainly those who achieve enduring distinction within the field seem to be those prepared by a liberal educational background for a life of active inquiry based upon an insatiable interest in the "international dimension."

Nicholas J. Spykman, among the first to propose a rigorous definition, used the term *interstate relations,* which, however, he did not expect would gain wide acceptance: "International relations are relations between individuals belonging to different states, . . . international behavior is the social behavior of individuals or groups aimed at . . . or influenced by the existence or behavior of individuals or groups belonging to a different state."[41] Loosely defined, the term *international relations* could encompass many different activities—international communications, business transactions, athletic contests, tourism, scientific conferences, educational exchange programs, and religious missionary activities. International relations scholars have never agreed on where the boundaries of their field lie. Frederick S. Dunn once warned that the word *scope* is dangerously ambiguous because it implies the existence of clearly discernible boundary lines as readily identifiable as a surveyor's mark.

> A field of knowledge does not possess a fixed extension in space but is a constantly changing focus of data and methods that happen at the moment to be useful in answering an identifiable set of questions. It presents at any given time different aspects to different observers, depending on their point of view and purpose. The boundaries that supposedly divide one field of knowledge from another are not fixed walls between separate cells of truth but are convenient devices for arranging known facts and methods in manageable segments for instruction and practice. But the foci of interest are constantly shifting and these divisions tend to change with them.[42]

He went on to suggest, quite sensibly, that the "subject-matter of international relations consists of whatever knowledge, from any sources, may be of assistance in meeting new international problems or understanding old ones."[43]

For more than a decade after World War II, scholars debated whether international relations could be called a discipline with a methodology and substantive content of its own, or whether it was so encyclopaedic as to belong to several disciplines. Quincy Wright regarded it as "an emerging discipline," one in the process of formation, and argued that it meets the definitional criteria of its critics as well as most academic disciplines, in the development of which history has played as much a part as logic.[44] Morton

A. Kaplan, insisting that international relations lacks the character of a discipline because there is "no common disciplinary core to be enriched as there had been in the companion subject-matter of political science," no set of unique skills and techniques, and no developed body of theoretical propositions, preferred to recognize international politics merely as a subdiscipline of political science.[45]

Frederick S. Dunn states that international relations may "be looked upon as the actual relations that take place across national boundaries, or as the body of knowledge which we have of those relations at any given time."[46] This is a fairly standard approach, but is it adequate? It is comprehensive, and it does not limit the subject to official relations between states and governments. But is this delineation too broad, and would it be better to include transnational relations on the basis of their political significance, for example, by focusing upon the influences that they exert on the world's political units? As students of politics, we are concerned with relationships between or among all of the actors—state and nonstate, international and transnational—to the extent that they contribute to an understanding of political phenomena. We define international politics as the effort of one state, or other international actor, to influence in some way another state, or other international actor. An influence relationship may encompass the actual or threatened use of military force, or it may be based entirely or partly on other inducements, such as political or economic ones. International politics, moreover, like all politics, represents the reconciliation of varying perspectives, goals, and interests. Thus international politics includes many but not necessarily all transactions or interactions that take place across national frontiers.

Stanley Hoffmann found that "debates which try to determine the scope of a social science are rather pointless" because there are no immutable essences in social relationships. In his view, all definitions are bound to involve ambiguities and difficulties, especially in the case of a field marked by constant flux. Preferring a formula that leads to perceptive investigations and does not violate common sense, Hoffmann suggests an operational definition of the field to encompass "the factors and the activities which affect the external policies and the power of the basic units into which the world is divided."[47] He warns, however, against trying to gather everything within the fold, noting that "a flea market is not a discipline."

The prudent international theorist will avoid the Scylla and Charybdis of either including trivia or excluding significant phenomena. A field that is too broad or cluttered cannot be comprehended by the human mind, and may seem to outsiders in other academic disciplines to be intellectually arrogant, if not downright imperialistic. On the other hand, if something can be shown to be relevant to a full understanding of an issue that belongs to international relations, it should not be "kept outside the walls" on the grounds that it is part of a different academic preserve. Much depends, of course, upon the nature of the problem under investigation and upon the degree to which material from another field can be incorporated and handled competently. As for the scope of our field, more will be said below when we take up "The Level-of-Analysis Problem" and the "units" or "actors" on which we should focus attention.

Should international theory focus on the contemporary scene? There is an inescapable attractiveness about the present, bounded by what has recently happened and what is imminently about to happen. Fascination with the contemporary is heightened by the attention it receives in the news media, by the preoccupation of policymakers, and by the fact that research funding is more readily available for topics of current interest and concern. Nevertheless, most experienced scholars in international relations realize that a knowledge of history is essential because it broadens immensely the data base from which extrapolations into the future are to be made, and it also refines our ability to formulate hypotheses that approximate social reality. Morton Kaplan opens his principal work on the international system with a tribute to history: "There is one respect in which a science of international politics must always be indebted to history. History is the great laboratory within which international action occurs."[48] Kaplan calls for investigations into the ancient Greek city-state system, the Italian state system of the Renaissance period, and the balance-of-power system that dominated Europe during the eighteenth and nineteenth centuries, so that typical system behaviors in different eras might be compared.[49] In his view, international theorists should be interested in all systems—past, present, future, and hypothetical.[50] (Kaplan's theory will be examined in Chapter 4.) If we limit our attention exclusively to the existing nation-state system, and ignore the vast record of the past out of which present reality evolved, we seriously restrict our ability to imagine possible futures. The history of international relations is *not* an international theory, but as the primary source of empirical data it *is* the essential raw material with which the theoretician works.[51] One can hardly grasp, for example, the functionalist theory of economic sector integration (cf. Chapter 10) without accurate historical knowledge of the European Community's formative years.

The Nature and Function of Theory

A theory—any theory, in any field—is a general explanation of certain selected phenomena set forth in a manner satisfactory to someone acquainted with the characteristics of the reality being studied. It need not be acceptable to all experts; indeed, it may satisfy the expounder and horrify all others. Powerful theories are those that exercise great influence upon the thinking of large numbers, perhaps the overwhelming majority, of knowledgeable persons for a long time before being replaced by new theories. (Among the enduring theories are those of the economists pertaining to the division of labor and the principle of comparative advantage; those of social theorists pertaining to the ethnocentricism of groups—the preference for traditional over new and alien ways—and the relationship between external conflict and internal cohesiveness; those of physicists pertaining to the conservation of energy and the relativity of the time-space continuum; and those of international theorists in the realist school pertaining to the nearly universal tendency of states to seek their interests as defined in terms of power.) In the social sciences, however, not even the most powerful theories command unquestioning assent within a disciplinary field. As we survey throughout this text a variety of theories in the academic discipline of international relations, it will become clear that no single generalization, principle, or hypothesis has yet been demonstrated with sufficient force to serve as the foundation for a universally accepted comprehensive theory of international relations.

A theory is an intellectual tool that helps us to organize our knowledge, to ask significant questions, and to guide the formulation of priorities in research as well as the selection of methods to carry out research in a fruitful manner. In other words, theory—although not to be confused with scientific method—enables us to apply the methods of scientific inquiry in an orderly rather than a haphazard way. It helps us to relate knowledge in our own field to that of other fields. Finally, it provides a framework for evaluating the policy recommendations, either explicit or implicit, that abound in all the social sciences. We are often in a better position to judge the soundness of specific policy recommendations if we know something about the theoretical assumptions on which they are based, and if we are also familiar with alternative theories that might lead to different policy recommendations.

In literature on the philosophy of science the term *theory* has assumed a specific meaning. A theory is defined as a symbolic construction, a series of interrelated hypotheses together with definitions, laws, theorems, and axioms. A theory sets forth a systematic view of phenomena by presenting a series of propositions or hypotheses that specify relations among variables in order to present explanations and make predictions about the phenomena. In the physical sciences a theory may be viewed as a system consisting of the following elements: (1) a set of axioms whose truth is assumed and can be tested only by testing their logical consequences—an axiom cannot be deduced from other statements contained in the system; (2) statements, or theorems, that are deduced from the axioms, or from other theorems and definitions; and (3) definitions of descriptive terms contained in the axioms.[52] A theory is a group of laws that are deductively connected. Some of the laws are premises from which other laws are deduced. Those laws deduced from the axioms are the theorems of the theory. Whether or not a law is an axiom or a theorem depends on its position in a theory.

A theory does not depend necessarily upon empirical referents for validity; it need only state logically deduced relationships among the phenomena with which the theory is concerned.[53] According to Abraham Kaplan, the ability to apply the theory successfully is not a necessary condition for its success, since the failure of the application may be traceable to many factors external to the theory itself.[54] But the development of empirical referents makes possible the testing of a theory. Carl Hempel has offered the following analogy:

> A scientific theory might therefore be likened to a complex spatial network: Its terms are represented by the knots, while the threads connecting the latter correspond, in part, to the definitions and, in part, to the fundamental and derivative hypotheses contained in the theory. The whole system floats, as it were, above the plane of observation and is anchored to it by rules of interpretation. These might be viewed as strings which are not part of the network but link certain parts of the latter with specific laces in the plane of observation. By virtue of those interpretive connectors, the network can function as a scientific theory. From certain observational data, we may ascend, via an interpretive string, to some point in the theoretical network, thence proceed, via definitions and hypotheses, to other points from which another interpretive string permits a descent to the place of observation.[55]

In the field of international relations, as in all the social sciences, theory is somewhat more diffuse and less precise than one finds in the physical sciences (for reasons to be explained later), and may assume several different forms. In international relations, the term *theory* has been used, like so many other terms, in distinctive and often confusing ways. Among the most important usages are the following. Theory has been equated with a philosophy, ideology, hypotheses, a set of interrelated concepts, a set of interrelated hypotheses, a set of interrelated hypotheses with a requisite amount of supporting evidence, and a set of axioms and concepts from which hypotheses may be derived. Theory may be deductive or inductive, a distinction to be elaborated below. It may be a taxonomy—a classification scheme or a conceptual framework that provides for the orderly arrangement and examination of data. It may be a description and analysis of the political behavior of rational actors, based upon a single dominant motive such as power. Or, instead of describing how rational actors *do* in fact behave, it may be *normative,* indicating how they *ought* to behave—a subject on which more will be said subsequently. Finally, as suggested above, it may be a set of policy recommendations for following a particular course of action.

Relation Between Theory and Practice

Despite their complementarity, basic differences exist between academic social science theory and political-diplomatic practice. There are also differences, perhaps less basic, between general theoretical approaches to international relations and the "policy sciences" that deal with the foreign policy problems of particular states, just as there are differences between the "policy sciences" and the actual conduct of diplomacy. Each of the several levels of knowledge and action has a legitimacy of its own that ought not to be disparaged by one who happens to be operating at another level. In all cases it is useful to keep in mind the distinction between the scholar who seeks to achieve a theoretical understanding of phenomena and to formulate generalizations about political behavior based on a high level of probability, and the decision-maker who has to choose a specific course of action in a concrete set of circumstances in which probability analysis may not be helpful.

Long ago Aristotle differentiated between knowing and doing, between the speculative intellect and the practical intellect.[56] David Hume drew a sharp contrast among three classes of knowledge: (1) deductive reasoning, which relates to the logical and necessary truths of mathematics and metaphysics; (2) empirical knowledge, which pertains to apparently causal relationships that are not really rationally necessary; and (3) value judgments, which derive from an accumulation of historical facts as they have affected human emotion and intuition. For Hume, politics and morals must always be inextricably bound with value judgments and hence can be neither deductive nor empirical.[57] To state the problem of theory and practice in Humean terms, we might say that whereas the pure theorist is usually concerned principally with deductive thought processes to generalized formulations, the policymaker has a principal interest in the empirical, inductive knowledge derived from one's own personal experience rather than from any systematic research effort. The policymaker is concerned also with the subtle details of the political values, forces, and preferences operating in a particular situation in all its existential reality rather than to a universal abstraction or probability. Whereas the social theorist wishes to concentrate primarily upon elements common to many situations, the decision-maker invariably wants detailed information about those elements that are unique to the case at hand.

However, lest anyone receive the wrong impression, we stress that the differing emphases of theorist and practitioner do not alter the desirability that each should try to appreciate the modes of knowledge peculiar to the other. Neither can afford to dismiss generalized or particularized knowledge. Leaders in the late twentieth century must weigh and mix different theories in their ongoing efforts to understand developments, choose appropriate policies, and predict outcomes. They will be likely, however, to continue to prefer their own "intuitional theories"—the cumulative effect of their own education and political experience whether in elected, appointed, or usurped offices, executive, legislative, or diplomatic—as more reliable guideposts to policy choices than abstract theoretical constructs developed in academic circles and often couched in terminology unfamiliar to policymakers. Academic theoreticians aim at understanding; practical politicians must choose courses of action. The former try to prescind from day-to-day events; the latter cannot.

Finally, we must remember that political leaders are usually preoccupied with shaping the foreign policies of their own countries vis-à-vis major allies and adversaries. Their span of attention in the international realm is limited by the greater amount of time and effort they must devote to domestic matters. They can seldom afford the luxury of thinking about the entire international system. The international theorist may be deeply interested in the foreign policies of a number of states, depending upon the precise phenomenon being investigated, but realizes that "international relations" are more than merely the sum of the foreign policies of nations. Even though there is a strong linkage between international and domestic politics and economics,[58] there is an "inwardness" to the making of foreign policy that requires a nationally specific perspective. The academic scholar who deals with international theory views the subject from a larger perspective and focuses upon the net results of interactive processes that national policymakers may try to understand and influence, but not always completely or successfully. Lest we be misunderstood, let us quickly add that a great deal of our substantive knowledge about international relations has always come and will continue to come from studies of national and comparative foreign policies.[59] The two approaches intersect in many places but are not identical.

Deductive and Inductive Theorizing

Two eminent theorists in the field—Quincy Wright and James N. Rosenau—offered, at an interval of two decades, some useful advice to would-be theorists of international relations. According to Wright, "a general theory of international relations means a comprehensive, coherent and self-correcting body of knowledge contributing to the understanding, the prediction, the evaluation and the control of the relations among states and of the conditions of the world."[60] Wright's mandate is quite ambitious: He has a "grand theory" in mind, one that covers all aspects of the field. It should be expressed in generalized propositions as clear, as accurate, and as few as possible. It should not be cluttered up with a lot of exceptions. In short, the theory should be parsimonious—that is, it should state an important truth as accurately, elegantly, and briefly as possible. Scientists have always been disposed to equate scientific truth with esthetic beauty, and the latter with intellectual simplicity. Every part of the theory should be logically consistent with every other part. The theory should be formulated in a manner conducive to continual updating and improvement in the light of new evidence. Thus it should be capable of constant verification and refinement. It should contribute to an objective understanding of international reality, rather than one distorted by national perspective. Theory, said Wright, should enable us to predict at least some things, and also help us to arrive at value judgments—even if the process of moral assessment may not be entirely consistent with the value-free tradition of Western science.[61] Wright himself agrees, and we agree with him, that a theory fulfilling all these ideal requirements would be extremely difficult, and perhaps impossible, to achieve.

Rosenau agrees with Hoffmann that being able to define "theory" precisely furnishes no guarantee that one will be able to theorize imaginatively or creatively. He would distinguish more sharply than Wright between empirical and normative (or ethical) theory. He considers both types important, but fears that both can be distorted if "what is" and "what ought to be" are mixed too closely together.* The theorist, Rosenau insists, must assume that in human affairs there is an underlying order, that things do not happen randomly, but that their causes can be explained rationally (even when what we call "irrational behavior" is involved). He urges the theorist to seek not the unique but the general, and to sacrifice detailed descriptions of the single case in favor of the broader, more abstract patterns that encompass many instances. The theorist should be ready to tolerate ambiguity and to be contented with probabilities rather than certainties and absolutes. One must give the mind free rein to "play" with unusual, even absurd, ideas that may produce insights into previously unthought-of explanations. International phenomena should be looked upon as "puzzles" or "mysteries" awaiting solution by the inquisitive mind. Finally, the theorist must always be ready to be proven wrong.[62] (Most are, sooner or later.)

The summaries just given make it clear that Wright had general deductive theory in mind, while Rosenau's advice seems pointed somewhat more toward empirical, inductive, and middle-range theories. These are the two basic approaches to theorizing in the Western intellectual tradition. The deductive method can be traced to Plato, who used it to construct his Ideal Republic. One begins with an abstract concept, model, or major premise—flowing from a set of definitions and assumptions drawn more from "wisdom" than from systematically collected evidence—and then proceeds by plausible, logical steps to deduce ("draw out") subordinate propositions and necessary conclusions. Deduction is a *formal* process of deriving hypotheses from axioms, assumptions, and concepts logically integrated. The hypothesis so derived, in a "scientific" conception, should be tested with data that are not impressionistic, but systematically and carefully selected. Take, for example, the notion that all political communities are concerned in one way or another with *power*—acquiring, consolidating, or expanding power, projecting an image of power to preserve it, balancing power for security, or accommodating to the power of another political community. This is an example of a deductive theory. Theorists of power have not pulled it out of thin air. Far from disdaining empirical data, they have developed their ideas on the basis of one highly credible reading and interpretation of historical evidence. It is a mistake, therefore, to equate deductive theory with nonempirical theory. The de-

---

*The subject of disarmament provides an example of what Rosenau means. Those who assign the highest priority and urgency to disarmament on the international agenda may underestimate the political, psychological, technical, and strategic problems involved. Those who have specialized in studying the empirical-historical-technical data on disarmament may have reached such pessimistic conclusions as to overestimate the difficulties of ever reaching arms limitation agreements.

ductive differs from the inductive method in the way historical factual evidence is collected, converted into usable data, analyzed, and interpreted for purposes of theory. The deductive thinker may arrive at a concept, model, or major premise in an "impressionistic," "intuitive," or "insightful" manner rather than according to strict methodological criteria for selecting cases, rigorous coding rules for classifying events, or mathematically precise ways of determining correlations.

The inductive approach entails a different route toward generalizing from experience. Instead of leaping to a conclusion by way of an "inner mental light," as it were, the inductive empiricist is more careful about observing, categorizing, measuring, and analyzing facts. This method is traceable to Aristotle, who wrote his *Politics* after examining the constitutions of some 150 Greek city-states. The inductive thinker may consider the deductive method excellent in mathematics, logic, and metaphysics, but prefers to investigate physical and social phenomena by observing a number of instances in the same class, and by describing in detail both the research procedures followed and the substantive results, so that others (who may be skeptical) can replicate, or repeat, the work if they wish. The inductive method produces no certainties, only probabilities, and in the social sciences (as contrasted with physics or chemistry) these are usually not of a very high order—nor does the deductive method, nor do methods utilized by chemists, physicists, or biologists. Newton was the greatest physicist of his age, but Einstein demonstrated that his work was partial and flawed, just as eventually even Einstein's work may be superseded by a new theory. In international politics research, it is a rare thing to obtain statistical correlations at high levels of significance—such, for example, that there would be only one chance in a thousand that they were due to coincidence.

Deduction and induction should not be regarded as either competitive or mutually exclusive approaches. Some scholars will prefer one over the other and will make better progress with one than the other. Theory-building requires a fruitful combination of the two, plus something more, to be discussed in a moment. The argument that in the nuclear age a bipolar international system is more stable than a multipolar one, and vice versa, not being amenable to empirical proof, usually proceeds by logical deduction from assumed premises regarding the amount of uncertainty in the system and the number of actors to whom the states must allocate their attention. (See the reference to Singer, Waltz, and Bueno de Mesquita in Chapter 8.) On the other hand, the middle-range theoretical proposition that governments find it relatively easy to pursue policies of regional economic integration in periods of prosperous growth and tend to retrench toward national particularism at times of recession can be arrived at by deduction and can then be tested by reference to the evaluation of the European Economic Community. (See Chapter 10.)

Kenneth N. Waltz distinguishes theories from empirical data, statistical correlations, hypotheses, and inductively arrived-at laws or generalizations. Statistical correlations, even when significant, are not facts, and they can never establish causal connections. We can arrive at laws and empirical generalizations through inductive methods, and these may identify invariable or probable associations, but cannot explain them. The ancient Babylonians were familiar with the laws of tidal movements, which they could observe, measure, and predict, but they could not explain those laws. That is the function of theory, which cannot be arrived at by deduction alone, for deduction merely proceeds logically from initial premises and thus can provide no powerful new explanations. Theories have to be invented by a creative intellectual process that takes a number of disparate laws and generalizations, simplifies them by isolating a few key factors, abstracting them from what is not relevant, aggregating them in a previously unknown way, and synthesizing them in a new, ideal, quasi-perfect explanatory system. Such a process can hardly be taught. A textbook can do no more than show how others have theorized. Students can judge for themselves whether a particular theory is insightful, satisfying, and promising. Hopefully a survey of many theories will inspire those who study them to embark on their own road to theorizing.[63]

The "Level-of-Analysis" Problem: Who Are the Actors?

In all the social sciences—politics, economics, and sociology, for example— one cannot help wondering where to begin, where to focus attention, where to try to "get a handle" on the subject. In all these fields the "micro" and "macro" perspectives have their ardent partisans. Determining the proper "fulcrum point" is particularly difficult in international relations because of the comprehensiveness of the field. On which of many possible levels of analysis should we focus our attention? Which are the proper units of study—or "actors"? From the "micro" to the "macro" level, one can draw up a lengthy inventory of logical candidates.

Individuals Although most international theorists would probably reject the notion that individuals are international actors (somewhat as nearly all legal authorities have denied them any status as subjects of international law), a classical liberal would argue that the individual should be the foundation for any social theory, since only individuals are real, while society is an abstraction. Although few theorists would agree with that position, and most would probably tend to think that social forces produce the heroic figure more often than the other way around, it cannot be denied that scholars in the fields of history, politics, and international relations do pay attention to leaders who have played a prominent role on the world stage. Moreover, those who survey, for example, the attitudes of voters on international issues are, for all practical purposes, placing the individual at the center of their investigations. It bears repeating, however, that most theorists do not do this, but subsume individuals into a nation-state or other organizational context.

Subnational Groups   These may take many forms: political parties; the communications media; and organized interest groups of a nongovernmental nature that seek to influence foreign policies by lobbying or shaping public opinion. These actors fall primarily within the scope of foreign policy studies, national and comparative. International theorists, however, while not placing them at the center of their attention, are obliged to recognize their relevance because of the undoubtedly significant linkage between domestic and international politics. Numerous important examples will come to mind if one thinks about the implications of the Iran-arms-hostages-Contras affair and the Greenpeace incident, the relation between media coverage and international terrorism, the effect upon foreign policies of governmental changes as a result of elections in democratic countries, and the impact that ethnic minorities can have in parliamentary systems upon the foreign policies of their countries, as for example when Greek constituents prompted Congress to cut off aid to Turkey for having invaded Cyprus in 1974—and in Gorbachev's Soviet Union.

Nation-states   Realist theorists subscribe to what is called the "state-centric" view of international relations, focusing upon the action of states and governments. They recognize other realities mentioned in this inventory, and take them into account as appropriate, but insist that all others, whether less or more extensive, are subordinate to nation-states, which are the principal actors at the international level. In recent centuries, the world was divided into imperialist powers and colonial territories or protectorates. The number of states claiming to be legally sovereign and politically independent has increased steadily in this century: Whereas there were only about 60 in the 1930s, there are more than 160 as we move into the decade of the 1990s. Throughout the various eras of history, the patterns of political organization have always reflected some relationship with political, military, economic, technological, cultural, and other forms of power (including religious and psychological). Realists do not assert that currently existing nation-state structures will endure forever, but they have no doubt that those structures are now firmly entrenched and are likely to constitute the basic units of international political reality for a long time to come.[64] Non-state actors derive their significance from states or from the degree to which they can influence the policies and behavior of states.

Transnational Groups and Organizations Not Made Up of States   This category includes all entities—political, religious, economic-commercial, and so on—that operate transnationally (across one or more international boundaries) but do not have governments or their formal representatives as members. For centuries the Catholic church was recognized as an indisputable example. In more recent times the category has included the World Zionist Organization, Communist parties, or national liberation movements that follow orders from foreign headquarters (Moscow, Beijing, or Havana, for example), the Palestine Liberation Organization (PLO), international terrorist groups (such as Haerzbollah), international arms dealers, and many international nongovernmental organizations.[65] In recent years there has been a growing awareness of Islamic fundamentalism (with its center in Shi'ite Iran) as a force of considerable transnational potential, regardless of the fact that historically Islam has not been characterized by either a priesthood or a hierarchical organization.

Among the transnational phenomena that have attracted academic attention during the last two decades is the multinational corporation (MNC)—a term that has been subjected to a variety of subtle definitional refinements by other scholars.[66] Multinational corporations, in contrast to nation-states, regard boundaries and territory as irrelevant. Despite the amount of concern expressed over their potential for politically intervening in host countries (especially in the Third World), they are primarily interested in profits rather than politics, except insofar as the latter affects the former. Apart from the deductive literature on dependency and interdependence (to be discussed below) and the limited number of case studies of specific MNCs in specific countries, there has not yet been an impressive amount of scientific research on the role of MNCs in the international political system, on their political power in comparison with that of host states, and on the degree to which they are controllable or uncontrollable by home countries, host countries, or international organizations. Much of the debate has been normative, turning on whether MNCs have been beneficial or harmful to less developed countries (or less advantaged social classes) in the Third World, a subject to be treated in greater detail in Chapter 6. There can be no doubt, however, that General Motors, Westinghouse, Royal Dutch Shell, British Petroleum, SONY, Volkswagen, and International Telephone and Telegraph are important transnational firms and international actors.

International Groups and Organizations with States or Their Representatives as Members   These include such principal universal international actors in this century as the League of Nations, the United Nations, and the World Court, as well as such specialized agencies as the United Nations Educational, Scientific and Cultural Organization (UNESCO); the World Health Organization (WHO); the Food and Agriculture Organization (FAO); the International Bank for Reconstruction and Development (IBRD); the International Monetary Fund (IMF); the International Civil Aviation Organization (ICAO); the International Telecommunications Union (ITU); the International Fund for Agricultural Development (IFAD); and other intergovernmental bodies that report to the UN Economic and Social Council. A study by the Union of International Associations estimated that the number of national representatives of more than 110 countries in more than 2,100 international organizations exceeded 54,000.[67] Most of these carry on routine administrative activities that do not attract the interest of the international theorist. On those occasions, however, when Arab and other countries attempt to expel Israel from UNESCO, or when the ICAO debates what to do about the hijacking of aircraft by terrorists, or when the adequacy of the IAEA safeguards system becomes an issue in regard to compliance with the provisions of the Non-Proliferation Treaty, the specialized agencies are removed from obscurity into the spotlight of international politics, and become for a time at least "bit players" if not full-fledged actors.

The International System   At the most comprehensive and abstract level, we come to the international or global system, which will receive detailed treatment in Chapter 4. The systems analyst contemplates the whole rather than focusing on the component parts (described in the five previous sections). In this global scheme, specific nation-states and other international actors are not absent, but they are present in blurred rather than sharp outline. J. David Singer has noted that the nation-state model produces richer descriptions and causal explanations (e.g., of how and why specific wars begin), whereas the systemic model is more conducive to broader generalizations about how all states normally behave. Singer sees Morgenthau's thesis that states seek their national interest defined in terms of power as a systemic theory, a general rule to which one might be able to find some exceptions that do not vitiate the rule.[68]

Generally speaking, those who favor an international systems level approach are convinced that the international system exerts a more profound effect upon the component parts than the other way around. This, of course, is a modern version of the ancient philosophical problem known as the "one and the many," one of those profound and recurring problems that seem always to defy solution but that make the intellectual life fascinating. In earlier historical periods, it was possible to recognize partial international systems (e.g., the Greek city-states, and the European balance-of-power system), but political communities could scarcely be said to be aware of the existence of a "global system" in the sense in which we now use that term. In fact, it is difficult to say precisely when the development of communications technology made possible the emergence of a truly global system. Nevertheless, it cannot be denied that the impact of "global" factors upon component units is perceived increasingly to be the international reality as we approach the close of the twentieth century.

There is no "official" list of international actors, nor can one be compiled. Realists continue to concentrate on the nation-state as the central figure in the *dramatis personae*. The nation-state is assumed to be a unitary, rational actor pursuing its national interest (viewed in terms of power) within an anarchical society, a system of self-help in which security remains the primary concern. Pluralists who study multinational corporations, international organizations, terrorist groups, and the burgeoning importance of economic interdependence insist that the realists are too narrow and single-minded in their approach, if not absolutist and simplistic. Foreign policy decisions that affect the international system are not really taken by nation-states, which are abstractions "reified" by the realists. Instead, decisions are taken by groups or individuals who can act with the authority of the state.[69] Moreover, they contend, many significant decisions are taken outside the framework of nation-states—by international organizations or by multinational corporations (which, invested with formidable economic resources, may pursue policies different from those of their home governments).[70] Marxists and many international systems analysts are convinced that global structures and processes (whether "capitalist" or other) predominate over those of states and that only the global system, therefore, is a worthy object of serious investigation.[71]

The international systems level provides a neat, manageable yet comprehensive model that assigns homogeneous goals to all national actors, but it also gives rise to simplistic images of "look-alike" nation-states, while underestimating their differences and exaggerating the degree to which the total system determines member/actor behavior. Focusing on the nation-states, by way of contrast, enables us to see the unique characteristics and situational circumstances of the actors, but it also involves the risk of excessive differentiation, which may obscure the general patterns for which the theorist is searching. Analyses of the international system and of the individual states as units focus on different, equally legitimate questions. Such questions cannot be adequately addressed except with different kinds of studies from one level to another. One question to be asked is "Which kind of actors are most important in the global system?" A second is "What kind of factors—characteristics of individual leaders, the differing structures of states, or states' relationships to the system—are the most important in their impact on the policies of states?" A third is "What is the relationship between studies that focus on different levels—that is, on different social entities? For example, what can one infer about the behavior of individual states from studies that focus on the entire international system?" States are undoubtedly the most important kind of entity, but that does not detract from the fact that their behavior may be most importantly influenced by individual leader characteristics or international system structure, or from the fact that studies on different levels are equally legitimate, while addressing different questions. Balance-of-power systems have operated for thousands of years, for example, and have operated in similar ways independent of the importance of states or of the aims of the constituent units. Basic to such analysis is the question of what is the logical relationship between system-level and national-level studies, and what inferences from one level can be made about another. Equally important is the question of which social entities (individuals, states, or the entire international system) one should look to for factors that have the greatest impact on the behavior of states. Stated somewhat differently, what independent variables at the international level shape the behavior of individual actors? What independent variables below the level of the state shape its foreign policies?

Politics, Economics, and Interdependence   Since World War II, the study of international relations in American universities has usually been organized within departments of political science, or else those departments have played a pivotal role in interdisciplinary programs. Political scientists traditionally have focused their attention on the policies and actions of governments, but in recent decades they have become interested in a broader range of phenomena that influence and are influenced by politics and diplomacy. In the international no less than the domestic field the tendency has been to expand the concept of "the political" to include trends in economics, science and technology, and even education, culture, and religion. Today, "international relations" encompass the operations of multinational corporations, trade balances, fluctuations in the value of currencies, satellite communications, the superconductivity revolution, environmental pollution, Islamic fundamentalism, and the Olympic Games insofar as they have political aspects.

No sensible observer would deny that the world has become progressively integrated in this century as a result of economic and technological developments that link together all parts of the global system. It has not become politically or culturally integrated, however. Indeed, many nations, regions, and subnational groups have sought to resist or limit integrative processes (discussed in Chapter 10) by asserting their own identity and independence against larger unifying or centralizing forces.[72] The powerful new transnational forces that have emerged on the international scene in the last quarter-century give rise to concern because it has not yet proved possible to subject them to control or regulation by effective political authority. One of the most frequently cited modern definitions of "politics"—that of David Easton, who described the process as that whereby societal values are authoritatively allocated[73]—is simply not suited to the international dimension. Since it presupposes the organization of a society under effective authority able to take decisions on values and priorities by way of the budget process, and able to enforce its laws by holding in the background the threat of sanctions, the model of the national political system cannot be extended to the international realm because there is no effective authority in existence at this level. Easton himself admitted that "decisions and actions performed by international systems rely for their acceptance upon accord with the perceived self-interest of the participating members" among whom "the impact of a sense of legitimacy is still extremely low."[74] Raymond Aron, Stanley Hoffmann, Roger D. Masters, Kenneth N. Waltz, and several other theorists in the realist school have frequently warned against losing sight of the crucial difference between national societies in which values, law, and power are often quite highly centralized, and the international system in which they are so decentralized that each state, taking into account its own interest, can decide which norms it will observe and which ones it will ignore.[75]

During the last fifteen years, several international theorists have sought to bridge the wide gap, as it were, between national and international systems, between the political and economic orders, and between the realists and pluralists/globalists by spotlighting the concepts of "interdependence" and "international regimes." Both concepts will be discussed more fully in the chapters on realism and systems. Here it is sufficient to note that "interdependence" carries the connotation that nation-states are becoming increasingly sensitive and vulnerable to economic-technological changes in other nation-states and in the global system as a whole, and that they are slowly adjusting their policies accordingly.[76] International regimes, discussed more fully in Chapter 3, are those sets of governing arrangements—procedures, norms, rules, and, in some cases, special functional institutions—designed to regulate and control certain kinds of transnational activity, where such regulation and control would seem to be a matter of common interest (or at least coincident interest) among several or many states.[77] Examples would be the international regimes designed to manage monetary rates (in the International Monetary Fund), to remove impediments to international trade (in the periodically revised General Agreement on International trade, or GATT, which began its eighth round of negotiations in Punta del Este in 1986), and to prevent the proliferation of nuclear weapons through the Non-Proliferation Treaty, the safeguards system of the International Agency for Atomic Energy (IAEA), and various agreements among nuclear-supplier countries to regulate their exports.

The Controversy Between Traditionalists and Behaviorists

The 1960s witnessed a "great debate" between traditional advocates of a "classical" approach to international relations and those who preferred the methods of the newer behavioral sciences that placed emphasis on quantification. Both schools, as Norman Palmer noted, tended at that time to accept the basic assumptions of state-centric realism.[78] The acerbity of that debate has now worn off, and the controversy seems less relevant in the contemporary field of international relations theory. At the time, however, it reflected a fundamental dichotomy in the American discipline of political science that disturbed Europeans. A summary of the principal arguments on each side can still contribute to an understanding of how our field has developed. The two perspectives are less polarized than they once were, but by no means can they be said to have merged synthetically.

Hedley Bull called "classical" that "approach to theorizing that derives from philosophy, history, and law, and that is characterized above all by explicit reliance upon the exercise of judgment and by the assumption that if we confine ourselves to strict standards of verification and proof there is very little of significance that can be said about international relations."[79] Traditionalists are usually skeptical of the effort to predict or to apply probability analysis to human affairs. They will occasionally use quantitative data to illustrate a point they are trying to make in an otherwise discursive presentation, but they are critical of the proclivity of some contemporary analysts to quantify in order to demonstrate by tortuous statistical analysis a proposition that ought to be obvious to a person of common sense. Traditionalists are typically but not rigidly interested in the single and unique event, case, situation, or problem, which they seek to understand in the subtlety of detail, including relationships with other relevant phenomena. Often the traditionalist will study several cases of a similar nature, drawing appropriate comparisons and contrasts along the way. (Scientists, too, of course, may rely on a small number of case studies to develop, illustrate, or test a general model.) Traditionalists would insist that they are at least as meticulous in gathering, sifting, weighing, and interpreting evidence as any social scientists. They would not deny that they make use of judgment, intuition, and insight in arriving at their conclusions, after having reviewed and digested all the data that they deem relevant and reliable.

The behavioral-quantifying approach places considerable emphasis upon what it regards as scientifically precise methods. Different social scientists stress different methods or combinations of methods—attitude surveys, content analysis, simulation and gaming, statistical correlations, model-building, and the use of quantitative analysis as well as computers as a basis for achieving precision in measurement.[80] The scientific approach is not to be fully equated with quantitative methodology, but the latter is much more likely to be employed, and certain to be utilized on a grander scale, in the scientific than in the traditional approach. Although scientific scholars cannot avoid using personal judgment in the selection of their problems, the formulation of their hypotheses, and the development of their classification schemes, they attempt to go beyond personal judgments and to launch into deductive or inductive methods that are independent of personal bias,[81] and that invoke either logic or mathematics to serve as substitutes for intuitive interpretation.

The traditionalist often criticizes the behavioralist for allegedly being too confident of the ability to generalize, to convert problematic statements into causal propositions, and to use these propositions to predict behavior in an area in which things are not predictable; for attributing to abstract models a congruence with reality that they do not have; for avoiding the substantive issues of international politics because, in the zeal for scientific method, he or she may never have really mastered those issues in all their complexity; and for succumbing to a "fetish for measurement" that ignores crucially important qualitative differences among the quantities being measured.[82]

Behavioralists assert that when they test for statistical correlation between two factors, they are determining whether the relationship between the two might be merely coincidental, and when they engage in multivariate analysis they are trying to find out which of several factors constitutes the most reliable predictor of a particular outcome.[83] The scientific analyst regards the traditionalist's distrust of precise method, quantification, and verification through statistical testing as irresponsible and arrogant.[84] Traditionalists retort that in their own way they perform a careful "content analysis" of the primary and secondary sources (documentary and otherwise) that they adduce as evidence—speeches, press statements, government reports, diplomatic messages, personal memoirs, newspaper accounts and commentaries, interviews, scholarly studies, and so on—and intuitively select what they deem important and relevant without a systematic counting of words and phrases. The traditionalist remains convinced that the *essence* of politics is the qualitative difference—that subtle shade or nuance of meaning that can be communicated in the choice of a single word or phrase but does not lend itself to quantification.

TRADITIONAL THEORY: BALANCE OF POWER

The oldest, most persistent, and most controversial of all theories of international politics—the balance of power—was recognized at least implicitly in ancient India and in ancient Greece, although it was never formally articulated. David Hume noted that although the term *balance of power* may be modern, "the maxim of preserving the balance of power is founded so much on common sense and obvious reasoning that it is impossible it could altogether have escaped antiquity," concluding that it had been practiced from ancient times to the eighteenth century.[85]

Insofar as it could be called a formal theory of international politics, the modern concept of balance of power was associated with the Newtonian conception of a universe in equilibrium. (Frequently a social science theory has been adapted from a physical science theory or at least influenced by development of one.) Actually, the notion of equilibrium is basic to many sciences. Chemists speak of a solution in stable equilibrium. Economists perceive a balance of countervailing forces, such as supply and demand. Biologists warn against human activities that disturb the "balance of nature" between organisms and environment. Political writers often analyze the interaction of interest groups or of governmental branches within national society in terms of "checks and balances."[86] Naturally, theorists of international social reality employ "balance" as a central organizing concept for the power relations of nation-states, and then assume that the latter are driven, almost by a law of their own nature, to seek their security by some form of power-balancing.

Balance of Power: Problems and Definition

The term *balance of power* has been roundly criticized for causing considerable semantic confusion. Ernst B. Haas found at least eight distinct meanings for the term: (1) any distribution of power, (2) equilibrium or balancing process, (3) hegemony or the search for hegemony, (4) stability and peace in a concert of power, (5) instability and war, (6) power politics in general, (7) a universal law of history, and (8) a system and guide to policymakers.[87] "The trouble with the balance of power," says Inis L. Claude, Jr., "is not that it has no meaning, but that it has too many meanings." The term has been used to connote equilibrium and disequilibrium, or any distribution of power whether balanced or unbalanced, or as both policy and system (either automatic and self-regulating or wholly dependent upon manipulation by shrewd statesmen). Claude concludes that the concept of the balance of power is extremely difficult to analyze because those who write about it not only fail to provide precise clues as to its meaning but often "slide blissfully from one usage of the term to another and back again, frequently without posting any warning that plural meanings exist."[88]

It is true that the concept of balance of power is riddled with ambiguity. Many statesmen have sought a unilateral superiority rather than an objective bilateral balance with their principal rival. Nevertheless, it is theoretically possible to conceive of the balance of power as a situation or condition, as a universal tendency or law of state behavior, as a guide for statesmanship, and as a mode of system-maintenance characteristic of certain types of international systems. As long as we think in terms of equilibrium rather than of superiority, these four usages need not be inconsistent with each other.

Conceived as a situation or a condition, balance of power implies an objective arrangement in which there is relatively widespread satisfaction with the distribution of power. The universal tendency or law describes a probability, and enables one to predict, that members of a system threatened by the emergence of a "disturber of the balance"—that is, a power seemingly bent upon establishing an international hegemony—will form a countervailing coalition. Balance of power as a policy guide prescribes to statesmen who would act "rationally" that they should maintain eternal vigilance and be prepared to organize a countervailing coalition against the disrupter of equilibrium. Balance of power as a system refers to a multinational society in which all essential actors preserve their identity, integrity, and independence through the balancing process.[89]

Balance of Power: Purposes and Functions

Various purposes and functions were attributed to the balance of power in classical theory as expounded by Bolingbroke, Gentz, Metternich, and Castlereagh. It was supposed to (1) prevent the establishment of a universal hegemony, (2) preserve the constituent elements of the system and the system itself, (3) ensure stability and mutual security in the international system, and (4) strengthen and prolong the peace by deterring war, that is, by confronting an aggressor with the likelihood that a policy of expansion would meet with the formation of a countercoalition. The traditional methods and techniques of maintaining or restoring the balance were (1) the policy of divide and rule (working to diminish the weight of the heavier side), (2) territorial compensations after a war, (3) creation of buffer states, (4) the formation of alliances, (5) spheres of influence, (6) intervention, (7) diplomatic bargaining, (8) legal and peaceful settlement of disputes, (9) reduction of armaments, (10) armaments competition or races, and (11) war itself.

A review of the list of objectives and methods will show that there were internal inconsistencies in the theory and in the practice. These were probably unavoidable, given the historic oscillation between stable and unstable equilibria within the nation-state system. If the balance of power had worked perfectly as all statesmen expected, and if the existing distribution of power had posed no threat to their national security, then the balance of power as situation, law, policy, and system would almost certainly have contributed to the prolongation of peace. But the dynamics of the international political system were conducive neither to serene stability nor to prudent rational decision-making at all times. Moreover, statesmen pursuing only what they considered their own legitimate national interest—a term closely associated with the balance-of-power system—may have appeared in the eyes of other statesmen as conspiring to overturn the international system and gain predominance. Conversely, a government embarked upon a hegemonial path might not provoke the formation of a countercoalition until it was too late to prevent a large-scale war declared to restore the balance. In theory the balance helped preserve the peace and identity of member-states, but in practice balance-of-power policy sometimes led to war and to the partitioning of "less essential" actors (such as Poland in the 1790s). But keeping the peace and preserving all the lesser members intact were subordinate to the more fundamental aims of preserving the multistate system by observing the maxim expressed by Friedrich Gentz: "That if the states system of Europe is to exist and be maintained by common exertions no one of its members must ever become so powerful as to be able to coerce all the rest put together."[90]

Another key concept in the classical theory must be mentioned. Under normal circumstances, with several nations seeking to maximize their power position through the various methods and techniques of balance-of-power politics, no one nation gains hegemony, and a precarious equilibrium is maintained. But for various reasons the balance might be on the verge of breaking down. At this point an impartial and vigilant "holder of the balance" emerges, which is strong enough to restore the balance swiftly once it is disturbed. Historically, England played this role in the European state system. In a famous memorandum published on January 1, 1907, Sir Eyre Crowe wrote that it had "become almost a historical truism to identify England's secular policy with the maintenance of this balance by throwing her weight now in this scale and now in that, but ever on the side opposed to the political dictatorship of the strongest single state or group at a given time.[91] Winston Churchill reiterated this as a fundamental tenet of British foreign policy in 1936.[92] Perhaps the theory of the balance of power, as a policy guide to statesmen, is a distinctively British theory, at least in modern times.

Critiques of Balance of Power

In recent decades, the balance-of-power theory has encountered much criticism even from traditional analysts, and for reasons other than the semantic vagueness mentioned earlier. Nicholas J. Spykman held that the theory inadequately explained the practice:

> The truth of the matter is that states are interested only in a balance (imbalance) which is in their favor. Not an equilibrium, but a generous margin is their objective. There is no real security in being just as strong as a potential enemy; there is security only in being a little stronger. There is no possibility of action if one's strength is fully checked; there is a chance for a positive foreign policy only if there is a margin of force which can be freely used.[93]

Hans J. Morgenthau finds the balance of power deficient on several grounds. It has failed on a number of occasions since the end of the eighteenth century to preserve the independent existence of states. The multistate system precluding a single state from achieving universal dominion has been preserved only at the price of frequent and costly wars. He finds the balance of power (1) *uncertain* because no completely reliable means of measuring, evaluating, and comparing power exist; (2) *unreal* because statesmen try to compensate for its uncertainty by aiming for superiority; and (3) *inadequate* for explaining national restraint during most of the years from 1648 to 1914 because it does not give credit to the restraining influence of the basic intellectual unity and moral consensus then prevailing in Europe.[94]

Ernst B. Haas has observed that using the balance of power as a policy guide assumes a high degree of flexibility in national decision-making. The vigilant political leader must engage in a constant power calculus and be ready to enter into a countervailing coalition, regardless of ideological differences, economic interests, and domestic political attitudes. Haas had questioned the degree to which policymakers, especially in democratic countries, can enjoy the kind of flexibility that the balance-of-power theory would seem to demand.[95] It should be pointed out, however, that the Anglo-American democracies managed to overcome their aversion to Soviet communism in World War II against Nazi Germany, and in more recent decades the United States has apparently sought to play a balance-of-power game *vis-à-vis* the People's Republic of China and the Soviet Union.

Kenneth N. Waltz has defended the balance-of-power theory against critics who, in his view, have misunderstood certain crucial points. Every theory, he argues, must begin with some assumptions. He assumes that states are unitary actors that seek, at a minimum, to preserve themselves and, at a maximum, to dominate others if possible. They strive to achieve their objectives through internal efforts (e.g., increasing capabilities) and external efforts (e.g., strengthening their own alliance and weakening that of the adversary). He then adds the condition that states are operating in a self-help system with no superior referee. Those who do not help themselves as well as others do will become disadvantaged. Assumptions, Waltz points out, are neither true nor false, but they are essential for the construction of a theory. In Waltz's theory of structural realism, the balance of power is rooted inescapably and necessarily in the international system of states. Thus he parts company with other theorists of the balance of power—Hume, Churchill, Organski, Morgenthau, Haas, Kissinger, and others—who have held that the balance-of-power policy is something to be followed voluntarily by wise and prudent political leaders. For Waltz, the tendency toward equilibrium is automatic, regardless of whether "some or all states consciously aim to establish and maintain a balance, or whether some or all states aim for universal domination." If the results to be produced (i.e., balance) depend upon some or all states' consciously working for it, then international politics can be explained by theories of national bureaucratic policymaking, and an international balance-of-power theory would have nothing to explain. Waltz wants a theory applicable to the international system irrespective of the behavior of particular states.[96]

Balance of Power: Contemporary Models

Even aside from Waltz's trenchant analysis, it would be erroneous to suggest that the balance-of-power theory is obsolete. Several "modern," "nontraditional," and "scientific" theoreticians have found it to be worthy of attention. Morton A. Kaplan makes it one of his six heuristic models of international systems. He devotes more space to the balance-of-power system with its essential rules than to any of the other systems.[97] (For a discussion of Kaplan's system models, see Chapter 4.) Arthur Lee Burns, after studying the problem of the system in stable balance, concludes that "the most stable arrangement would seem to be a world of five or some greater odd number of Powers, independent and of approximately equal strength," since these would not be readily divisible into two equal sides.[98] For simplicity in calculating relationships, and for the certainty and stability that such simplicity would yield, Burns holds that, optimally, the most stable system would be a world of "five roughly equal blocs, each including a family of exchangeable client nations."[99]

More recently, R. Harrison Wagner has argued that any number of actors from two through five can produce a stable system, but that the most stable system is one with three actors.[100] Several analysts in the field of nuclear deterrence and arms control theory have updated and cast into highly sophisticated forms the categories of balance-of-power thinking.[101] And although many intellectuals and academicians regard the balance-of-power theory as a crude, unsophisticated, naively simplistic, or obsolete theory of international politics, large numbers of statesmen, politicians, diplomats, pundits, journalists, and people-in-the-street still regard it as an adequate explanation of what actually happens in the international system and the basis on which foreign policy ought to be formulated and conducted. The theory retains a charm and a validity for analysts of strategic arms limitations and the relationship of the United States, the Soviet Union, China, Western Europe, Japan, and other power centers in the global system.

A Case Study in Quantitative Methodology

During the past three decades, scholars have turned to the computer, with its capacity for the statistical manipulation of vast amounts of data, for the building of theories of international relations. "Quantitative international relations," according to Harvey Starr, "does not constitute a substantive subfield of international relations, but merely a common methodological approach to the diverse substance that makes up international relations."[102] Using the computer can greatly speed up the performance of complex statistical analyses and may even suggest correlations that might not otherwise have occurred to scholars. Advanced technologies of information storage and retrieval, as well as of data analysis, have already enhanced our ability to manipulate huge amounts of data. Some writers have suggested that the time has come to establish a global monitoring system for the international measurement of various phenomena.[103] Throughout this book, we shall have occasion to refer to the use of quantitative methods in several areas of theory-building—for example, integration, arms races, and decision-making. Here, we discuss just one case to illustrate the utility of the computer in our field—in analyzing the relationship between intranational and international conflict.

In a project designed to find recurrent political patterns within and between nations, Rudolph J. Rummel collected data for 236 variables about 82 nations for the year 1955. These data were analyzed through a technique known as factor analysis.[104] In the first phase of the Dimensionality of Nations (DON) Project, three separate analyses were applied to the data: (1) the foreign conflict behavior variables were intercorrelated and factor-analyzed separately, (2) the foreign conflict behavior variables were regressed upon dimensions of national characteristics and domestic conflict dimensions (to "regress" means to determine how well data on one variable can be predicted from data on a set of variables), and (3) the foreign conflict and domestic conflict variables were factor-analyzed together.

Of the 236 variables, 94 were measures of such aspects of international relations as trade, membership in international organizations, treaties signed, aid given and received, and votes with the United States in the United Nations.

It was found that conflict behavior did not correlate with the degree of a nation's involvement in foreign affairs. Stated differently, nations may be heavily engaged in foreign affairs without necessarily resorting to conflict. In factor analysis of all variables, domestic conflict variables appeared in patterns distinct from foreign conflict variables.

However, these conclusions were based upon a method that does not differentiate among the nations under consideration. Jonathan Wilkenfeld reevaluated Rummel's data using a different method that involved "the rearrangement of the nations under consideration into groups, according to type of nation, in an effort to determine whether type of nation has any bearing on the relationship between internal and external behavior.[105] A group of 74 nations was divided into three groups, based on differences in leadership: personalist (or dictatorial), centrist (centralized government), and polyarchic. All possible pairs of domestic conflict between domestic and foreign conflict behavior dimensions were correlated for these groups. Moreover, the possibility of time lags was considered. The results indicated that there is a relationship between internal and external conflict behavior. The nature of the relationship depends upon the type of nation and the dimension of conflict: "As we shift our attention from the personalist, to the centrist, and finally to the polyarchic group, the particular dimensions of conflict behavior which are related change. Indeed, there is no one particular relationship between any pair of internal and external conflict dimensions which holds for all groups equally well. . . . Nations in the international system do not behave solely on the basis of the givens of the international situation. Depending upon the type of nation, we must look beyond the international sphere to the internal situation in the participating nation, to determine that nation's reaction."[106]

Rummel owes a considerable intellectual debt to Quincy Wright, who developed a field theory for the analysis of international relations. Field theory, which had its origins in physics, had been taken over into psychology by Kurt Lewin, who influenced Wright.[107] The field theorist emphasizes the total situation or "life space" of organism-in-environment viewed as a constellation of interdependent factors. Wright, Rummel, and other international field theorists view the behavior of nations in relation to similarities and differences in national attributes—all within the context of a geographic-social field defined by time-space coordinates. Wright's geographic-social field represents a description of the real world, with its distribution of population, resources, agricultural and industrial production, and political and economic power, as well as their changes over time. Wright overlays the geographic-social field with an analytic one consisting of values and capabilities, because he assumes that decision-makers formulate and pursue policies (both foreign and domestic) that relate values to capabilities. By locating each state or other acting unit at a point in these multidimensional fields that reflects to each coordinate employed its position in respect to each field, Wright seeks not only to describe the international field at any moment in history, but also to provide a basis for explaining the past and predicting the future.[108] In the value field, for example, Wright's coordinates define a range of behavior from a narrow to a broad conception of national interest, from the politics of passivity to strategies of foreign intervention.[109]

Field theorists assume that systems of action within each field may move over time to new positions in the field and thus form new relationships with each other. Field theory is essentially a form of spatial analysis in which relative position accessibility, connectivity, and the direction of movement are studied. R. J. Rummel in particular stresses attribute distance as a central concept, because "nation attribute similarities and differences are field forces creating social space-time motion; attribute distance between nations cause international behavior."[110]

In Rummel's study, the foreign conflict variables were regressed upon other dimensions of national characteristics. The findings were that the magnitude of a nation's characteristics or attributes has little relationship to its foreign conflict behavior. In other words, such factors as the level of economic or technological development, international communications, totalitarianism, power, instability, military capabilities, ideology, or values of any individual nation were not found to correlate importantly with its foreign conflict behavior.

Can There Be a "Scientific" International Theory?

The meaning of "scientific" is relative. The term *science* connotes nothing more than a body of knowledge and a way of discovering new knowledge. Whatever satisfies intelligent human beings in any age as the optimum means of enlarging their intellectual frontiers will pass muster as "scientific."

Genuine scientific progress is usually made when one starts out by accepting that knowledge of the field already generally accepted by scholars. Individuals may wish to reorganize somewhat the existing body of knowledge to enhance their own working comprehension of it. But the individual must take something as given—something already based upon empirical observation, experience, and human reflection. If learning is social, the individual cannot begin every day to create the universe *de novo*.

Once the investigator has mastered the existing knowledge, and organized it for his or her purposes, the investigator pleads a "meaningful ignorance": "Here is what I know; what do I not know that is worth knowing?" This is a very important question. Once an area has been selected for investigation, the question should be posed as clearly as possible, and it is here that quantification can prove useful,[111] provided that mathematical methods are combined with carefully constructed taxonomic schemes. Achieving a satisfactory merger of appropriate tools of statistical analysis with solid typologies is one of the most difficult aspects of formulating a worthwhile and testable hypothesis in the realm of political reality, where the names we call things and the words we use are of crucial importance. Surveying the field of international relations, or any sector of it, we see many disparate elements and keep sifting them through various permutations in our minds, wondering whether there may be any significant relationships between A and B or between B and C. By a process that we are compelled to call "intuition" until we learn much more about it than we now know, we perceive a possible correlation, hitherto unsuspected or not firmly known, between two or more elements. At this point, we have the ingredients of a hypothesis that can be expressed in measurable referents and that, if validated, would be both explanatory and predictive. (In the strictest scientific sense, what we cannot predict we cannot fully explain,[112] but that is an extremely demanding criterion of explanation in the social sciences.)

From here on, the scientific method becomes more familiar. The hypothesis must be tested. This demands the construction of an experiment or the gathering of data in other ways. In either case every effort must be made to eliminate the influence of the unknown, and to make certain that the evidence sought pertains to the hypothesis and to nothing else. The results of the data-gathering effort are carefully observed, recorded, and analyzed, after which the hypothesis is discarded, modified, reformulated, or confirmed. Findings are published, and others are invited to repeat, or replicate, this knowledge-discovering adventure, and to conform or deny. This, very roughly, is what we usually mean by "the scientific method." At every step of the way there is emphasis upon precision of thought and language and upon a distinction between what is assumed and what is empirically testable.

Application of scientific method during the past 250 years has produced impressive results in the physical sciences in the form of generalized laws. In physics, astrophysics, chemistry, biology, and certain areas of psychology a high degree of predictability has been achieved. But even the "exact" sciences, with all their powerful methodologies, reach limits to what can be known at any given moment. According to Werner Heisenberg's principle of indeterminacy, for example, it is not possible to determine simultaneously both the position and the movement of a particle of matter.[113] In all the sciences, physical and social, we find that our efforts to measure a phenomenon may dislocate or change the thing we are trying to measure.

The Search for Recurring Patterns

Anyone claiming to be a "scientific" theorist, whether "traditional" or future-oriented "behaviorist," is bound to search for regularities. But we should remember that there are peculiar difficulties confronting all social scientists, and if we keep these in mind we are more likely to make intellectual progress than if we ignore or forget them.

The social scientist studying human affairs encounters problems concerning the relation of the observer to the observed to a greater degree than the scientist studying atoms, molecules, or stars. The physical scientist requires certain instruments and techniques that are fairly standardized and that work in the same way for all. Physical scientists, no matter how excited they might be about their work, usually avoid the kind of emotional involvement with the observed phenomenon that might influence their perception and their judgment. In the investigation of human society, objective observation is much more likely to be infused with subjective purpose. A physicist or a chemist who happens to be an ardent pacifist in personal outlook is not prone to be swayed by this conviction in the analytic approach to the more fissionable atoms as compared with other atoms. But social scientists who have strong preconceptions about such subjects as war, guerrilla terrorism, national values, world population and hunger, disarmament, and international organization or the conflict between democracies and dictatorships are much more likely to run into difficulty in their efforts to achieve the complete detachment that the scientific method presupposes. (There is, in the view of the authors, no need for social scientists to apologize for this "human involvement.") Although the method is supposed to be "value-free," the phenomenon being examined is often overladen with value implications that influence the intellectual and psychological set of the observer-analyst. Social scientists hardly agree on which of these two attitudes produces the greater perceptual distortion in the study, let us say, of the problems of war and peace: a purely neutral or nonethical desire to "understand" human aggressiveness for the purpose of explaining it and predicting its manifestations, or a moral commitment to study war with a view toward abolishing it in order to make the world a better place. Undoubtedly the effort to build a scientific international theory will continue to be characterized by the interpenetration of these two distinct purposes, both within individual minds and within the field as a whole.[114]

The peculiarities of the observer-observed relationship in the social sciences give rise to additional difficulties. Some of these are well known and frequently cited, such as the inability to conduct controlled experiments in order to isolate the factors being studied. Even the most ruthless totalitarian regime, whatever the efficiency of the technical means of social control at its disposal, would be extremely hard pressed to conduct a strictly controlled scientific experiment with a single nation, not to mention two or more. The point is that in attempting to study any large social aggregates scientifically, the conditions of control for the sake of exactitude must be established primarily through the clarification of one's own thought processes, rather than in the confusing and uncontrollable social universe.

Other problems are less readily recognized. Given the comprehensibility of the field, the sheer mass of pertinent data seems to exceed the bounds of human mastery. Many data are inaccessible and remain so either for a very long time (in governmental archives) or forever (in the minds of individuals who forget or die before they transmit to scholars all that they know about what really happened). The scholar and theorist, therefore, often arrive at generalized conclusions from sketchy evidence that might be unreliable on grounds quite apart from its incompleteness.

Finally, we come to the problem of language, in which all theory must be couched. Even the exact sciences have not been immune from difficulties in relating language to observation, or verbal symbols to experience. It is inaccurate to say that the exact sciences require quantitative symbols, whereas the social sciences rely on qualitative symbols: Every physical science and every social science require some empirical foundation, and the method is not empirical unless it entails the essential functions of naming and counting. In all the sciences, counting is a very simple thing. An important separator between the physical sciences and the social sciences is the realm of qualitative language, or the naming process. No one debates the meaning of such terms as *liquid, vapor, magnetic, electrically charged, sodium chloride,* or *nuclear fission.* But in analyzing the social universe, we constantly face terms such as *democratic, aggressive, revolutionary, illegal, discriminatory,* and *violent.* Not one of these terms is invested with scientific objectivity. Thus although all social scientists can count, and a great many understand the process of statistically correlating dependent and independent variables, or of performing factor analysis, there is reason to believe that the basis of agreement on what is being counted or measured in the field of international relations is very narrow and precarious indeed.

CONCLUSION

Our purpose in this chapter has been to show generally how the study of international relations has evolved, in order to set the stage for examining the major theories, past and present, in detail.

In Quincy Wright's major work, *A Study of International Relations,* after admitting that international relations is still "an emerging discipline manifesting little unity from the point of view of method and logic,"[115] he suggests that the field might best be understood if approached through four basic intellectual perspectives. In his opinion, all social reality can be conveniently divided into four categories: (1) the *actual* (what was or what is, known through the method of description); (2) the *possible* (what can be, known through the method of theoretical speculation); (3) the *probable* (what will be, known through the method of prediction); (4) the *desirable* (what ought to be, known through the method of ethical, valuational, or normative reflection). These four categories, says Wright, correspond to history, art, science, and philosophy.[116] The authors find this a categorization worth pondering—one that is useful in all the social sciences.

To sum up, the essential function of international theory is to enable us to improve our knowledge concerning international reality, whether for the sake of "pure understanding" or for the more active purpose of changing that reality. Theory helps us to order our existing knowledge and to discover new knowledge more efficiently. It provides a framework of thought in which we define research priorities and select the most appropriate available tools for the gathering and analysis of data. Theory directs our attention to significant similarities and differences, and suggests relationships not previously perceived. At its best, theory serves as a proof that the powers of the human mind have been applied to a problem at hand with prevision, imagination, and profundity, and this proof inspires others to further efforts for purposes either of agreeing or disagreeing.

There is no one model for theory. Social theorizing occurs at many levels and through many discipline-perspectives, with several experiments at interdisciplinary approaches under way. International theory, which goes beyond "foreign policy" theory, contains components that are descriptive, speculative, predictive, and normative. A single scholar may stress any one of these, but the more highly developed the field of international theory as a whole becomes, the more likely will it involve a synthesis of "what is," "what might be," "what probably will be," and "what ought to be." Good theory may be inductive or deductive; micro or macro; highly specific, midrange, or "grand" in the sense of being as comprehensive as the state of our knowledge at any given time permits and explaining as wide a number of phenomena with as few variables as possible. All of these approaches are valid and useful when handled with intelligence and methodological care and when applied to the appropriate level, or levels, of analysis in the study of international relations.

NOTES*

1. Thucydides, *The History of the Peloponnesian War,* trans. Rex Warner (Harmondsworth: Penguin Books, 1954). See also William T. Bluhm, *Theories of the Political System: Classics of Political Thought and Modern Political Analysis* (Englewood Cliffs, N.J.: Prentice-Hall, 1965), chap. II; John H. Finley, Jr., *Thucydides* (Cambridge: Harvard University Press, 1942); Charles Norris Cochrane, *Thucydides and the Science of History* (London: Oxford University Press, 1929); Peter J. Fliess, *Thucydides and the Politics of Bipolarity* (Baton Rouge: Louisiana State University Press, 1966).

---

*Editor's note: Harper & Row's policy is to cite the names of publishers in their contemporary form in most instances even though the original edition cited by the authors may have been published under a different company name.

2. Niccolo Machiavelli, *The Prince and the Discourses* (New York: Random House [Modern Library], 1940); James Burnham, *The Machiavellians* (New York: John Day, 1943); Herbert Butterfield, *The Statecraft of Machiavelli* (New York: Macmillan, 1956); Friedrich Meinecke, *Machiavellism: The Doctrine of Raison d'Etat and Its Place in Modern History,* trans. Douglas Scott (New Haven: Yale University Press, 1957).

3. Dante Alighieri, *On World Government,* trans. Herbert W. Schneider, 2nd ed. rev. (New York: Liberal Arts Press, 1957); Etienne Gilson, *Dante and Philosophy,* trans. David Moore (New York: Harper & Row [Torchbooks], 1963), part III.

4. See Daniel S. Cheever and H. Field Haviland, *Organizing for Peace* (Boston: Houghton Mifflin, 1954), chap. 2. For additional reading on the history of international political theory, see F. H. Hinsley, *Power and the Pursuit of Peace: Theory and Practice in the History of Relations Between States* (Cambridge: Cambridge University Press, 1967), pp. 13–149; Frank M. Russell, *Theories of International Relations* (New York: Appleton, 1936), pp. 99–113 and chap. XI; Kenneth N. Waltz, "Political Philosophy and the Study of International Relations," in William T. R. Fox, ed., *Theoretical Aspects of International Relations* (Notre Dame: University of Notre Dame Press, 1959).

5. Martin Wight, "Why Is There No International Theory?" *International Relations,* II (April 1960), 35–48, 62.

6. Ibid., pp. 37–38.

7. See in Chapter 6 the section on the Marxist-Leninist theories of imperialism.

8. Martin Wight, op. cit., p. 40.

9. Grayson Kirk, *The Study of International Relations in American Colleges and Universities* (New York: Council on Foreign Relations, 1947), p. 4; Foster Rhea Dulles, *America's Rise to World Power, 1898–1954* (New York: Harper & Row, 1963), pp. 158–161. For an excellent treatment of the dichotomy, see Robert E. Osgood, *Ideals and Self-Interest in America's Foreign Relations* (Chicago: University of Chicago Press, 1953).

10. Kenneth W. Thompson, "The Study of International Politics: A Survey of Trends and Developments," *Review of Politics,* XIV (October 1952), 433–443.

11. James L. Brierly, *The Law of Nations,* 2nd ed. (New York: Oxford University Press, 1936); Clyde Eagleton, *International Government* (New York: Ronald Press, 1932); Charles G. Fenwick, *International Law,* 2nd ed. (New York: Appleton, 1934); Norman L. Hill, *International Administration* (New York: McGraw-Hill, 1931); Hersch Lauterpacht, *The Function of Law in the International Community* (New York: Oxford University Press, 1933); J. B. Moore, *A Digest of International Law* (Washington: Government Printing Office, 1906); Lassa F. L. Oppenheim, *International Law: A Treatise,* 4th ed. (London: Longmans, 1928); Pitman B. Potter, *An Introduction to the Study of International Organization,* 3rd ed. (New York: Appleton, 1928).

12. Sidney B. Fay, *The Origins of the World War,* 2nd ed. (New York: Macmillan, 1930); G. P. Gooch, *History of Modern Europe, 1878–1919* (New York: Holt, Rinehart and Winston, 1923); R. B. Mowat, *European Diplomacy, 1815–1914* (London: Longmans, 1922); Bernadotte E. Schmitt, *The Coming of the War, 1914* (New York: Scribner's, 1930); Raymond J. Sontag, *European Diplomatic History, 1871–1932* (New York: Appleton, 1933); G. P. Gooch and Harold W. Temperly, *British Documents on the Origins of the War, 1989–1914* (London: His Majesty's Stationery Office, 1928). For an historiographical appraisal of the

work of American historians, see Warren I. Cohen, *The American Revisionists: The Lessons of Intervention in World War I* (Chicago: University of Chicago Press, 1967).

13. Carlton J. H. Hayes, *Essays on Nationalism* (New York: Macmillan, 1926); Hans Kohn, *A History of Nationalism in the East* (London: George Routledge, 1932), *Nationalism in the Soviet Union* (London: George Routledge, 1933), and *The Idea of Nationalism* (New York: Macmillan, 1944).

14. Philip J. Noel-Baker, *Disarmament* (New York: Harcourt Brace Jovanovich, 1926); James T. Shotwell, *War as an Instrument of National Policy* (New York: Harcourt Brace Jovanovich, 1929); J. W. Wheeler-Bennett, *Disarmament and Security Since Locarno, 1925–1931* (New York: Macmillan, 1932).

15. Parker T. Moon, *Imperialism and World Politics* (New York: Macmillan, 1926); Herbert I. Priestley, *France Overseas: A Study of Modern Imperialism* (New York: Appleton, 1938).

16. Harold Nicolson, *Peacemaking, 1919* (Boston: Houghton Mifflin, 1933), and *Diplomacy* (London: Oxford University Press, 1939).

17. Carl J. Friedrich, *Foreign Policy in the Making: The Search for a New Balance of Power* (New York: Norton, 1938); Alfred Vagts, "The United States and the Balance of Power," *Journal of Politics,* III (November 1941), 401–449.

18. James Fairgrieve, *Geography and World Power* (New York: Dutton, 1921); Nicholas J. Spykman, "Geography and Foreign Policy, I," *American Political Science Review,* XXXII (February 1938), 213–236; and the following two books: *America's Strategy in World Politics* (New York: Harcourt Brace Jovanovich, 1942) and *The Geography of Peace* (New York: Harcourt Brace Jovanovich, 1944). Spykman also wrote two articles with Abbie A. Rollins, "Geographic Objectives in Foreign Policy I," *American Political Science Review,* XXXIII (June 1939), 391–410, and "Geographic Objectives in Foreign Policy II," ibid. (August 1939), 591–614. The theories of Mahan and Mackinder are treated in Chapter 2 in this text; for a discussion of Spykman's theories, see Chapter 3.

19. Frank M. Russell, *Theories of International Relations* (New York: Appleton, 1936).

20. Sir Norman Angell, *The Great Illusion* (New York: G. P. Putnam's Sons), 1933. See also J. D. B. Miller, *Norman Angell and the Futility of War: Peace and the Public Mind* (London: Macmillan, 1986), especially chaps. 2 and 3.

21. E. H. Carr, *The Twenty-Years' Crisis, 1919–1939: An Introduction to the Study of International Relations* (London: Macmillan, 1939; Harper & Row [Torchbooks], 1964).

22. Arnold Wolfers, "Statesmanship and Moral Choice," *World Politics,* I (January 1949), 175–195, and "Political Theory and International Relations," in Arnold Wolfers and Laurence Martin, eds., *The Anglo-American Tradition in Foreign Affairs* (New Haven: Yale University Press, 1956); Kenneth W. Thompson, "The Limits of Principle in International Politics: Necessity and the New Balance of Power," *Journal of Politics,* XX (August 1958), 437–467. George F. Kennan has commented as follows on the American legalistic-moralistic approach to international problems: "Our national genius, our sense of decency, our feeling for compromise and law, our frankness and honesty—had not these qualities succeeded in producing on this continent a society unparalleled for its lack of strain and violence . . . ? There was no reason why the outside world, with our assistance, should not similarly compose itself to a life without vio-

lence." From *Realities of American Foreign Policy*, excerpted in David L. Larson, ed., *The Puritan Ethic in United States Foreign Policy* (Princeton: Van Nostrand, 1966), p. 34.

23. Adam Smith and other eighteenth-century economists, following in the individualistic steps of John Locke, taught that people in a competitive system, when they seek their own private gain, are led by an "invisible hand" to promote the interest of the whole society.

24. E. H. Carr, *The Twenty Years' Crisis, 1919–1939: An Introduction to the Study of International Relations* (London: Macmillan and Company Ltd., 1962), p. 9.

25. Ibid., p. 5.

26. G. Lowes Dickinson, *Causes of International War* (London: The Swarthmore Press Ltd., 1920). Other major works that are illustrative of the literature of international relations in its utopian phase include. Norman Angell, op. cit.; Nicholas Murray Butler, *Between Two Worlds: Interpretations of the Age in Which We Live* (New York: Charles Scribner's Sons, 1934); Nicholas Murray Butler, *A World in Ferment: Interpretations of the War for a New World* (New York: Charles Scribner's Sons, 1917); G. Lowes Dickinson, *The International Anarchy, 1904–1914* (New York and London: The Century Company, 1926; Harold Josephson, *James T. Shotwell and the Rise of Internationalism in America* (Cranbury, N.J.: Associated University Presses, Inc., 1975); Gilbert Murray, *The Ordeal of This Generation* (New York and London: Harper & Row, 1929); James T. Shotwell, *The Autobiography of James T. Shotwell* (New York: The Bobbs-Merrill Company, Inc., 1961; James T. Shotwell, *The History of History* (New York: Columbia University Press, 1939); Alfred Zimmern, *America & Europe and Other Essays* (Freeport, N.Y.: Books for Libraries Press, 1929, reprinted 1969); Alfred Zimmern, *The League of Nations and The Rule of Law, 1918–1935* (New York: Russell & Russell, 1939, reissued 1969). See Alfred Zimmern, "The Problem of Collective Security" in *Neutrality and Collective Security,* Harris Foundation Lectures, 1936 (Chicago: University of Chicago, 1936), pp. 3–89.

27. E. H. Carr, op. cit., p. 62; see especially chaps. 1–6. For a fuller exposition of the realist theories, see Chapter 3 in this text.

28. Ibid,. p. 92.

29. Ibid., pp. 5–6.

30. Ibid., pp. 10, 20–21, 93–94.

31. Martin Wight, *Power Politics,* "Looking Forward," Pamphlet No. 8 (London: Royal Institute of International Affairs, 1946), p. 11.

32. Hans J. Morgenthau, *Politics Among Nations* (New York: Knopf, 1948, 1954, 1960, 1967); Frederick L. Schuman, *International Politics: An Introduction to the Western State System,* 4th and 5th eds. (New York: McGraw-Hill, 1948, 1953); Robert Strausz-Hupé and Stefan T. Possony, *International Relations* (New York: McGraw-Hill, 1950, 1954); Norman D. Palmer and Howard C. Perkins, *International Relations* (Boston: Houghton Mifflin, 1953, 1957, 1969); Norman J. Padelford and George A. Lincoln, *The Dynamics of International Politics* (New York: Macmillan, 1962); Ernst B. Haas and Allen S. Whiting, *Dynamics of International Relations* (New York: McGraw-Hill, 1956); Harold and Margaret Sprout, *Foundations of National Power* (Princeton: Van Nostrand, 1945, 1951) and *Foundations of International Politics* (Princeton: Van Nostrand, 1962); Quincy Wright, *The Study of International Relations* (New

York: Appleton-Century-Crofts, 1955), pp. 23–24; Charles P. Schleicher, *Introduction to International Relations* (Englewood Cliffs, N.J.: Prentice-Hall, 1954) and *International Relations: Cooperation and Conflict* (Englewood Cliffs, N.J.: Prentice-Hall, 1962); Frederick H. Hartmann, *The Relations of Nations* (New York: Macmillan, 1957, 1962); A. F. K. Organski, *World Politics* (New York: Knopf, 1958); Lennox A. Mills and Charles H. McLaughlin, *World Politics in Transition* (New York: Holt, Rinehart and Winston, 1956); Fred Greene, *Dynamics of International Relations* (New York: Holt, Rinehart and Winston, 1964); W. W. Kulski, *International Politics in a Revolutionary Age* (Philadelphia: Lippincott, 1964, 1967). The reader's attention is called to the following reviews of the earlier international relations texts: Richard C. Snyder, "Toward Greater Order in the Study of International Politics," *World Politics*, VII (April 1955), 462–478; Fred A. Sondermann, "The Study of International Relations: 1956 Version," *World Politics*, X (July 1958), 639–647; Kenneth E. Boulding, "The Content of International Studies in College: A Review," *The Journal of Conflict Resolution*, VIII (March 1964), 65–71; and Dina A. Zinnes, "An Introduction to the Behavioral Approach: A Review," *The Journal of Conflict Resolution*, XII (June 1968), 258–267. For a content analysis of more recent textbooks and other teaching materials, see James N. Rosenau et al., "Of Syllabi, Texts, Students and Scholarship in International Relations: Some Data and Interpretations on the State of a Burgeoning Field," *World Politics*, XXIX (January 1977), 263–340.

33. Georg Schwarzenberger, *Power Politics: A Study of World Society* (New York: Praeger, 1951), pp. 13–14. (The third edition of this work appeared in 1964.) For recent discussions of efforts to clarify the notion of power, see David V. J. Bell, *Power, Influence and Authority* (New York: Oxford University Press, 1975); Jack H. Nagel, *The Descriptive Analysis of Power* (New Haven: Yale University Press, 1975); and David A. Baldwin, "Power Analysis and World Politics," *World Politics*, XXXI (January 1979), 161–194.

34. Horace V. Harrison, writing in 1964, criticized not only the textbooks but nearly all writing in international theory as being partial, implicit rather than explicit, too narrowly focused, designed to serve particular professional interests, and incapable of providing a guide either to research or to action. He added, however, that some progress toward more general theories had begun since the latter 1950s. See his introduction to the book he edited, *The Role of Theory in International Relations* (Princeton: Van Nostrand, 1964), pp. 8–9.

35. William T. R. Fox and Annette Baker Fox, "The Teaching of International Relations in the United States," *World Politics*, XIII (July 1961), 339–359. See also Quincy Wright, op. cit., chaps. 3 and 4; Grayson Kirk, op. cit.; Waldemar Gurian, "On the Study of International Relations," *Review of Politics*, VIII (July 1946), 275–282; Frederick L. Schuman, "The Study of International Relations in the United States," *Contemporary Political Science: A Survey of Methods, Research and Training* (Paris: United Nations Educational, Scientific, and Cultural Organization, 1950); Frederick S. Dunn, "The Present Course of International Relations Research," *World Politics*, II (October 1949), 142–146; Kenneth W. Thompson, op. cit.; L. Gray Cowen, "Theory and Practice in the Teaching of International Relations in the United States," in Geoffrey L. Goodwin, ed., *The University Teaching of International Relations* (Oxford: Basil Blackwell, 1951); John Gange, *University Research on International Relations* (Washington: American Council on Education, 1958); Richard N. Swift, *World*

Affairs and the College Curriculum (Washington: American Council on Education, 1959); Edward W. Weidner, *The World Role of Universities,* The Carnegie Series in American Education (New York: McGraw-Hill, 1962) especially the chapters dealing with student-abroad programs, exchange programs, and international programs of university assistance.

36. The appearance of several anthologies in international theory in the early 1960s attested to a burgeoning interest in the field. See William T. R. Fox, ed., *Theoretical Aspects of International Relations* (Notre Dame: University of Notre Dame Press, 1959); Charles A. McClelland, William C. Olson, and Fred A. Sondermann, eds., *The Theory and Practice of International Relations* (Englewood Cliffs, N.J.: Prentice-Hall, 1960); Ivo D. Duchacek, ed., with the collaboration of Kenneth W. Thompson, *Conflict and Cooperation Among Nations* (New York: Holt, Rinehart and Winston, 1960); Klaus Knorr and Sidney Verba, eds., *The International System: Theoretical Essays (World Politics,* XIV [October 1961]) (Princeton: Princeton University Press, 1961); James N. Rosenau, ed., *International Politics and Foreign Policy: A Reader in Research and Theory* (New York: The Free Press, 1961); Horace V. Harrison, ed., op. cit.

37. Glenn H. Snyder and Paul Diesing, *Conflict Among Nations: Bargaining, Decision-making, and System Structure in International Crises* (Princeton: Princeton University Press, 1977), pp. 21–22.

38. Kenneth E. Boulding, *Ecodynamics: A New Theory of Societal Dynamics* (Beverly Hills, Calif.: Sage Publications, 1978), p. 9.

39. Alfred North Whitehead, *Science and the Modern World* (New York: Macmillan, 1925) (New York: New American Library, 1948), p. 30.

40. Alfred Zimmern, "Introductory Report to the Discussions in 1935," in Alfred Zimmern, ed., *University Teaching of International Relations,* Report of the Eleventh Session of the International Studies Conference (Paris: International Institute of Intellectual Cooperation, League of Nations, 1939), pp. 7–9. Later, C. A. W. Manning prepared a pamphlet for UNESCO on the university teaching of international relations in which he took a similar position. There is an international relations complex that has to be viewed from a "universalistic angle," and none of the established disciplines as traditionally taught can be relied upon to supply this necessary perspective. See P. D. Marchant, "Theory and Practice in the Study of International Relations," *International Relations,* I (April 1955), 95–102.

41. Nicholas J. Spykman, "Methods of Approach to the Study of International Relations," *Proceedings of the Fifth Conference of Teachers of International Law and Related Subjects* (Washington: Carnegie Endowment for International Peace, 1933), p. 60.

42. Frederick S. Dunn, "The Scope of International Relations," *World Politics,* I (October 1948), 142.

43. Ibid., p. 144.

44. Quincy Wright, *The Study of International Relations* (New York: Appleton-Century-Crofts, 1955), pp. 23–24.

45. Morton A. Kaplan, "Is International Relations a Discipline?" *The Journal of Politics,* XXIII (August 1961), p. 463.

46. Frederick S. Dunn, op. cit., p. 143.

47. Stanley Hoffmann, ed., *Contemporary Theory in International Relations* (Englewood Cliffs, N.J.: Prentice-Hall, 1960), pp. 4–6. Raymond Aron has similarly noted that, although the definitional difficulty is real, it should not be exag-

gerated, since every scientific discipline lacks precise outer limits. More important than knowing where phenomena become or cease to be data of international relations, says Aron, is the field's principal focus of interest. For him, this is on interstate relations. *Peace and War: A Theory of International Relations,* trans. Richard Howard and Annette Baker Fox (New York: Praeger, 1968), pp. 5–8.

48. Morton A. Kaplan, *System and Process in International Politics* (New York: Krieger, 1976), p. 3. In an article written as a rejoinder to Bull's criticism of the scientific writers (see note 79), Kaplan accused the traditionalists of using history ineptly, of falling into the trap of "over-particularization and unrelated generalization," and of being unaware that many writers in the modern scientific school regard history as a laboratory for the acquisition of empirical data. See his "The New Great Debate: Traditionalism vs. Science in International Relations," *World Politics,* XIX (October 1966), 15–16.

49. Morton A. Kaplan, "Problems of Theory Building and Theory Confirmation in International Politics," in Knorr and Verba, eds., op. cit., p. 23; Morton A. Kaplan, *New Approaches to International Relations* (New York: St. Martin's, 1968), pp. 399–404. See also George Modelski, "Comparative International Systems," *World Politics,* XIV (July 1962), 662–674, in which he reviews Adda B. Bozeman, *Politics and Culture in International History* (Princeton: Princeton University Press, 1960). See also Hoffmann, op. cit., pp. 174–180.

50. Morton A. Kaplan, *System and Process,* chap. 2.

51. "The substance of theory is history, composed of unique events and occurrences. An episode in history and politics is in one sense never repeated. It happens as it does only once. . . . In this sense history is beyond the reach of theory. Underlying all theory, however, is the assumption that these same unique events are also more concrete instances of more general propositions. The wholly unique, having nothing in common with anything else, is indescribable. . . ." Kenneth W. Thompson, "Toward a Theory of International Politics," *American Political Science Review,* XLIX (September 1955), 734.

52. See Fred N. Kerlinger, *Foundations of Behavioral Research* (New York: Holt, Rinehart and Winston, 1966), p. 11, and Robert Brown, *Explanation in Social Science* (Chicago: Aldine, 1963), p. 174.

53. Gustav Bergman, *The Philosophy of Science* (Madison: University of Wisconsin Press, 1958), pp. 31–32.

54. Abraham Kaplan, *The Conduct of Inquiry* (San Francisco: Chandler, 1964), p. 319.

55. Carl G. Hempel, *Fundamentals of Concept Formation in Empirical Science* (Chicago: University of Chicago Press, 1952), p. 36.

56. *The Ethics of Aristotle,* trans. D. P. Chase (New York: Dutton, 1950), Book VI, p. 147. Hans J. Morgenthau, echoing Aristotle, stressed the difference between "what is worth knowing intellectually and what is useful for practice." "Reflections on the State of Political Science," *Review of Politics,* XVII (October 1955), 440.

57. David Hume, *A Treatise of Human Nature,* Part III, "Of Probability and Knowledge," in *The Essential David Hume,* Introduction by Robert P. Wolff (New York: New American Library, 1969), pp. 53–99. See Sheldon S. Wolin, "Hume and Conservatism," *American Political Science Review,* XLVII (December 1954), 999–1016. Michael Polanyi, too, has treated the difference between the theory of affairs and the practice of affairs. *Personal Knowledge* (Chicago: University of Chicago Press, 1958), pp. 49ff.

58. For analyses of linkages between domestic political structures and processes on the one hand and foreign policy on the other, see: James Rosenau, *Linkage Politics* (New York: The Free Press, 1969); Henry A. Kissinger, "Domestic Structure and Foreign Policy," in *American Foreign Policy: Three Essays* (New York: Norton, 1969); Wolfram Hanreider, "Compatibility and Consensus: A Proposal for the Conceptual Linkage of External and Internal Dimensions of Foreign Policy," in Hanreider, ed., *Comparative Foreign Policy: Theoretical Essays* (New York: McKay, 1971); and Jonathan Wilkenfeld, ed., *Conflict Behavior and Linkage Politics* (New York: McKay, 1973).

59. Fred A. Sondermann, "The Linkage Between Foreign Policy and International Politics," in James N. Rosenau, ed., op. cit., pp. 8–17.

60. Quincy Wright, "Development of a General Theory of International Relations," in Horace V. Harrison, ed., op. cit., p. 20.

61. Ibid., pp. 21–23.

62. James N. Rosenau, *The Scientific Study of Foreign Policy*, rev. ed. (London: Frances Pinter, 1980), pp. 19–31.

63. Kenneth N. Waltz, *Theory of International Politics*, chap. 1, "Laws and Theories."

64. See J. David Singer, "The Level-of-Analysis Problem in International Relations," in Knorr and Verba, eds., op. cit., pp. 77–92. Reprinted in James N. Rosenau, ed., *International Politics and Foreign Policy: A Reader in Research and Theory*, rev. ed. (New York: The Free Press, 1969), pp. 20–29. K. J. Holsti concedes that the classical paradigm, postulating sovereign states as principal actors in an anarchic global system, has been much pilloried in recent decades, but he insists that it remains the dominant paradigm and still commands the allegiance of most international theorists. *The Dividing Discipline: Harmony and Diversity in International Theory* (Boston, Mass.: Allen & Unwin, 1985), p. 11.

65. The subject of other-than-state actors is fully explored in Richard W. Mansbach, Yale H. Ferguson, and Donald E. Lampert, *The Web of World Politics: Non-State Actors in the Global System* (Englewood Cliffs, N.J.: Prentice-Hall, 1976).

66. Samuel P. Huntington, "Transnational Organizations in World Politics," *World Politics*, XXV (April 1973); Joseph S. Nye, Jr., "Multinational Corporations in World Politics," *Foreign Affairs*, 53 (October 1974); Robert Gilpin, *U.S. Power and the Multinational Corporation* (New York: Basic Books, 1975); David E. Apter and Louis Wold Goodman, eds., *The Multinational Corporation and Social Change* (New York: Praeger, 1976); Raymond Vernon, *Storm over the Multinationals: The Real Issues* (Cambridge, Mass.: Harvard University Press, 1977); George Modelski, ed., *Transnational Corporations and World Order* (San Francisco: Freeman, 1979); Charles W. Kegley, Jr., and Eugene R. Wittkopf, eds., "The Rise of Multinational Corporations: Blessing or Curse?" in chap. 5 of their *World Politics: Trend and Transformation* (New York: St. Martin's, 1981); Joan Edelman Spero, *The Politics of International Economic Relations*, 3rd ed. (New York: St. Martin's, 1985), chaps. 4 and 8; and Robert T. Kudrle, "The Several Faces of the Multinational Corporation," in Jeffrey A. Frieden and David A. Lake, eds., *International Political Economy* (New York: St. Martin's, 1987).

67. Kegley and Wittkopf, eds., op. cit., p. 106.

68. J. David Singer, in Rosenau, ed., op. cit., p. 23.

69. The pluralists' critique of the realists is well described in Paul R. Viotti and Mark V. Kauppi, *International Relations Theory: Realism, Pluralism, Globalism* (New York: Macmillan, 1987), pp. 7–8, 192–193.

70. Ibid., p. 204; Kegley and Wittkopf, eds., op. cit., p. 139.

71. Viotti and Kauppi, p. 9.

72. Cf. Joseph S. Nye, ed., *International Regionalism: Readings* (Boston: Little, Brown, 1968); Walker Connor, "Nation-Building or Nation-Destroying?" *World Politics,* XXIV (April 1972).

73. David Easton, *The Political System* (New York: Knopf, 1959), pp. 129–131.

74. David Easton, *A Systems Analysis of Political Life* (New York: John Wiley and Sons, 1965), p. 284. Nevertheless, Easton holds that in some small degree at least, it is proper to consider decisions taken through appropriate international structures and procedures as "authoritative." Ibid., and also pp. 484–488. Even in some rare cases, however, of United Nations Security Council resolutions that are considered by international law authorities to be legally binding, states remain politically free to decide for themselves whether to comply, because no effective enforcement mechanism exists.

75. Raymond Aron, "What Is a Theory of International Relations?" *Journal of International Affairs,* XXI, No. 2 (1967), 190; Stanley Hoffmann, *The State of War* (New York: Praeger, 1965), chap. 2; Roger D. Masters, "World Politics as a Primitive Political System," *World Politics,* XVI (July 1964); Kenneth N. Waltz, *Theory of International Politics,* p. 113.

76. Robert O. Keohane and Joseph S. Nye, *Power and Interdependence: World Politics in Transition* (Boston: Little, Brown, 1977), chap. 1.

77. Ibid., pp. 5, 19–22; Ernst B. Haas, "On Systems and International Regimes," *World Politics,* XXVII (January 1975) and "Why Collaborate? Issue-Linkage and International Regimes," *World Politics,* XXXII (April 1980); Stephen D. Krasner, "Transforming International Regimes: What the Third World Wants and Why," *International Studies Quarterly,* 25 (March 1981); and the special issue of *International Organization,* XXXVI (Spring 1982) devoted to international regimes and edited by Stephen D. Krasner.

78. See Norman D. Palmer, "The Study of International Relations in the United States: Perspectives of Half a Century," *International Studies Quarterly,* Vol. 24, No. 3 (September 1980), pp. 343–344. Cf. also Klaus Knorr and James N. Rosenau, "Tradition and Science in the Study of International Politics," in the book they edited, *Contending Approaches to International Politics* (Princeton: Princeton University Press, 1970), p. 13; John J. Weltman, "The American Tradition in International Thought: Science as Therapy," in Timothy Fuller, ed., *The Prospects of Liberalism,* Colorado College Studies 20 (1984), Proceedings of a Symposium, pp. 127–144; John J. Weltman, "On the Interpretation of International Thought," *Review of Politics,* Vol. 44, No. 1 (January, 1982), pp. 27–41.

79. Hedley Bull, "International Theory: The Case for a Classical Approach," *World Politics,* XVIII (April 1966), 361. Bull's essay is reprinted in the volume by Knorr and Rosenau, eds., op. cit.; cf. p. 20.

80. Klaus Knorr and James N. Rosenau, op. cit., p. 14.

81. Ibid., p. 15.

82. All of these and other criticisms are presented by Hedley Bull, op. cit.

83. J. David Singer, "The Incompleat Theorist: Insight Without Evidence," in Knorr and Rosenau, eds., op. cit., pp. 72–73.

84. Klaus Knorr and James N. Rosenau, op. cit., p. 16.
85. David Hume, *Essays and Treatises on Several Subjects* (Edinburgh: Bell and Bradfute, and W. Blackwood, 1925), Vol. I, pp. 331–339. Reprinted in Arend Lijphart, ed., *World Politics* (Boston: Allyn & Bacon, 1966), pp. 228–234.
86. All these examples are cited in Hans J. Morgenthau, *Politics Among Nations,* op. cit., pp. 161–166.
87. Ernst B. Haas, "The Balance of Power: Prescription, Concept or Propaganda?" *World Politics,* V (July 1953), 442–477.
88. Inis L. Claude, Jr., *Power and International Relations* (New York: Random House, 1962), pp. 13, 22.
89. This paragraph and the one following constitute a synthesis from several different sources. For fuller treatment of the balance of power, see Inis L. Claude, Jr., op. cit.; Edward V. Gulick, *Europe's Classical Balance of Power* (Ithaca: Cornell University Press, 1955); Sidney B. Fay, "Balance of Power," in *Encyclopedia of the Social Sciences,* Vol. II (New York: Macmillan, 1930); Alfred Vagts, "The Balance of Power: Growth of an Idea," *World Politics,* I (October 1948), 82–101; and Paul Seabury, ed., *Balance of Power* (San Francisco: Chandler, 1965).
90. Quoted in Edward V. Gulick, op. cit., p. 34.
91. "Memorandum on the Present State of British Relations with France and Germany," in G. P. Gooch and Harold V. Temperly, eds., op. cit., III, 402.
92. Winston S. Churchill, *The Gathering Storm* (Boston: Houghton Mifflin, 1948), pp. 207–210.
93. Nicholas J. Spykman, *American Strategy and World Politics* (New York: Harcourt Brace Jovanovich, 1942), pp. 21–22.
94. Hans J. Morgenthau, op. cit., chap. 14.
95. Ernst B. Haas, "The Balance of Power as a Guide to Policy-Making," *Journal of Politics,* XV (August 1953), 370–398.
96. Kenneth N. Waltz, *Theory of International Politics,* op. cit., pp. 117–123.
97. Morton A. Kaplan, *System and Process,* op. cit., pp. 22–36. Particularly important to his theory is the list of six essential rules of the balance-of-power system on p. 23.
98. Arthur Lee Burns, "From Balance to Deterrence: A Theoretical Analysis," *World Politics,* IX (July 1957), 505. Whereas Burns prefers five as the optimal number required for security, Kaplan says that five is the minimal number required for security, but that security increases with the number of states up to some as-yet-undetermined upper limit. "Traditionalism vs. Science in International Relations," op. cit., p. 10.
99. Arthur Lee Burns, op. cit., p. 508.
100. R. Harrison Wagner, "The Theory of Games and the Balance of Power," *World Politics,* July, 1986, p. 575.
101. See Glenn H. Snyder, "Balance of Power in the Missile Age," *Journal of International Affairs,* XIV, No. 1 (1960); John H. Herz, "Balance Systems and Balance Policies in a Nuclear and Bipolar Age," ibid.; and the books and articles cited below in the extended discussion on deterrence and arms control in Chapter 9, this text.
102. Harvey Starr, "The Quantitative International Relations Scholar as Surfer," *The Journal of Conflict Resolution,* vol. 18 (June 1974), 337.
103. J. David Singer, "Data-making in International Relations," *Behavioral Scientist,* 10 (1969).

104. Developed in mathematics and used first in psychology, later in economics, and more recently in political science, factor analysis is a statistical technique by which a large number of variables can be clustered on the basis of their intercorrelation. Factor analysis enables the researcher to identify patterns among variables. The results of factor analysis, the factors defining the different patterns, are often termed "dimensions," hence the use of the word "dimensionality" in the DON Project. For a detailed discussion of factor analysis, see Harry H. Harmon, *Modern Factor Analysis* (Chicago: University of Chicago Press, 1967); R. J. Rummel, *Applied Factor Analysis* (Evanston, Ill.: Northwestern University Press, 1970); and L. L. Thurstone, *Multiple Factor Analysis* (Chicago: University of Chicago Press, 1965).

105. Jonathan Wilkenfeld, "Domestic and Foreign Conflict Behavior of Nations," *Journal of Peace Research*, I (1968), 57.

106. Ibid., p. 66.

107. Kurt Lewin's contributions in determining the methodological and conceptual prerequisites for a science of human behavior are said to be relevant to all the social sciences. The psychological field theorist sees human behavior as a function not of the internal characteristics of the person, nor of a historical claim of causation, but of the interaction of the person and the contemporary events in the environment. He argued, therefore, that the determinants of human behavior should be treated in a single unified field rather than separated into traditional disciplines. According to Lewin, all behavior can be conceived as change occurring in some state of a field in a given unit of time. By focusing on the dynamics of motivation, conflict, and change, he developed a field theory similar in several respects to systems theory. He showed how living systems seek an equilibrium in relation to their environments through recurring processes of goal-setting, tension-arousal, locomotion of the person within the psychological environment or a change in the structure of the perceived environment, and tension reduction. See Kurt Lewin, *Field Theory in Social Science* (New York: Harper & Row, 1951), p. 45; and the article on "Field Theory" by Morton Deutsch in the *International Encyclopedia of the Social Sciences*, David L. Sills, ed. (New York: Macmillan and The Free Press, 1972), vol. 5, pp. 407–417.

108. Quincy Wright, "Development of a General Theory of International Relations," in Horace V. Harrison, ed., *The Role of Theory in International Relations* (Princeton: Van Nostrand, 1964), p. 38, and *The Study of International Relations* (New York: Appleton, 1955), pp. 524–569.

109. For a more complete examination of coordinates in field theory, see Quincy Wright, *A Study of International Relations*, op. cit., pp. 540–567.

110. R. J. Rummel, "A Status Field Theory of International Relations," *Dimensionality of Nations Project Report No. 50* (Honolulu, 1971), p. 5.

111. For examples of quantitative studies in international relations, see Morton A. Kaplan, ed., *New Approaches to International Relations* (New York: St. Martin's Press, 1968); Richard L. Merritt and Stein Rokkan, eds., *Comparing Nations: The Use of Quantitative Data in Cross-National Research* (New Haven: Yale University Press, 1966); John E. Mueller, ed., *Approaches to Measurement in International Relations: A Non-Evangelical Survey* (New York: Appleton, 1969); James N. Rosenau, ed., *International Politics and Foreign Policy* (New York: The Free Press, 1969); Rudolph J. Rummel et al., *Dimensions of Nations* (Evanston, Ill.: Northwestern University Press, 1967);

Bruce Russett, *International Regions in the International System* (Chicago: Rand McNally, 1967); and J. David Singer, *Quantitative International Politics: Insights and Evidence* (New York: The Free Press, 1968).

112. Carl G. Hempel and Paul Oppenheim, "Studies in the Logic of Explanation," *Philosophy of Science,* XV (1948), 135–175.

113. Werner Heisenberg, *Physics and Philosophy* (New York: Harper & Row, 1958), pp. 179, 183, 186. It should be pointed out that the principle of indeterminancy is often referred to less accurately by social scientists as "the uncertainty principle."

114. See Quincy Wright, *A Study of International Relations,* chap. 7, "Educational and Research Objectives," *Western Political Quarterly,* XI (September 1958), 598–606. Another penetrating discourse on the role of normative theory in contrast to a purely value-free approach to international relations is to be found in Charles A. McClelland, "The Function of Theory in International Relations," *Journal of Conflict Resolution,* IV (September 1960), 311–314.

115. Quincy Wright, *A Study of International Relations,* op. cit., p. 26.

116. Ibid., p. 11 and chaps. 8–11.

Chapter
2

Environmental Theories

THE ROLE OF ENVIRONMENT IN INTERNATIONAL RELATIONS

Especially since the 1960s there has been a revival of interest, among scholars and policymakers, in environmental theories of political behavior. Factors such as geography, demography, resource distribution, and technological development are now seen as increasingly important to the study, as well as to the practice, of international politics. Indeed, Harold and Margaret Sprout have suggested that the international political milieu cannot be fully understood without reference to the "whole spectrum of environing factors, human as well as nonhuman, intangible as well as tangible."[1] Still, this manifestation of interest in the impact of geographical and broader environmental factors upon politics is but the most recent phase of an age-old focus of attention that extends back to the ancient world. Aristotle, for example, believed that people and their environment are inseparable, and that they are affected by both geographical circumstances and political institutions. Location near the sea stimulated the commercial activity upon which the city-state was based; temperate climate favorably affected the development of national character, human energy, and intellect.[2] Jean Bodin, too, maintained that climatic circumstances influence national characteristics as well as the foreign policies of states. According to Bodin, the extremes of northern and temperate climates offer conditions most favorable to building a political system based on law and justice. Northern and mountainous regions were said to be conducive to greater political discipline than southern climes, which fail to spark initiative.[3] Montesquieu also pointed to various climatic factors that he felt influenced the political divisions of Western Europe, in contrast to the great plains of Asia and Eastern Europe, and contributed to a spirit of political independence. According to Montesquieu, islands could preserve their freedom more easily than continental countries because they are isolated from foreign influences.[4] Here, Montesquieu had in mind Britain, which had evolved unique political institutions that he greatly admired and had withstood invasion from Continental Europe since 1066.

In American history, Frederick Jackson Turner hypothesized that the existence of the frontier, pushed westward by succeeding generations of settlers until the last decade of the nineteenth century, shaped the American character and intellect—"that practical, inventive turn of mind, quick to find expedients; that masterful grasp of material things, lacking in the artistic but powerful to affect great ends; that restless, nervous energy; the dominant individualism, working for good and evil, and withal that buoyancy and exuberance which comes with freedom—these are the traits of the frontier, or traits called out elsewhere because of the existence of the frontier."[5] The use of Social Darwinian analysis in the late nineteenth century also provided an important intellectual stimulus to environmentally oriented studies of international affairs, insofar as it transferred to the social order a scientific perspective in which the evolutionary development of a species was a function of its ability to adjust to its physical habitat. The concept of the "survival of the fittest" was adapted from living organisms to the state, as exemplified in the geopolitical writings of Friedrich Ratzel, discussed later in this chapter.

The physical habitat encompasses resources and population, as well as the impact of population upon resources, including the availability of food supplies. The notion that there are severe "limits to growth" is central to the thought of Thomas Robert Malthus and to many of the writings on imperialism. Beginning in 1798, with his *Essay on the Principle of Population as it Affects the Future Improvement of Society,* Malthus hypothesized that population growth will always outpace the increase in food supplies. If unchecked, population will rise in geometric progression, although the means of subsistence will be augmented only in arithmetic progression. As a result, poverty will be the inevitable fate of mankind, unless population growth is checked by war, famine, and disease. J. A. Hobson and Lenin, in their respective analyses of imperialism, saw a quest for access to markets and raw materials leading capitalist states to become imperialistic. For Lenin, the ultimate effect of capitalism, as noted in Chapter 6, would be a struggle among capitalist states for the world's remaining markets and raw materials. In a contemporary study, Nazli Choucri and Robert C. North hypothesized that there is an inextricable relationship between population growth and resource demand, and that the more advanced the level of technology, the greater will be the need for resources. A population increase of 1 percent is said to make necessary a 4 percent increase in national income merely to maintain living standards at their existing level.[6] As technology advances, together with population growth, societies seek greater access to resources. As societies attempt to extend their interests outward in light of resource needs, the likelihood of conflict is enhanced. Here, Choucri and North draw linkages among resource factors, domestic growth, and foreign policy. Their hypotheses will be examined in greater detail in Chapter 8, along with the writings of Quincy Wright, who emphasized the relationship between cultural, political, institutional, and technological change and conflict.

Peace is said to be dependent upon an "equilibrium among many forces" and to be jeopardized by a transformation in forces such as demography. Rapid increases in population in the past century have produced cultural interpenetration and have greatly increased communication as what Quincy Wright terms *technological distance* has narrowed, but they have also enlarged the opportunities for friction and for conflict among peoples.[7] Wright postulated that the growth in size of states had made it more necessary and more likely that conflict would be resolved without violence, but it had also made more severe those conflicts that could not be settled by peaceful means.[8]

Thus, in the late twentieth century, population, as well as resource and technology factors—the so-called global issues of the present era—have contributed to a burgeoning literature focused upon the implications of population growth for resource scarcity, the implications of resource scarcity for potential conflict, the relationship between resources and geography, and the impact of technology upon resources and geography. Technology has made possible the exploitation of resources in inhospitable environments, such as the seabed, and in the years to come in outer space. At the same time, technology has created the great need for resources that has contributed to their depletion and has raised the specter of resource scarcity unless alternative sources or substitutes are found. The political significance of one or another geographical location has been influenced decisively by technology and by resource issues. In historic context the importance of the seas—in the writings of Alfred Thayer Mahan, for example—stemmed from the mobility they conferred, by virtue of the ability of the sailing vessel and later the steamship to move military resources most effectively from one point to another. Subsequent changes in technology have enhanced the importance of other geographical elements. In the late twentieth century, the increased dependence of industrialized states upon resource imports, especially energy, once again gave renewed significance to the oceans. As Saul B. Cohen has suggested, "The essence of geopolitical analysis is the relation of international political power to the geographical setting. Geopolitical views vary with changing geographical setting and with man's interpretation of the nature of this change."[9] According to Raymond Aron, the term *geopolitical* encompasses a "geographical schematization of diplomatic-strategic relations with a geographic-economic analysis of resources, with an interpretation of diplomatic attitudes as a result of the way of life and of the environment (sedentary, nomadic, agricultural, seafaring)."[10] In Colin Gray's perspective, "Physical geography alone, while providing important constraints and opportunities, is given specific strategic meaning only with reference to time, technology, relative national effort, and choices effected among strategies and tactics."[11]

Both "utopians" and "realists" in international relations (examined in Chapters 1 and 3, respectively) discussed man in relation to the environment. But they broadened the notion of "environment" to include the products of human culture as well as the physical features of the earth. Drawing upon the writings of theorists of the Enlightenment, utopian theory claimed that international behavior could be altered by transforming the institutional setting. Schemes for international organization and world government, as well as for establishing norms for international conduct, were designed to alter human behavior by changing the international political environment. In contrast, as the analysis undertaken in Chapter 3 reveals, realists in international relations often held that the geographical location of states conditions, if not determines, political behavior. If the political behavior of national units is in large part the product of environmental circumstances, including geography, in which nations find themselves, the statesman's perennial task is to work within the parameters established by the environment.

Our relationship with the environment remains a focal point of analysis. Such studies, exemplified by the writings of Harold and Margaret Sprout, have emphasized multiple factor analysis, embracing a variety of environmental conditions and trends in addition to geography. Moreover, writers who have utilized the constructs of systems theory in the study of politics including international relations have emphasized environment. Systems, discussed in Chapter 4, may be "open" or "closed." The open systems, both biological and social, by definition are susceptible to, and dependent for their survival on, inputs from, and outputs into, their environment. In so-called closed or self-contained systems inputs from an external environment have been eliminated, although environmental factors have often been incorporated into closed systems.

Buckle and Huntington: Climatic Factors

Many nineteenth- and twentieth-century scholars were as convinced as the classical writers of the importance of climate as a conditioner of political behavior. Henry Thomas Buckle (1821–1862), a British historian, suggested that climate, food, and soil depend closely on each other. Climate influenced the kinds of crops grown; the quality of the food depended on the soil. Buckle explained the alleged vigor of the northern laborer as a result of the food supply available in a cold climate. In nations in cold climates, "there is for the most part displayed, even in the infancy of society, a bolder or more adventurous character, than we find among those other nations whose ordinary nutriment, . . . is easily obtained, and indeed is supplied to them, by the bounty of nature, gratuitously and without a struggle." Furthermore, Buckle contended that:

The food essential to life is scarcer in cold countries than in hot ones; and not only is it scarcer, but more of it is required; so that on both grounds smaller encouragement is given to the growth of that population of whose ranks the labor-market is stocked. To express, therefore, the conclusion in its simplest form, we may say that there is a strong and constant tendency in hot countries for wages to be low, in cold countries for them to be high.[12]

Civilizations with hot climates, and therefore low wages, are said to produce large and depressed working classes, with attendant social and economic consequences. Great inequality in the distribution of wealth, political power, and social influence, according to Buckle, led many ancient civilizations to reach a "certain stage of development and then to decline."

Ellsworth Huntington (1876–1947), the American geographer and explorer, found climate a determinant not only of health, activity, level of food production, and other resource availabilities, but of the migration of peoples and their racial mixtures as well. Only the most physically fit, intelligent, and adventurous survive migration. And only those subject to economic distress due to poor harvest and food shortages attempt to migrate to more desirable climates. To support this view, Huntington cited as an example the desiccation of central Asia at different periods of history, which led to the invasion of Europe by the barbarians, the Dorian and Ionian invasions of ancient Greece, and the Mongol incursion into Southwest Asia. The Arab migration led by Mohammed and strengthened by religious fervor represented a movement from parched deserts to more fertile lands. Improved economic conditions, stimulated by climatic factors, liberated large parts of a population from the tasks of gathering and producing food, and permitted them to develop new and advanced ideas in the fields of art, literature, science, and political life. Huntington concluded that most of the world's major civilizations had developed in climates where the annual average temperature neared the optimum necessary for maximum human productivity (65°–70° Fahrenheit).[13] Great civilizations within the tropic zones have risen only on temperate plateaus or along cool seacoasts in which the temperature in no season far exceeded the optimum level—for example, the Mayas in Mexico and in Guatemala, and the ancient Javanese and Singhalese.

TOYNBEE: ENVIRONMENTAL CHALLENGE AND RESPONSE

Arnold Toynbee held that civilizations are born in environments that pose difficult challenges.[14] The challenged civilization develops an *élan vital*, which carries it through equilibrium toward another challenge, thereby inspiring another response. The challenge-response cycle is potentially infinite, although it is retrospective, thus not allowing us to predict the potential response to a challenge. He examined five types of challenging stimuli. Two were physical: hard country—that is, country possessing a harsh climate, terrain, and soil—and new ground—that is, the exploration, opening up, and development of a wilderness into productive land. The three nonphysical stimuli include (1) those challenges emanating from another state, (2) continuous external pressure against a state, and (3) a stimulus of penalization—that is, if a state loses the use of a particular component, it is likely to respond by increasing correspondingly the efficiency of another component. Toynbee adds that overly severe physical challenge can arrest the development of civilization. The Polynesian, Eskimo, Nomad, Spartan, and Osmanli civilizations were retarded as a result of physical challenges they could not meet.

The breakdown of civilizations results from the degeneration of the creative minority into a "dominant minority which attempts to retain by force a position that it has ceased to merit." This in turn provokes a "secession of a proletariat which no longer admires and imitates its rulers and revolts against its servitude."[15] Thus the society loses its social cohesiveness. Vertical schisms between geographically segregated communities and horizontal schisms between classes or groups that are geographically contiguous but socially segregated characterize the disintegration of a civilization. The horizontal schism may occur when a dominant minority retains its ruling position by force, but loses its right to that role as a result of its loss of complexity. Toynbee's schema is related to modern, more complex theories of social revolution, treated in Chapter 8.

GEOGRAPHICAL FACTORS OF NATIONAL POWER

With the advent of modern communication-transportation technologies, increased attention was given to geography, focusing upon population/resource distribution, the strategic location of states, and the forward projection of national power. Because geopolitics has as its focal point national power and the control of territory, it follows that those political entities most able to project their capabilities over greater distances constitute the dominant states of any time in the history of the international system. According to numerous writers—including, for example, Kenneth Boulding and subsequently Patrick O'Sullivan—there is an inverse relationship between power and distance from its core area.[16] In O'Sullivan's words: "Most of the conflicts of the last 30 years have arisen in the crush zone between the great powers. The force fields of the hegemonies may be thought of as extending out from their cores, overwhelming smaller nations with their power, surrounding the spheres of influence of lesser powers and lapping against each other at the edges."[17] To be sure, the impact of technology has been of such importance, as noted elsewhere in this chapter, that the political significance of geography has been altered but not eliminated. To the extent that weapons of mass destruction can be launched from any point on earth, from under the oceans, or from outer space, to strike a target anywhere on earth, the distinction between greater power at its core compared with the periphery has lost previous meaning.[18]

However, the capabilities available to political entities are numerous, with some more easily moveable than others, and the geographic objectives on whose behalf they are used are raised. At an abstract level, the relationship between geography and power—geopolitics—resides in the ability, at any time, of one state or another to move power in order to influence or control desired territory deemed to be of strategic importance.

For the most part, those writers concerned with the environment have tended to stress the importance of such factors as determinants, or at least conditioners, of political behavior. Environment not only limits human conduct, but it also provides opportunities. Of particular importance are climatic and geographical factors. Uneven distribution of resources as well as differences in geographical and climatic endowments affects the potential power of a state. The size of the country influences the availability of indigenous natural resources, and the climate affects the mobilization of human resources necessary for exploiting those natural resources. Variations in those factors may crucially affect the structure of political systems, even influencing their capacity for survival under stress.

If political behavior is affected by environment, individuals have some capacity for choice even within the constraints furnished by environing circumstances. Of particular importance to writers such as Alfred Thayer Mahan (1840–1914), an American naval officer and historian; Sir Halford Mackinder (1861–1947), a British geographer; and Giulio Douhet, an Italian advocate of air power; as well as the Sprouts, is the impact of technological change upon our environment. Technology, it is suggested, does not render environmental factors unimportant or obsolete. Rather, it replaces one set of environmental factors with still another set. Mahan saw naval capabilities as the key to national power; Mackinder considered the technology of land transportation as crucial; Douhet focused upon the technology of air power as it was altering the conduct of warfare earlier in the twentieth century by extending our capacity for projecting power far beyond historic confines. The advent of the new technologies of the late twentieth century for the extension of control both on the earth's surface and in inner and outer space has enhanced the interest of scholars and policymakers in geopolitical relationships. Thus, for example, in this age of intercontinental ballistic missiles (ICBMs), analysts engaging in the constant calculus of deterrence consider such geographic factors as a country's size and population distribution, together with weapon deployments on land or sea, as relevant to targeting strategies.

Although possessing a limited capacity to change our environment, we remain circumscribed in our behavior by environmental factors. Central to geopolitical theories has been the question of the extent to which environmental factors can be modified to suit human needs. This question is not new. It long separated Anglo-American and French theorizing about geopolitical relationships. A French school of geographical "possibilist" thought, represented by Lucien Febvre and Vidal de la Blache, rejected the determinism of Anglo-American and German environmental theories. Drawing upon the intellectual heritage of the Enlightenment,

French students of geography suggested that the natural environment could be modified. In fact, human free will was said ultimately to determine the options available. Environment, and geography in particular, is but one of many forces governing the development of human activity.[19] Twentieth-century geopolitical writers fall somewhere between a strictly determinist and a possibilist interpretation. If environment does not determine the boundaries of human conduct, it nevertheless provides an important, if not crucial, conditioning influence. As Ladis K. D. Kristof has suggested, "The modern geopolitician does not look at the world map in order to find out what nature compels us to do but what nature advises us to do, given our preferences."[20]

We turn now to the writings of representative geopolitical theorists from the United States and Europe. Among the Americans, we focus on Mahan and the Sprouts. Mahan concentrated on the impact of naval power upon national political potential. The Sprouts probed the implications of a broad range of environmental factors for political behavior. In addition to Mahan and the Sprouts, a list of the most eminent American students of geopolitical relationships includes such diverse writers as Isaiah Bowman, James Fairgreave, Richard Hartshorne, Stephen B. Jones, George F. Kennan, Owen Lattimore, Homer Lea, General William Mitchell, Ellen Churchill Semple, Alexander P. de Seversky, Nicholas J. Spykman, Robert Strausz-Hupé, Frederick Jackson Turner, Hans A. Weigert, Karl A. Wittfogel, Derwent Whittlesey, and Quincy Wright. Moreover, as noted in Chapter 3, geopolitical relationships have been integral to the realist theory of international relations.

MAHAN, THE SEAS, AND NATIONAL POWER

Mahan wrote during the period of the last great wave of European imperial expansion and the rise of the United States to the status of a world power. His ideas greatly influenced Theodore Roosevelt who, first as Assistant Secretary of the Navy and later as President, contributed decisively to the rise of the United States as a leading naval power. Mahan's analysis of maritime history, particularly the growth of British global influence, led him to conclude that control of the seas, and especially of strategically important narrow waterways, was crucial to great power status.[21] Mahan based his theory on the observation that the rise of the British Empire and the development of Britain as a naval power had occurred simultaneously. The world's principal sea routes had become the Empire's internal communications links. Except for the Panama Canal, Britain controlled all of the world's major waterways and narrow seas or choke points—those bodies of water to which access, or passage through, could be controlled relatively easily from either shore: Dover, Gibraltar, Malta, Alexandria, the Cape of Good Hope, the Strait of Malacca at Singapore, the Suez Canal, and the entrance to the St. Lawrence River.

The ocean commerce of Northern Europe passed either through the narrow Strait of Dover under British guns or around the northern tip of Scotland, where the British navy maintained constant vigil. Britain and the United States enjoyed greater access to the oceans than Germany and Russia. Movement by sea was easier than over land, and the land masses were surrounded by oceans. States with ready access to the oceans had greater potential for major power status than states that were landlocked. Islands had an advantage over states sharing land boundaries with other states. Maritime states formed alliances more for purposes of commerce than of aggression.

In Mahan's analysis, sea power was crucially important to national strength and prosperity. The capacity of a state to achieve such status was dependent upon its geographic position, land configuration, extent of territory, population, national character, and form of government. For example, nations such as Britain or Japan, isolated by water, must maintain large naval forces if they are to be great powers, because for nations with long coastlines, the sea is a frontier and their position relative to other states is a function of their capacity to operate beyond that frontier. Geographical position contributed to Britain's power—with sufficient proximity to Continental Europe to strike potential enemies and adequate distance from Continental Europe to be reasonably safe from invasion. By focusing sea power in the Northeastern Atlantic and the Channel, Britain could control the world commerce of European powers, since there were no rivals to British sea power until the rise after 1890 of German, Japanese, and U.S. naval forces.

Such an option was not open to France, whose power had to be divided to protect its eastern frontier and Mediterranean and Atlantic coastlines. In Mahan's analysis the length of the coastline and the quality of harbors were important factors, although the extent of territory may constitute a source of weakness if the land does not have adequate levels of population and natural resources. Mahan held that the size and character of population and an aptitude for commercial pursuits, particularly those of international trade, indicated a capacity in a nation to become a major power. A nation with a large portion of its population skilled in maritime pursuits, especially shipbuilding and trade, had the potential to become a great maritime state. In sum, Mahan correlated national power and mobility over the seas, because at the time he wrote, transportation over land was primitive in contrast to the relative facility of movement over the "frictionless" oceans.

Mackinder and the Heartland

Like Mahan, Mackinder saw an intimate relationship between geography and technology. If the technology of the earlier era had enhanced the mobility of sea power over land power, the technology of the early twentieth century gave to land power the dominant position. The railroad, and subsequently the internal combustion engine and the construction of a modern highway and road network, made possible rapid transportation within much of the land mass of Eurasia. Until then the inner regions of Eurasia had been landlocked. Mackinder noted that Eurasia's river systems drain into none of the major seas of the world. The Arctic freezes much of the northern Eurasian coast. But with the advent of the railroad, the Middle East was becoming as accessible to Germany by land in the early twentieth century as it had been to Britain by sea. Although Britain, as a small island, was what Mackinder termed the legatee of a depreciating estate, the major Eurasian powers sat astride the greatest combination of human and natural resources. Mackinder saw the struggle between land power and sea power as a unifying theme of history. The first cycle in the evolution of sea power was completed in the closing of the Mediterranean Sea by the Macedonians. In the next cycle in the evolution of sea power, Mackinder noted that Rome, a land power, had defeated maritime Carthage and once again the Mediterranean had become a "closed sea."[22] In both these cycles in the ancient era—the Macedonian-Greek and the Roman-Carthaginian—a land power had successfully challenged a sea power. In modern times Britain found it difficult, if not impossible, to withstand pressures from land powers. Technology, once favorable to sea power, was said to be tipping the advantage in the early twentieth century to land power.

First, in a famous paper read before the Royal Geographic Society of London in 1904, and later, just after World War I, in his book *Democratic Ideals and Reality,* Mackinder suggested that the "pivot area" of international politics was that vast expanse of territory stretching from the East European and Siberian plains:

> As we consider this rapid review of the broader currents of history, does not a certain persistence of geographical relationship become evident? Is not the pivot region of the world's politics that vast area of Euro-Asia which is inaccessible to ships, but in antiquity lay open to the horse-riding nomads, and is today about to be covered with a network of railroads?[23]

This area, which coincided with the czarist Russian Empire, "occupies the central strategical position" and possesses "incalculably great" resources. (This "pivot area" Mackinder called the *Heartland.*) The region, he suggested, was surrounded by the "inner crescent," which includes such countries on the periphery of Eurasia as Germany, Turkey, India, and China. This region in turn is surrounded by the "outer crescent," which includes such countries as Britain, South Africa, and Japan.

Mackinder formulated the famous dictum:

Who rules East Europe commands the Heartland
Who rules the Heartland commands the World Island [Eurasia]
Who rules the World Island commands the World.[24]

Mackinder feared the rise of Germany and later the Soviet Union as mighty land states capable of becoming great naval powers. While emphasizing the growing importance of land power, Mackinder did not deprecate the role of sea power. Sea power was as vital to world power as it had ever been. In the twentieth century, however, broader land bases were necessary for sea power than had been needed in the nineteenth century.

✳ The World Island had the potential to become the greatest sea power, even though its Heartland would remain invulnerable to attack by sea power. In the twentieth century the state controlling the Heartland and hence the World Island would become a leading sea power in the same way as Macedonia and Rome, although primarily land powers, had eventually gained control of the seas. In fact, Mackinder correctly foresaw international politics in the first half of the twentieth century as being principally a struggle between Germany and Russia for control of the Heartland and adjacent areas on the Eurasian land mass. Such a conception has influenced the thought of other writers, including many of the realist school considered in Chapter 3, who have posited that the state capable of dominating Eurasia would have within its grasp the means to control remaining portions of the world.

Without necessarily referring to Mackinder or stating their assumptions as explicitly, American policymakers have had as a principal objective to prevent the domination of the Eurasian land mass by a hostile power—hence, the American interest in alliances with Western Europe and Japan and in security commitments elsewhere on the rimlands of Eurasia, including the Middle East. From this conception derives the American diplomacy, especially evident in the Nixon-Kissinger foreign policy and subsequently, to strengthen links between the United States and the People's Republic of China, and thus to help prevent a reconciliation between the two largest land powers of Eurasia.

During World War II Mackinder revised his theory to include in an Atlantic community a counterpoise to the aggregation of power in Eurasia. Although the Soviet Union would emerge from World War II as the "greatest land power on the globe" and "in the strategically strongest defensive position," the nations of the North Atlantic basin would form a counterpoise, which in fact occurred with the formation of the Atlantic Alliance in 1949 as East-West tensions deepened in the early post–World War II period.[25] Together, Britain, France, and the United States, Mackinder held, could provide power adequate to prevent a resurgence of Germany and to balance the Soviet Union. Other writers, such as Nicholas J. Spykman and Stephen B. Jones, suggested that the "rimland" of Eurasia might prove strategically more important than the Heartland if new centers of industrial power and communications were created along the circumference of the Eurasian land mass. The "rimland" hypothesis is a central theoretical foundation of George F. Kennan's famous postwar proposal for a "policy of containment" of the Soviet Union, which became the philosophical basis for the American foreign policy of internationalism beginning with the Truman Doctrine and the Marshall Plan in 1947.[26]

The advent of the airplane, and subsequently the means to penetrate outer space, provided a whole new dimension to geopolitics. Once again, technology had the effect of altering the significance of specific geopolitical relations. Just as Mahan and Mackinder had based their geopolitical theories on an analysis of the implications, respectively, of technologies facilitating movement over the seas and the land, Giulio Douhet, writing in the 1920s, saw the airplane as conferring unprecedented possibilities for the conduct of warfare against targets previously invulnerable to attack and destruction. As long as human activities were restricted to the earth's surface, they were subject to constraints imposed by the terrain. Although the seas are uniform in character, man's mobility via the oceans is limited by virtue of the coastlines that surround them. No such impediments to mobility exist in the air. Writing with great foresight in 1921, Douhet concluded: "The airplane has complete freedom of action and direction; it can fly to and from any point of the compass in the shortest time—a straight line—by any route deemed expedient. . . . By virtue of this new weapon, the repercussions of war are no longer limited by the farthest artillery range of surface guns, but can be directly felt for hundreds and hundreds of miles over all the lands and seas of nations at war. . . . There will be no distinction any longer between soldiers and civilians."[27] It followed that the wars of the future would differ radically from those of the past, and that control of the air would confer upon states unprecedented mobility of power and the capacity to inflict devastation upon an adversary's military forces and industry.

Writing during World War II, and building upon the writings of Douhet and the ideas of General Billy Mitchell, Alexander de Seversky emphasized the implications of advances in technology for rapid increases in the range of aircraft. This would render unnecessary the aircraft carrier, he predicted, because planes could operate from land bases to attack targets in the enemy's homeland. Thus, the unprecedented mobility conferred by manned flight, noted by Douhet, was given even greater emphasis by Alexander de Seversky. Air power made possible not only greater mobility, but also freed man to an unprecedented extent from dependence on an extensive ground organization, including bases for refueling, as the range of aircraft, and thus their operating radius, grew.[28] Control of air space became as complex a problem as control of the land and the sea.

GEOPOLITICS: THE POLITICAL SIGNIFICANCE OF SPATIAL FACTORS

Friedrich Ratzel (1844–1904), a German geographer, coined the term *Anthropogeographie,* which meant a synthesis of geography, anthropology, and politics. Thus the new discipline of political geography was born in Germany in the nineteenth century. This new discipline was directed to the study of man, the state, and the world as organic units. The state was seen as a living organism that occupies space and that grows, contracts, and eventually dies, although Ratzel himself stopped short of imputing to the state an objective reality, asserting instead that states "are not organisms properly speaking but only aggregate-organisms," the unity of which is forged by "moral and spiritual forces."[29]

Political geographers addressed themselves to the question of man's relationship to nature. They concerned themselves with the implications of climate, topography, and natural resources for civilization. In fact, Ratzel attributed the development of superior civilizations, which he identified principally with Europe, to favorable climatic conditions. He contended that mankind was engaged in an unending struggle for living space, an idea that later was integrated in the form of the term *lebensraum* into the thought of Haushofer and Hitler. A state's land area indicates its power position. States strive to extend their territorial frontiers. The urge to territorial expansion is greatest among strong states. Boundaries therefore are constantly shifting. They form the zones of conflict between states as "dynamic frontiers." In twentieth-century German geopolitical writings and in Spykman's work,[30] boundaries or "dynamic frontiers" are viewed as demarcations of zones in which expansion has temporarily ceased.

Rudolf Kjellen (1864–1922), a Swedish geographer, first used the term *geopolitics* to describe the geopolitical bases of national power. Adhering to an organic theory of the state, he held that states, like animals in a Darwinian theory, engage in a relentless struggle for survival. States have boundaries, a capital, and lines of communication, as well as a consciousness and a culture. Although Kjellen wrote metaphysically and imputed to the state the quality of a living organism, he nevertheless concluded that "the life of a state is, ultimately, in the hands of the individual."[31] He considered the emergence of a few great powers as a result of efforts of strong states to expand.

In the interwar period, the followers of Kjellen and Ratzel used geopolitics to develop a framework for German national expansion. Karl Haushofer (1869–1946) founded the German Academy at the University of Munich in 1925, together with the journal *Zeitschrift für Geopolitik*. Both received active support from the Third Reich.[32] Haushofer's influence was considerable in military circles and became the basis for many of Hitler's conceptions of Nazi expansion.

For Haushofer, geopolitics represented the relationship of political phenomena to geography. Geopolitics enabled German leaders to establish national objectives and policies. The purpose of geopolitics, in Haushofer's conception, was to place the systematic study of geography at the disposal of a militarized Reich by relating national power to geographic factors, collecting relevant geographical information, and presenting a propaganda rationale for Nazi expansion and aggression. Thus, for Hau-

shofer and his followers, geopolitics and power politics became synonymous. The geopolitical concepts developed by Haushofer (including *lebensraum* and "dynamic frontiers"), to the extent that they shaped Hitler's view of the world, contributed to the outbreak of World War II. In
this respect, they stand in sharp contrast to other types of geopolitical
analysis based upon a scientific knowledge of geography and its relationship to technology, resources, and population.

German geopolitical thinking, from Ratzel to Haushofer, expressed
the need for great states to enlarge their frontiers; to obtain *lebensraum;*
to gain self-sufficiency in raw materials, industry, and markets; and to
achieve population growth. Extensive geographical space and national
power were synonymous. Haushofer drew upon Ratzel's writings on the
relationship between space and power. Moreover, Haushofer based his
recommendations for achieving *lebensraum* on Japan's successful imperial expansion in the 1930s. He was indebted to Mackinder's conception
that the Heartland was the key to global mastery. Haushofer himself was
deeply influenced by the writings of Mackinder and in particular, by the
Heartland theory, which for him became a basis for Nazi Germany's continued expansion in quest of *lebensraum.*[33] Warning of the danger posed
by an expansionist Nazi Germany, Robert Strausz-Hupé, referring to Haushofer rather than Mackinder, suggested that geopolitics "represents a
revolutionary attempt to measure and to harness the forces which make
for expansionism."[34] German geopolitical theorists considered conflict
among leading states to be inevitable, and so perhaps it was if nations
adopted policies for imperial expansion as espoused by Haushofer and his
followers. This conflict would pit a continental European grouping dominated by Germany in alliance with a Pacific grouping led by Japan against
an Atlantic grouping under the leadership of Britain and the United
States. Thus the world would be divided into various pan regions that
themselves would have been formed either in anticipation, or as a result,
of war.

Haushofer's organic theory of boundaries contained a second major
component of German geopolitical thinking. He proposed in this theory
that a state strives to achieve a frontier that contains a zone of sparse
settlement—a zone outside the living space, separating the state from
neighboring states. Haushofer and his followers considered the world to
consist of renovating and decadent states. British "decadence" was exemplified by Britain's inability to halt tendencies in its empire toward self-
government. In another war, Haushofer believed, Britain could not be
assured of the loyalty and support of the self-governing parts of the British
Empire, although he acknowledged that the British Empire would probably constitute a formidable obstacle to the development of new pan regions. Finally, the German geopolitical theorists developed geostrategy as
a military science. All relevant information about an opponent was gathered so that "blitzkrieg," a quick and decisive attack, could be mounted.

In brief, German geopolitical writings contained five concepts: (1)

*autarchy, or national economic self-sufficiency, precluding the need for foreign products; (2) *lebensraum,* or sufficient land area and natural resources to support the population of a nation; (3) pan regions, or broader geographical areas, to replace narrow national frontiers; (4) the assumption that the land mass of Eurasia-Africa, being the most populous and the largest combination of land power and sea power, has therefore the potential for world domination; and (5) the right of the state to "natural frontiers or boundaries set forth by nature."[35]

[handwritten: Jefferson would say this is wrong. Because the state has no rights]

THE SPROUTS AND MAN-MILIEU RELATIONSHIPS

Harold Sprout (1901–1980) and Margaret Sprout (1903–) made the greatest contribution of the mid-twentieth century toward the development of hypotheses for examining environing relationships. Although the Sprouts long believed in the importance of geography in examining political behavior,[36] they contended that most, if not all, human activity is affected by the uneven distribution of human and nonhuman resources.[37] The Sprouts rejected unidimensional, geopolitical theories in favor of an "ecological perspective" because it appeared to provide a more integrated, holistic view of the international environment that took account of its physical and nonphysical features. The environment, or milieu, was viewed as a multidimensional system, in which the perceptions held by political leaders of environmental conditions (the psychomilieu) as well as the conditions themselves were the objects of study and analysis. Such research emphasized the *interrelationship* of geography, demography, technology, and resources, and focused upon the importance of perceptual variables, as well as quantitative factors such as population and territorial size.

The milieu is said to affect human activities in only two respects. First, it can influence human decisions only if human beings perceive factors related to the milieu. Second, such factors can limit individual performance or the outcome of decisions based upon perceptions of the environment.[38] Thus, decisions may be taken on the basis of erroneous perceptions of the environment with potentially disastrous consequences. The task confronting the decision-maker, therefore—to link the Sprouts' analysis to decision-making theories considered in Chapter 11—is to narrow the gap between the perceived and the real environment.

The Sprouts regarded geography as "concerned with the arrangement of things on the face of the earth, and with the association of things that give character to particular places." They believe that geography affects all human and nonhuman, tangible and intangible phenomena that "exhibit areal dimensions and variations upon or in relation to the earth's surface."[39] Every political community has a geographical base. Each political community is set on a territory that is a unique combination of location, size, shape, climate, and natural resources. Thus must transactions among nations entail significant, even crucial, geographical considerations. The Sprouts noted that international statecraft exhibits in all periods "more or less discernible patterns of coercion and submission, influence and deference; patterns reflected in political terms with strong geographic connotations."[40]

Cognitive Behavioralism and the Operational Milieu

Important to the Sprouts is the concept of cognitive behavioralism. This concept assumes that a person consciously responds to the milieu through perception "and in no other way."[41] Erroneous ideas of the milieu may be just as influential as accurate ideas in forming moods, preferences, decisions, and actions. The Sprouts proceed to distinguish, somewhat imprecisely, between the environment as the observer perceives it and the environment as it actually exists. The so-called psychomilieu may be compared to Plato's shadows in the cave—"images or ideas which the individual derives from interaction between what he selectively receives from his milieu, by means of his sensory apparatus, and his scheme of values, conscious memories, and subconsciously stored experience."[42] Failure to perceive the limiting condition may result in severe consequences. Inflated illusions about and misinterpretations of geographic circumstances may have similar unfortunate effects.[43] Popular attitudes, as well as the decisions of statesmen, are based upon geographical conceptions that "depend in no small degree upon the kinds of maps to which they are accustomed," as is noted in greater detail in a later section of this chapter. Therefore, an analysis of political behavior must take account of assumptions that political leaders make about their milieu.

The decisional entity, acting within the operational milieu and having a psychomilieu,[44] is an environed organism (an individual or a population) rather than an abstraction (the state). It is this decisional entity that is a principal concern of the social scientist and a particular interest of the student of international relations and of decision-making, as noted in Chapter 11. Thus, the Sprouts object to terminology such as the "state's motivation" and the "state's needs." They do not apply psychoecological concepts to social organization for much the same reason that they reject giving human attributes to the national or international system. They attribute these concepts only to human beings. They believe that political discussion on such an abstract level muddies rather than clarifies one's understanding of the workings of international politics.[45]

Although political decisions are based on the statesman's perceptions of the milieu, the results of these decisions are limited by the objective nature of the operational milieu—that is to say, by "the situation as it actually exists and affects the achievements and capabilities of the entity in question (whether a single individual, group, or community as a whole)."[46] In short, the operational milieu exists, even though it may not be fully discernible by the political actor. So far as decision-making is concerned, the Sprouts do not see the milieu as inevitably "conditioning," "drawing," or "compelling" the policymaker and "dictating" his choices.

Thus the ecological perspective provides a framework for the consideration of three types of phenomena: (1) the perceived, or psychomilieu; (2) the actions of individuals or groups; and (3) the outcomes of their actions.[47] The three fundamental concepts of importance to the Sprouts include environment, environed entities, and entity-environmental relationships.[48]

Limitations of Geopolitical Theorizing

The Sprouts emphasize that technology and social change play a large role in environmental relationships. Although technology has obviously not altered the physical layout of lands and seas, it has added new dimensions to the international milieu. Although geopolitical speculation has enriched our understanding of the international system, the most serious defect has been the "almost universal failure of the geopolitical theorists to anticipate and allow for the rate of technological and other changes." An accurate assessment of the tools, skills, and technological innovations available to the interacting communities is crucial to all geopolitical theorizing. The Sprouts adduce the ecological principle that substantial change in one sector of the milieu can be expected to produce "significant, often unsettling, sometimes utterly disruptive consequences in other sectors."[49]

Geography, environed organisms, the psychomilieu, technology, the operational milieu, and beliefs all affect each other. "Substantial changes either in the environment or in the genetic makeups of the organisms involved are likely to start chain reactions that ramify throughout the entire 'web-of-life' within the 'biotic community.' "[50] The interrelatedness of the ecological paradigm has grown increasingly with the mounting complexity of modern society resulting from expanding populations and advanced technology. It is increasingly difficult to "isolate and classify human political events as merely domestic matters or foreign affairs, or as political, sociological, or economic." In fact, the complexity of interrelatedness "within and between national communities, and the increasing irrelevance of the time honored distinction between domestic and international questions, constitute major datum points in the ecological perspective on international politics."[51] The focal point for empirical analysis in the past decade has increasingly been the "linkage" between domestic politics and foreign policy.

In their study of environmental relationships, the Sprouts have drawn four major conclusions. First, the ecological perspective and frame of reference provide a fruitful approach to the analysis of foreign policy and the estimation of a state's capabilities. Second, it is helpful to distinguish analytically between the relation of environmental factors to policy decisions and to the operational results of decisions. In the Sprouts' judgment, much of the confusion clouding the discussion of environmental factors in international politics stems from the failure to make this distinction explicit. Third, the ecological approach is a useful complement to the study of both the foreign policy and the international capabilities of states. The Sprouts' paradigm entails the examination of such limiting conditions as the level of available technology, cognition of essential factors, and the ratio of available resources to commitments.[52] Finally, they see the ecological approach as broadening the study of international politics by integrating into it relevant theories and data from geography, psychology, sociology, and other systems of learning.

CURRENT RESEARCH ON ENVIRONMENTAL FACTORS

Some scholars have focused on the relationship between environment and political behavior. Writing in the mid-1970s, George Liska examined the nature of equilibrium in the international system with specific reference to conflict and geopolitical factors. He concluded that conflict between continental and maritime states has been a recurrent phenomenon in international relations, especially in the European system.

> The qualitative disparity between principally land-based and sea-oriented states proved commonly incapable of assimilation by competitive or other interactions. . . . The schism was conspicuously manifest whenever a strong land power staged, and the dominant maritime power resisted to the point of vetoing, a drive for seaborne outreach that would expand the scope of the balance of power and adapt its functioning to overseas extensions of the system's continental core.[53]

In an effort to determine the impact of insular status on nations, two other authors—Robert Holt and John Turner—have compared the policies of Britain, Ceylon, and Japan.[54] Their analysis revealed that insular polities have a "more active involvement" with other countries than noninsular polities. Insular polities are more limited than noninsular states in the range of foreign policies available to them. These authors found similarities in the foreign policies of Britain and Japan. Both countries attempted to occupy sections of the Eurasian mainland, especially those areas from which invasions might be mounted against them. Both tried to maintain a balance of power among mainland nations by supporting the weaker coalition. Both sought alliances with powers outside the region to strengthen their position with respect to more proximate continental national units.

In assessing the effect of noncontiguity on the integration of political units, Richard Merritt's study of territorially discontiguous polities indicated that centrifugal forces increased with the distance.[55] There was greater communication with neighboring than with physically distant peoples. The noncontiguous polity depends on the external environment to preserve communication links among its physically separated parts. Daily dependence upon communications makes noncontiguous polities sensitive to shifts in the international environment that affect communications. Such polities have been concerned with the application of international law to internal waters, territorial and high seas, air rights, and land access, to cite only the modern history of problems experienced by such states as Malaysia, Pakistan (1947–1974), the United Arab Republic (Egypt-Syria) (1958–1962), and the now-defunct West Indies Federation.

CRITIQUES OF ENVIRONMENTAL THEORIES

Critics of environmental theories, including the Sprouts, take issue with writers who engage in "environmentalistic rhetoric" and assume that attitudes or decisions are "determined" or "influenced" or in some other way causally affected by environmental factors.[56] Although the Sprouts reject environment as a determinant of politics, they conceive as crucial (1) the actor's perception of environmental factors and (2) limitations to human activity posed by the environment.[57]

According to Strausz-Hupé, geographic conditions have been modified by man throughout history: "Geographic conditions determine largely *where* history is made, but it is always man who makes it."[58] Although deriving his own work from the geopolitical concepts in Mackinder's writings, Spykman criticized Mackinder for overestimating the potentialities of the Heartland and underestimating those of the Inner Crescent. "If there is to be a slogan for the power politics of the Old World, it must be 'Who controls the Rimland rules Eurasia; who rules Eurasia controls the destinies of the world.' "[59] Spykman also noted that a combination of sea powers had never been aligned against a grouping of land powers. "The historical alignment has always been in terms of some members of the Rimland with Great Britain and Russia together against a dominating Rimland power."[60] In his analysis of the German geopolitical school Strausz-Hupé asserts that "there is, in short, no historical evidence in support of the causal nexus alleged by the advocates of *lebensraum* . . . to exist between population pressure and national growth in space."[61] Historically, national expansion has resulted from conditions other than population pressure. For example, Japanese expansionism in Asia antedated the upsurge in Japan's population. Nor does large space necessarily equate with national power, although "whenever large space was thoroughly organized by a state, small nations . . . were not able to withstand its expansive force."[62] According to Derwent Whittlesey, Haushofer's conception of geopolitics was illogical in that it based the need for *lebensraum* upon Germany's high birth rates. Since the birth rates of the Slavic territories to the East were even higher, their need for territory should have been greater than that of Germany.[63]

Finally, it is often asserted that technological change has rendered both Mackinder's Heartland concept and Haushofer's geopolitical theory obsolete. In the discussion following Mackinder's presentation of his paper, "The Geographical Pivot of History," to the Royal Geographic Society, Leopold Amery asserted, "Both the sea and the railway are going in the future . . . to be supplemented by the air as a means of locomotion, [and] when we come to that, a great deal of this geographical distribution must lose its importance, and the successful powers will be those who have the greatest industrial basis."[64] According to Strausz-Hupé, "If it [the Heartland] ever was a valid concept (for which there is no convincing evidence), there is no guarantee that modern technology will not invalidate it. It may, indeed, have done so already."[65] The Sprouts criticize the theories of both Mahan and Mackinder as being outmoded as a result of innovations in military technology and "paramilitary and nonmilitary forms of political interaction."[66] Kristof faults geopolitical writers for having "marshaled facts and laws of the physical world to justify political demands and support political opinions. One of the best examples of the hopelessly contradictory arguments to which this may lead is a concept akin in spirit to that of the 'natural boundary,' namely, the concept of the 'harmonic state.' "[67]

If the psychomilieu—the world as it is perceived—is central to the work of writers such as the Sprouts, others have focused specifically upon the effects of alternative types of maps—the visual presentation of spatial and geographical relationships—as they relate to the formation of images about the world. Since World War II, special emphasis has been placed upon the distortion introduced into political analysis by reliance upon Mercator equator-based projections. Such maps failed to present the idea of the earth as a sphere and therefore as having geographical unity and continuity. The Mercator projection provided an erroneous conception of distances—for example, the proximity of the United States to the Soviet Union across the Arctic. Viewing the world as a sphere makes evident that, for example, Buenos Aires is farther from the United States than every European capital including Moscow.

The advent of air power, and its indispensable contribution to the Allied victory in World War II, contributed decisively to the alteration in traditional Mercator-type conceptions of geography, for the shortest distance by air between two points lay in a line that followed the contour of the earth. In its place came asymmetrical projections based for the most part upon spherical pole-centered maps. Numerous writers during World War II pointed to the need for such alternative maps. The need for such maps became apparent also because, as Richard E. Harrison and Hans W. Weigert, writing in the 1940s, pointed out:

> We continued using it (the Mercator projection) when land power and land-based air power became pivotal in the greatest of all world conflicts. In a world war that is mainly being fought in the northern hemisphere this proved to be

an almost fatal misjudgment; for the Mercator projection whose center of accuracy is along the equator cannot possibly show the relationship between the power spheres of the contending great Powers.[68]

If maps shape a person's perceptions of the world, they also reflect the shared constructs of geographic and spatial relationships that are prevalent. Maps are drawn and redrawn to take account of "those geographical" factors deemed to be important at a given point in time. As Alan Henrikson has written, "One can regard such things as maps as pure subjective ideographs, or as constructs with only a mathematical relation to objective reality, or even as mere reflections of the material processes of history, in which case they would have no independent determining power. . . . The global maps that helped to guide and explain the war effort (World War II)—and were thus an essential part of the war's intellectual history—were traces on the human mind, etched there not only by man's experience but by man's imagination."[69] This idea is reflected in the works of Richard Edes Harrison and Robert Strausz-Hupé, who went so far as to suggest that the "psychological isolationism" of the United States resulted from the deficiencies of maps, notably the utilization of two-dimensional (Mercator) projections instead of those representing the earth as a globe.[70] According to W. H. Parker, Mackinder viewed the "map of the world" not as "the physical or political map found in an atlas, but a mental map in which the various horizontal distinctions and movements of global phenomena are vertically integrated in dynamic interaction."[71]

The changing importance of other geographic relationships has contributed, over the past generation, to the development of additional conceptions of the world etched in maps. Some writers have suggested the emergence of global trends that are leading to a new set of geostrategic, and geopolitical, relationships. Of special importance are resources and the increased vulnerability of oil supplies and vital raw materials to disruption either at their source or in transit from producer to consumer states. The growth of resource-import dependence by industrialized states, together with the increase in vulnerability of such resources to interdiction, has contributed to a revival of interest in geopolitical analysis, but in the present context, the potential for conflict over scarce resources is increasing at a time of diffusion of military technologies to a variety of state and nonstate actors.[72] Such trends take place in context of the emergence of a new maritime regime as a result of the growing importance of resources in the seas and/or the seabed, and changing patterns of Western and Soviet overseas base access—more detrimental to the United States than to the Soviet Union. A "new strategic map" is said to have come into existence, whose "practical effects are to resurrect the importance of geography and resources as a factor in military thinking. . . . Thus knowledge about the whereabouts of food, energy, and universal resources, the location of small islands, patterns of sea and air lines of communication, and the impact of arms transfers on regional power balances may become as necessary tools for strategic analysis as familiarity with the acronyms of nuclear warfare has been in the recent past."[73]

This revival of interest in geopolitical analysis has extended beyond resource issues, per se, to an effort to update concepts drawn from such earlier writers as Mahan and Mackinder to the international system of the late twentieth century. In present context, the Soviet Union represents a vast land power whose traditional Eurasian focus has expanded both into the rimlands and into regions far from Eurasia. The superpower relationship of our age pits the Soviet Union, as the leading land power, against the United States, the principal maritime power. Historically, the internal lines of communication between the Soviet Union and its allies have been in the Eurasian land mass. The links between the United States and its allies on the rimlands of Eurasia lie across the oceans. The growth of Soviet naval power, together with the projection of Soviet influence and capabilities far from Eurasia, poses a threat of growing proportions to the United States and its allies. According to Colin S. Gray:

> The strength of geopolitical grand theory is that it places local action, or interaction, within a global framework. . . . Just as those who wish to understand nuclear strategy have no choice other than to master the essential concepts of the nuclear strategist (first strike/second strike, counterforce, and countervalue, and so forth), so those seeking to comprehend the geopolitical realities of international security questions need to master the essential concepts of the geopolitician.[74]

In Gray's view, the geopolitics of Mackinder "provide an intellectual architecture, far superior to rival conceptions, for understanding the principal international security issues[.] . . . Mackinder's geopolitical work is grand theory at its best."[75] According to W. H. Parker, the "originality and brilliance" of Mackinder's work, and in particular his "Geopolitical Pivot of History," results from "the way it related the fact of the world having become a closed system to technological changes in communications, with the balance of advantage oscillating between land power and sea power, between centre and periphery. It thus reduced the complex interplay of historical event and geographical fact to an astonishing simplicity."[76] In operational terms, geopolitical theorizing, in present context, leads to the conclusion that the United States and its allies must prevent the expansion of Soviet power into the rimlands of Eurasia. For this purpose alliances with West European states and Japan are crucially important.

At the same time, the reestablishment of a close Sino-Soviet relationship would unify the two largest land powers of Eurasia—the Heartland about which Mackinder wrote. Thus geopolitics, Colin Gray suggests, "is not simply one set of ideas among many competing sets that help to illuminate the structure of policy problems. Rather, it is a meta- or master framework that, without predetermining policy choice, suggests long-term factors and trends in the security objectives of particular, territorially organized security communities."[77]

TECHNOLOGY, POPULATION GROWTH, AND ENVIRONMENTAL ISSUES

Technological changes may have altered the significance of the theorizing of certain of the writers examined in this chapter, although advanced technology has rendered environmental relationships ever more important. As many writers have suggested, modern science and technology have transformed the environment in intended, but also in unintended ways.[78] Science and technology have brought "uninvited guests" in such forms as air pollution, traffic congestion, and resource scarcity. In the twentieth century, the pace of scientific-technological innovation has quickened beyond any historical precedent, and people in all parts of the globe have been drawn into the orbit of modern technology. Whether changes wrought by technology are affecting the environment in ways beyond the means of coping with them remains an unanswered question. What is certain is that inextricable relationships or linkages exist among technology, geography, and international politics.

The pollution of the environment has become an enduring concern for the late twentieth century. As Zbigniew Brzezinski has pointed out, those societies that are most advanced technologically—the United States, Western Europe, and Japan—have spawned the most vocal groups in support of issues related to the "quality of life." This is characteristic of the "technetronic age" into which such societies are said already to have entered, or are on the threshold of entering.[79] Population growth, urbanization, and the chemical wastes of products of industrial civilization—all of which are more prevalent in the more advanced societies than in the less developed—are held to be causing changes in the balance of nature from the oceans to the ozone layer.

Thus in the late twentieth century, the focus on the milieu in the literature of international relations represents a convergence of several principal interests of scholars and policymakers. These include resource scarcity, population growth, and the relationship of geography to political power. In short, a new set of geopolitical or geostrategic relationships has come into existence largely as a result of the pervasive impact of technology on international relations generally and, specifically, on the foreign policies of states. Because the perception of the milieu, and the impact of the milieu itself, is central to decision-making and to political behavior generally, those concerned with the development of theories of political behavior at the international level have taken renewed interest in environmental relationships. Political systems have been hypothesized to be open systems—susceptible to inputs from, and making outputs to, their environments. Last but not least, the issues of pollution and ecology and of population growth and food supply have led to efforts both to forecast trends and to develop models often neo-Malthusian in nature. The milieu then provides a unique focal point not only for older and contemporary theorizing, but for analytical and normative theory in international relations in the years ahead, for in the final analysis all foreign policies and other patterns of international interaction are set within a political, social, cultural, and geographic environment.

NOTES

1. Harold and Margaret Sprout, *The Ecological Perspective on Human Affairs with Special Reference to International Politics* (Princeton: Princeton University Press, 1965), p. 27. The Sprouts set forth the following definitions: Environment may be defined as a generic concept under which are subsumed all external forces and factors to which an organism or aggregate of organisms is actually or potentially responsive; or environment may be limited to the material and spatial aspects of the surrounding world, to the exclusion of the melee of human social relations.
2. Aristotle, *The Politics of Aristotle,* trans. Ernest Barker (Oxford: Clarendon, 1961), pp. 289–311.
3. Jean Bodin, *Six Books of the Commonwealth,* trans. F. J. Tooley (New York: Macmillan, 1955), pp. 145–157.
4. Baron de Montesquieu, *The Spirit of Laws* (Worcester, Mass.: Isaiah Thomas, 1802), vol. I, pp. 154–159, 259–274.
5. Frederick Jackson Turner, "The Significance of the Frontier in American History," in Donald Sheehan, ed., *The Making of American History,* Book II (New York: Dryden, 1950), p. 200.
6. Nazli Choucri, "Population Resources and Technology: Political Implications of the Environmental Crisis," in David A. Kay and Eugene B. Skolnikoff, eds., *World-Eco-Crisis: International Organizations in Response* (Madison: University of Wisconsin Press, 1972), p. 24. See also the discussion in Chapter 8, pp. 344–346 and notes 127ff.
7. Quincy Wright, *A Study of War* (Chicago and London: The University of Chicago Press, 1965), p. 1144.
8. Ibid., p. 1285.
9. Saul B. Cohen, *Geography and Politics in a World Divided,* 2nd ed. (New York: Oxford University Press, 1973), p. 29.
10. Raymond Aron, *Peace and War* (Garden City, N.Y.: Doubleday, 1966), p. 191.
11. Colin S. Gray, *The Geopolitics of Super Power* (Lexington: The University Press of Kentucky, 1988), p. 45.
12. Henry Thomas Buckle, *History of Civilization in England* (London: Longmans, 1903), vol. I, pp. 39–151.
13. Ellsworth Huntington, *Mainsprings of Civilization* (New York: Wiley, 1945), especially pp. 250–275; and *Civilization and Climate* (New Haven: Yale University Press, 1924), esp. pp. 1–29, 387–411.
14. For an examination of Toynbee's challenge-response hypothesis, see *A Study of History,* abridgement of vols. I–IV by D. C. Somervell (London: Oxford University Press, 1956), pp. 60–139. Andrew M. Scott has proposed the challenge-response concept as a central approach to the study of international affairs, closely related to the balance-of-power idea. "Challenge and Response: A Tool for the Analysis of International Affairs," *Review of Politics,* XVIII (1956), 207–226.

15. Toynbee, op. cit., p. 246. Toynbee defines breakdown as the termination of growth.
16. Kenneth D. Boulding, *Conflict and Defense* (New York: Harper & Row, 1963); Patrick O'Sullivan, *Geopolitics* (New York: St. Martin's Press, 1986).
17. Ibid., p. 69.
18. See, for example, Albert Wohlstetter, "Illusions of Distance," *Foreign Affairs*, 46, No. 2 (1968), 242–255.
19. See Harold and Margaret Sprout, *The Ecological Perspective on Human Affairs*, pp. 83–98; Lucien Febvre, *A Geographical Introduction to History* (New York: Knopf, 1925), pp. 358–368; P. W. J. Vidal de la Blache, *Principles of Human Geography*, Emmanuel de Martonne, ed. (New York: Holt, Rinehart and Winston, 1926); O. H. K. Spate, "How Determined Is Possibilism?" *Geographical Studies*, IV (1957), 3–8; George Tatham, "Environmentalism and Possibilism," in Griffith Taylor, ed., *Geography in the Twentieth Century* (New York: Philosophical Library, 1951), pp. 128ff, 151ff.
20. Ladis K. D. Kristof, "The Origins and Evolution of Geopolitics," *Journal of Conflict Resolution*, IV (March 1960), 19. See also R. J. Johnston, *Geography and State: An Essay in Political Geography* (New York: St. Martin's Press, 1982), esp. pp. 1–28, 120–187; J. R. V. Prescott, *Political Geography* (New York: St. Martin's Press, 1972), esp. pp. 1–75; Kliot, Nurit, and Waterman, eds., *Pluralism and Political Geography: People, Territory and State* (New York: St. Martin's Press, 1983), esp. pp. 9–36.
21. Alfred Thayer Mahan, *The Influence of Seapower Upon History, 1660–1783* (Boston: Little, Brown, 1897), esp. pp. 281–329. See also Margaret Tuttle Sprout, "Mahan: Evangelist of Sea Power," in Edward Mead Earle, ed., *Makers of Modern Strategy: Military Thought from Machiavelli to Hitler* (Princeton: Princeton University Press, 1943), pp. 415–445; Harold and Margaret Sprout, *The Rise of American Naval Power* (Princeton: Princeton University Press, 1942); William Reitzel, "Mahan on Use of the Sea," and James A. Field, Jr., "The Origins of Maritime Strategy and the Development of Seapower," in B. Mitchell Simpson III, ed., *War, Strategy and Maritime Power* (New Brunswick, N.J.: Rutgers University Press, 1977), pp. 77–107.
22. Halford Mackinder, *Democratic Ideals and Reality* (New York: Norton, 1962), pp. 35–39.
23. Halford Mackinder, "The Geographical Pivot of History," *Geographical Journal*, XXIII (April 1904), 434. For an extended discussion and critique of Mackinder's thought and writings on geography and geopolitics, within the broader context of his life and times, see W. H. Parker, *Mackinder: Geography as an Aid to Statecraft* (Oxford: Clarendon Press, 1982), esp. chs. 5–8.
24. Halford Mackinder, op. cit., p. 150. See also Hans W. Weigert, "Mackinder's Heartland," *The American Scholar*, XV (Winter 1945), 43–45.
25. Halford J. Mackinder, "The Round World and the Winning of the Peace," *Foreign Affairs*, XXI (July 1943), 601.
26. See Stephen B. Jones, "Global Strategic Views," *Geographic Review*, XLV (October 1955), 492–508; Nicholas J. Spykman, *The Geography of the Peace* (New York: Harcourt Brace and Company, 1944), p. 43; and George F. Kennan, "The Sources of Soviet Conduct," *Foreign Affairs*, XXV (July 1947), 566–582. Spykman, in discussing the value of the "Heartland's interior lines" with respect to the periphery or "rimland," suggested that the relations between center and circumference are of one sort if the maritime powers are trying to

apply their leverage around the rimland from afar; but these relations are changed if local centers of power and communications are developed around the rimland. Op. cit., p. 40.

27. Giulio Douhet, *The Command of the Air,* trans. Dino Ferrari (New York: Coward-McCann, 1942), pp. 10–11.

28. Alexander P. de Seversky, *Victory Through Air Power* (New York: Simon & Schuster, 1942).

29. Friedrich Ratzel, *Anthropogeographie,* 2nd ed. (Stuttgart: J. Engelhorn, 1899), part I, p. 2. See Kristof, op. cit., p. 22.

30. See, in particular, Nicholas J. Spykman and Abbie A. Rollins, "Geographic Objectives in Foreign Policy I," *American Political Science Review,* XXXIII (June 1939), 391–393.

31. Rudolf Kjellen, *Der Staat als Lebensform,* trans. M. Langfelt (Leipzig: S. Hirzel Verlag, 1917), pp. 218–220. See Kristof, op. cit., p. 22.

32. For a discussion of the development of the German Academy, see Donald H. Norton, "Karl Haushofer and the German Academy, 1925–1945," *Central European History,* I (March 1958), 82. According to its rules and regulations, the objectives of the Academy were "to nourish all spiritual expressions of Germandom and to bring together and strengthen the unofficial cultural relations of Germany with areas abroad and of the Germans abroad with the homeland, in the service of the all-German folk-consciousness." Ibid.

33. W. H. Parker, op. cit., p. 159. According to Parker, Haushofer had used Mackinder's 1904 paper ("The Geographical Pivot of History") as early as 1921, and continued to do so throughout the interwar period.

34. Robert Strausz-Hupé, *Geopolitics: The Struggle for Space and Power* (New York: Putnam's, 1942), p. vii. Ladis K. D. Kristof suggests the following definition: "Geopolitics is the study of political phenomena (1) in their spatial relationship and (2) in their relationship with, dependence upon, and influence on earth as well as on all those cultural factors which constitute the subject matter of human geography (anthropogeography) broadly defined. In other words, geopolitics is what the word itself suggests etymologically: geographical politics, that is, politics and not geography—politics geographically interpreted or analyzed for its geographical content." Kristof, op. cit., p. 34.

35. Derwent Whittlesey, "Haushofer: The Geopolitician," in Edward Mead Earle, ed., *Makers of Modern Strategy: Military Thought from Machiavelli to Hitler* (Princeton: Princeton University Press, 1943), pp. 398–406.

36. Harold and Margaret Sprout, *The Ecological Perspective on Human Affairs,* p. 9.

37. Harold and Margaret Sprout, *An Ecological Paradigm for the Study of International Politics* (Princeton: Center for International Studies, 1968). Monograph No. 30, p. 21.

38. Ibid., p. 11.

39. Ibid., p. 13. The definition is quoted by the Sprouts from Preston F. James et al., *American Geography: Inventory and Prospect* (Syracuse: Syracuse University Press, 1954), p. 4.

40. Harold and Margaret Sprout, *The Ecological Perspective on Human Affairs,* p. 15.

41. Ibid., p. 140.

42. Ibid., p. 28.

43. See Harold and Margaret Sprout, *An Ecological Paradigm for the Study of International Politics*, pp. 39–41. For the implications of perception in foreign policy decision-making, see Chapter 11.

44. Ibid., p. 11.

45. Ibid., p. 42.

46. Ibid., p. 34.

47. Harold and Margaret Sprout, *The Ecological Perspective on Human Affairs*, p. 8.

48. Harold and Margaret Sprout, *An Ecological Paradigm for the Study of International Politics*, p. 62.

49. Ibid., p. 55.

50. Ibid., p. 20.

51. Ibid., p. 56.

52. Ibid., p. 64.

53. George Liska, *Quest for Equilibrium: America and the Balance of Power on Land and Sea* (Baltimore and London: Johns Hopkins Press, 1977), p. 4.

54. Robert T. Holt and John E. Turner, "Insular Polities," in James N. Rosenau, ed., *Linkage Politics* (New York: The Free Press, 1969), pp. 199–236.

55. Richard L. Merritt, "Noncontiguity and Political Integration," ibid., pp. 237–272.

56. Harold and Margaret Sprout, *Foundations of International Politics* (Princeton: Van Nostrand, 1962), p. 54. Examples of such rhetoric include "The mountains of Japan have pushed the Japanese out upon the seas *making* them the greatest seafaring people of Asia." "England, *driven* to the sea by her sparse resources to seek a livelihood and to find homes for her burgeoning population, and sitting athwart the main sea routes of Western Europe, seemed *destined by geography* to command the seas." (Italics in original.)

57. Harold and Margaret Sprout, *The Ecological Perspective on Human Affairs*, p. 11.

58. Robert Strausz-Hupé, *Geopolitics*, p. 173.

59. Nicholas Spykman, *The Geography of the Peace*, p. 43.

60. Ibid., p. 181.

61. Robert Strausz-Hupé, op. cit., pp. 164–165.

62. Ibid., p. 181.

63. Derwent Whittlesey, "Haushofer: The Geopolitician," in Edward Mead Earle, ed., op. cit., p. 400.

64. *Geographical Journal*, XXIII (April 1904), 441.

65. Robert Strausz-Hupé, op. cit., pp. 189–190. A half-century after Leopold Amery made his comment about the airplane, long-range bombers carrying nuclear bombs had become prime symbols of international power, and analysts were still arguing, not quite conclusively, as to whether the advent of air power and nuclear energy had rendered the Heartland concept obsolete. See W. Gordon East, "How Strong Is the Heartland?" *Foreign Affairs*, XXIX (October 1950), 78–93; and Charles Kruszewski, "The Pivot of History," *Foreign Affairs*, XXXII (April 1954), 338–401.

66. Harold and Margaret Sprout, *Foundations of International Politics*, pp. 338–339.

67. Ladis Kristof, op. cit., p. 29.

68. Richard E. Harrison and Hans W. Weigert, "World View and Strategy," in Hans W. Weigert and Vilhjalmut Stefansson, eds., *Compass of the World: A Symposium on Political Geography* (New York: Macmillan, 1947), p. 76.
69. Alan K. Henrikson, "The Map as an 'Idea': The Role of Cartographic Imagery During the Second World War," *The American Cartographer,* 2, No. I (1975), 46–47.
70. Richard Edes Harrison and Robert Strausz-Hupé, "Maps, Strategy and World Politics," in Harold and Margaret Sprout, eds., *Foundations of National Power* (Princeton: Princeton University Press, 1945), pp. 64–68.
71. W. H. Parker, op. cit., p. 133. The phenomena to which Mackinder referred are lithosphere (land); hydrosphere (water); atmosphere (air); photosphere (light); biosphere (life); and psychosphere (mind) (pp. 133–134).
72. See, for example, Geoffrey Kemp, Robert L. Pfaltzgraff, Jr., and Uri Ra'anan, eds., *The Other Arms Race: New Technologies and Non-Nuclear Conflict* (Lexington, Mass.: D. C. Heath, 1975).
73. Geoffrey Kemp, "The New Strategic Map," *Survival,* XIX, No. 2 (March-April, 1977), 52. See by the same author, "Scarcity and Strategy," *Foreign Affairs,* 56, No. 2 (January 1978), 396–414.
74. Colin S. Gray, *The Geopolitics of the Nuclear Era: Heartland, Rimlands and the Technological Revolution* (New York: Crane, Rusak, for the National Strategy Information Center, 1977), p. 65.
75. Colin S. Gray, *The Geopolitics of Super Power,* p. 4.
76. W. H. Parker, op. cit., p. 162.
77. Colin S. Gray, op. cit., p. 11.
78. See, for example, Robert Strausz-Hupé, "Social Values and Politics: The Uninvited Guests," *Review of Politics,* XXX (January 1968), 59–78. Another writer, George F. Kennan, who, like Strausz-Hupé, is examined in the following chapter, has suggested the need for an international organization for the collection, storage, and retrieval and dissemination of information and the coordination of research and operational activities on environmental problems at the international level. See George F. Kennan, "To Prevent a World Wasteland," *Foreign Affairs,* XLVIII (April 1970), 404.
79. Zbigniew Brzezinski, *Between Two Ages: America's Role in the Technetronic Era* (New York: Viking, 1970), p. 14.

Chapter
3

Power and Realist Theory

REALIST THEORY VERSUS UTOPIANISM

Realist theory dominated the study of international relations in the United States from the 1940s to the 1960s. Moreover, what is termed the traditional paradigm of the international system is based upon the assumptions found in realist theory: (1) that nation-states, in a "state-centric" system, are the key actors; (2) that domestic politics can be clearly separated from foreign policy; (3) that international politics is a struggle for power in an anarchic environment; (4) that there are gradations of capabilities among nation-states—greater powers and lesser states—in a decentralized international system of states possessing legal equality, or sovereignty. Nevertheless, since the 1970s, there has been not only a revival of interest in realism but the emergence of a broadly based neorealist approach, described in this chapter. Textbooks by realist scholars and their other writings, often policy-oriented, especially in the generation after World War II, have had wide currency both in official and academic circles. The influence of such works remains substantial in the late twentieth century. Realist theory, like utopianism in this respect, is normative and policy-oriented, although its proponents purport to present an analysis based upon a theoretical framework drawn from the history of the international system, especially the era of Europe's classical balance of power. In part, realist theory stands as a critique of utopianism, whose normative emphasis is the possibility of transforming the nation-state system through international law and organization. In marked contrast, realism posits that the prospects for effecting a dramatic and fundamental transformation in the international system are not great. The international system is shaped by numerous forces, many of which are unchanging and unchangeable. Unlike utopians, realists assume that there is no essential harmony of interest among nations. Instead, they suggest that nation-states often have conflicting national objectives, some of which may lead to war.

The capabilities, but also the posited policy goals, of states are crucial for the outcome of international conflict and for one state's ability to influence another's behavior. Yet seldom, if ever, is the notion of capabilities, or power, synonymous in realist theory with strictly military force levels. Power is said to be a multidimensional phenomenon with both military and nonmilitary components, and realist theorists have developed frameworks for classifying the elements of national power. Such capabilities include not only military forces, but also levels of technology, population, natural resources, geographical factors, form of government, political leadership, strategy, and ideology. In short, power consists of qualitative *and* quantitative factors. Its efficacy as a set of capabilities bears a necessary relationship to the goals for which it is to be utilized, as well as to the means available to other actors in harmony with, or against, whom power is to be utilized.

Realist theorists assume that certain largely immutable factors such as geography and the nature of human behavior shape international conduct. In contrast to utopianism, realism holds that human nature is essentially constant, or at least not easily altered. In the utopian framework human behavior was said to be improvable, and perhaps even perfectible. Utopianism is based on the idea that politics can be made to conform to an ethical standard. Norms of behavior, such as those specified in international law and organization, can be established and, later if not sooner, can be made the basis for international behavior. In contrast, the realist posits that there are severe limitations in the extent to which political reform or education can alter human nature: Humankind is evil, sinful, and power-seeking. According to realist theory, human nature is not innately good or perfectible. The task of the statesman lies in fashioning political frameworks within which the human propensity to engage in conflict can be minimized. Hence the realist writers emphasize regulatory mechanisms such as the balance of power, discussed in greater detail in Chapter 1. Because of the difficulty of achieving peace through international law and organization, or even by means of world government, it is necessary to devise other arrangements for the management of power. The balance of power is said to furnish an important regulatory device to prevent any one nation or other political group from achieving hegemony.

Realist writers generally agree that a state's location affects its national capabilities and its foreign policy orientation. Geography is said to shape the options available to states and to impose limitations—often severe—upon the choices open to states in their foreign policies. Because of geography certain states are more vulnerable than others to foreign conquest. Some nations occupy more strategically important geographical positions than others. Access to key waterways and the extent to which the configuration of frontiers exposes a state to, or affords protection from, hostile neighbors are held to influence its foreign policy. Geographical location affects the climate and length of the growing season for crops, as well as the ability to mobilize against other nations. Such variables are discussed more fully in Chapter 2. In sum, geographic, demographic, resource, and geopolitical factors are central to realist theory of international relations.

Realists assume, moreover, that moral principles in their abstract formulation cannot be applied to specific political actions. The statesman operates in an international environment that is distinguishable from the environment within the state by the absence of authoritative political institutions, legal systems, and commonly accepted standards of conduct. Therefore, the standards of conduct at the international level differ from those governing behavior within a national unit. In the words of George F. Kennan, "Government is an agent, not a principal. Its primary obligation is to the *interests* of the national society it represents, not to the moral impulses that individual elements of that society may experience."[1]

Although not all realists consider the statesman *qua* statesman as amoral, they nevertheless often place less emphasis upon abstract standards of behavior in international conduct than in utopian theory. The statesman acting on behalf of state interests necessarily embodies a standard of conduct substantially different from that of the individual within a civilized political unit and from that of the individual *qua* individual. The statesman is sworn, by oath of office, to safeguard the political unit from external threat. In a world of nation-states, over whom there is no legally and politically superior authority, the power of the nation-state becomes the ultimate arbiter. The protection of the nation-state from its enemies, in an international system containing revolutionary, expansionist, revisionist powers, inevitably leads the statesman to adopt or to countenance policies that would be legally and morally repugnant in behavior among individuals or groups within a civilized state. However, as Robert E. Osgood suggests in his analysis of the relationship between self-interest and ideals:

> It is man's reluctance to face the inevitable moral dilemmas of social existence that robs him of his moral perspective and leads him to an easy identification of his own nation's self-interest with high moral purpose and the welfare of mankind. It is the common conceit that persuades men to view the inevitable moral compromises of international relations as good things in themselves rather than as unfortunate expedients designed to maximize ideal values in a society where partial morality is the best morality attainable.[2]

According to the realist, politics is not a function of ethical philosophy. Instead, political theory is derived from political practice and historical experience. Finally, the realist seeks to reconcile national interest with supranational ideals, although it is posited in realist theory that the former has, or should have, primacy over the latter.

POWER AS A DETERMINANT OF INTERNATIONAL BEHAVIOR

Power is one of the words most frequently used in the study of political science, especially in international relations. The absence at the international level of adequate institutions and procedures for resolving conflict comparable to those in most domestic political systems makes the so-called power element more obvious than at the domestic level. In a textbook first published in 1933, Frederick L. Schuman held that in an international system lacking a common government, each unit "necessarily seeks safety by relying on its own power and viewing with alarm the power of its neighbors."[3] According to Nicholas J. Spykman, "All civilized life rests in the last instance on power." Power is the ability to move the individual or the human collectivity in some desired fashion, through "persuasion, purchase, barter, and coercion."[4] Hans J. Morgenthau even defined international politics, and indeed all politics, as a "struggle for power." Thus power has been conceptualized—with some confusion—as both a means and an end. Morgenthau held that power is "man's control over the minds and actions of other men."[5] Robert Strausz-Hupé maintained that international politics is "dominated by the quest for power," and that "at any given period of known history, there were several states locked in deadly conflict, all desiring the augmentation or preservation of their power."[6] Arnold Wolfers argued that power is "the ability to move others or to get them to do what one wants them to do and not to do what one does not want them to do." Moreover, he deemed it important "to distinguish between power and influence, the first to mean the ability to move others by the threat or infliction of deprivations, the latter to mean the ability to do so through promises or grants of benefits."[7] John Burton, himself clearly not an exponent of the realist school of theory or of *Realpolitik,* suggests that "there is probably no greater common factor in all thinking on international relations than the assumption that States depend for their existence upon power, and achieve their objectives by power, thus making the management of power the main problem to be solved."[8] According to Robert Gilpin power encompasses the military, economic, and technological capabilities of states, while prestige consists of the "perceptions of other states with respect to a state's capacities and its ability and willingness to express its power."[9]

As noted elsewhere in this chapter, the power of a state is said to consist of capabilities, some of which are economic in nature—such as levels of industrialization and productivity, gross national product, national income, and income on a per capita basis. In an analysis of the economic dimensions of international politics and the political aspects of international economics, Charles P. Kindleberger assesses power in its intertwined economic and political contexts. He defines power as "strength capable of being used efficiently," that is, "strength *plus* the capacity to use it effectively"[10] in support of some objective. Thus, like several other writers, Kindleberger distinguishes between means and ends, or the use of means for the attainment of ends. Thus strength is a means that exists even in the absence of its use for some goal, whereas power is the use of strength for a particular purpose. According to Kindleberger, "Prestige is the respect which is paid to power. Influence is the capacity to affect the decisions of others. Force is the use of physical means to affect those decisions. Dominance is defined as the condition under which A affects a significant number of B's decisions without B affecting those of A."[11] Power thus conceptualized is related in Kindleberger's analysis to adaptability and flexibility in a nation's economy. Such is the meaning of efficiency in the use of power. Thus, power is dynamic and changing, rather than static in nature. Those states or other entities best able to adjust to change are likely to possess power, and to make most effective use of it in support of posited goals.

According to Klaus Knorr, power, influence, and interdependence are inextricably related. Two states can be in conflict over some issues while cooperating on others. "When they cooperate, they benefit from the creation of new values, material or nonmaterial. When they are in conflict, they attempt to gain values at each other's expense. In either case, they are interdependent."[12] Power becomes important in conflictual situations, whereas influence is central both in circumstances of conflict and in cooperative relationships. Power may be used coercively or noncoercively. "When power is used coercively, an actor (B) is influenced if he adapts his behavior in compliance with, or in anticipation of, another actor's (A) demands, wishes, or proposals." Knorr suggests that the term *power* is employed by some writers to identify all influence, whether coercive or noncoercive. He prefers to invoke the term *power* to designate "only the exercise of coercive influence."[13] Developing a model for the analysis of the utility of military power by one actor (A) against another actor (B), Knorr identifies four basic factors: (1) B's estimate of the costs of complying with A's threat, (2) B's estimate of the costs of defying A's threat, (3) B's bargaining skill relative to A's, and (4) B's propensity to act rationally and to assume risks.[14] Knorr holds that many variables "intervene in determining whether or not a military threat will be effective, and to what extent."[15]

Interdependence is said to connote the ability of one state to influence another in some way. If the interdependence is mutual, each could damage both the other and itself by severing the relationship that exists between them. Thus the costs and the benefits of exercising power by each party in an interdependent relationship increase as the level of interdependence grows. According to David Baldwin, dependency relationships represent a form of influence in which one actor's ability, for example, to cut off the supply of a critical resource such as oil to another actor may furnish the basis for influence of the disadvantaged party in other areas as well.[16] Clearly related is the issue of cost in analyzing the relationship between power and dependency. The level of dependency is determined either by the opportunity costs of forgoing the object at issue—for example, oil—or by the extent to which the dependent state can substitute another supplier or another source of energy for oil.[17] Similarly, James A. Caporaso maintains that the nature of dependence would include (1) the magnitude of the dependent state's interest in a desire for a good, (2) the extent of the control of the good in question by the party exerting influence, and (3) the ability of the dependent state to find an alternative source for the commodity for which there exists a particular level of dependence.[18]

Power exists to a certain extent in the eyes of the beholder. The element of perception, or subjective assessment, may be high in calculating the resolve of an adversary to use effectively the power at its disposal. Similar considerations are operative in deterrence theory (see Chapter 9), which in turn is closely related to power as discussed here. The perceptual dimension of power has been studied by the scoring and ranking of 103 nations in terms of power perception. It was concluded that perceived national power is some function of military expenditures if the state has not been at war recently.[19] Another study developed a multidimensional conception of influence for comparing the perceived power of seven nations: China, the Federal Republic of Germany, France, Japan, the Soviet Union, the United Kingdom, and the United States.

The attributes of influence consisted of (1) human resources; (2) economic strength, or wealth; (3) technology; (4) trade; and (5) military strength. States were ranked in accordance with numerical values attached to each attribute by the use of expert judgment. The authors concluded that wealth and military strength, in themselves, are not necessarily sufficient to gain for a nation the status of superpower, although developing military capabilities may provide a "convenient and relatively inexpensive way" toward influence, especially for poor states, in a relatively short period of time.[20] Yet another writer asks, "Given the highly psychological nature of power relationships, is it ever possible to use available information to measure power?"[21] Beyond the actual quantitative measures of power itself, perceptions held by allies and adversaries alike form a necessary component of power measurement. Moreover, self-perception may constitute for a state yet another ingredient in its power calculation. For example, in the late twentieth century the discussion of federal deficits and trade imbalances enters into estimates of U.S. power: How actually to measure such variables, and how to relate them to specific types of power, such as military capabilities, remains a formidable and unresolved problem.

Power has usually been viewed as an influence relationship—the ability of one actor to induce another to act in some desired fashion, or to refrain from undesired behavior.[22] According to Michael P. Sullivan, "Power may not only be distinguished from sheer capabilities, it can also be differentiated from the use of force. Power can be present in situations where force is not used. Indeed, some argue that such instances are illustrations of ultimate power—when one party influences the other to act without even possessing the supposed necessary capabilities. 'Power,' then, can become *psychological control* over others."[23] The ability to exert influence over another, it has been suggested, without the actual expenditure of capabilities, represents the most effective employment of power. In such a conception, it is not the use of power, as in a military campaign, that is important but rather the political shadow alleged to be cast by its perceived possession. Thus, power becomes the "cutting edge" of diplomacy.

Also viewing power as an influence relationship, K. J. Holsti suggests that power is a multidimensional concept consisting of (1) the acts by which one actor influences another actor, (2) the capabilities utilized for this purpose, and (3) the response solicited. Holsti conceptualizes power as a means to an end, even though some political leaders may seek influence as an end in itself, just as some people may value money not only for what it can buy but for its own sake. In short, Holsti defines power as the "general capacity of a state to control the behavior of others."[24] Stated differently, answers are sought to the following questions: In light of our goals, what kind of behavior do we seek to obtain from another actor, and how can such an actor be induced to do what we want? What capabilities are available for use in support of our goal? What is likely to be the response to our effort to influence the behavior of the other actor?[25] In such an analysis of power, the idea of causation is implicit. Possessing power is said to be conducive to its threatened or actual use to produce a desired result. Those who object to causally based theories of political behavior logically fault power theory that is based on causation.[26] In such a critique, we are brought back to one of the enduring questions of power and political behavior: Stated simply, to what extent can the intentions of states as political actors be inferred from the capabilities in their possession?

Of special concern has been the estimation and measurement of power. According to Robert J. Lieber, power is said to be the

> currency of the political system in the way that money is the currency of the economy. That is, we cannot eat or dress or shelter ourselves with money, but money permits access to the goods and services with which we can be fed, clothed, and housed. And just as the flows of currency are well suited to quantitative analysis by economists, so too this conception of power should provide the opportunity for quantification.[27]

Karl Deutsch views power as a

> symbol of the ability to change the distribution of results, and particularly the results of people's behavior. In this respect, power can be compared in some ways to money, which is our usual standardized symbol of purchasing power—that is, of our ability to change the distribution of goods and resources.[28]

David A. Baldwin holds that power is situationally specific. Although power is far less fungible than money, some aspects of power are more fungible than others and might be so rank-ordered. If power must be related to the situation in which it is used, or available for use, Baldwin maintains, categorizing states as "great powers" or "small powers" is inadequate if not misleading, since such terms relate to a generalized, rather than to a specific, situational context, or to a particular issue area.[29] The need exists, it is suggested, for students of international politics to examine the "multiple distributional patterns" of power in a large number of issue areas, while recognizing the limitations of power analysis resulting from the absence of a common denominator of political value for comparing different forms and uses of power.

According to Jeffrey Hart, power can be observed and measured by reference to three approaches: (1) control over resources, (2) control over actors, and (3) control over events and outcomes. The latter approach—events and outcomes—is said to constitute the most promising focal point for observing and measuring power in international relations, even though most analysis of power, as noted elsewhere in this chapter, has been based on control over resources, such as military expenditures, size of military capabilities, population, and level of economic development.[30] It may be inferred that power measured as control over events and outcomes becomes in the final analysis situational. But the measurement of an outcome is related, in turn, to the preferences of actors in a power relationship.

Jack H. Nagel has suggested that the "measurement and observation of preferences will be a fundamental difficulty in the study of power, severely restricting outcomes over which power can be measured."[31] Nagel argues for power analysis based on data that relate preferences causally to explanations of outcomes. He contends that this problem extends to motivation theory in psychology as well as to game theory and to decision theory. According to Herbert Simon and Roderick Bell, the essential prerequisite for the measurement of power is a theoretical framework or theory of power.[32] The use of cardinal numbers to measure power implies that the observed or measured units have the same properties as, or are isomorphic to, the cardinal numbers. Thus the problem of power measurement relates more to the deficiencies inherent in existing theory than in the measurement techniques themselves, however formidable these techniques remain. In yet another approach to power measurement, Jacek Kugler and William Domke have constructed a framework based on the resources available to a government and its ability to extract, mobilize, and utilize them in support of a specific goal. National strength is defined as the sum of a state's internal capabilities (societal base) and external resources (in the form of help from allies or assistance of other lands from abroad). States that are directly threatened are likely to be more able than other states to mobilize resources. States under stress of war are capable of mobilizing vast resources. According to this analysis, differences in the form of government—pluralistic or totalitarian—did not decisively shape the level of resource mobilization. These authors also found that, while richer nations can mobilize greater amounts of societal resources, poorer states are more effective in raising their levels of extraction because of greater political "slack" in less developed countries that can be mobilized during times of stress.[33]

The problems of quantifying power have proven great indeed. The inability of political scientists and others to develop adequate means for the quantification of power accounts, to no small extent, for the failure of theories of international relations based upon quantification to be widely accepted, as contrasted with theories of economic behavior, and econometrics in particular. In international relations, power has been considered relative to the goals for which it is being used. As we have already seen, power has been conceptualized to include tangible factors such as military capabilities and intangible elements such as political will. Measuring both actual and potential power, however difficult, has been and remains a central concern of governments in all parts of the world, which promises to gain in importance as the capabilities of states increase with a diffusion of technologies in the late twentieth century. Power measurement will also become more complex as a result of the increased salience of its economic dimensions and as a greater variety of weapons systems of unprecedented accuracy and range become available to a larger number of actors.

Especially in the last generation, numerous indicators of relative military capabilities have been developed. If the strategic-military relationship between the United States and the Soviet Union remains central to international politics in the late twentieth century, the ability to assess trends in relative superpower force levels will concern scholars and policymakers alike. The complexity inherent in measuring this important dimension of power derives from differences, or asymmetries, in strategic-military doctrines, which state strikes first, the accuracy of strategic-nuclear missiles, the size and number of warheads, the ability of one side or the other to defend against a strategic-nuclear attack—that is, to safeguard its retaliatory strategic forces from a disarming strike, and to protect its population, especially those segments most important for postattack recovery.[34] There are numerous conceptual relationships between the analysis of strategic-military force levels and theories of conflict and deterrence, discussed in Chapter 9. In short, measuring the military capabilities of states, both at the superpower level and among other states in the process of acquiring unprecedented means of destruction, is both a pressing conceptual problem for the scholar and a practical issue of great importance for the policymaker and for the management of power in the late twentieth century.

Among the concepts in which the capacity for power measurement is implicit is that of parity, which in the strategic-military literature is related to deterrence theory. Parity represents what has been termed *strategic equivalence*—that is, the presumed possession by both the United States and the Soviet Union of capabilities that in the aggregate are equal or adequate for the deterrence of strategic warfare, although specific components of such forces might favor one side or the other.

Whether parity can be said to exist depends upon the relative capabilities of states. In the absence of agreed-upon methodologies for power measurement, we cannot conclude definitively that a condition of parity does or does not exist. As George Liska has written,

> Parity is, in the last analysis, along with several other key normative and strategic political concepts (such as intervention and the balance of power itself) essentially and fruitfully a metaphysical notion. It is such in both the literal sense, of being above the physical aspect of hardware calculations (if not above the physics of power dynamics), and in the wider sense, of being a concept with a debatable concrete meaning but also with meaningful and objectively self-evident connotations (differing thus favorably from, say, the notion of sufficiency in mere weaponry).[35]

Efforts have been made to measure power, and especially influence, by reference to communications—who communicates with whom, who consults with whom. (Such measures have also been utilized in the study of political integration, to be discussed in Chapter 10.) It is hypothesized that the more a person, group, or nation is the recipient rather than the originator of communications, the greater the influence of that entity over others. Steven Brams has hypothesized that two nations have an influence relationship with each other that is symmetrical if the transactions between them are approximately equal.[36] If one nation receives the preponderant number of transactions, especially official level visits, it exercises asymmetrical influence over the other.[37] Such a proposition can be, and has been, tested with the use of international visit data, but without conclusive results. Research utilizing such data forms part of a broader emphasis in the past generation upon events/data analysis considered in Chapter 4.

ANTECEDENTS OF REALISM

Like utopianism in international relations theory, realism has its intellectual roots in the older political philosophy of the West and in the writings of non-Western ancient authors such as Mencius and the Legalists in China and Kautilya in India, as well as Thucydides in ancient Greece. In his celebrated history of the Peloponnesian War, Thucydides wrote: "What made war inevitable was the growth of Athenian power and the fear which this caused in Sparta."[38] His conception of the importance of power, together with the propensity of states to form competing alliances, places Thucydides well within the realist school. Just as Thucydides had developed an understanding of state behavior from his observation of relations between Athens and Sparta, Machiavelli analyzed interstate relations in the Italian system of the sixteenth century.

Machiavelli is clearly linked to realist theory by his emphasis on the ruler's need to adopt moral standards different from those of the individual in order to ensure the state's survival, his concern with power, his assumption that politics is characterized by a clash of interests, and his pessimistic view of human nature.

Thomas Hobbes, like Machiavelli, viewed power as crucial in human behavior: Man has a "perpetual and restless desire of power after power that ceaseth only in death."[39] Hobbes believed that "covenants, without the sword, are but words and of no strength to secure a man at all."[40] Without a strong sovereign, chaos and violence follow: "If there be no power erected, or not great enough for our own security; man will and may lawfully rely on his own strength and art for caution against all other men."[41]

Like other modern realists, Hobbes concerned himself with the underlying forces of politics and with the nature of power in political relationships. Although Hobbes believed that a strong sovereign was mandatory for maintaining order within the political system, he saw little prospect for fundamentally changing human behavior or the environment. In his emphasis on strong political institutions for managing power and preventing conflict, Hobbes paradoxically was closer to proponents of world government or, to be more precise, world empire than to realists who stress a balance of power among major political groups. Hobbes regarded the latter condition as analogous to an anarchical state of nature, but he doubted the possibility of establishing a world empire.

Hegel, more than any other political philosopher, elevated the position of the state. Although realist writers are usually by no means Hegelian, Hegel's belief that the state's highest duty lies in its own preservation is found in realist theory. Hegel reasoned that "since states are related to one another as autonomous entities and so as particular wills on which the validity of treaties depends, and since the particular will of the whole is in content a will for its own welfare it follows that welfare is the highest aim governing the relation of one state to another."[42] Moreover, Hegel held that the state has an "individual totality" that develops according to its own laws. The state has objective reality; that is, it exists apart from its citizens. Hegel held that the state has moral standards different from and superior to those of the individual—a theme that is found in many realist writings.

Among the antecedents of realist theory is the work of Max Weber (1864–1920), whose writings dealt extensively not only with the nature of politics and the state, but also with power as central to politics. Although the richness of Weber's political thought cannot be encompassed in a short analysis, suffice it to suggest that, with respect to realist theory, many of the formulations contained in his work shaped subsequent generations of writing and scholarship. For Weber as for later realists, the principal characteristic of politics is a struggle for power. The power element of political life is especially evident at the international level because "every political structure naturally prefers to have weak rather than strong neighbors. Furthermore, as every big political community is a potential aspirant to prestige, it is also a potential threat to all its neighbors; hence, the big political community, simply because it is big and strong, is latently and constantly endangered."[43] Among the dimensions of politics as a struggle for power, moreover, is that of economics. In Weber's thought, economic policy stands in a subordinate relationship to politics inasmuch as the "power political interests of nations" encompass an economic struggle for existence.

Among the concerns of realists with which Weber before them was preoccupied is the ethical problem of intention versus consequences, or what is also termed the absolute ethic of conviction and the ethic of responsibility. To adhere to an absolute ethic is to take actions in keeping with that ethic without regard for their consequences. However, according to Weber, leaders in an imperfect world confront the need to behave by a political ethic in which the achievement of "good" ends may make necessary the utilization of less than morally acceptable means. For Weber the ethic of conviction cannot be separated from an understanding of the consequences of such action, which in turn gives concrete meaning to an ethic of responsibility. In contemporary realist thought the meaning of the ethic of responsibility comes forth in the notion that each political action must be judged on specific merits rather than in accordance with some abstract, universal standard. Such an idea strikes a familiar chord in much of the realist thought assessed in this chapter.

REALISM IN TWENTIETH-CENTURY INTERNATIONAL RELATIONS THEORY

Reinhold Niebuhr

Although many scholars past and present have shaped the development of realist international relations theory, the writings of the Protestant theologian Reinhold Niebuhr (1892–1971) have had a major and indeed a unique impact on realist theory.[44] Crucial to Niebuhr's theory is his biblical concept of man who is tainted by original sin and therefore capable of evil. Man's sinfulness stems from his anxiety. "Anxiety is the inevitable concomitant of the paradox of freedom and finiteness in which man is involved."[45] Man is said to be sinful because he denies his finiteness, pretending to be more than he really is.[46]

Man's effort to usurp God's position "inevitably subordinates other life to its will and thus does injustice to other life." Moreover, humans have a "will-to-live" that leads to a "will-to-power." Since our "will-to-live" transcends a mere will to assure physical survival, we invariably seek security against the perils of nature and history by enhancing our individual and collective power.

> The conflicts between men are thus simple conflicts between competing expressions of power and pride. Since the very possession of power and prestige always involves some encroachment upon the prestige and power of others, this conflict is by its very nature a more stubborn and difficult one than the mere competition between various survival impulses in nature.[47]

Moral behavior is difficult but possible for the individual: It is extremely difficult or impossible for groups, especially large groups. Discussing the nature of power in groups and nations, Niebuhr asserts that national power is the projection of the individual's "will-to-power." When there are fewer moral restraints upon the individual as a member of a group or a nation than as an individual, greater violence results at the group or national level. An individual acting as a member of a group loses his or her identity, becoming instead a member of an anonymous mass.[48] Thus the tendencies toward power become magnified at the group or national level. (The hypothesis that individual aggressiveness is eventually displaced to the national level is treated in Chapter 7.)

Charting a course that such intellectual disciples as George F. Kennan, Charles Burton Marshall, and Hans J. Morgenthau would follow, Niebuhr criticized what he considered historic American attitudes toward foreign policy. In particular, as he saw it, Americans have been unaware of the power motive in international politics because their nation enjoyed a long period of isolation from the power confrontations of other nations. The "irony" of American history is that the Founding Fathers' dreams of the United States developing into a uniquely virtuous nation have been shattered. Instead, the United States entered into a struggle for world power. "Our age," wrote Niebuhr, "is involved in irony because so many dreams of our nation have been so cruelly refuted by history."[49] The "irony" is heightened by the "frantic efforts of some of our idealists to escape this hard reality by dreaming up schemes of an ideal world order which have no relevance to either our present dangers or our urgent duties."[50]

In criticizing proponents of world government, Niebuhr suggested that political theory derives from political practice:

> Governments cannot create communities for the simple reason that the government is not primarily the authority of law nor the authority of force, but the authority of the community itself. Laws are obeyed because the community accepts them as corresponding, on the whole, to its conception of justice.[51]

Because the forces of cohesiveness are minimal, the prospects for world government are not promising.

Although believing that conflict is inherent in intergroup and international relations, Niebuhr did not agree that the statesman *qua* statesman is amoral. He suggested, instead, that realism must be tempered with morality, that "nations must use their power with the purpose of making it an instrument of justice and a servant of interests broader than their own."[52] Moreover, he criticized those realists who overemphasize the "national interest," because at the national as well as the individual level, "egotism is not the proper cure for an abstract and pretentious ideal-ism."[53] Since each nation interprets justice from its own perspective rather than that of a competing state, it becomes difficult to give opera-tional meaning to the rule that statesmen must always frame policies based upon the "national interest." For Niebuhr, the balance of power is the organizational device for achieving a semblance of justice: "Some balance of power is the basis of whatever justice is achieved in human relations. Where the disproportion of power is too great and where an equilibrium of social forces is lacking no mere rational or moral demands can achieve justice."[54]

Niebuhr maintained that political leaders constantly face moral am-biguities. The United States, for example, must contain the expansion of communism and at the same time prevent nuclear war. He held that constitutional democracy, for all its shortcomings, is a clearly superior form of political organization to communist oligarchy, which, by un-scrupulously centralizing absolute power, promotes far greater injustices than those communists attribute to the free society.[55] But Niebuhr fre-quently warned Americans against thinking that they were innocent of the power drives that have motivated other peoples of the world. The United States has engaged in its own imperialist ventures, but a demo-cratic nation with a strong sense of international mission is always reluc-tant to admit to itself that its actions spring from any but the noblest of motives. Niebuhr contended that although the mission of preserving and extending democratic self-government had greater validity than some other forms of national messianism, Americans must abandon their illusion of a special national innocence and righteousness and must resist the temptation to "claim more virtue for the exercise of power than the facts warrant."[56]

Nicholas J. Spykman

Several realist writers support the idea that conflict rather than coopera-tion is more typical of international relations than of intrastate relations. Nicholas J. Spykman (1893–1943) assumed that only those conditions that characterize intrastate relations during crises and breakdowns of central authority are normal for relations among states in the international sys-tem. States exist because they are strong or have other states protecting them. In the international system, as in other social groupings, Spykman saw several basic processes operating: cooperation, accommodation, and opposition. To assure their survival, states "must make the preservation or improvement of their power position a principal objective of their foreign policy."[57] Because power is ultimately the ability to wage war, states have always emphasized building military establishments.

Spykman's geopolitical and balance-of-power concepts are crucial to his realism. According to Spykman, expansion follows the line of least resistance: "New territories are conquered, held, assimilated, and serve as a starting point for a new advance. It is therefore not surprising to find a correlation between amount of expansion and ease of movement." The limits to expansion are set up by natural barriers such as oceans, rivers, and mountains, as well as the tendencies to expand up and down river valleys, to seek access to the sea, and to dominate strategic points near communications routes. At any time in history, the frontiers of states indicate their relative power relationship. The potential for conflict increased, Spykman held, as the world became more densely populated and nations encroached upon each other.

Drawing upon Mackinder's geopolitical theory, Spykman advanced his conception of the goals that should guide American foreign policy during and after World War II. Because the Western hemisphere did not contain economic, military, and technological resources capable of withstanding the combined resources of the Eurasian land mass, it was crucial for the United States to preserve a balance of power in Europe and Asia.[58] Writing before the United States entry into World War II, Spykman concluded that just as the German-Japanese alliance represented a threat to America's security, other powers—namely, Russia and China—would pose security problems for the United States in the postwar period. "A Russian state from the Urals to the North Sea can be no great improvement over a German state from the North Sea to the Urals."[59] In Asia, Spykman suggested, the United States may face a "modern, vitalized, and militarized China" that would threaten not only the position of Japan but also that of the Western powers in Asia. Just as the United States twice came to the aid of Britain so "that the small offshore island might not have to face a single gigantic military state in control of the opposite coast of the mainland," the United States would "have to adopt a similar protective policy toward Japan" to preserve a balance of power in Asia. Moreover, Spykman acknowledged that an "equilibrium of forces inherently unstable, always shifting, always changing" is an "indispensable element of an international order based on independent states."[60]

Implicit in Spykman's thought is the pursuit of limited national objectives. He urged the United States to seek only the removal of the then-existing regimes of Germany and Japan, not to have as an objective their destruction as states, because they must play a major role in restraining other powers that one day would vie for hegemony in the Eurasian landmass. Thus, he related the pursuit of limited national interest to balance of power and geopolitical concepts.

Hans J. Morgenthau

Hans J. Morgenthau (1904–1980) set forth six principles of realist theory. First, he suggested that political relationships are governed by objective rules deeply rooted in human nature. Since these rules are "impervious to our preferences, men will challenge them only at the risk of failure."[61] If these rules themselves cannot be changed, Morgenthau's determinism held that society can be improved by first understanding the laws that govern society and then by basing public policy on that knowledge.

In theorizing about international politics it is necessary to employ historical data for examining political acts and their consequences. In systematizing these vast amounts of historical data, the student of politics should empathize with "the position of a statesman who must meet a certain problem of foreign policy under certain circumstances," and ask "what the rational alternatives are from which a statesman may choose who must meet this problem under these circumstances (presuming always that he acts in a rational manner), and which of these rational alternatives this particular statesman, acting under these circumstances, is likely to choose. It is the testing of this rational hypothesis against the actual facts and their consequences that gives meaning to the facts of international politics."[62]

Second, Morgenthau posited that statesmen "think and act in terms of interest defined as power" and that historical evidence proves this assumption.[63] This concept, central to Morgenthau's realism, gives continuity and unity to the seemingly diverse foreign policies of the widely separated nation-states. Moreover, the concept "interest defined as power" makes it possible to evaluate actions of political leaders at different points in history. To describe Morgenthau's framework in more contemporary language, it is a model of interaction within an international system. Using historical data, Morgenthau compared the real world with the interaction patterns within his model.

In his view, international politics is a process in which national interests are adjusted.

> The concept of the national interest presupposes neither a naturally harmonious, peaceful world nor the inevitability of war as a consequence of the pursuit by all nations of their national interests. Quite to the contrary, it assumes continuous conflict and threat of war to be minimized through the continuous adjustment of conflicting interest by diplomatic action.[64]

Third, Morgenthau acknowledged that the meaning of "interest defined as power" is an unstable one. However, in a world in which sovereign nations vie for power, the foreign policies of all nations must consider survival the minimum goal of foreign policy. All nations are compelled to protect "their physical, political, and cultural identity against encroachments by other nations." Thus, national interest is identified with national survival. "Taken in isolation, the determination of its content in a concrete situation is relatively simple, for it encompasses the integrity of the nation's territory, of its political institutions, and of its culture."[65] As long as the world is divided into nations, Morgenthau asserted, the "national interest is indeed the last word in world politics." Interest, then, is the essence of politics.

Once its survival is assured, the nation-state may pursue lesser interests. Morgenthau assumed that nations ignore the national interest only at the risk of destruction. Yet in twentieth-century foreign policy formulation, lesser interests sometimes preceded the national interest.[66] Had Great Britain in 1939–1940 based its policy toward Finland upon legalistic-moralistic considerations, backed with large-scale military aid against Soviet aggression, then Britain's position might have been weakened sufficiently to assure its destruction by Nazi Germany. Britain would have neither restored Finland's independence nor safeguarded its own most vital national interest, that of physical survival. Only when the national interest most closely related to national survival has been safeguarded can nations pursue lesser interests.

Fourth, Morgenthau stated that "universal moral principles cannot be applied to the actions of states in their abstract, universal formulation, but that they must be filtered through the concrete circumstances of time and place."[67] In pursuit of the national interest, nation-states are governed by a morality that differs from the morality of individuals in their personal relationships. In the actions of statesmen *qua* statesmen, the political consequences of a particular policy become the criteria for judging it. To confuse an individual's morality with a state's morality is to court national disaster. Because the primary official responsibility of statesmen is the survival of the nation-state, their obligations to the citizenry require a different mode of moral judgment from that of the individual.

Fifth, Morgenthau asserted that political realism does not identify the "moral aspirations of a particular nation with the moral laws that govern the universe."[68] In fact, if international politics is placed within a framework of defining interests in terms of power, "we are able to judge other nations as we judge our own."[69] This aspect of Morgenthau's realism bears resemblance to Niebuhr's thought and in turn to Augustinian theology.

Sixth, and finally, Morgenthau stressed the autonomy of the political sphere. Political actions must be judged by political criteria. "The economist asks: 'How does this policy affect the welfare of society, or a segment of it?' The lawyer asks: 'Is this policy in accord with the rules of law?' The realist asks: 'How does this policy affect the power of the nation?' "[70]

In power struggles, nations follow policies designed to preserve the status quo, to achieve imperialistic expansion, or to gain prestige. In Morgenthau's view, domestic and international politics can be reduced to one of three basic types: "A political policy seeks either to keep power, to increase power, or to demonstrate power."[71]

Although the purpose of a status quo policy is to preserve the existing distribution of power, the nation adopting such a policy does not necessarily act to prevent all international change. Instead, status quo nations seek to thwart change that may produce fundamental shifts in the international distribution of power. Morgenthau cites the Monroe Doctrine as an example of a status quo policy that fulfills his two criteria. First, it was designed to maintain the prevailing power balance in the Western hemisphere.

Second, it expressed the unwillingness of the United States to prevent all change. Instead, the United States would act only against change that threatened the existing distribution of power. Likewise, treaties concluded at the end of wars invariably codify the then-prevailing status quo.

Imperialism is the second major alternative available to nations. This is a policy designed to achieve a "reversal of existing power relations between nations."[72] The goals of imperialist powers include local preponderance, continental empire, or world domain. Nations may adopt imperialistic policies as a result of victory, defeat, or the weakness of other states. A state whose leaders expect victory may alter its objectives from the restoration of the status quo to a permanent change in the distribution of power. Moreover, a defeated nation may adopt an imperialistic policy to "turn the scales on the victor, to overthrow the status quo created by his victory, and to change places with him in the hierarchy of power."[73] Finally, the existence of weak states may prove irresistible to a strong state.

To attain imperialistic objectives, states may resort to military force or to cultural and economic means. Military conquest is the oldest and most obvious form of imperialism. Economic imperialism is not as effective a technique as military conquest, but if one imperialistic state cannot gain control over another by military means, it may attempt to do so by economic capabilities. Cultural imperialism represents an attempt to influence the human mind "as an instrument for changing the power relations between two nations."[74] (For an examination of theories of imperialism, see Chapter 6.)

According to Morgenthau, states may pursue a policy of prestige. This may be "one of the instrumentalities through which the policies of status quo and of imperialism try to achieve their ends."[75] Its objective is to "impress other nations with the power one's own nation actually possesses, or with the power it believes, or wants other nations to believe, it possesses."[76] Morgenthau suggested two specific techniques of this policy: diplomacy and display of force. A policy of prestige succeeds when a nation gains such a reputation for power that the actual use of power becomes unnecessary—the political shadow allegedly cast by military power noted earlier in this chapter.

Morgenthau was concerned not only about the quest for power, but also with the conditions for international peace. His concept of international order is closely related to his concept of national interest. The pursuit of national interests that are not essential to national survival contributes to international conflict. In the twentieth century, especially, nations have substituted global objectives for more limited goals that, in Morgenthau's view, constitute the essence of national interest. Modern nationalism, combined with the messianic ideologies of the twentieth century, has obscured the national interest. In the guise of extending communism or "making the world safe for democracy," nations intervene in the affairs of regions not vital to their security. For example, Morgenthau, like Kennan, opposed American military intervention in South Vietnam because Southeast Asia allegedly lay beyond the most vital interests of the United States, and because the United States would find it impossible, except perhaps with a vast expenditure of resources, to maintain a balance of power in Southeast Asia. In contrast, he expressed great concern about Soviet influence in Cuba because of its geographic location in close proximity to the United States.

Even in an international system without ideologically motivated foreign policies, competition between opposing nation-states is likely. Like many other realists, Morgenthau viewed the balance of power as the most effective technique for managing power in an international system based on competitive relationships among states. He defined balance of power as (1) a policy aimed at a certain state of affairs, (2) an actual state of affairs, (3) an approximately equal distribution of power, and (4) any distribution of power. However, it is not the balance of power itself, but the international consensus upon which it is built that preserves international peace. "Before the balance of power could impose its restraints upon the power aspirations of nations through the mechanical interplay of opposing forces, the competing nations had first to restrain themselves by accepting the system of the balance of power as the common framework of their endeavors." Such a consensus "kept in check the limitless desire for power, potentially inherent, as we know, in all imperialisms, and prevented it from becoming a political actuality."[77]

The international consensus that sustained the balance of power before the twentieth century no longer exists. Structural changes in the international system have drastically limited, if not rendered ineffective, the classical balance of power. In Morgenthau's view, the balance of world power through the early 1960s rested with two nations, the United States and the Soviet Union, rather than with several great powers. He contended that allies of one superpower could shift their alignment to the other superpower, but they could not alter significantly the distribution of power because of their weakness relative to either the United States or the Soviet Union, nor was any third power of sufficient strength as to be capable of intervening on either side and greatly changing the power distribution.

Like the balance of power, diplomacy plays a crucial role in the preservation of peace. In fact, a precondition for the creation of a peaceful world is the development of a new international consensus, in the twentieth century. The diplomat's role has been diminished by the development of advanced communications, by public disparagement of diplomacy and diplomats, and by the tendency of heads of government to conduct their own negotiations in summit conferences. The rise in importance of international assemblies, the substitution of open diplomacy for secrecy, and the inexperience on the part of the superpowers contributed to the decline of diplomacy during much of the twentieth century. Morgenthau clearly preferred a diplomacy similar to that of the international system before the twentieth century. His views on traditional diplomacy as a means for adjusting national interests resembled those of Sir Harold Nicolson, a leading twentieth-century British diplomat and theoretician of diplomatic practice.[78]

If it is to be revived as an effective technique for managing power, diplomacy must meet four conditions: (1) It must be divested of its crusading spirit, (2) foreign policy objectives must be defined in terms of national interest and must be supported with adequate power, (3) nations must view foreign policy from the point of view of other nations, and (4) nations must be willing to compromise on issues that are not vital to them. If diplomacy can be restored to a position of importance, Morgenthau believed, it may not only contribute to "peace through accommodation," but also to creating an international consensus upon which more adequate world political institutions can be built.

George F. Kennan

Much like Morgenthau, George F. Kennan (1904–   ) bases his theory of international relations upon historical analysis, especially from the eighteenth and nineteenth centuries. However, Morgenthau's model was derived largely from a European context, whereas Kennan's is based for the most part on American diplomacy from 1776 to 1812. Kennan divided United States foreign policy into two periods: the first from the American Revolution to the middle nineteenth century, and the second from that time to the present.

In the first period, for which Kennan clearly shows preference, the United States evolved basic goals that found expression in such documents as the Declaration of Independence and the Constitution. American statesmen developed a foreign policy designed to achieve their objectives. In defining and shaping the limits of foreign policy, American leaders concluded that

> the first and obvious answer was: that one ought to protect the physical intactness of our national life from any external or political intrusions—in other words, that we ought to look to the national security. . . . Secondly, one could see to it that insofar as the activities of our citizens in pursuit of their private interests spilled beyond our borders and into the outside world, the best possible arrangements were made to promote and protect them.[79]

According to Kennan, American goals were fixed, limited, and devoid of pretensions of international benevolence or assumptions of moral superiority or inferiority on the part of one nation or another. Like Morgenthau, he derived his model from the historical data of an era when limited, rather than universalist, concepts of the national interest prevailed.

Erroneously, in Kennan's estimation, Americans projected to the international arena assumptions based upon their own national experience.

Because they believed that the political and legal framework of the United States had contributed decisively to domestic tranquility, American spokesmen focused on creating a comparable international order in an effort to minimize the likelihood of conflict.

> I see the most serious fault of our past policy formation to lie in something that I might call the legalistic-moralistic approach to international problems. This approach runs like a red skein through our foreign policy of the past fifty years [1900–1950]. It has in it something of the old emphasis on arbitration treaties, something of the Hague Conferences, and schemes for universal disarmament, something of the more ambitious American concepts of international law, something of the Kellogg Pact, something of the idea of a universal "Article 51," something of the belief in World Law and World Government. . . . It is the belief that it should be possible to suppress the chaotic and dangerous aspirations of governments by the acceptance of some system of legal rules and restraints.[80]

Moreover, Kennan asserts that American statesmen in this first period frankly and confidently dealt with power realities.[81] Recognizing the importance of power factors in international politics, the United States strove to restrain the European powers in their territorial ambitions in the Western hemisphere. The United States encouraged movements toward political independence and gave guarantees to new countries that had severed their links with European powers. "All of this involved power considerations. Yet none of it was considered evil or Machiavellian, or cynical. It was simply regarded as a response to the obvious and logical requirements of our situation."[82]

In contrast, Kennan assesses U.S. policy in a later period, when America allegedly lost sight of the power factor and substituted legalistic-moralistic assumptions and objectives for earlier foreign policy goals. If Americans forgot the power factor in the nineteenth century, this was only "natural and inevitable." Geographically separated from Europe, shielded by the British navy from continental European powers, and preoccupied with domestic development, Americans especially in the second half of the nineteenth century cultivated a spirit of romanticism:

> We were satisfied, by this time, with our own borders; and we found it pleasant to picture the outside world as one in which other peoples were similarly satisfied with theirs, or ought to be. With everyone thus satisfied, the main problem of world peace, as it appeared to us, was plainly the arrangement of a suitable framework of contractual engagements in which this happy status quo, the final fruit of human progress, could be sealed and perpetuated. If such a framework could be provided, then, it seemed, the ugly conflicts of international politics would cease to threaten world peace.[83]

In addition to criticizing the American assumption of an international harmony of interests, Kennan asserts that Americans lost sight that the rules governing the behavior of individuals are likely to differ drastically from those that exist in relations between states. Governmental behavior at the international level cannot be subjected to the same moral standards that are applied to human behavior:

> Moral principles have their place in the heart of the individual in the shaping of his own conduct, whether as a citizen or as a government official. . . . But when the individual's behavior passes through the machinery of political organization and merges with that of millions of other individuals to find its expression in the actions of government, then it undergoes a general transformation, and the same moral concepts are no longer relevant to it. A government is an agent, not a principal; and no more than any other agent may it attempt to be the conscience of its principal.[84]

Nevertheless, even though the use of force in international affairs cannot be completely ruled out, this "does not constitute a reason for being indifferent to the ways in which force is applied—to the moral implications of weapons and their use."[85] Finally, Kennan objects to a concept of international affairs that leads one nation to consider its own purposes moral and those of its opponent immoral. "A war fought in the name of high moral principle finds no end short of some form of total domination."[86] Thus the introduction of moralistic principles leads nations to pursue unlimited national objectives, to choose total war, and to impose laws of unconditional surrender upon defeated opponents. In sum, the pursuit of moralistic principles is incompatible with the pursuit of essentially limited foreign policy objectives.

Like most other writers examined in this chapter, Kennan believes that human nature is "irrational, selfish, obstinate, and tends to violence."[87] It is difficult if not impossible to effect basic changes in the individual, and few people will ever "have an abstract devotion to the principles of international legality capable of competing with the impulses from which wars are apt to arise."[88] Moreover, it is by no means certain that governments in their foreign policies express the aspirations of their peoples. "Every government represents only the momentary product of the never-ending competition for political power within the respective national framework. In the most direct sense, therefore, it speaks only for a portion of the nation: for one political faction or coalition of factions."[89] In foreign policy, public opinion cannot play a role similar to its role in national politics, since "international affairs are, after all, a matter of relations between governments and not peoples."[90]

The many and varied causes of international conflict are not easily eliminated by human action. Lack of uniformity in the cultural, political, economic, and social development of nations contributes to conflict. Moreover, Kennan believes that "just as there is no uncomplicated personal relationship between individuals, so . . . there is no international relationship between sovereign states which is without its elements of antagonism, its competitive aspects."[91]

Like Morgenthau, Kennan assigns to diplomacy a major role in the mitigation of international conflict, although he is highly critical of the widespread use of summit diplomacy in the late twentieth century because it leads to imprecision in international discourse and accords, makes difficult the conduct of delicate negotiations in private, raises unwarranted expectations among public opinion, and reduces the effectiveness of professional ambassadors and diplomats whose knowledge, training, and temperament equip them more fully than most democratic political leaders to deal with the complex issues of foreign policy. Through diplomacy, nations have usually been able to adjust differences and to achieve peaceful international change. In fact, Kennan is critical of schemes for world government and international law because

> the function of a system of international relationships is not to inhibit this process of change by imposing a legal straitjacket upon it but rather to facilitate it; to ease its transition; to temper the asperities to which it often leads; to isolate and moderate the conflict to which it gives rise, and to see that these conflicts do not assume forms too unsettling for international life in general.[92]

Moreover, to expect the United Nations to play a major role in the resolution of East-West problems is to impose on it burdens it cannot bear.[93] Even to assume that international organizations can cope effectively with global environmental problems is to assign to them tasks beyond their political competence. Instead, Kennan advocates that "leading industrial and maritime nations—the nations which created the most serious problems of pollution, which had the resources to study the problem, and which had it in their power to remedy most of the evils in question" should play the principal role in their resolution.[94]

Like most other realist theorists, Kennan bases his realism on geopolitical concepts. He assumes that military strength on a scale capable of reaching the United States can be mobilized only in a few parts of the world, namely, in "those regions where a major industrial power, enjoying adequate access to raw materials, is combined with large reserves of educated and technically skilled manpower." These geographically important regions include the Atlantic Community, Japan, and the Soviet Union.[95] For Kennan, the relationship between Germany and Russia is crucial to United States security.

Both as a diplomat and a scholar, Kennan has been preoccupied largely with East-West problems. As chairman of the State Department's Policy Planning Staff in the early post–World War II period, he played a major role in developing United States policy toward the Soviet Union. It was his assumption that the Soviet leaders were influenced in large part by communist ideology. Because of their ideology, the Soviets were in no hurry to administer a *coup de grace* to the West, since capitalism supposedly contained the seeds of its own destruction. In fact, Lenin's teachings advise caution and flexibility in pursuing foreign policy objectives. The Soviet Union, Kennan reasoned, would press its advantage and seek to fill any apparent power vacuum. Given their belief in the inevitability of the triumph of communism, together with Lenin's strategic principles, the Soviets have "no compunction about retreating in the face of superior force," although Kennan, as discussed subsequently, views military power as an element subordinate to diplomacy in containment.[96]

The immediate problem confronting the United States was to prevent the extension of Soviet power into regions of the world that were threatened in the early post–World War II period. In the longer run, the United States faced the difficult problem of effecting change within the Soviet Union. If the Soviet leadership could be induced to abandon its ideology, the Soviet Union might substitute limited foreign policy objectives for universalist goals. By a policy of containment, Kennan concluded, the United States could respond as effectively as possible to the formidable problems of Soviet-American relations. By denying the Soviet Union foreign policy gains, the United States would eventually lead Soviet leaders not only to question and reject their ideology, but also to adopt limited foreign policy objectives.

A decade after his formulation of the rationale for containment, Kennan discerned changes within the Soviet Union itself and in the communist states of East Central Europe. In calling for the disengagement of U.S. forces in the Federal Republic of Germany, Kennan reasoned, the Soviet Union would be prepared to agree to a similar withdrawal of forces from East Central European countries. The removal of Soviet troops would contribute to internal liberalization of communist regimes as well as to greater independence from the Soviet Union in foreign policy. Thus Soviet influence in this region would be reduced.[97] Of course, the Soviet Union has intervened with massive military power—in Hungary in 1956 and Czechoslovakia in 1968—to prevent unacceptable changes in the status quo in East Central Europe. By the late 1970s, Kennan had concluded that the Soviet Union, despite its vast military buildup and increasing interest in Africa, was essentially a power whose "reactions and purposes are much more defensive than aggressive."[98]

In Kennan's conception of international politics, military power is difficult to measure because of the problems of inferring intentions from capabilities: "All depends on the time, the place, the purpose, and the manner, at which, for which, or in which, these weapons or units are employed. A weapon effective in defense may be relatively ineffective in offense. A weapon effective on the plains may be useless in mountainous territory. A weapon in the hands of a highly trained and motivated unit may have a wholly different value than it has in the hands of a differently trained and motivated one. Mere numerical comparisons do not reflect these variables."[99] In Kennan's perspective, a democracy finds it difficult to maintain and actually use military power in a rational and limited fashion.[100] Kennan views military power as inappropriate, if not irrelevant, to the major issues confronting the United States in the world of the late twentieth century—the organization of global society, a food-population crisis, and the environmental problem.[101] Instead, such political systems in wartime are prone to employ force in a massive effort that loses sight of political goals. Here, he has been criticized for having failed, according to Uri Ra'anan, to reflect the voluminous Soviet literature on the nature and utility of military power, including nuclear weapons, and for having embraced "action-reaction" models and "mirror-imaging" concepts in his analysis of the Soviet Union.[102]

Nevertheless, given the importance of the German-Soviet relationship and his belief in the pursuit of limited foreign policy objectives, Kennan, both in his earlier and more recent writings, has seen no great urgency about the problems of less developed areas.[103] As in the case of economic assistance, the United States has had no overriding interest in responding around the world to communist wars of national liberation. In fact, Kennan views disdainfully subsequent efforts to extend the containment doctrine from Europe to other geographic regions. He objects to the universalization of containment to situations and times different from those during which he formulated it, just as he opposed in his writings other efforts to develop and apply abstract principles to all foreign policy problems.[104] The United States, he maintains, is largely unable to effect fundamental change in the Third World because of the "enormity of the problems in relation to our resources" and because of the "necessity of concentrating our resources elsewhere."[105]

Writing in the mid-1970s and a decade later as well, Kennan reaffirmed his commitment to a United States foreign policy based upon strictly limited capabilities and goals. "In an age of nuclear striking power, national security can never be more than relative; and to the extent that it can be assumed at all, it must find its sanction in the intentions of rival powers as well as in their capabilities."[106] His conception of United States national interest in the late twentieth century is narrowly defined—perhaps, according to one reviewer, verging on isolationism.[107] His global conception of the role of the United States was based upon the reduction of external commitments to an indispensable minimum: "the preservation of the political independence and military security of Western Europe, of Japan, and—with the single reservation that it should not involve the dispatch and commitment of American armed forces—of Israel."[108]

Arnold Wolfers

There are, of course, important differences among the realist theorists. Although Arnold Wolfers (1892–1968) may, for example, be included in a survey of realist thought, his focus differed from that of other proponents of realism. While acknowledging that central to the study of international relations is the "behavior of states as organized bodies of men," he called for "concentration on human beings upon whose psychological reactions the behavior credited to states ultimately rests."[109] The international behavior of states is the amalgam of conflicting pressures. Moreover, subnational, transnational, and supranational actors intrude into international politics, and must be the object of scholarly analysis.

In their relationships nation-states exhibit various kinds of behavior from amity to enmity, depending upon their international goals. Nations set for themselves differing sets of objectives: (1) "possession" goals, such as national independence, physical survival, and territorial integrity; or (2) "milieu" goals, designed to affect the environment beyond a nation's boundaries. Moreover, Wolfers delineated three basic clusters of foreign policy objectives, namely, those related to (1) national self-extension, (2) national self-preservation, and (3) national self-abnegation, such as international solidarity, lawfulness, or peace. Goals of self-abnegation transcend, although they do not necessarily conflict with, goals of national self-interest. For example, the United States in 1918 was powerful enough to permit President Wilson to indulge in self-abnegation goals without harm to its vital national interests. A nation's foreign policy thus includes overlapping goals. The pursuit of objectives related to national self-preservation often makes necessary the pursuit of goals of national self-extension. In fact, increasing international interdependence contributes to the pursuit among nations of goals of national self-extension in order to achieve goals of national self-preservation, thus rendering difficult the return to foreign policies based upon limited objectives, as Kennan, Kissinger, and Morgenthau have urged.

According to Wolfers, a nation's foreign policy is the amalgam of many factors. Although policymakers are guided by their conception of the national interest, this concept holds differing meanings for different peoples. At the minimum, national interest encompasses a nation's territorial integrity, independence, and national survival, yet the goal of "national survival itself is given a wide variety of interpretations by countries facing different conditions."[110] According to Wolfers, "security is a value some countries prize to greater extent than others. The level of security sought by states is not always identical. In fact, political leaders are often confronted with other values."[111] Decision-makers are constantly confronted with difficult choices in which they are unable to separate interest from morality. In fact, their calculus of interest is based upon a hierarchy of values, since "the 'necessities' in international politics, and for that matter in all spheres of life, do not push decision and action beyond the realm of moral judgment; they rest on moral choice themselves. If a statesman decides that the dangers to the security of his country are so great as to make necessary a course of action that may lead to war, he has placed an exceedingly high value on an increment of national security."[112]

Henry A. Kissinger

Another scholar who has drawn from history—in this case, diplomatic history—is Henry A. Kissinger (1923–). Kissinger's theory of international relations is derived from his analysis of early nineteenth-century Europe. In *A World Restored,* based on his doctoral dissertation, Kissinger wrote:

The success of physical science depends on the selection of the "crucial" experiment; that of political science in the field of international affairs, on the selection of the "crucial" period. I have chosen for my topic the period between 1812 and 1822, partly, I am frank to say, because its problems seem to me analogous to those of our day. But I do not insist on this analogy.[113]

Kissinger's fascination with this period lies in the insights that might be provided into the exercise of power by statesmen such as Castlereagh and Metternich for the development of an international structure that contributed to peace in the century between the Congress of Vienna and the outbreak of World War I. Kissinger studied the nature and quality of political leadership, the impact of domestic political structures upon foreign policy, and the relationship between diplomacy and military policy in stable and revolutionary international systems.

As Stephen R. Graubard has written:

Kissinger saw choice as fundamental to the whole political process. It was of the greatest consequence to him that a given state opted for a specific policy for one reason rather than another: because its bureaucracy determined that here was only one safe course; because its leaders were anxious to test the adversary's reactions; because domestic opinion demanded a specific policy; because the political leadership was confused and saw the necessity of creating the illusion that it was still capable of action.[114]

Drawing heavily upon the 1815 to 1822 period, Kissinger postulates that peace is achieved not as an end in itself, but instead emerges as the result of a stable, contrasted with a revolutionary, international system. Therefore Kissinger develops two models for the study of international politics: first, a stable system; and second, a revolutionary system. He contends that stability has resulted not "from a quest for peace, but from a general accepted legitimacy."[115] By Kissinger's definition, legitimacy means "no more than an international agreement about the nature of workable arrangements and about the permissible aims and methods of foreign policy."[116] Legitimacy implies an acceptance of the framework of the international order by all major powers. Agreement among major powers upon the framework of international order does not eliminate international conflicts, but it limits their scope. Conflict *within* the framework has been more limited than conflict *about* the framework. Diplomacy, which Kissinger defines as "the adjustment of differences through negotiation," becomes possible only in international systems where "legitimacy obtains."[117] In Kissinger's model the primary objective of national actors is not to preserve peace. In fact, "wherever peace—conceived as the avoidance of war—has been the primary objective of a power or a group of powers, the international system has been at the mercy of the most ruthless member of the international community."[118] In contrast, "whenever the international order has acknowledged that certain principles could not be compromised even for the sake of peace, stability based on an equilibrium of forces was at least conceivable."[119]

An understanding of the characteristics of a revolutionary world order can be derived from Kissinger's model of stability. Any order in which a major power is so dissatisfied that it seeks to transform that order is revolutionary. In the generation before 1815, revolutionary France presented a major challenge to the existing order.

> Disputes no longer concerned the adjustment of differences within an accepted framework, but the validity of the framework itself; the political contest had become doctrinal: the balance of power which had operated so intricately throughout the eighteenth century suddenly lost its flexibility and the European equilibrium came to seem an insufficient protection to powers faced by a France which proclaimed the incompatibility of its political maxims with those of the other states.[120]

Tracing the diplomacy of European powers between 1812 and 1822, Kissinger concludes that the restoration of a stable order depends on several factors: (1) the willingness of supporters of legitimacy to negotiate with a revolutionary power while at the same time being prepared to use military power; (2) the ability of supporters of legitimacy to avoid the outbreak of "total" war, since such conflict would threaten the international framework that status quo powers wish to preserve; and (3) the capacity of national units to use limited means to achieve limited objectives. No power is compelled to surrender unconditionally; powers defeated in limited war are not eliminated from the international system. No power, whether victorious or vanquished, is completely satisfied or completely dissatisfied. Limitations placed upon means and goals make possible the restoration of a balance of power between the victorious and the vanquished.

In other writings Kissinger has applied concepts derived from his study of early nineteenth-century European diplomatic history to the contemporary international system. The problems posed by the great destructive potential of nuclear weapons have been of great concern to him. As in the past, it is necessary for nations to develop limited means to achieve limited objectives. "An all or nothing military policy will . . . play into the hands of the Soviet strategy of ambiguity which seeks to upset the strategic balance by small degrees and which combines political, psychological, and military pressures to induce the greatest degree of uncertainty and hesitation in the mind of the opponent."[121] If United States policymakers are to have a choice other than "the dread alternatives of surrender or suicide,"[122] they must adopt concepts of limited war derived from the experience of nineteenth-century warfare. At that time the objective of warfare "was to create a calculus of risks according to which continued resistance would appear more costly than the peace terms sought to be imposed."[123] A strategy of limited warfare would provide the United States with the means "to establish a reasonable relationship between power and the willingness to use it, between the physical and psychological components of national policy."[124]

Writing in the 1960s, Kissinger contended that if the United States was to avoid the stark alternatives of suicide or surrender, it must have both large-scale conventional forces and tactical nuclear weapons. Kissinger established three requirements for limited war capabilities:

1. The limited war forces must be able to prevent the potential aggressor from creating a fait accompli.
2. They must be of a nature to convince the aggressor that their use, although invoking an increasing risk of all-out war, is not an inevitable prelude to it.
3. They must be coupled with a diplomacy which succeeds in conveying that all-out war is not the sole response to aggression and that there exists a willingness to negotiate a settlement short of unconditional surrender.[125]

If nations are to evolve a limited war strategy, they must develop an understanding of those interests that do not threaten national survival. Decision-makers must possess the ability to restrain public opinion if disagreement arises as to whether national survival is at stake. Given a tacit understanding among nations about the nature of limited objectives, it is possible to fight both conventional conflicts and limited nuclear wars without their escalation to total war.

In the adjustment of differences among nations, Kissinger, like most other realists, assigns an important role to diplomacy. Historically, negotiation was aided by the military capabilities a nation could bring to bear if diplomacy failed. The vast increase in destructive capabilities has contributed to the perpetuation of disputes. "Our age faces the paradoxical problem that because the violence of war has grown out of all proportion to the objectives to be achieved, no issue has been resolved."[126]

Moreover, the reduction in the number of powers of approximately equal strength has increased the difficulty of conducting diplomacy.

> As long as no nation was strong enough to eliminate all the others, shifting coalitions could be used for exerting pressure or marshaling support. They serve in a sense as substitutes for physical conflict. In the classical periods of cabinet diplomacy in the eighteenth and nineteenth centuries, a country's diplomatic flexibility and bargaining position depends on its availability as a partner to as many other countries as possible. As a result, no relationship was considered permanent and no conflict was pushed to its ultimate conclusion.[127]

Although wars occurred, nations did not risk national survival and were able instead to use limited means to achieve limited objectives.

Like Morgenthau, Kissinger views with disfavor the injection of ideology into the international system. Ideology not only contributes to the development of unlimited national objectives, but it also eventually creates states whose goal is to overthrow the existing international system. In the absence of agreement among powers about the framework for the system—or its legitimacy—the conduct of diplomacy becomes difficult, even impossible. Hence the emphasis in the Nixon-Ford-Kissinger foreign policy upon creating a stable structure for the international system: "All nations, adversaries and friends alike, must have a stake in preserving the international system. They must feel that their principles are being respected and their national interests secured. They must, in short, see positive incentive for keeping the peace, not just the dangers of breaking it."[128]

Such a conception for the late twentieth century drew heavily upon the theoretical framework developed by Kissinger in *A World Restored*. His quest for a stable international system as a policymaker, moreover, drew upon a belief in the need for a "certain equilibrium between potential adversaries," namely, the United States and the Soviet Union. In his memoir, Kissinger wrote: "If history teaches anything it is that there can be no peace without equilibrium and no justice without restraint."[129] But the global system of the 1970s differed substantially from that of the early nineteenth century described by Kissinger in *A World Restored*.

> The classical concept of balance of power included continual maneuvering for marginal advantages over others. In the nuclear era, this is not realistic because when both sides possess such enormous power, small additional increments cannot be translated into tangible advantage or even usable political strength. And it is dangerous because attempts to seek tactical gains might lead to confrontation which would be catastrophic.[130]

Nevertheless, the balance-of-power concept pervaded the foreign policy of the United States in this period: The "opening" to China was a means, in part at least, of exerting leverage upon the Soviet Union to mitigate tensions between Washington and Moscow in the so-called détente diplomacy; "tilting" toward Pakistan in the war with India of 1971; and pressing for a cease-fire and disengagement of forces in the October 1973 war, when Israel was on the verge of destroying what remained of the Egyptian army. Each of these examples illustrates a central element of balance-of-power theory, as noted in Chapter 1—that is, to support the weaker of two protagonists in order to forestall the ascendancy of the stronger.

As Secretary of State, Kissinger proposed several initiatives designed to enhance the cohesiveness of the Atlantic Alliance, although his conception of a world of several power centers, the emphasis placed upon diplomatic flexibility and surprise, and the perceived need to develop a form of détente diplomacy both with the Soviet Union and the People's Republic of China created formidable problems in the early 1970s for United States alliance relationships, both with Western Europe and Japan. The dilemma was that of maintaining and strengthening partnerships with allies, while seeking new bilateral relationships with adversaries, against which the alliances were originally formed. Especially in the aftermath of the October 1973 war, moreover, Kissinger saw the need to develop among the United States, Western Europe, and Japan frameworks for the resolution of such problems as energy supply and other global issues of the late twentieth century. Between 1973 and 1977, the United States took initiatives toward establishing the International Energy Agency, convening multilateral trade negotiations, and creating a dialogue between industrialized and developing countries, between producer and consumer states, and among industrialized states, symbolized in summit meetings of heads of government to discuss important economic issues.

Realist writers, Kissinger included, have often sought to separate domestic politics from foreign policy. The conduct of an effective diplomacy is said to be difficult, if not impossible, if it must be subject, both in its conception and execution, to the continuous scrutiny of public opinion in a democracy such as the United States. Flexibility, characteristic of Kissinger's style of diplomacy, can be achieved in secrecy more easily than in a policy process open to the glare of publicity.

But the relationship between domestic politics and foreign policy has another dimension for realists, and especially for Kissinger. Unlike those who subscribe to Wilsonian idealism or utopianism, Kissinger does not seek to transform domestic political structures in the belief that democratic political systems are a prerequisite for a peaceful world:

> We shall never condone the suppression of fundamental liberties. We shall urge humane principles and use our influence to promote justice. But the issue comes down to the limits of such efforts. How hard can we press without provoking the Soviet leadership into returning to practices in its foreign policy that increase international tensions? . . . For half a century we have objected to Communist efforts to alter the domestic structure of other countries. For a generation of Cold War we sought to ease the risks produced by competing ideologies. Are we now to come full circle and *insist* on domestic compatibility of progress?[131]

Here Kissinger's theory of international relations contrasts sharply with the view that a precondition for the development of a stable relationship with the Soviet Union is the transformation of its political system to conform with principles of human rights and political freedom cherished in the West. At most, the easing of tensions between states is a complex process, dependent upon diplomacy, mutual interest, and "a strong military balance and flexible defense posture." In short, foreign policy should be based on national power and interest, rather than abstract moralistic principles or political crusades.[132]

Nevertheless, in Kissinger's theory of international relations the domestic political structure of states is a key element. His stable and revolutionary system models of international politics, noted earlier, are linked to the domestic political structures of the states in either system. Stable international systems are characterized by actors whose domestic political structures are based on compatible notions about the means and goals of foreign policies. By definition, governments with stable domestic political structures do not resort to revolutionary or adventuristic foreign policies to restore or preserve domestic cohesion. In contrast, revolutionary systems contain actors whose domestic political structures contrast sharply with each other. Kissinger contends that

> when domestic structures—and the concept of legitimacy on which they are based—differ widely, statesmen can still meet, but their ability to persuade has been reduced for they no longer speak the same language. . . . But when one or more states claims universal applicability for their particular structure, schisms grow deep indeed.[133]

Thus Kissinger, in effect, links his conception of domestic political structure not only to his models of stable and revolutionary systems, but also to the notion of legitimacy set forth in *A World Restored.* Presumably, domestic political structures that are compatible are conducive to the development of consensus, or legitimacy, at the international level. Those eras of stability among states coincide with the presence, at the national level, of compatible political structures based on a modicum of stability.

Robert Strausz-Hupé

Although prescriptions for action by the statesman can be found in most realist writings, the works of Robert Strausz-Hupé, in particular, have emphasized the relationship between power and values, between power and the transformation of the international system. Strausz-Hupé (1903–   ) has had as a major concern the nature of power as well as its exercise and control. In his study of international relations, he contends: "Power is the staff of orderly government. Without the exercise of power, political order could neither be established nor maintained. Power guards society against anarchy. Yet power spawns tyranny and violence, corrupts the mighty and crushes freedom."[134]

Although international conflict is attributable to several causes, it stems largely from the human "urge for power," which is "derived from the more basic urge of self-aggrandizement or self-assertion."[135] The power urge may take any one of several forms: "personal ambition, a quest for prestige and gratification, or simply a desire to profit from other people's work."[136] In the modern world, power is more important than ever. Population growth, the emergence of organizational structures with intermediate layers of power holders, and the growth of the physical force of power have all enhanced the importance of power. Moreover, the religious and metaphysical limitations that once restrained power-holders have broken down. Deification of the state and development of Darwinian theories have strengthened the power urge. Rapid social change, together with the alienation of people from older collectives, has produced states of anxiety and anomie, which often stimulate in individuals and groups suicidal tendencies and increase the incidence of war and aggressiveness.[137]

The individual's quest for power has the effect of making the entire society more aggressive. Domestic power struggles spill over into the international system. In international politics, the power urge reveals itself in several kinds of conflict: the attempt of one state to impose its political ideology on another state; psychological differences, especially fear, hatred, or divergent manners or customs; differences in social structure and culture; population pressures; conflicts over economic issues; territorial claims; conflicting security interests; and differences between political systems. As a result, a state may seek one of several kinds of objectives: the redrawing of its own borders; the modification of another state's political, social, and cultural system; or an increase in its security by removing possible threats and establishing its own power superiority.

In achieving foreign policy objectives, decision-makers must choose among alternative means. Their choice depends upon their degree of motivation to achieve a particular goal, the time available for its attainment, the cost, the risk, and the extent to which one goal conflicts with other goals. Conflict management has many aspects. Four basic techniques are available for shaping an opponent's behavior: evolution (the gradual transformation of an opponent's intention or ruling class), revolution from above, revolution from below, and war.

Like several other theorists examined in this chapter, Strausz-Hupé is concerned with geographical location, manpower, and natural resources, as well as scientific and technological proficiency, national psychology, and political institutions as elements of national power. Size and structure of population are vital measurements of national power. A decline in population usually precedes a decline in a nation's international position. Those countries that are most powerful "possess an adequate supply of all 'essential,' 'strategic,' and 'critical' materials or . . . are able, by virtue of their mastery over transportation routes, to import, in time of war, materials inadequately supplied at home."[138] Political, economic, and military organization "transforms these elements of power into world-political realities."[139]

Despite changes in technology, geography remains an important factor in the power equation. As a student of geopolitical relationships, Strausz-Hupé attached particular significance to Sir Halford Mackinder's concept of the Heartland. "If domination of the landlocked plains-lands of European Russia is joined to the domination of east central Europe between the Baltic, Adriatic, and Aegean, then the condition obtains which Sir Halford Mackinder conceived as the final step to the mastery of Europe."[140] Because the "political unification of the European continent under a single power would profoundly alter the distribution of technological and economic potentials,"[141] the defense of Western Europe remains vital to the security of the United States.

Conflict can be traced to the conditions that attend the breakdown of political systems. It is possible to trace a series of "systemic" revolutions that have transformed political institutions and practices. According to Strausz-Hupé, the first systemic revolution "started with the Peloponnesian War and reached its climax in the Roman Civil Wars which pitted first Pompey against Caesar and then Caesar's heirs against one another. The revolution . . . was not confined to any one city or country It rolled over the entire Mediterranean region—the universe of the ancients. When it had run its course of four centuries, the state system had changed from one of many city-states into one of a single universal empire."[142] With the dawn of the modern period during the Renaissance and the Reformation, the feudal system gave way to the nation-state system. This system in turn is in decline. In the twentieth century, the world once again is passing through a systemic revolution. The nation-state is no longer adequate to the demands imposed upon it. Ultimately, the systemic revolution ushers in the development of larger political units, and even possibly the eventual unification of the globe. The struggle between the United States and the Soviet Union is but the contemporary expression of pervasive conflict that encompasses all lands, all peoples, and all levels of society. The systemic revolution obeys a law of the dialectic. Within each period there are forces that contend with and eventually lead to the destruction of the existing system. One system gives way to another system, which in turn contains forces that lead eventually to its transformation. Upon the outcome of the systemic revolution depends the future of political organization in the world.

Raymond Aron

Because of his attempt in the monumental work *Peace and War* to synthesize much of the past and contemporary writings in international relations, Raymond Aron (1904–1983), noted French social philosopher, does not fall easily into a realist category of international theorists. Aron engaged in what he termed a fourfold analysis of international relations: theory, sociology, history, and praxeology. What he called theory corresponds to "ordering of data, selection of problems, and variables."[143] His conceptualization included the development of propositions about diplomacy and strategy, the nature of power, notions of equilibrium, and models of multipolar and bipolar international systems and homogenous and heterogeneous systems.

In Aron's view, theory provides an enumeration of "effect-phenomena, the determined factors, for which the sociologist is tempted to seek cause-phenomena, the determinant."[144] In the section of his work termed sociology, he was concerned with causality and the determinants of international behavior. In particular, Aron addressed himself to the problems of spatial relationships, population, resources, and the origins of war, as well as what he termed the nation, the civilization, and humanity as collectives that affect conduct at the international level. Aron's examination of history, his third level of conceptualization, consisted of an effort to relate his theory and sociology to the international system since 1945.

Finally, to use a term that appears frequently in his work, praxeology represented Aron's attempt to formulate both a normative theory (asking what the goals of states should be) and a series of prescriptions for international conduct (asking how statesmen should act to achieve those goals).

According to Aron, international relations consists of relations among the political units into which the world is divided at any given time, from the Greek city-state to the modern nation-state. Although a science or philosophy of politics would include the study of international relations, the case for the uniqueness of international relations stems from the fact that it deals with "relations between political units, each of which claims the right to take justice into its own hands and to be the sole arbiter of the decision to fight or not to fight."[145]

Because of the existence of several or many autonomous political units, the principal objective of each unit is to ensure its safety, and ultimately its survival. Given this preoccupation, the political leader can never develop a fully rational diplomatic-strategic behavior. Nevertheless, Aron sought to develop a "rational type of theory, proceeding from fundamental concepts (strategy and diplomacy, means and ends, power and force, power, glory, and idea) to systems and types of systems."

In international relations, diplomat-strategists face the risk of war since they confront opponents in a situation of "incessant rivalry in which each side reserves the right to resort to the ultimate ratio, that is, to violence."[146] In Aron's conceptualization, relations among nations are often marked by conflict, although the essence of politics does not lie, in his view, exclusively in a struggle for power. Essentially, relations among political units consist of the alternatives of war and peace, since every collectivity exists among friends, enemies, neutrals, or indifferent parties. The status of political units is determined by the material or human resources that they can allocate to diplomatic-strategic action. The extent to which political units mobilize such resources depends upon many factors, including, of course, accessibility to them, but also the objectives that political leaders choose to pursue. Aron asserted that political units do not desire power for its own sake, but rather as a means toward achieving some goal, such as peace or glory, or in order to influence the future of the international system. Many kinds of circumstances, such as changes in military or economic technique and the transformation of institutions or ideologies, affect the goals of political leaders. Technological innovations modify previously held spatial concepts, including the strategic value of geographical positions and the economic importance of certain natural and human resources. But Aron acknowledged that political units that have the greatest influence on others are not always those that most consciously attempt to impose themselves on others. Although it is possible, as Aron attempted, to examine or even quantify elements of national power, it is more difficult to assess their effectiveness in attaining the goals set by political leaders.

Moreover, the conduct of nations toward each other is the product not only of their relative power, but also of the ideas and emotions that influence the actions of decision-makers. It is necessary, as Aron himself did in his theory, to provide for geographical relationships, alliances, and military structures. But it is essential as well to assess the relationship between the capabilities of political units and the objectives sought by political leaders.

Here Aron introduced two models of the international system, the so-called homogeneous system and the heterogeneous system. In the homogeneous system "states belong to the same type, obey the same conception of policy." In the heterogeneous system, the "states are organized according to different principles and appeal to contradictory values."[147] In homogeneous systems political leaders are in agreement about the kinds of objectives to be pursued; conflict occurs within the system, but the continued existence of the system itself is not at stake. Thus Aron suggested that from the end of the Thirty Years' War in 1648 until the French Revolution, and again from 1815 until the early twentieth century, the international system was largely homogeneous. Especially since 1945, however, the international system has been heterogeneous, because much of the conflict has been concerned with the system itself, not just the attainment of goals within the system.

Although Aron gave great prominence in his theory to power as a means toward attaining national objectives, he set forth explicitly a systems framework for the analysis of international politics. An international system, he suggested, is "the ensemble constituted by political units that maintain regular relations with each other and that are capable of being implicated in a generalized war."[148] In addition to homogeneous and heterogeneous systems, it is possible to distinguish bipolar and multipolar systems, depending on whether the majority of political units are grouped around two sites of far greater strength, or the system includes several political units relatively similar in strength.

Both the bipolar and multipolar systems contain equilibrating mechanisms. At its highest level of abstraction, equilibrium consists of the tendency, found also in other theories, of a state or combination of states to attempt to restrain a state or coalition that seems capable of achieving preponderance. Although this rule, according to Aron, is applicable to all international systems, it is necessary to construct models according to a configuration of forces in order to elaborate rules for the operation of equilibrium. In the multipolar system the essential rule of equilibrium is that "the state whose forces are increasing must anticipate the dissidence of certain of its allies, who will rejoin the other camp in order to maintain the balance."[149] In the bipolar system, the most general law of equilibrium is that "the goal of chief actors is to avoid finding themselves at the mercy of a rival."[150] The principal goal of each of the chief actors is that of preventing the other from acquiring capabilities superior to its own. The chief actor, the leader of a coalition, seeks simultaneously to prevent the growth of the opposing coalition and to maintain the cohesiveness of its own coalition.

In Aron's theory, there are three types of peace: equilibrium, hegemony, or empire. In any historical period the forces of the political units are in one of three conditions: (1) they are in balance, (2) they are dominated by those of one of the units, or (3) they are outclassed by the forces of one of the political units. Between peace by equilibrium and peace by empire, Aron placed what he termed peace by hegemony. The incontestable superiority of one political unit is acknowledged by other members of the international system. Although the smaller states are unable to change the status quo, the hegemonic state does not attempt to absorb them. Germany, for example, in the period after the Franco-Prussian War of 1870 to 1871, possessed a kind of hegemony on the continent, which Bismarck sought to make acceptable to other European states.

If peace is the "more or less lasting suspension of violent modes of rivalry between political units," conflict, in Aron's theory, consists of the dialectics of antagonism—deterrence, persuasion, and subversion.

Deterrence is related both to the material means that a state possesses to prevent action by another political unit and to the perception of resolution one state is able to convey to another that threatens it. "Today as yesterday, the essential problem of deterrence is both psychological and technological. How can the state diplomatically on the defensive convince a state diplomatically on the offensive that it will carry out its threat?"[151] If the credibility of a threat depends upon the perceived intention of the state making a threat to carry it out, the threat becomes less convincing as its execution appears to be contrary to the interests of those who make it. The advent of weapons of mass destruction increases the risk of executing a threat and thus reduces the interests for which the use of force can be credibly threatened. Aron outlines a system, similar to Morton Kaplan's unit veto system, in which each state will be in a position to exterminate all others. Thus, in this model, technology affects the credibility of threats made by political actors. (For theories of deterrence, see Chapter 9.)

What Aron termed persuasion, in his dialectics of antagonism, consists of methods designed to modify behavior in some desired fashion and, indeed, includes the strategy of subversion. What Aron described as subversion is the use of violence to attain an objective. "Abstractly," he suggested, "the goal of subversion is to withdraw a population from the administrative and moral authority of an established power and to integrate it within other political and military frameworks, sometimes in and by conflict."[152]

According to Aron, conflict, in the most general sense, results whenever two individuals, social groups, or political units covet the same property or seek incompatible goals. Aron held that the human animal is aggressive, but that humanity does not fight by instinct. War is an expression of human aggressiveness. Although, given human nature, it is impossible to eliminate all conflict, it is not "proved that these conflicts must be manifested in the phenomenon of war, as we have known it for thousands of years, with organized combatants, utilizing increasingly destructive weapons."[153]

Although Aron's theoretical framework is similar in many respects to those of American realists, he contrasted American realism with the work of earlier European scholars such as the German historian Heinrich von Treitschke (1834–1896). In contrast to Treitschke, "the American authors who are commonly regarded as belonging to the realist school declare that states, animated by a will-to-power, are in permanent rivalry, but that they are not self-congratulatory about the situation and do not regard it as a part of the divine plan. The refusal of states to submit to a common law or arbitration seems to them incontestable, intelligible, but not sublime, for they hold neither war nor the right to draw the sword as sublime."[154] But American realists, according to Aron, are "located on the margin of the idealist situation" since, although they criticize the utopian or idealist conception, the realists unconsciously "follow the example of those whom they oppose." Realists, too, develop a normative theory of international relations.

In the portion of his work entitled praxeology, Aron himself engaged in normative theorizing. He believed that the political leader ought to remember that international order is the result of a balancing of forces that support the preservation of the system with those that seek its transformation. If statesmen are unable to calculate such forces correctly, they fail to perform their primary responsibility—for the security of the persons and values entrusted to their care. For the statesman, immorality in Aron's conception is a condition in which the political leader "obeys his heart without concerning himself with the consequences of his acts." Thus Aron suggested, as American realists have held, that the morality of the political leader as a political leader differs from that of the citizen within a political unit.

As Stanley Hoffmann has pointed out, the normative implications of Aron's theory lie in the "contradiction between the constraints which weigh on the statesman, responsible for his country's interests in a world in which the use of force remains possible and legitimate, and moral conscience, which protects against the bloody anarchy of the international milieu and demands universal peace."[155] Aron expressed skepticism about the efficacy of international law, world government, or arms control— about the ability of international politics to be transformed from a world of anarchy to one of consensually based order. Yet Aron preferred an international community based on world law and order. Such a community is not possible without what he terms a homogeneity of states and a similarity of constitutional practices. Under such circumstances, states would reduce their levels of armaments, cease to suspect each other of the worst intentions, abandon the resort to force to resolve disputes, and give respect to the same legal and moral ideas. However worthy such a goal,

Aron remained convinced that such a world was beyond human grasp and that the threat to use force, or its actual employment, in the world as it exists furnishes the ultimate basis for preserving political pluralism against the threat of militant totalitarianism.

NEOREALISM

The realist tradition has furnished an abundant basis for the formation of what is termed a neorealist approach to international relations theory. Neorealism purports to refine and reinvigorate classical realism by developing propositions based upon the disaggregation of independent and dependent variables, and by integrating what is termed classical realist theory into a contemporary framework based upon comparative analysis. A neorealist theory would inject greater rigor into the realist tradition by defining key concepts more clearly and consistently, and developing a series of propositions that could be subjected to empirical testing and investigation. Neorealism has embraced work that is termed structural realism, identified with recent writings of Kenneth Waltz,[156] as well as the effort explicitly to build upon the writings of Hans Morgenthau by Gott-fried-Karl Kindermann.[157] For neorealism, power remains a key variable, although it exists less as an end in itself than as a necessary and inevitable component of a political relationship. According to Kindermann, "just as the instrument of power and of sanctions does not exhaust the nature of law, the nature of Politics is also not exhausted by primarily referring to power as its most important tool."[158]

Indeed, the neorealist approach represents an effort not only to draw from classical realism those elements of a theory adequate to the world of the late twentieth century, but also to link conceptually other theoretical efforts. Thus the structural realism of Kenneth Waltz draws heavily upon systems constructs and the neorealism of Kindermann's Munich School of Neorealism has as its basis a constellation, or configuration, consisting of a "system of interaction—relations between states and other action-systems of international politics at a given moment or within a defined period of history past or present." This neorealist approach contains as interdependent categories of inquiry (1) system and decision (leadership), (2) interest and power, (3) perception and reality, (4) cooperation and conflict (behavioral strategy), and (5) norm or advantage. Thus neorealism posits the existence of an international system consisting of interactive elements that are to be studied by reference to concepts derived from classical realist theory, but also based on variables drawn from cross-cultural comparative analysis. To quote again from Kindermann's description: "Neorealism, in other words, proceeds from the assumption that a much higher degree of concrete and quasi-institutionalized cross-disciplinary cooperation is required before essential progress can be made in our ability to analyze and, if possible, to predict political action processes of systems as complex as, for instance, the nation-state and its structurally essential subsystems."[159]

If the flawed nature of man forms a crucially important point of departure for classical realist analysis, neorealism has as its focus the international system. Stated differently, it is the structure that shapes the political relationships that take place among its members. For structural realism, international politics is more than the summation of the foreign policies of states and the external balance of other actors in the system. Thus, Waltz argues for a neorealist approach based on patterned relationships among actors in a system that is anarchical. In this respect, drawing upon the paradigm of international politics of classical realism, structural realism contains an emphasis on those features of the structure that mold the way in which the components relate to one another. According to Waltz, the term *structure* connotes the way in which the parts are arranged. In domestic politics there is said to be a hierarchical relationship, in which units stand in formal differentiation from one another by reference to their degree of authority or the function that they perform. By contrast, the international system lacks comparable governmental institutions. Actors stand in a horizontal relationship with each other, with each state the formal equal (sovereignty) of the other. Waltz defines structure by the principle (hierarchical or anarchic) by which it is organized. Furthermore, Waltz defines structure by the specification of functions of the units. The more hierarchical the system, the greater the differentiation of functions; the more anarchical, the greater the similarity in function among the units.[160] Finally, structure is defined by the distribution of capabilities among the units, including, for example, the extent to which it consists of actors who are similar to or widely different from each other as to the means in their possession. In keeping with classical realism, Waltz treats states as "unitary actors who, at a minimum, seek their own preservation and, at a maximum, drive for universal domination." Therefore, in the realist tradition, he points to the necessary emergence of a balance of power.

The focus of structural realism is the arrangement of the parts of the international system with respect to each other. According to Waltz, "The concept of structure is based on the fact that units differently juxtaposed and combined behave differently and in interacting produce different outcomes."[161] Basic to an anarchic system, by virtue of its structure, is the need for member units to rely on whatever means or arrangements they can generate in order to ensure survival and enhance security. In such a system, based as it is on the principle of self-help, states pursue one or both of two basic courses of action, in keeping with Waltz's approach to structure as a variable conditioning, or circumscribing, political behavior. They engage in internal efforts to increase their political, military, and economic capabilities and to develop effective strategies. They also undertake external attempts to align, or realign, with other actors. The structure of the system, notably the number of actors and their respective capabilities, shapes the patterns of interaction that will take place, including the number of states aligned with each other in opposing groupings as part of a balance of power. In the anarchical structure all units confront the minimal need or functional requirement for security, although there are wide variations among them in their respective capabilities for this purpose. Indeed, differences among states in the means possessed for security represent the principal distinguishing characteristic separating one from the other. In Waltz's perspective, international systems are transfigured by changes in the distribution of capabilities among its units. As structures change, so do interactive patterns among its members as well as the outcomes that such interactions can be expected to produce. Although the capabilities constitute attributes of units, their distribution among the various units forms a defining characteristic of the structure of the system, and in this case, of structural realism. In sum, central to structural realism, and especially to the approach developed by Waltz, is the proposition that only a structural transformation can alter the anarchical nature of the international system.

If structure defines the arrangement of the parts of the international system in the structural realism of Waltz, what accounts for change in the structure? According to Waltz, structures emerge from the coexistence of the primary political units of a given era. They may be city-states, nations, or empires. His approach to structural realism does not address the question of how and why such political units come into existence at a particular time in history. His concern is not with the units or combinations of units at the national or subnational levels. Stated differently, Waltz's structural realism does not approach international relations theory from a reductionist theoretical perspective. In contrast to structural realism, a reductionist theory would explain international phenomena principally by reference to the actions of the separate states and their internal characteristics. Structural realism in itself, Waltz admits, does not furnish a comprehensive theory of international relations; this would require, for example, a theory of domestic politics because the units shape the system's structure, just as the structure affects the units. Changes in systems, including their transformation, originate not in their structure, but in their parts. Unit-level forces are said to shape the possibilities for systemic change.[162]

Other contemporary neorealist analysis has as its focus change at the international level based upon a reinterpretation of classical realist theory. According to Robert Gilpin, states engage in cost-benefit calculations about alternative courses of action available to them.[163] To the extent that the anticipated benefits exceed the costs, states are likely to attempt to make changes in the system. In this respect, Gilpin attempts to refine the rationality assumption that is contained in classical realist theory. In Gilpin's formulation, a state will attempt to change the international system by means of territorial, political, or economic expansion until the marginal costs of additional change become equal to or exceed the marginal benefits. An international system is in a condition of equilibrium to the extent that its major actors are satisfied with the territorial, political, and economic status quo. It is acknowledged that every state or group in the system could benefit from some form of change; therefore, the costs of changing form the principal barriers to disruptive or destabilizing action. The distribution of power represents the principal means for controlling the behavior of states. Dominant states maintain a network of relationships within the system for this purpose. In deciding upon foreign policies that would produce change in the international system, Gilpin suggests, states usually make trade-offs among various objectives. They do not attempt to achieve one goal at the sacrifice of all others, but instead engage in a "satisficing" approach designed to attain various combinations of desired results. Historically, states have had as their goal the conquest of territory that, before the Industrial Revolution and the advent of advanced technology, represented the principal means for enhancing security or wealth. Furthermore, states strive to increase their influence over other states by means of threats, coercion, alliances, and spheres of influence. Finally, an increasingly important goal of states lies in the extension of influence in the global economy. In keeping with the "satisficing" principle, subgoals are by no means mutually exclusive. Among the objectives of states, Gilpin asserts, those considered to be most important are defined as vital interests on whose behalf the state is willing to go to war.

International systems are said to undergo essentially three types of change. First and of fundamental importance is an alteration in the nature of the actors or the types of entities—empires, states, or other units—that comprise a particular international system, which Gilpin terms systems change. Examples include the rise and decline of the Greek city-state system, the medieval European state system, and the emergence of the nuclear state system leading to the present era. What, it is asked, are the particular sociopolitical, economic, and technological factors that give rise to the organizational framework with which groups or individuals advance their interests? A system changes as the cost-benefit ratio of membership in the existing system is altered.

A second dimension of change has as its focus not the system itself but instead the components, within which change takes place. All international systems are characterized by the rise and fall of powerful states that shape patterns of international interactions and establish the rules by which the system operates. Thus the distribution of power within the system is altered. Here, the emphasis is placed not on the rise and fall of international systems but instead on the growth and decline of their constituent elements—that is, the greater or lesser powers and, in particular, the replacement of one dominant entity by another such actor. Whereas classical realist theory was derived largely from the European state system, a comparative study of international systems including earlier, non-Western systems would yield an understanding of how and why systemic change takes place. Finally, the third element of this neorealist theory of change has as its focus the nature of its members' political, economic, or sociocultural interactions. In sum, the study of change embraces the system itself, its constituent elements, and the interactive process among them.

The propensity of states, or other actors, to seek to extend their territorial control, political influence, and economic domination is said to be a function of their power. Such a process, according to Gilpin, continues until the marginal costs of further change equal or exceed the marginal benefits. As the size of the state and the extent of its control grow, there eventually comes a point at which the cost expansion relative to the derived benefits limits the capacity for control and for further expansion. A system in which the cost of expansion equals or exceeds the perceived benefits is said to be in equilibrium. By the same token, an equilibrium, once reached, is itself subject to change, since there is a tendency for the economic costs of maintaining the status quo to increase faster than the economic capacity to support it. Therefore, disequilibrium represents a gap between the units of the international system and the capacity of the dominant states to maintain the existing system. Such is the condition that results in the decline of a principal actor, a phenomenon that can be observed historically in the Roman, Byzantine, Chinese, and British empires in successive ages. In place of the one dominant actor, there eventually arises a new equilibrium reflecting the altered distribution of power. As its relative power grows, a rising state attempts to extend its control of territory and to increase its influence, usually at the expense of the dominant, but declining, power. The power in decline has essentially several options: to attempt to increase capabilities to match the rising unit; to reduce commitments and thus to acquiesce, gracefully, in altered circumstances; to enter into alliances or other arrangements with other powers; or to make concessions to the rising power. However, Gilpin suggests, the primary means by which the issue of disequilibrium has been resolved throughout history has been by war, the result of which has usually been a redistribution of power between the victorious and the vanquished. Thus international politics consists of forces leading to conflict or accommodation in a succession of international systems marked by change. "Ultimately," Gilpin concludes,

> international politics still can be characterized as it was by Thucydides: the interplay of impersonal forces and great leaders. . . . World politics is still characterized by the struggle of political entities for power, prestige, and wealth in a coalition of global anarchy. Nuclear weapons have not made the resort to force irrelevant; economic interdependence does not guarantee that cooperation will triumph over conflict; a global community of common values and outlook has yet to displace international anarchy.[164]

REALISM: ITS LIMITATIONS AND CONTRIBUTIONS

No theoretical approach to the study of international relations is without its critics. Realism evoked criticism in part because of the boldness with which its proponents stated assumptions about political behavior, as well as the assumptions themselves and the policy proposals issuing from them. Although each theorist has supporters and critics, the following critique relates principally to concepts shared by more than one, but not necessarily by all, of those surveyed in this chapter.

Fundamental to the critique of realist theory was the questioning, rejection, or modification of the traditional paradigm of international relations on which realism in its classical formulation was based. Politics, defined as a struggle of power in a state-centric system based on actors whose foreign polemics could clearly be separated from domestic politics, had given way by the 1960s to a newer and more complex paradigm, or model, of the international system.[165] In place of the Eurocentric realist paradigm came an international system global in scope and containing an unprecedented number of states and nonstate actors. To the extent that domestic politics shapes foreign policy, the clearly defined separation assumed in realist theory became at least blurred and at most a gross distortion of the complex process by which state action takes place. According to John A. Vasquez,

> *realpolitik* explanations do not provide a theory of world politics, but merely an image that decision makers can have of the world. Power politics is not so much an explanation as a description of one type of behavior found in the global political system. If this is correct, then power politics behavior itself must be explained; it does not explain.[166]

Reflecting on other research of the 1970s as well as his own effort to test propositions derived from realist theory, Vasquez concluded that those that are "based on realist assumptions do not do as well as those that reject realist assumptions."[167]

For several reasons, the "national interest" concept has been the object of criticism. According to one critique, "That national interest is a necessary criterion of policy is obvious and unilluminating. No statesman, no publicist, no scholar would seriously argue that foreign policy ought to be conducted in opposition to, or in disregard of, the national interest."[168] Moreover, it is difficult to give operational meaning to the concept of national interest. Statesmen are constrained, or given freedom, by many forces in interpreting the national interest. They are often the captive of their predecessors' policies. They interpret national interest as a result of their cultural training, values, and the data made available to them as decision-makers. According to Stanley Hoffmann,

> The conception of an objective and easily recognizable national interest, the reliable guide and criterion of national policy, is one which makes sense only

in a stable period in which the participants play for limited ends, with limited means, and without domestic kibbitzers to disrupt the players' moves. In a period when the survival of states is at stake to a far greater extent than in former times, the most divergent courses of action can be recommended as valid choices for survival. Ordinarily less compelling objectives, such as prestige, or an increment of power in a limited area, or the protection of private citizens abroad, all become tied up with the issues of survival, and the most frequent argument against even attempting to redefine a hierarchy of national objectives so as to separate at least some of them from survival is the familiar fear of a "chain of events" or a "row of dominoes."[169]

Therefore, in the absence of empirically based studies, it is difficult to determine what "national interest" means at any specific time. According to Michael Joseph Smith, realists, having adopted Weber's ethic of responsibility, have not presented a competent set of criteria for judging responsibility. Although, and perhaps because, they minimize the relevance of ethics to international relations, they appear not to recognize that "their judgment of morality and their definition of the national interest rested on their own hierarchy of values."[170]

Among the focal points of neorealist analysis is an effort to reformulate and refine the national interest concept to encompass a perceived calculus of benefits and losses in accordance with alternative posited goals for the state. Specifically, the regime concept (described in Chapter 4) includes an attempt to adapt national interest to a theoretical framework related to state motivation in the formation of what are defined as international regimes for collaboration or cooperation. (See the further discussion in Chapter 11.)

Realist writers, it has been noted, have been criticized for their efforts to draw from the Eurocentric system of the past a series of political concepts for the analysis of a vastly different contemporary global international system. The pursuit of limited national objectives, the separation of foreign policy from domestic politics, the conduct of secret diplomacy, the use of balance of power as a technique for the management of power, and the pleas for nations to place reduced emphasis on ideology as a conditioner of international conduct have little relevance to the international system today. By urging that nations return to the practices of an earlier period, some realist writers overestimate the extent to which such change in the present international system is possible. If nations obey laws of nature, which the realist purports to have discovered, why is it necessary to urge them, as realists do, to return to practices supposedly based upon such laws?[171] Although history provides many examples of international behavior that substantiate classical realist theory, historical data offer deviant cases. In calling upon statesmen to alter their behavior, the realist becomes normative in theoretical orientation and fails to provide an adequate explanation as to why political leaders sometimes do not adhere to realist tenets in foreign policy.

In emphasizing power as the principal motivation for political behavior, realists have made themselves the object of criticism. Critics have suggested that realist writers, for the most part, have not clearly conceptualized power. There are formidable problems of measuring power, as noted earlier in this chapter. There is no common unit into which power is converted for measurement in realist writings. Moreover, power must be related to the objective for which it is to be used. The amount and type of power vary with national goals. In addition, realists have been criticized for allegedly having placed too much emphasis on power, to the relative exclusion of other important variables. In Hoffmann's view, "It is impossible to subsume under one word variables as different as: power as a condition of policy and power as a criterion of policy; power as a potential and power in use; power as a sum of resources and power as a set of processes."[172]

As discussed in Chapter 1, Ernst Haas and Inis L. Claude, Jr., have criticized the realists' use of the term *balance of power* as being fraught with many inconsistent meanings.

Neorealism and, specifically, structural realism, have encountered several criticisms, including an alleged disregard for history as a process that is continually undergoing redefinition, in which individuals contribute to the molding of each successive era. In this respect, the neorealist is considered to have departed from classical realism, which held that the statesman was shaped by but also had an important influence on history. Far from being the captives of a particular system—itself a reification—the individual person holds the potential to be the master of structures, not simply the object. Moreover, neorealism is faulted for having presumably reduced politics to those dimensions that are conducive to interpretation by reference to rational behavior under various structural constraints. Because of its focus on structure, neorealism is said to have ignored the social basis and social limits of power. Power cannot be reduced to capabilities; instead, power consists also of psychological factors such as public morale and political leadership, as well as situational factors and the extent to which power is exercised within a consensual, contrasted with a conflictual, framework. The "state-as-actor" world of neorealism is faulted for having imputed to the state the role of unitary actor whose behavior is shaped by the structure of the international system. Neorealism, it is suggested, was statist before it was structuralist.[173] In response, neorealists deny that realism is, in fact, structural determinism. Although structural elements exert a powerful constraining influence on political behavior, the neorealist does not consider all of human political conduct to be determined by the structure within which the polity is organized, nor does the neorealist accept the criticism that the "state-as-actor" world represents a negation of the role of those individuals or groups who act as the actual decision-makers.[174]

Despite its critics, realism ranks as the most important attempt thus far to isolate and focus on a key variable in political behavior—namely, power—and to develop a theory of international relations. If only as a result of having stated its premises in such bold fashion, realism has painted a sharply contoured global theoretical landscape that can be (as it has been) modified by another generation of theory builders. In Robert O. Keohane's words: "Realism provides a good starting point for the analysis of cooperation and discord, since its tautological structure and its pessimistic assumptions about individual and state behavior serve as barriers against wishful thinking."[175] According to R. B. J. Walker, political realism should be viewed "less as a coherent theoretical position in its own right than as the site of a great many contested claims and metaphysical disputes."[176] For example, realism, Walker points out, and as this chapter illustrates, contains structural and historicist traditions. To a far greater extent than their predecessors, realist students of international relations attempted to construct theory from historical data. In addition to their efforts to determine how national actors in fact behaved, realists developed a body of normative theory with prescriptions addressed particularly to policymakers. Having isolated what they considered to be the important determinants of political behavior in the past, they compared contemporary international politics with a model based on their study of history. The problems to which realist thought has addressed itself—of the interaction and behavior of human beings as decision-makers, the nature of power, the foreign policy goals, the techniques for measuring and managing power, the impact of environmental factors upon political behavior, the purposes and practices that ought to guide political leaders, and the impact of structures of alternative international systems—are central both to the study of international politics and to the practice of statecraft.

Other approaches are addressed to similar problems. Social-psychological theories of international behavior have focused on the study of power. In systems theory the study of demand-response relationships encompasses the efforts of one national unit to influence one or more other national units in either conflictual or collaborative situations. The study of decision-making is essentially an examination of the interpretation in a given instance of the national interest. The decision-making system, like all social systems, is "open"—that is, it is subject to a variety of inputs from its environment. Hence, environment, or political ecology, becomes important not only to the realist, but also to the student of systems theory as a potential conditioner of political behavior. In summary, in addition to its contribution to international relations theory, realism provides a large number of propositions about political behavior that can be subjected to further examination with the use of other frameworks and methodologies. Nevertheless, academicians and policy analysts have felt compelled to search for theory beyond realism. One result has been the adaptation in political science generally, and international relations specifically, of the concept of "system." To this we now turn.

NOTES

1. George F. Kennan, "Morality and Foreign Policy," *Foreign Affairs*, Winter 1985/1986, 206.
2. Robert E. Osgood, *Ideals and Self-Interest in America's Foreign Relations* (Chicago: University of Chicago Press, 1953), p. 22.
3. See Frederick L. Schuman, *International Politics*, 4th ed. (New York: McGraw-Hill, 1969), p. 271; Klaus Knorr, *The War Potential of Nations* (Princeton: Princeton University Press, 1956). For an analysis of the various components of national power, see Klaus Knorr, *Power and Wealth: Military Power and Potential* (Lexington, Mass.: D. C. Heath, 1970).
4. Nicholas J. Spykman, *America's Strategy in World Politics* (New York: Harcourt Brace Jovanovich, 1942), p. 11.
5. Hans J. Morgenthau, *Politics Among Nations*, 4th ed. (New York: Knopf, 1967), pp. 25–26.
6. Robert Strausz-Hupé and Stefan T. Possony, *International Relations* (New York: McGraw-Hill, 1954), pp. 5–6.
7. Arnold Wolfers, *Discord and Collaboration* (Baltimore: Johns Hopkins Press, 1962), p. 103.
8. John. W. Burton, *International Relations: A General Theory* (New York: Cambridge University Press, 1967), p. 46.
9. Robert Gilpin, *War and Change in World Politics* (New York: Cambridge University Press, 1981), p. 33.
10. Charles P. Kindleberger, *Power and Money: The Politics of International Economics and the Economics of International Politics* (New York: Basic Books, 1970), pp. 56, 65.
11. Ibid., p. 56.
12. Klaus Knorr, *The Power of Nations: The Political Economy of International Relations* (New York: Basic Books, 1975), p. 3. See also by the same author, *Power and Wealth: Military Power and Potential* (Lexington, Mass.: D. C. Heath, 1970); *On the Uses of Military Power in the Nuclear Age* (Princeton: Princeton University Press, 1966).
13. Klaus Knorr, *The Power of Nations: The Political Economy of International Relations*, op. cit., p. 4.
14. Ibid.
15. Ibid., p. 10.
16. David A. Baldwin, "Power Analysis and World Politics: New Trends versus Old Tendencies," *World Politics*, XXXI, No. 2 (January 1979), 177. See also Oran R. Young, "Interdependencies in World Politics," *International Journal* (Autumn 1969), 726–750.
17. David Baldwin, "Interdependence and Power: A Conceptual Analysis," *International Organization*, Vol. 34, No. 4 (Autumn 1980), 499.
18. James A. Caporaso, "Dependence, Dependency, and Power in the Global System," *International Organization*, Vol. 32 (Winter 1978), 32.
19. Norman Z. Alcock and Alan G. Newcombe, "The Perception of National Power," *Journal of Conflict Resolution*, XIV, No. 3 (September 1970), 342.
20. Thomas L. Saaty and Mohamad W. Khowja, "A Measure of World Influence," *Journal of Peace Science*, 2, No. 1 (Spring 1976), 44–45.

21. Jeffrey Hart, "Three Approaches to the Measurement of Power in International Relations," *International Organization,* 30, No. 2 (Spring 1976), 293.
22. See, for example, K. J. Holsti, "The Concept of Power in the Study of International Relations," *Background,* 7 (February 1964), 182.
23. Michael P. Sullivan, *International Relations: Theories and Evidence* (Englewood Cliffs, N.J.: Prentice-Hall, 1967), p. 160.
24. K. J. Holsti, *International Politics: A Framework for Analysis* (Englewood Cliffs, N.J.: Prentice-Hall, 1967), p. 193.
25. Ibid., pp. 194–195.
26. See, for example, Jack H. Nagel, *The Descriptive Analysis of Power* (New Haven and London: Yale University Press, 1975), p. 11; Robert A. Dahl, "Cause and Effect in the Study of Politics," in Daniel Lerner, "Power," in *International Encyclopedia of the Social Sciences* (New York: The Free Press, 1968).
27. Robert J. Lieber, *Theory and World Politics* (Cambridge, Mass.: Winthrop, 1972), p. 93.
28. Karl W. Deutsch, *The Analysis of International Relations,* 2nd ed. (Englewood Cliffs, N.J.: Prentice-Hall, 1978), pp. 45–46.
29. David A. Baldwin, "Power Analysis and World Politics: New Trends versus Old Tendencies," *World Politics,* XXXI, No. 2 (January 1979), 161–194.
30. Jeffrey Hart, "Three Approaches to the Measurement of Power in International Relations," *International Organization,* Vol. 30, No. 2 (Spring 1976), 289, 303.
31. Jack H. Nagel, *The Descriptive Analysis of Power,* p. 122.
32. Herbert Simon, "Notes on the Observation and Measurement of Power," and Roderick Bell, "Political Power: The Problem of Measurement," in Roderick Bell, David V. Edwards, and R. Harrison Wagner, eds., *Political Power: A Reader in Theory and Research* (New York: The Free Press, 1969), pp. 26–27, 73–78.
33. Jacek Kugler and William Domke, "Comparing the Strength of Nations," *Comparative Political Studies,* Vol. 19, No. 1 (April 1986), 39–69.
34. There have been various efforts to measure the respective force levels of the United States and the Soviet Union. They include John M. Collins, *America and Soviet Military Trends Since the Cuban Missile Crisis* (Washington: The Center for Strategic and International Studies, Georgetown University, 1978); Ray S. Cline, *World Power Assessment* (Boulder, Colo.: Westview Press, 1977); *The Military Balance* (London: International Institute for Strategic Studies, published annually); *Jane's Ships* and *Jane's Missile Systems* (London: *Jane's Yearbooks,* published annually); *Strategic Survey* (London: International Institute for Strategic Studies, published annually).
35. George Liska, *Quest for Equilibrium: America and the Balance of Power on Land and Sea* (Baltimore and London: Johns Hopkins University Press, 1977), p. 212.
36. Steven Brams, *Superpower Games: Applying Game-Theory to the Superpower Conflict,* (New Haven: Yale University Press, 1985). See also Klaus Knorr, *The Power of Nations: The Political Economy of International Relations,* p. 11. See also by the same author, *Power and Wealth: Military Power and Potential; On the Uses of Military Power in the Nuclear Age* (Princeton: Princeton University Press, 1966). Wayne H. Ferris, *The Power Capabilities of Nation-States: International Conflict and War* (Lexington, Mass.: D. C. Heath, 1973).

37. Brams, op. cit., p. 267.

38. Thucydides, *History of the Peloponnesian War,* ed. M. I. Finley; trans. Rex Warner (Harmondsworth: Penguin, 1972), p. 49.

39. Thomas Hobbes, *Leviathan,* edited and with an introduction by Michael Oakeshott (Oxford: Basil Blackwell, 1946), p. 64.

40. Ibid., p. 109.

41. Ibid.

42. G. W. F. Hegel, *Philosophy of Right* (Oxford: Clarendon, 1942), p. 264; Friederich Meinecke, *Machiavellism: The Doctrine of Raison d'Etat and Its Place in Modern History* (New York: Praeger, 1965), p. 360.

43. Max Weber, *Economy and Society,* ed. Guenther Roth and Claus Wittich (2 vols.) (Berkeley and Los Angeles: University of California Press, 1978), p. 911.

44. In discussing the realist intellectual debt to Niebuhr, Kennan referred to him as "the father of us all." See Kenneth W. Thompson, *Political Realism and the Crisis of World Politics: An American Approach to Foreign Policy* (Princeton: Princeton University Press, 1960), pp. 23–25.

45. Harry K. Davis and Robert C. Good, eds., *Reinhold Niebuhr on Politics: His Political Philosophy and Its Application to Our Age as Expressed in His Writings* (New York: Scribner's, 1960), p. 75.

46. "In the Christian view, then, for man to understand himself truly means to begin with a faith that he is understood from beyond himself, that he is known and loved of God and must find himself in terms of obedience to the divine will. This relation of the divine to the human will makes it possible for man to relate himself to God without pretending to be God and to accept his distance from God as a created thing, without believing that the evil of his nature is caused by this finiteness." Davis and Good, *Christianity and Power Politics* (New York: Scribner's, 1940), p. 64; and his *Christian Realism and Political Problems* (New York: Scribner's, 1953).

47. Harry K. Davis and Robert C. Good, eds., op. cit., p. 77.

48. Reinhold Niebuhr, *Moral Man and Immoral Society* (New York: Scribner's, 1947), pp. xi–xii.

49. Reinhold Niebuhr, *The Irony of American History* (New York: Scribner's, 1952), p. 2. See also Gabriel Fackre, *The Promise of Reinhold Niebuhr* (Philadelphia: Lippincott, 1970), pp. 60–64; Charles Burton Marshall, *The Limits of Foreign Policy* (New York: Holt, Rinehart and Winston, 1954).

50. Ibid., p. 2.

51. Reinhold Niebuhr, "The Illusion of World Government," *Bulletin of the Atomic Scientists,* V (October 1949), 290. See also Charles Burton Marshall, op. cit., p. 122. "Legitimate government, let us remember, must rest on a tradition of kingship or aristocracy, or on a popular consensus. . . . Thus proposals to solve all the problems by the magic of world government are invariably hazy on the most serious underlying question of government—how to make it legitimate."

52. Reinhold Niebuhr, *The Irony of American History,* op. cit., p. 40.

53. Ibid., p. 148.

54. Davis and Good, eds., op. cit., p. 65.

55. Reinhold Niebuhr, *Christian Realism and Political Problems,* op. cit., p. 36; and Reinhold Niebuhr, "Coexistence or Total War," *Christian Century,* LXXI (August 18, 1954), 972–974.

56. Reinhold Niebuhr, *The Irony of American History,* op. cit., p. 35; Reinhold Niebuhr and Alan Heimert, *A Nation So Conceived* (New York: Scribner's,

1963), pp. 129–139, 144 (where the above quotation appears); and Reinhold Niebuhr, "American Hegemony and the Prospects for Peace," *Annals of the American Academy of Political and Social Science*, CCCXLII (July 1962), 156.

57. Nicholas J. Spykman, op. cit., p. 7; Nicholas J. Spykman and Abbie A. Rollins, "Geographic Objectives in Foreign Policy," *American Political Science Review*, XXXIII (June 1939), 392.

58. "The Old World is two and one-half times as large as the New World and contains seven times the population. It is true that, at present, industrial productivity is almost equally divided, but in terms of self-sufficiency, the Eurasian Continent with the related continents of Africa and Australia is in a much stronger position. If the land masses of the Old World can be brought under the control of a few states and so organized that large unbalanced forces are available for pressure across the ocean fronts, the Americas will be politically and strategically encircled." Spykman, op. cit., pp. 447–448.

59. Ibid., p. 460.

60. Ibid., p. 472. The view that the balance of power in Asia, as well as in Europe, is an essential ingredient of the national interest of the United States was subsequently advanced by Walt W. Rostow in *The United States in the World Arena* (New York: Harper & Row, 1960), Appendix A, pp. 543–550.

61. Hans J. Morgenthau, *Politics Among Nations,* 5th ed., rev. (New York: Knopf, 1978), p. 4. For a retrospective assessment of Morgenthau's political philosophy, see Kenneth Thompson and Robert J. Myers, eds., *Truth and Tragedy: A Tribute to Hans J. Morgenthau,* Augmented edition [New Brunswick (USA) and London (U.K.): Transaction Books, 1984].

62. Ibid., p. 5.

63. Ibid.

64. Hans J. Morgenthau, "Another 'Great Debate': The National Interest of the United States," *American Political Science Review,* LXVI (December 1952), 961.

65. Ibid. See also Hans J. Morgenthau, *In Defense of the National Interest* (New York: Knopf, 1951); Charles A. Beard, *The Idea of the National Interest* (New York: Macmillan, 1934). The idea of the national interest as a basis for decision-making is examined in Chapter 11.

66. Hans J. Morgenthau, *Politics Among Nations,* pp. 11–14.

67. Ibid., p. 10.

68. Ibid., p. 11.

69. Ibid.

70. Ibid., p. 12.

71. Ibid., p. 36.

72. Ibid., p. 43.

73. Ibid., p. 58.

74. Ibid., p. 64.

75. Ibid., p. 77.

76. Ibid., p. 78.

77. Ibid., pp. 226–227.

78. See, for example, Harold Nicolson, *Diplomacy,* 3rd ed. (New York: Harcourt, Brace and Company, 1963); *Evolution of Diplomatic Method* (New York: Macmillan, 1962); *The Congress of Vienna* (London: Constable, 1946); Morgenthau, *Politics Among Nations,* pp. 540–548.

79. George F. Kennan, *Realities of American Foreign Policy* (Princeton, N.J.: Princeton University Press, 1954), p. 11.
80. George F. Kennan, *American Diplomacy, 1900–1950* (New York: Mentor Books, 1957), pp. 93–94. See also Charles Burton Marshall, op. cit., p. 56: ". . . Our national experience has been such as to root in our minds an excess of confidence in the political efficacy of documents—in the capability of statesmen to resolve the future by agreement on the written word."
81. George F. Kennan, *Realities of American Foreign Policy*, p. 13.
82. Ibid., p. 14.
83. Ibid., p. 16.
84. Ibid., p. 48.
85. George F. Kennan, "World Problems in Christian Perspective," *Theology Today,* XVI (July 1959), 155–172.
86. George F. Kennan, *American Diplomacy*, p. 87.
87. George F. Kennan, *Realities of American Foreign Policy*, p. 48.
88. Ibid., p. 36.
89. George F. Kennan, "History and Diplomacy as Viewed by a Diplomatist," *Review of Politics,* XVIII (April 1956), 173.
90. George F. Kennan, "World Problems in Christian Perspective," p. 156.
91. George F. Kennan, *Russia and the West under Lenin and Stalin* (New York: Harper & Row, 1958), p. 367.
92. George F. Kennan, *American Diplomacy*, p. 96.
93. George F. Kennan, *Russia, the Atom and the West* (New York: Harper & Row, 1958), p. 27.
94. George F. Kennan, *The Cloud of Danger: Current Realities of American Foreign Policy* (Boston: Little, Brown, 1977), p. 34.
95. George F. Kennan, *Realities of American Foreign Policy*, pp. 63–64.
96. George F. Kennan, "X," "The Sources of Soviet Conduct," *Foreign Affairs,* XXV (July 1947), 514. Charles Burton Marshall was in substantial agreement when he wrote: "The best hope lies in creating the circumstances for a heightening of the dilemma within the Soviet framework, eventually to move it along the course of accommodation and thereby toward its own transformation," op. cit., p. 97.
97. George F. Kennan, *Russia, the Atom and the West,* pp. 41–45.
98. Ibid., p. 200. The aging Soviet leadership is "not given to rash or adventuristic policies. It commands, and is deeply involved with, a structure of power, and particularly a higher bureaucracy" (pp. 199–200) that would not easily conflict with the United States.
99. George F. Kennan, *The Cloud of Danger: Current Realities of American Foreign Policy,* pp. 159–160.
100. Barton Gellman, *Contending with Kennan: Toward a Philosophy of American Power* (New York: Praeger Special Studies, 1985), p. 121.
101. Ibid., p. 27.
102. Uri Ra'anan, "Elder Statesman's Primer," *Strategic Review* (Winter 1978), 80–81.
103. George F. Kennan, *Russia, the Atom and the West,* pp. 676–71.
104. George F. Kennan, *Memoirs, 1925–1950* (Boston: Little, Brown, 1967), p. 367.
105. Ibid., p. 230.
106. George F. Kennan, "Morality and Foreign Policy," *Foreign Affairs* (Winter 1985/1986), 206.

107. See Richard Rovere, "Containers," *The New Yorker* (August 8, 1977), 70–73.

108. George F. Kennan, *The Cloud of Danger: Current Realities of American Foreign Policy*, p. 229.

109. Arnold Wolfers, *Discord and Collaboration: Essays on International Politics* (Baltimore: Johns Hopkins University Press, 1962), p. 9.

110. Ibid., p. 73.

111. Ibid., pp. 147–165.

112. Ibid., p. 58.

113. Henry A. Kissinger, *A World Restored—Europe After Napoleon: The Politics of Conservatism in a Revolutionary Age* (New York: Grosset and Dunlap, 1964).

114. Stephen R. Graubard, *Kissinger: Portrait of a Mind* (New York: Norton, 1974), p. 11. Graubard points out that Kissinger's doctoral dissertation "could not have been written in many other universities in America, not because the others lacked a library of the distinction of Harvard's, but because they had neither the tradition nor the self-assurance that permitted them to let many of their students run free. . . . In a more conventionally organized department, questions might have been raised about the appropriateness of the subject Kissinger chose for his dissertation or about the research procedures that he intended to employ. Neither question was even bruited in the Government Department, which, then in the early 1950s was a loose confederation of several disparate disciplines, presided over by men who did not much interfere with what their colleagues consented to" (p. 15).

115. Henry A. Kissinger, op. cit., p. 1.

116. Ibid., p. 2.

117. Ibid., p. 1.

118. Ibid.

119. Ibid., p. 4.

120. Henry A. Kissinger, *Nuclear Weapons and Foreign Policy* (New York: Harper & Row, 1961), p. 16.

121. Henry A. Kissinger, *The Necessity for Choice* (New York: Harper & Row, 1961), p. 63.

122. Henry A. Kissinger, *Nuclear Weapons and Foreign Policy*, p. 89.

123. Ibid., p. 84.

124. Henry A. Kissinger, *The Necessity for Choice*, p. 65.

125. Ibid., p. 65.

126. Ibid., p. 170.

127. *U.S. Foreign Policy for the 1970s: Shaping a Durable Peace.* A report to the Congress by President Nixon, President of the United States, May 3, 1973 (Washington: U.S. Government Printing Office, 1973), pp. 232–233. For an assessment of Kissinger as policymaker, see Sayom Brown, *The Crises of Power: Foreign Policy in the Kissinger Years* (New York: Columbia University Press, 1979), esp. pp. 107–153.

128. Henry A. Kissinger, *White House Years* (Boston: Little, Brown and Company, 1979), p. 55.

129. Ibid., p. 232.

130. "The Nature of the National Dialogue," Address to the Pacem in Terris III Conference, Washington, October 8, 1973. Reprinted in Henry A. Kissinger, *American Foreign Policy*, 3rd ed. (New York: Norton, 1977), p. 126.

131. Ibid., p. 125.

132. Peter W. Dickson, *Kissinger and the Meaning of History* (Cambridge: Cambridge University Press, 1978), p. 20.
133. Henry A. Kissinger, "Domestic Structure and Foreign Policy," in *American Foreign Policy,* p. 12.
134. Robert Strausz-Hupé, *Power and Community* (New York: Praeger, 1956), p. 3.
135. Robert Strausz-Hupé and Stefan T. Possony, *International Relations,* p. 11.
136. Ibid.
137. Ibid., p. 18.
138. Robert Strausz-Hupé, *The Balance of Tomorrow* (New York: Putnam's, 1945), p. 119.
139. Ibid., p. 173.
140. Ibid., p. 262.
141. Ibid., p. 234.
142. Robert Strausz-Hupé, William R. Kintner, James E. Dougherty, and Alvin J. Cottrell, *Protracted Conflict* (New York: Harper & Row, 1959), pp. 8–9.
143. Raymond Aron, *Peace and War* (New York: Doubleday, 1966), p. 2. For contrasting analyses of Aron's writings on international relations, see Stanley Hoffman, *The State of War: Essays in the Theory and Practice of International Relations* (New York: Praeger, 1965), pp. 22–53; Klaus Knorr and James N. Rosenau, eds., *Contending Approaches to International Politics* (Princeton: Princeton University Press, 1969), pp. 129–143. For an examination of Aron as an intellectual, see Milton Viorst, "Talk with 'a Reasonable Man,'" *New York Times* Magazine (April 5, 1970), 341.
144. Ibid., p. 178.
145. Ibid., p. 8.
146. Ibid., p. 16.
147. Ibid., p. 100.
148. Ibid., p. 94.
149. Ibid., p. 128.
150. Ibid., p. 36.
151. Ibid., p. 405.
152. Ibid., pp. 166–167.
153. Ibid., p. 366.
154. Ibid., p. 592.
155. Stanley Hoffmann, "Raymond Aron and the Theory of International Relations," *International Studies Quarterly* (March 1985), 21.
156. Kenneth M. Waltz, *Theory of International Politics* (Reading, Mass.: Addison-Wesley Publishing Company, 1979).
157. Gottfried-Karl Kindermann, "The Munich School of Neorealism in International Politics," unpublished manuscript, University of Munich, 1985.
158. Kindermann, pp. 10–11.
159. Kindermann, p. 12.
160. Waltz, *Theory of International Politics,* pp. 93–101.
161. Ibid., p. 81. For additional analysis of the concept of anarchy and system structure, see Barry Buzan, "Peace, Power, and Security: Contending Concepts in the Study of International Relations," *Journal of Peace Research,* Vol. 21, No. 2 (1984), 109–125; Joseph M. Grieco, "Anarchy and the Limits of Cooperation: A Realist Critique of the Newest Liberal Institutionalism," *International Organization,* Vol. 42, No. 3 (Summer 1988), 485–507.

162. Waltz, *Theory of International Politics,* pp. 60–67.

163. Robert Gilpin, *War and Change in World Politics* (New York: Cambridge University Press, 1981), pp. 9–11.

164. Ibid., p. 230.

165. See, for example, Richard W. Mansbach and John A. Vasquez, *In Search of Theory: A New Paradigm for Global Politics* (New York: Columbia University Press, 1981), chs. 1–3.

166. John A. Vasquez, *The Power of Power Politics: A Critique* (New Brunswick: Rutgers University Press, 1983), p. 216.

167. Ibid., p. 223.

168. Thomas I. Cook and Malcolm Moos, "The American Idea of International Interest," *American Political Science Review,* XLVII (March 1953), 28.

169. Stanley Hoffmann, *Contemporary Theory in International Relations* (Englewood Cliffs, N.J.: Prentice-Hall, 1960), p. 33.

170. Michael Joseph Smith, *Realist Thought from Weber to Kissinger* (Baton Rouge and London: Louisiana State University Press, 1986), p. 235.

171. Cecil V. Crabb, *American Foreign Policy in the Nuclear Age* (New York: Harper & Row, 1965), pp. 458–459.

172. Hoffmann, op. cit., p. 32. For a more recent critique of realist theory, see Stanley Hoffmann, *Janus and Minerva: Essays in the Theory and Practice of International Politics* (Boulder, Colo., and London: Westview Press, 1987), esp. pp. 70–85.

173. Richard K. Ashley, "Poverty of Neorealism," in Robert O. Keohane, ed., *Neorealism and its Critics* (New York: Columbia University Press, 1986).

174. Robert G. Gilpin, "The Richness of the Tradition of Political Realism," in Robert O. Keohane, ed., op. cit., pp. 316–321.

175. Robert O. Keohane, *After Hegemony: Cooperation and Discord in the World Political Economy* (Princeton, N.J.: Princeton University Press, 1984), p. 245.

176. R. B. J. Walker, "Realism, Change, and International Political Theory," *International Studies Quarterly,* Vol. 31 (March 1987), 67.

Chapter
4

Systemic Theories of Politics and International Relations

DEFINITION, NATURE, AND APPROACHES TO SYSTEMS THEORY

System is probably the term most widely used today in political science and international relations literature. System describes (1) a theoretical framework for the coding of data about political phenomena; (2) an integrated set of relationships based on a hypothetical set of political variables—for example, an international system involving world government; (3) a set of relationships among political variables in an international system alleged to have existed—for example, the international system of the 1950s; and (4) any set of variables in interaction.

Systems analysis describes a variety of techniques, such as cost-effectiveness studies, which are designed to allow rational choice decisions regarding the allocation of resources. In the literature of political science, however, "systems analysis" has often been used interchangeably with "systems theory" insofar as it is employed to describe conceptual frameworks and methodologies for understanding the operation of political systems. As Robert J. Lieber has suggested, "Systems analysis is really a set of techniques for systematic analysis that facilitates the organizing of data, but which possesses no ideal theoretical goals. By contrast, general systems theory subsumes an integrated set of concepts, hypotheses, and propositions, which (theoretically) are widely applicable across the spectrum of human knowledge."[1] We define systems theory, or general systems theory, as a series of statements about relationships among independent and dependent variables in which changes in one or more variables are accompanied, or followed, by changes in other variables or combinations of variables. As Anatol Rapoport has defined it, "A whole which functions as a whole by virtue of the interdependence of its parts is called a system, and the method which aims at discovering how this is brought about in the widest variety of systems has been called general systems theory."[2] John Burton has written that the concept of system connotes "relationships between units. The units of a system are of the same 'set,' by which is meant that they have features in common that enable a particular relationship."[3] The human nervous system, a car motor, the Hilton Hotel chain, an Apollo spacecraft, the Federal Reserve system, a fishtank in a marine ecology experimental project, and the "balance of power"—all of these are systems.

A system can be described in its successive states. It may be loosely or tightly organized, stable or unstable. A stable system requires an input of relatively considerable power to upset it; an unstable system is more precarious and its balance is more easily disturbed. Every system seeks to establish, maintain, and return after disturbance to some sort of equilibrium. The equilibrium itself may be stable or unstable. A stable equilibrium is capable of absorbing new components and processing a variety of inputs while continuing to function normally, adjusting to changes, and correcting its behavior by making appropriate reactions to "negative feedback" (i.e., information that it is deviating from course).

Smaller systems (or subsystems) may exist within larger systems. According to John Burton, "Whereas the subsystem is a system in itself that can be isolated (though in isolation its functional relevance will not always be apparent) a system level refers to a complex of relationships comprising all units at that level. Systems have different features at different levels."[4] Every system has boundaries that distinguish it from its operating environment. Every system is, in some sense, a communications net that permits the flow of information leading to a self-adjusting process. Every system has inputs and outputs; an output of a system may reenter that system as an input, or what is termed feedback.

Closely related to systems theory has been the term *interdependence*, used to characterize relationships in a global international system. In such a conception, the emergence for the first time in history of a truly global system calls forth the need for a "geocentric" rather than an "ethnocentric" approach to the study of international relations.[5] J. David Singer suggests, "By a social system . . . I mean nothing more than an aggregation of human beings (plus their physical milieu) who are sufficiently interdependent to share a common fate . . . or to have actions of some of them usually affecting the lives of many of them."[6] Quoting approvingly Singer's definition of system, Ernst Haas holds that systems are simply "taxonomies devised by the researcher to permit the specification of hypothesized nonrandom events and trends in the hope of gradually mapping reality. If everyone used the construct in this sense, we would have no problem."[7]

According to Robert O. Keohane and Joseph S. Nye, interdependence always carries with it costs, "since interdependence restricts autonomy, but it is impossible to specify *a priori* whether the benefits of a relationship will exceed the costs. This will depend on the values of the actors as well as on the nature of the relationship."[8] The same authors conceptualize interdependence as having two dimensions: sensitivity and vulnerability. "Sensitivity involves degrees of responsiveness within a policy framework—how quickly do changes in one country bring costly changes in another, and how great are the costly effects?"[9] They suggest that "vulnerability can be defined as an actor's liability to suffer costs imposed by external events even after policies have been altered."[10] Interdependence, with its sensitivity and vulnerability dimensions, can be social, political, economic, military, or ideological in nature, as Keohane and Nye demonstrate in their analysis. It follows that interdependence is not symmetrical. As R. Harrison Wagner suggests, an interdependent relationship between parties that are not equal is likely to be characterized either by "dependence," defined as need, and by "asymmetry," which refers to a situation in which "one party needs the benefits derived from a relationship more than the other."[11] In turn, interdependence as a concept is closely related to power and dependency theory, discussed respectively in Chapters 3 and 6.

Also widely used in international relations studies, and especially in systems theory, is the term *interaction*. The greater the level of interdependence, the greater the amount of interaction. Systems are hypothesized patterns of interaction. As the level of interdependence and the amount of interaction grow, the complexity of the system increases. Interdependence and interaction in turn, like systems theory itself, are closely linked to integration theory, which is discussed in Chapter 10. Interaction consists not only of the demands and responses—the actions—of nation-states, international organizations, and other nonstate actors, but also the transactions across national boundaries, including trade, tourism, investment, technology transfer, and the flow of ideas more broadly.

Examining the international system of the late twentieth century, Andrew M. Scott characterizes interaction in the following way:

> Hundreds of actors are pouring actions into the international arena at the same time, and those actions are being variously deflected and aggregated and combined with one another. . . . In an undirected aggregative process, the behavior of individual actors is purposive, but the process as a whole knows no purpose and is under no overall direction. . . . A process that is only partly under control does not become quiescent because the control element has ceased to be adequate, but rather, continues to function and produces results only some of which are intended.[12]

In short, problems, or inputs, in the international system are multiplying faster than solutions can be found, thus leading to systems overload. Patterns of interdependence and interaction grow more complex as a result of the pervasive impact of technology upon the international system.

Under such conditions, it is hypothesized, the "structural requisites"—that is, those needs that must be satisfied for a system to function effectively—become more numerous.[13]

Interdependence and interaction provide focal points for many writers in explaining systems transformation. The formation in the late twentieth century of a global international system for the first time in history, in place of the Eurocentric system that endured from the Treaty of Westphalia in 1648 until World War II, is related to the global diffusion of technology. Edward L. Morse refers to the twofold effects of modernization as "the emergence of certain forms of interdependence among a large set of states and the transnational nature of the international system."[14] Here, interdependence is defined as "the outcome of specified actions of two or more parties (in our case, of governments) when the outcomes of these actions are mutually contingent." Morse sets forth a series of propositions about interdependence within the international system. For example, the greater the degree of interdependence, the greater the likelihood of crisis. "Interdependence does not only breed crises and various forms of linkage, it also increases the potential for any single party to manipulate a crisis for its own domestic or foreign political ends."[15]

Other writers have sought to define interdependence and to ascertain the extent to which, especially in the late twentieth century, levels of interdependence are rising or declining. According to Hayward Alker, a "synthetic, multifaceted definition of interdependence is possible." Interdependence is a "social relationship among two or more cross-state actors observable in terms of actual or anticipated interactions among them."[16] Richard Rosecrance and Arthur Stein view interdependence, in the most general sense, as consisting of "a relationship of interests such that if one nation's position changes, other states will be affected by that change" or, in an economic sense, "interdependencies are present when there is an increased national 'sensitivity' to external economic developments."[17] They take issue with the conclusion of Karl Deutsch and his associates (see Chapter 10) that levels of transactions, especially trade, in the international stage, relative to those within states, have been declining in much of the twentieth century. The growth in the service sector, most pronounced in highly industrialized states, has been underestimated in GNP calculations for earlier periods, especially the previous century. The authors note a paradox in the contemporary international system: "The vertical integration of nationalist processes has moved to a new peak. The horizontal interaction of transnational processes is higher than at any point since World War I."[18]

Although in the past generation, systems theory has had a major influence upon the study of politics, the idea of systems was not unknown to earlier political writers. For example, Thomas Hobbes, in Chapter 22 of his *Leviathan,* writes of systems.[19] Modern students of politics have adapted the concept of systems from the physical sciences and the social sciences, on which systems theory has had a major impact.

One of the most important exponents of general systems theory (GST) is Ludwig von Bertalanffy, who was for a long time professor of theoretical biology at the University of Alberta, Canada; his work in this field dates from the 1920s. He suggests that the ever-increasing specialization within modern science begets fragmentation among disciplines: "The physicist, the biologist, the psychologist and the social scientist are, so to speak, encapsulated in a private universe, and it is difficult to get a word from one cocoon to the other."[20] The growth of disciplines and greater academic specialization threaten to fragment the scientific community into isolated enclaves unable to communicate with each other. General systems theory represents a response to this problem. Rapoport suggests that systems theory has the potential of reestablishing approaches that emphasize the functional relationship between parts and whole without sacrificing scientific rigor. The analogies established or conjectured in systems theory are not mere metaphors. According to Rapoport, they are rooted in actual correspondences between systems or theories of systems.[21] Bertalanffy discerns similar viewpoints and conceptions in various fields.

Disciplines such as physics and chemistry study phenomena in dynamic interaction. In biology there are problems of an organismic nature. In such seemingly diverse disciplines, it is essential, according to Bertalanffy, to "study not only isolated parts and processes, but the essential problems that are the organizing relations that result from dynamic interaction and make the behavior of parts different when studied in isolation or within the whole."[22]

In short, Bertalanffy, like Rapoport, sees structural similarities or isomorphism[23] in the principles that govern the behavior of intrinsically dissimilar entities. This is because they are in certain respects "systems"— that is, "complexes of elements standing interaction." Because of such similarities, general systems theory offers a "useful tool *providing* on the one hand, models that can be used in, and transferred to, different fields, and *safeguarding,* on the other hand, from vague analogies which have often marred the progress in these fields."[24] According to Peter Nettl, general systems theory "is an attempt to explore structural isomorphisms and homeomorphisms between systems."[25]

As Jerone Stephens has noted, the value of systems theory, in the strictest sense, lies in the extent to which isomorphisms, or structural identities, among political phenomena and between social, physical, and biological systems can be found. "In international relations, as well as in political science, no isomorphisms have been established, and the changes that have been made in GST since its inception have not been any more beneficial in helping us find isomorphic relations than the original formulation was."[26] Therefore the value of systems theory has derived from the conceptualization it is said to provide for assessing the capacity of alternative structures to fulfill various functions. Such structures, many writers have observed, may include nonstate actors such as alliances, multinational enterprise, religious organizations, and other groups that, in their membership and outreach, transcend state frontiers.[27]

Systems and Cascading Interdependence

In the late twentieth century, the international system is said to have entered an era of what James M. Rosenau terms "cascading interdependence," based upon rapidly changing patterns of interaction among such phenomena as "resource scarcities, subgroupism, the effectiveness of governments, transnational issues, and the aptitudes of publics."[28] Taken together, the rise to political consciousness and assertiveness of previously quiescent groups and their coalescence; the extensive impact of technology in such forms as the information and communications revolution; the widening availability, or diffusion, of technologies for war or peace; the widening and deepening of economic and other forms of transactions resulting both in conflictual and cooperative solutions point to what Rosenau calls "interlocking tensions that, being interlocked, derive strength and direction from each other and cascade throughout the global system."[29] The rise of subgroups means that the loyalties of individuals have been transferred from the larger to a smaller entity, with a consequent weakening of the authority of the established nation-state. The "crisis of authority" to which Rosenau refers diminishes the utility of conceiving of the state as an appropriate focal point for theory-building. It is both inadequate and misleading to refer to a "state system." Instead, the effect of cascading interdependence is to distribute power in erratic fashion among state entities and numerous subsystems at many levels.[30] Such is the meaning of cascading interdependence that individuals and groups occupy various roles in differing systems, including systems of which they may previously have been members as well as those in which they are currently participating as official policymakers or in a private capacity. The resultant patterns of interaction create what Rosenau calls role conflicts, reflected in the "values, capabilities and histories that differentiate the various systems in which the policy-making position is situated."[31] Roles are viewed as containing expectations held by the participants both of themselves and of others with whom they are dealing. The fact that role occupants as policymakers envisage a variety of results from the interactive process in which they are engaged on a policy issue lends importance to scenarios as relevant focal points. To quote Rosenau,

> They [role scenarios] are . . . the basis on which publics participate in global life, with choices among various scenarios underlying the degree to which they are active and the direction which their collective actions take. Stated more emphatically, role scenarios are among the basic understandings and values that are transmitted through political socialization and that sustain collectivities across generations. . . . Put in still another way, the task of leadership is that of selling action scripts, of getting publics to regard one set of scripts as more viable and valid than any other they may find compelling.[32]

In Rosenau's formulation, it is the existence of shared action scripts about how collectivities, or systems, resolve their problems that holds them together. It is the emergence of a cascade of disparate interacting action scripts based on changing role scenarios that lies at the center of the crisis of authority depicted by Rosenau. If the cohesiveness of groups and systems is measured by the extent to which the role scenarios of its members are compatible or congruent, it is the cascading of subgroups across the world that characterizes and contributes to disaggregation. As Rosenau states it,

> The more crises of authority cascade subgroupism across the global landscape, the more extensive is the disaggregation of wholes into parts that, in turn, either get aggregated or incorporated into new wholes. That is, cascading interdependence can readily be viewed as continuous processes of systemic formation and reformation.[33]

Thus Rosenau posits the existence of open systems subject to inputs based on recurrent phenomena whose cumulative effect is to yield patterns of disorder. Cascading interdependence is a function of interaction dynamics producing not necessarily cooperation but also the conflict that is inherent in systemic breakdown. Hence, the concept of cascading interdependence is said to furnish a basis for analyzing authority relationships, the dynamics of sociopolitical aggregation, and the adaptive mechanisms of systems in which the threat or actual use of force or the prospect for cooperative behavior represents points along a continuum.

Kenneth Boulding

From his work in economics and general systems theory, Kenneth Boulding has attempted to classify systems according to levels of increasing complexity: mechanical, homeostatic, biological, equivalent to higher animals, and human.[34] The process of gathering, selecting, and using information essential to preservation is far more complex in the human system than in a simple system. A thermostat, for example, reacts only to changes in temperature and ignores other data. The simpler the system, the fewer the data essential for survival. In contrast to simple systems, humans have a capacity for self-knowledge, which makes possible the selection of information based on a particular cognitive structure, or "image." The image can furnish the basis for the restructuring of the information, or stimulus, into something fundamentally different from the information itself. The resulting human behavior is a response not to a specific stimulus, but to a knowledge structure effecting a comprehensive view of the environment. Difficulties in the prediction of system behavior arise to account for the image's intervention between stimulus and response. To a far greater extent than simple systems, complex systems have a potential for collapse because the image has screened out information essential for survival.

Social and political systems are structured from the images of participant human actors. Boulding gives the term *folk knowledge* to the collective images of the members of political systems. The decisions of political leaders conform to the dictates of folk knowledge, screening out conflicting information. The information-gathering apparatus of both national and international systems usually serves to confirm both the images of the leading decision-makers and also the folk knowledge of the systems. Boulding is convinced that eliminating the influence of folk knowledge in decision-making would have as great an effect on international behavior as removing medieval notions about cosmology had on developing modern science. Boulding considers the idea of image crucial in understanding systems and in studying such political phenomena as conflict and decision-making. Thus, general systems theory contributes to conceptualization at a level "between the highly generalized constructions of pure mathematics and the specific theories of the specialized disciplines."[35]

Talcott Parsons

In sociology, Talcott Parsons was the foremost student of systems theory. Parsons postulated the existence of an actor oriented toward attaining anticipated goals by means of a normatively regulated expenditure of energy.[36] Since the relationships between actors and their situation have a recurrent character or system, all action occurs in systems. Although Parsons recognizes that there can be action between an individual and an object, he is more concerned with action in a societal context, or with what he calls an "action system." Parsons's action system places persons in the role of subjects and in the role of objects. Subject (alter) and object (ego) interact in a system. If actors gain satisfaction, they develop a vested interest in the preservation and functioning of the system. Mutual acceptance of the system by the actors creates an equilibrating mechanism in the system.

At any given time, a person is a member of several action systems such as family, employer, and nation-state. Three subsystems comprise the Parsonian system: (1) the personality system, (2) the social system, and (3) the cultural system. These subsystems are interconnected within the "action system" so that each affects the other. In summary, Parsons conceives of society as an interlocking network of action systems. A change in one subsystem affects the other subsystems and the whole action system.

It is possible, Parsons suggests, to distinguish and study the actions that persons, or actors, perform as members of a specific system of action. Action is based on the choices among alternative courses that actors believe to be open to them. In Parsons's view, action is "a set of oriented processes," in which there are two major "vectors," the motivational orientations and the value orientations. Supposedly, the course of action that actors adopt is based on a previous learning experience as well as on their expectations about the behavior of the persons with whom they are interacting. According to Parsons, interaction makes the development of culture possible at the human level, and provides culture with a significant determinant of patterns of action in a social system.[37]

Parsons proposed a set of five dichotomous pattern variables as constituting the basic dilemmas that actors face in all social action. These variables describe the alternatives available to actors confronted with problematic situations. The pattern variables are grouped as follows: (1) universalism-particularism; (2) ascription-achievement; (3) self-orientation–collectivity-orientation; (4) affectivity-affective neutrality; and (5) specificity-diffuseness. The universalism-particularism dichotomy distinguishes between judging objects in a general frame of reference and judging them in a particular scheme. Whereas the impartial dispensation of justice under law is universalistic, kinship behavior is particularistic. The ascription-achievement dichotomy refers to values governing human advancement in social and political systems—whether, for example, birth and wealth count for more than intellectual ability and education. The self-orientation–collectivity-orientation dichotomy categorizes action as being taken on behalf of the unit initiating action or as initiated on behalf of other units. Businesses, for example, tend to be self-oriented, whereas governments are collectivity-oriented. The affectivity-affective neutrality variable indicates an individual's sensitivity or insensitivity to emotional stimuli. The specificity-diffuseness variable distinguishes between those relationships that are diffuse and all-encompassing, such as a marriage, and those that are specific and highly structured, such as interaction between a sales clerk and customer. Although diffuseness characterizes traditional societies, specificity of function is a mark of modernized societies.

Parsons's pattern variables provide a framework for describing recurring and contrasting patterns in the norms of social systems. Many authors deem the Parsonian pattern variables as useful in examining social and political systems. For example, Parsons suggests that a bureaucracy is built on universalistic and achievement norms, and that the contractual relationships among business corporations are based on norms of specificity. Such variables may be used either in a discussion of international relations or of political parties at the national or local level in the United States.

In his theory, Parsons attaches great importance to equilibrium as a means of measuring fluctuations in the ability of a social system to cope with problems that affect its structure.[38] Systems theory assumes the interdependence of parts in determinate relationships, which impose order upon the components of the system. Although equating order with equilibrium, Parsons asserts that equilibrium is not necessarily equated with "static self-maintenance or a stable equilibrium. It may be an ordered process of change—a process following a determinate pattern rather than random variability relative to the starting point. This is called a moving equilibrium and is well exemplified in growth."[39] Social systems are characterized by a multiple equilibrium process, since social systems have many subsystems, each of which must remain in equilibrium if the larger system is to maintain equilibrium.

✷Parsons is concerned with how social systems endure stress, how they enhance their position, and how they disintegrate. If societal equilibrium ✷ and ultimately the social system itself are to be maintained, four functional conditions are prerequisite: (1) pattern maintenance—the ability of a system to ensure the reproduction of its own basic patterns, values, and norms; (2) adaptation to the environment and to changes in the environment; (3) goal attainment—the capacity of the system to achieve whatever goals the system has accepted or set for itself; and (4) integration of the different functions and subsystems into a cohesive, coordinated whole. In Parsons's social system, families and households are the subsystems that serve the function of pattern maintenance. Adaptation occurs in the economy and in areas of scientific and technological change. The polity—the government in particular—performs the function of goal attainment. The integrative function is fulfilled by the cultural subsystems, which include ✷ mass communications, religion, and education. Parsons's functional prerequisites have been adapted, in varying forms, to the study of politics, which is itself one of his subsystems, and they have influenced those international systems writers who are considered in this chapter.[40] Although Parsons briefly addresses himself to the concept of international systems, he sees in the international system patterns of interaction similar to those within the action system at the domestic level. The major problem for the international system, as well as for the domestic system, is that of maintaining the equilibrium, which is important if a system is to manage its inner tensions.[41]

The existence of a bipolar international system increases the difficulty of maintaining equilibrium. According to Parsons, the formulation of common values that cut across national boundaries is essential to international order. Although the international system is deficient in such values, the importance attached to economic development and national independence in many parts of the world over the past generation represents their emergence, at least in rudimentary form, as consensus-building forces at the global level. Parsons sees the need for procedural consensus-agreement among participants in international politics about the institutions and procedures for the settlement of problems and differences. He also calls for the differentiation of interests among peoples in a pluralistic fashion so that they will cut across the historic lines of partisan differentiation. In domestic political and social systems, peoples achieve greater unity as a result of their cross-cutting cleavages—that is, some Protestants being Democrats and others being Republicans. Such pluralistic differentiation at the international level would enhance the prospects for international stability. Central to Parsons's writings is the problem of building a social and political community.[42] His action system has influenced the thought of students of integration at the international level, as discussed in Chapter 10.

David Easton and Others

Several political scientists have developed, adapted, and employed systems theory. These scholars have concerned themselves with the "political system," which has been defined by Gabriel Almond as "that system of interactions to be found in all independent societies which performs the functions of integration and adaptation (both internally and vis-à-vis other societies) by means of the employment, or the threat of employment, of more or less legitimate physical compulsion."[43] Karl Deutsch, who also adheres to the functional prerequisites of Parsons, holds that a system is characterized by transactions and communications. He is concerned with the extent to which political systems are equipped with adequate facilities for collecting external and internal information as well as for transmitting this information to the points of decision-making. Those political systems that survive stress can receive, screen, transmit, and evaluate information.[44] According to David Easton, systems theory is based on the idea of political life as a boundary-maintaining set of interactions imbedded in and surrounded by other social systems that constantly influence it.[45] Further, political interactions can be distinguished from other kinds of interactions by the fact that they are oriented principally toward the "authoritative allocation of values for a society."[46]

Scholars such as Almond, Deutsch, and Easton share an interest in functions performed by the political system—an interest in the means by which the system converts inputs into outputs. Easton in particular has been identified with what is termed input-output analysis. In his scheme, the principal inputs into the political system are demands and supports, whereas the major outputs are the decisions allocating system benefits. Almond addresses himself to the question of how political systems engage in political socialization, interest articulation and aggregation, and political communication. Such factors represent means for making demands on the political system; therefore, they are input functions. Almond is concerned particularly with political output functions involving rule-making, rule application, and rule adjudication. His output functions, in the case of the American political system, correspond to the executive, legislative, and judicial branches.

The system represents an effort to cut across the boundaries separating seemingly discrete disciplines. Easton, for example, maintains that at the international level no less than at the national level, it is possible to find sets of relationships through which values are authoritatively allocated. Unlike certain other systems, however, the international system lacks universal or even strongly held feelings of legitimacy; nevertheless, its members make demands with the expectation that these will be converted into outputs. According to Easton, authorities in this case are much "less centralized than in most modern systems, less continuous in their operation and more contingent on events, as in the case of primitive systems. But, nonetheless, historically the great powers and, more recently, various kinds of international organizations, such as the League of Nations and the United Nations, have been successful, intermittently, in resolving differences that were not privately negotiated and in having them accepted as authoritative."[47] Employing his systems model, Easton suggests the possibility of studying and categorizing political systems, at both the national and international levels, according to their capacity for authoritatively allocating values. In Herbert Spiro's framework, the political process consists essentially of four phases: (1) the formulation of issues arising from problems, (2) the deliberation of issues, (3) the resolution of issues, and (4) the solution of the problem that provoked the issue.[48] Although all political systems perform these functions, they vary widely, depending on the political style of the actors. In turn, political style is derived from four basic goals toward which political systems are more or less deliberately directed: stability, flexibility, efficiency, and effectiveness.[49] The effective political system achieves an equilibrium among these goals. Spiro views problems as constituting the inputs, and solutions as the outputs, of political systems.

Systems theory—in particular, the work of Gabriel Almond—and comparative studies of political systems all share a basic concern with structural-functional analysis that attempts to examine the performance of certain kinds of functions within such seemingly different entities as a biological organism and a political system. Contemporary scholars who employ structural-functional analysis are indebted to the early twentieth-century work of anthropologists Bronislaw Malinowski (1884–1942) and A. R. Radcliffe-Brown (1881–1955). Subsequently, Robert K. Merton developed a framework for structural-functional analysis in the field of sociology.[50] Proponents of structural-functional analysis assume that it is possible, first, to specify a pattern of behavior that satisfies a functional requirement of the system and, second, to identify functional equivalents in several different structural units. Structural-functional analysis contains as concepts structural and functional requisites. A functional requisite is a generalized condition, given the level of generalization of the definition and the unit's general setting.[51] A structural requisite is a pattern or observable uniformity of action necessary for the continued existence of the system.[52] Moreover, an effort is made to distinguish between functions (or what Levy calls eufunctions) and dysfunctions. According to Merton, "eufunctions are those observed consequences which make for the adaptation or adjustment of the system."[53] Thus structural-functional analysis may enable the researcher to avoid the pitfall of associating particular functions with particular structures and, for this reason, may prove useful in comparative research and analysis. According to John Weltman, the utilization of systems theory in the study of international relations represents a "mode of analysis growing out of, and conditioned by, two pervasive currents of thought—functional sociology and general systems theory." He suggests that functional sociology and general systems theory, taken together, are mutually reinforcing. "The functional sociologists are more concerned with activity than with the entity within which this activity occurs, to which it is related, and in terms of which it is assessed." In contrast, for general systems theory he proposes: "The nature of the entity within which activity occurs is paramount, often to the exclusion of direct concern with the concrete activity itself."[54]

Both the Parsonian functional prerequisites and the functions set forth by Almond and Easton can be located and described within a given political system. Such functions relate to the system's goals, to the system's maintaining an equilibrium, and to the system's ability to interact with and adapt to changes within the environment. Structural-functional analysis provides, at the minimum, a classificatory scheme for examining political phenomena.[55]

Systems concepts have been applied to studies in international integration, foreign policy decision-making, and conflict. Systems theory has been used at several analytical levels of immediate interest to the student of international politics:

- the development of models of international systems in which patterns of interaction are specified;
- the study of the processes by which decision-makers in one national unit, interacting with each other and responding to inputs from the domestic and international environment, formulate foreign policy—although, as Raymond Tanter has suggested, "international systems approaches may imply interaction models, whereas foreign policy approaches may suggest decision-making models";[56]
- the study of interaction between a national political system and its domestic subsystems—such as public opinion, interest groups, and culture—in order to analyze patterns of interaction;
- the study of external "linkage groups," that is, other political systems, actors, or structures in the international system with which the national system under examination has direct relations; and
- the examination of the interaction between external "linkage groups"[57] and those internal groups most responsive to external events, such as foreign affairs elites, the military, and business people engaged in world trade.

These analytic foci are by no means mutually exclusive: Understanding decision-making processes and systems at the national level is essential to understanding interaction between the national units of the international system. To focus on national decision-making is to study a subsystem of the international system; the international system has as a focal point investigating interaction among the foreign policies of a series of national units. In this chapter we are concerned in particular with those theorists who concentrate on the international system and its regional subsystems. In subsequent chapters on decision-making and integration theory, we shall examine other applications of systems theory.

THE NATURE OF SYSTEMS AT THE INTERNATIONAL LEVEL

In the study of international relations, Morton A. Kaplan suggests the existence of a system of action that he defines as "a set of variables so related, in contradistinction to its environment, that describable behavioral regularities characterize the internal relationships of the set of individual variables to combinations of external variables."[58] According to another student of international relations, Charles A. McClelland, systems theory is a technique for developing an understanding of relationships among nation-states:

> The strategy, first of all, of conceiving of many kinds of phenomena in terms of working relations among their parts, and then labeling the systems according to a definition of what part of the problem is most relevant, is the key to the approach. Then, the procedures of bypassing many complexities in order to investigate relationships between input and output, of systematically moving to different levels of analysis by recognizing the link of subsystems to systems, of being alert to "boundary phenomena" and the ranges of normal operations of subsystems and systems, and of taking into account both "parameters" and "perturbations" in the environments of systems are other major parts of the general systems apparatus.[59]

In McClelland's work, systems theory is simply a framework for an event/interaction model or a technique for identifying, measuring, and examining interaction within a system and its subsystems. Systems theory provides for the examination of linkages, or recurrent sequences of behavior that originate in one system and are reacted to in another. If such sequences can be isolated and examined, it may be possible to gain theoretical insights into the nature of the interdependence of national and international systems.

George Modelski defines an international system as a social system having structural and functional requirements. International systems consist of a set of objects, together with the relationships between these objects and between their attributes. International systems contain patterns of action and interaction between collectivities and between individuals acting on their behalf.[60] Richard N. Rosecrance concludes that a system comprises disturbance inputs, a regulator that undergoes changes as a result of the disturbing influence, and environmental constraints that translate the state of the disturbance and the state of the regulator into stable or unstable outcomes.[61]

Hedley Bull drew a basic distinction between international systems as a concept over international society. It is possible, as in the case of the history of relations among the basic political units of the world, to have an international system without the existence of an international society. Whenever there is interaction—in the form, for example, of diplomatic communications, the exchange of ambassadors, and the conclusion of agreements—there is said to be an international system. In Hedley Bull's view, however, an international society decides when a group of states "conceive themselves to be bound by a common set of rules in their relations with one another, and share in the working of common institutions . . . such as the forms of procedures of international law, the machinery of diplomacy and general international organization, and the customs and conventions of war."[62] An international society has as its prerequisite an international system. Among the international societies of the past, Hedley Bull included the classical Greek city-state system, the Hellenistic states in the era from the collapse of Alexander's empire and the Roman conquest, China in the Period of Warring States, the state system of ancient India, and the modern state system from its Eurocentric origins to its present global structure.[63]

The systems approach has had many adherents because supposedly it furnishes a framework for organizing data, integrating variables, and introducing materials from other disciplines. Kaplan has suggested that systems theory permits the integration of variables from different disciplines.[64] Rosecrance believes that systems theory helps link "general organizing concepts" with "detailed empirical investigation." In his work the concept of system provides a framework for studying the history of a particular period and enhances the prospects for developing a "theoretical approach which aims at a degree of comprehensiveness."[65] Dissatisfied with past approaches to the study of international relations, McClelland favors a systems approach because there is a need "to gather the specialized parts of knowledge into a coherent whole."[66] Other writers, especially in the 1970s, have suggested that, by virtue of the inherent complexity of global politics, there exists no entity known as an international system. Instead, there are "multiple issue-based systems." International politics is hypothesized as consisting of "many distinctive and overlapping systems that differ from each other in terms of their structural properties and in terms of the purposes of the individuals and groups that constitute them. If we allow that these multiple systems can overlap and/or become linked, then it becomes apparent that there is more than a single relevant global system as well as many that are less than global in domain."[67]

Writers on international systems develop what are termed concrete or physical systems and analytic systems. A concrete system describes a pattern of interaction among human actors that supposedly exists, or existed, in the real world. In contrast, an analytic system is a heuristic device for the analysis of possible future systems, for comparison between some existing systems and a kind of ideal or analytical system.[68] Kaplan's systems are models in the same sense in which a theory of molecular structure could be translated into a model that, if correct, would relate to the observable real world. They are theoretical models that can be applied to real systems, but that in principle can also be expressed in purely logical form. Modelski's models, Agraria and Industria, are analytic systems; Rosecrance's international systems derived from the analysis of historical data are concrete systems.

Just as there are similarities in their definitions of systems, those writers discussed in this chapter whose work has dealt primarily with the international level have common elements in their respective international systems frameworks. First, each has an interest in those factors that contribute to stability or instability in the international system. Second, there is a common concern with the adaptive controls by which the system remains in equilibrium or "steady-state." Such preoccupation in the study of political and social systems is analogous to the interest of biologists in homeostasis in living organisms. Third, there is a shared interest in assessing the impact upon the system of the existence of units with a greater or lesser ability to mobilize resources and to utilize advanced technology. Fourth, there is a consensus among writers that domestic forces within the national political units exert a major effect on the international system. Fifth, they are concerned, as part of their interest in the nature of stability, with the capacity of the international system to contain and deal effectively with disturbances within it. This leads the writers to share an interest in the role of national and supranational actors as regulators of the system. They are in accord that the international system is characterized by change, rather than by static qualities.

All are concerned with the role of elites, resources, regulators, and environment as factors that enhance or detract from stability in the system. Moreover, the flow of information is crucial to the functioning and preservation of the system. In fact, systems theory owes much to principles of cybernetics developed by Norbert Wiener and applied by scholars such as Karl W. Deutsch to the study of politics (see Chapter 10). Interaction among the units of a system occurs as a result of a communications process.

In short, writers who use systems theory are concerned in varying degree with several categories of questions, concepts, and data:

- the internal organization and interaction patterns of complexes of elements hypothesized or observed to exist as a system;
- the relationship and boundaries between a system and its environment and, in particular, the nature and impact of inputs from and outputs to the environment;
- the functions performed by systems, the structures for the performance of such functions, and their effect upon the stability of the system;
- the homeostatic mechanisms available to the system for the maintenance of steady-state or equilibrium;
- the classification of systems as open or closed, or as organismic or nonorganismic systems; and

- the structuring of hierarchical levels of systems, the location of subsystems within systems, and the patterns of interaction both among
subsystems and between subsystems and the system itself.

This last category may be restated as the problem of level of analysis,
including international subsystems, or "subordinate state systems," to
which students of international relations have addressed themselves at
considerable length over the past generation.[69] (Reference has previously
been made to the level-of-analysis problem in Chapter 1.) Several scholars
have attempted to specify patterns of interaction within models and
within actual political units in the North Atlantic area, the Middle East,
and Asia. Regions have been treated as subsystems of the international
system, and efforts have been made to link integration theory to general
systems theory. Research on international subsystems has had several focal
points: (1) an attempt to specify as precisely as possible patterns of interaction among units in one international subsystem, (2) an effort to compare
two or more international subsystems, and (3) studies of relationships
between a subsystem and the international system.[70]

Charles A. McClelland and Events Data Analysis

Charles A. McClelland has attempted to link systems theory explicitly to
the problem of delineating levels of analysis for the study of international
relations, and in doing so has provided the basis for a growing literature
focused on events/data interaction—the recording and analysis of data
about a variety of relationships among states, including trade patterns,
levels of foreign aid, diplomatic exchanges, and communications flows.
Events data are defined as "single action events of nonroutine, extraordi-
nary, or newsworthy character that in some clear sense are directed across
national boundaries and have in most instances a specific foreign target."
Visits of heads of state, diplomatic warnings, and participation in international conferences provide examples of such nonroutine single action
events. Such data, used either separately or in conjunction with transaction data, may yield a more precise understanding of patterns of interaction among states in carefully defined circumstances. For example, does
a shift in foreign policy by Country A toward Country B lead each country
to alter its foreign policy toward Country C? If so, what types of transactions and events precede, accompany, or follow such changes?

McClelland's model of the international system is an expanded version of two interacting states. The international system is multidimensional in character. In order to understand McClelland's systems framework, it is necessary to imagine nations of the world having a wide range
of official and unofficial contacts with each other—demand-response relationships, in which an action by one nation elicits a response from another, in turn calling forth a response from the nation that initiated the
action. According to McClelland, conditions and events in the interna-

tional system result from sources generated within nations, and from subsystems within the national unit such as public opinion, interest groups, and political parties. Therefore McClelland's model includes not only interaction at the international level, but also interaction between the national unit and its subsystems. He suggests that a nation's "international behavior is a two-way activity of taking from and giving to the international environment. All the giving and taking, when considered together and for all the national actors, is called the international system."[71] A systems framework, McClelland contends, provides an orderly procedure for shifting perspective from one level to another in the study of international politics.

Although the international system is multidimensional, the most promising prospect for theory-building is said to lie in the focus of attention upon one level of analysis at a time. McClelland concentrates on interaction between the national units, rather than interaction between the national unit and its domestic subsystems. He is concerned only with interaction observable outside the "black-boxes" that constitute the national units, with their complex and obscure decision-making processes. In McClelland's scheme, transactions between the national units are recorded and analyzed. Both routine and nonroutine activity between nations may be studied, since the "performance of the participants—the interaction sequences—are reliable indicators of active traits of participating actors. . . . Our basic assumption is that the kind of social organization developed in a nation-state fundamentally conditions its crisis behavior."[72]

In McClelland's own work the "acute international crisis," as a subsystem of the international system, is the object of examination by interaction analysis. He asks the following research questions: Is it possible to detect a "change of state" in the activities of a system in the transition from a noncrisis to a crisis period? Is a designated subsystem that is part of a more general system of action responsive to major disturbances in the general system? McClelland offers three propositions for examination: (1) that acute international crises are "short burst" affairs and are marked by an unusual value and intensity of events; (2) that the general trend in acute international crises will be toward "routinizing" crisis behavior—that is, dealing with problems by means of increasingly "standard" techniques; and (3) that participants will be reluctant to allow the level of violence to increase beyond that present at the onset of the crisis.

Since the early 1960s, numerous efforts have been made to collect and utilize events data in the study of international interaction. As McClelland notes, a major portion of events data studies has focused on crisis behavior, not unlike the emphasis in his own research. (Definitions of "crisis" and a discussion of crisis behavior will be found in Chapter 11.) McClelland suggests that anticrisis early warning systems may be developed from "current intelligence analyses in the policy community and event monitoring and indexing from the flow of the news by the academic community."[73] Thus, he sees the need, and the prospect, for theory and research utilizing events data that would serve the interests of both the scholar and the policymaker. The objects of study have been hypotheses about the structure, patterns, and performance of the international system and its subsystems; political behavior in alignments and under conditions of non-alignment; negotiating behavior; the causes, outcomes, and dynamics of crisis and conflict; and relationships between domestic political variables and foreign policy. The results of such analyses are, for the most part, inconclusive. To be sure, the extensive testing of hypotheses has illustrated a continuing and broadening effort to validate theoretical frameworks. But differing and often incomplete data sources, as well as statistical techniques, have hampered the development of cumulative knowledge. Sophia Peterson has concluded that, in the area of conflict, in which the greatest research effort has been concentrated: "Four factors have received the most emphasis: previous foreign conflict, domestic conflict, political structure, and power. Of these, findings have been more or less consistently pointing in the direction of the importance of previous foreign conflict and domestic conflict. The findings on power and political structure are contradictory as are the findings on several of the other factors."[74]

Richard N. Rosecrance

Although students of international relations have traditionally turned to historical materials for the construction and validation of theories, their work has been faulted often for its noncomparability or for the failure to develop adequate criteria for the selection of data. Proponents of systemic theories of politics, such as Rosecrance and Kaplan, have made use of historical materials in an effort to construct and validate models of international behavior. Rosecrance bases his systems analysis on the study of nine historical systems.[75] He divides European history between 1740 and 1960 into nine periods or systems, each which is demarcated by significant changes in diplomatic techniques and objectives. Rosecrance discerns the existence of recurring phenomena in the nine international systems periods, from which he develops two models. Concerned with the conditions for international stability, he selects as his basic elements disturbance input, the regulator mechanism that reacts to the disturbance, the environmental restraints that influence the range of possible outcomes, and finally the outcomes themselves. Disturbance input includes such forces as ideologies, domestic insecurity, disparities between nations in resources, and conflicting national interests. The regulator mechanism consists of capabilities such as those deriving from the Concert of Europe, the United Nations, or an informal consensus that, it is often pointed out by historians, the major European nations shared in the eighteenth century. The third element, the presence of environmental restraints, limits the range of possible outcomes. He judges systems to be equilibrial or disequilibrial, depending upon whether the regulator or the disturbance was stronger. From these elements, Rosecrance develops and examines four basic determinants for each of his nine systems: elite direction (attitudes), degree of elite control, resources available to the controlling elites, and the capacity of the system to contain disturbances. Given his choice of determinants, it is evident that Rosecrance attaches considerable importance to the domestic sources of international behavior.

Among his domestic determinants Rosecrance emphasizes the elites of national units. First, was the elite satisfied with its position domestically or did it feel threatened by events in the international system? Second, the control or security of the elite within the society that it commanded was a determinant in each of the international systems: Did the elites perceive a weakening in their internal position? Third, emphasis is placed upon the availability of disposable resources to the elite and its ability to mobilize them. Finally, Rosecrance views the system's capacity to mitigate and contain disturbances as a determinant of equilibrium.[76]

From Rosecrance's work, it is possible to construct essentially two models of the international system. The first is a model with characteristics of stability. A stable system is based on a comparison of systems I, Eighteenth Century (1740–1789); III, Concert of Europe (1814–1822); IV, Truncated Concert (1822–1848); VI, Bismarckian Concert (1871–1890); and IX, Postwar (1945–1960). In these systems the amount of disturbance was at a minimum and the regulator, be it Concert League or informal consensus, was able to cope with actor disturbance. The elites were satisfied with the status quo, both within their own respective national units and in the international system in general. In their political views they were not strongly influenced by ideology except, perhaps, in system IX (1945–1960). Even in this system, however, the elites were willing for the most part to resolve problems by means short of war.

The characteristics of an unstable system may be derived from a comparison of systems II, Revolutionary Imperium (1789–1814); V, Shattered Concert (1848–1871); VII, Imperialist Nationalism (1890–1918); and VIII, Totalitarian Militarism (1918–1945). In these systems, actor disturbance was high relative to the ability of the regulator to cope with it, and the variety of means at the disposal of the regulator was minimal. The elites were dissatisfied with the status quo and harbored feelings of insecurity. They sought to improve their own internal and external positions with respect to the international system and other actors. Elites were able to mobilize resources through appeals to nationalism and ideology. Because of their feelings of insecurity, governing elites often could not resist the urge to resort to such appeals. Environmental constraints failed to play a role in restricting disturbances. Rosecrance's major conclusion is that there is a correlation between international instability and the domestic insecurity of elites[77]—a subject that will be treated further under macrocosmic theories of the causes of war.

Morton A. Kaplan

Of all writers, Morton A. Kaplan has made the greatest effort to specify rules and patterns of interaction within models of alternative international systems. According to Kaplan, the classic statement of systems theory is to be found in the work of W. Ross Ashby on the human brain.[78] Although Ashby is concerned with the human brain and Kaplan with international politics, both are preoccupied in their respective fields with a system as a set of interrelated variables, distinguishable from its environment, and with the manner in which the set of variables maintains itself under the impact of disturbances from the environment.

Accordingly, Kaplan has constructed six models of hypothetical international systems that provide a theoretical framework within which hypotheses can be, and have been, generated and tested.[79] Within each model he has developed five sets of variables: essential rules, transformation rules, actor classificatory variables, capability variables, and information variables. The so-called essential rules are essential because they describe the behavior necessary to maintain equilibrium in the system.[80] The transformation rules specify the changes that take place as inputs other than those necessary for equilibrium to enter the system. The actor classificatory variables set forth the structural characteristics of actors. Capability variables indicate armament levels, technologies, and other elements of power available to actors. Information variables refer to the levels of communication within the system. The rules refer to the kinds of actors; their capabilities, motivations, and goal orientations; their styles of political behavior; and the structural characteristics of each of Kaplan's six systems—the balance of power, loose bipolar, tight bipolar, universal-international, hierarchical, and unit veto. These six systems can be ranged along a scale of integrative activity, with the unit veto system as least integrated and the hierarchical system as most integrated.

In Kaplan's models, changes in the system are the result of changes in the value of the parameters or constants. He acknowledges that few if any existing international systems conform fully with any of his models of hypothetical systems. Nevertheless, he is prepared, so long as the theory set forth in the model explains behavior when "suitable adjustments are made for the parameters of the system," to continue to employ that model. The system has changed when a different theory, or systems model, is needed to account for its behavior. Thus the utility of Kaplan's models lies in the extent to which they permit the student to compare behavior within any given existing international system with one or another of the six models. Moreover, by specifying rules for system change, a step-level function (that is, a system response to a disturbance input of such a nature as to transform the system itself), Kaplan claims to have built into his models a means of understanding how international systems are transformed.

Kaplan's models represent a spectrum ranging from more loosely to more tightly organized international system models. Moreover, in his scheme national actors are classified according to structural categories—directive or nondirective systems, which in turn may be system dominant or subsystem dominant. Kaplan is concerned with (1) the organizational focus of decisions, including the nature of actors' objectives and the instruments available to attain them; (2) the allocation of rewards, including the extent to which they are allocated by the system or by the subsystem; (3) the alignment preferences of actors; (4) the scope and direction of political activity; and (5) the flexibility or adaptability of units in their behavior.

Historical materials have been used to test propositions drawn from models of international systems. In one such endeavor, Kaplan's models were tested for formal logical consistency with the use of mathematical tools and the computer.[81] The models were then applied to historical periods such as the Chinese warlord system of the early twentieth century and the Italian city-state system of the fourteenth and fifteenth centuries. The author of a study of the Chinese warlord system found that this was "basically a 'balance of power' system operating under many unfavorable parameters." Moreover, this was a "balance of power system in which the actors either deliberately or unwittingly violated many of the essential behavioral rules that are necessary for the stability of such a system."[82] Among the conclusions of a study of the Italian city-state system were that, by and large, essential rules contained in the "balance-of-power" model were not violated, essential and even nonessential actors were preserved, the territorial capabilities of actors did not change greatly, equilibrium became both less static and less stable, and inevitably the system disintegrated.[83]

Utilizing an approach similar to events data, but drawing upon diplomatic history rather than current events, Patrick J. McGowan and Robert M. Rood examined the rate of alliance formation in the period between 1814 and 1914 in order to test hypotheses drawn from Kaplan's balance-of-power model. Specifically, they hypothesized that "in a balance of power international system, a decline in the systemic rate of alliance formation precedes system changing events, such as general war."[84] They tested hypotheses concerning the formation of alliances as a stochastic process. "That is, in a balance of power system alliances occur from time to time, and these events over time are subject to probability laws because the past behavior of the alliance process has no influence on future behavior."[85] There was a tendency, in the nineteenth-century European balance-of-power system, for alliances to be formed "quickly upon one another or with a lag of about three and one-half years." They note that "a clear cut decline in systems flexibility occurred after 1909, and that this period immediately preceded an event (World War I) that destroyed the European balance of power, perhaps forever."[86] They conclude that the data analyzed strongly supported Kaplan's balance-of-power model. The subject of how alliances relate to the amount of war in the international system is taken up in the following section and in Chapter 8.

Thus Kaplan's models, although less complex than the international system of the real world, are designed to facilitate comparisons with the real world to contribute to a meaningful ordering of data, and to build theory at the macrolevel. Only two of them—the balance of power and the loose bipolar—can be clearly discerned in history. However, the case can be made that a third model (the unit veto system) is partially validated in the contemporary role of the nuclear powers, while a fourth model (the universal-international system) exists in normative theory and in the aspirations of those scholars and practitioners, past and present, who seek to create such a global system.

THEORIES OF BIPOLARITY, MULTIPOLARITY, AND INTERNATIONAL STABILITY

The relationship between the distribution of power and the incidence of war has been the object of theorizing both in traditional and contemporary writings. Although Kaplan, in his models, has focused on "essential rules" for the operation of several international systems, other scholars, including Karl W. Deutsch, J. David Singer, Kenneth N. Waltz, and Richard N. Rosecrance, have theorized about the implications of multipolarity and bipolarity for the frequency and intensity of war. Deutsch and Singer contend that "as the system moves away from bipolarity toward multipolarity, the frequency and intensity of war should be expected to diminish."[87] They assume that coalitions of blocs of nations reduce the freedom of alliance members to interact with outside countries. The greater the number of actors who are not alliance members, the greater the number of possible partners for interaction in the international system. Although alliance membership minimizes both the range and intensity of conflict among those countries that are alliance members, the range and intensity of conflicts with actors outside the alliance are increased.

Although interaction among nations is as likely to be competitive as it is to be cooperative, the more limited the possibility for interaction, the greater the potential for instability. Deutsch and Singer assume that the international system is but a special case of the pluralism model—namely, that "one of the greatest threats to the stability of any impersonal social system is the shortage of alternative partners." Interaction with a great number of nations produces cross-cutting loyalties that induce hostility between any single dyad of nations.

Another hypothesis in support of a correlation between the number of actors and war is based on the "degree of attention that any nation in the system may allocate to all of the other nations or to possible coalitions of nations."[88] The greater the number of dyadic relationships, the less attention that an actor can give to any one dyadic relationship. If some minimal percentage of a nation's external attention is needed for "behavior tending toward armed conflict, and the increase in the number of independent actors diminishes the share that any nation can allocate to any other single actor, such an increase is likely to have a stabilizing effect upon the system."[89] Multipolarity is said to reduce the prospects for an arms race, since a country is likely to respond only to that part of the increase in armaments spending of a rival power that appears to be directed toward it.

SYSTEM STRUCTURE AND STABILITY

Although there is, as we have seen, little agreement among writers on this subject, some contend that a multipolar world is likely to be less stable than a bipolar system. With fewer important actors and greater certainty in military and political relationships, the prospects for misunderstandings and conflict are said to be less under conditions of bipolarity than in a multipolar world. Stanley Hoffmann, for example, sees the existence of the five uneven power centers, as hypothesized to exist in the early 1970s, to be not only undesirable, but also dangerous since the "balance of uncertainty" is increased and might lead to an arms race.[90] Another writer, Ronald Yalem, sees an emerging tripolar world (United States, Soviet Union, and China), in which two powers would tend to coalesce against the third. Because of the tripling of the number of bilateral interactions in comparison with the more simple interaction pattern in a bipolar world, and the additional patterns of potential conflict, there is a greater possibility for conflict in a tripolar world. Stability in such a system depends upon each state's preventing the emergence of a bipolar alignment against itself. Each must resist the temptation to form bipolar alignments against the third major power. Yalem writes, "Without any 'balancer' of power to affect the inherent tendency of two of the principals to combine against the third, or a strong supranational actor to regulate tripolarity, the system is likely to be susceptible to continual instability."[91]

Empirical studies by Singer and Melvin Small yielded conclusions not fully in support of the hypothesis about bipolarity-multipolarity and the outbreak of war. Analyzing historical data for the period 1815 to 1945 for possible correlations between alliance aggregation and the onset of war, Singer and Small tested the following hypotheses: (1) the greater the number of alliance commitments in the system, the more war the system will experience; and (2) the closer the system is to bipolarity, the more war it will experience.[92]

For the entire period under examination, the hypothesis about alliance aggregation and the outbreak of war was not confirmed. In the nineteenth century, alliance aggregation and occurrence of war correlated inversely, whereas in the twentieth century the variables covaried. In addition, the authors discovered that regardless of "whether we measure amount of war by numbers of wars, the nation-months involved, or battle deaths incurred, alliance aggregation and bipolarity predict strongly away from war in the nineteenth century and even more strongly toward it in the twentieth."[93] In short, for the period 1815 to 1899, the evidence presented by Singer and Small failed to support the theory about bipolarity and conflict presented earlier by Deutsch and Singer.

Although such a study using aggregate data can show the existence of correlations, it cannot, as Singer and Small acknowledge, establish a causal relationship. Conceivably, a third variable, such as the perception of national decision-makers, is the causal factor affecting the other two variables. For example, leaders may "step up their alliance-building activities as they perceived the probability of war to be rising."[94]

Another study tested hypotheses about the balance of power for a much shorter period—1870 to 1881. Drawing upon international events data, specifically a coded compilation of significant diplomatic events drawn from diplomatic histories, Brian Healy and Arthur Stein found that the alliances of the period—the Three Emperors' League of 1873 and the Dual Alliance of 1879—did not lead to an increase in cooperation among allies and an increase in conflict between allies and other states. In the case of the Three Emperors' League, Germany was the object of sharply increased hostility by an ally, Russia, and even by Austria. The authors conclude that there was a decrease in cooperation between members of the Three Emperors' League and outside states, although this decrease was less than what occurred within the League itself. Similarly, the period following the formation of the Dual Alliance of 1879 between Germany and Austria was marked by a deterioration in relations between the two signatories, together with an improvement in relations with Russia, against which the Dual Alliance was directed.

These findings point to a modification of the Singer-Small hypothesis, as well as the proposition advanced by Arthur Lee Burns and others, that the alignment of two or more states with each other heightens the opposition of others and enhances the risk of war. Moreover, the formation of the Three Emperors' League was followed by a decline in interactions among allies, from which Healy and Stein conclude that interactions between members of the League and outside states probably increased. But the findings of this study supported the proposition that there was a tendency toward equilibrium in this international system based on a multipolar balance of power, with the inference that "unbalanced relationships are more likely to be unstable than are balanced relationships," and "the tension caused by the unbalanced relationship induces a change in interaction behavior."[95]

There is little agreement among scholars about the relationship between multipolarity-bipolarity and international stability. In marked contrast to Deutsch and Singer, Kenneth Waltz argues that a bipolar international system, with its inherent disparity between the superpowers and the lesser states, is more stabilizing than a multipolar system. Having the capacity to inflict and control violence, the superpowers are "able both to moderate other's use of violence and to absorb possibly destabilizing changes that emanate from uses of violence that they do not or cannot control."[96] Both superpowers, following their instinct for self-preservation, continually seek to maintain a balance of power based upon a wide range of capabilities, including military and technological strength. Military power is most effective when it deters an attack. Hence Waltz sees utility in the maintenance of strength by each of two competing superpowers in a bipolar system, since states "supreme in their power have to use force less often."[97] According to Waltz, "Bipolarity is expressed as the reciprocal control of the two strongest states by each other out of their mutual antagonism. . . . [E]ach is very sensitive to the gains of the other."[98]

Offering an alternative system, Richard N. Rosecrance is critical of both the Deutsch-Singer and Waltz models, respectively, of multipolarity and bipolarity, and argues instead for bimultipolarity. Criticizing Waltz's formulation of bipolarity, Rosecrance contends that a bipolar world in which the two superpowers are intensely and vitally interested in the outcome of all major international issues is essentially a zero sum game. Hence the motivation for expansion and the potential for conflict between the bloc leaders are said to be greater in a bipolar system than in a multipolar world.[99]

Although the intensity of conflict may be lower in a multipolar world than in a bipolar system, Rosecrance suggests that the frequency of conflict will be greater because of a greater diversity of interests and demands. "If a multipolar order limits the consequences of conflict elsewhere in the system, it can scarcely diminish their number. If a bipolar system involves a serious conflict between the two poles, it at least reduces or eliminates conflict elsewhere in the system."[100] Another criticism is that, while reducing the significance of any change in the power balance, multipolarity increases the uncertainty as to what the consequences will be. Thus it makes policymaking complex and the achievement of stable results difficult.

The alternative system proposed by Rosecrance combines the positive features of bipolarity and multipolarity without their attendant liabilities. In bimultipolarity, "the two major states would act as regulators for conflict in the external areas; but multipolar states would act as mediators and buffers for conflict between the bipolar powers. In neither case would conflict be eliminated, but it might be held in check."[101] The bipolar nations, and in particular the superpowers, would seek to restrain each other from attaining predominance while acting together from a mutual interest in minimizing conflict or challenge in the multipolar region of the globe. The multipolar states, although having rivalries stemming from a diversity of national perspectives and interests, would have a common interest in resisting the ambitions of the bipolar powers. Therefore the probability of war would be lower in a bimultipolar system than in either a strictly bipolar or multipolar system. Rosecrance concludes that the increase of multipolarity would enhance the prospects for détente between the superpowers, and thus for collaboration between them on the resolution of problems of a multipolar nature.

As an alternative to each of the foregoing models, Oran R. Young suggests the need for a model that emphasizes "the growing interpenetration of the global or systemwide axes of international politics on the one hand and several newly emerging but widely divergent regional areas or subsystems on the other hand."[102] Critical of the bipolar and multipolar models for their focus on essentially structural problems to the neglect of the dynamics of international systems, Young develops a "discontinuities model" that encompasses the concurrent influence of global and regional power processes in patterns that are strongly marked by elements of both congruence and discontinuity.[103] Young uses the concepts of congruence and discontinuity to refer to the degree to which "patterns of political interests and relationships of power are similar or dissimilar as between the global area and various regional areas and as between the different regional areas themselves."[104] Young's conception of "discontinuities" is similar to the model of a world of "multiple issue-systems" noted earlier.[105] The crisscrossing, overlap, and linkage phenomena entail acute boundary identification problems: Where does system X end and system Y begin?

No final answer can be given to such questions because system boundaries, like systems themselves, are imposed by analysts for particular research purposes and are constantly changing. Some actors, including the superpowers, and certain issues—such as communism, nationalism, and economic development—are relevant throughout the international system. Yet the regional subsystems of the international system have unique features and patterns of interaction. Young proposes a model in which the existence of discontinuities is emphasized. The discontinuities model is designed to generate useful insights about the variety and complexity of interpenetration among subsystems, the trade-offs and the possibilities for manipulation across subsystems, the problems of incompatibility of the actors with systemwide interests, and the relationships between various subsystems and the global patterns of international politics.

REGIONAL SUBSYSTEMS IN THE INTERNATIONAL SYSTEM

As part of the systems perspective in international relations theory, the interest of scholars in delineating subsystems has increased substantially in the past generation. It has been noted elsewhere in this chapter and in Chapter 10 that systems theory and integration theory have been closely associated in the literature of international relations theory. Because much of the theorizing about integration has focused on the regional level, it follows that integration studies and the regional subsystem have also been linked in the writings of scholars, especially since the early 1960s. As Michael Banks noted in 1969, "A number of attempts have been made to approach regional subsystems from the traditionally ideographic standpoint of area studies, but in a way which employs at least some of the more cogent of the systems' insights into the patterns of world politics."[106] According to Louis Cantori and Steven Spiegel the regional subsystem consists of "one state, or of two or more proximate and interacting states which have some common ethnic, linguistic, cultural, social, and historical bonds, and whose sense of identity is sometimes increased by the actions and attitudes of states external to the system."[107] The systems are delineated by four "pattern variables":

1. the nature and level of cohesion, or the "degree of similarity or complementarity in the properties of the political entities being considered and the degree of interaction between these units";
2. the nature of communications within the region;
3. the level of power in the subsystem, with power defined as the "present and potential ability and the willingness of one nation to alter the internal decision-making processes of other countries in accordance with its own policies"; and
4. the structure of relations within the region.[108]

In order to take account of overlap between subsystems and boundary diffuseness in regional membership, it is necessary, as the authors suggest, to divide each subsystem into first, a core sector, or principal focus of international politics within a given region; second, a peripheral sector, including states that play a role in the political affairs of the region but are separated from the core as a result of social, political, economic, organizational, or other factors; and third, an intrusive system that takes account of external powers whose participation in the subsystem is important.

Another scholar, William R. Thompson, has reviewed and synthesized the literature of international subsystems. According to Thompson, the attributes set forth in the literature of international subsystems include proximity of actors to each other; patterns of relations or interactions exhibiting regularity; intrarelatedness, with a change in one part of the subsystem affecting other parts; internal and external recognition as distinctive units of power that are relatively inferior to those of the dominant system; the effects of change in the dominant system being greater upon the subsystem than vice versa; a certain (unspecified) degree of shared linguistic, cultural, historical, social, or ethnic bonds; a relatively high level of integration, including perhaps explicit institutional relations; intrasystem actions that are predominant over external influences; distinctive military forces; a form of regional equilibrium; and a common level of development.[109] Thus, one can say that the level of consensus on the attributes of a subsystem is low.

Thompson concludes: "Strictly speaking, regional subsystems need not be geographical regions per se. Rather, the subsystems consist of the interactions of national elites, not the physical entities of political units, of which interactions are observed to have more or less regional boundaries. In this sense, it should only be necessary to employ the minimal regional criterion—namely, general proximity."[110] From his analysis, the author infers that the "necessary and sufficient conditions for a regional subsystem include: regularity and intensity of interactions so that a change in one part affects other parts; general proximity of actors; internal and external recognition of the subsystem as distinctive; and provision of at least two, and probably more, actors in the subsystem."[111]

Utilizing such criteria, it is possible to identify many subsystems, although their boundaries may differ for different purposes. From an institutional perspective, we may identify the European Economic Community as a subsystem. From a geographic and cultural perspective, we may view Western Europe as yet another subsystem. The existence of a state such as Great Britain, France, or Germany within each of these subsystems provides a series of inputs from the international environment into its foreign policy. Elsewhere in the world, we could develop a series of regional subsystems that help to shape the foreign policies of the states that are core or peripheral members, or that are located outside the subsystem.

World System Analysis

Central to the analysis of systems is the study of their structures and processes. World system analysis represents an attempt to assess the relationships of structure and process within contemporary and historic contexts. Of fundamental importance is the assumption that the origins of the modern world system can be traced to as long ago as the late fifteenth century. For several centuries, therefore, the present world system, together with its various subsystems, has been evolving from lesser to greater levels of complexity based on increasing forms of interaction. It is possible to observe and to analyze a series of structures and processes in the world system that display elements of continuity over a period of at least 500 years. Indeed, the world system of the late twentieth century, however distinctive it may appear from that of earlier eras, nevertheless is based on modifications of the same structures and processes found in previous centuries. In this sense, world system analysis represents an intellectual reaction to what have been deemed to be excessively abstract, ahistorical social science models. History is deemed to be a vital ingredient not merely as a basis for descriptive narrative—not the principal goal of the proponents of world system analysis—but instead as the crucially important means of discerning and comparing repetitive phenomena and, in particular, cyclical phases, to be described in greater detail below.

World system analysis forms an effort, in keeping with much of the study of international phenomena, to cut across traditional disciplinary boundaries. It is based on the assumption that the world system contains a series of interdependent political-military, economic, and cultural subsystems, and that it is difficult, if not self-defeating, to examine, for example, patterns of political and economic interaction in isolation from each other. World system analysis shares with structural realism the fundamental assumption that, as William R. Thompson puts it, "behavior within the system can best be explained in terms of world system structure and its critical processes."[112] However, for world system analysis, structures exist at many levels. Thus, to quote Thompson again: "The operating assumption is that analysts must at some point decipher the pervasive structural context within which all behavior is conducted, regardless of the level of interaction."[113] Such processes and structures should be studied in integrated fashion, by which is meant within a context that not only cuts across academic disciplinary boundaries, but also brings into focus what is termed world system time.

In world system analysis, it is posited that rhythms and cycles in the processes of the system can be identified and examined. The world system of the past half-millenium contains a series of such phenomena. Of importance are not years and decades themselves, but instead the longer-term fluctuations that may be seen in the system. A large number of cycles are identified by various contributors to the world system analysis literature. According to Immanuel Wallerstein, the world system has been characterized historically by the development of a division of labor between the core area and its periphery, and by the rise and fall of hegemonic powers and the gradual territorial expansion of such states and their eventual decline, together with successive periods of growth and stagnation in the world economy.[114] In economic terms, at any time the core area encompasses those states having the most efficient agricultural-industrial production together with the highest level of capital accumulation. With such a frame of reference Wallerstein discerns a first stage (1450–1600) in the development of the modern world economy, during which time the core area shifted from the Mediterranean to northwest Europe. This was a period, of course, in which the economy was primarily agrarian. This was followed by an era of systemwide stagnation in a second stage beginning in about 1600 and extending as long as 150 years. Only in a third stage, beginning in 1750 and extending into the twentieth century, did the industrial dimension become predominant, followed in turn by global economic expansion and consolidation.

Of central importance in Wallerstein's analysis for students of international politics is the relationship that is drawn between the core-periphery division of labor in economic terms and the concentration or diffusion of power with respect to more or less dominant states. There have been only brief periods of hegemonic power associated with the world system of the past 500 years. These included the Netherlands (1625–1672/75); Great Britain (1763–1815/ca. 1850–1873); and the United States (1945–1965/67). According to Wallerstein, such eras are characterized by the concentration within the hegemonic state of agriculture and industry, as well as financial resources. The shortness of such periods is attributed to the high cost of preserving hegemony and the eventual spread of economic capabilities to rival core states. With the cyclical decline of hegemonic control there follows a period of power diffusion and competition among rival core powers.

Since the mid-1970s, George Modelski has developed a form of world system analysis based on what he terms "long cycles of world leadership."[115] Such phenomena represent a pattern of regularity in balance in the world system. According to Modelski, the basic unit of the modern world system (since 1500) is a world region. Before the modern period, such regions existed in relative isolation from each other. It was only with the Age of Exploration that such interaction intensified. The greater the extent and scope of interregional interaction, the more complex is the world system—a characteristic of the modern world contrasted with that of the premodern period. In an examination of interactive patterns that bears some resemblance to traditional geopolitical analysis (see Chapter 2), Modelski views the development of the contemporary world system as the direct result of sea power. By means of increasing mobility over the oceans, a complex international system was forged in place of the premodern system in existence for more than a millenium before 1500 and based on a single path of interaction—namely, the Silk Road, linking China with Europe through Central Asia and the Middle East. Based on sea power, a succession of leading states came into existence. They included the Iberian order, in turn under the Portuguese and Spanish hegemony, followed by a period of Dutch supremacy that was superseded by the maritime dominance of Great Britain and ultimately by the United States. Rejecting the realist thesis of endemic and pervasive anarchy, Modelski instead suggests that periods of global leadership under leading maritime states have been accompanied by international stability. It is in the interval between the decline of one hegemonic maritime state and the rise of another that international conflict increases. Leading world states have shown a remarkable capability to forge mechanisms such as alliances and coalitions for collaborative behavior within various forms of a balance of power.

The long cycle to which Modelski refers contains a pattern that begins in the aftermath of a major war. For example, the Italian wars at the end of the sixteenth century, together with the conflicts between France and Spain, were followed by the rise of Iberian dominance in place of the Italian states of the previous era. Succeeding cycles, featuring the rise and decline of leading states, were punctuated by the wars that, in their time, were systemwide or global in nature, culminating of course in World War II. At the height of its capabilities a leading world state possesses power in excess of 50 percent of that generally available in the system as a whole. Of central importance as theoretical antecedents for Modelski are the balance of power, sea power, and transnationalism. Within the balance of power, leading states pursued strategies designed to preserve, or restore, stability—for example, by aiding a weaker state threatened by the power of a stronger one. The literature of sea power, and in particular that of Alfred Thayer Mahan, represents an important contribution to the study of interactive patterns of direct importance to world system analysis. Finally, transnationalism, as to totality of the forces conducive to interdependence, represents a focal point for world system analysis because, in Modelski's words, "it sets up a useful tension between the nation-state, a creation of the modern world, and the forces supplementing it or possibly transcending it in a post-modern system."[116] Modelski regards the long cycle theory of world system analysis as having potentially important predictive power, even though skepticism and caution are justified. If, for example, system time can be clearly delineated from one cycle to the next, it might be possible not only to discern recurring patterns of cyclical behavior but also to assess the position of various states in the present cycle. To the extent that such an assessment is deemed possible, the world system of the decades that lie ahead is said to be characterized by a tendency toward increased fragmentation together with greater competition among major powers in a system of heightened complexity.

In the world system concept, it is the level of concentration of power—political, military, and economic—that shapes the structure of the system. In this respect world system analysis resembles other theories in which structural elements provide defining characteristics of the relationships among entities within the system. It follows that rules for the operation of the system are formulated during periods of high power concentration under the leadership of a dominant state. The rhythm of the system is that of alterations in the concentration of capabilities followed by major wars. In the wake of a fragmentation of power comes a period of warfare, succeeded in turn by a reconcentration of capabilities in the hands of a newly emergent leading state. According to Kenneth Organski, for example, the international system is divided into two tiers of major powers—a dominant state and the lesser of great powers. Taken together such states are divided between those that are satisfied with the status quo and those that seek to change the existing distribution of capabilities. The erosion of the position of the dominant power, part of the cyclical evolution of world system analysis, leads dissatisfied actors to threaten or actually to resort to using force in order to effect changes in their favor.

International Regimes

Since the mid-1970s, the concept of international regimes has emerged as a focal point for research and analysis. The result has been a substantial literature that has had an interdisciplinary focus in keeping with the nature of international regimes, which encompass issue areas as diverse as defense, trade, monetary policy, law, and food policy. Such entities are said to represent efforts within the international system to develop collaborative arrangements, either by formal or by informal means. According to John Ruggie, who introduced the concept in 1975, an international regime is "a set of mutual expectations, rules and regulations, plans, organizational energies and financial commitments, which have been accepted by a group of states."[117] Subsequently, international regimes have been defined as "principles, norms, rules, and decision-making procedures around which actor expectations converge in a given issue area."[118] Furthermore, regimes may be categorized according to function on a continuum extending from specific or single issues to a diffuse, multi-issue level.[119] As Stephen D. Krasner suggests, international regimes have been said to consist of "intervening variables standing between basic causal factors on the one hand and outcomes and behavior on the other." According to Krasner, principles represent "beliefs of fact, causation, and rectitude. Norms are standards of behavior defined in terms of rights and obligations. Rules are specific prescriptions or proscriptions for action. Decision-making procedures are prevailing practices for making and implementing collective choice."[120] According to Oran R. Young, regimes consist of "social institutions governing the actions of those interested in specifiable activities (or meaningful sets of activities)," with the core element of regimes lying in a collection of rights and rules that are "more or less extensive or formally articulated, but some such institutional arrangements will structure the opportunities of the actors interested in a given activity, and that exact content will be a matter of intense interest to these actors."[121] Included in the idea of international regimes is the decision-making process with respect to a particular form of activity. Thus, the regime concept encompasses both structural and process elements. Stated differently, inquiry focuses on questions associated with how and why regimes are established and what organizational or structural form they take, as well as the process by which decisions are taken within them and the resulting outputs.

Regimes may be formal in nature or they may consist of informal arrangements. Formal regimes may be the result of legislation by international organizations. Such regimes may possess governing councils and bureaucratic structures. Informal regimes may be based simply on a consensus of objectives and mutual interests among participants, resulting in ad hoc agreements. Regimes may be based on a conception of common interest in which collaboration represents an optional strategy for participants. At the minimum, collaboration entails agreed rules to work together for certain goals and to abstain from certain actions. However, just as regimes may be based on common interest, they may also be the product of what Ernst Haas has termed "common aversion." In such regimes, "the actors do not agree on a jointly preferred outcome, but they do agree on the outcome all wish to avoid; such regimes merely require policy coordination, not collaboration."[122] Regimes may result from voluntary collaboration or cooperation. They may be based on the imposed will of a dominant power. Thus, we may speak of colonial or imperial regimes, or of the *ancien régime* in the prerevolutionary France of the eighteenth century. Oran Young distinguishes between negotiated regimes characterized by explicit consent on the part of the participants and imposed regimes that are "deliberately established by dominant actors who succeed in getting others to conform to the requirements of those orders through some combination of cohesion, cooperation, and the manipulation of incentives."[123] Regimes may come into existence as a result of an agreement or contract among the participants. Alternatively, regimes may be created either in evolutionary fashion or by dramatic unilateral action by one party that is accepted by others. Finally, actors who have formed one regime may engage in what Oran R. Young describes as "a process of task expansion or 'spillover' that will lead over time to the emergence of a more comprehensive and coherent regime."[124] In this respect there exists a process similar to that described in neofunctionalist integration literature.

In this concept, regimes may be the result of the direct imposition of institutional arrangements upon subordinate elements coerced into compliance. Imperial and feudal systems are said to be illustrative of such regimes. In an alternate conception, a dominant power may exert leadership in the formation and preservation of regimes that serve its interests but are also widely accepted in the international system. Thus Robert Keohane develops a regime concept based on hegemonic stability, cooperation, and collaboration. Focusing on the world political economy of the two generations after World War II, Keohane defines hegemony as possession of a preponderance of material resources—raw materials, sources of capital, control over markets, and a competitively advantageous position in the production of goods in great demand.[125] Central to Keohane's concept is what he terms cooperation "after hegemony"[126]—at a time when the hegemonic power has declined in power and influence. A large number of international regimes were formed under the leadership of the United States in the decades after World War II. What happens, it is asked, to such regimes when a hegemonic power loses its preponderant position? How and why do regimes that were formed as part of a relationship between a dominant power and lesser units endure after the hegemonic power has ceased to play a determinant role? According to Keohane, the answer lies in the fact that regimes are more easily preserved than created. In his words: "Cooperation is possible after hegemony not only because shared interests can lead to the creation of regimes, but also because the conditions for maintaining existing regimes are less demanding than those required for creating them."[127] Moreover, whether or not there exists a hegemonic power, international regimes, in Keohane's formulation, depend for their existence on perceived interests that are common or complementary in nature. As the hegemonic power's position is diminished, a growth in interaction among at least a few of the units of the regime may serve as a replacement or supplement leading to posthegemonic cooperation. International regimes arise from shared interests. The greater the incentives to cooperation, the more likely it is that such regimes will survive the decline of a hegemonic power.

Keohane draws a distinction between cooperation and harmony as the indispensable basis for the international regimes that he describes. Harmony is illustrated by the situation in which the pursuit of self-interest by all actors leads automatically to the achievement of all the participants' goals—much as in the case of the harmony of interest concept discussed in utopian theory (see Chapter 1). International regimes, especially those lacking formal structures, may be based simply on harmony, as with the market competition of the invisible hand of a classical economics model. However, cooperation represents a condition in which actor participants take steps to adapt their behavior to the needs of others by means of a process of policy coordination. Harmony may exist even in the absence of communication among actors; cooperation is political in nature because it requires adjustment on the part of participants to the needs and interests of each other. Hence, cooperation does not assure that conflict is absent from the relationship. Instead, cooperation forms either a reaction to existing conflict or part of an effort to avoid future conflict. According to Keohane, the international regime concept enhances our ability both to describe and to account for patterns of cooperation, and to understand the basis for discord. Such analysis leads Keohane to view international regimes as reflecting patterns of cooperation and discord over a period of time. Within the international regime concept, such relationships can be treated as longer-term patterns of behavior rather than as isolated actors or events. According to Keohane: "By investigating the evolution of the norms and rules of a regime over time, we can use the concept of international regime both to explore continuity and to investigate change in the world political economy."[128] Thus the regime, in keeping also with the concept articulated by Krasner earlier in this chapter, can be hypothesized as a set of intermediate factors, or "intervening variables," that stand between the landscape of international politics, including especially the distribution of power, on the one hand, and the actual behavior of the basic entities, be they state or nonstate actors, on the other. To the extent that such actors, in a horizontally organized, decentralized international system, seek to evolve solutions to problems of disparate kinds, they form various types of international regimes. Thus the emphasis of regime analysis is the state actor, inasmuch as regimes evolve within an international system in which power is diffused or concentrated. Regimes are found in international systems in which there is a broadly based distribution of capabilities—a balance of power—among a large number of states. Regimes exist, it has already been noted, in international systems in which, as was the case with Britain in the nineteenth century (Pax Britannica) or the United States in the twentieth century (Pax Americana), there is a hegemonic state. To the extent that such powers create a basis for peace and stability while furnishing rewards for cooperative behavior, they contribute to the formation of international regimes.

To the extent that its focus is state-centric, the regime concept draws upon and contributes to neorealist theory. (See Chapter 3.) Classical realism holds that international behavior is based principally on interests and power, and that world politics is anarchic. The regime concept represents an effort not necessarily to reject such an assumption but instead to modify it. In the original realist formulation, states with competing interests may resort to conflict and ultimately war to achieve a resolution compatible with perceived needs. While realist theory did not reject the possibility of accommodation as a means of resolving differences, the regime concept adds an explicit and extended analysis of national interest and politics in which competitive elements produce cooperative behavior. In the regime concept, national interest is based on a calculus of benefits and costs, of perceived gains and risks inherent in complying with or violating the provisions, rules, and procedures set forth in a given international regime. As Oran Young points out: "Like other social institutions, international regimes are products of human interactions and the convergence of expectations among groups of interested actors."[129] Thus the regime concept may be viewed in part as an attempt to refine the realist idea of national interest to encompass the notion that, as Keohane suggests, "cooperation is explicable even on narrowly self-interested, egoistic assumptions about the actors in world politics."[130] To the extent that contributors to the literature of regimes attribute the behavioral characteristics of members of regimes to the distribution of power among them (for example, the study of hegemonic regimes), they adopt a structural realist perspective. By the same token, to the extent that such theorists attempt to account for the persistence of regimes created during the period of a hegemonic power, they search for alternative explanations for the behavior of regimes.

If regime analysis draws upon the realist tradition, it has equally important intellectual antecedents and links to the literature of systems and integration at the international level. According to Ernst Haas: "Regimes are supposed to help solve problems, but the problem itself is a function of how one manages the system in which something problematical is taking place."[131] Although they are in need of clarification in the regime literature, there exist such concepts and terms (familiar to systems theory) as type of regime structure, equilibrium, causation, adaptation, and learning. How do regimes, like systems, come into existence, adapt to changing environing circumstances, and engage in patterns of growth, preservation, and decline? As in the case of systems theory, such questions are posed in regime literature. Regimes are said to arise as expectations converge on a new focal point that, in turn, furnishes the basis for new institutional arrangements—a process familiar to students of neofunctionalist integration theory, described earlier in this chapter. Deeply embedded in the regime concept, as in systems and integration theory, is the idea of interdependence among the entities constituting the regime. The greater the level and range of interdependence, it has been hypothesized, the more extensive will be the shared interest in cooperation or collaboration, and hence the need to utilize existing regimes or to create new ones. Moreover, international regimes, in keeping with much of integration theory, are likely to enhance the prospects for increasing transnational flows, although the international regime itself may arise from the prior existence of such flows rather than being in itself a determining factor in their creation.

If the international system within which regimes are formed is state-centric, in the realist tradition, the regimes themselves may be said to represent nonstate actors, be they security systems such as NATO and the

Organization of American States, or economic arrangements such as the International Monetary Fund or the European Community. Although such entities are creations of the state system, they exist as actors, or regimes, in themselves. According to Krasner: "Regimes may assume a life of their own, a life independent of the basic causal factors that led to their creation in the first place."[132] Because regimes function as intervening variables, a change in the relative power of states may not always be reflected in outcomes. This is to suggest that once regimes are created, they may themselves alter the distribution of power among the entities that originally formed them—or changes in the power balance may not immediately be reflected in the structure and operation of the regime. Moreover, regimes may contribute to strengthening or weakening the capabilities of their members—for example, by transferring resources from one unit to another. As nonstate actors and entities furnishing a framework for cooperative or collaborative behavior, regimes have attracted the interest of students of integration at the international level. In sum, the regime concept represents an attempted refinement of realist theory but also an effort to address the basis for international collaborative structures and processes of immediate relevance to integration theory.

To what extent, it has been asked, does the concept of regimes represent an extension of the frontier of theory? Or is it simply a reformulation of existing approaches? Does it furnish a long-term contribution to knowledge or instead form a fad that is likely to be cast aside by an emerging generation of scholars, just as its progenitors have rejected certain earlier approaches? According to Susan Strange, regime analysis contains several serious flaws. They are said to include an extensive emphasis on the states and an inadequate appreciation of the dynamic element of change at the international level. Its normative preoccupation is alleged to lie with the basis for order, or for the status quo, rather than with concepts such as justice. There is the criterion, familiar to realist theory as well, that the state-centric model is inadequate for the study of the complex and rapidly changing international system of the late twentieth century—even though the analysis of regimes represents in itself an effort to grapple with such phenomena. The concept of regimes has been faulted as well for its alleged lack of sufficient definitional precision. Regime has been used to describe explicitly agreed arrangements, decision-making procedures, international frameworks based on institutions, forms of cooperation lacking such institutional frameworks, and distributions of power with resulting forms of cooperation or collaboration among states relatively equal in capabilities between hegemonic and lesser powers.[133]

CRITIQUES OF SYSTEMS THEORY

Although systems theory has become one of the major approaches to the study of politics, it has also been the object of major criticism. According to Harold and Margaret Sprout, some systems theorists (of whom they cite

McClelland as an example) "explicitly introduce the 'organismic' concept (reminiscent of Hegelian doctrine) into their discussions of the state and the international system." Although they acknowledge that "most systems theorists would stop far short of claiming that social and biological structures and functions are isomorphic in any but a purely metaphysical sense," the Sprouts question "whether one derives clearer and richer insights into the operations of political organizations by endowing them even metaphorically with pseudobiological structures and pseudopsychological functions."[134] The Sprouts caution against the reification of abstractions.

Another critic, Stanley Hoffmann, contends that systems theory does not provide a framework for achieving predictability. By combining the ideal of a deductive science with the desire to achieve predictability, Hoffmann claims that system theorists become tautological.

> If one builds a model of the behavior of certain groups (for instance, nations) based on a set of hypotheses about the variables which are supposed to determine the behavior of the groups, if, further, some of these hypotheses are highly questionable, and if, finally, the model rests on the assumption that these groups are interchangeable, then the "predictions" about the groups' behavior will be a mere restatement in the future tense of the original hypotheses, and thus comprise a totally arbitrary set of propositions about the groups concerned. Such is the danger of "formal models of imaginary worlds, not generalizations about the real world." It is the triumph of form over substance.[135]

In Hoffmann's critique is the contention that systems theorists use inappropriate techniques borrowed from other disciplines such as sociology, economics, cybernetics, biology, and astronomy. At the same time, Hoffmann faults models that posit specific patterns of interaction, such as those of Kaplan and Modelski, for being deficient in empirical referents.

> The construction of purely abstract hypotheses based on a small number of axioms, from which a number of propositions are deduced, either is a strange form of parlor game, too remote from reality to be "testable," or else rests on postulates about the behavior of the included variables, which are either too arbitrary or too general: the choice is between perversion and platitude.[136]

Hoffmann contends that systems models, because they aim at a high level of generalization and use tools from other disciplines, do not "capture the stuff of politics." The emphasis of many systems models on communications theory reduces individuals and societies to communications systems, to the relative neglect of the substance of the messages that these networks carry. Stated differently, measuring the quantity of transactions, or interactions, without reference to the qualitative dimension is inadequate. What the transactions, or interactions, contain is likely to be as important, and probably more important, than their number. Moreover, the tendency to reduce a theory to as few hypotheses as possible "and to prefer a single hypothesis to a complex one", because such simplicity makes a theory easier to use even though it might imply sheer formalism and the tendency to reduce politics to what it is not, entails a loss of such vital elements as institutions, or the "stuff of politics." However, this is not to conclude that systems theorists necessarily hold that such studies have no place in the field of international relations. For the quantitative study of politics, systems theory has presented problems of operationalization. It is often difficult to develop operational indicators for verifying concepts contained in systems theory, although events data studies have represented an important effort since the 1960s to validate propositions about interaction between and among states, as discussed earlier in this chapter. Moreover, there is disagreement about the extent to which, in the relative absence of empirical studies using hypotheses from systems theory, it is possible to develop criteria of significance in order to judge isomorphic relationships.

Other writers such as Jerone Stephens and George Modelski are critical of systems theory. Stephens calls for research on the requisites that international systems must fulfill and the ranges within which they can be fulfilled without transforming the system. He maintains that international relations scholars must avoid a further proliferation of works that merely advocate systems theory and systems analysis in favor of empirical studies of the requisites of international systems. Stephens writes, "We have had enough heuristic formulations already to last most students of politics a lifetime, and it is now time to ask for results of this heuristic deluge, and if none are forthcoming, to move on to other ways of studying politics."[137] Similarly, George Modelski believes that systems theory has been "devoid of significant insights" in international relations. "System is a concept of high generality and what is true of all systems, while relevant to world politics, is usually not specific enough to add greatly to our appreciation of that narrowly circumscribed field. What is more, for some practitioners of what has come to be known as systems theory, the mere utterance and frequent repetition of the magic term system has become a ritual act of special potency, expected to confer upon the utterer instant admission not only to the circle of the initiated, but also to a sesame of political wisdom." Modelski concludes "that the usefulness of a specific systems approach to international relations may now be approaching its end, despite the fact that the influence expected by it will undoubtedly prove to have been a lasting one."[138] In the same vein, Steven J. Brams has stated: "Verbal formulations abound of the functions systems perform, but notably lacking in most of these systems paradigms is what empirical referents the concepts employed have that would allow propositions linking them to be tested empirically."[139]

Because of its emphasis upon notions of stability, equilibrium, steady-state, and pattern maintenance, systems theory has been criticized for its alleged ideological bias in favor of the status quo, although equilibrium theory does not necessarily connote a bias against change. This criticism has been leveled against structural-functionalism in particular, although in response Robert K. Merton has argued that its proponents could be accused of having a bias in favor of change because of the essentially mechanistic nature of structural-functional analysis and its susceptibility, therefore, to social engineering.[140]

Systemic studies have been faulted for having failed allegedly either to specify or to clarify adequately their epistemological bases. Without such preliminary investigation, writers on systems theory have turned at an early stage of their work to substantive statements about power and stability without having set forth definitions or clearly specified variables. According to Oran Young, such a tendency to dispense with preliminaries "leads to obscurity with regard to conceptual choices" and to ambiguities and confusion within the works of single writers.[141] For example, there is confusion about the distinction between concrete and analytical constructs, the relevance of concepts such as environment, and the use of organismic analogies. There is disagreement among students of systems theory about deductive and inductive studies, quantitative techniques for the manipulation of data, and the relative merits of comparative analyses and historical studies.[142] According to John Weltman, "systems theory has not been applied in any uniform fashion." In this perspective, "The context of the applied (systems) theory ranges from stylistic allusion to a full display of its complex conceptual paraphernalia."[143] Thus the problems of definition, scope, and method that divide proponents of systems theory resemble those that beset the study of international relations and political science. Because of such discord among students of systems theory, its contribution to the methodological and conceptual advances of international relations is uncertain. But undoubtedly systems theory will continue to attract interest until more adequate and promising approaches are found for the development of macrolevel theory.

NOTES

1. Robert J. Lieber, *Theory and World Politics* (Cambridge: Winthrop, 1972), p. 123. See also Oran R. Young, *Systems of Political Science* (Englewood Cliffs, N.J.: Prentice-Hall, 1968), p. 19; Michael Banks, "Systems Analysis and the Study of Regions," *International Studies Quarterly*, 13, No. 4 (December 1969), 345–350.
2. Anatol Rapoport, "Foreword," in Walter Buckley, ed., *Modern Systems Research for the Behavioral Scientists* (Chicago: Aldine, 1968), p. xvii. (Italics added in text.) See also James E. Dougherty, "The Study of the Global System," in James N. Rosenau, Kenneth W. Thompson, and Gavin Boyd, eds., *World Politics: An Introduction* (New York: The Free Press, 1976), pp. 597–623.
3. J. W. Burton, *Systems, States, Diplomacy and Rules* (Cambridge: Cambridge University Press, 1968), p. 6.
4. Ibid., p. 14.
5. See George Modelski, "The Promise of Geocentric Politics," *World Politics*, XXII, No. 4 (July 1970), 633–635. According to Modelski, "The rapidly mount-

ing problems of the earth as a whole no longer are amenable to attack with the ethnocentric conceptual equipment inherited from the nineteenth century. Although this holds true for all the social sciences and although they all need a reorientation in the direction of geocentricity, nowhere is the need more compelling than it is in political science, still basically the science of the state, and in international relations, still under the spell of the conventional diplomatic wisdom of Metternich and Bismarck" (p. 635).

6. J. David Singer, *A General Systems Taxonomy for Political Science* (New York: General Learning Press, 1971), p. 9.

7. Ernst B. Haas, "On Systems and International Regimes," *World Politics,* XXVII, No. 2 (January 1975), 150.

8. Robert O. Keohane and Joseph S. Nye, *Power and Interdependence: World Politics in Transition* (Boston: Little, Brown, 1977), pp. 9–10.

9. Ibid., p. 12.

10. Ibid., p. 13.

11. R. Harrison Wagner, "Economic Interdependence, Bargaining Power, and Political Influence," *International Organization,* 42, No. 3 (Summer 1988), 461. For an extended treatment of the economic dimensions of interdependence, see John Gerard Ruggie, ed., *The Antinomies of Interdependence: National Welfare and the International Division of Labor* (New York: Columbia University Press, 1983).

12. Andrew M. Scott, "The Logic of International Interaction," *International Studies Quarterly,* 21, No. 3 (September 1977).

13. According to Scott, they consist of environmental and resource requisites, system flow requisites (materials, people, energy, technology, information), trained personnel and their services, and control and guidance requisites. Ibid., p. 445.

14. Edward L. Morse, *Modernization and the Transformation of International Relations* (New York: The Free Press, 1976), p. 14.

15. Ibid., p. 130.

16. Hayward R. Alker, Jr., "A Methodology for Design Research on Interdependence Alternatives," *International Organization,* 31, No. 1 (Winter 1977), 31.

17. Richard Rosecrance and Arthur Stein, "Interdependence: Myth or Reality?" *World Politics,* XXVI, No. 1 (October 1973), 2.

18. Ibid., p. 21.

19. Hobbes defines systems as follows: "By systems I understand any numbers of men joined in one interest or one business of which some are regular and some irregular." Thomas Hobbes, *Leviathan,* Introduction by Michael Oakeshott (Oxford: Basil Blackwell, 1946), p. 146.

20. Ludwig von Bertalanffy, "General Systems Theory," in *General Systems,* I (1956), pp. 1–10; reprinted in J. David Singer, ed., *Human Behavior and International Politics: Contributions from the Social-Psychological Sciences* (Chicago: Rand McNally, 1965), p. 21. See also Roy R. Grinker, ed., *Toward a Unified Theory of Human Behavior* (New York: Basic Books, 1956).

21. Anatol Rapoport, op. cit., p. xxi.

22. Bertalanffy, op. cit., p. 21. He has suggested that a "system" implies any arrangement or combination of parts or elements in a whole, which may apply to a cell, a human being, or a society. "General Systems Theory: A New Approach to United of Science," *Human Biology,* XXIII (1951), 302–304.

23. Isomorphism may be defined as "a one-to-one correspondence between objects in different systems which preserves the relationship between the ob-

jects." A. Hall and R. Fagen, "Definition of a System," *General Systems,* I (1956), 18.

24. Ibid., p. 22. (Italics in original.)
25. Peter Nettl, "The Concept of Systems in Political Science," *Political Studies,* 14 (September 1966), 305–338.
26. Jerone Stephens, "An Appraisal of Some System Approaches in the Study of International Systems, " *International Studies Quarterly,* 16, No. 3 (September 1972), 328.
27. See, for example, Andrew M. Scott, *The Functioning of the International System* (New York: Macmillan, 1967), p. 27.
28. James M. Rosenau, "A Pre-Theory Revisited: World Politics in an Era of Cascading Interdependence," *International Studies Quarterly,* Vol. 28, No. 3 (September 1984), 255.
29. Ibid., p. 262.
30. Ibid., p. 264.
31. Ibid., p. 268.
32. Ibid., p. 272.
33. Ibid., p. 281.
34. Kenneth E. Boulding, *The Image: Knowledge in Life and Society* (Ann Arbor: University of Michigan Press, 1956), p. 8; "Political Implications of General Systems Research," *General Systems Yearbook,* VI (1961), 1–7. For a treatment of image theory and international conflict, see Chapter 7, pp. 290–298.
35. Kenneth E. Boulding, *Beyond Economics* (Ann Arbor: University of Michigan Press, 1968), p. 83.
36. Talcott Parsons and Edward A. Shils, eds., *Toward a General Theory of Action* (New York: Harper & Row [Torchbooks]), p. 53.
37. Parsons defines a social system as a "system of interaction of a plurality of actors, in which the action is oriented by rules which are complexes of complementary expectations concerning roles and sanctions. *As a system,* it has determinate internal organization and determinate patterns of structural change. It has, furthermore, as a system, a variety of mechanisms of adaptation to changes in the external environment. These mechanisms function to create one of the important properties of a system, namely, a tendency to maintain boundaries. A total social system which, for practical purposes, may be treated as self-sufficient—which, in other words, contains within approximately the boundaries defined by membership all the functional mechanisms required for its maintenance as a system—is here called a *society.* " (Italics in original.) Parsons and Shils, ibid., pp. 195–196.
38. Talcott Parsons, "An Outline of the Social System," in Talcott Parsons, Edward A. Shils, Kaspar Naegele, and Jesse R. Pitts, eds., *Theories of Society* (New York: The Free Press, 1961), p. 37.
39. Talcott Parsons and J. Edward Shils, *Toward a General Theory of Action,* in Parsons et al., eds., op. cit., p. 107. Parsons defines "process" as "any mode in which a given state of a system or a part of a system changes into another state," *An Outline of the Social System,* op. cit., p. 201.
40. According to Parsons, the traditional focus of political science has been on such concrete phenomena as government and constitutions rather than on conceptual schemes such as system. Classical political theory has consisted primarily of the normative and philosophical problems of government instead of empirical analysis of its processes and determinants. Parsons acknowledges that gov-

ernment, which is "one of the most strategically important processes and foci of differentiated structures within social systems," forms therefore one of the most crucial disciplines of the social sciences. But Parsons calls for a shift in focus of the study of political science from the concrete phenomena of government to a more sharply theoretical and empirical emphasis (ibid., p. 29).

41. Talcott Parsons, "Order and Community in the International Social System," in James N. Rosenau, ed., *International Politics and Foreign Policy* (New York: The Free Press 1961), pp. 120–121. For the implications of Parsons's work for sociological theories of conflict, see Chapter 8, Note 1.

42. Talcott Parsons, *Sociological Theory and Modern Society* (New York: The Free Press, 1967), pp. 467–488.

43. Gabriel Almond, "Introduction," to Gabriel Almond and James S. Coleman, eds., *The Politics of the Developing Areas* (Princeton: Princeton University Press, 1960), p. 7. See also Gabriel A. Almond and G. Bingham Powell, Jr., *Comparative Politics: A Developmental Approach* (Boston: Little, Brown, 1966), especially ch. 2.

44. Karl W. Deutsch, *The Nerves of Government* (New York: The Free Press, 1964), pp. 250–254.

45. David Easton, *A Framework for Political Analysis* (Englewood Cliffs, N.J.: Prentice-Hall, 1965), p. 25.

46. Ibid., p. 50.

47. David Easton, *A Systems Analysis of Political Life* (New York: Wiley, 1965), pp. 284–285, 484–488. See also N. B. Nicholson and P. A. Reynolds, "General Systems, the International System and the Eastonian Analysis," *Political Studies*, XV, No. 1 (1967), 12–31.

48. Herbert J. Spiro, *World Politics: The Global System* (Homewood, Ill.: Dorsey, 1966), p. 51.

49. Ibid.

50. See Robert K. Merton, *Social Theory and Social Structure* (New York: The Free Press, 1957).

51. Marion J. Levy, Jr., "Functional Analysis," *International Encyclopedia of Social Sciences*, VI (New York: Macmillan and The Free Press, 1968), 23.

52. Ibid.

53. Robert K. Merton, op. cit., p. 51. In addition, Merton distinguishes between manifest and latent functions. Manifest are those whose patterns produce consequences that are both intended and recognized by the participants. Latent functions consist of patterns whose results are unintended and unrecognized by participants.

54. John J. Weltman, *Systems Theory in International Relations: A Study in Metaphoric Hypertrophy* (Lexington, Mass.: Lexington Books, 1973), p. 14.

55. See A. James Gregor, "Political Science and the Uses of Functional Analysis," *American Political Science Review*, LXII (June 1968), 434–435. Even though the point is not central to international theory, the student should be aware of the important distinction drawn in recent years by scholars of comparative politics between static or equilibrium models of the system with dynamic or developmental models. See Gabriel A. Almond, "A Developmental Approach to Political Systems," *World Politics*, XVII (January 1965), 182–214.

56. Raymond Tanter, "International Systems and Foreign Policy Approaches: Implications for Conflict Modeling and Management," in Raymond Tanter and Richard A. Ullman, eds. *Theory and Policy in International Relations* (Princeton: Princeton University Press, 1972), p. 8.

57. James Rosenau has defined "linkage" as "any recurrent sequence of behavior that originates in one system and is reacted to in another." "Toward the Study of National-International Linkages," in James N. Rosenau, ed., *Linkage Politics* (New York: The Free Press, 1969), p. 45.

58. Morton A. Kaplan, *System and Process in International Politics* (New York: Wiley, 1962), p. 4.

59. Charles A. McClelland, "System Theory and Human Conflict," in Elton B. McNeil, ed., *The Nature of Human Conflict* (Englewood Cliffs, N.J.: Prentice-Hall, 1965), p. 258.

60. George Modelski, "Agraria and Industria: Two Models of the International System," in Klaus Knorr and Sidney Verba, eds., *The International System: Theoretical Essays* (Princeton: Princeton University Press, 1961), pp. 121–122.

61. Richard N. Rosecrance, *Action and Reaction in World Politics* (Boston: Little, Brown, 1963), pp. 220–221.

62. Hedley Bull, *The Anarchical Society: A Study of Order in World Politics* (New York: Columbia University Press, 1977), p. 13.

63. Ibid., pp. 15–16.

64. Morton A. Kaplan, op. cit., p. xii.

65. Richard Rosecrance, op. cit., p. 267.

66. Charles A. McClelland, "Systems History in International Relations: Some Perspectives for Empirical Research and Theory," *General Systems, Yearbook of the Society for General Systems Research,* III (1958), 221–247.

67. Donald E. Lampert, Lawrence S. Falkowski, and Richard W. Mansbach, "Is There an International System?" *International Studies Quarterly,* 22, No. 1 (March 1978), 146.

68. According to Oran Young, "membership (i.e., concrete) systems are those whose basic components are human beings and that can therefore be thought of as collections of individuals. Analytic systems, on the other hand, are abstractions that focus on selected elements of human behavior. In this context we may distinguish a wide range of types of analytic systems such as political, economic, or religious systems." *Systems of Political Science* (Englewood Cliffs, N.J.: Prentice-Hall, 1968), pp. 37–38. Haas writes: "Systems theories can be divided into deterministic and heuristic constructs. Determinists see the components as relatively unchangeable and arrange them in an eternal pre-programmed dance; the rules of the dance may be unknown to the actors and are specified by the theorist. The recurrent patterns discovered by him constitute a superlogic which predicts the future state of the system. Deterministic systems are 'concrete' in the sense that their designers believe them to be real; such systems are the reality out there. Certainty about them facilitates prescription. Heuristic constructs follow the Durkheim-Weber pattern. They are analytic rather than concrete because they do not profess to represent the real world faithfully and accurately, but select for intensive investigation of certain features deliberately isolated by the theorist as presumptively crucial in explaining a variety of events or trends." Ernst B. Haas, "On Systems and International Regimes," *World Politics,* XXVII, (January 1975), 151–152.

69. See J. David Singer, "The Level-of-Analysis Problem in International Relations," in Klaus Knorr and Sidney Verba, eds., op. cit., pp. 77–92. *See International Studies Quarterly* (special issue on international subsystems), XIII (December 1969).

70. For studies on international subsystems, see Michael Brecher, *The States of Asia: A Political Analysis* (New York: Oxford University Press, 1963), pp.

88–111; Leon N. Linkberg, "The European Community as a Political System," *Journal of Common Market Studies*, V (June 1967), 348–386; Karl Kaiser, "The U.S. and EEC in the Altantic System: The Problem of Theory," ibid., pp. 388–425; Stanley Hoffmann, "Discord in Community: The North Atlantic Area as a Partial International System," in Francis O. Wilcox and H. Field Haviland, Jr., eds., *The Atlantic Community: Progress and Prospects* (New York: Praeger, 1963), pp. 3–31; see *International Studies Quarterly* (special issue on international subsystems), XIII (December 1969).

71. Charles A. McClelland, *Theory and the International System* (New York: Macmillan, 1966), p. 90.

72. Charles A. McClelland, "The Acute International Crisis," in Knorr and Verba, eds., op. cit., p. 194.

73. Charles A. McClelland, "The Anticipation of International Crises: Prospects for Theory and Research," *International Studies Quarterly*, 21, No. 1 (March 1977), 35. Other contributions to this special issue on "International Crisis: Progress and Prospects for Applied Forecasting and Management," Robert A. Young, ed., include Stephen J. Andriole and Robert A. Young, "Toward the Development of an Integrated Crisis Operations," pp. 181–199; and Richard W. Parker, "An Examination of Basic and Applied International Crisis Research," pp. 225–247. For other studies utilizing events data, see Charles A. McClelland and G. D. Hoggards, "Conflict Patterns in the Interactions Among Nations," in J. N. Rosenau, ed., *International Politics and Foreign Policy* (New York: The Free Press, 1969), p. 713. See also Edward Azar, Richard Brody, and Charles A. McClelland, *International Events Interaction: Some Research Considerations* (Beverly Hills, Calif: Sage Professional Papers, 1972); Edward E. Azar, *Probe for Peace: Small-State Hostilities* (Minneapolis: Burgess, 1973), especially pp. 45–72; Charles A. McClelland, "Access to Berlin: The Quantity and Variety of Events, 1948–1963," in J. David Singer, ed., op. cit., pp. 159–186. See also Jonathan Wilkenfeld, ed., *Conflict Behavior and Linkage Politics* (New York: McKay, 1973); Edward Azar, "Analysis of International Events," *Peace Research Reviews*, 4, No. 1 (1970); P. M. Burgess and R. W. Lawton, *Indicators of International Behavior: An Assessment of Events Data Research*, Sage Professional Paper in International Studies, 02–010 (Beverly Hills, Calif. and London: Sage Publications, 1973); Charles W. Kegley, Jr., G. A. Raymond, R. M. Rood, and R. A. Skinner, eds., *International Events and the Comparative Analysis of Foreign Policy* (Columbia: University of South Carolina Press, 1975); and James N. Rosenau, ed., *In Search of Global Patterns* (New York: The Free Press, 1976).

74. The findings of such research conducted between 1961 and 1972 are summarized succinctly by Sophia Peterson, "Research on Research: Events Dates Studies," 1961–1972, in Patrick J. McGowan, ed., *Sage International Yearbook of Foreign Policy Studies*, vol. 3 (Beverly Hills, Calif.: Sage Publications, 1975), pp. 263–309. This volume together with volumes 1 and 2 in the same series, also edited by Patrick McGowan, contains numerous other chapters reporting on research using events data.

75. Richard Rosecrance lists past international systems as follows: (1) Eighteenth Century, 1740–1789; (2) Revolutionary Imperium, 1789–1814; (3) Concert of Europe, 1814–1822; (4) Truncated Concert; 1822–1848; (5) Shattered Concert, 1848–1871; (6) Bismarckian Concert, 1871–1890; (7) Imperialist Nationalism, 1890–1918; (8) Totalitarian Militarism, 1918–1945; (9) Postwar, 1945–1960.

76. Richard Rosecrance, op. cit., pp. 280–296.

77. Ibid., p. 304.

78. W. Ross Ashby, *Design for a Brain* (New York: Wiley, 1952). Kaplan makes this assertion in "Systems Theory," in James C. Charlesworth, ed., *Contemporary Political Analysis* (New York: The Free Press, 1967), p. 150.

79. According to Kaplan, "The conception that underlies System and Process is fairly simple. If the number, type, and behavior of nations differ over time, and if their military capabilities, their economic assets, and their information also vary over time, then there is some likely interconnection between these elements such that different structural and behavioral systems can be discerned to operate at different periods of history. This conception may turn out to be incorrect, but it does not seem an unreasonable basis for an investigation of the subject matter. To conduct such an investigation requires systematic hypotheses concerning the nature of the connections of the variables. Only after these are made can past history be examined in a way that illuminates the hypotheses. Otherwise the investigator has no criteria on the basis of which he can pick and choose from among the infinite reservoir of facts available to him. These initial hypotheses indicate the areas of facts which have the greatest importance for this type of investigation; presumably if the hypotheses are wrong, this will become reasonably evident in the course of attempting to use them." Morton A. Kaplan, "The New Great Debate: Traditionalism vs. Science in International Relations," *World Politics,* XX (October 1967), 8.

80. According to Kaplan, "The models are not equilibrium models in the Parsonian sense. Thus they are not static but respond to change, when it is within specified limits, by maintaining or restoring system equilibrium. Equilibrium does not have an explanatory function within such systems. Rather it is the equilibrium that is to be explained; and the model itself constitutes the explanation by indicating the mechanisms that restore or maintain equilibrium." Morton A. Kaplan, "The Systems Approach to International Politics," in Morton A. Kaplan, ed., *New Approaches to International Relations* (New York: St. Martin's, 1968), p. 388.

81. See Donald L. Reinken, "Computer Explorations of the 'Balance of Power': A Progress Report," in Morton A. Kaplan, ed., *New Approaches to International Relations,* pp. 459–481.

82. Hsi-Sheng Chi, "The Chinese Warlord System as an International System," ibid., p. 449.

83. Winfried Franke, "The Italian City-State System as an International System," ibid., p. 449.

84. Patrick J. McGowan and Robert M. Rood, "Alliance Behavior in Balance of Power Systems: Applying a Poisson Model to Nineteenth Century Europe," *American Political Science Review,* LXIX, No. 3 (September 1975), 862. The authors note that Poisson sampling, as utilized in their study, "consists of observing the process over a predetermined amount of time, length, or other dimensions, and counting the number of events which occur." Quoted from Howard Raiffa and Robert Schlaifer, *Applied Statistical Decision Theory* (Cambridge: M.I.T. Press, 1961), p. 283.

85. Ibid., p. 861.

86. Ibid., p. 869.

87. Karl W. Deutsch and J. David Singer, "Multipolar Power Systems and International Stability," *World Politics,* XVI (April 1964), 390. For an earlier theoreti-

cal analysis of multipolarity and international stability, see Arthur Lee Burns, "From Balance to Deterrence: A Theoretical Analysis," *World Politics,* IX (July 1957), 494–529. Burns examines several propositions, including the following: The closer the alliance between any two or more powers, the greater the increase of opposition or "pressure" (other things being equal) between any one of the two and any third power or group powers: other things being equal, considerations of long-run security determine an optimum degree of short-run security; any system embodying the balance of power has some intrinsic tendency to increase that number; a deterrent state or system will emerge from a power-balancing system whenever the development of military technology makes (1) the physical destruction of all of an opponent's forces impossible and (2) the physical destruction of the economy very easy.

88. Karl Deutsch and J. David Singer, op. cit., p. 392.

89. Ibid., p. 400.

90. Stanley Hoffmann, "Weighing the Balance of Power," *Foreign Affairs,* 50 (July 1972), 618–643.

91. Ronald Yalem, "Tripolarity and the International System," *ORBIS* (Winter 1972), 1055.

92. International wars (in which at least one participant on each side is an independent and sovereign member of the international system) with total battle-connected deaths of more than 1000 were included in the data. To "operationalize" the dependent variable, the duration and magnitude of each war were measured by "the nation-months-of-war measure; the sum of the months which all nations individually experienced as participants in the war." Furthermore, a distinction was made between major and minor powers, and their wars and nation-months were calculated separately. To operationalize and quantify this independent variable, namely, "the extent to which alliance commitments reduced the interaction opportunities," two dimensions were considered: (1) the nature of the obligation (whether it was a defense pact, neutrality pact, or entente); and (2) the nature of the signatories' power status (whether it was between two major, two minor, or one major and one minor power). After the alliances were discovered and classified, the data on each type of alliance for each year were converted into a percentage figure as follows: (1) percent of all in any alliance; (2) percent of all in defense pact; (3) percent of majors in any alliance; (4) percent of majors in defense pact; and (5) percent of majors in any alliance with minor. J. David Singer and Melvin Small, "Alliance Aggregation and the Onset of War," in J. David Singer, ed., *Quantitative International Politics* (New York: The Free Press, 1968), pp. 246–286.

93. Ibid., p. 283.

94. Ibid., p. 284.

95. Brian Healy and Arthur Stein, "The Balance of Power in International History: Theory and Reality," *The Journal of Conflict Resolution,* XVII, No. 1 (March 1973), 57.

96. Kenneth N. Waltz, "International Structure, National Force, and the Balance of World Power," *Journal of International Affairs,* XXI, No. 2 (1967), 220.

97. Ibid., p. 223.

98. Ibid., p. 230.

99. Richard N. Rosecrance, "Bipolarity, Multipolarity, and the Future," *Journal of Conflict Resolution,* X (September 1966), 318.

100. Ibid., p. 319.
101. Ibid., p. 322. Another study, whose focus is the relationship between polarity and armed conflict, concludes in similar vein: Based on the research contained in this volume, it may well be that the best prospects for stability in the emerging international order reside in a continuation of "power bipolarity," and "cluster multipolarity," not unlike Rosecrance's bimultipolarity whose political expression was the Nixon Doctrine itself. Alan Ned Sabrosky, "Beyond Bipolarity: The Potential for War," in Alan Ned Sabrosky, ed., *Polarity and War: The Changing Structure of International Conflict* (Boulder, Colo., and London: Westview Press, 1985), p. 217.
102. Oran R. Young, "Political Discontinuities in the International System," *World Politics,* XX (April 1968), 369.
103. Ibid., p. 370.
104. Ibid.
105. Donald E. Lampert, Lawrence S. Falkowski, and Richard W. Mansbach, "Is There an International System?" *International Studies Quarterly,* 22, No. 1 (March 1978), 150.
106. Michael Banks, "Systems Analysis and the Study of Regions," *International Studies Quarterly,* 13, No. 4 (December 1969), 357. Other early efforts to study regional subsystems include Mario Barrera and Ernst B. Haas, "The Operationalization of Some Variables Related to Regional Integration," *International Organization,* 23, No. 1 (Winter 1969), 150–160; Joseph S. Nye, Jr., ed., *International Regionalism Readings* (Boston: Little, Brown, 1968); Stanley Hoffmann, "Discord in Community: The North Atlantic Area as a Partial International System," *International Organization,* 17, No. 3 (Summer 1963), 521–549; Michael Brecher, "International Relations and Asian Studies: The Subordinate State System of Southern Asia," *World Politics,* 15, No. 2 (January 1963), 213–235; Larry W. Bowman, "The Subordinate State System of Southern Africa," *International Studies Quarterly,* 12, No. 3 (September 1968), 231–261; Michael Brecher, "The Middle East Subordinate System and Its Impact on Israel's Foreign Policy," *International Studies Quarterly,* 13, No. 2 (June 1969), 117–139; see *International Studies Quarterly,* 13, No. 4 (December 1969), Special Issue on International Subsystems, prepared by Peter Berton, especially articles by John H. Sigler, "News Flow in the North African International Subsystem"; Thomas W. Robinson, "Systems Theory and the Communist System"; Donald C. Hellmann, "The Emergence of an East Asian International Subsystem"; Leonard Binder, "The Middle East as a Subordinate International System," *World Politics,* X (1958), 408–429. See also Michael Banks, "Systems Analysis and the Study of Regions," *International Studies Quarterly,* 13 (1969), 335–360; Karl Kaiser, "The Interaction of Regional Subsystems: Some Preliminary Notes on Recurrent Patterns and the Role of Superpowers," *World Politics,* XXI (1968), 84–107; and Kathryn D. Baols, "The Concept 'Subordinate International System': A Critique," in Richard A. Falk and Saul H. Mendlovitz, eds., *Regional Politics and World Order* (San Francisco: Freeman, 1973).
107. Louis J. Cantori and Steven L. Spiegel, *The International Politics of Regions: A Comparative Approach* (Englewood Cliffs, N.J.: Prentice-Hall, 1970), p. 607.
108. Ibid., pp. 7–20.

109. William R. Thompson, "The Regional Subsystem: A Conceptual Explication and a Propositional Inventory," *International Studies Quarterly,* 17, No. 1 (March 1973), 93. This article contains an extensive list of propositions about regional subsystem behavior drawn from the literature of the past generation.

110. Ibid., p. 96.

111. Ibid., p. 101.

112. William R. Thompson, "Introduction: World System Analysis With and Without the Hyphen," in William R. Thompson, ed., *Contending Approaches to World System Analysis* (Beverly Hills, Calif.: Sage Publications, 1983), p. 9.

113. Ibid.

114. Immanuel Wallerstein, *The Modern World-System: Capitalist Agriculture and the Origins of the European World Economy in the Sixteenth Century* (New York: Academic Press, 1974); *The Modern World-System II: Mercantilism and the Consolidation of the European World-Economy, 1600–1750* (New York: Academic Press, 1980).

115. George Modelski, "Long Cycles of World Leadership," in William R. Thompson, ed., op. cit., p. 115.

116. Ibid., p. 131.

117. John Gerard Ruggie, "International Responses to Technology: Concepts and Trends," *International Organization,* Vol. 29, No. 3 (Summer 1975), p. 570.

118. Stephen D. Krasner, "Structural Causes and Regime Consequences: Regimes as Intervening Variables," in Stephen D. Krasner, ed., *International Regimes* (Ithaca and London: Cornell University Press, 1985), p. 1.

119. Donald L. Puchala and Raymond F. Hopkins, "International Regimes: Lessons from Inductive Analysis," ibid., p. 64.

120. Ibid., p. 2.

121. Oran R. Young, "International Regimes: Problems of Concept Formation," *World Politics,* Vol. XXXII, No. 3 (April 1980), 332–333.

122. Ernst B. Haas, "Words Can Hurt You; or, Who Said What to Whom About Regimes," in Stephen D. Krasner, ed., op. cit., p. 27.

123. Oran R. Young, "Regime Dynamics: The Rise and Fall of International Regimes," in Stephen D. Krasner, ed., op. cit., p. 100.

124. Oran R. Young, "International Regimes: Problems of Concept Formation," *World Politics,* Vol. XXXII, No. 3 (April 1980), 349–350.

125. Robert O. Keohane, *After Hegemony: Cooperation and Discord in the World Economy* (Princeton, N.J.: Princeton University Press, 1984), p. 32.

126. Ibid., p. 49.

127. Ibid., p. 50.

128. Ibid., p. 64.

129. Oran R. Young, op. cit., p. 348.

130. Robert O. Keohane, op. cit., p. 109.

131. Ernst B. Haas, op. cit., p. 30.

132. Stephen D. Krasner, op. cit., p. 357.

133. Susan Strange, "Cave! Hic Dragones: A Critique of Regime Analysis," in Stephen D. Krasner, ed., op. cit., pp. 337–354.

134. Harold and Margaret Sprout, *The Ecological Perspective on Human Affairs with Special Reference to International Politics* (Princeton: Princeton University Press, 1965), p. 208; Harold and Margaret Sprout, *An Ecological Paradigm for the Study of International Politics,* Research Monograph No.

30, Center of International Studies (Princeton: Princeton University Press, 1968), pp. 2–10.

135. Stanley Hoffmann, "Theory as a Set of Questions," in Stanley Hoffmann, ed., *Contemporary Theory in International Relations,* p. 44. The quotation in this excerpt is from Ralph Dahrendorf, "Out of Utopia: Toward a Reorientation of Sociological Analysis," *American Journal of Sociology,* LXIX (September 1958), 120.

136. Stanley Hoffmann, "International Relations: The Long Road to Theory," in James N. Rosenau, ed., *International Politics and Foreign Policy* (New York: The Free Press, 1961), p. 426.

137. Jerone Stephens, "An Appraisal of Some System Approaches in the Study of International Systems," *International Studies Quarterly,* 16, No. 3 (September 1972), 348.

138. George Modelski, "The Promise of Geocentric Politics," *World Politics,* 22, No. 4 (July 1970), 631; *Principles of World Politics* (New York: The Free Press, 1972), p. 8.

139. Steven J. Brams, "The Search for Structural Order in the International System: Some Models and Preliminary Results," *International Studies Quarterly,* 13, No. 3 (September 1969), 278.

140. See Robert K. Merton, *Social Theory and Social Structure,* pp. 37–42.

141. Oran B. Young, *A Systemic Approach to International Politics,* Research Monograph No. 33, Center of International Studies (Princeton: Princeton University Press, 1968), p. 1.

142. Ibid., pp. 2–3.

143. John J. Weltman, *Systems Theory in International Relations: A Study in Metaphoric Hypertrophy,* op. cit., p. 311.

Chapter
5

The Older Theories
of Conflict

PREREQUISITES OF A GENERAL THEORY OF CONFLICT

All theorists of international relations recognize the problem of war as a central one. The stability of the international system is usually defined in terms of its proximity to or remoteness from the occurrence or likelihood of large-scale war. Scholarly works probing the causes of war continue to be published.[1] Prior to the Great War of 1914, writes Michael Howard, historians were interested in the causes of specific wars but devoted little attention to the quest for the causes of war in general. War as a recurring phenomenon was taken for granted. In Howard's view, the causes of war have not changed fundamentally throughout the centuries. Just as Thucydides had written that the causes of the Peloponnesian War were "the growth of Athenian power and the fear this caused in Sparta," so were some of the principal causes of the Great War the growth of Germany's power and the fear this aroused in Britain. War, according to Howard, does not happen by accident nor does it arise out of subconscious, emotional forces, but rather from a "superabundance of analytic rationality."[2] The fears of those who take the decision for war may be rational or irrational, or both in combination. If fear is a basic cause of war, then we are forced to conclude that war is the product of irrational as well as rational factors, and that an understanding of its causes—as well as of ways to prevent, control, limit, regulate, and terminate it—would seem to require a comprehensive approach to the problem. Whether war as an institutionalized form of state behavior can ever be totally abolished from the international system is a larger question that cannot be answered until we understand the causes of war.

Unfortunately, we still do not know what those causes are, or if we do know them, we are far from being in agreement about them. No single general theory of conflict and war exists that is acceptable to social scientists in their respective disciplines, or to authorities in other fields from which social scientists borrow insights. If a comprehensive theory is ever to be developed, it will probably require inputs from biology, psychology, social psychology, anthropology, history, political science, economics, geography, theories of communications, organization, games, decision-making, military strategy, functional integration, and systems, as well as philosophy, theology, and religion. Such a vast synthesis of human knowledge may be impossible to achieve. Merely to contemplate the need for it, however, serves to warn us against what Alfred North Whitehead called "the fallacy of the single factor." We cannot identify any single cause of conflict or war; the causes are not only multiple but they have kept multiplying throughout history.

The term *conflict* usually refers to a condition in which one identifiable group of human beings (whether tribal, ethnic, linguistic, cultural, religious, socioeconomic, political, or other) is engaged in conscious opposition to one or more other identifiable human groups because these groups are pursuing what are or appear to be incompatible goals. Lewis A. Coser defines conflict as a "struggle over values and claims to scarce status, power, and resources in which the aims of the opponents are to neutralize, injure, or eliminate their rivals."[3] Conflict is an interaction involving humans; it does not include the struggle of individuals against their physical environment. Conflict implies more than mere competition. People may compete with each other for something that is in shortage without being fully aware of their competitors' existence, or without seeking to prevent the competitors from achieving their objectives. Competition shades off into conflict when the parties try to enhance their own position by reducing that of others, try to thwart others from gaining their own ends, and try to put their competitors "out of business" or even to destroy them. Conflict may be violent or nonviolent (i.e., in terms of physical force), dominant or recessive, controllable or uncontrollable, resolvable or insoluble under various sets of circumstances. Conflict is distinct from "tensions" insofar as tensions usually imply latent hostility, fear, suspicion, the perceived divergence of interests, and perhaps the desire to dominate or gain revenge; however, tensions do not necessarily extend beyond attitudes and perceptions to encompass actual overt opposition and mutual efforts to thwart one another. They often precede and always accompany the outbreak of conflict, but they are not the same as conflict, and are not always incompatible with cooperation. The "causes" of tension, however, are probably closely related to the "causes" of conflict. Moreover, if tensions become powerful enough, they themselves may become contributory or preliminary "causes" of the occurrence of conflict insofar as they affect the decision-making process.

What Coser provides above is a sociological definition. He is interested in conflict between groups. Other analysts insist that the term must embrace not only intergroup but interpersonal and intrapersonal phenomena. Society would not have to be concerned about conflict within the individual if it were not for the plausible assumption that there is a significant relationship between conflicts within the inner structure of the individual and conflicts in the external social order. No theory of conflict can ignore this relationship. The internal and the external can never be completely separated. Neither can the one ever be reduced completely to the other and derived solely from it. Psychological states alone cannot explain social behavior, and social conditions alone cannot explain individual behavior.

Conflict is a universally ubiquitous and permanently recurring phenomenon within and between societies. It is not necessarily continuous or uniformly intense. Many societies experience periods of relative peace, both internal and external. Quite probably, however, a certain amount of low-level, muted, almost invisible conflict goes on constantly in all societies, even those apparently most peaceful. (Individual criminal behavior is certainly considered a form of violent conflict.) Conflict, as we said above, need not issue in violent behavior—it may be carried on by subtle political, economic, psychological, and social means. Politics itself is a process for resolving conflict. Whether or not large-scale, organized international warfare can ever be eliminated from human affairs—as were the institutions of slavery and human sacrifice, also considered natural at one time—remains a subject for debate.

Perhaps the most that can be realistically hoped for at the present time is that the most destructive forms of organized international violence (such as nuclear war and conventional wars that might escalate to the level of nuclear war) can be deterred indefinitely as a result of intelligent policies of mutual restraint on the part of governments until effective methods of international arms limitation emerge. But it is too much to expect that all social conflict can ever be abolished, or even that political violence at all levels can be permanently ruled out. H. L. Nieburg has argued that violence is a natural form of political behavior; that the threat of inflicting pain by resorting to violence will always be a useful means of political bargaining within domestic and international society; and that the threat of resorting to force demonstrates the seriousness with which the dissatisfied party sets forth its demands against the satisfied, the establishment, the defender of the status quo in order to confront the latter starkly with the alternatives of making adjustments or risking dangerous escalation of violence.[4] Many social scientists, including several identified with the peace movement, recognized that total elimination of conflict from the human situation is not only impossible but undesirable, because conflict in some forms is a condition of social change and progress.[5]

MICRO- AND MACROTHEORIES OF CONFLICT

Most social sciences can be roughly divided into two groups, depending upon whether they adopt the "micro" or the "macro" approach to the study of the human universe. Do we seek the origins of conflict in the nature of human beings or in their institutions? Generally speaking, psychologists, social psychologists, biologists, games theorists, and decision-making theorists take as their point of departure the behavior of individuals, and from this they draw inferences to the behavior of the species. Moreover, sociologists, anthropologists, geographers, organization and communication theorists, political scientists, international relations analysts, and systems theorists typically examine conflict at the level of groups, collectivities, social institutions, social classes, large political movements, religious or ethnic entities, nation-states, coalitions, and cultural systems. Some scholars—economists, for example—might divide their efforts between the macro- and microdimensions. One historian might prefer to study the clash of nation-states, while another might prefer to concentrate on the unique factors in the personality, background, and crisis behavior of an individual statesman that prompted the statesman to opt for war or peace in a specific set of circumstances.

Historically, the intellectual chasm between the macro- and the microperspectives of human conflict was nowhere better illustrated than in the earlier polarity of psychology and sociology. The former analyzed conflict from a knowledge of the individual, the latter from a knowledge of collective behavior. Psychologists tended to approach human problems as arising from the inner psychic structure of the individual, whence they assumed that complexes, tensions, and other disorders were projected into the external social situation. Conversely, sociologists were disposed to conduct their analysis of all human problems at the level of social structures and institutions, and to trace the effects of disorders at that level back to the psychic life of individuals. The sharpness of the cleavage as it was perceived around the turn of the century is reflected in Emile Durkheim's statement that "every time that a social phenomenon is directly explained as a psychic phenomenon, one may be sure that the explanation is false."[6] The long-standing antipathy of Freudian analysis toward the Marxian dialectic (so severe that for several decades Freudian psychology was completely taboo in the Soviet Union) provides a well-known if somewhat extreme example of the divergent perspectives of the two fields.[7]

In the twentieth century, especially in the past two decades, the distance between the two fields has narrowed. Psychologists have recognized the importance in shaping the individual's psychic life of institutions, groups, and the total cultural environment. For their part, sociologists have paid increasing attention to the role of psychic factors in social processes. Social psychologists, in particular, have sought to bridge the gap between the two parent disciplines. While it would be going too far to conclude that the gap has yet been fully bridged, increasing numbers of social scientists are becoming convinced that it is impossible to construct an adequate theory of conflict without fusing the macro- and the microdimensions into a coherent whole.[8] In recent years, as Michael Haas has noted, social scientists, armed with statistical methods and aided by computers, have begun for the first time to study international conflict systematically and to accumulate a definitive body of scientific knowledge about the subject. But theory on international conflict, he concludes, remains at a primitive level partly because "most empirical researchers have been bulldozing exhibitionistically without attempting to put the subject in order analytically."[9]

INTERPERSONAL CONFLICT AND INTERNATIONAL CONFLICT

Social psychologists are more hesitant today than were their predecessors two or three decades ago to extrapolate the explanations of complex social behavior, particularly at the level of international relations, from their knowledge of individual psychic behavior. In the past, some psychologists who were concerned with the problem of conflict assumed too readily that the explanation of group aggression is a mere corollary of the explanation of individual aggression. They took the Platonic notion that the state is the individual "writ large" and converted this into a pseudoscientific analogy under which society came to be uncritically regarded as the psychological organism "writ large." Social psychologists are now much less confident in this respect. Stephen Withey and Daniel Katz have warned against the attempt to "explain the functioning of social systems by a simple reduction of a macroscopic process."[10] Herbert C. Kelman has also pointed out that many earlier writings on war and peace by psychologists and psychiatrists were not germane to the interactions of nation-states. Kelman holds that the earlier writers tended to overemphasize individual aggressive impulses. These writers took it for granted that the behavior of states is merely the aggregate of individual behaviors, ignoring the fact that individuals differ widely in their roles, interests, and ability to influence final decisions. The behavior of such a large collectivity as a nation, according to Kelman, cannot be considered a direct reflection of the motives and personal feelings of either its citizens or its leaders.

Only by analyzing international relations, not by automatically applying psychological findings about the individual, can we identify those points at which such application is relevant. Kelman defines war as a societal and intersocietal action conducted within a national and international political context. Of crucial importance in the study of international relations is the process by which nations develop their national policies and decide upon war. In part, such an explanation includes the motivations and perceptions of individuals as policymakers and relevant publics playing various roles as part of a larger society. But Kelman cautions that psychological analysis is useful to the study of aggressive behavior in an international context only if we know where and how such individuals fit into the larger political and social framework of the nation and the international system, as well as the constraints under which they operate.[11]

Most specialists in the fields of political science and international relations would heartily endorse Kelman's conclusion. Psychological factors alone might go a long way toward explaining instances of anomic violence (i.e., apparently spontaneous and irrational outbursts by either a crowd or an individual), but even in these cases social scientists are now more wary of the "fallacy of the single factor." At more complex levels of politicized conflict, where violence reflects to a much greater degree planning, organization, management, and even institutionalization, the need for circumspection in explaining phenomena by reference to purely psychological factors becomes commensurately greater.

CONFLICT AND SOCIAL INTEGRATION

Social scientists are divided on the question of whether social conflict should be regarded as something rational, constructive, and socially functional or something irrational, pathological, and socially dysfunctional. Most Western psychologists and social psychologists seem to regard all violent forms of individual, group, and politicized aggression as irrational departures from normal, desirable behavior. By way of contrast, most sociologists and anthropologists in Europe and America (with the notable exception of the Parsonian school, which, like a majority of psychologists, stresses the importance of compromise and adjustment) have been willing to attribute a constructive purpose to conflict, insofar as it helps to establish group boundaries, strengthens group consciousness and sense of self-identity, and contributes toward social integration, community-building and socioeconomic change in a progressive direction.[12] Marx, of course, who was more sociologist than economist, placed the greatest emphasis on class conflict and the final conflict between the proletariat and the bourgeoisie as the forceps that is supposed to give birth to a just social order. Many social scientists tend to divide on the issue, some regarding violent conflict as irrational, while others judge it "good" or "bad" depending upon the context in which it arises; the political, economic or social values at stake; the costs incurred in comparison with anticipated gains; and the net outcome for the group, the nation, or the international system.

VARIETIES OF CONFLICT   Historicism

Several salient questions occur at the outset of our inquiry. Should we study the phenomenon of conflict in terms of conscious motivations? Do people really fight about what they say they are fighting about? Or must we go beyond stated reasons, regard them with suspicion as mere self-rationalizations, and try to penetrate to the "real"—that is, unconscious, murky, and sordid impulses that drive people to aggressive behavior? Is this a false dichotomy? If we look carefully, we shall see that microscientists are more inclined to probe beneath the surface into the unconscious, the innate, the "instinctive" (to use an obsolete term), whereas macroscientists are somewhat more willing to lend credence to conscious motivations, for these motivations pertain to thought, language, and communications patterns, which, in contrast to internal psychic forces, are products of society. Given that the human being is a symbolic animal, words are crucial links between the unconscious and the conscious, between micro and macro.

International war is one form of social conflict—undoubtedly the most important single form in terms of its potential consequences for the individual in the nuclear age. But there are many other forms of social conflict: civil war, revolution, coup, guerrilla insurgency, political assassination, sabotage, terrorism, seizure of hostages, prison riots, strikes and strikebreaking, sit-ins, threats, displays of force, economic sanctions and reprisals, psychological warfare, propaganda, tavern brawls, labor-management disputes, flare-ups at collegiate or professional sports events, divorce contests and legal wrangling over the custody of children, intrafamily fights, and felonious crimes.

A crucial question that arises frequently in the social sciences regardless of the phenomenon under investigation is whether we are dealing with the one or the many. Can we understand war as a separate conflict phenomenon in isolation, or must we study it as one highly organized manifestation, at a specific social-structural level, of a general phenomenon? Social scientists are far from agreement as to whether human conflict can be satisfactorily explained as a continuum in which violent outbursts differ only by such accidents as the nature of the parties, the size, the duration, the intensity, the nature of the issues and the objectives sought, the processes and modes of conflict, and the weapons employed, but not in their underlying "causes"; or whether human conflict is an indefinite series of discrete phenomena, each of which, despite a superficial external resemblance to the others, requires its own unique theoretical explanation.

In sum, social scientists have yet to come forth with a generally accepted taxonomy for classifying and arranging coherently the various types of conflict. What we cannot satisfactorily classify, we cannot accurately count, measure, correlate, or organize into a general pattern.

THE OLDER THEORIES OF WAR AND ITS CAUSES

There exists a considerable body of literature pertaining to the older theories of war and its causes. Most of these theories we would now call "prescientific," even though some of them were based upon "empirical evidence" drawn from history and human experience. Several of the ear-

lier theories contain perceptive insights that continue to merit our attention as part of our cultural heritage. They enable us to see how the problem of war was looked upon in other historical epochs, and why it was not
always regarded as the greatest of evils; they reflect conscious motivations
for and rationalizations of war, which at the level of human decision-
making can be "causal"; they provide philosophical, religious, political,
and psychological arguments for and against war, both in general and in
specific circumstances.

In virtually all the ancient religious-ethical civilizations, the problem
of war was approached not only as one of political-military strategy, but
also as one of spiritual and moral dimensions. It was assumed that human
beings enjoyed freedom of choice, that they were responsible for their
decisions in a moral universe of rational causality created by God, and that
the causes of war lay deep in the wills of individuals whose motives were
good or bad.

In ancient China, the theories ranged from Mo-Ti's doctrine of universal love, with which the waging of war was deemed incompatible, to the
view of realists (including the authors of *The Book of Lord Shang*), who
in a more Machiavellian vein stressed the strategic approach to power,
foreign policy, and war.[13] A similarly broad spectrum of views is to be
found in ancient India, but it is worth noting that the Buddhist doctrine
of *ahimsa* (harmlessness toward all living things), famous in modern times
as one of the sources from which Gandhi derived the creed of nonviolent
resistance, was not originally taken to forbid the waging of war.[14]

In Islam, the Prophet Muhammad preached the holy war (*jihad*) as a
sacred duty and a guarantee of salvation, and for several centuries Moslem
theorists assumed that the world was divided into the *dar al-Islam* (the
peaceful abode of the true believers and those who submitted to their
tolerant rule) and the *dar al-harb* (the territory of war).

Inasmuch as Islam was an universalist system of belief, the two territories were always theoretically at war with each other, since war was the
ultimate device for incorporating recalcitrant peoples into the peaceful
territory of Islam. The *jihad,* therefore, was more a crusade than the
bellum justum ("just war"), familiar to medieval Christian writers. The
concept of the *jihad* as a permanent state of war against the non-Moslem
world had become almost obsolete in modern times, at least prior to the
emergence of Muammar Qhaddhafi in Libya, Ayatollah Khomeini in Iran,
and various radical fundamentalist groups (e.g., the Muslim Brotherhood)
and militant terrorists (e.g., *Jihad*) who call for a holy war against enemies
of Islam. Several modern writers have stressed that the term refers not
only to international war, but also to the spiritual struggle for perfection
within the heart of individuals.[15] Mahatma Gandhi declared that he was
able to perceive the origins of the doctrine of nonviolence and love for all
living things not only in the sacred Hindu and Buddhist writings and the
Bible, but also in the Koran.[16]

The predominant historical attitudes toward war that are found in

Western culture are a product of several different sources, including the Judeo-Christian religious tradition, Greek philosophy, Roman legalism, European feudalism, Enlightenment pacifism, and modern scientism, humanitarianism, and other ideologies. The ancient Jewish scriptures reflect the paradox of human yearning for a peaceful existence amidst the constant recurrence of war. Surrounded by hostile peoples, the Israelites relied heavily upon a combination of religious prophetism and military organization for nation-building, defense, and territorial expansion. In the earlier history of the Jews, Yahweh often appeared as a warrior-god. Joshua, Gideon, Saul, and David fought wars for His honor and glory, to demonstrate His power as well as His special relationship to the chosen people. Once the Promised Land had been won from the Canaanites, and Kings took over from Judges, the wars of Israel and Judah became less ferocious, and themes of love, justice, and peace became more prominent in the Jewish scriptures.[17]

War and Christianity

The early Christians were divided in their attitude toward the use of military force by the state. During the first three centuries of the Church's history, when Christianity was regarded an an alien and subversive creed within the Roman Empire, there was a strong tendency toward pacifism, especially among the intellectuals, many of whom believed that the Christian both as private person and as a citizen should respond to injury by turning the other cheek, regardless of the consequences for the state. Pacifism, however, did not become the orthodox Christian doctrine. The dominant view among the Fathers of the Church was that political authority was divinely instituted for the benefit of the individual, and that when force was used justly it was a good, not an evil. People are enjoined to turn the other cheek when their own rights are violated, because they seek a salvation beyond history, but the state, which must safeguard the temporal social good here and now, may have to resort to force at times. Saint Ambrose and Saint Augustine, writing after Christians in the West had begun to assume responsibility for the social order, "baptized" the ancient Roman doctrine of the "just war" as a "sad necessity in the eyes of men of principle."[18]

Scholastic philosophers in the Middle Ages considerably refined the "just war" doctrine. The decision to initiate violent hostilities could not be taken by a private individual, but only by public authority. Rulers were enjoined against resorting to war unless they were morally certain that their cause was just (*jus ad bellum*), that is, that their juridical rights had been violated by a neighboring ruler. Even then, they were exhorted to exhaust all peaceful means of settling the dispute before initiating the use of force, and this usually meant arbitration. Furthermore, there had to be a reasonable prospect that the resort to force would be more productive of good than of evil and would restore the order of justice. The war had to be waged throughout with a right moral intention, and had to be conducted by means that were not intrinsically immoral (*jus in bello*), for what begins as a just war could become unjust in its prosecution. These were the common teachings of such medieval writers as Antoninus of Florence and St. Thomas Aquinas. Emphasis was placed on what would later be called the principles of proportionality and discrimination. Under the first, the suffering and destruction caused by the war should not be disproportionate to the cause justifying resort to war; under the second, "innocent" populations were considered "immune" as targets of military action.[19]

Throughout the Middle Ages, the Church attempted to impose ethical controls upon the conduct of war by specifying times when fighting could not be carried on, sites where battle was prohibited, types of weapons that could not legitimately be employed, and classes of persons that were either exempted from the obligation of military service or protected against military action. This effort to "soften" the cruelty of warfare was by no means new in Western culture. The ancient Greeks and Romans had been familiar with such agreed rules of war as those forbidding wanton destruction of populations, the burning of cities, and the severance of water supplies. Many circumstances of medieval European culture, including the common values of Christendom, the nature of feudalism, prevailing economic conditions, the Teutonic tradition of the chivalric warrior, and the crude state of the military sciences, actually reinforced the moral efforts of the Church to mitigate the harshness of warfare during the medieval period.[20]

In the period of transition from medieval to modern Europe, three outstanding exceptions to the dominant theory and practice of morally limited warfare can be identified. These were invariably expressions of ideological conflict that ran counter to the distinctive tendencies of medieval culture: (1) the Crusades of the twelfth and thirteenth centuries, fought against an alien and infidel civilization; (2) the wars of the fourteenth and fifteenth centuries, especially between the French and English, in which the forces of national feeling made themselves felt for the first time on a large scale; and (3) the religious wars that followed the Reformation. In all of these cases, war ceased to be a rational instrument of monarchical policy for the defense of juridical rights. The concept of war as a small-scale affair of skirmish and maneuver lost its primacy when large numbers of nonprofessional (i.e., nonchivalric) warriors, both volunteers and mercenaries, became enmeshed with cultural, national, or religious antipathies. When a cherished set of values or a way of life was thought to hinge upon the outcome of an encounter, war became an all-consuming psychological and moral experience. Hence the battles of Antioch, Crécy, Poitiers, Agincourt, and Magdeburg were bitter and bloody in the extreme. In the Thirty Years' War between Catholics and Protestants (1618–1648), the population of Germany was reduced from 21 to 13 million.[21]

The Philosophical Theories of the Nation-State Period

During the classical period of the balance of power that was ushered in by the Peace of Westphalia in 1648, the concept of limited war regained currency in Europe. At the beginning of the modern nation-state period in the sixteenth and seventeenth centuries, the traditional Western doctrine of the "just war" was reaffirmed by scholastic theologians and philosophers, such as Victoria and Suarez, as well as by the earliest systematic expounders of international law—Grotius, Ayala, Vattel, Gentilis, and others. For these writers, the just war emerged as a substitute juridical proceeding—a sort of lawsuit in defense of the legal rights of the state, prosecuted by force in the absence of an effective international judicial superior capable of vindicating the order of justice. Virtually all the classical European writers on international war insisted upon the necessity of sparing the lives of the innocent in war. The slaying of the guiltless could never be directly intended; at best, it was permitted as incidental to the legitimate operations of a just war.[22]

In the latter half of the seventeenth century, after the violence of the religious wars had subsided, the pendulum swung back again toward more moderate forms of warfare. From then on through most of the eighteenth century, the Age of Reason, wars were less ideological and more instrumental in the traditional sense. Armies were larger, but also better organized, supplied, disciplined, and trained, officered largely by aristocrats who tried, not very successfully, to imbue lower-class ranks with the ideals of the old chivalric code. Professor John U. Nef suggests a number of factors that influenced the trend toward greater restraint: a growing distaste for violence; a raising of the comfort level among the European bourgeoisie; the refinement of manners, customs, and laws by an aristocracy that now admired gentility, agility, and subtlety more than prowess in battle; the pursuit of commerce; and the growth of the fine arts, combined with zealous efforts to apply reason to social affairs. All these factors, Nef concludes, helped to weaken the will for organized fighting.[23]

Down to the time of the French Revolution, the nations of Europe were not willing to pursue objectives that required inflicting a great deal of destruction upon the enemy. This period witnessed the emergence of economic motivations for conflict, but, although it is true that colonial and commercial rivalries were added to dynastic feuds as causes of international disputes, the rise of the bourgeoisie helped buttress pacifist rather than militarist sentiments, for the bourgeoisie desired more than anything else an orderly international community in which conditions of trade would be predictable. The very fact that the leading commercial nations of Western Europe were also developing naval power helped to soften the effects of warfare in the eighteenth century insofar as naval forces could carry on hostile engagements without directly involving land populations. Such land warfare as did take place was usually characterized by adroit maneuver, surprise, march and countermarch, and rapier thrusts at the enemy's supply lines, as exemplified in the campaigns of Turenne, Saxe, and Marlborough. War, in the century of "drawing room culture," was not entirely unrelated to the game of chess or the minuet. The prevailing sense of restraint probably led to a slowdown in the innovation rate of military technology. Encounters between armies in the field were often looked upon as mere adjuncts to the diplomatic process, designed to strengthen or weaken the bargaining positions of envoys during prolonged negotiations.

THE ORIGINS OF MODERN PACIFISM

Meanwhile, the post-Renaissance and Enlightenment periods had witnessed the rise in Europe of a school of pacifist thought that rejected the medieval moral-legal doctrine of war. The pacifist writers—Erasmus, More, Comenius, Crucé, Fenelon, Penn, Voltaire, Rousseau, and Bentham—took their stand either on Stoic and early Christian radical positions or on the newer European ideals of cosmopolitanism, humanitarianism, and bourgeois internationalism. Practically all of them exhibited a pronounced skepticism in their attitudes toward war and the military profession. It was particularly fashionable to compare unfavorably the destructive life of the soldier with the useful life of the merchant. The abolition of force from international politics came to be looked upon as the noblest objective of statesmen. The quest for human happiness unmarred by any trace of the tragic became for European intellectuals the great goal of life.[24]

The philosophers were not agreed among themselves as to whether happiness was to be achieved through the application of scientific and technical reason or through people's return to nature and rediscovery of their original simplicity. But rationalists and romantics alike were convinced that society was about to break the shackles of traditional authority and superstition; dispel the historic curses of ignorance, disease, and war; and embark—in the vision of Condorcet—upon the absolutely indefinite perfectibility of humanity, which knows no limit other than the duration of the globe upon which nature has placed us.[25] "The people, being more enlightened," wrote Condorcet, "will learn by degrees to regard war as the most dreadful of all calamities, the most terrible of all crimes."[26] The era was marked by a bitter cynicism concerning the concept of the "just war," which was regarded as mere propaganda calculated to cloak the aggressive urges of ambitious kings. No one at the time denounced the stupidity and incongruities of war with more scathing sarcasm than Voltaire, who poked fun at the two kings, each of whom had *Te Deums* sung in his own camp after the battle.[27] There was an anticipation, reflected in the writings of Montesquieu and others, that the transition from monarchical to republican institutions would be accompanied by a shift from the spirit of war and aggrandizement to that of peace and moderation. The period abounded in projects for abolishing war and establishing perpetual peace.[28]

The hopes of the Enlightenment writers proved ill-founded at the end of the eighteenth century. Liberal nationalist ideology was born in France during the Revolution and its Napoleonic aftermath, eventually sparking nationalist reactions elsewhere in Europe. The French introduced the *levée en masse,* the citizen conscript army—the "nation at arms," backed by all the organizable resources of a newly industrializing society. Thus France became the prototype of economic regimentation, large-scale factory production for war, and the mobilization of popular opinion in support of national expansionist policies. The charismatic "Little Corsican" was virtually the first to wage "total war" in modern times. For a while, his powerful army was unconquerable. Military casualties reached unprecedented proportions.[29]

Napoleon, however, had left the European balance of power in a shambles. The conservative reaction of 1815 and thereafter, masterminded by Metternich and Talleyrand and based on the principle of a return to monarchical legitimacy, restored the classical idea of the balance of power—a Newtonian notion of an international universe in equilibrium—to a central place in the thinking of European statesmen.[30] This restoration helped to limit war and, with the exception of the Franco-Prussian War, minimize the harsh effects of a developing military technology for a hundred years. Standing armies were reduced in size everywhere outside of Russia and Prussia. In Western Europe the conviction grew that science, industry, communications technology, the growth of liberal parliamentary institutions, education, and international trade were all combining to make war obsolete and perhaps impossible. The era of the "Concert of Powers," of which the Pax Britannica was an important feature, was marked by astute diplomacy and short wars rather than by lengthy, destructive engagements between military forces. Bismarck, the most canny manipulator of war as an adjunct of his diplomacy toward Denmark, Austria, and France in his efforts to unify Germany under Prussia's leadership, preferred to wield "an iron fist in a velvet glove."[31] Throughout the nineteenth century, Europe experienced no conflict as bloody as the American Civil War, which was in several respects a prototype of modern "total war" in which powerful political and ideological motivations pitted the industrial technology of emerging capitalist liberalism against the traditional values of an agrarian, slave-holding aristocracy.[32]

Appearances in Europe, however, were somewhat deceptive. Despite the return to limited war, fought for limited political objectives (e.g., the unification of Germany), the latter decades of the nineteenth century witnessed the spread of universal conscription in Europe, the mass production of new automatic weapons, armaments races, the creation of alliances, increasing colonial and commercial rivalries among the powers, and the growth of a popular press that could be converted into a powerful instrument for stirring belligerent sentiments. The rise of modern war industry had an ambiguous significance. On the one hand, it served to make war more frightful and more unprofitable, and hence less readily undertaken. On the other hand, it served to make it much more likely that war, when it did come, would be total in nature, absorbing all available energies. The closely packed battle, in which mass is multiplied by velocity, became a dominant feature in modern European military thought.[33] Emphasis was placed upon means of rapid mobilization—the telegraph for ordering up reserves, the railroad for transporting troops and equipment to the front, and steamships for getting them to the colonial territories of Asia and Africa. The speed of mobilization was so critical that the decision to mobilize became tantamount to a declaration of war by 1914.[34]

Pacifist Theories

Throughout the nineteenth century, the pacifist movement slowly extended its influence in England and the United States. Jonathan Dymond, an English Quaker, argued that war, like the slave trade, would begin to disappear when people would refuse to acquiesce in it any longer and begin to question its necessity. Dymond denied that the patriotic warrior celebrated in song and story for having laid down his life for his country deserves such praise. The officer, he said, enters the army in order to obtain an income, the private because he prefers a life of idleness to industry. Both fight because it is their business, or because their reputation is at stake, or because they are compelled to do so. Dymond anticipated the contentions of the socialists and the later exponents of the "devil theory of war" by insinuating that the industrialists who profit from war combine forces with the professional military for the purpose of promoting war. He declared that the Christian scriptures require the individual to refrain from violence under all circumstances. All distinctions between just and unjust war, between defensive and aggressive war he dismissed as being in vain. War must be either absolutely forbidden or else permitted to run its unlimited course.[35] Dymond is one of the early voices of that modern movement of uncompromising pacifism that seeks not only to give religious advice to the conscience of the individual, but also to exert an influence upon the policy of states—or at least those states in which the climate of opinion is sufficiently liberal to permit the propagation of the pacifist doctrine.

The aversion of modern intellectual pacifists to war cannot be explained purely in terms of religious and humanitarian factors. Since the nineteenth century, economic considerations, either liberal or socialist in their foundation, have entered into the thinking of most pacifists on the subject of war and peace. From Richard Cobden's era in the mid-nineteenth century down to very recent times, many liberal pacifists have been convinced that there exists an intrinsic and mutually causal relationship between free trade and peace, and that the abolition of trade barriers is the only means of effecting permanent peace. To a certain extent, the heirs of this intellectual tradition in the contemporary era are the interdependence theorists.

Sir Norman Angell and War as an Anachronism

The liberal view that war represents the greatest threat to the economic health of modern industrial civilization reached its culmination in the writings of Norman Angell, an English publicist who achieved prominence in the 1920s and 1930s and whose work formed part of the utopian phase of international relations described in Chapter 1. Shortly before World War I, Angell argued that warfare in the industrial age had become an unprofitable anachronism. The economic futility of military power, he declared, had been amply demonstrated by recent history, which showed that even when victory in war seems at first glance to bring with it substantial economic gains, such appearances are misleading and illusory. Nearly everyone thought that the Germans had reaped an advantage from the huge indemnity that France was forced to pay after being defeated in the Franco-Prussian War of 1870 to 1871, but, Angell argued, the indemnity actually induced an inflation that hurt the German economy. No nation, he went on to say, can genuinely improve its economic position either through war or through those imperialistic operations that involve costly preparations for military defense. Angell was convinced that "the factors which really do constitute prosperity have not the remotest connection with military or naval power, all our political jargon notwithstanding."[36]

In the final analysis, Angell was a rationalist who believed that war could be eliminated through the growth and progressive application of human reason to international affairs. The modern technical state could no longer expect to profit from waging war, but could only anticipate the disintegration of its own society. Once people become convinced that war has lost its meaning except as a form of mutual suicide, thought Angell, disarmament and peace would be possible. He was confident that peace was primarily a matter of educating the publics of democratic societies, and he chose to couch his homilies in terms of the economic self-interest of an interdependent European community, rather than in terms of traditional religious morality. But he had no doubt that once human beings fully realized the irrelevance of military force for the attainment, promotion, and preservation of prosperity or socioeconomic well-being, then political wars would cease as religious wars did in the West a long time ago. It is worth noting the parallel between the thought of Norman Angell with Herbert Spencer in the nineteenth century and George Liska in the middle of the twentieth, all of whom held that industrial nations are bound to eschew war.[37] Moreover, most contemporary strategic theorists (to be surveyed in Chapter 9), who come from a great diversity of perspectives, have concluded that nuclear war makes no sense, that no gain could be worth its cost, that it is unwinnable, and that nuclear weapons can have no use except a deterrent one. Deterrence theorists, it might be said, think that Angell's theory could not be demonstrably validated until after the advent of nuclear weapons on a large scale, producing a balance of terror.

BELLICIST THEORIES

Modern Western theories of conflict and war, including those of utopian pacifism, cannot be understood without some reference to the appearance, following the French Revolution, of a militarist school of thought within the West. Bellicism, as this school might be called, developed at least partly in conscious reaction to idealistic pacifism. Perhaps it would be more accurate to say that the two tendencies in Western thought fed upon each other as polar opposites. Western culture has never lacked thinkers who stressed conflict and tension over cooperation and harmony in social reality.

Most Western theorists of military strategy from the period of the French Revolution until the latter 1950s (when the emphasis shifted from conventional and nuclear strategies to the study of guerrilla warfare and counterinsurgency) showed a distinct preference for direct over indirect strategies, for the bludgeoning attack of the massed army over the graceful rapier thrust, for the frontal assault and the quick decision over the more patient strategy of maneuver, encirclement, attrition, and negotiation. The concept of total war has often been traced to the writings of Karl von Clausewitz, who at times expressed quite vividly the idea of war as an act of force pushed to its utmost bounds, as he did in the following passage:

> Now philanthropic souls might easily imagine that there was an artistic way of disarming or overthrowing our adversary without too much bloodshed and that this was what the art of war should seek to achieve. However agreeable this may sound, it is a false idea which must be demolished. . . . He who uses this force ruthlessly, shrinking from no amount of bloodshed, must gain an advantage if his adversary does not do the same. Thereby he forces his adversary's hand, and thus each pushes the other to extremities to which the only limitation is the strength of resistance on the other side. . . . Never in the philosophy of war can we introduce a modifying principle without committing an absurdity. . . . So we repeat our statement: War is an act of force, and to the application of that force there is no limit.[38]

Yet according to an eminent twentieth-century strategist of limited war and opponent of total war thinking, Sir Basil H. Liddell Hart, Clausewitz has often been misinterpreted. As a student of Immanuel Kant, Clausewitz appreciated the difference between the ideal and the real, between the tendency of thought for the sake of clarity to carry an idea to an extreme, abstract form and the significant modifications that practical reality imposes upon the abstraction. Clausewitz spoke of "absolute war" as a logical extreme to which military combat can be carried within the mind—a context in which each side strives for perfection of effort to break the other's will to resist—but he also recognized that there is no such thing in the real world, where war should be and is an instrument of state policy, "a continuation of politics by other means." Thus, war is always subordinate to and limited by politics. Human beings always fall short of absolute efforts; they can never devote all of their resources to war because there is a continuing demand that many other needs be met. The aims for which a war is undertaken and the means used to wage it are to be controlled by a political intelligence. Echoing the ancient Chinese strategist Sun Tzu, the Prussian theorist suggested that the decisive battle need not always be fought. Especially when the two warring sides are relatively equal in capabilities, they may wish to avoid a mutually destructive war of attrition, more costly than any political objective to be gained would be worth. Clausewitz was willing to contemplate limited war not for any moral or humanitarian reasons in the sense of the medieval "just war" doctrine, but rather for reasons concerning the interests of the state.[39]

Other philosophers of the nineteenth century—Hegel, Nietzsche, Treitschke, and Bernhardi—seemed at times to exalt power and war as ends in themselves. Hegel, for whom reality was the dialectical clash of ideas, regarded the nation-state as the concretization of the absolute in history, "the march of God in the world." On the subject of war, he has perhaps been misunderstood. He did not glorify war and its brutality, but since he valued the nation so highly he accepted war as a phenomenon that could contribute to national unity. Hegel left himself open either to misunderstanding or to justifiable criticism when he said that through war "the ethical health of nations is maintained . . . just as the motion of the winds keeps the sea from the foulness which a constant calm would produce."[40]

The harshest nineteenth-century critic of the values that underlay not only the Western Christian civilization of his day but even those of pure original Christianity was Friedrich Nietzsche. Emphasizing as he did the "will-to-power" as the basic determinant of human behavior, Nietzsche looked upon the Christian ethos, marked by self-denial, resignation, humility, respect for weakness, and the renunciation of power, as the foe of the truly creative impulses in a person—a religion of failure that inhibits the full development of "Superman."[41] Even more than for Hegel, war for Nietzsche plays an indispensable role in the renewal of civilizations. In the following passage, published in 1878, the German philosopher seemed to adumbrate in a very stark way the theory of the "moral equivalent of war" that William James would express more optimistically in 1912:

> For the present, we know of no other means whereby the rough energy of the camp, the deep impersonal hatred, the cold-bloodedness of murder with a good conscience, the general order of the system in the destruction of the

enemy, the proud indifference to great losses, to one's own existence and that of one's friends, the hollow earthlike convulsion of the soul, can be as forcibly and certainly communicated to enervated nations as is done by every great war. . . . Culture can by no means dispense with passions, vices and malignities. When the Romans, after having become Imperial, had grown rather tired of war, they attempted to gain new strength by gladiatorial combats and Christian persecutions. The English of today, who appear on the whole to have also renounced war, adopt other means in order to generate anew those vanishing forces; namely, the dangerous exploring expeditions, sea voyages, and mountaineerings, nominally undertaken for scientific purposes, but in reality to bring home surplus strength from adventures and dangers of all kinds. Many other such substitutes for war will be discovered, but perhaps precisely thereby it will become more and more obvious that such a highly cultivated and therefore necessarily enfeebled humanity as that of modern Europe not only needs wars, but the greatest and most terrible wars—consequently occasional relapse into barbarism—lest, by the means of culture, it should lose its culture and its very existence.[42]

Lesser minds than Nietzsche's followed in his tracks. The German historian Treitschke, who spoke for the Prussian military caste, drew his inspiration from such figures as Machiavelli and Bismarck. Convinced that the independent sovereign nation-state is the highest political achievement of which the individual is capable, he rejected as intolerable the concept of a genuine universal political community. War is frequently the only means available to the state to protect its independence, and thus the ability and readiness to wage war must be preserved in a carefully honed condition. The state ought to be oversensitive in matters of national honor, so that the instinct of political self-preservation can be developed to the highest possible degree. Whenever the flag is insulted, there must be an immediate demand for full satisfaction, and if this is not forthcoming, "war must follow, however small the occasion may seem."[43] There is nothing reprehensible in this, for in Treitschke's eyes war itself was majestic and sublime.[44]

The ideas voiced by Clausewitz, Hegel, Nietzsche, and Treitschke were echoed by several philosophers of military history in Europe and in the United States. General Friedrich von Bernhardi, strongly influenced by the Darwinian concept of "survival of the fittest" (which he understood only superficially), correlated war with human progress, holding that "those intellectual and moral factors which insure superiority in war are also those which render possible a general progressive development [among nations]."[45] The geopolitical writings of Kjellen and Ratzel, as well as the twentieth-century German students of geopolitics represented by Haushofer, were indebted intellectually to Darwinian concepts. (See Chapter 2, in which the geopolitical theories are discussed.)

Alfred Thayer Mahan also saw history as a Darwinian struggle in which fitness is measured in terms of military strength. The habits of military discipline, he thought, are necessary underpinnings of an orderly civilian structure. He viewed the nations of the world as economic corporations locked in a fierce survival competition for resources and markets. Unlike the Marxists, however, he attributed this not merely to the impulses of competition, but rather to human nature and the fact that the supply of economic goods is finite. Contradictions of national self-interest, along with wide and irreducible discrepancies of power, opportunity, and determination, produce the conditions of permanent conflict and render it unrealistic to expect violence to be eliminated from international affairs. Mahan deemed futile all efforts to substitute law for force, since all law depends upon force for its efficacy. Finally, Mahan defended the institution of war against the accusation that it was immoral and un-Christian. He argued that war is the means whereby nation-states carry out the mandates of their citizens' consciences. A state should go to war only when it is convinced of rightfulness, but once it has committed its conscience, there is no choice but war (not even arbitration), for "the material evils of war are less than the moral evil of compliance with wrong."[46] (Mahan's views on the geopolitics of maritime power were treated in Chapter 2.)

BELLICISTS AND ANTIDEMOCRATIC THEORISTS

As the nineteenth century gave way to the twentieth, the intellectual polarization of Western pacifists and bellicists became complete. The bellicists and their doctrines may be classified as follows.

1. Realistic positivism, represented by such turn-of-the-century Italian writers as Vilfredo Pareto (1848–1923) and Gaetano Mosca (1858–1941). Pareto, an economist and sociologist, and Mosca, a political scientist, both expounded the concepts of rule by the elite, the importance of coercive instruments in the maintenance of social unity and order, and the inevitable recurrence of revolution. Mosca was not as antihumanitarian and antidemocratic as Pareto, but he shared Pareto's prejudice against pacifism, fearing that if war should be eliminated nations would grow soft and disintegrate.[47]

2. Social Darwinists and nationalists with proclivities toward social Darwinism, such as the sociologists William Graham Sumner and Ernst Haeckel and the jurist Oliver Wendell Holmes.[48]

3. Certain pessimistic philosophers of history, including Oswald Spengler (1880–1936) and Bendetto Croce (1866–1952). Spengler, a German historian, was particularly fascinated by the will-to-power, the virility of barbarians, the subjugation of weaker peoples, and the law of the jungle, while he suffered from a special dread of a worldwide revolution of the nonwhite people against the whites.[49] Croce, an Italian philosopher and statesman, although a critic of the excesses of militarism, regarded war as a necessary tragedy of the human condition, indispensable to human progress, and the dream of perpetual peace as fatuous.

4. The forerunners and cryptorepresentatives of racist theory and/or fascism, as well as the actual archetypes of those ideologies. Writers in these categories included Houston Stewart Chamberlain, Arthur de Gobineau, Giovanni Gentile, Alfredo Rocco, Georges Sorel, Gabriel d'Annunzio, and Benito Mussolini.[50]

It would be unfair to insinuate that all the foregoing schools of thought should be linked with the fascists, or even that all fascists were or are racists, but all exalted, in varying degrees, the role of force and virile action in social processes. The individuals mentioned above are more appropriately treated in works on political theory or intellectual (and anti-intellectual) history, but serious students of international relations cannot afford to ignore the impact these writers had on the thinking of their time, nor should they overlook the influential role of conscious ideas and persisting attitudes in decision-making and social conflict.

ANARCHISM AND THE MARXIST SOCIALISTS

Finally, there were the anarchists and the Marxian socialists. These two movements of an extremist nature, antithetical in many respects, produced contrary offshoots, some theoretical and some practical. Both movements helped dialectically to strengthen the theory of pacifism and the practice of politicized violence as an instrument either of abolishing the state or of promoting class revolution as a prelude to establishing a cooperative or a socialist order. The Marxist-socialist theory of imperialism and war will be examined in the next chapter. Here, a brief word about anarchism is in order, because it is often misunderstood by the public at large and because it constitutes a more significant tendency of the contemporary mind, especially the minds of Western youth and anti-Western "liberationists," than is generally recognized.

Anarchism is the doctrine that opposes established political authority in all its forms. Anarchists view life as a moral drama in which the individual is arrayed against the state and all the oppressive instruments of coercion that they associate with government—bureaucracies, courts, police, and the military, as well as the institutions of private property and religion. They seek liberation from these and all forms of external constraint upon human freedom. Firmly convinced of humanity's innate goodness and reasonableness, a benign anarchist who follows Kropotkin believes that the basic law of society is not conflict but mutual aid and cooperation. The anarchist, according to Irving Louis Horowitz, in addition to being antipolitical is also antitechnological and antieconomic.[51] Thus anarchists are essentially foes of capitalist and socialist alike: If the former keeps government merely to protect their bourgeois interests and manage their affairs, the latter would replace capitalist tyranny with socialist tyranny—the "dictatorship of the proletariat."

Some branches of anarchism—notably collectivist, communist, syndicalist, and conspiratorial—openly espoused the use of violence both in theory and as a tactical necessity. Sergei Nechaev (1847–1882), a disciple of the Russian revolutionary agitator Mikhail Bakunin (1814–1876), adopted a creed of "propaganda by deed" and "universal pan destruction." He advocated the nihilistic tactic of assassination for its effects of psychological terror and the demolition of existing institutions.[52] Enrico Malatesta (1850–1932), an Italian journalist, regarded well-planned violence as an apt means of educating the working classes as to the meaning of the revolutionary struggle.[53] Similarly, the French journalist Georges Sorel (1847–1922) perceived value in proletarian acts of violence that serve to delineate the separation of classes. Such violence, he maintained, helps to develop the consciousness of the working class and keeps the middle class in a chronic state of fear, always ready to capitulate to the demands made upon it rather than run the risk of defending its position by resorting to force.[54]

Not all anarchists have been advocates of violence. Individualist anarchists in America, such as Henry David Thoreau (1817–1862) and Benjamin R. Tucker (1854–1939), eschewed violence as unrespectable. They preferred to emphasize nonviolent civil disobedience. The two most influential pacifist anarchists of modern times—Mahatma Gandhi (1869–1948) and Leo Tolstoi (1828–1910)—radically opposed a pure religious ethic to a person's willingness to submit to the state, which they excoriated for brutalizing the masses and converting military heroism into a virtue. Deeming it imperative that the law of force be superseded by the law of love, yet finding this impossible within the framework of the existing nation-state system, they insisted that the latter must give way to a universal society.[55]

Anarchism has sometimes been quite trenchant in its moral criticism of existing institutions, but it has not made a significant contribution toward a scientific understanding of the sources of human conflict. Where one finds in anarchist writings a keen insight into group sociology (e.g., in Sorel's awareness of the group-integrating function of externally directed violence), this usually reflects borrowing from more dispassionate social scientists (e.g., Sorel was strongly influenced by Durkheim). In recent decades, the chief appeal of anarchist theories in the United States, which have a long history in this country, has been to intellectuals, artists, black militants, students, youth, and others identified with the "counterculture," and, especially in the late 1960s, the protest against the Vietnam War. On the international plane, anarchist thought has been reflected in an increasing incidence of terroristic acts of hijacking, bombings, guerrilla raids, kidnappings, assassinations, the taking of hostages, and other violent deeds designed nihilistically to transform society by delivering random, indiscriminate blows regardless of the guilt or innocence of those targeted, thus producing widespread insecurity and senseless shocks that shake society to its foundations. "Propaganda by deed" remains the preferred strategy of nihilists who, like Verloc in Joseph Conrad's novel, *The Secret*

Agent, ask what response can be made "to an act of destructive ferocity so absurd as to be incomprehensible, inexplicable, almost unthinkable; in fact, mad? Madness alone is truly terrifying, inasmuch as you cannot placate it either by threats, persuasion, or bribes."[56]

THE "JUST WAR" THEORY IN THE NUCLEAR AGE

Considerable attention was devoted earlier in this chapter to the "just war" doctrine as a set of normative constraints limiting the way a state may act in pursuit of its "necessities" (survival, independence, the preservation of its common good, and the defense of its rights). Debate over the ethics of warfare has been revived with great vigor in the twentieth century, particularly since the advent of nuclear weapons.

Several writers have argued that in view of the destructive power of modern military technology, especially nuclear weapons, the conditions of the "just war"—specifically, the requirement that the amount of force employed must be proportionate to the political objectives sought—can no longer be validated. According to the "nuclear pacifist" school, even though it may have been theoretically possible to justify the use of force by states in earlier historical periods, nuclear war is potentially fraught with such monstrous consequences that it cannot be deemed politically or morally justifiable under any circumstances. Moreover, the fact that political leaders in all states and at all times have invoked the justice of their cause when they went to war, combined with the fact that history furnishes scant evidence of religious leaders in any nation questioning or denying the justice of their government's policies during wartime, has contributed to a growing skepticism toward the "just war" theory even in respect to nonnuclear war. Finally, the inhumanity of modern warfare has prompted increasing numbers of theologians and ethicists to ask whether waging war can ever be made compatible with the imperatives of the Christian conscience.[57]

Typical contemporary pacifists are appalled by what they regard as the stupidity, futility, or immorality of nuclear war. They allege that such conflict threatens not only mutual extinction for the nations engaging in a large-scale nuclear exchange, but also grave dangers of widespread radioactive fallout and genetic mutations for the rest of humanity. The pacifist is usually skeptical of all theories of nuclear deterrence and of the decision-makers' presumed rationality, on which deterrence is supposed to be based. Pacifists abhor the international competition in armaments (or "arms race"), which in their view, even if it does not lead inevitably to war, supposedly piles up an "overkill" capability, produces an international climate of neurotic fear, wastes vast amounts of economic and scientific-technological resources that could otherwise be channeled into other uses, and generally dehumanizes individuals, stifling their impulse to love others. Some writers, after contemplating the tragic situation into which the nations have drifted, advocate unilateral disarmament and nonviolent resistance as the only ways of breaking through the vicious circle. Erich Fromm, Mulford Q. Sibley, and Gordon Zahn have seen nonviolent resistance less as a form of helpless passivity than as a psychic or spiritual "soul" force capable of effecting a significant attitude change or "conversion" on the part of the aggressor.[58]

Even in the nuclear age with all its potential horrors, the mode of rational analysis embodied in the "just war" tradition has not lacked advocates. Without denying that the theory has often been abused in history, its modern proponents generally take the position that past distortions, while they should make us wary of the self-rationalizing tendency of nations, do not warrant our discarding an intellectual type of ethical analysis that seeks to chart a middle course between the extremes of pacifism and bellicism. Theorists in this group have included John Courtney Murray, Paul Ramsey, Robert E. Osgood, Richard A. Falk, William V. O'Brien, Michael Walzer, and others.[59]

The "just war" writers are convinced that, no matter how far efforts in this area may fall short of an ideal model of moral action, it is still better for people to engage in this kind of evaluation than to try to achieve a sense of inner purification by washing their hands of advanced weapons technology and military strategy, thereby allowing them to develop according to their own dialectic. That nuclear power exists is a fundamental fact of contemporary political reality that cannot be conjured away by pious rhetoric or wishful thinking. This massive power, wrote the Jesuit theologian John Courtney Murray in 1959, demands a master strategic concept based upon a high sense of moral and political direction.

> This sense of direction cannot be found in technology; of itself, technology tends toward the exploitation of scientific possibilities simply because they are possibilities. . . . It is the function of morality to command the use of power, to forbid it, to limit it; or, more in general, to define the ends for which power may or must be used and to judge the circumstances of its use.[60]

The general consensus of the "just war" writers can be summed up in the following propositions.

1. In the absence of effective international peacekeeping institutions, the moral right of states to resort to war under certain circumstances cannot be denied. Within the "self-help" international system, which is admittedly deficient but nevertheless real, it is probable that states will continue to feel constrained to resort to the use of military force. An ethical doctrine to govern and limit war, therefore, remains essential.

2. Although aggressive war (which was permitted under the traditional doctrine to punish offenses and to restore justice) is no longer considered a lawful means available to states for the vindication of violated rights, there still exists the right to wage defensive war against aggression and to give aid to another party who is a victim of aggression.[61]

3. Modern military technology cannot be allowed to render entirely meaningless the traditional distinction between "combatant forces" and "innocents" even in strategic war. (This issue arose in the somewhat inconclusive strategic debate during the 1960s over "counterforce" versus "countercity" or "countervalue" strategies, during the 1970s over "selective targeting" and "limited nuclear options," and during the 1980s over the morality of nuclear deterrence strategy and "warfighting" doctrines.)

4. The "just war" theorist denies that in war the end justifies the means and that once a war starts a government may employ any and every instrument at its disposal in an unlimited quest for victory. Even when the state has the moral right to wage war (*ius ad bellum*), there is an obligation to adhere to the law governing the means used in war (*ius in bello*).[62]

5. Although there is reason to hope that deterrence will succeed and nuclear war will not occur, the "just war" writers insist that a posture of massive deterrence through the threat of massive retaliation against urban centers is not sufficient. There is a heavy moral obligation upon political leaders to assure an operational readiness, in case deterrence fails, to wage war (including nuclear war) in a limited and discriminating rather than an all-out manner. Ramsey argues that "traditional and acceptable moral teachings concerning legitimate military targets require the avoidance of civilian damage as much as possible even while accepting this as in some measure an unavoidable indirect effect."[63]

6. Thus, the "just war" theorists insist, nuclear weapons cannot be held intrinsically evil (*malum in se*). According to Ramsey, their strictly controlled use against primarily military targets, under conditions calculated to avoid escalation to uncontrollable levels, is morally conceivable, especially where this seems necessary to contain aggression quickly and bring about early negotiations. But he contends that their indiscriminate use against whole cities cannot be morally justified—not even in retaliation.[64]

The debate over war and morality will go on indefinitely. Pacifists of various persuasions, absolutist or relativist, will argue that it is either logically absurd or ethically monstrous to analyze warfare in terms of "rationality" or "justice." Other theorists will contend that in a global system that lacks an effective global peacekeeping authority—that is, an international force organized in support of international justice—independent national governments and other political entities are likely to be disposed from time to time to resort to the use of force, and that the world will be better off if those who advise governments—regardless of whether they are pacifists or "just war" theorists—can have recourse to an intellectually credible code of rational, moral, civilized behavior that enjoins decision-makers, in an age of intrinsically inhumane technological possibilities, to observe humane limits in their strategizing. Despite frequent assertions that the "just war" doctrine has become obsolete in a nuclear era of unlimited destructive capability, there have been numerous instances of limited conventional and unconventional warfare, as well as of efforts to develop new systems of advanced weapons technology, to which the traditional analysis of the conditions required for the moral justification of deterrence and force remains quite relevant and—what is more—is still applied with remarkable frequency in the public political debate.[65] Much of the intellectual controversy over U.S. military involvement in Vietnam was carried on within the framework of the traditional conditions required for a just war. Moreover, writers on the religious left who sought during the 1970s to develop theologies of liberation and revolution appropriated some of the elements of the just-war doctrine, even while shifting the presumption of justice away from incumbent governments (attempting to maintain internal peace and order) to insurgent revolutionary groups (attempting to overthrow incumbent governments that they deemed oppressive).[66]

Perhaps no student of the "just war" has dealt more intricately with the paradox confronted by strategists and moralists in the nuclear age than Michael Walzer. The human mind seems unable to devise a coherent conceptual framework—political policy, strategic doctrine, and operational military plan—that neatly combines effective deterrence with workable defense, and that is widely acceptable on grounds of rationality, credibility, and morality. Walzer reminds us that superpower governments are deterred from risking even conventional war, not to mention limited nuclear war, by the specter of ultimate horror—the danger that it might escalate to an uncontrollable nuclear exchange. In an era of plentiful nuclear stockpiles, he says, any imaginable strategy is likely to deter a "central war" between the giants. Once we understood what the strategists of deterrence were saying, it became unnecessary to adopt any particular strategy for fighting a nuclear war.[67] (Many strategic theorists, of course, would deny this.) It was deemed sufficient merely to pose the ultimate nuclear threat. Deterrence is frightening in principle when we stop to ponder the ultimate, but in actuality deterrence is easy to live with because it has been a bloodless strategy. It causes no pain or injury to its hostages, unless they stop to think it through, which not many people do. Walzer puts distance between himself and most "just war" theorists when he propounds the view that all nuclear war is immoral.[68]

In the era of nuclear deterrence, the debate among ethicists has shifted subtly from one involving the morality or immorality of war and strategic policy to one that pits the immorality of large-scale nuclear war against the probability that nuclear war will occur and spin out of control. Virtually all moral theologians and philosophers have long agreed that, if nuclear deterrence should break down, carrying out the strategy of assured destruction (which is described in Chapter 9) would constitute a moral evil of historically unprecedented magnitude. Concerning that strategy itself, writers who deal with the ethics of strategy have been in serious disagreement on four points:

1. What is the intention underlying the strategy of assured destruction? Is it the good intention of preventing nuclear war or the reprehensible intention to wreak catastrophic death and destruction in retaliation? If the two intentions are combined in one, how is it to be judged?

2. Is it possible to distinguish the public threat embodied in a strategic deterrent policy, designed to prevent war, from the plan that would actually be executed if the deterrent failed? (This question also causes problems for strategic analysts, government policymakers, and military leaders who are concerned with keeping the threat credible.)

3. For purposes of moral evaluation, can we predicate intention of a government, just as we would of an individual in a legal case? In matters of governmental policy, especially in a pluralist constitutional democratic system, who can be held responsible for intending to do what?

4. Is it morally permissible, for the sake of preserving peace, to confront the adversary with a strategic threat that would be immoral to execute? (On this issue the American Catholic Bishops answered in the negative; the French Catholic Bishops, in the affirmative.)

A compelling argument can be made that the more frightful the threat, the more effective it should be as a deterrent, provided that it is credible. That is why the strategy of assured destruction was considered so politically successful, and also why it was so roundly condemned by many church leaders and other moralists who fixed their attention on the implicit, conditional intention embodied in it to destroy urban population and industrial complexes. Some argued that it was justifiable to hold nuclear weapons for purposes of deterrence, but that these weapons could never be used in war. This argument contravened the requirement of deterrent credibility, because it deprived deterrence of an operational doctrine. (Whether it is possible for a democratic government to have one doctrine for deterrence and a more limited one in case of deterrence failure is debatable.)

Presumably, any effort to render the threat less immoral and more limited might also seem, at least logically, less effective as a deterrent (even though some would argue that this could enhance its credibility— i.e., its certainty of being applied). When U.S. defense officials have appeared to be considering responses to aggression more measured than all-out massive retaliation with strategic nuclear missiles—for example, "limited nuclear options," "selective targeting," "counterforce" rather than "countercity" strategies, "battlefield or tactical nuclear weapons," "horizontal escalation," or "conventional deterrence"—they have often been criticized by moralists for making nuclear war "less unthinkable" or more likely to occur as a result of escalation. Thus indirectly the moralists, whether wittingly or not, have been indicating their concern with regard not only to the morality of deterrence but also to its effectiveness. Even though they might not condemn every conceivable use of nuclear weapons, and might reluctantly approve the possibility that retaliatory use in a limited and discriminating manner against military targets could be theoretically justified, nevertheless the moralists have exhibited a great deal of skepticism that a nuclear war could be kept limited, regardless of efforts to control it. Fearing the escalatory process, they have generally opposed any first use of nuclear weapons.[69]

The prolonged debate about the morality of nuclear war, which has gone through several phases, has served amply to demonstrate that the concept of deterrence, which may well constitute the most significant theoretical development in the international relations of the twentieth century, represents something quite new in history. It seems to defy adequate evaluation in terms of the two traditional Western categories of thought on the subject of war and peace—"just war" and pacifism—and requires a unique, rather paradoxical mode of ethical analysis.

NOTES

1. Since the second edition of this present text was written, several books on war and its causes have appeared. Those worth noting include J. David Singer, ed., *Correlates of War II: Testing Some Balance-of-Power Models* (New York: The Free Press, 1980); Francis A. Beer, *Peace Against War: The Ecology of International Violence* (San Francisco, Calif.: Freeman, 1981); Bruce Bueno de Mesquita, *The War Trap* (New Haven, Conn.: Yale University Press, 1981); Richard Ned Liebow, *Between Peace and War: The Nature of International Crisis* (Baltimore, Md.: The Johns Hopkins University Press, 1981); Robert G. Gilpin, *War and Change in World Politics* (Cambridge: Cambridge University Press, 1981); James A. Schellenberg, *The Science of Conflict* (New York: Oxford University Press, 1982); Michael Howard, *The Causes of Wars and Other Essays* (Cambridge, Mass.: Harvard University Press, 1983); Robert J. Art and Kenneth N. Waltz, eds., *The Use of Force: International Politics and Foreign Policy* (Lanham, Md.: University Press of America, 1983); Melvin Small and J. David Singer, eds., *International War* (Homewood, Ill.: Dorsey Press, 1985); John G. Stoessinger, *Why Nations Go To War*, rev. ed. (New York: St. Martin's, 1985); Seyom Brown, *The Causes and Prevention of War* (New York: St. Martin's, 1987).

   Noteworthy articles include Miles Kahler, "Rumors of War: The 1914 Analogy," *Foreign Affairs*, 58 (Winter 1979/1980); Charles F. Doran and Wes Parsons, "War and the Cycle of Relative Power," *American Political Science Review*, 74 (December 1980); Bruce Bueno de Mesquita, "Risk, Power Distributions, and the Likelihood of War," *International Studies Quarterly*, 25 (December 1981), "The Costs of War: A Rational Expectations Approach," *American Political Science Review*, 77 (June 1983), and "The War Trap Revisited: A Revised Expected Utility Model," *American Political Science Review*, 79 (March 1985); Charles W. Kegley, Jr. and Gregory A. Raymond, "Alliance Norms and War," *International Studies Quarterly*, 26 (December 1982); Jack

S. Levy, "Historical Trends in Great Power War, 1945–1975," ibid., 26 (June 1982), "Misperception and the Causes of War," *World Politics,* 36 (October 1983), and "Theories of General War," ibid., 37 (April 1985).

2. Michael Howard, op. cit., pp. 7–22, quoted at p. 14. J. David Singer has noted that, with the possible exception of Jean de Bloch's *Future of War* (1899), which predicted with surprising accuracy what the next European war would look like, and Pitirim Sorokin, whose 1937 work *Social and Cultural Dynamics* correlated war with cycles in cultural patterns, Quincy Wright's *A Study of War* (1942), and Lewis Richardson's studies of the statistics of arms races, published in 1960 on the basis of earlier research (and discussed in Chapter 8) "mark the first traceable efforts to bring scientific method to bear on international conflict." He adds: "While physical phenomena had been studied in an essentially scientific fashion for several centuries, and biological phenomena for nearly a century, social phenomena had remained largely the domain of theological speculation, moral imperative and conventional folklore." "Accounting for International War: The State of the Discipline," *Journal of Peace Research,* No. 1, Vol. XVIII (1981), p. 1. Singer's judgment may be a bit unfair to the philosophers and social, political, and legal theorists who reflected prior to the twentieth century on the problem of war without employing quantitative methodologies and whose views can hardly be dismissed as "conventional folklore." It is correct, nevertheless, to say that the sustained effort to study wars in a systematic, scientific way, employing the methods of the behavioral disciplines, did not get under way until after the First World War.

3. Lewis A. Coser, *The Functions of Social Conflict* (New York: The Free Press, 1956), p. 3.

4. H. L. Neiburg, *Political Violence* (New York: St. Martin's, 1969).

5. Seymour Martin Lipset has noted that both Tocqueville and Marx emphasized the necessity for conflict among social units, and Lipset defines the "existence of a moderate state of conflict" as "another way of defining a legitimate democracy." *Political Man: The Social Bases of Politics* (Garden City, N.Y.: Doubleday-Anchor, 1963), pp. 7 and 71. "Conflict is an essential aspect of growth, one that we can neither fully control nor prevent, nor should we wish to do so." H. L. Nieburg, op. cit., pp. 16–17. "Human existence without conflict is unthinkable. Conflict gives life much of its meaning, so that its elimination, even if attainable, would not be desirable." Jerome D. Frank, "Human Nature and Nonviolent Resistance,"in Quincy Wright et al., eds., *Preventing World War III* (New York: Simon & Schuster, 1962), p. 193. Kenneth Boulding has suggested that "in a given situation there may be too much or too little conflict, or an optimal amount which lends to life a certain dramatic interest." *Conflict and Defense* (New York: Harper & Row, 1962), pp. 305–307.

6. Quoted in Abram Kardiner and Edward Preble, *They Studied Man* (New York: New American Library [Mentor Books], 1963), p. 102. Elsewhere Durkheim wrote: "Social facts do not differ from psychological facts in quality only: They have a different substratum; they evolve in a different milieu; they depend on different conditions. . . . The mentality of groups is not the same as that of individuals; it has its own laws." Introduction to S. A. Solvay and J. K. Mueller, *The Rules of Sociological Method,* 2nd ed., trans. G. E. G. Catlin, ed. (New York: Free Press, 1938), p. xix.

7. See Reuben Osborn, *Freud and Marx* (London: Victor Gallancz, 1937), and *Marxism and Psycho-Analysis* (London: Barrie and Rockliff, 1965).

8. See, for example, the collection of essays from various social science disciplines in Elton B. McNeil, ed., *The Nature of Human Conflict* (Englewood Cliffs, N.J.: Prentice-Hall, 1963); also J. David Singer, "Man and World Politics: the Psycho-Cultural Interface," *Journal of Social Issues,* XXIV (July 1968), 127–156.

9. Michael Haas, *International Conflict* (New York: Bobbs-Merrill, 1974), p. 4.

10. Stephen Withey and Daniel Katz, "The Social Psychology of Human Conflict," in Elton B. McNeil, ed., *The Nature of Human Conflict* (Englewood Cliffs, N.J.: Prentice-Hall, 1965), p. 65.

11. Herbert C. Kelman, "Social-Psychological Approaches to the Study of International Relations," in Herbert C. Kelman, ed., *International Behavior: A Social-Psychological Analysis* (New York: Holt, Rinehart and Winston, 1965), pp. 5–6. See also the references to the work of Werner Levi in Chapter 7 on the microcosmic theories of war.

12. See M. Jane Stroup, "Problems of Research on Social Conflict in the Area of International Relations," *Journal of Conflict Resolution,* IX (September 1965), 413–417. See also Coser, op. cit., pp. 15–38; Jessie Bernard, "Parties and Issues in Conflict," *Journal of Conflict Resolution,* I (June 1957), 111–121; and Raymond W. Mack and Richard C. Snyder, "The Analysis of Social Conflict— Toward an Overview and Synthesis," ibid., I (June 1957), 212–248. For the argument that Talcott Parsons's "structural-functional" approach, relegating conflict to the realm of the abnormal, deviant, and pathological, renders itself incapable of explaining social change and conflict, see Ralf Dahrendorf, "Toward a Theory of Social Conflict," *Journal of Conflict Resolution,* II (June 1958), 170–183. According to Dahrendorf, Parsons was more interested in the maintenance of social structures and order than in change. The Parsonians focused attention upon problems of adjustment rather than of change. For them, social conflict was essentially disruptive and dysfunctional. Dahrendorf in his sociology stresses change rather than persisting configurations, conflict rather than consensus. He presents his postulates not to overturn the Parsonian view, but rather to complement it with an organic model of different emphases. He believes that neither model alone, but only the two taken synthetically, can exhaust social reality and supply us with a complete theory of society in its changing as well as in its enduring aspects. For the earlier views of the German sociologist Georg Simmel, see Nicholas J. Spykman, *The Social Theory of Georg Simmel* (New York: Atherton, 1966), especially pp. 3–127; Lewis Coser, ed., *Georg Simmel* (Englewood Cliffs, N.J.: Prentice-Hall, 1965), especially pp. 1–77. See also "Conflict," trans. Kurt H. Wolff, in *Conflict and the Web of Group Affiliations* (New York: The Free Press, 1955), p. 13. Simmel wrote: "Just as the universe needs 'love and hate,' that is, attractive and repulsive forces, in order to have any form at all, so society, too, in order to attain a determinate shape, needs some quantitative ration of harmony and disharmony, of association and competition, of favorable and unfavorable tendencies." Ibid., p. 15. "A certain amount of discord, inner divergence and outer controversy is organically tied up with the very elements that ultimately hold the group together" (pp. 17–18). Even in relatively hopeless situations, the opportunity to offer opposition can help to render the unbearable bearable: "Opposition gives us inner satisfaction, distraction and relief, just as do humility and patience under different psychological conditions" (p. 19). See also R. C. North et al., "The Integrative Functions of Conflict," *Journal of*

Conflict Resolution, IV (September 1960), 355–374; Lewis A. Coser, "Some Social Functions of Violence," *Annals of the American Academy of Political and Social Science,* CCCLXIV (March 1966), 8–18; and Charles Lockhart, "Problems in the Management and Resolution of International Conflicts," *World Politics,* XXIX (April 1977), 370.

13. See the excellent chapter on "Ancient China," in Frank M. Russell, *Theories of International Relations* (New York: Appleton, 1936); Mousheng Lin, *Men and Ideas: An Informal History of Chinese Political Thought* (New York: John Day, 1942); Arthur Waley, *Three Ways of Thought in Ancient China* (London: Allen and Unwin, 1939 [Anchor edition, 1956]); H. G. Creel, *Chinese Thought from Confucius to Mao Tse-tung* (New York: New American Library, 1960), especially pp. 51–53, 113–121, and 120–130; and Ch'u Chai and Winberg Chai, eds., *The Humanist Way in Ancient China: Essential Works of Confucianism* (New York: Bantam, 1965). Jacques Gernet pointed out that Mo-Ti's followers sought to avoid wars but were willing to defend by force of arms cities subject to unjust attack. *A History of Chinese Civilization,* trans. J. R. Foster (Cambridge: Cambridge University Press, 1983), p. 88.

14. In other words, *ahimsa* promoted vegetarianism long before it promoted pacifism in India. For further discussion of historic Indian attitudes toward war, see D. Mackenzie Brown, *The White Umbrella: Indian Political Thought from Manu to Gandhi* (Berkeley: University of California Press, 1953), especially part one; U. N. Goshal, *A History of Hindu Political Theories* (London: Oxford University Press, 1923); A. L. Basham, "Some Fundamentals of Hindu Statecraft," in Joel Laurus, ed., *Comparative World Politics: Readings in Western and Pre-Modern Non-Western International Relations* (Belmont, Calif.: Wadsworth, 1964), especially pp. 47–52; and the chapter on "Ancient India," in Frank M. Russell, op. cit.; Norman D. Palmer, "Indian and Western Political Thought: Coalescence or Clash?" *American Political Science Review,* XLIX (September 1955), 747–761; George Modelski, "Kautilya: Foreign Policy and International System in the Ancient Hindu World," ibid., LVIII (September 1964), 549–560.

15. Hamilton A. R. Gibb, *Mohammedanism: An Historical Survey* (New York: New American Library, 1955), pp. 57–58. Majid Khadduri has written two very fine expositions of the subject: *War and Peace in the Law of Islam* (Baltimore, Md.: Johns Hopkins Press, 1955) and "The Islamic Theory of International Relations and its Contemporary Relevance," in J. Harris Proctor, ed., *Islam and International Relations* (New York: Praeger, 1965), pp. 24–39; and Bernard Lewis, "The Return of Islam," in Michael Curtis, ed., *The Middle East Reader* (New Brunswick, N.J.: Transaction Books, 1986), esp. pp. 79–82.

16. D. Mackenzie Brown, op. cit., p. 143.

17. For the beliefs and practices of the Israelites in the ages of the prophets and judges, before the rise of political kings, see Exod. 15:1–21; Deut. 20:1–9, 10–20 and 23:15; Josh. 1:1–9, 2:24, 3:5–10 and 6:1–19; Judg. 7:2–22 and 2 Sam. 5:24. See also Everett F. Gendler, "War and the Jewish Tradition," in James Finn, ed., *A Conflict of Loyalties* (New York: Pegasus, 1968); George Foot Moore, *Judaism* (Cambridge: Cambridge University Press, 1966), vol. 2, pp. 106–107; Roland de Vaux, *Ancient Israel: Its Life and Institutions* (New York: McGraw-Hill, 1961), pp. 213–267; "War," Article in the *Jewish Encyclopaedia* (London: Funk and Wagnall's, 1905), Vol. 12, pp. 463–466; Y. Yarden, "Warfare in the

Second Millenium B.C.E." in Benjamin Manzar, ed., *The History of the Jewish People* (New Brunswick, N.J.: Rutgers University Press, 1970); and "Peace (*shalom*)," Article in *The Encyclopaedia Judaica* (Jerusalem: Keter Publishing Company. and New York: Macmillan, 1971), vol. 13, pp. 274–282. For the later themes of love, justice, and peace, see the Books of Isaiah, Jeremiah, Hosea, and Amos.

18. In the New Testament Scriptures, see Matt. 26:7 and 52; Luke 14:31–33 and 22:38. See also John Cadoux, *The Early Church and the World* (Edinburgh: T & T Clark, 1925), pp. 36 and 51–57; Roland H. Bainton, *Christian Attitudes Toward War and Peace* (Nashville: Abingdon Press, 1960), chs. 4, 5, and 6; Peter Brock, *Pacifism in Europe to 1914* (Princeton, N.J.: Princeton University Press, 1972), pp. 3–24; Edward A. Ryan, S. J., "The Rejection of Military Service by the Early Christians," *Theological Studies,* 13 (March 1952); Knut Willem Ruyter, "Pacifism and Military Service in the Early Church," *Cross Currents,* 32 (Spring 1982); Joan D. Tooke, "The Development of the Christian Attitude Toward War Before Aquinas," Chapter 1 in *The Just War in Aquinas and Grotius* (London: SPCK, 1965); G. I. A. D. Draper, "The Origins of the Just War Tradition," *New Blackfriars* (November 1964); F. Homes Dudden, *The Life and Times of Saint Ambrose* (Oxford: Clarendon Press, 1945), Vol. 2, pp. 538–539; Saint Augustine, *The City of God,* trans. Demetrius B. Zema, S. J. and Gerald G. Walsh, S. J. (New York: Fathers of the Church, Inc., 1950), Book 4, Chapter 15, and Book 19, Chapter 12; James E. Dougherty, *The Bishops and Nuclear Weapons: The Catholic Pastoral Letter on War and Peace* (Hamden, Conn.: Archon Books, 1984), pp. 18–42.

19. St. Thomas Aquinas, *Summa Theologica,* 2–2ae, Quest. 40, Art. 1 in Aquinas, *Selected Political Writings,* trans. J. G. Dawson (Oxford: Blackwell, 1948), p. 159; Joan D. Tooke, op. cit., pp. 21–29; James E. Dougherty, op. cit., pp. 42–47.

20. Coleman Phillipson, *The International Law and Custom of Ancient Greece and Rome* (New York: Macmillan, 1911), Vol. 2, pp. 5–8; James Turner Johnson, *The Just War Tradition and the Restraint of War: A Moral and Historical Inquiry* (Princeton, N.J.: Princeton University Press, 1981); Frederick Russell, *The Just War in the Middle Ages* (Cambridge: Cambridge University Press, 1975); E. B. F. Midgley, *The Natural Law Tradition and the Theory of International Relations* (New York: Barnes and Noble, 1975), pp. 62–93; James R. Childress, "Just War Theories," *Theological Studies,* 39 (September 1978). Since medieval society exalted cavalry over infantry, only a limited number of full-fledged warriors was available. Given the low level of the armor-making arts, the fully equipped mounted knight represented a considerable investment. Monarchs lacked the financial and organizational resources to raise and maintain large professional armies. Europe, with population sparse and agricultural methods poor, was usually preoccupied with basic problems of survival. Furthermore, the intricate feudal network of land-loyalty relationships gave rise to many conflicts of fealty among vassals and lords. In a society of delicately balanced bargaining relationships, wars were frequent but they were waged on a small scale for strictly limited objectives. See Henri Pirenne, *Economic and Social History of Medieval Europe* (New York: Harcourt Brace Jovanovich, 1937); Joseph R. Strayer and Rushton Coulborn, *Feudalism in History* (Princeton: Princeton University Press, 1956); F. L. Ganshof, *Feudalism* (London: Longmans, 1952); and Richard A. Preston, Sydney F. Wise, and

Herman O. Werner, *Men in Arms: A History of Warfare and Its Interrelationships with Western Society* (New York: Praeger, 1962), chs. 6 and 7. For an account of the rules of warfare laid down by the Church during the twelfth century under the "Truce of God" and the "Peace of God," see Arthur Nussbaum, *A Concise History of the Law of Nations* (New York: Macmillan, 1954), p. 18.

21. Gwynne Dyer, *War* (New York: Crown, 1985), p. 60.
22. See Francisco de Victoria, *De Indis et De Iure Belli Relectiones,* trans. John P. Bate (Washington: Carnegie Endowment for International Peace, 1917); Francisco Suarez, *De Triplici Virtute Theologica,* Disp. VIII, "De Bello," in *Selection from Three Works* (Oxford: Clarendon, 1925); Balthazar Ayala, *Three Books on the Law of War, the Duties Connected with War and Military Discipline* (Washington: Carnegie Institute, 1912); Emerich Vattel, *Le Droit des Gens* (Washington: Carnegie Institute, 1916); and Albericus Gentilis, *De Iure Belli,* trans. John C. Rolfe (Oxford: Clarendon, 1933). All of these works are in the Classics of International Law Series, edited by James Brown Scott.
23. John U. Nef, *War and Human Progress* (Cambridge: Harvard University Press, 1950), pp. 250–259; Richard A. Preston et al., *Men in Arms,* chap. 9; Dyer, op. cit., p. 67.
24. Paul Hazard, *European Thought in the Eighteenth Century,* trans. J. Lewis May (New York: World, 1963), p. 18.
25. Kingsley Martin, *French Liberal Thought in the Eighteenth Century,* 2nd ed. (New York: New York University Press, 1954), ch. XI.
26. *Outlines of an Historical View of the Progress of the Human Mind,* 1794. Excerpts from an English translation of 1802 in Hans Kohn, *Making of the Modern French Mind* (Princeton: Van Nostrand [Anvil Books], 1955), pp. 97–98.
27. Candide, ch. 3, in Edmund Fuller, ed., *Voltaire: A Laurel Reader* (New York: Dell, 1959), pp. 13–14.
28. William Penn wrote an *Essay Toward the Present and Future Peace of Europe;* Abbé de St. Pierre, *A Project for Making Peace Perpetual in Europe;* Jean-Jacques Rousseau, *A Lasting Peace Through the Federation of Europe;* Immanuel Kant, *Perpetual Peace;* and Jeremy Bentham, *Plan for a Universal and Perpetual Peace.*
29. Dyer, op. cit., pp. 68–72. The death toll in the Revolutionary and Napoleonic wars came to four million, most of them soldiers. The total number killed was only half that of the Thirty Years' War, when most of the deaths were civilian, caused by famine, plague, murder, and socioeconomic breakdown. Ibid., p. 72.
30. See Henry A. Kissinger, *A World Restored—Europe After Napoleon: The Politics of Conservatism in a Revolutionary Age* (New York: Grosset and Dunlap [Universal Library], 1964). See also Charles Breunig, *The Age of Revolution and Reaction* (New York: W. W. Norton, 1970), chs. 3–5.
31. David W. Zeigler, *War, Peace and International Politics,* 4th ed. (Boston: Little, Brown, 1987), ch. 1, "The Wars for German Reunification;" Gordon A. Craig, *Germany 1866–1945* (New York: Oxford University Press, 1978), ch. 1.
32. In the American Civil War 622,000 soldiers died. That total was greater than the combined total for U.S. military personnel in the two world wars plus Korea and Vietnam, although the population of the country was much larger in the 1980s. Gwynne Dyer, op. cit., p. 77.

33. R. A. Preston et al., *Men in Arms: A History of Warfare and Its Interrelationships with Western Society,* 4th ed. (New York: Holt, Rinehart and Winston, 1979), ch. 15, "Approach to Total Warfare."

34. Dyer, op. cit., pp. 78, 150; Preston et al., op. cit., pp. 244–245, 250–253; Barbara Tuchman, *The Guns of August* (New York: Dell, 1962), pp. 91–95.

35. Jonathan Dymond, *An Inquiry into the Accordancy of War with the Principles of Christianity and an Examination of the Philosophical Reasoning by Which It Is Defended,* 3rd ed. (Philadelphia: Brown, 1834).

36. Norman Angell, *The Great Illusion: A Study of the Relation of Military Power to National Advantage* (New York: Putnam's, 1910), p. 71. One of the arguments employed by Angell to prove that economic prosperity can be separated from military capability was that the national bonds of small nonmilitary states were sought after by investors as more secure than bonds of the larger military powers. In rebuttal to Angell, Professor J. H. Jones of the University of Glasgow pointed out that it was the military expenditures of the larger powers that created the conditions of international stability and security on which smaller nations depended, in *The Economics of War and Conquest* (London: King and Son, 1915), p. 25. For a skeptical critique of the view that railways, steamships, and international commerce promote friendship among nations and were responsible for long periods of peace in nineteenth-century Europe, see Geoffrey Blainey, *The Causes of War* (New York: Macmillan-Free Press, 1973), esp. ch. 2, "Paradise Is a Bazaar."

37. Norman Angell, ibid., p. 335. For Herbert Spencer's view that war is too costly and destructive for industrial societies, see his *Principles of Sociology* (New York: Appleton, 1898), Vol. II, pp. 568–642. George Liska's views are discussed in ch. 4.

38. Karl von Clausewitz, *On War,* trans. O. J. Mathhias Jolles (New York: Modern Library-Random House, 1943), pp. 3–4, 5, 30; cf. also Sir Basil H. Liddell Hart, "The Objective in War," in B. Mitchell Simpson, ed., *War, Strategy and Maritime Power* (New Brunswick, N.J.: Rutgers University Press, 1977), p. 33 and Hans Rothfels, "Clausewitz," in Edward Mead Earle, ed., *Makers of Modern Strategy* (Princeton: Princeton University Press, 1943), pp. 93–94.

39. Clausewitz wrote: "The smaller the sacrifice we demand from our adversary, the slighter we may expect his efforts to be to refuse it to us. . . . Furthermore, the less important our political object, the less will be the value we attach to it and the readier we shall be to abandon it. . . . Thus the political as the original motive of the war will be the standard alike for the aim to be attained by military action and for the efforts required for this purpose." *On War,* p. 9. In another passage, he said that the abstract object of disarming the enemy "by no means universally occurs in practice, nor is it a necessary condition to peace." Ibid., p. 20. See also Sun Tzu, *The Art of War,* trans. and with Introduction by Samuel B. Griffith (Cambridge: Clarendon Press, 1963), pp. 40–45.

40. G. W. F. Hegel, *Philosophy of Right and Law,* par. 324, in Carl J. Friedrich, ed., *The Philosophy of Hegel* (New York: Random House-The Modern Library, 1953), p. 322.

41. "What is good? All that enhances the feeling of power, the Will-to-Power, and power itself in man. What is bad? All that proceeds from weakness. What is happiness? The feeling that power is increasing—that resistance has been overcome. Not contentment, but more power; not peace at any price, but war;

not virtue, but efficiency. . . . The weak and the botched shall perish: first principle of our humanity. And they ought even to be helped to perish. What is more harmful than any vice? Practical sympathy with all the botched and the weak—Christianity." From *The Twilight of the Idols* (1888), in Geoffrey Clive, ed., *The Philosophy of Nietzsche* (New York: New American Library, 1965), p. 427.

42. *Human, All Too Human,* vol. I (1878), pp. 372–373. According to William James, peaceful activities involving a challenge to strenuous exertion and sacrifice could serve as a substitute for war in providing the "social vitamins" generated by war. The philosopher-psychologist recognized that war and the military life met certain deep-rooted needs of societies and summoned forth human efforts of heroic proportions. He did not think it possible to attenuate the proclivity to war until these same energies could be redirected—for example, by training young men to fight not other human beings but such natural forces as diseases, floods, poverty, and ignorance. If the nation is not to evolve into a society of mollycoddles, youth must be conscripted to hardship tasks to "get the childishness knocked out of them." See William James, "The Moral Equivalent of War," in his *Memories and Studies* (London: Longmans, 1912); and *A Moral Equivalent for War* (New York: Carnegie Endowment for International Peace, 1926). Later, Aldous Huxley was to popularize the hypothesis that many people find an exhilaration in war because their peacetime pursuits are humiliating, boring, and frustrating. War brings with it a state of chronic enthusiasm, and "life during wartime takes on significance and purposefulness, so that even the most intrinsically boring job is ennobled as 'war work.' " Prosperity is artificially induced; newspapers are filled with interesting news; and the rules of sexual morality are relaxed in wartime. But Huxley, writing just before World War II, conceded that the conditions of modern war have become so appalling that not only the civilians on the home front, but "even the most naturally adventurous and combative human beings will soon come to hate and fear the process of fighting." *Ends and Means* (New York: Harper & Row, 1937). Excerpted in Robert A. Goldwin et al., eds., *Readings in World Politics* (New York: Oxford University Press, 1959), pp. 13–14.

43. Heinrich von Treitschke, *Politics* (New York: Macmillan, 1916), II, 595.

44. "We have learned to perceive the moral majesty of war through the very processes which to the superficial observer seem brutal and inhuman. The greatness of war is just what at first sight seems to be its horror—that for the sake of their country men will overcome the natural feelings of humanity, that they will slaughter their fellowmen who have done them no injury, nay whom they perhaps respect as chivalrous foes. Man will not only sacrifice his life, but the natural and justified instincts of his soul; . . . here we have the sublimity of war." Ibid., pp. 395–396.

45. Quoted in Russell, op. cit., p. 245.

46. Alfred Thayer Mahan, *Armaments and Arbitration* (1912), p. 31. Quoted in Charles D. Tarlton, "The Styles of American International Thought: Mahan, Bryan, and Lippmann," *World Politics,* XVII (July 1965), 590. The foregoing summary of Mahan is based largely upon Tarlton's analysis.

47. Vilfredo Pareto, *The Mind and Society,* trans. A. Bongiorno and A. Livingston (New York: Harcourt Brace Jovanovich, 1935), vol. IV, pp. 2170–2175 and 2179–2220; Gaetano Mosca, *The Ruling Class,* trans. H. D. Kahn (New York:

McGraw-Hill, 1939). For interesting and valuable assessments of both Pareto and Mosca, see parts III and VI of James Burnham, *The Machiavellians: Defenders of Freedom* (New York: John Day, 1943).

48. Holmes glorified war as a romantic adventure and as a necessary corrective for the irresponsible and sybaritic tendencies of modern youth. See Edward McNall Burns, *Ideas in Conflict: The Political Theories of the Contemporary World* (New York: Norton, 1960), p. 54.

49. Oswald Spengler, *The Decline of the West,* trans. Charles F. Atkinson (New York: Knopf, 1926–1928), 2 vols.; and *The Hour of Decision,* trans. Charles F. Atkinson (New York: Knopf, 1934).

50. See A. James Gregor, *The Fascist Persuasion in Radical Politics* (Princeton: Princeton University Press, 1974); Anthony James Joes, *Fascism in the Contemporary World: Ideology, Evolution, Resurgence* (Boulder, Colo.: Westview, 1978), ch. 3; H. S. Harris, *The Social Philosophy of Giovanni Gentile* (Urbana: University of Illinois Press, 1960).

51. Irving Louis Horowitz, ed., *The Anarchists* (New York: Dell, 1964), from the editor's Introduction, p. 22.

52. See the excerpt from Thomas G. Masaryk, ibid., pp. 469–473.

53. Irving Louis Horowitz, op. cit., pp. 44–55.

54. Georges Sorel, *Reflections on Violence* (New York: Macmillan, 1961), pp. 77–79, 115. See his ch. 2, "Violence and the Decadence of the Middle Classes." See also part IV, "Sorel: A Note on Myth and Violence," in Burnham, op. cit.; and William Y. Elliott, *The Pragmatic Revolt in Politics: Syndicalism, Fascism and the Constitutional State* (New York: Howard Fertig, 1968), pp. 111–141.

55. Irving Louis Horowitz, op. cit., pp. 53–54; Francis W. Coker, *Recent Political Thought* (New York: Appleton, 1934), ch. VII, esp. pp. 223–225.

56. Quoted in Daniel Bell, *The Cultural Contradictions of Capitalism* (New York: Basic Books, 1976), p. 6. Contemporary terrorists often select at random, for kidnapping or murder, "typical" members of the group or class they seek to terrorize (e.g., business personnel, diplomats, air travelers, or restaurant diners). See Edward Hyams, *Terrorists and Terrorism* (New York: St. Martin's, 1974); Paul Wilkinson, *Political Terrorism* (New York: Wiley, 1974); and J. Bowyer Bell, "Trends on Terror: The Analysis of Political Violence," *World Politics,* XXIX (April 1977), 476–488.

57. For a representative sample of the voluminous literature reflecting these attitudes, see Roland H. Bainton, *Christian Attitudes Toward War and Peace* (Nashville: Abingdon Press, 1960); John C. Bennett, ed., *Nuclear Weapons and the Conflict of Conscience* (New York: Scribner's, 1962); Gordon Zahn, *An Alternative to War* (New York: Council on Religion and International Affairs, 1963); James Finn, ed., *Peace, the Churches and the Bomb* (New York: Council on Religion and International Affairs, 1965); Donald A. Wells, *The War Myth* (New York: Pegasus, 1967); James W. Douglass, *The Non-Violent Cross* (New York: Macmillan, 1968); John H. Yoder, *Politics of Jesus* (Grand Rapids, Mich.: Erdmans, 1972); Gene Sharp, *The Politics of Non-Violent Action* (Boston: Sargent, 1973); Joseph Fahey, *Justice and Peace* (Maryknoll, N.Y.: Orbis Books, 1979); Thomas Merton, *The Non-Violent Alternative* (New York: Farrar, Straus and Giroux, 1980); *The Church and the Bomb: Nuclear Weapons and the Christian Conscience,* A report of a working party under the chairmanship of the Bishop of Salisbury (London: Hodder and Stoughton, 1982).

58. See Erich Fromm, "The Case for Unilateral Disarmament," in Donald G. Brennan, ed., *Arms Control, Disarmament and National Security* (New York: Braziller, 1961), pp. 187–197; Mulford Q. Sibley, "Unilateral Disarmament," in Robert A. Goldwin, ed., *American Armed* (Chicago: Rand McNally, 1961), pp. 112–140; Gordon Zahn, op. cit.

59. See John Courtney Murray, *Morality and Modern War* (New York: Church Peace Union, 1959) and republished as "Theology and Modern War" in *Theological Studies*, XX (March 1959), 40–61; Paul Ramsey, *War and the Christian Conscience* (Durham, N.C.: Duke University Press, 1961) and *The Limits of Nuclear War* (New York: Council on Religion and International Affairs, 1963); Robert E. Osgood, "The Uses of Military Power in the Cold War," in Robert A. Goldwin, ed., op. cit., pp. 1–21; Richard A. Falk, *Law, Morality and War in the Contemporary World*, Princeton Studies in World Politics No. 5 (New York: Praeger, 1963); Robert W. Tucker, *The Just War* (Baltimore: Johns Hopkins University Press, 1960) and *Just War and Vatican II: A Critique* (New York: Council on Religion and International Affairs, 1966); William V. O'Brien, *Nuclear War, Deterrence and Morality* (Westminster, Md.: Newman Press, 1967), and *The Conduct of Just and Limited War* (New York: Praeger, 1981); Michael Walzer, *Just and Unjust Wars* (New York: Basic Books, 1977); James T. Johnson, *Just War Tradition and the Restraint of War* (Princeton: Princeton University Press, 1981).

60. Murray, op. cit., p. 61.

61. O'Brien, *Nuclear War, Deterrence and Morality*, pp. 34–41.

62. Ibid., pp. 23–26 and ch. 5, "Morality and Nuclear Weapons Systems."

63. Ramsey, *The Limits of Nuclear War*, p. 10.

64. This point was made by Pope Pius XII in 1954 and was reiterated by the Second Vatican Council in 1965.

65. See Ralph B. Potter, *War and Moral Discourse* (Richmond, Va.: John Knox Press, 1969); Robert Ginsberg, ed., *The Critique of War* (Chicago: Regnery, 1969); Richard A. Wasserstrom, *War and Morality* (Belmont, Calif.: Wadsworth, 1970); Morton A. Kaplan, ed., *Strategic Thinking and Its Moral Implications* (Chicago: University of Chicago Center for Policy Study, 1973); James T. Johnson, "The Cruise Missile and the Neutron Bomb: Some Moral Reflections," *Worldview*, 20 (December 1977); Robert L. Phillips, *War and Justice* (Oklahoma City: University of Oklahoma Press, 1984); John D. Jones and Marc F. Griesbach, eds., *Just War Theory in the Nuclear Age* (Lanham, Md.: University Press of America, 1985); William V. O'Brien and John Langan, S. J., eds., *The Nuclear Dilemma and the Just War Tradition* (Lexington, Mass.: D. C. Heath, 1986).

66. For the debate over the "theology of liberation" and the morality of revolutionary violence, see the October 1968 issue of *Worldview*, devoted to "Revolution and Violence"; Gustavo Guttierez, "Liberation and Development," *Cross Currents* 21 (1971); Philip E. Berryman, "Latin American Liberation Theology," *Theological Studies*, 34 (December 1973); Guenter Lewy, *Religion and Revolution* (New York: Oxford University Press, 1974), esp. ch. 20; Francis P. Fiorenza, "Political Theology and Liberation Theology," in Thomas M. McFadden, ed., *Liberation, Revolution and Freedom: Theological Perspectives* (New York: Seabury Press, 1975); Gustavo Guttierez, *A Theology of Liberation*, trans. Caridad Inda and John Eagleson (Maryknoll, N.Y.: Orbis Books, 1978); Dennis P. McCann, *Christian Realism and Liberation Theology*

(Maryknoll, N.Y.: Orbis Books, 1981); and Quentin L. Quade, ed., *The Pope and Revolution: John Paul II Confronts Liberation Theology* (Washington, D.C.: Ethics and Public Policy Center, 1982).

67. Michael Walzer, op. cit., p. 278.

68. Ibid., p. 274.

69. Concerning the ethics of the strategy of nuclear deterrence, see (in addition to the works cited in notes 57, 59, and 65): Geoffrey Goodwin, ed., *Ethics and Nuclear Deterrence* (New York: St. Martin's Press, 1982); German Grisez, "The Moral Implications of a Nuclear Deterrent," *Center Journal,* 2 (Winter 1982); Francis X. Winters, S. J., "Nuclear Deterrence Morality: Atlantic Community Bishops in Tension," *Theological Studies,* 43 (September 1982); John Langan, "The American Hierarchy and Nuclear Weapons," ibid.; David Hollenbach, S. J., "Nuclear Weapons and Nuclear War: The Shape of the Catholic Debate," ibid. (December 1982); *The Challenge of Peace: God's Promise and Our Response,* U.S. Catholic Bishops' Pastoral Letter on War and Peace, Text in *Origins,* NC Documentary Service 13 (May 19, 1983); L. Bruce van Voorst, "The Churches and Nuclear Deterrence," *Foreign Affairs,* 61 (Spring 1983); Albert Wohlstetter, "Bishops, Statesmen and Other Strategists on the Bombing of Innocents," *Commentary* (June 1983); Donald L. Davidson, *Nuclear War and the American Churches: Ethical Positions on Modern Warfare* (Boulder, Colo.: Westview, 1983); Jim Castelli, *The Bishops and the Bomb: Waging Peace in the Nuclear Age* (Garden City, N.Y.: Doubleday-Image, 1983); Michael Novak, *Moral Clarity in the Nuclear Age* (Nashville, Tenn.: Thomas Nelson, 1983); Philip F. Lawler, ed., *Justice and War in the Nuclear Age* (Lanham, Md.: University Press of America, 1983); Judith A. Dwyer, S. S. J., ed., *The Catholic Bishops and Nuclear War* (Washington, D.C.: Georgetown University Press, 1984); James E. Dougherty, *The Bishops and Nuclear Weapons* (Hamden, Conn.: Archon Books, 1984), esp. chs. 5 and 6; Bruce M. Russett, "Ethical Dilemmas of Nuclear Deterrence," *International Security,* 8 (Spring 1984); Michael Fox and Leo Groarke, *Nuclear War: Philosophical Perspectives* (New York: Peter Land, 1985); George Weigel, *Tranquillitas Ordinis: The Present Failure and Future Promise of American Catholic Thought on War and Peace* (New York: Oxford University Press, 1987); *The Nuclear Dilemma,* Statement of the Commission on Peace, Episcopal Diocese of Washington, 1987. The more technical questions of deterrence strategy, the controllability of nuclear war, a NATO policy of "no first use," the possibility of substituting conventional for nuclear deterrence, and related issues will be discussed in Chapter 9. See also Robert K. Tucker, *The Nuclear Debate: Deterrence and the Lapse of Faith* (New York: Holmes and Meier, 1985).

Chapter
6

Theories of Imperialism and the Economic Causes of International Conflict

*I*n the study of the essential conditions for world peace and the causes of international conflict, economic factors have held a position of considerable importance. Implicit, if not explicit, in many theories of international relations is the assumption that rising living standards and national economic growth contribute to peace among nations. In modern liberal thought, writers such as Adam Smith, John Stuart Mill, and Richard Cobden considered free trade to be a guarantor of peace. Free trade ✱ would create a division of labor based on international specialization in an international economy in which nations were so interdependent as to make virtually impossible the resort to war. The growth of individual and national prosperity would divert public attention from military ventures because of their potentially disruptive effects on economic growth and prosperity. In marked contrast to the proponents of free trade based upon economic competition, other writers have argued that free competition is a principal determinant of international conflict.

There is a widespread disposition to explain all international political relations by reference, more often gratuitously asserted than scientifically demonstrated, to forces associated with the quest for economic gain or advantage. The most significant trends in world politics and the most significant decisions of governments are said to be traceable to such economic forces as complex, powerful multinational corporations; the ruthless competition (or sinister collusion) of European Community, Japanese, and American manufacturing, agricultural, labor, trading, and banking-financial interests; the divergence of economic interests between the industrialized countries of the North and the less developed countries of the South, with the richer exploiting the poorer; and the systemic rivalry between free-market economies and centrally directed socialist economies.

Central to economic theories of imperialism and war is the assumption (rejected by the authors) that all international issues are reducible to issues of economic gain rather than political power. The strength of such an assumption, dubious as it may be, lies in the considerable influence of the philosophical system propounded originally by Karl Marx and Friedrich Engels, as well as of the pronouncements, whether consistent or contradictory, of their numerous socialist and communist descendants. Generations of academic and journalistic theoreticians, as well as would-be political practitioners, who never lived under a communist or a socialist regime, have expounded an essentially Marxist analysis of the world.[1] Large numbers of otherwise bourgeois teachers, students, politicians, and writers, and even business people have adopted an economic interpretation of history based at least in part on Marxian analysis. In nearly all Third World countries, elites take for granted the validity of Lenin's notion of imperialism, and this powerfully influences their attitude toward the West. The main elements of the Marxist theory date back to 1848. Yet the theory has shown a remarkable survivability into the final quarter-century that has often proved brutally critical of abstractions inherited from the past. The Marxist analysis of international relations, especially of imperialism and war, and of social conflict and revolution, has survived more as faith than science.

THE MARXIST THEORY

Marxism is an admixture of metaphysics (dialectical materialism), theory of history (economic determinism), economic and sociological science, political ideology, theory and strategy of revolution, social ethics, and an eschatological moral theology that looks toward a secular salvation: the advent of a classless social order of perfect justice in which conflict ceases and the psychology of a "new man" is generated. Marx more than any other individual strengthened the idea that conflict arises inevitably out of the life-and-death struggle of socioeconomic classes. Capitalism is the bondage from which people strive to be liberated, and this will be accomplished through knowledge of the inexorable dialectical laws of historical-social change. Up to now, class conflict has been the motor of social change. Once class conflict comes to an end with the establishment of communism, social change will occur only as a result of rational planning, debate, and decision-making.

Karl Marx (1818–1883) evolved a theory of history based on dialectical materialism, in which the system of economic production determines the institutional and ideological structures of society.[2] Whoever controls the economic system also controls the political system. Marx and Engels's study of history and of nineteenth-century Britain led them to conclude that each period of history contains clashing forces, or a dialectic, from which a new order emerges. "In ancient Rome, we have patricians, knights, plebeians, slaves; in the Middle Ages, feudal lords, vassals, guild-master, journeymen, apprentices, serfs; in almost all of these classes, again, subordinate gradations."[3]

All history is the history of class struggle between a ruling group and an opposing group, from which comes a new economic, political, and social system. Marx's model for the study of society and its transformation contains a thesis (ruling group) and an antithesis (opposing group), which clash and produce a synthesis (a new economic, political, and social system).

Like the systems that preceded it, capitalism contains the seeds of its own destruction. Marx believed that the growing impoverishment of the working class, or proletariat, would lead to a revolution to overthrow the ruling capitalist class. The lower strata of the middle class are absorbed into the proletariat, since they do not have the capital to compete on the scale of their more fortunate confreres, and their specialized skills become worthless as a result of new methods of production. As the ranks of the proletariat increase, the struggle with the bourgeoisie grows in intensity. Initially the struggle is conducted by individual members of the exploiting capitalist class. Marx envisaged a series of clashes of increasing intensity between the proletariat and the bourgeoisie, until the eruption of a revolution finally resulting in the overthrow of the bourgeoisie.

In Marx's doctrine of surplus value, the socially useful labor that produces a commodity is considered to be the only measure of its worth. Capitalists themselves produce nothing. Instead, they live like parasites from the labor of the producing class. The capitalist pays the laborer a subsistence wage and keeps the rest. According to Marx, the vast mass of the population is reduced to wage slavery in a capitalist society. The proletariat produces goods and services for which it receives little or no return. In a capitalist system, the bourgeoisie, which controls the means of production, exploits the worker and widens the gap, or surplus value, between the price paid workers for their labor and the price obtained by the bourgeoisie in the marketplace.[4]

The coming clash between the capitalist, bourgeois class (thesis) and the proletariat (antithesis) would lead to a socialist order. There would be a period of extensive government controls over production and distribution until the last vestiges of capitalism were removed. Marx predicted the withering away of the state with the development of a communist economic, political, and socialist order.

Orthodox Marxists view all political phenomena, including imperialism and war, as projections of underlying economic forces. All forms of consciousness are subordinated to the economic. Religious, humanitarian, political, cultural and military-strategic motives for any kind of power relationship between a stronger and a weaker community are explained by the Marxist as rationalizations designed to disguise the economic substructure. This has been essentially true throughout history, Marx held, but it becomes most apparent in the era of capitalism. In a passage written avowedly for polemicist purposes rather than to display social science objectivity, Marx and Engels declared:

> The bourgeoisie . . . has left no other bond between man and man than naked self-interest, than callous cash payment. It has drowned the most heavenly ecstacies of religious fervor, of chivalrous enthusiasm, of philistine sentimentalism, in the icy water of egotistical calculation. . . . The bourgeoisie has stripped of its halo every occupation hitherto honored and looked up to with reverent awe. It has converted the physician, the lawyer, the priest, the poet, the man of science, into its paid wage-laborers.[5]

Marx had a vision of peace—the peace of the self-alienated man restored to himself as a result of the "negation of the negation," the revolutionary self-appropriation by the proletariat, taking that which rightfully belongs to itself.[6] He did not project an image throughout his writings of a man bent upon violent revolution. Especially in his earlier years, he may have preferred or hoped that the inevitable victory of socialism could be achieved through a nonviolent working out of the dialectic. But as he grew older, Marx's youthful philosophical idealism gave way to the thought modes of a frustrated, impatient, professional revolutionary. John Plamenatz has put well the case for avoiding extremes in interpreting Marx—insisting either that Marx was pathologically bent upon violence or that he abhorred violence as a pacifist might:

> Logically, violence, the shedding of blood, is no essential part of revolution as Marx and Engels conceived it. True, they thought there would be violence when the proletariat took over power, in most countries if not in all. They even at times, I suspect, took pleasure in the thought that there would be.
>
> They were not very gentle persons; nor did they believe, as certain other socialists and communists of their day did, that violence is wrong or that it corrupts those who use it. But all this takes nothing away from the point I am making: revolution, as Marx and Engels conceived of it, does not necessarily involve violence.[7]

It was Lenin, coming out of a tradition of Russian revolutionary conspiratorial activity that had become a mirror image of the czarist oppressiveness it fought, who more than anyone else imparted to twentieth-century Marxist communism its predilection for violence and terror. Lenin was reacting in part against the Revisionism of such German Marxists as Karl Kautsky (1854–1938) and Eduard Bernstein (1850–1932), who realized that some of Marx's predictions had gone awry and that the achievement of socialism might be a long, gradual process utilizing education, psychological intimidation, and the ballot box. Lenin insisted that the appeal of violence was inherent in the makeup of the true revolutionary, and that the bourgeois state cannot be replaced by the proletarian state through a withering away but, as a general rule, only through a violent revolution.

Although Marx fully appreciated the worldwide scope of capitalist operations for acquiring raw materials and marketing manufactures, he himself did not elaborate a theory of imperialism. This task was left to his twentieth-century intellectual heirs—Rudolph Hilferding (1877–1941), a German Social Democrat; Rosa Luxembourg (1870–1919), a German Socialist agitator; and, of course, Lenin.

HOBSON ON IMPERIALISM

Curiously enough, most of the clues to the communist theory of imperialism in this century were provided by the English economist John A. Hobson (1858–1940). Hobson, an Oxford graduate, was a journalist, essayist, and university lecturer who had been influenced toward liberalism by John Stuart Mill and toward the science of society by Herbert Spencer. Attracted to idealist, humanitarian, and ethical causes of social reform, he became a self-designated religious and economic heretic, and gravitated toward a Fabian-type socialism as he grew increasingly disenchanted with "mechanized capitalism." During the Boer War he went to South Africa as a correspondent for *The Manchester Guardian.* His coverage of that conflict, which he saw as a concoction of diamond monopolists and other economic exploiters, moved him further in the direction of an anticapitalist, antimilitarist polemic that was not free of anti-Semitic overtones. Perhaps he was merely appealing to an anti-Semitism that was then on the rise in Western Europe, just as he was to socialist and pacifist thought trends. In any event it is not too much to say that Hobson practically invented the modern theory of imperialism, and did a great deal to create an intellectual-moral revulsion against it in the English-speaking world.[8] (Liberal opinion in the United States was already manifesting a guilt feeling over Cuba and Pacific expansionism in the wake of the Spanish-American War.[9])

More than 60 years later, two scholars would conclude that "the worldwide misinterpretation of the Boer War as a capitalist plot . . . became the basis of all subsequent theory of imperialism."[10] The very word *imperialism,* which had hitherto been invoked proudly to imply what Britain had contributed toward civilizing the parts of the world once or still controlled by Britain—the rule of law, parliamentary institutions, a rational administration of civil servants with some sense of public responsibility (hitherto a rather rare phenomenon in many regions), and a conviction of the worth and rights of human beings (even rarer)—became in England "a recognized symbol of a strong moral revulsion on the part of a minority with Liberal, Radical, and Labor leanings, or with strong religious scruples."[11]

Hobson argued that imperialism results from maladjustments within the capitalist system, in which a wealthy minority oversaves while an impoverished or "bare subsistence" majority lacks the purchasing power to consume all the fruits of modern industry. Capitalist societies are thus faced with the critical dilemma of overproduction and underconsumption. If capitalists were willing to redistribute their surplus wealth in the form of domestic welfare measures, there would be no serious structural problem. The capitalists, however, seek instead to reinvest their surplus capital in profit-making ventures abroad. The result is imperialism, "the endeavor of the great controllers of industry to broaden the channel for the flow of their surplus wealth by seeking foreign markets and foreign investments to take off the goods and capital they cannot sell or use at home."[12]

Hobson was aware that there were noneconomic factors at work in late nineteenth-century European expansion abroad—forces of a political, military, psychological, and religious-philanthropic character. He insisted, however, that the essential ingredient in imperialism is finance capitalism, which galvanizes and organizes the other forces into a coherent whole:

> Finance capitalism manipulates the patriotic forces which politicians, soldiers, philanthropists and traders generate; the enthusiasm for expansion which issues from these sources, though strong and genuine, is irregular and blind; the financial interest has those qualities of concentration and clearsighted calculation which are needed to set imperialism at work.[13]

In Hobson's view, imperialism in the case of Britain had not been necessary to relieve population pressure, for Britain was not overpopulated and its growth rate at the turn of the century was declining toward a stationary level. Furthermore, he noted, Englishmen did not seem at all anxious to resettle in most areas of the Empire acquired after 1870.[14]

Hobson condemned late nineteenth-century imperialism as irrational and as bad business policy for the nation as a whole, even though it was rational and profitable for certain groups—bourses, speculative miners, engineers, the shipbuilding and armaments industries, the export industries, contractors to the military services, and the aristocratic classes that sent their sons to be officers in the army, navy, and colonial service.[15] Although the economic activities of these classes constituted but a small fraction of Britain's total enterprise, the groups benefiting from imperialism were well organized for advancing their interests through political channels. Imperialism, said Hobson, involves enormous risks and costs to the nation compared with its relatively meager results in the form of increased trade, and hence the rationale for it must be sought in the advantages it brings to special groups within the society: "To a larger extent every year Great Britain is becoming a nation living upon tribute from abroad, and the classes who enjoy this tribute have an ever-increasing incentive to employ the public policy, the public purse, and the public force to extend the field of their private investments."[16] E. M. Winslow (1896–1966), evaluating the significance of Hobson's study, concluded: "No other book has been so influential in spreading the doctrine of economic imperialism."[17] Lenin would later clearly acknowledge his indebtedness to Hobson's work.

Hobson anticipated the later Leninist attack upon capitalist profiteering as a major factor in causing international war. Policies of aggressive imperialism and war lead to vast arms budgets, public debts, and the fluctuation of the securities values from which the skilled financier benefits most. "There is not a war, a revolution, an anarchist assassination, or any other public shock, which is not gainful to these men; they are harpies who suck their gains from every new forced expenditure, and every sudden disturbance of public credit."[18] To be sure, Hobson is not saying here that the capitalists are responsible for the wars from which they profit. Almost certainly he would not contend that capitalists lurked behind every anarchist assassin. But the unmistakable thrust of his reasoning, which would be made more explicit by Lenin, was that if the behavior of capitalists is primarily motivated by the desire to gain profits, and if certain segments of capitalist society can profit from imperialistic wars, then these elements can be expected to bend every effort to bring about war when the circumstances call for it. In the last passage quoted, the tone of Hobson's moral indignation becomes less scholarly and more ideological, not unlike that which runs through the writings of Marx and his followers.

Lenin: Imperialism and International Conflict

Rosa Luxembourg, a theoretic German Socialist agitator, closely followed Hobson's analysis, while Hilferding sought to refine it by attributing the export of capital to the operation of cartel and monopoly systems that limit domestic investment possibilities. The best-known theorist of imperialism in modern times, of course, was Lenin. The architect of the Bolshevik Revolution was neither the scholar nor the original thinker that Hobson was. In addition to borrowing ideas from Hobson, Lenin relied upon Hilferding's analysis of the role of monopoly capitalism:

> Imperialism is capitalism in the stage of development in which the dominance of monopolies and finance capital has established itself; in which the export of capital has acquired pronounced importance; in which the division of the world among the international thrusts has begun; in which the division of all territories of the globe among the great capitalist powers has been completed.[19]

Lenin derived monopoly capitalism, which he equated with imperialism, from four factors: (1) the concentration of production in combines, cartels, syndicates, and trusts; (2) the competitive quest for sources of raw materials; (3) the development of banking oligarchies; and (4) the transformation of the "old" colonial policy into a struggle for spheres of economic interest in which the richer and the more powerful nations exploit the weaker ones. Thus Lenin took strong exception to Karl Kautsky's thesis that imperialism was merely the "preferred policy" of capitalist states; for Lenin it was inevitable. Moreover, in the Leninist interpretation the receipt of monopoly profits by the capitalists of certain industries enables them to corrupt the workers in those industries, who for the sake of a higher standard of living ally themselves with the bourgeoisie against their fellow workers of the exploited, imperialized countries.

Since finance capitalism is the source of imperialism, it also becomes for the Marxist-Leninists the principal source of international wars in the capitalist era, or at least the only source in which they are interested. If there are other sources of conflict, Marxists prefer not to call much attention to them. Hobson, who was a liberal rather than a Marxist, had conceded that there are "primitive instincts" in the human race that played a part in nineteenth-century imperialism—the instinct for the control of land, the "nomadic habit" that survives as love of travel, the "spirit of adventure," the sporting and hunting instincts, and the "lust of struggle," which in the age of spectator sports is transformed into gambling on the outcome of athletic games and into jingoism in war.[20] But Hobson circumvented the theoretical difficulty implicit in the plurality of factors merely by accusing the dominant classes in capitalistic societies of advancing their own interests by playing upon the primitive instincts of the race and channeling them into imperialistic ventures.

Lenin's contribution to communism was twofold. First, he imparted an organizational theory in which the Communist party became the "vanguard of the proletariat" to hasten the coming of the revolution that Marx had foreseen as inevitable. Second, drawing heavily upon the work of Hobson described above, Lenin developed a theory of imperialism that ranks as the principal communist theory of international relations in a global system consisting of capitalist states.[21]

Looking back upon the history of Europe in the decades after Marx published his *Communist Manifesto,* Lenin concluded that the proletariat would not revolt spontaneously, as Marx had believed, against the ruling bourgeoisie. In his famous tract entitled *What Is to Be Done?,* Lenin held that a strong, tightly knit, highly motivated party of professional revolutionaries was essential to the success of the revolution against the capitalist order. To Lenin, the Communist party, the "vanguard of the proletariat," was the most class-conscious, devoted, and self-sacrificing part of the proletariat.[22] Lenin held that the Party must be centralized or hierarchical. It must be based on "democratic centralism"—that is, the Party must provide for discussion and debate of issues before a decision was taken, while adopting iron-clad discipline in executing policy after a decision had been made.

Lenin saw imperialism as a special, advanced stage of capitalism. In capitalist systems, competition is eventually replaced by capitalist monopolies.[23] Imperialism is the monopoly stage of capitalism. The countries that are the principal exporters of capital are able to obtain economic advantages based on the exploitation of peoples abroad. Moreover, the greater the development of capitalism, the greater the need for raw materials and markets, and hence the greater the scramble for colonies. The establishment of political control over territories overseas is designed to provide a dependable source of raw materials and cheap labor and to guarantee markets for the industrial combines of advanced capitalist countries. Lenin held that imperialist policies would enable capitalist powers to stave off the inevitable revolution, since conditions of the domestic proletariat would be ameliorated by the exploitation of the working class in colonial territories.

Writing in the spring of 1916, nearly two years after the outbreak of World War I, Lenin viewed the history of the previous generation as a struggle between the advanced capitalist powers for the control of colonies and markets. Capitalist countries have formed alliances for the exploitation of the underdeveloped areas. Especially in East Asia and Africa, the imperialist powers have claimed territories and spheres of influence. Such alliances are only "breathing spells" between wars, since the capitalist powers find it necessary to fight for control of limited overseas markets and raw materials. Because of the ultimate dependence of capitalist economic systems upon such markets and natural resources, international conflict is endemic in a world of capitalist states. The elimination of capitalist states, Lenin concluded, was the essential precondition to abolishing international conflict.

For Lenin, capitalism had developed at its own pace in each country— earlier in Holland, England, and France; later in Germany and the United States; and later still in Japan and Russia. As it developed, monopolistic capital engaged in a feverishly competitive search for new markets, sources of raw materials, and cheap labor. Lenin was of the opinion that by this time the cartels had virtually completed the process of parceling out the territories of the world for exploitation. Because the planet had already been divided up, further expansion by some capitalists could occur only at the expense of other capitalists, and thus capitalistic imperialism would provoke international wars.[24] Stalin, remembering the Allied intervention in Russia at the end of World War I, regarded the capitalist West with suspicion and hostility, and spoke often of those outside plotting aggression against the Soviet Union. But in his famous "last thesis," issued on the eve of the 1952 meeting of the Communist party of the Soviet Union, Stalin argued that the "frightful clashes" that Lenin had predicted between the capitalist and socialist camps were no longer inevitable, because such a war would jeopardize the very existence of capitalism. Stalin then went on to declare that contradictions within the capitalist systems made the recurrence of war among capitalist states inevitable.[25]

LENIN, STALIN, AND WAR

Orthodox Leninist-Stalinist reasoning led inescapably to the conclusion that modern war is a function of capitalist imperialism; that if war should occur between the two systems it would be as a result of capitalist aggression and it would lead to the destruction of capitalism and the universal triumph of socialism; and that in an all-socialist world, once the dangers of "capitalist encirclement" had been eliminated, war would disappear. Stalin declared: "In order to destroy the inevitability of wars, it is necessary to destroy imperialism."[26] Of course, he was not necessarily implying that the socialist camp must someday try to destroy the imperialist camp by carrying out an aggressive military attack across national boundaries. He was, if anything, a cautious, conservative strategist; he certainly was not calling for a socialist holy war against a technologically superior Western state system. Both he and his successor, Khrushchev, propounded the thesis that "capitalist encirclement" must eventually give way to "socialist encirclement." Khrushchev is rather widely thought to have had a better appreciation than did Stalin of the implications of nuclear weapons technology for the "inevitability of war" problem, inasmuch as he formally recognized that general nuclear war could very well destroy not only capitalist society but communist society as well. Thus, while pursuing limited-risk arms control agreements with the capitalist West in order to render more manageable the strategic-military environment as reflected in international armaments competition, while at the same time continuing to develop Soviet military capabilities, both strategic and tactical, Khrushchev and his successors (Kosygin and Brezhnev) lent support to "wars of national liberation" in the Third World—forms of warfare considered both "just" in terms of socialist ideology and "safe" from the standpoint of strategic analysis in an era of mutual nuclear deterrence.[27]

LENINIST THEORY SINCE THE 1950s

The history of international relations since World War II has not dealt too kindly with the Leninist theory of imperialism. That theory is hard-pressed to explain Soviet Communist imperialism in Eastern Europe. Stalin's "last thesis" concerning the inevitability of war within the capitalist camp has not been validated.

On the other hand, the communist state system itself has been torn by serious conflicts. Soviet troops suppressed the workers' revolt in East Germany in 1953 and crushed the Hungarian uprising in 1956. In 1961, as previously noted, Nikita Khrushchev pledged the Soviet Union to support "wars of national liberation" in the developing world, but when Czechoslovakia in 1968 experienced the liberation stirrings known as the "Prague Spring," it elicited a response in the form of an invasion by the armed forces of five Warsaw Pact countries. Leonid Brezhnev subsequently justified the action by enunciating the doctrine that bears his name. The Brezhnev Doctrine in effect reserved to the Soviet Union the right to intervene in socialist states to suppress counterrevolutionary threats. The operational passages were contained in a statement made at the Fifth Congress of the Polish United Workers' Party on November 12, 1968:

> The CPSU has always been in favor of every socialist country determining the concrete forms of its development along the road to socialism, taking into account the specific character of national conditions. But we know, comrades, that there are also general laws of socialist construction, deviations from which could lead to deviations from socialism as such. And when internal and external forces hostile to socialism try to turn the development of any socialist country back toward a capitalist restoration, when a threat arises to the cause of socialism in that country, a threat to the security of the socialist community as a whole, that is no longer a problem only for the people of the country in question, but a general problem, the concern of all socialist states.[28]

Throughout the decade of the 1960s, the relationship between the Soviet Union and the People's Republic of China became increasingly polarized over several issues—ideological purity, support for world revolution, foreign development assistance, nuclear proliferation, territorial disputes as a result of old "unequal treaties," and the foolhardiness of socialist states entering into disarmament and arms control negotiations with capitalist states while the latter remained militarily powerful. (This last point was the orthodox Leninist position.[29]) In 1969, when U.S.-Soviet Strategic Arms Limitation Talks (SALT) were getting under way at a time of rising Sino-Soviet tension and hostilities along the Amur-Issuri Rivers, Mao Zedong decried the "collusion" of the imperialist powers, both capitalist and socialist. Within a few years, as the United States prepared to disengage from Southeast Asia, the leadership of the PRC concluded that the growth of Soviet military power was becoming a greater danger than a waning U.S. imperialist power, and began to warn Japan and other Asian states against Soviet hegemonic aims within their region.[30] Although the Sino-Soviet relationship became less confrontational in the 1980s, Beijing continued to regard Moscow as the primary threat to world peace largely as a result of what was perceived to be its effort to encircle and contain China through political-military moves in Mongolia and along the common border, in Afghanistan and Southeast Asia, and in the growth of the Soviet Pacific Fleet as well as the deployment of intermediate-range missiles in the Far East.[31] On the Western front, the Polish military and police forces were compelled to exercise a severe disciplinary hand against the Solidarity Labor Movement in order to avoid a direct Soviet intervention and crackdown in the early 1980s. Some Marxists continued to explain Soviet interventions in Eastern Europe and Vietnam in terms of a moral struggle between the forces of good and evil, of socialism and capitalism. But such explanations have grown feeble with time, after the Vietnamese invasion of Cambodia in December 1978, the PRC attack on Vietnam in February 1979, and the Soviet invasion of Afghanistan in December 1979.

The Andropov-Chernenko interregnum (1982–1985) was a transitional period of unstable leadership without precedent in Soviet history. Since 1985, the Gorbachev era has given rise to a spirited debate throughout the West as to whether *glasnost* (openness) and *perestroika* (restructuring) are harbingers of fundamental change in the Soviet world outlook—change that would so transform Lenin's ideological-political heritage as to be tantamount to abandoning it.[32]

CRITICS OF THE ECONOMIC THEORIES OF IMPERIALISM

Modern critics of the economic theories of imperialism have taken strong exception to the conclusions of Hobson, Lenin, and their followers on grounds of both semantics and economic-political analysis. Generally speaking, the semantic attack has taken the shape of an accusation that the followers of Lenin have been so obsessed by an ideological aversion to finance capitalism as to confuse a particular historical manifestation of the imperialistic impulse with a much more comprehensive sociological political phenomenon—what St. Augustine called the *animus dominandi*—which has assumed many different shapes throughout history.

Within recent decades, the most important critic of the Hobson-Leninist theory of imperialism as a terminological perversion for narrow polemical and ideological purposes has been Hans J. Morgenthau. Morgenthau lamented the application of the term *imperialism* to any foreign policy that the user of the term found objectionable, and he urged the post–World War II generation of university students to accept an objective, ethically neutral definition of imperialism as "a policy that aims at the overthrow of the status quo, at a reversal of the power relations between two or more nations."[33] He denied that every increase in the international power of a nation is necessarily imperialistic. Moreover, he warned against the disposition to regard every foreign policy that aims conservatively at maintaining an already existing empire as imperialistic when the term should be properly reserved for the dynamic process of changing the international status quo by acquiring an empire.[34] The economic interpretation of imperialism, contends Morgenthau, errs in the attempt to build a universal law of history upon the limited experience of a few isolated cases. Such a theory, in his view, ignores the problem of precapitalist imperialism (including the ancient empires of Egypt, Assyria, Persia, and Rome; Arab imperialism of the seventh and eighth centuries; the European Christian imperialism of the Crusades; and the personal empires of such men as Alexander the Great, Napoleon, and Hitler).[35] Moreover, Morgenthau contended that the theory fails to provide a convincing explanation even of capitalist-age imperialism in the *belle epoque* of imperialism, 1870 to 1914.

In the following summary of arguments against the Hobson-Lenin interpretation, the Morgenthau refutation is joined with that of several other prominent theorists, including the French political sociologist Raymond Aron; the Austrian economist Joseph A. Schumpeter (1883–1950), who taught at Harvard University; the American diplomatic historian William L. Langer (1896–1978); and the American economist Jacob Viner (1892–1970), as well as with the findings of more recent scholars who have uncovered several anomalies in the Hobson-Lenin hypothesis.[36]

1. The followers of Marx, Hobson, and Lenin confuse a particular historical manifestation of the imperialistic impulse with a much more comprehensive, multifaceted political-sociological phenomenon that has assumed many different shapes throughout history. The "turn of the century" economic theory of imperialism is a distortion insofar as it subordinates international politics to international economics both rigidly and superficially. Those who are well versed in the modern history of international politics have little difficulty demonstrating that the political impulse is usually stronger than the economic one, and that economic interests are frequently only a rationalization for a nation's will-to-power. Jacob Viner argued that in most cases,

> the capitalist, instead of pushing his government into an imperialistic enterprise in pursuit of his own financial gain, was pushed, or dragged, or cajoled, or lured into it by his government, in order that, in its relations with the outside world and with its own people this government might be able to point to an apparently real and legitimate economic stake in the territory involved which required military protection.[37]

2. Schumpeter insisted that imperialism cannot be reduced to the mere pursuit of economic interest when history is replete with examples of societies "that seek expansion for the sake of expanding, war for the sake of fighting, victory for the sake of winning, dominion for the sake of ruling."[38] Wars are not fought in order to realize immediate utilitarian advantages, even if these are the professed purpose. Imperialism rather is "the objectless disposition on the part of a state to unlimited forcible expansion."[39] Like nationalism, it is irrational and unconscious, a calling into play of instincts from the dim past. Imperialism, in short, is an atavism in the social culture. If one wants to trace it to economic roots, it should be attributed to *past* rather than present relations of production. Undoubtedly it is the ruling classes in any state who take the decisions for war, but it is not the business bourgeoisie who constitute the principal foreign policy decision-makers in the modern world; it is the vestigial aristocratic classes of an earlier regime who still fill the important governmental, diplomatic, and military posts.[40]

3. Notwithstanding the "devil theory" of war, which traces the causality of war to munitions-makers and others who stand to reap financial gain from its outbreak, capitalists as a whole are not given to bellicosity. Since war involves the irrational and the unpredictable, whereas capitalism thrives best on rational foresight and planning in a stable international environment, most capitalists are partisans of peace rather than of war, simply because those who suffer from the disruption of war greatly out-

number those who profit from it.[41] Competitive enterprise in the capitalist system, according to Schumpeter, absorbs tremendous amounts of human energy in purely economic pursuits, leaving little excess to be worked off in war and even less tendency to welcome war as a diversion from unpleasant activities or from boredom.[42] Capitalist society creates the sociological basis for a substantial popular opposition to war and armaments, as well as to socially entrenched professional armies. Before the age of capitalism, pacifist principles had been taken seriously in the West only by a few minority religious sects. Modern pacifism as a significant political movement emerges only in capitalist society in which organized parties produce peace leaders, peace slogans, and peace programs, along with a popular aversion to imperialism and popular support for arbitration of disputes, disarmament, and international organization. In this respect Schumpeter was in basic agreement with Norman Angell and even with Karl Marx and Friedrich Engels, who had noted that national differences and antagonisms between peoples were daily vanishing, owing to the development of the bourgeoisie, to freedom of commerce, to the world market, and to uniformity in the modes of production.

✱ 4. The fundamental assumptions of the economic theory of imperialism are wrong. "Hobson's theory has not stood the test of critical examination. The examples given by him for the fateful influence of capital investments overseas—South African mines and Chinese concessions—proved of ephemeral significance."[43] The effort to produce a universal theory on the basis of such scant evidence leads to several glaring anomalies in regard to what it leaves unexplained. According to that theory, the most advanced capitalist nations should have been the most expansionist and colonialist in the era of the highest development of monopolies and finance capitalism. Yet actually Europe's acquisition of colonial territories in the late nineteenth and early twentieth centuries was less extensive than in the period from the sixteenth to the eighteenth centuries. European settlements in North and South America involved genuine colonization; European imperialism in Asia and later in Africa did not, except for relatively small areas. The logical corollary of the Lenin-Hobson theory is that less capitalist states should be less imperialist and colonialist. Yet Portugal, backward among capitalist countries, was a leading colonial power. In contrast, Sweden and Switzerland, two states profoundly imbued with the capitalist spirit, exhibited no instinct whatever for imperial-colonial ventures.[44]

Schumpeter points to the United States, a developing country in the first half of the nineteenth century and a rapidly rising capitalist power after the American Civil War (1861–1865). According to the theory, the United States should have tried to seize its two resource-rich but militarily weak neighbors Mexico and Canada; but it did not do so.[45] (The United States, or at least some decision-makers, may have been aiming at territorial expansion in the 1812 attack on Canada and the 1848 attack on Mexico, but those episodes both fell within the precapitalist phase of American history.) Finally, the theory ignores the role of Western capital in making Japan an independent power of formidable proportions by the early twentieth century and of the United States postwar policy of rebuilding Western Europe's and Japan's ability to compete in world markets.

5. We can now examine the economic bases on which the Hobson-Lenin theory rests. First, it can be noted, in refutation of Hobson's underconsumption-oversavings hypothesis, that the export of surplus capital was not absolutely essential for growth; as Revisionist Marxists such as Karl Kautsky and Eduard Bernstein realized, the capitalists were not playing Marx's "iron law of wages" game to bring about the increasing "immiseration" of the workers; actually the workers' standard of living was on the rise, and domestic purchasing power was increasing in real terms as a consequence of trade union activity and the enfranchisement of larger numbers of people.[46] Second, during the period from 1870 to 1914, more capital moved into England than out of it, and three-quarters of the capital exported from Britain did not come from monopoly companies but consisted of loans to governments and government-guaranteed public utilities.[47]

Third, the colonies were not as important in the trade and investment patterns of the capitalist countries as the theory indicated. No more than 10 percent of France's overseas investments prior to 1914 were directed to the Empire.[48] Apart from India, the colonies, especially those in Africa, were not a source of much profit to Britain. Aron writes: "The two nations which during the half century before the First World War conquered the largest territories, France and Great Britain, were also the nations which, economically, least needed to acquire new possessions."[49] Most of the capital exported from the advanced capitalist countries during that period went to other industrially advanced countries, or else to such countries as Russia that were just beginning to develop industrially—and that France was anxious to build up for political-strategic reasons against Germany.

6. Lenin's contention that imperialism as he defined it is the principal cause of war in the capitalistic era has not stood up well under the scrutiny of scholars. The major wars since 1870 have not been fought primarily for economic motives. The Boer War in South Africa and the Chaco War between Bolivia and Paraguay (1932–1935) were, but not the Franco-German War, the Spanish-American War, the Russo-Japanese War, or the Turko-Italian War, and certainly not the two World Wars, the Arab-Israeli Wars, the Korean War, the Indo-Chinese War, the Indo-Pakistani Wars over Kashmir and Bangladesh, or the Vietnam War (even though leftist critics of the war in the West sometimes tried unconvincingly to reduce the Southeast Asian conflict to a capitalist-imperialist plot, mainly because the United States was identified as the leader of the capitalist-imperialist system).[50]

In the background of World War I, Aron assigns a central place to Anglo-German rivalry, especially the naval arms race, but he denies that this had much to do with capitalism. The British were aware that Germany represented a threat to their prosperity, but they also knew that each country was the best customer of the other's goods. If capitalist imperialism had been the main motive for England's going to war in 1914, then the country should have arrayed itself against its major competitor since the turn of the century—the United States.[51] That such a course of action was unthinkable should serve to cast some doubt upon the explanatory power of the Leninist-Stalinist theory. Coming to more recent times, no one has ever bothered to try making a case for economic imperialism as the cause of the Korean War; such a task must strike even the most single-minded Marxist as futile. Kenneth Boulding wrote that any economic benefits the United States might have hoped to derive from the Vietnam War would hardly be worth the cost of waging that war for one day.[52] In the Arab-Israeli conflict since 1948, anyone who wishes to prove that American policy has been based upon considerations of economic imperialism is hard-pressed to explain why the United States has supported Israel even at the risk of alienating the oil-producing Arab states.

In a recent study, a young scholar complained that earlier theorists of imperialism, notably Hobson, Lenin, and Schumpeter, were less interested in producing scholarly explanations of a particular phenomenon in international relations than they were in presenting either a political condemnation or defense of capitalism.[53] Michael W. Doyle defined "imperialism" as "the actual process by which empires are formed and maintained," and "empire" as "a system of interaction between two political entities, one of which, the dominant metropole, exerts political control over the internal and external policy—the effective sovereignty—of the other, the subordinate periphery."[54] He distinguishes empire from two commonly encountered forms of international equality: (a) *hegemony*, in which one power controls or influences the foreign but not the internal policy of other states; and (b) *dependence*, a condition under which a state finds itself limited by constraints on its economic, social, and political autonomy.[55] He denies that the forces driving and shaping imperialism are either primarily economic or primarily military; rather, they are economic, military, political, social, and cultural. "Both the opportunities that give rise to imperialism and the motives that drive it are to be found in a fourfold interaction among metropoles, peripheries, transnational forces, and international systemic incentives."[56] Whereas Hobson, Lenin, and Schumpeter trace the causes to the metropoles—the desire for financial profit, the necessities of monopoly capital, the atavistic impulses of military elites—others, such as John Gallagher and Ronald Robinson, see the roots of imperialism in the crises of weak, vulnerable societies on the African, Asian, and Latin American peripheries. Benjamin Cohen, Kenneth Waltz, A. J. P. Taylor, Morton Kaplan, Edward Gulick, and other theorists of power explain imperialism as a normal concomitant of the structural dynamic implicit in an international system in which stronger states engage in a power-balancing process by exerting their sway over weaker states.[57]

Doyle notes that anomalies often arise when we try to assess the elements of political and economic control in our study of empires and imperialism. For the half-century from 1890 to the outbreak of World War II, *empire* implied conquered territory while *imperialism* reflected a "deep disposition" within the metropolitan society. Following postwar decolonization, *imperialism* was transmuted into *neoimperialism* or *neocolonialism*—terms that meant continued economic control by the West of territories that had been granted formal political-legal independence. (The concepts, of course, are Marxist in inspiration.[58]) In Doyle's view, the legal acquisition of territory does not necessarily imply effective control. From 1882 until 1914, Egypt was still legally part of the Ottoman Empire, yet it was completely controlled by Britain. Furthermore, he says, defining imperialism by reference to its alleged cause (monopoly capitalism) is tautological, not explanatory. Finally, political control does not inevitably produce economic exploitation; the metropolitan country "brings" as well as "takes." It is erroneous to assume that inequality of power must lead to exploitation, as the long, friendly relationship between England and Siam amply demonstrated.

MODERN MARXISTS AND THE THIRD WORLD

Contemporary Marxist writers who adhere, however vaguely, to the Leninist theory of imperialism often charge that Western colonialism suppressed the economic, social, and political development of the countries that now constitute the Third World, and that the West is still to blame for the poverty of those countries. Khrushchev had contended three decades ago that the economic advances made by some Western countries were due to the underdevelopment of Asia, Africa, and Latin America. Western governments have been faulted for having failed during the era of colonial rule to introduce central economic planning in their territories and to promote the growth of indigenous industry with protective tariffs. André Gunder Frank has denied that underdevelopment is attributable to the survival of archaic institutions and capital shortages in regions isolated from the mainstream of world history. "On the contrary, underdevelopment was and still is generated by the very same historical process which also generated economic development: the development of capitalism itself."[59]

Marxists generally accuse the West—or "the world capitalist system" (which will be discussed later)—of keeping the poor countries in a position of subordination, dependence, or bondage by limiting investments to the extractive (raw materials) industries and by Westernizing, subjugating, and bribing the new elites who have an interest in modernizing their societies. Before the period of decolonization, the Marxists predicted that once the colonial territories had gained political independence they would become masters of their own economic destiny, and thus the capi-

talists would fight to the end to prevent them from achieving self-government, because that would spell the collapse of the capitalist system. Marx
himself saw capital penetration and imperialism as progressive forces,
bringing civilization and capitalism, which he held to be the necessary
prerequisites to socialism.[60]

Most of Europe's colonies had gained their independence by the
1960s. The Western capitalists had not fought effectively to hold them.
The British and the Belgians—if not the French, the Dutch, and the
Portuguese—seemed almost eager at times to get rid of their empires, as
if the empires were millstones around their necks.[61] Conflict did indeed
attend the independence of some imperial possessions—Algeria, In-
donesia, Cyprus, the Congo, Kenya, India, and Pakistan (due, in the latter
cases, to historic religious divisions in the subcontinent)—yet more than
twoscore colonial territories in Asia and Africa achieved status as independent states with relatively little or no violence. Furthermore, since the
standard of living of the masses in the Western capitalist states had been
alleged by the Marxists to be artificially high because it had long been
based on the exploitation of native populations, disimperialism should
have led to a perceptible decline in the West's standard of living, but this
did not occur. To the contrary, the formation of the European Economic
Community or Common Market ushered in a period of unprecedented
economic growth and prosperity during the decade of decolonization.

Despite the steady movement of Asia and Africa toward political
decolonization, Nikita Khrushchev frequently warned that the Western
nations would "halt the disintegration of the colonial system of imperialism and strangle the national liberation movements of the peoples for
freedom and independence."[62] The West, said Khrushchev, was desperately seeking new forms for keeping the peoples of economically underdeveloped countries in a state of permanent dependence. If any politically
independent government in the Third World entered into a military assistance pact with a Western nation for defense against external attack or
internal guerilla subversion, this was simply a case, in Khrushchev's eyes,
of fastening another control upon nominally independent states and prop-
ping up their "corrupt regimes" under the pretext of saving them from
communism.[63] Khrushchev singled out the European Economic Community as an instrument of "neocolonialism" against which the new states had
to be particularly on their guard. Official communist theory, while conceding that some economic development was now taking place in the Third
World, still regarded the newly independent countries as part of the world
subject to exploitation by the capitalist monopolies.[64]

Following independence, development in Third World countries continued pretty much as before. It did not spurt ahead dramatically. This
historic reality of the process of decolonization and its aftermath neces-
sitated further modification of the Marxist-Leninist theory. Political independence for the former colonies was portrayed as a sham, because it led
to no significant improvement in their economic status. The poor coun-

tries, said the Marxists, are still locked into the capitalist system and are being impoverished by its "iron law of prices," much as Marx used to deplore the increasing "immiseration" of the workers in capitalist countries as a result of the operation of the "iron law of wages." (In Marxist theory, all laws are iron laws.) This new situation explains the failure of the prediction that the capitalists would fight tenaciously to hold on to their colonies: The capitalists knew that they would have no difficulty continuing their economic domination.

Thomas E. Weisskopf has noted several factors at work within the world capitalist system that in his view reinforce the subordination of poor to rich countries:

- Rising elites in the poor countries are persuaded to emulate the consumption patterns of the bourgeoisie in the rich countries and to create a demand for Western imports that satisfy elite consumers without contributing to economic development.
- The "brain drain" of scientists, engineers, managers, and other technically educated professionals from poor to rich countries increases the dependence of the less developed countries (LDCs) on the industrialized regions.
- Foreign private enterprise perpetuates the conditions that made foreign capital indispensable and discourages the growth of host country knowledge, technology, skills, and incentives that would enhance its independence.
- Western capitalists create a labor aristocracy in the poor countries by paying a smaller number of skilled workers higher wages rather than paying a larger number of unskilled workers lower wages.[65]

Weisskopf ignores the contradiction implicit in his third and fourth points above.

Marxists have generally held that the affluence of Western society has not been due to human energy, scientific inventiveness, technological proficiency, managerial and organizational efficiency, economies of scale, and a climate of political freedom in which economic decisions, while subject to public policy regulations, can be taken without excessive constraints being imposed by bureaucratic central planners. Instead, they have explained that affluence is attributable in large measure to the exploitation by European and American capitalism of the peoples of Asia, Africa, and Latin America—an exploitation in which even the "bourgeois workers" of the West participated. To offset the paradox of the continued rise in the West's standard of living when it should have declined after the loss of empire, Marxists laid increasing emphasis on the argument that the Western economies were being artificially stimulated by the "arms race."

The view that the military competition of the superpowers and their alliance systems is due to the economic interests of Western capitalists is too simplistic to warrant comment.[66] Moreover, the notion that colonial exploitation has been replaced by the "arms race" does not stand up too well under serious scrutiny. The United States, which, compared to the European nations, had a very meager overseas empire, would undoubtedly have become the principal military defender of Western civilization after World War II regardless of developments in the colonial world. The Western European nations, which renounced rather enormous colonial holdings, have consistently allocated a much lower percentage of their gross national product to defense than has the United States, and the case could be made that the West German, French, and Japanese standards of living have risen more rapidly than that of the United States during the past three decades.

Among Marxist theorists in the post–World War II period who have sought to link imperialism closely with American foreign policy, Harry Magdoff is one of the leading writers. Magdoff takes issue with those who contend that political aims and national security, rather than economic imperialism, have been the prime motivators of United States foreign policy. Such people, says Magdoff, rely on the argument that foreign trade and investment make up such a small part of the GNP of the United States (less than 5 percent in the case of total exports) that economic factors could not possibly determine American foreign policy. Magdoff denies that the size of ratios is by itself an adequate indicator of what motivates foreign policy. He further argues that the stake of American business abroad is many times larger than the volume of merchandise exports. He estimates that the size of the foreign market for all United States firms (domestic and those owned abroad) comes to about two-fifths of the domestic output of all farms, factories, and mines. He sees foreign economic activity as having growing importance to this country and its national security policy, usually justified in political-military terms, and as being designed to protect the economic interest of giant corporations abroad:

> The widespread military bases, the far-flung military activities, and the accompanying complex of expenditures at home and abroad serve many purposes of special interest to the business community: (1) protecting present and potential sources of raw materials; (2) safeguarding foreign markets and foreign investments; (3) conserving commercial sea and air routes; (4) preserving spheres of influence where United States business gets a competitive edge for investment and trade; (5) creating new foreign customers and investment opportunities via foreign military and economic aid; and, more generally, (6) maintaining the structure of world capitalist markets not only directly for the United States but also for its junior partners among the industrialized nations.[67]

Magdoff, like all Marxists, expresses indignation over the fact that the United States invests primarily in extractive industries in Third World countries, thus ensuring sources of raw material supplies to domestic monopolies on the most favorable terms. He implicitly assumes that dependence on primary product exports prevents real development.[68] This Marxist argument, by dint of constant repetition, has exerted an influence upon the thinking of non-Marxist analysts in the West, especially those who have sought to show that the contemporary pattern of international exchange relations based upon world division of labor—in which the less developed countries supply the basic raw materials for the industrially advanced countries to process—leads to dynamic growth at one pole of the world economy and to stagnation and impoverishment at the other.

The Norwegian theorist Johan Galtung is an eminent proponent of this point of view. Galtung sees trade relationships between the European Community and Third World countries as characterized by a threefold structural dominance—the already-mentioned vertical division of labor plus two additional means of perpetuating the exploitative status quo: (1) "fragmentation" (or the relative absence of horizontal economic relationships among the developing countries); and (2) "penetration" (which involves the growth, previously alluded to, of economic, educational, cultural, and other relationships between local rising elites in Third World countries and the former metropolitan powers).[69] Galtung faults the European Community for "permitting" the Associated States of Africa to produce only such processed goods as will no longer be competitive with European Community exports. Even by granting "Associated" status and selective tariff preferences to certain African states, he declares, the European Community gives them a privileged position vis-à-vis the rest of the Third World, and thus fragments the "Group of 77" in UNCTAD (the United Nations Conference on Trade and Development).[70] Galtung is not a Marxist, but in his structural theory of imperialism he employs several of the same categories of thought as do the Marxists.

CRITIQUE OF THE NEO-MARXISTS

Marxists and others who blame the West for the poverty of the LDCs have been roundly criticized for oversimplifying the situation. No matter how much good may be done, it is always easy (and usually true) to say that more should have been done. But to blame the European governments for failing to carry out a higher degree of development in their empires when they held the responsibility, says P. T. Bauer, is to "overstate the potentialities of state power as an instrument of economic progress."[71] Actually, Bauer insists, colonial status was not incompatible with economic development. Whereas there had been virtually no economic growth in Africa before the Europeans arrived, between 1890 and 1960 West African trade (particularly for the Gold Coast and Nigeria) increased by a factor of 100 or more. According to Bauer,

> It is highly probable that over the last century or so the establishment of colonial rule in Africa and Asia has promoted, and not retarded, material progress. With relatively little coercion, or even interference in the lives of the great majority of the people, the colonial governments established law and order, safeguarded private property and contractual relations, organized basic

transport and health services, and introduced some modern financial and legal institutions. The resulting environment also promoted the establishment or extension of external contacts, which in turn encouraged the inflow of external resources, notably administrative, commercial, and technical skills, as well as capital. . . . It is unlikely (though this cannot be proved conclusively) that in the absence of colonial rule, the social, political, and economic environment in colonial Africa and Asia would have been more congenial to material progress.[72]

Bauer makes the telling observation that the African states not subject to Western imperialism—Liberia and Ethiopia—are today more backward than those of their neighbors that had been colonized.[73] The relationship between the West and the colonial peoples was far from being one-sidedly exploitative. With Western domination came literacy and education, hospitals, hygiene, sanitary methods, and at least a rudimentary knowledge of science and technology. The political impact of the West upon the colonial lands was in some respects greater than the economic impact. The concepts of "independence," "self-determination," "freedom," and "sovereign equality" that the peoples of Asia and Africa employed with great effect after World War II to express their political aspirations were, as Hans Kohn pointed out, borrowed from the Western political vocabulary by native leaders who had received their university education in Western countries.[74]

Other non-Marxist analysts have argued persuasively that there is no necessary relationship between poverty and the reliance of Third World countries upon extractive and agricultural industries. Posing a serious challenge to the fundamental assumptions of this particular "iron law" thesis are the anomalies of Australia and New Zealand. Taking issue with Galtung, Andrew Mack writes:

> The economic exchange relationships which link Australia and New Zealand with the rich industrialized countries are precisely those which Galtung claims not only characterize Third World/EC relationships but which are also the root cause of the former's underdevelopment. Both countries depend on the export of primary commodities . . . characterized by nonexistent or very low degrees of processing. On the other hand, both countries depend on imports which are typically highly processed. . . . In other words, both countries lie at the lower end of the vertical division of international labor. . . . Yet both countries have experienced steady economic growth *and* a significant degree of domestic industrialization. This is indeed an anomaly which Galtung's theory cannot explain.[75]

Marxist analysts seem to believe that whatever capitalists do constitutes exploitation. At the same time, they condemn Western governments and entrepreneurs for not having done more to help the colonial territories and their successor independent states. Seldom do Marxists spell out what capitalists ought to have done for Third World economic development and failed to do. Perhaps they cannot do this, for the more active capitalists are, the more exploitative they are—by definition. Marxists also assume that the socialist system, by definition, cannot be exploitative. Here they prefer to ignore the Soviet Union's postwar record in Eastern Europe. For many years, elites in the LDCs were strongly attracted to the Soviet model of economic development. Whether they will continue to prefer state planning Soviet-style over foreign-assisted "capitalist-imperialist" development has become more doubtful since Gorbachev indicted the Brezhnev era for its "stagnation" and began trying to inject new production incentives into the Soviet economy.

IMPERIALISM AS POLITICAL SLOGAN

"Imperialism" has remained the principal slogan or shibboleth of world politics in the second half of the twentieth century. The Leninist theory has often been called narrowly Eurocentric, but the term has taken on a universal applicability since World War II. All of the leading powers have employed it to describe the policies of their rivals. For Stalin, imperialism stood for the conduct of any power unfriendly to communist policy.[76] He condemned the Marshall Plan as a plot of capitalist imperialism and branded the defector Tito as a tool of the imperialists. Arab nationalists railed against British and American-Zionist imperialism in the Middle East.[77] It was inevitable that the activities of United States oil companies in the Middle East and fruit companies in Latin America should be labeled prime examples of imperialism, and that trade agreements between the European Community and its Associated States of Africa and Asia should be characterized as instruments of neoimperialism. The Indonesian leader Sukarno and other Third World neutralists, in the late 1950s, excoriated the West for having subjugated all the peoples living along the "imperialist highway" from the Atlantic Ocean to the Indian Ocean and the South China Sea.[78] Until the late 1960s, when the Soviet Union replaced the United States as Beijing's principal enemy, Mao Zedong, adhering to a hard Stalinist line, made imperialism the main slogan in China's propaganda war against the United States.

Lenin, Stalin, and Mao all effectively used "imperialism" to arouse Third World resentment against the West for political-strategic reasons. Most Western theorists of international relations, as well as political leaders, regarded the Soviet domination of Eastern Europe as imperialism, even though Third World intellectuals were not greatly exercised over the Soviet suppression of the Hungarian uprising in 1956. Kenneth E. Boulding wrote:

> It is quite impossible to explain modern imperialism in economic terms. The only possible exception to this, paradoxically enough, is the socialist imperialism exercised by the Soviet Union on Eastern Europe and especially on East Germany after the Second World War. The Soviet Union probably extracted more goods from East Germany in the ten years after the Second World War than Britain did in two hundred years from India, and this was pure tribute.[79]

The neutralists of the Third World, for three decades after World War II, seemed to take it for granted, as many had earlier, that imperialists are people who come in ships from distant lands. Those who could impose their dominance simply by marching armies across borders were for a long time excluded from the definition of "imperialists." It was the People's Republic of China, which itself had engaged in some imperialistic adventures against India and Tibet, that began to accuse the Soviet Union of imperialism in a manner credible to leftist elites in the Third World. While trying to replace the Soviet Union as the leader of the forces of world revolution, Mao first accused Soviet leaders of revisionism, bourgeoisification, and betrayal of the revolution through arms control collusion with capitalist imperialists. Later the Chinese leaders condemned capitalist and socialist imperialism in one breath. Later still, they began to indicate that they regarded the socialist imperialism of the Soviet Union as a greater threat than the capitalist imperialism of the United States, and acted as if they would welcome a tacit alliance with the enemy farther away against the enemy nearer. At the same time, they encouraged the strengthening of NATO, urged Europe to unite, and warned the West not to take a Soviet-promoted détente too seriously. In July 1978, the foreign ministers of more than 100 nonaligned states, meeting in Belgrade, hinted for the first time that they were becoming more worried about Soviet expansion, especially in Africa, than they were about a waning Western imperialism.[80]

Nevertheless, despite its many theoretical deficiencies and failures of prediction and practice—for example, several countries organized along Marxist communist lines have found it harder to feed themselves than they did before—Marxism continues to exercise a worldwide appeal as a vehicle for the expression of criticism, resentment, and protest against the complexities and frustrations of contemporary social reality.[81] According to Adam B. Ulam, the Hobson-Leninist theory of imperialism, "because of its simplicity, because of its psychological appeal and because of the undoubted depredations and brutalities that accompanied the process of colonization," retains its influence by enabling the disadvantaged of the world to express their rage and to disturb the conscience of a guilt-ridden West.[82]

In the final analysis, the Leninist theory of imperialism does a disservice to the developing nations of the non-Western world. The simplistic, polemical urge to blame all or most of those countries' troubles on the exploitation of a few capitalistic states, as Anthony James Joes has noted, diverts the attention of planners who take the ideological explanation seriously from examining carefully the obstacles posed to modernization by indigenous political, cultural, economic, and geographic factors. The theory is also self-serving to some Third World leaders, says Joes, for "it exculpates dogmatic theorists, incompetent windbags, epauleted megalomaniacs, and 'village tyrants' from all responsibility for the deplorable condition of their suffering countrymen even after two decades—or two centuries or two millenia—of political independence."[83]

THE NORTH-SOUTH DEBATE

For two decades or longer, political practitioners and academic theorists have been arguing that economic problems have come to rival the traditional security concerns of nations and that world politics is becoming increasingly meshed with issues of trade, aid, and monetary affairs. Many have gone so far as to contend that the North-South debate, which focuses on structural inequities in the international economy, has supplanted the East-West security preoccupation as the most urgent issue on the global agenda, at least in the eyes of more than two-thirds of the countries of the world—especially those of Asia, Africa, and Latin America. The Third World with persistent vehemence has condemned the "arms race" between the First (or Western) World and the Second (Soviet Socialist Bloc) World (not including Communist China) and has pressed hard within the United Nations for disarmament of the nuclear-weapons powers as a principal means of freeing up what the Third World regards as resources wasted on the dangerous chimera of deterrence—resources that could be reallocated to intranational development.

It is gross oversimplification to identify the Northern industrial countries with "the rich" and the Southern less developed countries with "the poor." Both within and among states of the North we can note economic disparities—for example, between the northern part of Italy and the Mezzogiorno in the south, or between the slums and the suburbs of many cities in the United States, or between Portugal and Greece on the one hand and the more affluent northwestern Europe on the other. Since the oil price rise of the early 1970s, the Third World has been divided into two worlds, one of which was adversely affected by the increased cost of oil imports required for industrial and agricultural development, and a Fourth World that includes some countries that can, thanks to OPEC pricing and production policies, boast per capita incomes higher than those of a few Northern countries. Several of the more than 100 states that identify themselves with "the South" are themselves newly industrializing countries (NICs) with labor-intensive economies whose manufacturing exports have proved highly competitive in international markets against countries that enjoy a higher standard of living.* Finally, the gap between the wealthy and the poverty-stricken classes in the urban areas and countries of the South is often more glaring than in the North or in the global economic system as a whole between North and South. Indeed, Third World voices that are most scathing in their condemnation of the Western industrialized nations for consuming three-quarters of the world's resources to satisfy one-quarter of its population often condone glaring inequalities in the class structures of their own societies, which they usually blame on the capitalist West.[84]

---

*These include Argentina, Brazil, Mexico, India, South Korea, Taiwan, the Philippines, Hong Kong, Singapore, and, more recently, Malaysia and Thailand.

After all the caveats have been noted, no one can deny that the bulk of mankind living in the 100 countries (outside North America, West Europe, Japan, East Europe, OPEC, and the NICs) with the lowest per capita incomes is substantially much worse off in material terms (although perhaps not culturally or psychologically or spiritually) than the people who live in the 40 countries with the highest income levels. Analysts have been pointing to the unequal relationship between the richer and the poorer nations for decades. Some prefer to ignore the glaring differences that exist, but no intelligent person can disagree with the grim statistical comparisons that have been recited so many times that most people in the industrialized countries have grown virtually immune to them.

Not surprisingly, the perspectives of the global problem adopted by the North and South are poles apart. In 1976, Mahbub ul Haq, the Pakistani Director of Policy Planning and Program Review at the International Bank for Reconstruction and Development (or World Bank) in Washington, summed up the two points of view as follows:

> The poor nations are beginning to question the basic premises of an international order that leads to ever widening disparities between the rich and poor countries and to a persistent denial of equality of opportunity to many poor nations. They are, in fact, arguing that in the international order—just as much as within national orders—all distribution of benefits, credits, services, and decision-making gets warped in favor of a privileged minority and that this situation cannot be changed except through fundamental institutional reforms.
>
> When this is pointed out to the rich nations, they dismiss it casually as empty rhetoric of the poor nations. Their standard answer is that the international market mechanism works, even though not too perfectly, and that the poor nations are always out to wring concessions from the rich nations in the name of past exploitation. They believe that the poor nations are demanding a massive redistribution of income and wealth which is simply not in the cards. Their general attitude seems to be that the poor nations must earn their economic development, much the same way as the rich nations had to over the last two centuries, through patient hard work and gradual capital formation, and that there are no shortcuts to this process and no rhetorical substitutes. The rich, however, are "generous" enough to offer some help to the poor nations to accelerate their economic development if the poor are only willing to behave themselves.[85]

The World Bank official went on to draw an analogy between the global poor and the poor strata within a national society, for whom the market mechanism ceases to function equitably, since the wealthy classes can bend the market to their will while the poor lack power to influence its decisions. "This is even more true at the international level," he adds, "since there is no world government and none of the usual mechanisms existing within countries that create pressures for redistribution of income and wealth."[86] Churches, philosophers, theologians, social theorists, and others may argue with forceful eloquence that the fortunately situated peoples of this world have a high moral obligation to help those much less fortunate. They are undoubtedly right. Even certain courageous politicians agree, despite the fact that such a message is never popular with taxpayers in democratic parliamentary countries (and it is practically never heard preached in the socialist bloc). People in affluent Western societies can exhibit extremely generous impulses when it comes to helping people whom they know in circumstances of chronic hardship (at home) or emergency needs (at home and abroad). It has never been easy for any government, however, to generate much enthusiasm for sustained, long-range, well-planned, and massive programs of international development assistance. Regardless of what the *moral* obligations of nations may be, there exists no effective world public authority to enforce the obligation by translating it into policy.

The Theory of *Dependencia* ✖

Most of the LDCs have emerged in the latter half of the twentieth century from a past in which either political colonialism, economic imperialism, or both predominated. Whereas all Western industrial countries and Japan experienced some problems in the transition from traditional to modern societies, for most of them the process has been gradual and phased over a longer period. Many Third World countries, suddenly caught up in rapid social change, have felt revolutionary pressures as a result of the modernization process. Most of them manifest glaring inequities in patterns of accumulated wealth and annual income distribution. Most suffer from high or above-average rates of population growth, infant mortality, malnutrition or hunger, contagious disease, and illiteracy, as well as inadequate programs of education, health, and welfare. Throughout the Third World, planning for coherent economic development is hampered by shortages of technical-administrative expertise, political instability, inflation, unfavorable terms of trade (because of dependence on the export of a few primary products and the import of costly capital and manufactures, plus large-scale indebtedness to foreign banking institutions, whether national or international), and pressures for consumption that more often than not outstrip domestic productivity.

Dependency theory originated during the 1970s as one school of structural-globalist thought, the object of which was to explain the gap between the rich and poor nations of the world. It was developed largely by Latin American analysts of the Economic Commission on Latin America (ECLA), and was quickly adopted by UNCTAD-oriented writers who were not satisfied with the explanations of those who attributed the development failure of Third World societies to the assumption that religious-cultural traditions acted as a bulwark against modernization. The basic thesis of the *dependentistas* is that dependency differs from the dependence that most contemporary scholars have in mind when they refer to an "interdependent" world, even when they acknowledge inequities in interdependent relationships. James Caporaso distinguished the two concepts as follows:

> The dependence orientation seeks to probe and explore the symmetries and asymmetries among nation-states. This approach most often proceeds from a *liberal* paradigm which focuses on individual actors and their goals and which sees power in decisional terms. The individual actors are usually internally unified states which confront the external environment as homogeneous units. . . . The dependency orientation, on the other hand, seeks to explore the process of integration of the periphery into the international capitalist system and to assess the developmental implications of this peripheral capitalism. This approach proceeds from a *structuralist* paradigm which focuses on the class structure and international capital, and the role of the state in shaping and managing the national, foreign, and class forces that propel development within countries. The dependency framework, in other words, explicitly rejects the unified state as actor as a useful conceptual building block of theory.[87]

In the view of dependency theorists, the relationship between the Northern "core" and the Southern "periphery," far from being a relationship of mutual-interest cooperation, connotes the subordination of the latter to and exploitation by the former. Thus, in the eyes of *dependentistas,* the poor countries do not lack capital and lag behind the rich because they lie outside or on the edge of the capitalist world but rather because they have been integrated into the international class structure of the capitalist system. In this respect, dependency theory is essentially a variant of the neo-Marxist perspective on the situation facing the erstwhile colonial territories. Tony Smith characterized dependency theory as follows:

> Put briefly, it holds that economic processes are the basic structural force of history, and that over the last several centuries it has been northern capitalism (first in its mercantile, then in its free trade, later in its financial, and today in its multinational guises) that has been history's locomotive. Those lands and peoples are "dependent" that are not "autonomous" (a favorite word of many of these writers that is never rigorously defined . . .) in the face of these external economic forces. . . .
>
> The major criticism to be made of dependency theory is that it exaggerates the explanatory power of economic imperialism as a concept to make sense of historical change in the south. Too much emphasis is placed on the dynamic, molding power of capitalist imperialism and the socioeconomic forces in league with it locally; too little attention is paid to political motives behind imperialism or to the autonomous power of local political circumstances in influencing the course of change in Africa, Asia and Latin America.[88]

J. Samuel and Arturo Valenzuela criticized the "modernization perspective" that economists, anthropologists, sociologists, and political scientists had developed in the postwar period to explain the failure of "new nations" to reach the "economic takeoff" point with an infusion of Western foreign aid. Such a perspective, in their view, was an outgrowth of the tradition-modernity dichotomy of nineteenth-century European sociology that saw culture itself, resistant to change, as the main obstacle to economic modernization. Traditional societies are marked by ascription, not achievement; by social status and not individual effort; by an extended kinship structure rather than the nuclear family. They manifest little occupational specialization and social mobility, a highly stratified system of upward deference, and an emphasis on elitism and hierarchical authority. By contrast, the features of "modern" society are conceptually quite different—indeed, polar opposites: high rates of social mobility; a complex occupational system; a predominance of secondary over merely primary economic activities (that is, manufacturing and service industries beyond agriculture and mining); differentiated political, legal, and social structures; and an institutionalized capacity for change rather than a rigid pattern calculated to preserve immemorial social, religious, and cultural values. Western modernizationists were faulted for assuming that unless traditional societies could learn to innovate and adopt Western ideas, techniques, organizational methods, incentives and institutions—a whole new set of attitudes and way of life—they must continue to languish on the fringe of poverty.

Dependency theorists, note the Valenzuelas, reject the modernizationist assumption that genuine development can result only through an appropriate response to stimuli from exogenous sources according to the uniquely successful Western model, as if development and Westernization were identical processes. They also reject the notion that the national society is the proper unit of analysis in this context. The Valenzuelas argue that different levels in the transition from tradition to modernity cannot explain differences in levels of economic growth achievement. Nations and regions can be analyzed only by reference to their locus in the world political-economic system—whether they are closer to the core or to the periphery. This is a central tenet running through all dependency literature. Dependency literature, unfortunately, is marred by such imprecise or inelegant concepts as "associated-dependent development," "inwardly [or outwardly] directed development," "global historical-structural processes," the "operationalization of dependency," and "diachronic analysis."[89]

Dependency theorists have had to deal with the undeniable fact that some LDCs have begun to produce manufactures for themselves on a substantial scale instead of importing them. These "newly industrializing countries" (NICs) include South Korea, Taiwan, Argentina, Brazil, India, the Philippines, Hong Kong, Singapore, Mexico, Venezuela, Thailand, and Malaysia. In some cases, the NICs themselves have become major exporters even to such countries as the United States, which in the 1980s had large balance of payments deficits with the emerging economic entities of the Republic of Korea and Taiwan. Dependency theorists admit that multinational corporations (MNCs) have been attracted to these countries and that some import-substitution has been going on, but it is because of cheaper labor costs and, in many cases, shorter supply lines for raw materials. Nevertheless, the *dependentistas* contend, such development as does occur is not really "autonomous," but is dictated by the global requirements of the world capitalist system. Neo-Marxists and dependency theorists prefer to emphasize the continued subordination of this "semiperiphery" to the core and ignore the fact that some entire countries are now better off than before.[90] In these as in other Third World countries, dependency theorists argue, a *comprador,* or national urban bourgeois class, has allied itself with foreign capitalists and aggrandizes itself by joining them in exploiting their less fortunate fellow nationals, particularly in rural areas and in the slums of modernizing cities.

The New International Economic Order (NIEO) ✘

The North-South debate about the real versus the ideal structure of world economic relations reached its maximum intensity during the 1970s in a series of specific demands by the Third World for global reform. These demands for a New International Economic Order were contained in several documents adopted by international conferences usually organized within the framework of the United Nations.[91] The success of the oil-producing countries in quadrupling the price of their product convinced many political leaders, along with their advisers, that the Third World could employ various forms of "commodity power" as leverage against what they regarded as the oppressive "global liberalism" of the industrialized West. They believed that they could flex their muscles through their voting power in the United Nations General Assembly, UNCTAD and UNCLOS III (the Third U. N. Conference on the Law of the Seas), and through their suasive rhetoric in the International Monetary Fund (IMF) and the World Bank. Their objectives were to speed up the pace of their own economic development and to shift the pattern of income distribution—less for the rich and more for the poor nations. By no means were all Third World states agreed on what had to be done, because of the divergences of interest that had become obvious within their own ranks—for example, between oil exporters and oil importers, between coastal and landlocked states, between agricultural-commodity-dependent states and the NICs. Generally, however, there was widespread agreement that the North must

- ensure a quickened rate of technology transfer (for most Third World countries were afraid that the technology gap would continue to widen rather than narrow);
- improve the terms of trade for the South and expand trade preferences for its manufactures;
- multilateralize foreign economic development assistance to insulate it against the attachment of political strings that often accompanied bilateral transactions;

- negotiate with UNCTAD and other Third World groups commodity price stabilization agreements to protect primary products exported to the North against wide price fluctuations in the world market;
- impose more stringent controls upon First World capital investment abroad and upon the operations of MNCs;
- grant debt relief by rescheduling or canceling Third World indebtedness to Northern banks and other North-dominated international financial institutions;
- accept price indexation, under which the prices of Third World primary products exported to the First World would be linked to the prices of manufactured goods imported from it; and
- accept a new international legal regime for the high seas that would recognize the mineral resources of the ocean bed as the "common heritage of mankind" and require that a portion of any economic benefits resulting from the exploitation of those resources by the technologically advanced First World go into an international fund for Third World development.

The South made no progress with the NIEO as such. The North was willing to hear it discussed, but refused to negotiate it. Modest progress has been made, however, toward the partial fulfillment of certain NIEO demands. Technology has moved to the NICs, which now produce textiles, clothing, shoes, steel and steel goods, machine tools, autos, radios and other audio equipment, toys, chemicals, medical supplies, and basic appliances—many items that the North, with high-cost labor, can no longer turn out efficiently. The North has approved a Generalized System of Preferences (GSP) for the manufactured (but not agricultural) exports of the South, and the EEC has granted, in the Lomé Convention, trading arrangements that discriminate in favor of the Third World. The IMF, the World Bank, and Northern private banks have become more sensitive to balance of payments and debt problems of Third World countries. Some oil producers, able to identify with the poor states and unable to absorb all their petrodollar wealth, initiated aid programs. The subsequent experience of OPEC from the late 1970s amply demonstrated that the solidarity of the South was becoming fragmented, along with its commodity power.

Stephen D. Krasner has shown that LDCs pursue simultaneously several different objectives in the international system, some of which may strike Western observers as inconsistent. He divides Third World political behavior into two general categories. The first he calls "relational power behavior," which accepts existing regimes and works through established economic institutions such as the IMF and the World Bank in order to alleviate foreign exchange difficulties and capital shortages, or through bilateral channels to conclude tax treaties and orderly marketing agreements. Such an approach may involve hard bargaining and reluctant submission to unpleasant conditions (e.g., debt service charges and pledges to reduce imports). The second type of political behavior, says Krasner, is "meta-power behavior," which aims at restructuring international regimes—altering institutions, rules, principles, values, and norms in favor of the weaker, poorer, more vulnerable states. The LDCs, lacking material-power capabilities (although these are growing in many areas), have relied more on political rhetoric and their voting power as formally equal sovereign communities in international organizations to effect fundamental changes in the way the international economy operates. Up to now, as we have seen, the changes have been far from fundamental in the eyes of the Third World, but there have been substantial changes and the process of change will undoubtedly continue, more through the exercise by the South of "relational power" than "meta-power."[92]

Multinational Corporations

One of the important shifts in the international climate of North-South relations during the last decade has taken place in the attitude of many Third World countries toward the MNCs. Whether the multinationals on balance have benefited or exploited host countries in the South has long been a subject of bitter controversy, but the debate has become somewhat less polemical and more economically complex of late. It should be realized first of all that well over two-thirds of the foreign affiliates of MNCs headquartered in the First World (that is, the United States, Western Europe, and Japan) also happen to be located in First World rather than Third World countries. The United States accounts for about a quarter of all MNCs; Britain and West Germany, another quarter. Approximately three-quarters of all First World foreign investments are in First World countries.[93]

By 1980, the annual volume of sales of the 10 largest MNCs was greater than the gross domestic product (GDP) of 87 countries (excluding Eastern European states). It has usually been inferred from this that MNCs can readily interfere, directly or indirectly, in the economic and political life of host countries, and even exercise a dominating influence in poorer Third World countries. (De Gaulle frequently complained about the "American challenge" posed by MNCs even to industrially advanced countries.) Exactly how economic capabilities of foreign corporations translate into domestic political power in either industrially advanced or less developed countries is seldom spelled out in specific terms, but rather it is readily assumed by those who take it for granted that politics is subordinate to economics. Corporations can, of course, serve the foreign policy interests of their host governments, just as they can contravene those interests. They can engage in intelligence-gathering activities; they can intervene legally or illegally in the domestic political affairs of the host (for example, by trying to influence the outcome of elections, or persuading the host government to alter certain policies); and they can pressure the parent state government to pursue legislatively enacted and foreign diplomatic policies that will promote the interests of MNCs, regardless of the consequences for host countries. The role played by International Telephone and Telegraph (IT&T) in Chile during the early 1970s, opposing and helping to overthrow the government of Salvatore Allende, can be cited as a classic case of MNC intervention, and other instances can be brought forward. The number of documentable cases, however, is not large enough to justify the elaboration of a general universally valid theory. The neo-Marxist assumption regarding the pernicious political significance of MNCs derives more from normative or ideological *a priori* judgments than from careful empirical analysis.

It is possible to present a balanced assessment of the positive and negative aspects of MNCs—their economic benefits and costs to the host countries.[94] Advocates argue that MNCs have served as a principal means of satisfying the overwhelming desire of most countries in the world to attract foreign investment capital and technological know-how. The initial inflow of capital improves the balance of payments picture; brings in advanced technology not available domestically; creates jobs locally; effects savings on research and development; enhances the technical, productive, and organizational-managerial skills of indigenous personnel; and exerts a continuing positive effect upon the balance of payments, both by elevating the host country's export capacity and by manufacturing for domestic consumption, thereby saving what would be spent on comparable imports. Multinational corporations also introduce, through their own personnel policies, higher standards of wages, housing, and social welfare, which eventually affect other segments of society.

Critics contend that MNCs are nothing but instruments of neocolonialist, profit-seeking capitalism, which absorb more local capital than they bring in from abroad; transfer in older, obsolescing technology that has become less efficient under the higher-cost labor conditions of the First World and that often has little relevance to the real needs of poorer countries; take advantage of local cheap labor while excluding host-country nationals from higher-paying technical-skill and management positions; reap higher profits than they could in their parent countries by locating where national taxes are low; import from parent-country affiliates instead of purchasing locally; and manipulate international differences in prices, licensing, interest rates, and other economic factors for their own advantage, and with minimal consideration for the economic interests of the host country.

During the 1950s and 1960s, rising nationalist sentiments made Third World elites, students, industrial workers, peasants, and displaced businessmen hostile toward MNCs. Faced with growing demands for jobs, housing, and social welfare policies, ruling elites began to realize that they could take advantage of the suspect corporations and put pressure on them to improve their performance in the host countries. Joan Edelman Spero (from whom the foregoing balance sheet was largely drawn) has trenchantly described how Third World governments manifested a learning curve in their response to MNCs as local elites developed technical, legal, managerial, and financial expertise. They also became aware that once MNCs had become established, the host country's bargaining power became stronger than it had been when the country was seeking to attract foreign investment. The host country could gradually adopt laws and administrative regulations to bring the corporations under greater control. Original investment agreements become subject to later revision on more favorable terms for the host country, especially as the number of foreign investors competing for entry into the South increases.[95] In really tough bargaining confrontations, the threat of expropriation may become more credible than the threat of disinvestment. At any rate, many governments within the "Southern periphery" have become confident that they can hold their own in dealing with the MNCs; that local control or ownership patterns are improving over time; and that most MNCs, even though they may take more than they give on current account, are becoming useful instruments of development and channels of ingress-egress into the global economic system. The process of exploitation often evolves into a mutual one.

The Capitalist World-Economy

Related to yet different from the theory of *dependencia* is the broader school of thought that looks beyond the current problems of the Third World in an effort to understand the uneven development of the world capitalist system as a whole, in its various political, economic, and social aspects, and to fit the historical evolution of each country or region into a global spatiotemporal perspective encompassing the capitalist world-economy since the sixteenth-century transition from feudalism. The principal spokesman for this *Weltanschauung* is Immanuel Wallerstein.

Wallerstein's analysis is essentially neo-Marxist, but he combines elements of realism and Marxism. He shares with such realists as Kenneth Waltz and Hedley Bull the view that the international system is characterized by anarchy—the absence of a single global political authority. It is precisely this condition that makes it impossible to regulate the capitalist mode of production across national boundaries. Consequently, there emerges an international economic division of labor consisting of a central core of powerful, industrially advanced capitalist states; a periphery made up of weak states, kept on a level of technological underdevelopment and subordinated to the status of provider of raw materials for the core; and a semiperiphery of states whose economic activities are a mixture in between those of core and periphery—those usually called NICs. Wallerstein avoids the excessive and exclusive emphasis that classical Marxists have placed upon the class struggle. He recognizes the important roles played within the capitalist world-economy by nation-states; ethnic, religious, racial, and linguistic groups; and even households. He realizes that the competition of bourgeoisie and proletariat has the effect of strengthening the state because both classes, regardless of whether they pursue exploitative status quo, reformist, or revolutionary strategies, work consciously or unconsciously to enhance the functional powers of government. Wallerstein readily concedes that the international distribution of power among states shifts constantly as one historic period gives way to another. In the end, however, he is more Marxist than realist when he insists that the balance of power is a function of economic processes that transcend purely national boundaries—such as those, for example, by which the United States replaced Britain as the world's premier power in the early decades of the twentieth century.[96] (Realists, of course, have always recognized the economic elements of power—population; geographical factors; and industrial, technological, and financial capacity—but they insist upon the importance of other noneconomic variables such as morale, political-diplomatic skills, form of government, strategic intelligence, and the ability to organize national resources for the purposes of solving domestic problems and pursuing foreign policy objectives that serve the national interest.)

Christopher Chase-Dunn, following Wallerstein, has inquired into the relationship between economic and political processes within the capitalist system. Some Marxists, he says, have joined such realists as Waltz and Modelski in reacting against the "economism" of Wallerstein by reemphasizing the autonomy of political factors, the interstate system, and geopolitical processes. Chase-Dunn contends that the interstate system and the capitalist mode of production and wealth accumulation are not only interdependent, but integrally unified. He attributes the separation of politics and economics in the past to the fact that economic phenomena seem more regular and more determined by mechanistic laws, whereas the order of political phenomena seems to be more influenced by free will and therefore less predictable. He notes that Adam Smith and his followers also attributed the separation to the public-private dichotomy, the state being equated with the public realm and economic activity with the private. Chase-Dunn rejects both the explanations of the separation and the separation itself.

Whether states pursue free enterprise and trade policies or impose strict controls over the economy depends on their position within the capitalist world-economy. (In this regard, Chase-Dunn agrees essentially with Wallerstein's assumption that socialist states cannot escape from the fact that, like it or not, they are a part of the capitalist world economy and cannot isolate themselves from it, try as they might.) Hegemonic core states possessing productive advantages, along with peripheral states dominated by capitalist producers of cheap-labor goods for export to the core both support free trade. Less favorably situated core states and semiperipheral states (NICs) seeking to improve their position relative to the core are usually characterized by centralized direction of the economy and protectionist policies. Chase-Dunn elaborates upon Wallerstein's view that the global system is anarchic. The capitalist world-economy prefers to preserve this condition, and opposes the emergence of a single power capable of acting as a universal hegemony or world state. Rival states engage in a balance of power that operates to prevent the establishment of a worldwide monopoly state strong enough to impose controls upon the global economic order, for capitalism could not then survive.[97] According to this theory, the liberal, decentralized state (such as the United States and Britain) was primarily a product of economic forces, especially the desire for unlimited material self-aggrandizement by capitalist entrepreneurs, rather than the fulfillment of a deep-rooted human spiritual impulse for freedom, equality, and dignity intrinsic to Western civilization, itself the outgrowth of Judeo-Christian, Greco-Roman ideas and ideals. In neo-Marxist no less than in Marxist theory, everything must ultimately be reduced to a purely material-economic explanation. Locke, Mill, de Tocqueville, Madison, Lincoln, Holmes, and other great liberal philosophers would smile at such naive reductionism.

The Brandt Commission Report

Several development problems of the Third World were treated with a mixture of sympathy and long-range realism in the Brandt Commission Report of 1980. The commission, named for the former West German chancellor who chaired it, sought to appeal to enlightened Western self-interest by avoiding extremes of leftist and rightist analysis. According to the report, it is not a question of expecting the North to make sacrifices for the South; what is needed, far from charitable aid, is a global restructuring to reflect a growing awareness that the world is a "fragile and interlocking system." The North has to be convinced that its own continuing economic well-being will depend upon future progress toward the development of the South. Unlike the pessimistic "limits of growth" studies conducted a decade earlier by the Club of Rome, the Brandt Commission did not demand curtailment of economic-technological growth rates within the industrialized countries. Rather, it prescribed additional growth to alleviate the problem of an expanding backlog of unemployment, more acute in the South than in the North.[98]

The report aroused little interest in the United States, but generated a debate in Europe. Graham Bird agreed essentially with its diagnosis and prescription for debt relief and the granting of credit on more generous terms to Third World countries, so that the latter can import needed energy and capital instead of using their foreign exchange largely to service loans. This, he argued, is the only way to expand world trade and solve the unemployment problem in the North and the South.[99] Susan Strange leaned toward those who were skeptical concerning certain aspects of the report, including its "pious tone," its proposals for disarmament, and its one-sided criticism of the West for selling arms but not of Third World governments for buying them. While acknowledging the need to recycle Third World debts and warning the West not to ignore the Commission's recommendations, she noted that the report's emphasis on mutuality of interest may have reflected the fact that its authors underestimated the complexity and depth of the conflict between the North and the South.[100]

CONCLUSIONS

Recent decades have witnessed a revival of interest in the study of international political economy. It is now widely agreed that the contemporary field divides into three broad schools of thought—liberal, Marxist, and realist.[101] Unlike the mercantilists who preceded them, liberals look upon politics and economics as two separate dimensions. Politics is a public affair; economic activity proceeds according to natural laws that are determined by the sum total of myriad private choices of production and consumption, saving and investment. The pure nineteenth-century liberal believed that if the economy could be insulated against interference by government, then the creative energies of individuals seeking their own good, unfettered by the artificial regulations of bureaucrats, would maximize the wealth of nations as if under the guidance of an "invisible hand," as Adam Smith had put it. Free trade in a market free of all political barriers would ensure both economic prosperity and international peace for all countries. Thus, in the liberal age, the academic disciplines of politics and economics were placed in distinct disciplinary compartments, each taking no more note of the other than was minimally unavoidable.

Whereas liberals usually idealize nineteenth-century British imperialism, based upon the European balance of power and international free trade, Marxists insist that the capitalist economy is essentially conflictual, given the irreducible antagonism between the capitalist bourgeoisie and the laboring proletariat. Classical Marxists had no doubt that *class* was a more fundamental sociological reality than *nation*. Stalin introduced a fissure into the sacred dogma with his "last thesis"—namely, that war was inevitable not between the socialist and capitalist camps, but rather within the capitalist camp itself, due to the cutthroat competition among capitalist nations. As we have seen, history has not borne out the Stalinist prognosis. Neo-Marxists have been compelled to acknowledge the coalescence of a single, mutually cooperating international free-market alliance. They have also participated enthusiastically in the effort to convert the political-strategic power rivalry of East versus West into an economic North-South dialectical conflict, thereby preserving in altered form some semblance of the "international class struggle" between the First World core and the Third World periphery, while playing down the exploitative activities of the Second (socialist bloc) World, as well as the awkward fact the Third World has splintered into three groups—the *nouveau riche* oil-exporting countries, the newly industrializing countries (NICs) of the semiperiphery, and the remaining LDCs, many of which languish in the most abject poverty. The socialist industrial countries make their contribution to the poorest countries of the world far less with food, capital, and technical development assistance than with their global political propaganda campaign that assesses all the blame for the socioeconomic and political ills of the globe upon the industrially advanced First World. One of the most serious defects in neo-Marxist and capitalist world-economy literature is its failure to recognize that the "capitalist world" of Karl Marx, Lenin, Stalin, and their disciples has to a large degree become an amalgam of social democracy and an economic mix of private enterprise with accountability to public control.

Whereas orthodox liberals contend that politics and economics are separate orders, neither of which should or does dominate the other, Marxists, neo-Marxists, and realists are relatively agreed that the two orders are much more closely related. Marxists and realists part company, however, in assigning dominance to one or the other. Realists, as shown in Chapter 3, regard the primary actors in the international system to be nation-states that pursue power objectives and subordinate economics to politics in this quest. Joan Edelman Spero has argued trenchantly that the political system shapes the economic system, that political concerns often shape economic policy, and that international economic relations are really political relations.[102] Realists have reason to suspect that when Marxist-Leninist communists come to power in any country—the Soviet Union, the People's Republics of Eastern Europe, Cuba, Vietnam, Ethiopia, Nicaragua, or elsewhere—they become "closet realists" in their determination to preserve, consolidate, and expand their power, while continuing to pay lip service to the thesis that economic interests are causal in the political behavior of capitalist states.

For a quarter-century following World War II, realists were the leading figures in the study of international relations. They focused largely upon political-strategic concepts and issues—national power, the Cold War, military security and alliances, decolonization, international organization, strategies of conflict and deterrence, and negotiating proposals for arms control and disarmament. Economic issues were certainly not ignored—economic recovery (the Marshall Plan), regional integration (the European Economic Community), foreign aid, and the promotion of international trade and monetary stabilization (through the Bretton Woods system and the subsequently created mechanisms of the International Monetary Fund, the International Bank for Reconstruction and Development, and the General Agreement on Tariffs and Trade). But economic matters were of a lower priority in the thinking of government policymakers and theoretical analysts, probably because they seemed less urgent in that "golden age" of unprecedented economic growth in the United States, Western Europe, and Japan. At a time when the American economy accounted for half of global production (as in the late 1940s), few doubted that the United States could, without straining itself, do whatever it deemed necessary for its own security and that of its allies overseas.

The international economic system and the position of the United

States in the global economy have undergone a gradual yet fundamental transformation since 1960. With the dissolution of the West's colonial empires, the number of legally independent states in the world has tripled and a nonaligned bloc has emerged. The EEC, Japan, and the OPEC countries have become major economic actors. Even before the oil-price crisis of the early 1970s, the international monetary system founded at Bretton Woods in 1944, with the U.S. dollar serving as the world's reserve currency, had come to an end in 1971 when a deteriorating balance of payments situation forced the United States to devalue the dollar. Henceforth, the international reserve would consist of a "basket" of currencies including the dollar, EEC monetary units, and the Japanese yen.

A fifteenfold increase in the price of oil between 1970 and 1980 wrought havoc with the foreign-exchange positions of many oil-importing countries, rich and poor, and shifted huge hard-currency surpluses to OPEC states. It also substantially compounded the pressure for global inflation caused by, *inter alia*, the Vietnam War, increased worldwide military expenditures (including those by OPEC governments), a faster rise in Third World population than in productivity, a variety of dislocations and shortages in primary commodity markets, and the demand for higher wages and extended social programs almost everywhere, especially in the Western democracies. The result was a phenomenon that baffled economists—stagflation, a paradoxical combination of rising price levels with increasing sluggishness in investment, production, and employment. Later, when oil prices went into a long decline down to a quarter of their peak levels, due to (1) the inability of OPEC members to fix prices by controlling production (leading to a glut on the world oil market) and (2) First World policies designed to conserve energy and pursue alternative sources, the Fourth World, its foreign earnings drastically reduced, found itself confronted with a heavy debt burden incurred when oil prices had been high. Several countries sought debt rescheduling by threatening debt repudiation. As the 1980s drew to a close, Japan led the way toward debt cancellation; Western Europe and the United States sought sound ways of rescheduling Third World debts in order to facilitate long-term development without prejudice to countries that were pursuing fiscally responsible policies.

The world has become more politically and economically complex during the last three decades. Despite the relative erosion of its position within the global economy, the United States continues to bear roughly the same major share of the international strategic-military security burden as it did 40 years ago; and questions have been raised as to whether the United States, given the large federal deficit and a sizable trade gap (which, in the late 1980s, did not appear to be closing at a rate commensurate with the fall of the U.S. dollar), should reduce its international security commitments and shift a larger share of the burden to its allies.[103]

The question of which is the determinant factor in international relations—politics or economics?—is one of the most important issues in international relations theory at the present time. No one can reasonably doubt that economics is of growing salience to international politics, but no matter how important economic considerations may become within the global system, they cannot—and should not be allowed to—replace political values, goals, and interests in the architectonic thinking of policymakers. In sum, the authors of this text, while fully recognizing the close reciprocal relationship between international politics and international economics, cannot accept either the Leninist or neo-Marxist explanation of imperialism. We are much more impressed, intellectually and scientifically, with such realists as Niebuhr, Morgenthau, Aron, Thompson, Waltz, and Gilpin, who harbor deep suspicions that, even in the unlikely eventuality that the whole world might someday adhere to the Marxist-Leninist model (hardly a paragon of economic success in this century), it cannot possibly solve the deeper perennial problem of power-motivated expansionist urges of human beings, particularly in their aggregate modes of behavior.

NOTES

1. These included Karl Kautsky and Eduard Bernstein (Germany); G. D. H. Cole, R. H. Tawney, Sidney and Beatrice Webb, Harold J. Laski, and Clement Attlee (England); Jules Guesde, Jean Jaurès, and Leon Blum (France); and Daniel DeLeon, Harry W. Laidler, Norman Thomas, Morris Hillquit, and Herbert Marcuse (United States). One could also list several Christian socialists, utopian socialists, anarchists, recent Revisionist historians, and advocates of a variety of New Left causes.
2. For a detailed examination of this concept, see Gustav A. Wetter, *Dialectical Materialism: A Historical and Systematic Survey of Philosophy in the Soviet Union* (New York: Praeger, 1963).
3. Karl Marx and Friedrich Engels, *Manifesto of the Communist Party* (New York: International Publishers, 1932), p. 9
4. See Karl Marx, *Capital: A Critique of Political Economy* (New York: Random House [Modern Library], n.d.), especially chs. 1, 7, 9, 11, 12, 16, 18, and 24 for Marx's most extensive treatment of the concept of surplus value.
5. Karl Marx and Friedrich Engels, *Manifesto of the Communist Party*, p. 11.
6. See Robert C. Tucker, *The Marxian Revolutionary Idea* (New York: Norton, 1970) and *Philosophy and Myth in Karl Marx* (Cambridge: Cambridge University Press, 1972); Vendulka Kubalkova and Albert Cruickshank, *Marxism and International Relations* (Oxford: Clarendon Press, 1985).
7. John Plamenatz, *Man and Society: Political and Social Theory*, vol. II, *Bentham Through Marx* (New York: McGraw-Hill, 1963), p. 310. Hannah Arendt notes in a similar vein that Marx was aware of the role of violence in history, but deemed it less important than the contradictions inherent in the old society in bringing about the latter's end, in *On Violence* (New York: Harcourt Brace Jovanovich, 1969), p. 11.
8. See Philip Siegelman's Introduction to J. A. Hobson, *Imperialism: A Study* (Ann Arbor: University of Michigan Press, 1965). Hobson's work was originally

published in London by George Allen and Unwin in 1902. Subsequent references will be to the 1965 edition.

9. Foster Rhea Dulles, *America's Rise to World Power, 1898–1954* (New York: Harper & Row, 1954), chs. 2 and 3.

10. Richard Koebner and Helmut Dan Schmidt, *Imperialism: The Story and Significance of a Political Word, 1840–1960* (New York: Cambridge University Press, 1964), p. 249. For a discussion of the anti-Semitic theme in Hobson's thought, see pp. 226–228. George Lichtheim notes that the American Founding Fathers, both Federalists and Republicans, had no qualms about calling the federal union an empire, and that in nineteenth-century England both Liberals and Tories employed the term *imperialism* for its popular appeal. *Imperialism* (New York: Praeger, 1971), chs 4, 5, and 6. For a thorough analysis of British "imperialism of free trade," see William Roger Louis, ed., *Imperialism: The Robinson and Gallagher Controversy* (New York: New Viewpoints, 1976).

11. Richard Koebner and Helmut Dan Schmidt, op. cit., p. 233.

12. J. A. Hobson, *Imperialism: A Study* (Ann Arbor: University of Michigan Press, 1965), p. 85.

13. Ibid., p. 59.

14. Ibid., pp. 41–45. Later, Italy and Germany employed the argument concerning population pressure to justify their quest for colonies in Africa prior to World War I, and the Japanese did likewise in their Manchurian venture in the early 1930s. But in all the cases where the *lebensraum* argument was employed, subsequent movement of population to the conquered areas proved negligible. See N. Peffer, "The Fallacy of Conquest," in *International Conciliation* (New York: Carnegie Endowment for International Peace, No. 318, 1938).

15. J. A. Hobson, op. cit., pp. 46–51.

16. Ibid., pp. 53–54.

17. E. M. Winslow, *The Pattern of Imperialism* (New York: Columbia University Press, 1948), p. 106.

18. J. A. Hobson, op. cit., p. 58.

19. V. I. Lenin, *Imperialism: The Highest Stage of Capitalism* (New York: International Publishers, 1939), p. 89. See the section, "Imperialism and Capitalism," by Alec Nove, "Lenin as Economist," in Leonard Schapiro and Peter Reddaway, eds., *Lenin: The Man, the Theorist, the Leader* (New York: Praeger, 1969), pp. 198–203.

20. "Jingoism is merely the lust of the spectator, unpurged by any personal effort, risk, or sacrifice, gloating in the perils, pains, and slaughter of fellow-men whom he does not know, but whose destruction he desires in a blind and artificially stimulated passion of hatred and revenge. . . . The arduous and weary monotony of the march, the long periods of waiting, the hard privations, the terrible tedium of a prolonged campaign play no part in his imagination; the redeeming factors of war, the fine sense of comradeship which common personal peril educates, the fruits of discipline and self-restraint, the respect for the personality of enemies whose courage he must admit and whom he comes to realize as fellow-beings—all those moderating elements in actual war are eliminated from the passion of the Jingo. It is precisely for these reasons that some friends of peace maintain that the two most potent checks of militarism and of war are the obligation of the entire body of citizens to undergo military service and the experience of an invasion." Hobson, op. cit., p. 215.

21. For the complete works of Lenin, see V. I. Lenin, *Collected Works* (Moscow: Foreign Languages Publishing House, 1963), 44 vols. For a biographical account of Lenin's life, see Louis Fischer, *The Life of Lenin* (New York: Harper & Row [Colophon Books], 1965); Robert Payne, *The Life and Death of Lenin* (New York: Simon & Schuster, 1946); Stefan T. Possony, *Lenin: The Compulsive Revolutionary* (Chicago: Regnery, 1964); Christopher Hill, *Lenin and the Russian Revolution* (London: English Universities Press, 1961); Bertram D. Wolfe, *Three Who Made a Revolution* (Boston: Beacon, 1955).

22. See V. I. Lenin, *Collected Works*, vol. V, pp. 425–529.

23. V. I. Lenin, *Imperialism: The Highest Stage of Capitalism*, pp. 16–30.

24. Lenin, *Collected Works*, vol. XIX, pp. 87 and 104.

25. Bernard Taurer, "Stalin's Last Thesis," *Foreign Affairs*, XXXI (April 1953), 374.

26. Ibid., p. 378.

27. See Herbert S. Dinerstein, *War and the Soviet Union* (New York: Praeger, 1959), pp. 68–69, 80–81; Frederick C. Barghoorn, *Soviet Foreign Propaganda* (Princeton: Princeton University Press, 1964), pp. 92–93; Frederic S. Burin, "The Communist Doctrine of the Inevitability of War," *American Political Science Review*, LVII (June 1963), 352–354; Walter C. Clemens, Jr., "Ideology in Soviet Disarmament Policy," *Journal of Conflict Resolution*, VIII (March 1964), 17–20.

28. L. I. Brezhnev, *Following Lenin's Course: Speeches and Articles* (Moscow: Progress Publishers, 1972).

29. Allen S. Whiting, "Foreign Policy of Communist China," in Roy C. Macridis, ed., *Foreign Policy in World Politics*, 3rd ed. (Englewood Cliffs, N.J.: Prentice-Hall, 1967), pp. 223–263; "The Disarmament Issue in the Sino-Soviet Dispute: A Chronological Documentation," Appendix in Alexander Dallin et al., *The Soviet Union, Arms Control and Disarmament* (New York: School of International Affairs, Columbia University, 1964), pp. 238–276; Walter C. Clemens, Jr., *The Arms Race and Sino-Soviet Relations* (Stanford, Calif.: Hoover Institute on War, Revolution and Peace, 1968), pp. 13–68; William E. Griffith, *Cold War and Co-Existence: Russia, China and the United States* (Englewood Cliffs, N.J.: Prentice-Hall, 1971).

Lenin wrote in 1916: "Only *after* the proletariat has disarmed the bourgeoisie will it be able, without betraying its world-historical mission, to throw all armaments on the scrap heap; and the proletariat will undoubtedly do this, but *only when this condition has been fulfilled, certainly not before.*" Passage from Lenin's *War Programme of the Proletarian Revolution*, quoted in PRC Letter of June 14, 1963. In Walter C. Clemens, Jr., *The Arms Race and Sino-Soviet Relations*, p. 227.

30. Alistair Buchan, "A World Restored?" *Foreign Affairs* (July 1972); W. A. C. Adie, "China's Strategic Posture in a Changing World," in *Royal United Services Institute and Brassey's Defence Yearbook 1974* (London: Brassey's Annual, 1974); John Gittings, *The World and China 1922–1972* (New York: Harper & Row, 1974), pp. 261–263; Francis O. Wilcox, ed., *China and the Great Powers: Relations with the United States, the Soviet Union and Japan* (New York: Praeger, 1974); Allen S. Whiting, "Foreign Policy of Communist China," in Roy C. Macridis, ed., op. cit., 5th ed. (Englewood Cliffs, N.J.: Prentice-Hall, 1976), pp. 223–263.

31. Steven I. Levine, "China in Asia: The PRC as a Regional Power," in Harry Harding, ed., *China's Foreign Relations in the 1980s* (New Haven, Conn.: Yale University Press, 1984), pp. 117, 124; and Jonathan D. Pollack, "China and the Global Strategic Balance," ibid., pp. 157, 166–169.

32. Stephen M. Meyer, "The Sources and Prospects of Gorbachev's New Political Thinking on Security," *International Security*, 13 (Fall 1988), 124ff; David Holloway, "Gorbachev's New Thinking" and Robert Legvold, "The Revolution in Soviet Foreign Policy," *Foreign Affairs*, 68, *America and the World 1988/89*, 66–81, 82–98.

33. Hans J. Morgenthau, *Politics Among Nations: The Struggle for Power and Peace*, 4th ed. (New York: Knopf, 1966), p. 42. This definition has been carried in all six editions of the book since 1948.

34. Ibid.

35. Ibid., p. 47. Cf. Raymond Aron, *Peace and War: A Theory of International Relations*, trans. Richard Howard and Annette Baker Fox (New York: Praeger, 1968), p. 259.

36. Raymond Aron, *The Century of Total War* (Boston: Beacon, 1955), ch. III, "The Leninist Myth of Imperialism," esp. p. 59; Morgenthau, *Politics Among Nations*, pp. 47–50; William L. Langer, "A Critique of Imperialism," *Foreign Affairs*, XIV (October 1935), 102–115.

37. Jacob Viner, "International Relations Between State-Controlled Economies," in *Readings in the Theory of International Trade*, American Economic Association (Philadelphia: Blakiston, 1949), vol. IV, pp. 437–458.

38. Joseph A. Schumpeter, *Imperialism and Social Classes*, trans. Heinz Norden, ed. Paul M. Sweezy (Oxford: Basil Blackwell, 1951), p. 5.

39. Ibid., p. 6.

40. Hans J. Morgenthau, op. cit., pp. 48–49.

41. Ibid., pp. 84–85. Kenneth E. Boulding has reiterated Schumpeter's view that imperialism was a form of social lag and, from an economic standpoint, unprofitable to the point of being a fraud. "Reflections on Imperialism," in David Mermelstein, ed., *Economics: Mainstream Readings and Radical Critiques*, 2nd ed. (New York: Random House, 1970), p. 201.

42. Joseph A. Schumpeter, op. cit., pp. 89–96. Schumpeter's own analysis of imperialism did not go unchallenged. He was faulted for defining imperialism as both "objectless" and "forcible," the expression of a warrior-class social structure that fights only because it is geared for fighting. He therefore excluded from the meaning of imperialism whatever is not warrior-class social structure. Murray Greene, "Schumpeter's Imperialism—A Critical Note," *Social Research* (An International Quarterly of Political and Social Science), XIX (December 1952), 453–463. Greene took issue with Schumpeter's thesis that because capitalism is nationalistic, it is antithetical to imperialism, militarism, and armaments.

43. Richard Koebner and Helmut Dan Schmidt, op. cit., p. 255.

44. Hans J. Morgenthau, op. cit., p. 47.

45. Joseph A. Schumpeter, op. cit., p. 57.

46. Andrew Mack, "Theories of Imperialism: The European Perspective," *The Journal of Conflict Resolution*, 18 (September 1974), 518.

47. Ibid., where Mack cites as authorities two Marxist critiques of the Leninist theory; Michael Barratt Brown, "A Critique of Marxist Theories of Imperial-

ism" and Harry Magdoff, "Imperialism Without Colonies," in Roger Owen and Bob Sutcliffe, eds., *Studies in the Theory of Imperialism* (London: Longmans, 1973).

48. Raymond Aron, *Peace and War: A Theory of International Relations,* p. 261. See also Langer, op. cit., p. 105, and Lichtheim, op. cit., p. 77.

49. Raymond Aron, op. cit., pp. 262–263.

50. Hans J. Morgenthau, op. cit., pp. 46–47; Aron, *The Century of Total War,* pp. 59–62. Referring to the Spanish-American War, Eugene Staley wrote: "The causes of this war, and of the expansionism exhibited in connection with it, have been laid at the door of private investment interests—on the whole, erroneously. Their role was slight compared with that of the interests of the 'yellow' press and of other internal influences in American life which made for chauvinism." *War and the Private Investor* (Chicago: University of Chicago Press, 1935), p. 433. Most diplomatic historians who studied the origins of World War I, including Sidney Bradshaw Fay, G. P. Gooch, A. J. P. Taylor, Bernadotte E. Schmitt, Nicholas Mansergh, and Raymond Sontag, have listed imperialistic rivalry (in its political more than its economic aspects) as *one* of the background causes of that war, but less important than the interaction of the European alliance systems and nationalisms in a framework dominated by balance-of-power thinking, security apprehensions generated by militarism and armaments competition, and the condition of international anarchy—that is, the absence of organization adequate to ensure peaceful settlement of disputes.

51. Raymond Aron, *The Century of Total War,* p. 65; *Peace and War,* p. 267. One additional anomaly might be mentioned. Canada took part in the Boer War, World Wars I and II, and the Korean War, not because her capitalistic interests were at stake in those wars but because she was part of a "political empire" (the British Empire/Commonwealth and the U.S. NATO alliance) in which the empire leader took the decision for war and Canada followed out of a sense of political loyalty. Gernot Kohler, "Imperialism as a Level of Analysis in Correlates-of-War Research," *The Journal of Conflict Resolution,* 19 (March 1975), 48.

52. Kenneth E. Boulding, "Reflections on Imperialism," p. 202.

53. Michael W. Doyle, *Empires* (Ithaca, N.Y.: Cornell University Press, 1986), p. 12. See also pp. 20 and 24.

54. Ibid., p. 12.

55. Ibid., pp. 12–13. Doyle notes that what characterizes empire is control of both foreign and domestic policy. Where only foreign policy is controlled, he uses the term *hegemony.* Ibid., p. 40.

56. Ibid., p. 19.

57. Ibid., pp. 25–28. Cf. also John Gallagher and Ronald Robinson, "The Imperialism of Free Trade," *Economic History Review,* 2nd ser., Vol. 6, No. 1 (1953), 1–15; Benjamin Cohen, *The Question of Imperialism* (New York: Basic Books, 1973); David Fieldhouse, *Economics and Empire, 1830–1914* (London: Weidenfeld and Nicholson, 1973); and Tony Smith, *The Pattern of Imperialism* (New York: Cambridge University Press, 1981).

58. Michael W. Doyle, op. cit., pp. 31–33. On this point see A. P. Thornton, *Doctrines of Imperialism* (New York: Wiley, 1963), p. 4, and J. Woodis, *Introduction to Neo-Colonialism* (New York: International Publishers, 1971), p. 56.

59. André Gunder Frank, "The Development of Underdevelopment," in Robert I. Rhodes, ed., *Imperialism and Underdevelopment: A Reader* (New York: Monthly Review Press, 1970), p. 9.

60. See, for example, Marx's comments about British rule in India in Lewis S. Feuer, ed., *Marx and Engels* (New York: Anchor Books, 1959), pp. 480–481.

61. Kenneth E. Boulding, op. cit., p. 201.

62. Nikita S. Khrushchev, *For Victory in Peaceful Competition with Capitalism* (New York: Dutton, 1960), p. 33; see also pp. 628–629.

63. Ibid., pp. 750–751.

64. G. Mirsky, "Whither the Newly Independent Countries?" *International Affairs* (Moscow), XII (December 1962), 2, 23–27.

65. Thomas E. Weisskopf, "Capitalism, Underdevelopment and the Future of the Poor Countries," in David Mermelstein, ed., op. cit., pp. 218–223.

66. Even though it is reasonable to expect that the cancellation of military contracts following upon a disarmament agreement would have an adverse multiplier effect upon prices, employment, public spending, and confidence in the health of a capitalist nation's economy, two important points must be made in this connection: (1) in terms of pure economics, the problem of disarmament is a soluble one; and (2) the primary obstacles to disarmament, far from being economic as the Marxists allege, are really technical, strategic, and political. The arms problem in the age of the nuclear missile can hardly be adequately explained by the old "devil theory" of war. It is not an aberration imposed upon the contemporary international system by the profiteering of certain militarists. It is rather an intrinsic part of the system, deeply rooted in the essential characteristics of modern science and technology, of the decision-making and diplomatic processes of governments, of the global ideological-sociopolitical competition, and of a world structure in which nation-states seem driven to seek their security by engaging in some form of power balancing. (The obstacles to disarmament are discussed in Chapter 9.)

67. Harry Magdoff, "The American Empire and the U.S. Economy," ch. 5 in *The Age of Imperialism* (New York: Monthly Review Press, 1969). Reprinted in Robert I. Rhodes, ed., op. cit., pp. 18–44; see especially pp. 18–28.

68. Ibid., pp. 28–29.

69. Johan Galtung, *The European Community: A Superpower in the Making* (London: Allen and Unwin, 1973).

70. Speaking of Europe as the economic center, Galtung writes: "Fragmentation means that whereas the center is well coordinated, even unified in the European Community, the periphery, the developing countries, are split in many ways." Ibid., p. 76. Economists who study the underdeveloped lands typically point out that the foreign trade of countries within the African, Arab, and Latin American regions is largely extraregional; usually less than 10 percent is intraregional.

71. P. T. Bauer, "The Economics of Resentment: Colonialism and Underdevelopment," *The Journal of Contemporary History*, vol. 4 (1969), p. 59.

72. Ibid., p. 56.

73. Ibid.

74. Hans Kohn, "Reflections on Colonialism," in Robert Strausz-Hupé and Harry W. Hazard, eds., *The Idea of Colonialism* (New York: Praeger, 1958), pp. 6–14.

75. Andrew Mack, "Theories of Imperialism," op cit., p. 526.

76. Richard Koebner and Helmut Dan Schmidt, op. cit., p. 316.
77. Ibid., p. 318.
78. Ibid., pp. 321–322.
79. Kenneth E. Boulding, "Reflections on Imperialism," p. 202.
80. *The New York Times*, July 31, 1978.
81. Robert G. Wesson, *Why Marxism? The Continuing Success of a Failed Theory* (New York: Basic Books, 1976).
82. Adam B. Ulam, *The Bolsheviks* (New York: Macmillan, 1965), p. 311. See also P. T. Bauer, op. cit., pp. 57–58.
83. Anthony James Joes, *Fascism in the Contemporary World: Ideology, Evolution, Resurgence* (Boulder, Colo.: Westview, 1978), p. 103.
84. See William C. Olson and David S. McLellan, "Population, Hunger and Poverty," in the book they coedited with Fred A. Sondermann, *The Theory and Practice of International Relations*, 6th ed. (Englewood Cliffs, N.J.: Prentice-Hall, 1983), p. 270.
85. Mahbub ul Huq, *The Third World and the International Economic Order*, Development Paper No. 22 (Washington, D.C.: Overseas Development Council, 1976). Reprinted in Olson, McLellan, and Sondermann, eds., op. cit., pp. 325–326.
86. Ibid., p. 326.
87. James Caporaso, "Dependence and Dependency in the Global System," *International Organization*, 32 (Winter 1978), 2.
88. Tony Smith, "The Logic of Dependency Theory Revisited," ibid., 35 (Autumn 1981), 756–757. Smith became less unsympathetic to dependency theory a few years later, conceding that it had prompted those in the "mainstream" to think in broader, more complex and normative terms about Third World development. "Requiem or New Agenda for Third World Studies," *World Politics*, XXXVII (July 1985).
89. J. Samuel Valenzuela and Arturo Valenzuela, "Modernization and Dependency: Alternative Perspectives in the Study of Latin American Underdevelopment," *Comparative Politics*, 10 (July 1978), 535–557. The Valenzuelas make it clear that they are criticizing the modernization perspectives of such writers as Sir Henry Maine, Ferdinand Tönnies, Emile Durkheim, Max Weber, Robert Redfield, Harry Eckstein, David Apter, Daniel Lerner, Neil J. Smelser, Alex Inkeles, Cyril Black, Gabriel Almond, James S. Coleman, Talcott Parsons, Seymour Martin Lipset, Kalvin H. Silvert, and others. Other representative works on dependency theory include Fernando Henrique Cardozo and Enzo Faletto, *Dependency and Development in Latin America* (Berkeley: University of California Press, 1979), and André Gunder Frank, *Crisis in the Third World* (New York: Holmes and Meier, 1981). For a critical view of dependency theory, see Tony Smith, "The Underdevelopment of Development Literature: The Case of Dependency Theory," *World Politics*, 31 (January 1979).
90. James A. Caporaso, "Industrialization in the Periphery: The Evolving Global Division of Labor," *International Studies Quarterly*, 25 (September 1981), 351. See also David B. Yoffie, "The Newly Industrializing Countries and the Political Economy of Protectionism," ibid., 25 (December 1981).
91. A full compendium of NIEO proposals over a 30-year period was compiled by Alfred George Moas and Harry N. M. Winton, librarians of the United Nations Institute for Training and Research (UNITAR): *A New International Economic*

Order, Selected Documents, 1945–1975, 2 vols. (New York: United Nations, 1977). See also Jagdish N. Bhaghwati, ed., *The New International and Economic Order: The North-South Debate* (Cambridge, Mass.: M.I.T. Press, 1977); Karl P. Sauvant and Hajo Hasenpflug, eds., *The NIEO: Confrontation or Cooperation Between North and South* (Boulder, Colo.: Westview Press, 1977); J. S. Singh, *A New International Economic Order* (New York: Praeger, 1977); D. C. Smyth, "The Global Economy and the Third World: Coalition or Cleavage?" *World Politics*, 29 (April 1977); Robert L. Rothstein, *Global Bargaining: UNCTAD and the Quest for a New International Economic Order* (Princeton, N.J.: Princeton University Press, 1979); Edwin Reuben, ed., *The Challenge of the New International Economic Order* (Boulder, Colo.: Westview Press, 1981); Jeffrey A. Hart, *The New International Economic Order: Cooperation and Conflict in North-South Economic Relations* (New York: St. Martin's Press, 1983); Craig N. Murphy, "What the Third World Wants: An Interpretation of the Development and Meaning of the New International Economic Order Ideology," *International Studies Quarterly*, 27 (March 1983); and Stephen D. Krasner, *Structural Conflict: The Third World Against Global Liberalism* (Berkeley: University of California Press, 1985).

92. Stephen D. Krasner, "Transforming International Regimes: What the Third World Wants and Why," *International Studies Quarterly*, 25 (March 1981). For additional discussions of North-South economic relations and the obstacles to achieving the NIEO, see Roger D. Hansen, *Beyond the North-South Stalemate*, for the Council on Foreign Relations (New York: McGraw-Hill, 1979); John Gerald Ruggie, ed., *The Antinomies of Interdependence* (New York: Columbia University Press, 1983); Robert O. Keohane, *After Hegemony: Cooperation and Discord in the World Political Economy* (Princeton, N.J.: Princeton University Press, 1984); and David A. Lake, "Power and the Third World: Toward a Realist Political Economy of North-South Relations," *International Studies Quarterly*, 31 (June 1987).

93. See Commission on Transnational Corporations, "Supplementary Material on the Issue of Defining Transnational Corporations," United Nations Economic and Social Council, March 23, 1979, pp. 8 and 11; *Transnational Corporations in World Development: A Re-Examination* (New York: United Nations, 1981), p. 286. Joan Edelman Spero has concluded that more than 95 percent of recorded direct foreign investment flows from countries that are members of the Organization of Economic Cooperation and Development (OECD), and that about three-quarters of this total is invested in other OECD countries. *The Politics of International Economic Relations*, 3rd ed. (New York: St. Martin's Press, 1985), p. 134. John R. Oneal and Frances H. Oneal, after comparing the rates of investment return in two groups of countries—LDCs and industrialized—that dependence results in systematic exploitation. "Hegemony, Imperialism and the Profitability of Foreign Investments," *International Organization*, 42 (Spring 1988), 373.

94. Among the earlier assessments of the pros and cons of MNCs, see Samuel Huntington, "Transnational Organizations in World Politics," *World Politics*, 25 (April 1973), and John Diebold, "Multinational Corporations—Why Be Scared of Them?" *Foreign Policy*, No. 12 (Fall 1973). In the early 1970s, there was some apprehension that the multinationals, because of their vast economic resources and because they could not be adequately controlled by national governments, much less by international organizations, might lead to the

erosion of the nation-state system as we have known it. See Raymond Vernon, *Sovereignty at Bay* (New York: Basic Books, 1971), and Robert Gilpin, "Three Models of the Future," *International Organization*, 29 (Winter 1979). Neither Vernon nor Gilpin agreed with the erosion hypothesis. For later assessments of the impact of MNCs on Third World countries, see Theodore H. Moran, "Multinational Corporations and Dependency: A Dialogue for Dependentistas and Non-Dependentistas," *International Organization*, 32 (Winter 1978); Joan Edelman Spero, op. cit., ch. 8.

95. For an account of how the Third World countries have adjusted, see Joan Edelman Spero, op. cit., pp. 285–287. Edith Penrose has argued that the presence of MNCs in Third World countries is likely to strengthen the governments of those countries politically and to improve their capabilities over time to control the foreign corporations. "The State and Multinational Enterprises in Less-Developed Countries," in Jeffrey A. Frieden and David A. Lake, eds., *International Political Economy: Perspectives on Global Power and Wealth* (New York: St. Martin's Press, 1987).

96. Immanuel Wallerstein, "The Future of the World Economy," in Terrence K. Hopkins and Immanuel Wallerstein, eds., *Processes of the World System* (Beverly Hills, Calif.: Sage Publications, 1980). Wallerstein's theory is to be found in two volumes: *The Modern World System I: Capitalist Agriculture and the Origins of the European World Economy in the Sixteenth Century* (New York: Academic Press, 1974), and *The Modern World System II: Mercantilism and the Consolidation of the European World-Economy, 1600–1750* (New York: Academic Press, 1980). See also his *Capitalist World-Economy* (Cambridge: Cambridge University Press, 1979).

97. Christopher Chase-Dunn, "Interstate System and Capitalist World-Economy: One Logic or Two?" *International Studies Quarterly*, 25 (March 1981). See the other articles in this special issue on "World System Debates," edited by W. Ladd Hollist and James N. Rosenau. Cf. also William R. Thompson, Christopher Chase-Dunn, and Joan Sokolovsky, "An Exchange on the Interstate System and the Capitalist World-Economy," ibid., 27 (September 1983).

98. Willy Brandt and Anthony Sampson, eds., *North-South: A Program for Survival, Report of the Independent Commission on International Development Issues* (Brandt Commission) (Cambridge: M.I.T. Press, 1980).

99. Graham Bird, "Beyond the Brandt Report: A Strategy for World Economic Development," *Millenium: Journal of International Studies*, 9 (Autumn 1983), 55–62. For a fuller economic analysis in a similar vein, cf. W. M. Corden, *Inflation, Exchange Rates and the World Economy: Lectures on International Monetary Economics* (New York: Oxford University Press, 1978); Graham Bird, *The International Monetary System and the Less Developed Countries* (London: Macmillan, 1978); and William R. Cline and Associates, *World Inflation and the Developing Countries* (Washington, D.C.: The Brookings Institution, 1981).

100. Susan Strange, "Reactions to Brandt: Popular Acclaim and Academic Attack," *International Studies Quarterly*, 25 (June 1981), 333–342.

101. See, for example, Jeffrey A. Frieden and David A. Lake, eds., op. cit., esp. pp. 1–17; Paul R. Viotti and Mark V. Kauppi, *International Relations Theory, Realism, Pluralism, Globalism* (New York: Macmillan, 1987); Kenneth Waltz, *Theory of International Relations* (Reading, Mass.: Addison-Wesley, 1979); and the works by Stephen Krasner, Immanuel Wallerstein, Christo-

pher Chase-Dunn, Michael W. Doyle, and others cited in this chapter. Rajan Menon and John R. Oneal have reviewed the debate about imperialism in terms of socialist and capitalist theories, realist theories, and the theory of imperialism as a result of lateral development pressure as expounded by Nazli Choucri and Robert North (treated in Chapter 8). "Explaining Imperialism: The State of the Art as Reflected in Three Theories," *Polity*, (Winter 1987).

102. Spero, op. cit., pp. 8–12.
103. Paul Kennedy, *The Rise and Fall of the Great Powers: Economic Change and Military Conflict from 1500 to 2000* (New York: Random House, 1987).

Chapter
7

Microcosmic Theories of Violent Conflict

HUMAN MOTIVATIONS AND CONFLICT

In his significant work *Man, the State and War,* Kenneth N. Waltz distinguished three images of international relations in terms of which we usually try to analyze the causes of war. According to the first image, war is traceable to human nature and behavior.[1] Partisans of the second image seek the explanation of war in the internal structure of the state, and this group includes both liberals (who believe that democracies are more peaceful than dictatorships) and Marxist-Leninists (who believe that capitalist states foment war while socialism leads to peace). The third image postulates the causes of war in the condition known to the classical political theorists (including Kant, Spinoza, Rousseau, and, in modern times, Hedley Bull) as "international anarchy"—that is, the absence of those instruments of law and organization that would be efficacious for peacekeeping. In other words, a deficiency in the state system makes it necessary for each state to pursue its own interests and ambitions, and act as judge in its own case when it becomes involved in disputes with another state, thereby making the recurrence of conflict, including occasional wars, inevitable and giving rise to "the expectation of war" as a normal feature of the state system.[2] It is a provocative thought—that the nonexistence of something (an effective peace enforcer) might be a cause of something else, namely, war. In this chapter, we shall be concerned initially with the "first image" explanations of conflict—those microcosmic theories pertaining to individual human nature and behavior—and subsequently with the macrocosmic theories that deal with larger social and political forces.

The historian is usually interested in the specific and unique events that lead to the outbreak of a particular war. The theorist of international relations cannot ignore the concrete circumstances in which wars occur; these have to be taken into account in the theory. But the theorist seeks to go beyond specific wars in an effort to explain the more general phenomenon of *war* itself—that is, large-scale fighting or other acts of violence and destruction involving the organized military forces of different states. The causality of international war may be, and probably is, related at least in part to the causality of other forms of violent political conflict, such as civil war, revolution, and guerrilla insurgency; but international war is a specific phenomenon, different from the others, and it requires a specific explanation of its own.

Waltz, in his treatment of first image theorists, noted that both optimists and pessimists, utopians and realists, agree in diagnosing the basic cause of war as human nature and behavior, but disagree in their answers to the question of whether that nature and behavior can be made to undergo a sufficient change to resolve the problem of war.[3] It is doubtful that either the traditionalists or the behavioral scientists will ever be able to isolate a single dominating causal factor adequate for explaining all violent conflict. Human life is much too diverse and complex to permit such an explanation. A more reasonable presumption is that all forms of violence, whether individual or social, have in common a few explanatory factors, related to what we refer to here as human nature. Microcosmic and macrocosmic theories of human aggression, violence, and war cannot be neatly separated from each other. International war cannot be adequately explained solely by reference to biological and psychological explanations of individual aggressiveness, nor can the latter phenomenon be comprehended purely "internally," without reference to social factors. In all fields that study human social behavior, micro and macro approaches must be appropriately blended.

Modern Studies of Motivations and War

In the twentieth century, social scientists have turned increasingly toward motives, reasons, and causal factors that may be operative both in individual human beings and in social collectivities even though people are not immediately aware of them and do not become consciously aware of them except as a result of scientific observation and methical analysis. Why do individuals behave aggressively? Why do states wage wars? The two questions are related, but they are not the same. The former pertains to the inner springs of action within individual human beings, the latter to the decision-making processes of national governments. Violent revolution constitutes yet another phenomenon, different from individual aggressiveness, which is rooted in the biological-psychological characteristics of human beings, and from international war, which is a highly politicized and institutionalized form of learned social behavior. Revolution itself, insofar as it requires organization, leadership, ideology and doctrine, propaganda, planning, strategy, tactics, communications, recruits and supplies, and very often a diplomacy for the acquisition of foreign support, assumes a highly politicized character with the passage of time. Thus it requires more of a *macrocosmic* than a *microcosmic* analysis.

Psychological and social psychological factors alone might go far to explain instances of anomic[4] violence, such as a food or language riot in India, an outbreak of fighting at a sports event, or a racial disorder at a public beach. But even in these cases, social psychologists would be wary of "the fallacy of the single factor," and social scientists would argue that some instances of apparently anomic violence might involve an element of political organization and can be adequately comprehended only when placed in their total sociological and political context. In all cases of social violence it is probably wise to assume the presence of multiple explanatory factors.

The phenomenon of international war is the most complex and difficult of all to explain. It is impossible to describe the causes of war purely in terms of individual psychology, as if it were a case of psychic tensions within individuals mounting to the breaking point and then spilling over into large-scale conflict. Analogies between psychologically based explanations of aggression by individuals and explanations of international war confront yet another problem. In the case of war, those who take the momentous decision to lead a state into war do not themselves do the fighting on the battlefield, even though in an age of total war the distinction between the battlefield and the home front has sometimes been blurred beyond distinction. Conversely, those who actually engage in battle are likely to have had little or nothing to do with the actual decision to fight. Feelings of hostility, moreover, might indeed be widespread within a nation vis-à-vis another nation and yet war might be averted by astute statesmanship. By the same token, a government can lead a people into a war for which there is little enthusiastic support, if not overt opposition. On this subject, Werner Levi suggests:

> When for instance will certain natural traits or psychological drives find outlets in war, and when in something more peaceful? . . . What these explanations fail to do is to indicate how these human factors are translated into violent conflict involving all citizens, regardless of their individual nature, and performed through a highly complex machinery constructed over a period of years for just such a purpose.
>
> There is always the missing link in these fascinating speculations about the psychological causes of war between the fundamental nature of man and the outbreak of war. . . . Usually, the psychological factors and human traits can be classified as conditions of war more correctly than as causes.[5]

BIOLOGICAL AND PSYCHOLOGICAL THEORIES

Conflict has an inside and an outside dimension. It arises out of the internal dimensions of individuals acting singly or in groups, and also out of external conditions and social structures. At all levels of analysis, larger organized aggregates of human beings affect smaller aggregates and individuals, and vice versa. Individuals and groups are in constant interaction. Which is more important, the larger or the smaller? Scientists from the many disciplines interested in conflict will probably never be able to agree on an answer to this fundamentally important question. The only available solution to this dilemma is to regard social situations and individual inner processes as an organic whole. We shall begin at the microcosmic level.

Peter A. Corning has noted that without an understanding of the evolutionary and genetic aspects of behavior, we cannot fully comprehend the inner principles by which human life is organized, and that social scientists must attend increasingly to the interaction between the organism and the environment.[6] It makes sense to begin with the biological foundations of behavior. Within recent years, a controversial new field has made its appearance in academe—sociobiology. Sociobiologists study the genetic roots of social behavior in insects, animals, and human beings, and seek to bridge the gap between the genetic inheritance of individuals on the one hand and social processes and institutions on the other. It is still too early to predict how the new discipline will fare.[7]

All living organisms have certain fundamental, species-specific biological requirements. Those of the members of human society are the most complex of all: "These needs include a reasonably pure atmosphere, numerous nutritional requirements, fresh water, sleep, . . . shelter and clothing (or, more generally, maintenance of body temperature), health care, including sanitation, physical security, procreation, and the nurture and training of the young."[8] Over the world as a whole, the greater part of all economic activity is devoted to meeting basic biological needs. Among humans, biological needs quickly shade off into higher psychological needs that are often even more difficult to satisfy—sense of belonging, self-esteem and prestige, self-actualization, and so forth.[9] Much of the political and economic competition and conflict among human societies is traceable to the fact that the demand for things required to satisfy biological *and* psychological needs always exceeds the supply.[10] This does not mean that any theory arising from a Darwinian evolutionary model of the natural selection process necessarily leads to the conclusion that nature is "red in tooth and claw" and that violent aggression and war are inescapable among human societies. Several biologists have insisted that fitness for survival dictates cooperation and mutual aid at least as often as aggressive conflict.[11]

INSTINCT THEORIES OF AGGRESSION

The key microcosmic concept developed by biologists and psychologists for the explanation of conflict is *aggression.* Normally, we think of aggression as a form of violent behavior directed toward injuring or killing a human being, or damaging or destroying a nonhuman entity. Some writers have distinguished between *hostile aggression,* the aim of which is to inflict injury, and *instrumental aggression,* the purpose of which is to secure extraneous rewards beyond the victim's suffering. This distinction has been criticized as misleading by Albert Bandura, who argues that most acts of hostile aggression serve ends other than the mere production of injury, and hence are instrumental.[12] Bandura defines aggression as behavior that results in personal injury (either psychological or physical) or in destruction of property, but he insists on the importance of the "social labeling process"—that is, on social judgments that determine which injurious or destructive acts are to be called "aggressive." Neither the surgeon who makes a painful incision nor the bulldozer operator who razes a condemned building is accused of committing aggression.[13]

Do human beings carry within their genetic or psychic structures an ineradicable "instinct" or predisposition for aggression? Given the way in which the debate about instinctive behavior has developed in this century, it will be useful to examine first the positions taken earlier by certain psychologists. Generally, psychologists have long agreed that aggression is to be understood in some sort of stimulus-response framework. A basic issue that arose in their field early in this century was whether aggressive tendencies are innate, instinctual, and ever-present in humans, or whether they appear only as a result of externally produced frustration.

Leading figures identified with the instinct theories of aggression during the early decades of the century were William James (1842–1910) and William McDougall (1871–1938). McDougall, the leading British psychologist of his day, considered instinct as a psychophysical process inherited by all members of a species; it was not learned, but could be modified by learning. McDougall took issue with the psychoanalysts who considered the aggressive impulse as ever-present in humans and constantly seeking release. McDougall insisted that the "instinct of pugnacity," as he called it (one of the 11 he identified), became operative only when instigated by a frustrating condition.[14] He did not look upon human aggressiveness as a built-in impulse constantly seeking release. Thus he placed himself midway between the pure "instinctivists" and the "frustration-aggression" school, seeking his understanding of aggression in neither the organism nor the environment alone, but in their interaction.

The most famous and most controversial of the "instinct" theories was that of the "death instinct," put forth by Sigmund Freud. Originally, Freud was inclined to the view that aggression results from frustration, especially the frustration of the sexual impulses.[15] But after World War I, Freud postulated the existence in the human being of a fundamental *eros,* or life instinct, and a fundamental *thanatos,* or death instinct. In no other way was the Austrian psychoanalyst able to explain why millions of men went to their death on the battlefield between 1914 and 1918.[16] For Freud, all instincts were directed toward the reduction or elimination of tension, stimulation, and excitation. The motivation of pleasure-seeking activity is to attain an unstimulated condition—a sort of Oriental Nirvana or absence of all desire. Death involves the removal of all excitation.

Hence all living things aspire to "the quiescence of the inorganic world."[17] But people go on living despite the death instinct, because the life instinct channels the annihilative drive away from the self toward others. Aggressive behavior thus provides an outlet for destructive energies that might otherwise lead to suicide. According to this hypothesis, the recurrence of war and conflict becomes a necessary periodic release by which groups preserve themselves through diverting their self-destructive tendencies to outsiders. This, in brief, is the psychoanalytic foundation for Freud's view, which he exchanged in correspondence with Albert Einstein—that is, a person carries within "an active instinct for hatred and aggression."[18]

Most contemporary psychologists reject Freud's hypothesis of the death wish as the basis for aggression theory. Professor Leonard Berkowitz called it "scientifically unwarranted."[19] He cited two principal grounds on which it is deemed deficient—one from positivist logic and one from modern experimental science. He maintained that Freudian theory is unacceptable because of its teleological character. In other words, the theory attributes the cause of present behavior to a future goal, that is, the reduction or removal of excitation.[20]

As for the experimental evidence, Berkowitz argued that research performed with animals (principally cats, rats, and mice) negates the validity of the notion that all behavior is aimed at tension-reduction, inasmuch as "organisms frequently go out of their way to obtain additional stimulation from their external environment."[21] It should be remembered that Freud never adduced any compelling body of evidence in support of his hypothesis; hence, there is no scientific need to disprove it. Yet Freud's position in the field of psychoanalysis is so dominant, and his influence on modern Western thought so pervasive, that psychologists sometimes seem anxious to discredit this particular aspect of his theory not only because of its scientific weakness but also because of its rather pessimistic connotations for society.[22]

ANIMAL BEHAVIOR STUDIES

In recent decades, one of the most rapidly advancing branches of biological science has been *ethology*—the study of animal behavior in all its aspects, with particular emphasis on the four basic animal drives of reproduction, hunger, fear, and aggression.

Human behavior and animal behavior are quite dissimilar; in some respects, though, they may be analogous, and a comparison of basic similarities and subtle differences can help us to avoid oversimplified single-factor explanations. From a knowledge of animal behavior we cannot directly infer anything about human behavior. "Work on one species," according to Elton B. McNeil, "can serve as a model only for the formation of *hypotheses* about other species."[23] Thus, although an examination of animal studies can furnish no direct proof as to the way human beings act, it can suggest fruitful areas for future research. The advantage of animal investigation is that it admits of a freedom of experimentation that would be impossible in the case of humans, and it permits the scientist to observe several generations of a species within a short time. The principal caveats to remember, of course, are that humans are vastly more complex than even the most highly developed animals, that the computing organism of the human nervous system lends itself to almost unlimited learning and adaptation, and that, above all, human beings exist in a moral-spiritual order.

The causes of aggressive behavior in animals are relatively few. Males, for example, fight over food, females, and territory; females, to protect the young. All exhibit hostility when strange members of their own species are introduced into their midst, when others make off with objects toward which they have become "possessive," and when their expectations have been first aroused and then frustrated. Researchers have found that there is a relationship between aggressiveness and the production of the male hormone (even though in a few species the female is more aggressive than the male); that within a species, some breeds may be more aggressive than others; that the so-called instinctive targets of aggression (such as the mouse for the cat) appear to be more a matter of learning than of heredity; that fighting within a species may produce intricate patterns of submission and dominance; that an animal will fight rather than be deprived of status; that repeated success in fighting can make an animal more aggressive; and that various forms of electrical, chemical, and surgical interventions into the brain can produce predictable alterations in animal aggressiveness.[24] Studies have also indicated that the same principles of learning on which the stimulation of conflict behavior is based may be applied in reverse, as it were, to control and reduce the aggressive urge.[25]

John Paul Scott, an experimental biologist who has based his study of individual aggression and its causes on animal research, denies that there is any physiological evidence pointing to a spontaneous "instinct for fighting" within the body. There is no need for the organism to fight, apart from happenings in the external environment. "There is, however, an internal physiological mechanism which has only to be stimulated to produce fighting."[26] As Scott sees it, aggression is the result of a learning process in which the motivation for fighting is increased by success; the longer success continues, the stronger the motivation becomes. He favors a multifactor theory of aggression, based on a complex network of physiological causes that eventually are traced to external stimulation. If the stimulation is sufficiently high, it may activate unconscious motor centers for fighting that, in the absence of the stimulus, are usually repressed as a result of training. Scott therefore roots the aggressive impulse in physiological processes, but demands a stimulus from the environment and rejects the concept of self-activation.

Generally speaking, biologists have been less reluctant than psychologists to speak of "instinct"—not so much as an explanation of an inherited pattern of behavior (through genetic transmission) as a short-hand description of those behavior differences that are determined by the interaction of heredity and environment.[27] However, a growing number of biologists now prefer the term *innate behavior* over the older term *instinct.*

Lorenz: Intraspecific Aggression

New light has been cast upon the nature of aggression by Konrad Lorenz, of the Max Planck Institute of Behavioral Physiology. Lorenz recognized that there is a subtle relationship between the two factors of evolutionary adaptation—innate behavior and learning in the environment. From studies of aggression in certain species of fish, dogs, birds, rats, deer, and farmyard animals, Lorenz concluded that aggression is something very different from the destructive principle expressed in the Freudian hypothesis of *thanatos.* According to Lorenz, "aggression, the effects of which are frequently equated with those of the death wish, is an instinct like any other and in natural conditions it helps just as much as any other to insure the survival of the individual and the species."[28]

Lorenz found that aggression, as he defined it, occurs primarily among members of the same species, not between members of different species. When an animal of one species kills an animal of another species for food, this is not aggression; in killing the prey, the food gatherer exhibits none of the characteristics of genuinely aggressive behavior. The typical aggressive instinct, according to Lorenz, is not *inter*specific but *intra*specific, and can best be illustrated by the tenacity with which a fish, an animal, or a bird will defend its territory against members of its own species. Aggression is seen as serving a species-preserving function in the Darwinian sense, because it prevents the members of a species from excessive bunching together and spaces them out over the available habitat.[29] Lorenz noted that among animals who hold sway over a particular territorial space, the readiness to offer combat to an intruder is greatest at the center of the individual's territory—the part of the habitat with which it is most familiar. This is the concept which Robert Ardrey has popularized (probably too simplistically and misleadingly, especially in its application to humans) as "the territorial imperative."[30] Paradoxically, as Lorenz noted, the sexual and family bond must overcome the tendency toward repulsion of others that is at the very heart of an individual's territory, where intraspecific aggression ought to be strongest.[31]

According to Lorenz, nonaggressive species do not form love bonds, while all species that exhibit bond behavior are highly aggressive. Some birds and animals are bonded only during the mating and rearing seasons, at which times they are aggressive. Bonding therefore protects the partners against each other and ensures the safe rearing of the young, but it increases the aggressiveness of the male against the territorial neighbor. Lorenz concluded that analogous processes play a significant role in the family and social life of many higher animals and of the human species.[32]

Besides helping to keep the species spread over the widest area, the aggressive urge as manifested in the rival fight, usually between males, contributes to the selection of the fittest for reproduction. But the aim of aggression, Lorenz insists, is to ward off the intruder, to take possession of the female, or to protect the brood. Its object is never to exterminate fellow members of the species. Among several species Lorenz observed a phenomenon he termed the *ritualization of aggression,* by which he means a fixed motor pattern involving a ceremonialized series of inciting or menacing gestures by one individual to ward off an interloping member of the same species. This form of aggressive expression seems to achieve the positive species-preserving purpose of the aggressive instinct without resort to actual violence.[33]

In summary, Lorenz depicts aggression as a benign instinct among animals. He points out that several animal species have developed some remarkable aggression-inhibiting mechanisms or appeasement gestures. The wolf, for example, is armed with such an array of powerful weapons that it had to develop strong aggression inhibitors (such as baring its neck to the fangs of a victorious foe, thus giving the latter pause); otherwise the species might have destroyed itself.[34] Lorenz and other scientists hope that humans will manage to ritualize and control their aggressive impulses as well as some of the lower orders of animals have done. But weak creatures (e.g., doves, hares, chimpanzees, and humans) that normally lack the power to kill a foe of their own size and that can rely upon flight or other forms of evasion have not been under much pressure to develop inhibitions against killing their own kind. Lorenz laments that human biological evolution did not include the development of similar inhibitory mechanisms.[35]

Lorenz's concept of the aggressive impulse should not be confused with that of the Freudians or others who subscribe to the notion of a self-stimulating urge to destroy. For Lorenz, the purpose of the instinct is to warn outsiders to keep their distance; it apparently comes into play only when the proper stimulus is applied, although it has been construed by some as a spontaneously operating urge.[36] Lorenz does not insist, as some writers do, that humans are uniquely vicious as killers of their own kind. We know that rats, ants, hyenas, and certain monkeys can be lethally aggressive against members of their own species. New male lions, when taking over a pride, are also likely to kill whatever cubs are already there in order to stimulate the reproductive processes of the females.[37] But Lorenz exhorts human beings to acquire a proper humility and to conquer the pride that prevents them from acknowledging their evolutionary origins and the natural causation of human behavior.[38] He has no doubt that humans represent the highest achievement of evolution, and that they are essentially more advanced and complex than all other primates, but he warns that the very faculties of conceptual thought and verbal speech that elevate them to a uniquely high level above all other creatures also pose the danger of extinction to humanity.[39]

Lorenz puts little faith in the power of reason alone to overcome the aggressive instinct in individuals. Nevertheless, he strikes a note of cautious optimism. Even though humans cannot develop aggression-inhibitors through biological evolution in time to save themselves (since this process might take hundreds of thousands of years), they are capable—by combining their rational calculus of the consequences of nuclear war, the dynamics of the instinctive drives of species preservation, compassion for the species, culturally ritualized behavior patterns, and the controlling, self-disciplining force of responsible politics and morality—of developing aggression-inhibitors in the form of sociopolitical structures within a relatively short time, once the major powers become genuinely convinced that large-scale nuclear war would be a mutually suicidal enterprise. Human beings possess a *culture,* and that means that when the cultural environment affecting human behavior changes, the acquired characteristic can be directly transmitted to the next generation.[40]

Lorenz's Critics

Lorenz and those who accept his explanation of biologically grounded aggression have drawn fire from analysts for whom "nurture" is more important than "nature" as a determinant of behavior. Erich Fromm strongly criticized the theory of such "instinctivists" as Lorenz, who hold that humans through the first million years have been hunters accustomed to the pleasure of killing, and that a streak of destructive cruelty has consequently become ingrained in their basic structure as a result of the selection process. Against such a view, Fromm cited the findings of Ruth Benedict and Margaret Mead, who insisted that cultures characterized by peacefulness and cooperation, like that of the Zunis, are just as "natural" as the hostile, cruel cultures of other peoples (even though they are much rarer). Fromm criticized what he perceived to be a political bias in the theories of all instinctivists, including Lorenz: "To stress the innate character of aggression corresponded to conservative or reactionary attitudes. If aggression was innate, there was little hope for lasting peace and radical democracy." Fromm's complaint was that the theory of an aggressive instinct serves to absolve human beings of a sense of responsibility for their self-destructive, belligerent behavior.[41] Behavioral psychologist B. F. Skinner and anthropologist M. F. Ashley Montagu also take issue with Lorenz. They admit that there is such a thing as instinct in human beings, but assert that as a component of human behavior it is much less important than conditioning and learning. Both Lorenz and Skinner may use the term *imprinting* to refer to messages encoded in the genetic system, but they do not mean the same thing. Lorenz locates the source of imprinting within the organism; Skinner finds it in the external environment.[42]

Social learning theorist Albert Bandura cites with approval those who fault Lorenz for weak scholarship, for errors of fact and questionable interpretations concerning animal behavior, and for failing to differentiate

inborn patterns of behavior from those resulting from experimental learning.[43] Fellow ethologists have criticized Lorenz not only for extrapolating
from his animal studies to humans, but also for reaching allegedly wrong
conclusions about animals in general after having studied a relatively small
number of species.[44]

Other biological factors appear to have some relationship to human
aggressive behavior. Prolonged hunger or chronic malnutrition is likely to
affect the operations of the brain and other organs, as well as the energy,
judgment, and behavior of humans. Francis A. Beer, however, probably
goes too far when he suggests that Third World governments, possessing
advanced military technology in the future and faced with mass starvation, may threaten, provoke, or launch nuclear war over the issue of
hunger.[45] In all likelihood, it is not the *leaders* of states experiencing mass
starvation who themselves will be hungry. Therefore, especially in cases
of authoritarian or totalitarian regimes, the impact of hunger on collectivities of *individuals* will be irrelevant to decisions by *leaders* to start a war.
Here again we confront the conceptual problem of inferring behavior at
the state level from the motivations, interests, and behavioral patterns of
individuals.

Still other writers have suggested that conditions of human overcrowding can cause hyperirritability, fighting, and interference with all
normal behavior patterns.[46] Moreover, it has been plausibly argued that
an international crisis can be a stress-inducing stimulus for political leaders
and decision-makers (even though some may feel a "sense of elation" in
the midst of crisis pressures), and that their performance under stress may
be significantly affected by such factors as health, age, fatigue (especially
sleep deprivation), circadian and diurnal rhythms, and the intake of tran-
quilizing drugs or other medication. Other examples could be drawn from
the field of biopolitics, but these few will serve to illustrate the variety of
ways in which biological factors are said to have a bearing upon human
conflict behavior and political decision-making.[47]

FRUSTRATION-AGGRESSION THEORY

Within recent decades, most psychological authorities have been inclined
to trace the source of aggression to some form of frustration. The psychological concept of frustration and its effects deserves close examination not
so much as an explanation of international war but rather because of a
widespread assumption that the high conflict potential of the developing
areas is a function of frustration caused by economic deprivation.[48]

The Dollard-Doob Hypothesis

The frustration-aggression theory is a relatively old one, suggested at one
time or another by McDougall, Freud, and others, but it received its classic
expression in the work of John Dollard and his colleagues at Yale Univer-

sity shortly before the outbreak of World War II. The Yale group took "as its point of departure the assumption that *aggression is always a consequence of frustration.*" More specifically they assumed that "the occurrence of aggressive behavior always presupposes the existence of frustration and, contrariwise, that the existence of frustration always leads to some form of aggression."[49] Frustration they defined as "an interference with the occurrence of an instigated-goal response at its proper time in the behavior sequence."[50] Whenever a barrier is interposed between persons and their desired goals, an extra amount of energy is mobilized. Such energy mobilization, said Ross Stagner, "if continued and unsuccessful, tends to flow over into generalized destructive behavior."[51] Abraham Maslow, however, pointed out a difference between mere deprivation that is unimportant to the organism and a threat to the personality or life-goal of the individual; only the latter, he said, causes aggression.[52]

According to the Dollard study, the strength of the instigation to aggression can be expected to vary with (1) the strength of instigation to the frustrated response, (2) the degree of interference with the frustrated response, and (3) the number of frustrated response-sequences.[53] Aggression occurs only if goal-directed activity is thwarted, not in cases of unperceived deprivation. Moreover, the Yale group pointed out that not every frustrating situation produces some overt aggression. Acts of aggression can be inhibited, especially when their commission would lead to punishment or other undesirable consequences. The expectation of punishment reduces overt aggression, and the greater the certainty and amount of punishment anticipated for an aggressive act, the less likely is that act to occur.[54]

The individual experiences an impulse to attack whatever barrier stands in the way of goal-directed behavior. The immediate barrier-target, however, may be physically, psychologically, or socially immune to attack: The persons who interpose themselves may be stronger, vested with an aura of authority, sacred in character, capable of retaliating with a socially approved punishment, or in some other way rendered invulnerable for all practical purposes. The Dollard group focused primarily on the threat of punishment. The expectation of punishment interferes with the act of aggression and thus gives rise to further frustration, which will intensify the pressure either for direct aggression against the interfering agent or for other, indirect forms of aggression.[55] There may occur a displacement of aggression, in which case the individual directs hostility toward someone or something not responsible for the original frustration. Alternatively, the individual who is both frustrated and inhibited may alter not the *object* but the *form* of aggression (e.g., by imagining or wishing injury to someone instead of actually harming the interfering agent). Another form that indirect aggression may take is self-aggression or *regression,* in which individuals castigate themselves, injure themselves, or, in the most extreme cases, commit suicide.[56] Dollard and his colleagues point to the "greater tendency for inhibited direct aggression to be turned against the self when it is inhibited by the self than when it is inhibited by an external agent." But they add that self-aggression is not the preferred type of expression.[57] Finally, it is assumed that any act of aggression (either direct or vicarious, e.g., fantasized physical assault) leads to catharsis—that is, a release of aggressive energy or tension and a reduction in the instigation to aggression.[58]

Modifications of the Dollard-Doob Hypothesis

The Dollard-Doob hypothesis has been modified and refined by other psychologists and social psychologists since the early 1940s. The crucial question is not whether frustration always leads to some form of aggression; researchers concede that it may be worked off in other ways and that a more accurate statement of the Dollard thesis is "that frustration produces instigation to different types of responses, one of which may be aggression."[59] Rather, the crucial question is whether all aggression is traceable to frustration. Several authorities, including Durbin and Bowlby, Karl Menninger, and J. P. Seward, have criticized the frustration-aggression hypothesis on the grounds that there are other causes of aggression besides frustration.[60] The studies of animal behavior made by Scott and Fredericson, as well as by Lorenz, also point to other causes such as dominance strivings, the sight of a strange animal of the same species, resentment at the intrusion of strangers, disputes over the possession of objects, pain, and interference with comfort. But the psychologists who subscribe to the Dollard-Doob hypothesis usually end up broadening the notion of frustration to encompass all these aggression-arousing factors, or by attempting to reduce these factors to forms of frustration.[61] Experimental studies have led to the conclusion that while thwarting goal-directed behavior may heighten aggressiveness, it sometimes exerts no significant influence in comparison with social-learning factors to be discussed later.[62]

Psychologists are not agreed as to whether the frustration-aggression nexus is a simple and virtually automatic stimulus-response pattern or whether such emotional states as anger and fear must be or can be interposed. Similarly, there is disagreement as to whether additional cues, releasers, or other triggering stimuli must be present for aggression actually to occur. What constitutes a frustration is not a completely objective matter; it often depends upon cognition and interpretation by the individual.[63] Various types of frustrations may lead to different kinds of aggressive reactions.[64] Although it may be relatively easy to see the operation of the frustration-aggression syndrome in children, it is considerably more ambiguous in adults. Finally, when aggressive behavior does occur, "it may be deflected from its original goal, disguised, displaced, delayed, or otherwise altered."[65]

The frustration-aggression theory is supported by a convincing body of experimental evidence, and it also appeals to the common sense of most people who know from personal experience that they have at times felt aggressive urges after being frustrated. There can be little doubt of its utility when it is applied to certain limited and simpler aspects of individual and small-group behavior. One can ask, however, whether it is appropriate to use it for the purpose of extrapolating from relatively simple stimulus-response experiments to an explanation of the more subtle and complex modes of human action, especially those that are politically organized at the nation-state level.

FROM INDIVIDUAL TO SOCIETAL AGGRESSION

How do we move from aggression in the individual to aggression in society? In view of Herbert C. Kelman's warning cited in Chapter 5 (pp. 190–191) such a transition should not be taken for granted. Yet the Dollard group transferred the lessons of individual frustration-aggression to the much broader level of collective social behavior—that of blacks against whites in the American South earlier in this century—without expressing any doubt as to the validity of the transfer and without offering any substantiating evidence or arguments that the transfer can in fact be made.[66] The Dollard study suggested that even the Marxist theory of the class struggle depends implicitly upon the frustration-aggression principle.[67]

Shifting the analysis of frustration from the plane of the individual to that of the society gives rise to a major "level of observation," or level of analysis, problem. Although it may be quite easy to see the frustration-aggression hypothesis validated in experiments with individuals, it is more difficult to verify the hypothesis at the level of large-group behavior. First, the time factor is quite different. The most clear-cut experimental evidence from the study of individuals would seem to indicate fairly rapid time sequences from the onset of frustration to the manifestation of aggressive responses—minutes or hours in most cases, and perhaps days or weeks in some. It seems reasonable to conclude that the longer the time interval between the interference with the goal-directed action and the commission of an aggressive act, the less certain is the connection between the frustration and the aggression, because other factors may have intervened in the meantime—inhibitions, displacements, substitute responses, and other outlets or adjustments.

No matter how the time factor for individual behavior is explained, it is reasonable to conclude that social psychological phenomena, apart from the behavior of a crowd that is deliberately incited to violence, usually develop at a slower rate. Frustrating situations are perceived more slowly; the perceptions are less uniform and the interpretations more diverse; the extended time frame provides greater opportunity for individuals to adjust; the variety of responses is broader for large groups than for individuals; responses to frustrating situations are likely to vary according to the cultural values of different groups within the social structure; and, perhaps most importantly, a whole complex of external sociological (rather than internal psychological) factors pertaining to crowd behavior contributes toward determining the response to frustration. Hence it may be possible to verify the frustration-aggression hypothesis in the behavior of smaller, unstructured groups (e.g., such anomic outbursts as the rioting of an unorganized mob), but it would seem much more difficult, and perhaps impossible, to apply the theory in any precise way to the behavior of larger, more highly institutionalized social entities.[68] Furthermore, it should be emphasized that most exponents of the frustration-aggression explanation are careful to exclude "learned aggression" from the scope of their theory. This is important to remember in any consideration of organized conflict (such as war, revolution, and guerrilla insurgency) in which training for aggressive conduct plays a significant role. The organized warfare that is characteristic of human societies has no counterpart among animals, and requires a high degree of social learning.

SOCIALIZATION, DISPLACEMENT, AND PROJECTION

The frustration-aggression school has attempted to move from the individual to the social level more by logical inference than by experimentation. The principal conceptual mechanisms by which the transfer is made are "the socialization of aggression," "displacement," and "projection"—all closely related notions.

Psychologists hold that the process of acquiring social habits invariably gives rise to frustrations, inasmuch as every forced modification of spontaneous behavior from childhood to adulthood interferes with goal-responses. This holds true for feeding habits, the suppression of crying, limitation of movement, cleanliness and toilet training, table and speech manners, sex behavior, sex typing, age grading, social behavior, the disciplines of schooling, restrictions on adolescents, and the various adjustments required in adulthood, such as marital, professional, or occupational requirements.[69]

Most of these examples, of course, are drawn from middle-class American family life. Frustration-aggression patterns are culture-bound; both the factors that make for frustration in human beings and the directions in which aggressive impulses are turned—or the "targets of aggression"—will depend largely upon the values of the specific cultural system. Every society imposes social controls upon the spontaneous behavior of individuals. Thus, every social system produces in its members frustrations that might eventually lead to fear, hatred, and violent aggression. Every culture must develop its own solution to the problem of socially managing the aggressive impulses of its members.[70] The "socialization of aggression" takes place in all human societies, attenuating hostile action among members of the "in-group" by directing aggressive impulses against "out-groups."[71]

A child who is frustrated by the decision of a parent may seek release by substituting a different object of aggression, such as a toy, a piece of furniture, a sibling, another child in the neighborhood, a teacher, a pet, or a neighbor's property. Targets may be invulnerable if aggression against them will lead to punishment. As one finds safer targets, they frequently bear less resemblance to the original objects. The repression of hostile impulses from the level of consciousness can help in the displacement process by allowing the individual to forget the identity of the original source of the frustration.[72] Repression can lead to projection, which involves attributing to, and exaggerating in, others the unfavorable qualities and malicious motives that one is reluctant to recognize in oneself. Individuals seek to reduce their guilt feelings by projecting their intolerable thoughts and feelings to others. Once they have fastened upon their target, perceptual distortion sets in; everything in the target's behavior confirms and justifies their suspicions.[73]

It is quite common for psychologists and social psychologists to cite the frustration-aggression-displacement syndrome as the explanation of hostile attitudes toward "scapegoat" groups within a society and toward foreign nations.[74] But it is not clear how the leap is made, or even whether it can logically be made, from individual psychological theory to the analysis of attitudes and behavior at the level of large sociological entities. One might readily agree that a system of rewards and punishments within a family structure will serve to deter overt aggression, which the growing child will then displace.[75] Psychologists call attention to the fact that the growing child assimilates the attitudes and prejudices of adults, especially parents, and thus the notion of "the enemy," whether internal or external, is perpetuated through transmission from one generation to another.

The mechanism by which individual psychic attitudes and complexes of a quasi-pathological character are translated into the concrete political decisions of leaders building up toward the actual outbreak of organized conflict has not yet been adequately defined and described, much less experimentally tested, in a manner intelligible to political scientists. Conceivably, such a mechanism has not been defined or described because no such mechanism exists. Undoubtedly the frustrations of human beings form an important part of the total matrix out of which social conflict arises. The presence of widespread frustration would seem to lend a conflict potential to any social situation. It might be said to constitute a prerequisite or a necessary condition, at least for some forms of collective aggression.[76] Nevertheless, the hypothesis remains uncertain. We do not understand the relationship between childhood frustration experiences (with their accompanying effects upon personality) and adult sociopolitical attitudes. The frustration-aggression-displacement syndrome alone cannot supply both the necessary and the sufficient conditions for collective aggression on a large scale. Frustration might supply the potential for conflict, but a trigger mechanism is required, and the potential must somehow be organized and given specific direction.

One of the most glaring deficiencies in the frustration-aggression-displacement theory is its failure to explain adequately why particular "foreign" groups are selected as targets of displaced aggression, especially when alternative targets are available.[77] At various times it has been suggested that they are chosen because they are "visible," because they are "different and strange," because they have been traditionally mistrusted and disliked, or because they are most feared. At the level of international relations, the selection of conflict targets has much more to do with macrocosmic factors—political, economic, ideological, and socio-cultural—than with the inner frustrations of individuals.

SOCIAL LEARNING THEORY

Social learning theorists such as Albert Bandura are skeptical of both the biological instinct theories of aggression and those psychological theories that postulate a frustration-aggression drive. Bandura denies that aggressive energy is cumulatively dammed up within the organism to be discharged without any external stimulus, and instead places emphasis on the environmental causes of aggression. He admits that the human being has a few inborn habits, but he sees them as less significant than the vast human potential for learning. He argues that human beings possess neurophysiological mechanisms that enable them to behave aggressively, but that these mechanisms are activated only by appropriate stimulation under conditions and in ways largely determined by social experience.[78]

Bandura cites anthropological evidence that in some cultures aggression is not the typical response to frustration. He contends that the definition of frustration has become so broad as to lose meaning—because it may include not only interfering with the achievement of desired goals, but also personal insults, subjection to pain, deprivation of rewards, and experience of failure. He sees frustration as only one, and not necessarily the most important, factor affecting the expression of aggression. He agrees that the threat of punishment on the other hand is more complex than originally believed. Convinced of the great complexity of human responsiveness in various situations, Bandura sets forth a sophisticated and somewhat intricate theory of aggressive behavior based not on inner impulses or drives, but on social learning, social contexts and roles, response feedback influences, modeling and reinforcement, and the learned ability to assess the rewarding and punishing consequences of any given action.[79]

LEARNED AGGRESSION AND MILITARY TRAINING

Those who have pondered the causes of war seem at times unable to make up their minds whether the frequency and ferocity of war in history are due to the fact that human beings like to fight, or whether most people actually hate to go to war but perform their soldierly duties out of a sense of obligation to serve their country, or to make a sacrifice for preserving ideals and loved ones, or simply because they are coerced by conscription or peer pressures, conditioned to fight during military training, and frightened at the prospect of death if they do not kill first.[80] Within two consecutive pages of a single work we are told, somewhat contradictorily, not only that people are naturally inclined to do battle, and to hurl themselves with profound passion into war on slight or nonexistent pretexts, but also that human beings find the sight of the gore of warfare so utterly repugnant, because resistance to killing is rooted in their whole psychic history, that hatred of the enemy is difficult to inculcate.[81]

Bandura has shown that the conversion of socialized individuals into effective military combatants requires a carefully conceived and executed training program. People who have been brought up to abhor killing as immoral and criminal must be made to accept killing in war as justified. Only in this way can they escape the self-condemnation consequent on taking human life in battle.[82] The soldier is taught that he is fighting for family and friends, for country and civilization, for a cherished way of life and moral values, and perhaps for other high ideals—for example, in defense of religion, democracy, freedom, or lasting peace.[83] Recruits to military service must be completely reoriented from familiar civilian ways. They are issued new, distinctive clothing and are indoctrinated with new beliefs and modes of behaving. Many behavioral patterns are regulated in accordance with a military code of discipline under which automatic compliance with orders is expected. Soldiers are given an intensive, practical training in the techniques of warfare, designed to inculcate a host of survival and combat skills, familiarize them with equipment and tactics, reduce the fear of battle, and enhance fighting unit solidarity, morale, and coordination.[84]

Despite the assertion of many social scientists that human beings "kill enthusiastically" for abstract ideas and theories, those who have made a careful, systematic study of the biological and psychological impulses to aggression do not argue that the typical soldier, in waging war, is working out any sort of aggressive instinct or frustration-aggression-displacement syndrome. If politically organized communities really thought that human beings are as innately aggressive as some intellectuals take them to be (perhaps thereby passing judgment on themselves rather than on humanity), societies in all probability would long ago have felt some need at the end of a war to devote a significant effort to the retraining of ex-soldiers to peacetime life—at least comparable to the kind of training required to inculcate a warlike spirit. A minority of veterans may be psychologically disturbed and prone to violent behavior as a result of wartime experiences,[85] although most veterans seem able to manage the transition from war to civilian life without special conditioning programs. This is a rather hopeful sign.

LEARNING, IMAGES, AND INTERNATIONAL CONFLICT

How do human beings form their attitudes about the world and other nations? Hadley Cantril, Harold Lasswell, and Kenneth Boulding were among the foremost political scientists who addressed themselves to this question. Cantril emphasized the importance of a government's understanding the state of mind of the people with whom it must deal at home and abroad—their feelings, hopes and aspirations, frustrations and fears, customs and traditions. Responding to the postwar call of UNESCO (the United Nations Economic, Scientific and Cultural Organization) for an inquiry into the influences that predispose to international understanding on the one hand and aggressive nationalism on the other, Cantril and associates concluded: "People in one nation are hostile to people in other nations not because they have unfavorable stereotypes; rather they have these unfavorable stereotypes because they think other people are interfering with their own or their nation's goals."[86]

Harold Lasswell, one of the first to suggest that international relations could be studied quantitatively, believed that growth of knowledge about trends would make possible predictions about wars that could be altered by "preventive politics." Such a theory could uncover the psychological and social roots of the human insecurities that cause wars. He defined politics in terms of the values of safety, income, and deference—very similar to Thucydides' basic motivating factors: fear, interest, and honor. Following such European political sociologists as Gaetano Mosca, Vilfredo Pareto, and Karl Mannheim, Lasswell impressed on his American colleagues the need for studying the attitudes and behaviors of elites, if they would understand politics and war. Since even key leaders may experience personal insecurity that may tempt them to consolidate their domestic positions by provoking foreign crises, Lasswell suggested that what is needed for a stable world is a "universal body of symbols and practices sustaining an elite which propagates itself by peaceful methods."[87]

Obviously the phenomena of "displacement" and "projection" are related to the concept of "national images," which reflects a process of selective perception (and some perceptual distortion) in the view of other nations transmitted through history, the educational system, folklore, the media, and other channels. Herbert Kelman defines the "image" simply as "the individual's conception of what the object is like."[88] Kenneth Boulding, an economist rather than a psychologist, has noted that the behavior of complex political organizations is determined by decisions which are in turn the functions of the decision-maker's *image*. The image is a product of messages received in the past—not a simple accumulation of messages but "a highly structured piece of informational-capital." Every nation is a complex of the images of the persons who think about it; hence the image is not one but many. The images of the decision-makers are more important than the images of the masses. For both groups, "Impressions of nationality are formed mostly in childhood and usually in the family group." He dismisses as a fallacy the notion that the image is imposed by the powerful on the masses. The "folk-image" is a mass image, shared by rulers and ruled alike.[89]

"Mirror Images"

The notion of mirror images is based on the assumption that the peoples of two countries involved in a prolonged hostile confrontation develop fixed, distorted attitudes that are really quite similar. Each people sees itself as virtuous, restrained, and peace-loving, and views the adversary nation as deceptive, imperialistic, and warlike. Arthur Gladstone described it in this way:

> Each side believes the other to be bent on aggression and conquest, to be capable of great brutality and evil-doing, to be something less than human and therefore hardly deserving respect or consideration, to be insincere and untrustworthy, etc. To hold this conception of the enemy becomes the moral duty of every citizen, and those who question it are denounced. Each side prepares actively for the anticipated combat, striving to amass the greater military power for the destruction of the enemy. . . . The approaching war is seen as due entirely to the hostile intentions of the enemy.[90]

According to social psychologists, the perception of the enemy, even though it may be erroneous, can help to shape reality and bring on the self-fulfilling prophecy: When suspicions run high, a "defensive" move by one side may look "provocative" to the other, evoking from the latter a further "defensive" reaction that serves only to confirm the suspicions of the former.[91]

Urie Bronfenbrenner argued that American and Russian citizens believe essentially the same things about each other's societies: *They* are the aggressors, *their* government exploits and deludes the people, the mass of *their* people are not really sympathetic to the regime, *they* cannot be trusted, and *their* policy verges on madness.[92] Even within the restricted context of Soviet-American relations, the concept of the mirror image has some serious problems, one of which is that it readily gives rise to pseudo-corollaries in the minds of untrained observers—corollaries that are not necessarily implicit in the concept itself but emerge by a process of insinuation:

1. The social and political values of the two sides are scarcely distinguishable from each other.
2. Neither party can properly be cast in the role of aggressor or defender.
3. Both sides are equally right, equally wrong, and equally responsible for pursuing policies that produce international tensions.
4. The strategic behavior of the two sides springs from thought processes that are essentially similar.

5. The reduction of image distortion can be accomplished with equal ease on both sides.

In fairness to the advocates of the mirror image theory, it should be pointed out that they often made some effort to dissociate themselves from these illogical inferences. Ralph K. White, for example, warned: "The proposition that 'there is probably some truth on both sides' should be distinguished from the quite different proposition that there is probably an equal amount of truth on both sides'. . . . [It is] entirely possible to attribute too much validity to the other's viewpoint, leaning over backward to avoid ethnocentrism."[93]

Urie Bronfenbrenner called attention to an important asymmetry:

> It proved far easier to get an American to change his picture of the Soviet Union than the reverse. Although showing some capacity for change, Soviet citizens were more likely than Americans to cling to their stereotypes and to defend them by denial and displacement. . . . I am persuaded that a comparative study of modes of adaptation in American and Soviet society would reveal a stronger predilection in the latter for black-and-white thinking, moral self-righteousness, mistrust, displacing of blame to others, perceptual distortion, and denial of reality.[94]

The concept of the mirror image in international relations was at the height of its popularity in the early 1960s, and was logically related to a number of suggestions put forth at that time for reducing the hostility of the Cold War as well as the risks of "hot" war between the superpowers through unilateral initiative by one side designed to reduce international tensions and evoke reciprocal gestures of cooperation from the other side. The basic idea, of course, was that the process of relating tensions, no less than the process of exacerbating them, is a reaction process, and that if one side can bring itself to break the vicious circle and take the initiative by making friendly gestures and concessions, the behavior of the other will sooner or later change for the better.[95]

AGGRESSION DIVERSION AND REDUCTION

Social psychologists often point out that the expression of aggression within a society may be either covert or overt. Physical aggression may be eschewed in favor of verbal aggression; that is, murder, suicide, and other forms of violence may be rather rare, while the culture sanctions malicious gossip, slander, and the use of sorcery as means of retaliating against those one dislikes. Elton B. McNeil pointed out that a relationship appears to exist between a high amount of freedom for the overt expression of aggression and a low degree to which it will take covert forms, and vice versa.[96] Political scientists have long been aware of the "safety valve" theory.

Societies may develop culturally acceptable ways of either reducing or working off aggressive impulses. In the search for social aggression-inhibitors or aggression-reducers one might logically look to such areas of life as religion, politics, business, sports, and education. In each one of these dimensions we find ourselves faced with ambiguities that prevent us from drawing definite conclusions. Religions that preach a doctrine of love and renunciation of self may significantly lessen the aggressiveness of those adherents who take the doctrine seriously, who apply it not selectively but universally, and who are sufficiently disciplined to follow it in practice. Yet throughout history religious differences themselves have often contributed to the occurrence and the ferocity of war. In the realm of politics, one might argue that, in comparison to authoritarian or totalitarian regimes, democratic states should be less aggressive because they provide a variety of outlets through which political frustrations can be released—free speech and press, election campaigning, voting, lobbying for a law, or organizing a protest. There is something to this "safety valve" theory of democratic government, but the democratic milieu also permits aggressive individuals and parties to play upon xenophobic attitudes and propagate nationalistic policies, whereas in more tightly controlled societies, promoting nationalism and organizing demonstrations is much closer to being a government monopoly. In free-market economies, business enterprise undoubtedly siphons off a considerable amount of creative aggression. However, although most business people prefer the conditions of peace and order for making their rational profit calculus, some may support trade, or investment, and other economic policies that increase international tensions. A minority might even hope to gain from war.

Behavioral and other scientists interested in controlling aggression have wondered whether a society might diminish its "funds" of pent-up aggressive energy by diverting them into harmless channels such as organized athletic contests. There is no clear consensus on the subject. According to Konrad Lorenz, all human sport is a form of ritualized fighting. Even though it contains an aggressive motivation absent in most animal play, it helps to keep people healthy and its main function consists in the cathartic discharge of aggression. Thus it provides a release for that dangerous form of collective militant enthusiasm that underlies aggressive nationalism.[97] Hebb and Thompson suggest that sports may be a useful means of creating and working off an optimum amount of frustration and thus of contributing to social stability.[98] Frank calls attendance at such spectator sports as prizefights and professional football games a vicarious discharge of aggression. He admits, however, that body-contact sports often involve inflicting pain and may arouse anger and hostility, but notes that the games themselves require the development of self-discipline to control the expression of anger.[99] Lorenz, Frank, and others have perceived much good in the Olympics as an exercise in promoting international cooperation and good sportsmanship,[100] although it cannot be denied that the Olympic Games have often been politicized—for example, being converted into an arena of international hostility (Berlin in 1936), violent conflict (Munich in 1972), protest over South Africa's apartheid

(Montreal in 1976), and intricate diplomatic maneuvering and boycott to express political opposition to the host country's policies (Moscow in 1980 and Los Angeles in 1984).[101]

Within recent years, writers have expressed concern that under some circumstances sports may get out of hand, possibly exacerbating both the aggressive impulses of individual players and spectators, and international tension, ill will, and hostility.[102] If there is such a thing as a "fund" of pent-up aggressive energy (a hypothesis never proven), competitive sports could represent on balance a healthy safety valve, because most sports contests are conducted peaceably and the losers, if they are "good sports," do not harbor lasting grudges. International sports competition, if approached purely as sports in a spirit of fair play, can contribute to strengthening international good will and amity, but sports contests, no less than religion and trade, are neutral from a political standpoint, and do not necessarily lead to peace, especially if governments, ideological movements, political organizations, or ethnic partisans attempt to exploit them for ends that have little to do with sports.[103] In the final analysis, we cannot be certain whether sports attenuate or stimulate aggression within individuals and among nations. The answer cannot be generalized, but must be given for each event, and probably depends less on the athletes themselves than on such factors as prevailing national or racial issues, the crowd behavior of fans, and media coverage.

The area to which a great many psychologists and social learning theorists attach their hopes for reducing human aggressiveness and fostering international standing is education. Changes in regard to education have been urged at two distinct levels. The first pertains to basic modifications in the method of rearing children, aimed at reducing the level of frustration, violence modeling, and aggression within a society. Some theorists who associate warlike cultures with asceticism, celibacy, and strict codes of sexual behavior advocate greater sexual permissiveness.[104] In medieval Europe, however, the celibate priestly class was forbidden to take part in warfare, and the knights who did fight were usually far from celibate. Some psychologists trace the problem to the readiness of parents to mete out physical punishment to children; they urge parents to be more tolerant of children's desire to "express themselves."[105] Still others argue that it is unhealthy to bottle up feelings of rage and anger, and that the "ventilation" of aggression can have a therapeutic effect, despite warnings to the contrary by experimental psychologists.[106] Others yet have called for eliminating violence in the mass media in order to decrease the incidence of violent behavior by imitation, and for banning the manufacture of toy guns.[107] The foregoing proposed remedies involve considerable cultural or social changes that may not be acceptable or easy to achieve. This represents a case of saying that if human beings behaved differently from the way they do, they would be less aggressive. There is no way of knowing, however, whether these changes—assuming that they could be achieved—would be relevant to the propensity toward international war.

The second proposed change pertains to the realm of formal educational efforts, calculated to attenuate international hostility and conflict by promoting understanding among societies. Theorists have long taken it for granted that courses in school that increase the student's knowledge about foreign cultures and countries—as well as international teacher, student, and cultural exchange programs that facilitate personal contacts and learning experiences across political boundaries—are bound to contribute to the growth of international good will and the strengthening of international peace.[108] But Kenneth N. Waltz has questioned whether misunderstandings among peoples of diverse cultural backgrounds have anything to do with the occurrence of most wars. "Conversely," he asks, "does understanding always promote peace, or do nations sometimes remain at peace precisely because they do not understand each other well?"[109] We probably cannot assume that increased communication leads inevitably to improved understanding, or that understanding necessarily makes for cooperation rather than conflict.

OTHER PSYCHOLOGICAL THEORIES

In addition to frustration-aggression and social learning theories, there are several other psychological theories of conflict with which the student of international relations should be familiar. These often serve to complement and in some cases to modify the theories treated in the foregoing sections. They include the studies of Allport, Klineberg, and others on such phenomena as bias, prejudice, and stereotypes, and the part played by educational and mass communications systems in the shaping of inter-group attitudes.[110] The student should be conversant with the phenomenon that Frenkel-Brunswik calls the "intolerance of ambiguity," or the tendency of human beings to reduce uncertainties and contradictions perceived as frustrating or anxiety-producing by reducing social reality to nice, neat, dichotomous categories—black and white, good and bad, friend and foe.[111] Adorno and his colleagues attempted to correlate a high degree of nationalistic feeling with an "authoritarian personality" that is characterized by neuroticism—an exaggerated fear of weakness, unquestioning submissiveness to authority, a heavy emphasis on conventional behavior, a conservative idea of a masculine-feminine dichotomy, and a preference for autocratic, punitive child-rearing methods.[112] A quarter-century later, two social psychologists, aware that the "authoritarian personality" hypothesis had received some harsh criticisms, reported that they had found evidence of a distinct type (of political leader) who displayed a consistent preference for belligerence and possessed certain recognizable personality traits which they related to the notion of compensatory masculinity and the archetype described by the Adorno group.[113]

Many writers have sought to probe the murky area of the influence that the personality of national leaders may have upon their foreign policy decisions. Michael P. Sullivan, after reviewing a fair sample of the voluminous literature on the subject, reaches the judicious conclusion that the personality characteristics or attributes of political leaders must undoubtedly have some effect at various times upon foreign policy decisions, but we are still far from sure what types of behavior can be accounted for by personality factors.[114] Also significant for understanding certain aspects of national and international politics is Erich Fromm's thesis concerning the desire of the modern human being to escape the burdens of freedom. Feeling alone and powerless in the face of gigantic entities and social forces that individuals cannot control, we are, according to Fromm, tempted to dissolve ourselves in the omnipotent state, to identify entirely with the state, and to seek satisfaction vicariously in the fortunes of the larger collectivity—to seek an "escape from freedom." Ready to submit to power within our nation, we want our nation to assert itself at the expense of the weak beyond its borders.[115] These psychological interpretations of political behavior cannot be examined here in detail; however, it should be obvious to the reader that if either national leadership groups or large segments of their publics should lapse into pronounced forms of the neuroticism these theories describe, it could have a profound impact upon the international behavior of states.

Related to Frenkel-Brunswik's "intolerance of ambiguity" is the psychological theory of cognitive dissonance and consistency advanced by Leon Festinger.[116] Stated simply, this refers to the normal tendency of the individual to reduce inconsistencies that may arise in the knowledge concerning one's values, environment, and behavior. Inconsistency might be reduced by modifying any one of the three. Festinger presents the fertile example of the mental processes and rationalizations that a "chain" smoker may go through to reduce cognitive dissonance by reconciling the values of health, long life, and love of family with the personal addiction to cigarettes that makes behavior modification the most difficult course to pursue.

The normal tendency of the individual to shift from cognitive dissonance to consistency may have significant implications for the study of conflict at the level of international relations, even though this is not empirically demonstrable. If it is operative at all, it will probably be within the minds of key decision-makers. A hypothetical example may illustrate the point. In a prolonged Cold War, leaders of a nation might be convinced ideologically that permanent security could not be achieved until the adversary had been destroyed by war. But with the growth of nuclear weapons stockpiles, leaders are compelled to realize that direct hostilities between the two rival powers will prove mutually suicidal. Leaders, therefore, reduce cognitive dissonance by restructuring their knowledge patterns concerning the world situation, focusing on such notions as "the balance of terror," "gradual convergence of social systems," "mutual deterrence," "limited adversary relationship," and so forth.

Other situations likely to produce cognitive dissonance among foreign policy decision-makers could include, for example, the desire to control inflation, thereby increasing unemployment, or the desire of OPEC countries to raise the price of oil without stimulating Western efforts to seek alternative energy sources, or the attempt to use nuclear civilian energy without abetting the proliferation of national nuclear weapons capabilities and polluting the human environment with waste materials from reactors.

The theory of cognitive dissonance might also cast light on the phenomenon of internal revolution within a society. It is often suggested that when human beings perceive an intolerably wide gap between their social ideals and the operating reality of the existing political system, they become alienated from the latter and seek to reduce their inner dissonance by gravitating toward revolutionary organization for the purpose of restructuring the external environment according to their ideal vision. In revolutionary situations, of course, many individuals will hover precariously on the borderline between continuing to grant the system minimal or passive support and withdrawing from the system to oppose it actively by violence. This is partly a matter of weighing prospective rewards and punishments, and thus falls under the heading of what psychologists call "approach-avoidance" conflict within the individual, in which the antagonistic tendencies are both sufficiently strong to produce ambivalent or neurotic behavior.[117]

PSYCHOLOGICAL FACTORS IN THE NUCLEAR AGE

The nuclear era is approaching the half-century mark. Psychologists and strategists have pondered the impact of nuclear weapons on the human psyche. The former dwell pessimistically upon the effect that nuclear weapons are said to have exerted upon the human mind. Most psychologists, and most political analysts who follow their lead, are convinced that nuclear weapons have brought humanity to the precipice of self-extinction and are responsible for the increase in alienation, morbidity, and neuroticism that they perceive in the world. Those who are loyal to Freud still discern an ultimate death wish in the maintenance of nuclear weapons stockpiles. They deem the major nuclear powers foolish in the extreme to base their security on the allegedly contradictory premises of the "deadly logic of deterrence,"[118] in which "assured destruction" and "mutual overkill" are implicit. Security policies that rely on the threat of nuclear war, they argue, can only aggravate international tensions, and their danger is heightened by a tendency—due to such psychological factors as defensive avoidance, apathy, and habituation—to seek escape from the anxieties of the nuclear age either by unconscious denial of the threat, or by an effort to blot its implications from consciousness by rationalizing them away with verbal nostrums: "They will never be used."[119]

Strategic analysts for the most part are less negative, and far less certain of disaster. They are concerned about nuclear weapons proliferation and about the need to develop and adhere to strategies that may prove stabilizing—that is, the need to deter or prevent the outbreak of war. Those who espouse the validity of nuclear deterrence contend that the growth of nuclear weapons arsenals has made the leading power governments more cautious than ever in resorting to the use of any kind of military force in international affairs, for the specter of large-scale nuclear destruction has compelled political decision-makers for the first time in history to face up squarely to the problem of war and to substitute the deterrence system for the war system. Whether deterrence has fundamentally and permanently (rather than merely temporarily) modified the war-proneness of great powers is one of the most crucial questions in international relations as we approach the end of the twentieth century and the beginning of a new millenium. (See Chapter 9.)

In the debate about deterrence, the same psychological factor—fear— is cited simultaneously by the two contesting sides as increasing and decreasing the probability of war. The issue is not a simple one. Some fears may be rational in the sense that they lead to rational calculations and decisions; some may be irrational, blocking rational judgment. Fears may operate with very different effects upon individuals, small groups, large groups, publics, elites, and policymakers. In an era of mass media, popular fears can quickly be whipped up to the point of hysteria, but governmental bureaucracies, which are essentially conservative, rational, and cautious calculators, can be disciplined to prudent action even in crisis.

Fear of and respect for nuclear power in all forms are healthy phenomena that should be neither denied nor discouraged. But only if the fear is kept rational will it remain politically viable so that the power of the atom can be used for beneficial rather than destructive purposes. The theory of nuclear deterrence as propounded by contemporary strategic analysts presupposes a high degree of "common sense" on the part of national political decision-makers. At this point, psychologists warn that in the lives and decisions of individuals, irrational, unconscious factors frequently prevail over rational, conscious factors. Sociologists who have been influenced by Max Weber rejoin by pointing to the inherently stabilizing rationality built into the political-administrative bureaucratic structures of modern states, in which the emotional preferences of individuals are subordinated to and neutralized by a complex network of institutionalized procedures that inhibit or screen out rash and erratic decisional behavior.[120]

CONCLUSION: MICROCOSMIC THEORIES IN PERSPECTIVE

All the theories discussed in this chapter—biological-instinctual, frustration-aggression, social learning, and others—have been modified over time, and the general direction of these modifications in an era of interdisciplinary research and theoretical integration has been toward conver-gence.[121] The various theories have been presented here in their clear, pristine form for the purpose of helping to explain the sources from which contemporary theories are evolving. Students are strongly encouraged to go back to the original theories, to trace these through subsequent modifications, and to formulate their own syntheses based upon reflection, analysis, and insights.

In summary, it is uncertain and even questionable that biological and psychological mechanisms within the individual that pertain to aggressive behavior can explain intersocietal warfare. To the extent that such a rela-tionship exists, it is probably indirect rather than direct, and may be rather remote at some times and more proximate at other times. Innate aggres-sive urges or drives may feed or reinforce belligerent political attitudes and give them an emotional basis. In the case of some individuals, highly developed inner aggressiveness may make them easier to train for fighting and killing in war. Aggressive impulses frequently indulged rather than controlled might contribute to a short temper in a political leader, and dispose the leader to resort readily to force in order to solve a problem that might be managed adequately through negotiation. Conversely, personal-ity factors can also make another leader vacillate and procrastinate in a state of Hamlet-like indecision until either war becomes inevitable or peace prevails by default. But despite these and several other linkages that could be drawn, it would be inaccurate to conclude that innate biological and psychological drives are the "cause" of wars or peace. They probably constitute one of the important *necessary* conditions for the emergence of aggressive discontents among individual leaders, elite groups, and masses that make the recurrence of war a possibility throughout human history. By themselves, however, they do not constitute a *sufficient* condi-tion of war. Fortunately, there is no compelling reason to think that hu-manity is being pushed inexorably toward nuclear cataclysm by an uncon-scious death wish or by some other innate biological/psychological urge to aggression.

NOTES

1. Kenneth N. Waltz, *Man, the State and War: A Theoretical Analysis* (New York: Columbia University Press, 1959), chs. 2 and 4.
2. Ibid., ch. 6. The anarchic character of the international system is discussed in ch. 1, pp. 60–62. See also "War and the Expectation of War," ch. 7 in Vernon Van Dyke, *International Politics,* 2nd ed. (New York: Appleton, 1966); Gordon W. Allport, "The Role of Expectancy," in Hadley Cantril, ed., *Tensions That Cause War* (Urbana: University of Illinois Press, 1950); and Werner Levi, "On the Causes of War and the Conditions of Peace," *Journal of Conflict Resolu-tion,* IV (December 1960), 411–420. Levi notes that war should be traced not to any specific factor but to a constellation of factors. Ibid., p. 418.

3. Kenneth N. Waltz, op. cit., pp. 18–20.

4. The word *anomic* here refers to a condition of normless violence flaring up rather unexpectedly.

5. Werner Levi, op. cit., p. 415. Here the reader should review the caution expressed by Herbert C. Kelman in the passage quoted in Chapter 5. See also the following statement by Kelman: "Any attempt to conceptualize the causes of war and the conditions for peace that starts from individual psychology rather than from an analysis of the relations between national-states is of questionable relevance." "International Relations: Psychological Aspects," in *International Encyclopedia of the Social Sciences* (New York: Macmillan, 1968), vol. 8, p. 76. See also Seymour Feshbach and Adam Fraczek, *Aggression and Behavior Change: Biological and Social Processes* (New York: Praeger, 1979).

6. Peter Corning, "The Biological Basis of Behavior and Some Implications for Political Science," *World Politics*, XXIII (April 1971), 339–340.

7. The founder of sociobiology is Edward O. Wilson, a professor of science and curator of entomology at Harvard University, who outlined the field in *Sociobiology: The New Synthesis* (Cambridge, Mass.: Harvard University Press, 1975). Since 1975, several works have appeared either attacking or defending the field or presenting the debate. These include David P. Barash, *Sociobiology and Behavior* (New York: Elsevier, 1977); Arthur L. Caplan, ed., *Sociobiology Debate* (New York: Harper & Row, 1978); Michael S. Gregaroy et al., eds., *Sociobiology and Human Nature: An Interdisciplinary Critique and Defense* (San Francisco: Jossey-Bass, 1978); George W. Barlow and James Silverberg, eds., *Sociobiology: Beyond Nature-Nurture* (Boulder, Colo.: Westview, 1979); and James H. Fetzer, ed., *Sociobiology and Epistemology* (Boston: D. Reidel, 1985).

8. Peter A. Corning, op. cit., pp. 339–340. See Thomas Landon Thorson, *Biopolitics* (New York: Holt, Rinehart and Winston, 1970); the essays in Albert Somit, ed., *Biology and Politics* (Paris: Mouton, 1976); and Roger D. Masters, "The Biological Nature of the State," *World Politics*, XXXV (January 1983). Cf. also additional references in note 47 below.

9. Abraham H. Maslow, *Motivation and Personality* (New York: Harper & Row, 1954), pp. 80–98. (A second edition was published in 1970.) Maslow argues that basic physical and safety needs demand satisfaction before the higher psychological needs emerge.

10. Robert C. North has shown that the shortages or scarcities that give rise to political conflict are due not only to objective physical causes (such as entropy) but also to psychological perceptions and anticipations of demand in excess of supply. "Toward a Framework for the Analysis of Scarcity and Conflict," *International Studies Quarterly*, 21 (December 1977), 569–591; see also David Novick et al., *A World of Scarcities: Critical Issues in Public Policy* (New York: Halsted, 1976).

11. See William Etkin, *Social Behavior from Fish to Man* (Chicago: University of Chicago Press, 1967), p. 33; George Gaylord Simpson, *The Meaning of Evolution* (New Haven: Yale University Press, 1967), p. 222; Theodosius Dobzhansky, *Mankind Evolving* (New Haven: Yale University Press, 1962), p. 134.

12. Albert Bandura, *Aggression: A Social Learning Analysis* (Englewood Cliffs, N.J.: Prentice-Hall, 1973), p. 3.

13. Ibid., p. 5. Corning, following the approach of the Committee on Violence of the Stanford University School of Medicine, defines aggressiveness as encompassing the entire spectrum of assertive and attacking behaviors found in humans and other animal species. "It includes overt and covert attacks, self-directed attacks, displacement attacks, dominance behavior, defamatory acts, and the motivational and emotional components of any determined attempt to accomplish a task." Op. cit., p. 345. Rollo May notes that, besides being physical, aggression may also be psychological, intellectual, spiritual, or economic. It may employ as its weapons words, artistic symbols, gestures, arguments *ad hominem,* insults, or even prolonged silence calculated to hurt or punish. *Power and Innocence: A Search for the Sources of Violence* (New York: Norton, 1972), pp. 148–152.

14. William McDougall, *An Introduction to Social Psychology* (Boston: Luce, 1926), especially pp. 30–45. See also his *Outline of Psychology* (New York: Scribner's 1923), pp. 140–141.

15. Sigmund Freud, *A General Introduction to Psychoanalysis,* trans. G. S. Hall (New York: Boni and Liveright, 1920), pp. 170–174.

16. See Urpo Harva, "War and Human Nature," in Robert Ginsberg, ed., *The Critique of War* (Chicago: Regnery, 1969), p. 48. "Aggression and necrophilia are the two deep sources from which war derives its motive energies." Ibid., p. 49.

17. Sigmund Freud, *Beyond the Pleasure Principle* (New York: Bantam, 1958), p. 198. See also Albert Bandura, op. cit., pp. 12–14.

18. "Why War?" in a letter from Sigmund Freud to Albert Einstein, written in 1932. Text in Robert A. Goldwin et al., *Readings in World Politics* (New York: Oxford University Press, 1950). After describing the "death instinct," Freud wrote: "The upshot of these observations . . . is that there is no likelihood of our being able to suppress humanity's aggressive tendencies. . . . The Bolshevists, too, aspire to do away with human aggressiveness by ensuring the satisfaction of material needs and enforcing equality between man and man. To me this hope seems vain." But then, paradoxically, he added that "complete suppression of a man's aggressive tendencies is not an issue; what we may try is to divert it into a channel other than that of warfare." Ibid., p. 29. This last statement seems to parallel William James's quest for a "moral equivalent of war." See also Freud's *Civilization and Its Discontents* (New York: Cap and Smith, 1930).

19. Leonard Berkowitz, *Aggression: A Social-Psychological Analysis* (New York: McGraw-Hill, 1962), p. 8; Rollo May, op. cit., p. 155. For a statement by one of Freud's own students rejecting his instinctivist theory of aggression, see Erich Fromm, *The Anatomy of Human Destructiveness* (New York: Holt, Rinehart and Winston, 1973).

20. Leonard Berkowitz, op. cit., p. 9.

21. Ibid., p. 10. D. O. Hebb has shown that there is an important relationship between excitation and the human being's mental development. Noting that a mere repetition of responses may weaken rather than strengthen them, he says that prolonged routinized learning has a negative, monotonous effect that often leads to a disturbance or reduction of motivation or loss of interest. Hebb argues that human behavior is dominated not by what is thoroughly familiar and arouses a "well-organized phase sequence," but rather

by the "thought process that is not fully organized." He insists upon "the continued need of some degree of novelty, to maintain a wakefulness of choice." He adds that "some degree of novelty, combined with what is predominantly familiar, is stimulating and exciting over a wide range of activities." He also refers to the human "preoccupation with what is new but not too new, with the mildly frustrating or the mildly fear-provoking." As examples he cites the case of children seeking controllably frightening situations, the addiction of adults to dangerous sports (such as mountain climbing and sky diving), or to "ghost stories," and the fascination of problem-solving challenges, even when they involve frustration. He concludes that conflict need not be regarded as "unpleasant and grossly disruptive of human behavior; on the contrary, some degree of conflict is stimulating and necessary to the maintenance of normal responsiveness to the environment." *The Organization of Behavior: A Neuropsychological Theory* (New York: Wiley, 1949), pp. 224–234. Human beings actively seek an optimum level of frustration. Cf. D. O. Hebb and W. R. Thompson, "The Social Significance of Animal Studies," in Gardiner Lindzey, ed., *Handbook of Social Psychology* (Reading, Mass.: Addison-Wesley, 1954). Reprinted in Leon Bramson and George W. Goethals, eds., *War: Studies from Psychology, Sociology, Anthropology* (New York: Free Press, 1968), p. 53.

22. Contemporary psychoanalytic writers have adhered to the aggressive instinct theory. A few, such as Karl Menninger, retain the notion of death instinct. Others, such as Hartmann, Kris, and Lowenstein, continue to postulate an aggressive instinct, but do not trace it to the death wish. Still others, including Fenichel, have shifted back toward the frustration explanation of aggression. See Berkowitz, op. cit., pp. 11–12.

23. See McNeil's chapter, "The Nature of Aggression," in Elton B. McNeil, ed., *The Nature of Human Conflict* (Englewood Cliffs, N.J.: Prentice-Hall), 1965, p. 15. Peter A. Corning has warned that it "would be fallacious to make an unqualified identification between any given human behavior and apparently similar behavior in lower animals." Op. cit., p. 331.

24. Students of animal behavior-physiology are producing some interesting insights into the problem of aggression, but they would be the first to admit difficulties in interpreting their data and to caution against the hasty application of their findings to the more mysterious realm of human affairs. A useful summary of findings on animal aggression can be found in McNeil, op. cit., pp. 15–27.

25. John Paul Scott, *Animal Behavior* (Garden City, N.Y.: Doubleday [Anchor Books], 1963), pp. 121–122. One should note that if human aggressiveness is to be reduced or inhibited, it will have to be by way of learning, since the avenues of electrical, hormonal, chemical, and surgical interventions into the human body are of necessity—and fortunately—quite limited.

26. John Paul Scott, *Aggression* (Chicago: University of Chicago Press, 1958), p. 62; Leonard Berkowitz, op. cit., p. 15.

27. John Paul Scott, *Animal Behavior,* op. cit., pp. 153–155.

28. Konrad Lorenz, *On Aggression,* trans. Marjorie Kerr Wilson (New York: Bantam, 1967), p. x.

29. Ibid., pp. 28–32.

30. Robert Ardrey, *The Territorial Imperative* (New York: Atheneum, 1966), p. 103; see also pp. 4–7, 110–117, as well as his book *African Genesis* (New York:

Dell, 1967), p. 174. For severe criticisms of Ardrey's work on territoriality as unscientific, see Geoffrey Gorer, "Ardrey on Human Nature," *Encounter, 28* (June 1967), and the essays by R. L. Holloway, Jr., P. H. Klopfer, Geoffrey Gorer, and J. H. Crook in M. F. Ashley Montagu, ed., *Man and Aggression,* 2nd ed. (New York: Oxford University Press, 1973).

31. Konrad Lorenz, op. cit., pp. 161–163.

32. Ibid., p. 164. Rollo May writes: "Lovemaking and fighting are very similar neurophysically in human beings." Op. cit., p. 151. See also Anthony Storr, *Human Aggression* (New York: Atheneum, 1968), p. 16.

33. Konrad Lorenz, op. cit., pp. 54–65, 69–81, and 99–110. He gives the familiar example of the ceremonial inciting by the female duck who will charge menacingly toward an "enemy couple" until, frightened by her own boldness, suddenly hurries back to her own protective drake to refurbish her courage before the next hostile foray. Thus without actually joining battle she delivers her warning message.

34. Ibid., p. 127. See also pp. 72–74, 122–132, and 232–233. For a further elaboration of Lorenz's views concerning the implications of biological findings for a knowledge of human social behavior, see "A Talk With Konrad Lorenz," Magazine Section, *The New York Times* (July 5, 1970), 4–5, 27–30. Lorenz's widely cited example of the wolf who submissively exposes his jugular vein to the adversary was later dismissed as having been based on faulty observation. R. Schenkel, "Submission: Its Features and Frustrations in the Wolf and Dog," *American Zoologist,* 7 (1967), 319–329. Most biologists, however, still subscribe to the concept of aggression-inhibiting mechanisms.

35. Konrad Lorenz, op. cit., p. 233. See also Jerome D. Frank, *Sanity and Survival: Psychological Aspects of War and Peace* (New York: Random House [Vintage Books], 1968), pp. 42–45 in his ch. 3, "Why Men Kill—Biological Roots." R. L. Holloway, Jr., suggests that the averting of eyes, cringing, and shedding tears may serve an inhibiting or appeasing function in humans, even though they are quite weak. "Human Aggression: The Need for a Species-Specific Framework," *Natural History,* LXXVI (December 1, 1967), 41.

36. John P. Scott, in reviewing the Lorenz book, criticized it for suggesting that destructive aggressive behavior arises from a spontaneous outburst of internal energy. "Actually," Scott reiterates, "there is no evidence that there is any physiological mechanism in any mammal which produces stimulation to fight in the absence of external stimulation. Rather there is much evidence indicating that mechanisms exist which are easily excited by external stimulation and which function to prolong and magnify the effect of this stimulation." "Fighting," *Science,* CLIV (November 4, 1966), 636–637.

37. Brian C. R. Bertram, "The Social System of Lions," *Scientific American,* 232 (May 1975), 65. See also H. Kruuk, "The Urge to Kill," *New Scientist, 54,* No. 802 (1972), 735–737.

38. Konrad Lorenz, op. cit., ch. 12.

39. The access of modern human beings to push-button remote-control weapons shields them from directly and emotionally experiencing the consequences of their destructive, warlike acts. Ibid., p. 234.

40. Alec Nisbett, *Konrad Lorenz: A Biography* (New York: Harcourt Brace Jovanovich, 1976), pp. 171–172.

41. Erich Fromm, "The Erich Fromm Theory of Aggression," Magazine Section, *The New York Times* (February 27, 1972), 74, and "Man Would as Soon Flee

as Fight," *Psychology Today,* 7 (August 1973), 35–45. A similar criticism may be found in Ralph L. Halloway, Jr., "Human Aggression: The Need for a Species-Specific Framework," op. cit., 41.

42. See B. F. Skinner, *Beyond Freedom and Dignity* (New York: Knopf, 1971), in ch. 1, "A Technology of Behavior"; Meredith W. Watts, "B. F. Skinner and the Technological Control of Social Behavior," *American Political Science Review,* LXIX (March 1975), ch. 1, "A Technology of Behavior."

43. Alec Nisbett, op. cit., pp. 131–135, 162–164, and 181–183; M. F. Ashley Montagu, ed., op. cit., p. 9; Albert Bandura, op. cit., pp. 16–31. See also T. C. Schneirla, "Instinct and Aggression," in Montagu, ed., op. cit., p. 61.

44. These criticisms are documented in Stephen D. Nelson, "Nature/Nurture Revisited. I: A Review of the Biological Bases of Conflict," *Journal of Conflict Resolution,* 18 (June 1974), especially pp. 296–302, and in Samuel S. Kim, "The Lorenzian Theory of Aggression and Peace Research: A Critique," in Richard A. Falk and Samuel S. Kim, eds., *The War System: An Interdisciplinary Approach* (Boulder, Colo: Westview, 1980), pp. 82–115.

45. Francis A. Beer, *Peace Against War: The Ecology of International Violence* (San Francisco: W. H. Freeman, 1981), p. 304.

46. George M. Carstairs, "Overcrowding and Human Aggression," in Hugh Davis Graham and Ted Robert Gurr, eds., *Violence in America,* Report to the National Commission on the Causes and Prevention of Violence, June 1969 (New York: New American Library, 1969), pp. 730–742. Cf. also Jonathan Freedman, *Crowding and Behavior* (San Francisco: Freeman, 1975); Susan Seagart, *Crowding in Real Environments* (Sage: Beverly Hills, Calif.: 1976); and Larry Severy, ed., *Crowding: Theoretical and Research Implications* (New York: Humanities Science Press, 1979).

47. Thomas C. Wiegele, "Decision-Making in an International Crisis: Some Biological Factors," *International Studies Quarterly,* 7 (September 1973), 295–335 and *Biopolitics* (Boulder, Colo: Westview, 1979); Meredith Watts, ed., *Biopolitics: Ethological and Physiological Approaches* (San Francisco: Jossey-Bass, 1981); Gerald W. Hopple and Lawrence Falkowski, *Biopolitics, Political Psychology and International Politics* (New York: St. Martin's, 1982).

48. See, for example, George Pettee, "Revolution—Typology and Process," in Carl J. Friedrich, ed., *Revolution* (New York: Atherton, 1966), p. 19. Pettee likens the prerevolutionary situation to one of frustration or cramp. Robert C. Williamson writes: "Internecine warfare has been the end result of social, political, and economic frustration as well as of personal anomie," in "Toward a Theory of Political Violence: The Case of Rural Colombia," *Western Political Quarterly,* XVIII (March 1965), 36. Robert L. Heilbroner, describing the problems of economic development in the emerging nations, writes: "Above all, the necessity to hold down the level of consumption—to force savings in order to free resources for the capital-building process will make for a rising level of frustration, even under the sternest discipline. This frustration will almost surely have to be channeled into directions other than that of economic expectations. . . . In a word, economic development has within it the potential, not alone of a revolutionary situation, but of heightened international friction." *The Great Ascent* (New York: Harper & Row, 1963), pp. 158–159. For a further discussion of the revolutionary economic deprivation and the development process in the light of the frustration-aggression hypothesis, see the section on revolution in Chapter 8 of this textbook.

49. John Dollard, Leonard W. Doob, Neal E. Miller, et al., *Frustration and Aggression* (New Haven: Yale University Press, 1939), p. 1. For another basic work in the field, see Norman R. F. Maier, *Frustration: The Study of Behavior Without a Goal* (New York: McGraw-Hill, 1949).

50. John Dollard et al., op. cit., p. 7.

51. Ross Stagner, "The Psychology of Human Conflict," in Elton B. McNeil, ed., *The Nature of Human Conflict*, p. 53.

52. Abraham H. Maslow, "Deprivation, Threat and Frustration," *Psychological Review*, XLVIII, No. 6 (1941); reprinted in J. K. Zawodny, ed., *Conflict*, vol. I of *Man and International Relations* (San Francisco: Chandler, 1966), pp. 17–19.

53. Ross Stagner, op. cit., p. 28. Minor frustrations and the residual instigations from them can become cumulative and lead to a stronger aggressive response than would ordinarily be expected from the frustrating situation that immediately triggers the response. Ibid., p. 31.

54. Ibid., pp. 32–38.

55. Norman R. F. Maier, from his study of the role of punishment in the learning process, was led to postulate a relationship between frustration and fixation. See "Frustration Theory: Restatement and Extension," *Psychological Review*, LXIII, No. 7 (1956), 370–399, in J. K. Zawodny, ed., op cit., pp. 20–29.

56. John Dollard et al., op. cit., pp. 39–47; Otto Klineberg, *Tensions Affecting International Understanding* (New York: Social Science Research Council, 1950), especially ch. 5, "Influences Making for Aggression," p. 196. Bernard Berelson and Gary A. Steiner also have noted that prolonged or intense frustration sometimes produces flight from the goal rather than a further struggle toward the goal. They suggest that when survival is not at stake, and occasionally even when it is, people may give up and abandon the situation, physically or psychologically. *Human Behavior: An Inventory of Scientific Findings* (New York: Harcourt Brace Jovanovich, 1965), p. 270. This phenomenon would seem to correspond to what the biologists describe as the "fight or flight" reactions of animals in states of anxiety. See Harley C. Shands, "Some Social and Biological Aspects of Anxiety," *Journal of Nervous and Mental Disease*, CXXV, No. 3 (1957); reprinted in J. K. Zawodny, ed., op. cit., especially pp. 9 and 15.

57. Ibid., p. 48.

58. According to a later reformulation of the concept of catharsis, aggressive action was thought to have three possible separable effects: reducing, increasing, or producing no observable change in the level of aggressive response. S. Feshbach, "Aggression," in P. H. Mussen, ed., *Carmichael's Manual of Child Psychology* (New York: Wiley, 1970), pp. 159–259. Cited in Bandura, op. cit., p. 37.

59. Elton B. McNeil, "Psychology and Aggression," *Journal of Conflict Resolution*, III (September 1959), 204. McNeil here is following N. E. Miller, "The Frustration-Aggression Hypothesis," *Psychological Review*, XLVIII (July 1941), 338.

60. Leonard Berkowitz, op. cit., p. 29.

61. Ibid., p. 30. Elton B. McNeil observes that "the contention that aggressive behavior always presupposes the existence of frustration has met with little resistance or criticism." Op. cit., p. 204.

62. Albert Bandura, op. cit., p. 167.

63. For an elaboration of these first two points, see Leonard Berkowitz, op. cit., pp. 32–48.
64. Sanford Rosenzweig, "An Outline of Frustration Theory," J. McV. Hunt, ed., *Personality and the Behavior Disorders* (New York: Ronald, 1944), pp. 381–382. Elton B. McNeil, following Rosenzweig, says: "The privation of being born into poverty poses a series of frustrations for the individual; but his reaction to them differs considerably from his responses to being deprived of wealth, once he has possessed it." "Psychology and Aggression," p. 203.
65. Ibid., p. 204.
66. John Dollard et al., op. cit., p. 2.
67. The Yale group noted that "when Marxists have described the dynamic human interrelationships involved in the class struggle and in the preservation and destruction of the state, they have introduced unwittingly a psychological system involving the assumption that aggression is a response to frustration." Ibid., p. 23. The frustrating agents, of course, are the bourgeoisie, and the aggressive response by the frustrated proletariat is the organization of a class that finally carries out a revolution. But most sociologists, including Marxist ones, would not use the term *frustration* except metaphorically and in a social context, not in the same sense in which psychologists use it.
68. Sociologists distinguish between the behavior of small groups and that of large groups. Herbert Blumer has called attention also to the differences between "collective behavior" (even by fairly large groups) in an "undefined or unstructured situation" and organized social behavior that follows culturally prescribed norms. "Collective Behavior," in J. B. Gitter, ed., *Review of Sociology: Analysis of a Decade* (New York: Wiley, 1957), p. 130. In the elementary forms of collective behavior, the individuals in the group stimulate each other and contribute toward the circular development of a sense of unrest and excitement. Blumer shows that elementary collective behavior can gradually develop into a more complex social movement as it "acquires organization and form, a body of customs and traditions, established leadership, an enduring division of labor, social rules, and social values—in short, a culture, a social organization, and a new scheme of life." Ibid., p. 199. Neil J. Smelser, while modifying some of Blumer's ideas, agrees with the distinction described above: "Collective behavior . . . is not institutionalized behavior. According to the degree to which it becomes institutionalized, it loses its distinctive character." *Theory of Collective Behavior* (New York: The Free Press 1963), p. 8. It is interesting to note that Smelser, in his chapter on "The Hostile Outburst," makes no mention of the frustration-aggression hypothesis in his efforts to explain aggression in society. Ibid., pp. 222–269.
69. John Dollard et al., op. cit., pp. 55–76. E. F. M. Durbin and John Bowlby contended that the conflict within the child arising out of the fear of punishment is an important source of aggressiveness in the adult, because aggression can be controlled but not destroyed. "The boy, instead of striking his father whom he fears, strikes a smaller boy whom he does not fear. Disguised aggression has made the boy into a bully. . . . And in the same way revolutionaries who hate ordered government, nationalists who hate foreign policies, individuals who hate bankers, Jews, or their political opponents, may be exhibiting characteristics that have been formed by the suppression of simple aggression in their childhood education." *Personal Aggressiveness and War* (New

York: Columbia University Press, 1939), excerpted in J. K. Zawodny, ed., op. cit., p. 97.

70. Martin Gold, "Suicide, Homicide and the Socialization of Aggression," in Bartlett H. Stoodley, ed., *Society and Self: A Reader in Social Psychology* (New York: The Free Press, 1962), pp. 281–282.

71. Robert R. Sears, Eleanor Maccoby, and Harry Levin, "The Socialization of Aggression," in Eleanor E. Maccoby, Theodore M. Newcomb, and Eugene L. Hartley, eds., *Readings in Social Psychology* (New York: Holt, Rinehart and Winston, 1958), pp. 350–352.

72. Elton B. McNeil, "Psychology and Aggression," p. 212. Albert Bandura notes that the fear of punishment produces an inhibiting or deterrent effect and causes the displacement of aggression from similar to dissimilar targets. *Aggression*, pp. 34–35.

73. Ibid., p. 213; Ross Stagner, op. cit., pp. 55–56.

74. Ibid., p. 54; and Ralph K. White, "Images in the Context of International Conflict," in Herbert C. Kelman, ed., op. cit., esp. pp. 267–268.

75. Frieda L. Bornston and J. C. Coleman, "The Relationship Between Certain Parents' Attitudes Toward Child Rearing and the Direction of Aggression of Their Young Adult Offspring," *Journal of Clinical Psychology*, XII (1956), 41–44.

76. Albert Bandura, op. cit., p. 170.

77. Leonard Berkowitz, op. cit., pp. 139, 149, and 193–264; cf. also his "Concept of Aggressive Drive," in Leonard Berkowitz, ed., *Advances in Experimental Social Psychology* (New York: Academic Press, 1965), vol. II, p. 312.

78. Albert Bandura, op. cit., pp. 29–30.

79. Ibid., pp. 32–36, 44. According to Jerome D. Frank, children can learn aggression as a result of punishment (either the infliction of pain or the withdrawal of affection) or by imitating aggressive behavior by parents or others, and exposure to violence in the mass media. *Sanity and Survival*, pp. 68–74. For a bibliography of the extensive experimental research by Bandura and his colleagues on the imitation of aggressive models, see Bandura, op. cit., pp. 327–329.

80. For a fascinating account and analysis of how soldiers in battle face the prospect of imminent death, see J. Glenn Gray, *The Warriors: Reflections on Men in Battle* (New York: Harper, 1967), esp. pp. 100–121, and John Keegan, *The Face of Battle* (New York: Penguin) 1983.

81. Donald A. Wells, *The War Myth* (New York: Pegasus, 1967), pp. 174–175. Within two pages that follow, Wells first suggests that "war is not so natural or so psychologically grounded in human nature as we have been led to believe," but then arrives at what appears to be an opposite conclusion: "The emptiness of the reasons men verbalize for war suggests that war really does not rest on any rationale. . . . After all, if people didn't like to fight, there are no good reasons why they should do so much of it." Ibid., pp. 176–177.

82. Albert Bandura, op. cit., p. 99.

83. Raymond Aron has noted that, as modern warfare technology has grown more frightful, industrially advanced societies have, by articulating ever more grandiose statements of war aims, sought to inspire their citizens to sustain the hardships and sacrifices of war. *The Century of Total War* (Boston: Beacon, 1955), p. 26.

84. John H. Faris, "The Impact of Basic Combat Training," in Nancy Goldman and David R. Segal, eds., *The Social Psychology of Military Service* (Beverly Hills, Calif.: Sage, 1976), pp. 14–15.

85. Francis A. Beer, op. cit., p. 128 and his documentation on p. 339.

86. Hadley Cantril, *The Human Dimension: Experiences in Policy Research* (New Brunswick, N.J.: Rutgers University Press, 1967), pp. 16, 156, and quoted at pp. 127–128. See also Hadley Cantril, ed., *Tensions That Cause Wars* (Urbana: University of Illinois Press, 1950), p. 7; Hadley Cantril and William Buchanan, *How Nations See Each Other* (Urbana: University of Illinois Press, 1953).

87. Harold D. Lasswell, *World Politics and Personality Insecurity* (New York: McGraw-Hill, 1935), pp. 3, 207, and 237. For the results of a study of foreign ministers as a small but strategically important segment of the world elite, made up of persons who exhibit a set of background similarities, who share some values regarding world order and professional diplomatic conduct, and who interact with each other enough to develop some friendships as a basis for elite cohesion, see George Modelski, "The World's Foreign Ministers: A Political Elite," *Journal of Conflict Resolution*, XIV (June 1970), 135–175. See also William T. R. Fox, "Harold D. Lasswell and the Study of World Politics," in Arnold A. Rogow, ed., *Politics, Personality, and Social Science in the Twentieth Century* (Chicago: University of Chicago Press, 1969), pp. 376–377.

88. Herbert C. Kelman in Kelman, ed., op. cit., p. 24.

89. Kenneth E. Boulding, "National Images and International Systems," *Journal of Conflict Resolution*, III (June 1959), 120–131. This and the previous quotations are on pp. 121–122. See also his book, *The Image: Knowledge in Life and Society* (Ann Arbor: University of Michigan Press, 1956); Ole R. Holsti, "The Belief System and National Images," *Journal of Conflict Resolution*, 16 (September 1962) and "Cognitive Dynamics and Images of the Enemy," *Journal of International Affairs*, 21 (1967); and Robert Jervis, *The Logic of Images in International Relations* (Princeton: Princeton University Press, 1970).

90. Arthur Gladstone, "The Conception of the Enemy," *Journal of Conflict Resolution*, III (June 1959), 132.

91. Ross Stagner, op. cit., p. 46.

92. "The Mirror Image in Soviet-American Relations: A Social Psychologists's Report," *Journal of Conflict Resolution*, XI (September 1967), 325–332; Charles E. Osgood, "Analysis of the Cold War Mentality," *Journal of Social Issues*, XVII, No. 3 (1961), 12–19.

93. Ralph K. White, op. cit., p. 240.

94. "Allowing for Soviet Perceptions," in Roger Fisher, ed., *International Conflict and Behavioral Science*, The Craigville Papers (New York: Basic Books, 1964), p. 172.

95. See, for example, the discussion of "Graduated and Reciprocated Initiative in Tension-Reduction," (GRIT) in Charles E. Osgood, *An Alternative to War or Surrender* (Urbana: University of Illinois Press, 1962), and his "Questioning Some Unquestioned Assumptions about National Defense," *Journal of Arms Control*, I (January 1963), 2–13. Cf. also Arthur I. Waskow, *The Limits of Defense* (Garden City, N.Y.: Doubleday, 1962), ch. IV.

96. Elton B. McNeil, "The Nature of Aggression," p. 35.

97. Konrad Lorenz, op. cit., pp. 271–272.

98. D. O. Hebb and W. R. Thompson, op. cit., p. 53.

99. Jerome D. Frank, op. cit., pp. 75, 87–88.

100. Konrad Lorenz, op. cit., p. 272; Jerome D. Frank, op. cit., pp. 88, 241.

101. Wilson Carey McWilliams, "The Political Olympics," *Worldview* (July 1984). See also Harry Edwards, *The Sociology of Sport* (Homewood: Ill.: Dorsey Press, 1973).

102. See Parton Keese, "Violence in Sports: What It Could Mean," *The New York Times* (January 26, 1975); Lowell Miller, "World Cup—Or World War?" Magazine Section, *The New York Times* (May 21, 1978).

103. For an interesting discussion of the implications of international athletic contests for diplomatic recognition, political protest, propaganda, and state prestige, as well as interstate cooperation and conflict, see Andrew Strenk, "The Thrill of Victory and the Agony of Defeat: Sport and International Politics," *Orbis,* 22 (Summer 1978), 453–469.

104. Elbert Russell, "Human Aggression," Paper presented at Canadian Peace Research Institute Summer School, Grindstone Island, Ontario, July 18, 1973; James W. Prescott, "Body Pleasure and the Origins of Violence," *The Bulletin of the Atomic Scientists,* XXXI (November 1975), 10–20.

105. Ibid.; Jerome D. Frank, op. cit., 68–69, 283. Bandura, however, while agreeing that punishment may have unfavorable consequences if it is excessive, ill-timed, erratic, or administered in a spirit of vengeance without providing constructive direction, nevertheless argues that punishment can, under certain conditions, effectively modify undesirable behavior. Op. cit., pp. 289, 304–308.

106. See Leonard Berkowitz, "The Case for Bottling Up Rage," *Psychology Today* (July 1973), 24, 31.

107. Jerome D. Frank, op. cit., pp. 72–74, 283–284; Bandura, op. cit., pp. 266–286. Bandura dismisses the disclaimers that, since behavior is determined by multiple factors, it is unfair to place blame on the mass media and that aggressive modeling affects only people who are already disturbed or predisposed to aggression. He argues that in the face of abundant experimental evidence for observational learning, continued equivocation on the aggressive modeling impact of television upon both children and adults cannot be justified. Ibid., pp. 266–271; see also "Toy Guns: Do They Fan Aggression?" *The New York Times* (June 16, 1988). Psychologists were reported debating whether toy guns encourage violent behavior among youngsters or acquaint them with the horrors and death of war. Some government officials have blamed toy guns for actual deaths when police officers mistook them for real weapons.

108. See, for example, Jerome D. Frank, op. cit., pp. 238–245; Ithiel DeSola Pool, "Effects of Cross-National Contact on National and International Images," in Herbert C. Kelman, ed., op. cit., pp. 106–129; J. Watson and R. Lippitt, "Cross-Cultural Experience as a Source of Attitude Change," *Journal of Conflict Resolution,* 2 (March 1958).

109. Kenneth N. Waltz, *Man, the State and War,* p. 48.

110. Gordon W. Allport, *The Nature of Prejudice* (Reading, Mass.: Addison-Wesley, 1954); and Otto Klineberg, *The Human Dimension in International Relations* (New York: Holt, Rinehart and Winston, 1964).

111. Else Frenkel-Brunswik, "Intolerance of Ambiguity as an Emotional and Perceptual Personality Variable," *Journal of Personality,* XVIII (September 1949), 108–143, and "Social Tensions and the Inhibition of Thought," *Social Problems,* II (October 1954), 75–81.

112. T. W. Adorno, Else Frenkel-Brunswik, Daniel J. Levinson, and R. N. Sanford, *The Authoritarian Personality* (New York: Harper & Row, 1950). For criticisms of the hypothesis, cf. Richard Christie and Marie Jahoda, eds., *Studies in the Scope and Methods of 'The Authoritarian Personality'* (Glencoe, Ill.: Free Press, 1954).

113. S. Griedlander and R. Cohen, "The Personality Correlates of Belligerence in International Conflict," *Comparative Politics*, 7 (January 1975).

114. Michael P. Sullivan, *International Relations: Theories and Evidence* (Englewood Cliffs, N.J.: Prentice-Hall, 1976), pp. 26–40. See also Alexander L. George, "Assessing Presidential Character," *World Politics*, XXVI (January 1974).

115. Erich Fromm, *Escape from Freedom* (New York: Holt, Rinehart and Winston, 1941), pp. 21, 22, 141–142, and 164–168.

116. Leon Festinger, *A Theory of Cognitive Dissonance* (Stanford: Stanford University Press, 1957), and *Conflict, Decision and Dissonance* (Stanford: Stanford University Press, 1964).

117. Judson S. Brown, "Principles of Intrapersonal Conflict," *Journal of Conflict Resolution*, I (June 1957), 137–138. For a different perspective of how psychological factors in the personal background of a political leader may affect his decision to "go revolutionary," see E. Victor Wolfenstein, *Violence or Non Violence: A Psychoanalytic Exploration of the Choice of Means in Social Change*, Monograph Series, Center for International Studies, (Princeton: 1965).

118. See Philip Green, *Deadly Logic: The Theory of Nuclear Deterrence* (New York: Schocken, 1968).

119. Jerome D. Frank, op. cit., pp. 26–33.

120. See H. H. Gerth and C. Wright Mills, trans. and eds., *From Max Weber: Essays in Sociology* (New York: Oxford University Press, 1946), pp. 196–203.

121. Peter Corning, op. cit., pp. 345–349.

Chapter
8

Macrocosmic Theories of Violent Conflict: Revolution and War

We now turn to those who theorize about war at the macrolevel—the level of societies, nation-states, and other large aggregates. Here we examine insights into large-scale social structural violence that can be obtained from the work of anthropologists, sociologists, political scientists, and international relations specialists. Whereas the microanalysts look within the individual member of the species for unconscious, aggressive drives, and tend to be somewhat skeptical of consciously articulated motives for social and international conflict, macroanalysts in general take seriously statements of conscious, verbal motives and reasons for people's resort to violence within, between, and among societies. They regard such statements as particularly important for explaining why specific conflicts break out between specific parties at specific times. They ascribe a certain validity to the dictum of Thucydides: If you want to know why people are fighting a war, ask them and they will tell you.

Social scientists, especially most sociologists and anthropologists, who adopt a macro approach to human phenomena tend to regard conflict as a normal concomitant of group existence, not as the disruptive, dysfunctional, or even pathological condition most psychologists take it to be. Those sociologists who follow Talcott Parsons in emphasizing social adjustment, "common-value orientation," and system maintenance are an exception. More interested in social order than social change, in social statics than dynamics, the Parsonians consider conflict as a disease with disruptive and dysfunctional consequences. However, most European sociologists from Karl Marx to Georg Simmel and Ralf Dahrendorf, and most American sociologists in the pre-Parsonian era (e.g., Robert E. Park, John W. Burgess, William Graham Sumner, Charles H. Cooley, E. A. Ross, and

Albion W. Small) and some in recent decades (e.g., Jesse Bernard and Lewis A. Coser) have viewed conflict as serving positive social purposes.[1] Even violent conflict sometimes is seen as a useful means of resolving disputes within society and between societies. Political scientists, economists, and game theorists, along with most rational political leaders, usually prefer to evaluate specific conflicts on the basis of probable or actual outcomes—that is, by weighing the gains of conflict in terms of values at stake versus the risks and cost of the conflict.

For "conflict-as-functional" theorists, conflict not only integrates, but it helps to establish group identity, clarifies group boundaries, and contributes to group cohesion. Nearly every sociologist and anthropologist postulates some degree of "in-group" hostility for the "out-group." When there are many out-groups, the political scientist can cast light upon the question of why a particular one may be singled out at a particular time as the target of hostility. Historians of nationalism often describe the importance of the external *bête noire* in the formative period of a nation's consciousness. The prime example in American history is the role played by Britain in the early formative period of national feeling. Beyond this well-known phenomenon, some social theorists contend that even within groups, discord and opposition help to hold the groups together by providing inner relief and making the unbearable bearable.[2] Thus many thinkers in modern times accept conflict as "the central explanatory category for the analysis of social change or progress."[3]

INSIDE VERSUS OUTSIDE DIMENSIONS OF CONFLICT

Many social theorists since Machiavelli have taken it for granted that a significant relationship exists between conflict *within* societies and conflict *between* societies. This gives rise to one of the most durable hypotheses in social conflict theory. The relationship can be formulated in two ways: (1) internal conflict varies inversely with external conflict; and (2) domestic cohesion correlates positively with involvement in foreign wars. Political rulers in all ages, faced with growing troubles and turmoil at home, have apparently been tempted to provoke foreign military adventures as a diversionary tactic.

William Graham Sumner advanced the theory that groups seek internal unity for strength in competition with external enemies; that the sentiments of peace and cooperation inside the group are complementary to sentiments of hostility toward outside groups; and that societies that experienced frequent and fierce wars developed governments and legal systems, and the whole societal system became more firmly integrated.[4] William James, too, saw war as "the gory nurse that trained societies to cohesiveness" in ancient times.[5]

Uncertainty over tenure of power among ruling elites, according to Richard Rosecrance, may make war more probable by bringing aggressive military and political personalities to the fore.[6] Clyde Kluckhohn writes: "If a nation's intragroup aggressions become so serious that there is danger of disruption, war, by displacing aggression against another group, is an adjustive response from the point of view of preserving national cohesion."[7] Students of primitive tribes have noted that where warfare once served those groups as a "safety valve institution," and intrasocietal aggressiveness was siphoned off by directing considerable hostility toward the outside world to promote the integration of the society, modernization and peace have led to community fission.[8] Simmel noted the reciprocity between social-political centralization and the aggressive impulse to war. War promotes inner cohesiveness, yet internal political centralization increases the probability that external release of tensions will be sought through war. According to Simmel, "War with the outside is sometimes the last chance for a state ridden with inner antagonisms to overcome these antagonisms, or else to break up indefinitely."[9]

Geoffrey Blainey, on the contrary, rejects what he calls the "scapegoat theory" of war despite its undoubted "universal glow" in the eyes of political scientists, historians, and anthropologists. Although admitting that more than half of all international wars from 1823 to 1937 studied by him were immediately preceded by serious disturbances in one of the fighting nations, he concluded that scapegoat theorists rely on dubious assumptions—for example, that war can be blamed on one side, that strife-torn nations are more likely to initiate war, and that every mild disturbance poses a threat of disintegration in the absence of war. If scapegoat theorists read the evidence of political history more carefully, he observed, they would cease to overlook two important facts: (1) The troubled nation can more easily suppress internal discontent if it does not become involved in international war; and (2) an external foe, seeing turmoil within a country as a sign of weakness, is more likely to try to exploit the situation by initiating war.[10]

The empirical evidence for the reciprocal relationship between internal and external conflict is not as conclusive as some advocates of the theory assert. It is plausible to suggest that political leaders faced with internal problems have often been tempted to be conciliatory toward foreign opponents in order to devote greater time and energy to internal problems. Since the mid-1960s, efforts to prove or disprove the correlation through applying quantitative methods have led to ambiguous and controversial results. Rudolph J. Rummel concluded that foreign conflict behavior is generally unrelated to domestic conflict behavior.[11] In a subsequent replication of the Rummel study, Raymond Tanter similarly found little positive relationship between foreign and domestic conflict behavior.[12] Later still, in a study of the United States domestic scene during the Vietnam War, Tanter suggested a positive correlation between a foreign war that continues without apparent success and the incidence of domestic turmoil.[13]

We do not interpret the traditional theory to mean either that external conflict *always* militates in favor of greater social cohesion or that in the prolonged absence of external conflict, internal disintegration *will necessarily* occur. Yet social scientists have been intrigued by the appearance of at least anecdotal evidence that seems to validate the connection. It has become the common stock of international relations writers during the past two decades to take note of a correlation between periodic thaws in U.S.-Soviet relations and a loosening of their respective alliances.[14] Mention can also be made of the case of Belgium. For more than a century, from 1830 to the late 1940s, a waning fear of France and a rising fear of Germany served to unite the Walloon and Flemish communities and contributed to Belgian national sentiment, but the post–World War II unification of Western Europe removed the German threat and led to rising tension between the two linguistic groups in Belgium.

Well-integrated communities, of course, are held together by more than fear, hostility, and external conflict. Shared beliefs and values, as well as the expectation of mutual benefits from living together as a community, can be important integrating factors. What the theory asserts is that external conflict can be *one* important integrating factor, but not the only one. It might be particularly significant when other factors are beginning to weaken. But if the process of internal consensus-disintegration has progressed too far, involvement in a foreign conflict, instead of reversing that process, might actually hasten it. It seems probable that any effort to correlate statistically internal and external conflict behavior will be inconclusive if it ignores such crucial questions as the degree of consensus that exists over the values of the political system and the societal beliefs about what is at stake in the conflict. Ruling elites cannot always be certain what effect their decision to undertake a foreign war will produce, and whether an unsuccessful war might lead to their overthrow.

In World War II, when the American people were almost unanimous in supporting the war against Nazi atrocities and tyranny, and presumed Japanese treachery and brutality, the press gave little, if any, coverage to those who criticized or resisted. In sharp contrast, the Vietnam War found the American people divided over the nature of the conflict (e.g., whether it was an "international" or a "civil" war), the purpose of the United States involvement (whether it was to carry out a treaty commitment, to contain Soviet and/or Chinese Communism, to preserve Vietnamese national independence, to promote democratic government, to establish a balance of power in Asia, or any, all, or none of these objectives), and the degree to which developments in Southeast Asia could seriously jeopardize the United States national interest. For policy reasons related to arms control and détente, and also because of the difficulties the military forces of an industrially advanced democracy encounter in combating insurgency, the U.S. government, instead of prosecuting the war in the all-out style of World War II, either imposed or accepted limits upon the conduct of its own military operations. The role played by the intellectuals, students, organized opposition groups, the media, and many politicians opened a gap between the government and substantial segments of the public, who were increasingly confused and frustrated by a war effort that was costly and yet seemed purposeless and futile. The Vietnam War provided an apt illustration of a point made by Jacek Kugler and William Domke: that the form of government (e.g., democracy versus a totalitarian regime) does not determine the political capacity of nations to mobilize their social resources under the stresses of war; poor nations are often better able to expand that capacity than rich nations.[15] The relation between internal and external conflicts can be evaluated only within a total political context that varies greatly from case to case. Although empirical studies in this area thus far leave much to be desired, it would seem that the theory of an inverse linkage between intrasocietal and extrasocietal conflict needs greater refinement and more differentiated research by students of international relations.

LESSONS FROM THE PRIMITIVES

The experience of primitive societies is not directly relevant for understanding contemporary international relations. Modern technologically advanced civilizations are not lineal descendants of primitive cultures. Ever since the age of discovery and exploration four centuries ago, Western philosophers and social theorists have been fascinated by primitive ways of social organization and life, and have sought to gain from them insights into the problems of civilization, including war. In earlier times, when there were abundant cases of societies unaffected by contact with the West, there were practically no trained scientific observers, and many superficial or erroneous conclusions were drawn. (Hobbes, Locke, and Rousseau, for example, apparently thought that the Indians of North America lived in a "state of nature," without government.) In the nineteenth century, as the science of cultural anthropology developed, the "purity" or authenticity of most primitive cultures had been diluted by the importation of Western religious and social beliefs, ideas, and practices. Considerable care must be exercised, therefore, in the interpretation of primitive institutions and customs. Because primitive societies are relatively uncomplicated and represent easy-to-see examples of self-contained social groups, often in interaction with other comparable groups, it is useful to study them for whatever general, rather than specific, lessons can be drawn concerning social structure, behavior, and interaction.

Anthropologists have not achieved any greater consensus among themselves than have scholars in any of the other social sciences. But after studying many specific societies, they are impressed by the variety in what they see. They avoid striving for a single generalization—for example, that primitives are basically warlike or that they are basically peaceful. Some primitives are extremely belligerent and always spoiling for a fight; others are almost exclusively peaceful. Clyde Kluckhohn writes:

Organized offensive warfare was unknown in aboriginal Australia. Certain areas of the New World seem to have been completely free from war in the pre-European period. . . . What is absolutely certain at present is that different types of social order carry with them varying degrees of propensity for war. The continuum ranges from groups like the Pueblo Indians who for many centuries have almost never engaged in offensive warfare to groups like some Plains Indians who made fighting their highest virtue.[16]

Where the word for war as a form of socially organized aggression or fighting is not even a part of some primitive languages—for example, of the Eskimos and the Andaman Islanders—we must hesitate to attribute this to the "inherently peaceful character" of the people, especially since they are in no proximate contact with well-defined societies. For technologically undeveloped societies, war, like violent crime, is usually a function of physical proximity. Prior to the era of the airplane and the missile, only maritime countries possessed the capabilities to mount offensive warfare at a distance.[17] In fact, even in recent decades most international wars have been waged between those communities that usually have the most frequent occasions and perhaps the strongest reasons for fighting—territorially adjacent states.

It would seem that the experience of most primitive societies is similar to that of many modern civilized states: They know alternating periods of war and peace, except that primitive wars (or raids) are more frequent and of shorter duration. Nearly all primitive societies seek to minimize *internal* violence by developing systems of law calculated to prevent the application of the *lex talionis,* which permits vindictive retaliation by individual victims of crime, from escalating out of control.[18] But most of these societies are willing from time to time to resort to external violent behavior for purposes they consider important. Andrew P. Vayda has pointed out that war among primitives serves as a regulating variable for the achievement of several different functions:

1. to remove inequalities in the possession of, or access to, certain economic goods and resources (land, camels, horses, water, hunting grounds, etc.) through redistribution;
2. to regulate such demographic variables as population size, sex ratios, and age distribution (as a result of war casualties), obtaining new sources of food and taking women and others captive;
3. to regulate relations with other groups (i.e., to deter certain types of undesirable behavior in the future by avenging and punishing offenses or wrongs committed);
4. to regulate psychological variables (anxiety, tension, and hostility) that are adverse to in-group cohesion by directing them outward.[19]

Some anthropologists stress singular explanatory variables such as the desire to revenge insults[20] or the determination to protect the tribal reputation against charges of weakness and cowardice that may invite attack.[21]

Vayda's analytic scheme synthesizes psychological, demographic, economic, and social variables, in which the regulation of each one depends upon the regulation of another. He refrains from insisting that his hypotheses about primitive war could be applied to warfare between civilized states. Moreover, he admits that more extensive data are needed to validate the hypotheses, and that some of the data needed are difficult to obtain.[22]

Finally, it is worth noting that primitive societies do not become involved in conflict over differing patterns of socioeconomic organization (e.g., private or communal property systems), probably because such societies do not develop elaborate "sentiment structures" or ideologies over such things. In some cases, the ferocity of conflict between neighboring primitives is attenuated by common religious beliefs, by endogamy (the practice of seeking wives from other tribes, thereby establishing blood ties), by imposing certain limits on warfare, by the conclusion of peace treaties and the exchange of hostages, and occasionally even by substituting "cold war" (the shouting of epithets and insults) for physical combat. But Vayda concedes that such intercommunity ties as intermarriage, commerce, and beliefs in common descent do not constitute a guarantee against the outbreak of hostilities.[23]

OTHER INSIGHTS FROM THEORISTS OF SOCIETY

Anthropologists and sociologists have formulated a great many hypotheses and partial theories relating to social conflict. It is not possible to examine all of them. Most of these hypotheses and theories have been suggested only in passing, without ever being subject to any thorough, systematic development and rigorous testing. All that can be done here is to present in summary form a sample of better-known hypotheses and theories, some of which are the stock-in-trade of so many writers that they cannot properly be attributed to any one.

1. Organized and collective fighting is distinct from individual, sporadic, and spontaneous acts of violence. The latter are antecedents of homicide and civil disorder, but not of war.[24] For anthropologists and sociologists, large-scale conflict and war arise more out of social structures and conditions than they do out of biological urges or psychological states. Warfare, said Margaret Mead, is a cultural invention, not a biological necessity.[25] William Graham Sumner argued that war originates from a struggle between groups, not individuals.[26] Bronislaw Malinowski held that war is not primeval or biologically determined, and makes its appearance late in human evolution. "Human beings never fight on an extensive scale under the direct influence of an aggressive impulse," Malinowski declared,[27] thereby severing the connection between psychological pugnacity and culturally determined fighting. Most cases of violent action are seen as the result of purely conventional, traditional, and ideological imperatives. Malinowski further stated, "All types of fighting are complex

cultural responses due not to any direct dictates of an impulse, but to collective forms of sentiment and value."[28] David Bidney has criticized Malinowski for adhering too rigidly to the view that war played no significant part in the earlier stages of human development. For Bidney, war can be an agent of cultural change and can bring about significant alterations in social structure.[29]

2. Discussion of international conflict in the abstract lacks cogency. Social scientists should not analyze the behavior of nations without reference to the intervening variable of culture, warn Margaret Mead and Rhoda Metraux, who cite as an example the impossibility of understanding conflict in Lebanon while ignoring the role of religious communities.[30] If Soviet behavior is to be at all intelligible and predictable, they say, one must understand the Russian preoccupation with the full use of strength, insistence on testing the limits, and willingness to be guided by them. "For example, in a situation in which Englishmen, Americans, and Russians are involved as participants, it is useful to know that the English regard compromise as a positive outcome, that Americans regard compromise negatively, and that Russians define behavior which, in English and American eyes, would be regarded as compromise, as a necessary and quite admirable strategic retreat after having put forth all available strength."[31]

3. The basic attitudes and values of societies are deeply embedded in an intricate system of cultural institutions and processes. Hence they cannot be easily or quickly changed. Clyde Kluckhohn has offered this advice to reformers: "Make haste slowly is usually a good motto for those who wish to institute or direct social change. Because of the enormous tenacity of nonlogical habits, the hasty attempt to alter intensifies resistance or even produces reaction."[32]

4. Whereas many social psychologists and political scientists in recent decades, in their desire to minimize the misleading and potentially dangerous consequences of "stereotyped" thinking in an era of mass communications, have become skeptical concerning the concept of "national character," anthropologists are more inclined to attribute a certain validity to it, provided that it is handled with appropriate care.[33]

5. Anthropologists and sociologists are for the most part suspicious of "psychopolitics" or "psychohistory"—the efforts to explain policy decisions made by such leaders as Wilson, Hitler, Stalin, de Gaulle, or Mao in terms of childhood experiences or psychological characteristics.[34] They do not, of course, deny that key individuals might play an important political role in the making of crucial conflict decisions, but they are disposed to explain those decisions in terms of social rather than psychological factors. (Although psychohistory has sometimes been severely criticized, it continues to have its defenders.[35])

6. Ethnocentrism, the overevaluation of one's own group in comparison with other groups, is virtually a universal phenomenon.[36]

7. The relative persistence of culture patterns does not mean that nations are incapable of undergoing significant behavioral changes over

time. Many writers have called attention to the striking alteration in the political outlook and behavior of Germany and Japan, and the substitution of democratic constitutional systems for dictatorial-militarist regimes, following defeat in World War II. These extreme cases might prompt us to formulate a "trauma" theory of rapid, fundamental social change. More gradual and more complex was the change in the world view, and the conception of its own role, that Britain underwent as a result of the profound political-technological-strategic shifts set in motion by the two world wars.

8. All through history, from the time Archimedes went to a mountain top near the sea and used a glass to focus the rays of the sun on the sails of an enemy ship, down to our own days of nuclear warheads and laser beams, war and technological change have been closely related. Preparations for war and waging war itself bring science, technology, industry, and medicine into cooperation with governments for purposes of military research and development, which may have "spinoff" applications in non-military dimensions. Scholars have shown how inventions from the canning of food and the sewing machine through chemicals down to jet engines, radar, nuclear energy, rockets, electronic communications, and blood plasma received their initial impetus from the military needs of the state.[37]

9. Some anthropological hypotheses may appear to be contradictory, but actually are not. We are told, for example, that both differences and similarities of peoples may lead to bitter conflicts. Substantial differences of an ethnic, linguistic, religious, racial, cultural, or ideological character are easily perceived and thus can give rise to animosity and a sense of threat, especially when different groups are physically close to each other, yet unequal in political and economic power. Differences that have been politically muted or controlled for a long time within a single nation may flare up and generate pressures for separatism or autonomy (e.g., Quebec in Canada, the Scots in the United Kingdom, the Walloons and the Flemish in Belgium, and the Basques in Spain).[38] On the other hand, it has often been noted that the closer the parties are together in belief systems, the more intense a conflict between them is likely to be.[39] Thus conflict is particularly intense when a group that was previously united undergoes schism and both groups henceforth claim to be the authentic heirs to the tradition. Examples include Catholic and Protestant Christians, Sunni and Shi'i Muslims, and Stalinists and Trotskyites.

10. Conflict may be studied by reference to the pattern of communications between conflict parties and the language employed in the conflict. As the conflict is developing, communication between the parties declines and intraparty communication (and cohesion) intensifies. Maximum conflict intensity coincides with minimal communication between the parties, as well as with intragroup propaganda of maximum hostility against the enemy. Changes in patterns of communication and propaganda usually signal a change in conflict intensity and a movement toward

conflict resolution. Every conflict has its unique structure, arising out of the nature of the parties, the issues at stake, the circumstances in which the conflict is waged, and the particular dynamic according to which it develops. In analyzing any specific conflict, a knowledge of the particular features of that conflict is just as important as, if not more important than, generalized knowledge of conflict processes.

SOCIOECONOMIC GAPS AND WORLD REVOLUTIONARY CONFLICT

In the late 1960s, American social scientists, largely in response to the Vietnam War, were preoccupied with the phenomenon of "revolution," especially guerrilla insurgency in the Third World. The advent of nuclear weapons technology appeared to have greatly reduced the likelihood of direct military hostilities between the possessors of such capabilities; the development of alliance systems had also helped to immunize the formal allies of the principal nuclear powers against the threat of overt military attack. Thus the international strategic-political situation since the end of World War II has resulted in a shift in the nature and locus of internationally significant conflict. At the same time, the conditions which social scientists usually cite as the source of human conflict potential—that is, socioeconomic discrepancies, the aggressive impulses resulting from frustration caused by measuring the actual against the ideal, withdrawal and alienation from existing social structures, and so forth—were apparently becoming more rather than less common on a world scale. Almost everywhere, thanks to communications technology, the gap between expected (or desired) need fulfillment and actual need fulfillment was (and still is) widening among large numbers of people. It may be that such a gap constitutes the single most important necessary (but not sufficient) condition for the occurrence of internal social conflict on a large scale.

Especially in the Third World (Asia, Africa, and Latin America), the process of social, economic, and political development is seldom able to provide increasing satisfactions at a pace commensurate with the expanding aspirations of peoples. Even the most advanced countries, including the United States, have problems associated with a so-called technetronic or postindustrial phase in their development. It seems that the development process always produces asymmetrical effects with respect to the benefits bestowed upon peoples. The mass media of technological communications facilitate drawing invidious comparisons not only between the "have" and the "have-not" nations, but also within national societies between privileged and disadvantaged groups. In most highly developed— and most rapidly developing—countries, segments of the privileged groups revolt against the conditions of "affluence," become alienated from the institutions that produced the affluence, and cast their lot with the disadvantaged to bring down The Establishment. Both in less developed and in highly developed societies, the breakdown of traditional mechanisms and agencies of social integration plays a crucial role in the growth of revolutionary conflict potential.

Revolution is an old concept in social theory. Classical political theorists were intensely interested in the problems of cyclical change, efforts to overthrow the government by violence, and the moral-political justifications of revolution. They usually attributed revolutionary feelings within a state to a discrepancy between people's desires and their perceived situation—a discrepancy that gives rise to profound political disagreement over the bases on which society ought to be organized. Contemporary theorists distinguish between genuine political revolutions and other phenomena that have often been called by the same name—for example, the coup d'etat (including "palace revolutions" by rival relatives of a monarch, executive coups or the illegal prolongation of a leader's term of office, military coups, and other relatively sudden seizures of power by small groups of high-status individuals);[40] various forms of peasant, urban, religious, and other revolts; and political breaking away known as *secession* (whether regional, colonial, ethnic, or religious). None of these need have the remotest connection with revolutionary change, says Mark N. Hagopian, who defines revolution as "an acute, prolonged crisis in one or more of the traditional systems of stratification (class, status, power) of a political community, which involves a purposive, elite-directed attempt to abolish or to reconstruct one or more of said systems by means of an intensification of political power and recourse to violence."[41]

Before the French Revolution, rebellion in Europe against the ruler usually implied no more than a personnel change in government—hardly an attack upon the established political order. Hannah Arendt has pointed out that modern revolutions are of a strikingly different genre, for they aim at a spirit of freedom and of liberation from an old order of things. Marked by a "pathos of novelty," revolution involves "the notion that the course of history suddenly begins anew, that an entirely new story, a story never known or told before, is about to unfold."[42] Modern revolution is normally characterized by a set of emotion-laden utopian ideas—an expectation that the society is marching toward a profound transformation of values and structures, as well as of personal behavior. Revolutionaries picture a vastly improved pattern of human relationships in a future realization, then impart their vision to the masses, hoping to motivate them to revolutionary action. The revolutionary describes a more perfect social situation—more freedom; more equality; more consciousness of community; more peace, justice, and human dignity; more of the transcendentals that appeal to human beings everywhere. Unlike the utopians of old, who posited their idyllic states in unreachable geographical places (utopia means "nowhere"), the modern revolutionaries locate their utopia in the future: Its eventual achievement is not only possible but inevitable.[43] The revolutionary credo strengthens the motives for enduring the hardships of the struggle. The vision of a life free from every form of oppression justifies the suffering, terror, and chaos revolution brings. It does not matter that the present generation of people must endure pain for the

sake of the cause: Without the revolution injustice will continue indefinitely, piling misery upon misery forever, but as a result of the revolution the human race, or a part of it, will be lifted up to a higher and nobler plane of existence. The present deprived masses suffer heroically so that the future fulfilled masses may be happy. Such has always been the ideological rationalization of revolutionaries.

James H. Meisel has presented a profound philosophical account of the role played by discontented intellectuals in historic revolutions. He suggests that the human mind is engaged in an endless quest for the triumph of reason in society, and this quest meets with both success and failure. Nearly every sudden intellectual leap forward seems to end up producing its own form of tyranny, liberating not the intellectuals but the barbarians, or the organization types and totalitarian bureaucrats. Throughout history, the intellectuals provide the breeding ground of revolution. Revolution begins when Mind proclaims some kind of new dispensation of freedom. But eventually mind becomes an enemy of Mind. Every revolution dies in overorganization, or terror, or oppression, or the restoration of the old order, or sheer boredom, or final alienation from technical culture.[44] John Roberts has shown that the revolution that rocked Europe from 1789 onward did not substantially change the social setting of most Europeans. To the extent that their way of life underwent any improvement, this was due much more to the process of industrialization than to revolution,[45] and thus was the result of economic rather than political forces.

According to pre–World War II theories of Crane Brinton and others, revolutions occur when the gap between distributed political power and distributed social power within a society becomes intolerable. Certain social classes that are experiencing some of the benefits of progress desire to develop more rapidly than the system will permit, and hence they feel cramped. Discontent spreads over the sharing of economic outputs, social prestige, or political power. Traditional values are openly questioned, and a new social myth challenges the old one. The intellectuals become alienated from the system. Gradually they move from mere criticism to a withdrawal of political loyalty. The governing elites begin to lose confidence in themselves, in their beliefs, and in their ability to command and to solve society's problems. The old elites become too rigid to absorb the emerging elites into their ranks, and this accelerates the polarization. Propagandists assume the intelligentsia's sophisticated criticisms of established institutions, translating them into slogans for mass consumption. The intellectuals join forces with the new and disaffected elites, and the demand for radical reforms increases. Moderate political elements prove too weak to strike viable compromises between those who agitate for rapid change and those who oppose all change. The breaking point is reached when the instruments of social control, especially the army and the police, collapse or shift their allegiance to the discontented elements, or when the incumbent government proves inept in using those instruments of social control. Such was the classic explanation of revolution advanced by Crane Brinton in 1938, of which it could be said three decades later that not much theoretical progress had been made beyond it.[46]

Social scientists have realized that the older theories of political revolution are not readily applicable to conflict in the Third World, where most of the guerrilla insurgencies that have occurred since World War II have arisen out of a very different social environment from the historic revolutions of the West. Nevertheless, the earlier and the later revolutions ought to have sufficient elements in common to permit at least a certain continuity in the development of conflict theory, with appropriate adjustments to take account of vastly different social circumstances and new social science knowledge.

Contemporary social scientists and policymakers generally look upon the high conflict potential of Asia, Africa, and Latin America as a function of widespread frustration traceable to economic deprivation. Ted Robert Gurr argues that "the necessary precondition for violent civil conflict is deprivation, defined as actors' perceptions of discrepancy between their value expectations and their environment's apparent value capabilities."[47] The disparity between aspirations and fulfillment can be conceived of either as mere economic deprivation or as a combination of various types of deprivation, including economic, psychological, social, and political. Perhaps the least sophisticated theory is that which makes poverty itself the prime frustrating agent. Efforts have often been made to correlate high conflict potential with absolutely low economic variables and with economic stagnation. According to this hypothesis, one can predict the highest incidence of violence in the most poverty-stricken countries measured in terms of per capita income. Such a hypothesis, however, contains several problems. Serious violence does indeed occur in many of the countries in the "very poor" category, but no more (and perhaps less) frequently in poorer countries than in more affluent Third World ones such as Lebanon, Iran, Argentina, South Korea, and the Philippines. Other factors besides the degree of poverty undoubtedly contribute to the incidence of conflict.

There is probably an oversimplification in the poverty-revolution nexus. Violence-proneness within a society declines only as a result of social development in many dimensions, of which the economic is but one and not necessarily always the centrally causative one. Furthermore, although conditions of poverty are frequently linked to criminal behavior and anomic conflict, it has often been pointed out that the most impoverished societies are usually not considered fertile breeding grounds for revolution.

> As Zawadzki and Lazarsfeld have indicated, preoccupation with physical survival, even in industrial areas, is a force strongly militating against the establishment of the community-sense and consensus on joint political action which are necessary to induce a revolutionary state of mind. Far from making people into revolutionaries, enduring poverty makes for concern with one's solitary self or solitary family at best and resignation or mute despair at worst.[48]

At any given time, one may be able to name several very poor countries in which a revolutionary upheaval is less likely to occur than in a relatively advanced economic system. Economic factors undoubtedly play an important part in many revolutions, but economic inequality is more relevant than sheer poverty.[49] Revolutions must be analyzed in relation to other important political, strategic, cultural, and social-psychological factors that are not reducible to pure economics.

SOCIOECONOMIC MODERNIZATION AND CONFLICT

A more interesting theory, somewhat better borne out by existing data, postulates conflict as a function not of poverty but of social development and change. James N. Rosenau contends that "the more rapid the rate of social change becomes, the greater the likelihood of intrasocietal violence."[50] Arnold Feldman has pointed out that "change contributes to revolutionary potential rather than eradicating dissatisfactions."[51] Many analysts now agree that social frustration and revolutionary potential are not as pronounced in the most backward areas as they are in areas economically and socially "on the move." A century and a third ago Alexis de Tocqueville recognized that abject poverty had not been the cause of the French Revolution. He contended that, despite a ramshackle, ill-regulated, and inefficient government, and despite burdensome tax and trade policies, France had experienced unprecedented economic growth and prosperity during the two decades immediately preceding the Revolution. This very fact, he said, promoted a spirit of unrest and hastened the outbreak, as people ignored the improvements that had taken place. Under Louis XVI, "the most trivial pin-pricks of arbitrary power caused more resentment than the thorough-going despotism of Louis XIV." People simply became more frustrated and impatient to precipitate events.[52] Regions of the world which are not undergoing "modernization" to some degree are becoming rare. Modernization may be imposed artificially from without, for example, by foreign investors, or it may grow organically from within as a result of a shift of attitude from a fatalistic acceptance of things as they are to an active desire for change. "When the Middle Eastern peasant," writes Manfred Halpern, "realizes for the first time that the structure of life can be concretely improved, and that he is being denied the opportunity to improve his own lot, then the seeds of revolution will have been planted."[53] As Crane Brinton noted in 1938, revolutionists are more likely to be children of hope than of despair.[54]

This does not mean, however, that the social-psychological states of the revolutionary leaders, of active revolutionary followers, and of the masses to whom the revolutionary appeals are addressed are necessarily all the same. In the interaction of these elements, there may be a dialectical relationship between the social psychology of despair and the revolutionary politics of hope. When people of "rising expectations" experience gradual progress at a sufficient rate to be able to perceive an improvement differential in their situation from year to year, they are not a likely target for the appeals of the revolutionary propagandist. But certain groups within the population may become frustrated as a result of asymmetrical change. Different sectors of the society, as they perceive the distribution of the benefits of development, are likely to be moving forward at different rates; some may perceive no motion or a loss of relative position.[55] This phenomenon occurs constantly in all developing societies, including the most advanced. The spread of technical communications facilitates the process whereby some groups become keenly aware of discrepancies and draw comparisons between their own position and that of others (within the community, the nation, and the world). Few groups in any country (even the most highly industrialized) experience real improvements commensurate with their mounting aspirations.[56]

James C. Davies has called attention to the fact that the gap between what people want and what they get may be tolerable or intolerable. Unfortunately, we cannot determine in advance the point at which the gap becomes so intolerable that revolution occurs, because this depends upon many other cultural, political, and psychological variables in addition to factors that are economically measurable. Perception of the gap may depend largely upon the way in which the revolutionary organization can utilize the communications nets to dramatize the discrepancies. Davies also suggests that the danger of revolutionary conflict becomes more acute when a society that is on the long-term path toward development suddenly experiences a downturn in the economic process.[57] His J-curve theory has been faulted for failing to specify how wide the gap must be between anticipated and actual need satisfaction before a revolution occurs, and for failing to explain why the J-curve pattern brings on revolution in some societies but not in others.[58] Although Davies's study pertained to economic trends within whole national societies, his J-curve theory might well be even more useful if applied to more than economics and to less than nations—that is, if it were applied to the way in which subnational groups perceive themselves as suffering a reversal of their total position within the social systems as a result of developmental change.

Political Instability and Frustration

Ivo K. and Rosalind L. Feierabend have identified political instability with aggressive behavior, which they attribute to unrelieved social frustration. In situations of systemic frustration, they contend, political stability may still be predicted if certain conditions are met—namely, that the society is a nonparticipant one; or that constructive solutions to frustrations are available; or that the government is sufficiently coercive to prevent overt acts of hostility against itself; or that the aggressive impulse can be displaced against minority groups or other nations; or that individual acts of aggression are sufficiently abundant to furnish an outlet. In the absence of these conditions, aggressive behavior can be expected to result from systemic frustration. In the more extreme cases, political instability is likely to take the form of riots, strikes, mass arrests, assassination of political figures, executions, terrorism and sabotage, guerrilla warfare, civil war, coups d'etat, and other forms of revolt.[59] Referring to the "essentially frustrating nature of the modernization process," the Feierabends offer the following generalization:

> Furthermore, it may be postulated that the peak discrepancy between systemic goals and their satisfaction, and hence the maximum frustration, should come somewhere in the middle of the transitional phase between traditional society and the achievement of modernity. It is at this middle stage that awareness of modernity and exposure to modern patterns should be complete, that is, at a theoretical ceiling, whereas achievement levels would still be lagging far behind. Prior to this theoretical middle stage, exposure can no longer increase, since it already amounts to complete awareness, but achievement will continue to progress, thus carrying the nation eventually into the stage of modernity. Thus, in contrast to transitional societies, it may be postulated that traditional and modern societies will be less frustrated and therefore will tend to be more stable than transitional societies.[60]

Is there such a thing as "complete exposure" to or awareness of modernization? Since increasingly rapid and profound social change is a permanent feature of the modernization process, there will always be, in every society, relatively traditional, transitional, and modernized sectors. Among the LDCs, as population is being drawn from rural to urban areas, traditional religious values and cultural patterns begin to break down among the intellectuals, professional classes, technically skilled groups, and sectors of the urban masses. Technology is imported; transport and communication nets grow; literacy rates rise; social mobility is enhanced. Family and other social ties that formerly bound individuals together disintegrate. New socioeconomic classes of a functional nature begin to emerge, but they are weaker than the structures they replace when it comes to giving the individual a sense of belonging to a community.

This is what the German sociologist Ferdinand Tönnies referred to in the late nineteenth century as the movement from *Gemeinshaft* (community) to *Gesellschaft* (association).[61] The contrast was perhaps overdrawn, and Tönnies's theory is one of the roots of those Western "developmentist" sociological theories that, as shown in Chapter 6, are repudiated by *dependentistas*. Yet it is not without some validity. Partially uprooted individuals move more rapidly and receive more varied impressions of the world from the communications media. They are forced to make profound adjustments, but probably can find no satisfactory set of norms to guide them. Both fascinated and frightened by the changes they see, they become psychologically troubled. Edward Shils has shown that the intellectuals in underdeveloped countries have an ambivalent attitude toward things foreign and Western: They appreciate foreign culture but have a sense of inferiority with respect to their own.[62] Moreover, as intellectuals abandon traditional religious and cultural values, acting differently from the way they were taught in their youth, they may develop feelings of guilt from which they may try to escape by projecting hostility against the external agents of social change—the Western imperialist system. Assertive nationalism becomes a means of restoring self-respect.

Incumbent governments in the developing countries, lacking experience in economic planning, find it difficult to impress the unsophisticated masses with the need to accept present deprivations in order to promote long-range economic expansion. Development demands patience in many dimensions: the acquisition of technical skills, improvements in the educational system, the modification of social incentives, the emergence of managerial capabilities, the willingness of traditional elites to admit the new functional elites to a fair share of the system's benefits, responsible fiscal policies, administrative reforms, and so forth. All these imperatives are frustrating to the impatient. Even gradual progress is frustrating to those whose appetites have been whetted to insist upon rapid and far-sweeping changes—instant progress. Meanwhile, population growth places added pressures upon developing systems, cutting into annual GNP growth rates and compounding the demands placed upon inexperienced planners in countries often faced with deteriorating terms of international trade.[63]

Sociologists and anthropologists consider the likelihood of internal social conflict to be on the increase when the integrating mechanisms of a society break down. As immemorial religious-cultural traditions give way to secularization, emergent nationalism as expressed by a charismatic leader might prove powerful enough to preserve domestic solidarity, especially if there is an external *bête noire* against which aggressive feelings can be directed. So long as national integration remains high, enemy groups do not become salient to each other within the society. In the absence of an integrating principle, the changes wrought by development increase the potential for group conflict within nations. As new groups emerge, they forge their own consciousness of group interests and values; they establish their self-identity by directing hostility outward. Since hostility may be aimed outward in many different directions and randomly distributes itself among so many targets as to become dissipated without the occurrence of serious politicized violence in a conflict with a single enemy, it is the function of political organization to channel the aggressive hostility inherent in discontented groups into one coherent direction. An incumbent government might attempt to divert it against a neighboring adversary. (In some regions of the world, such as Latin America, this is difficult to do, because of the cultural similarity of most members of the regional state system, and therefore it is more easily aimed at the culturally different imperialist power in the Northern hemisphere.) A revolutionary organization will attempt to mobilize and channel discontent against the incumbent government.[64] Neither external wars nor internal revolutions are typically spontaneous or accidental happenings; both require a high degree of organization and planning.

Charles Tilly, a Marxian sociologist-historian, has analyzed the phenomenon of revolution according to the theoretical systems of Karl Marx, Emile Durkheim, John Stuart Mill, and Max Weber.[65] Marx, as we saw in Chapter 6, treated all social conflict in terms of class structures and interests arising out of the pattern of relations determined by the organization of production. Emile Durkheim saw collective action (i.e., the mobilization of large numbers of people for the waging of social conflict) as a response to the interactive processes of integration and disintegration within a whole society. Industrialization leads to differentiation, which in turn leads to a breakdown in shared beliefs. Anomie results from excessive social differentiation and individual disorientation. As the gap widens before the pace of structural change and the institutionalization of social control, pressures increase toward collective action to restore shared beliefs.[66]

Last, says Tilly, Max Weber, the political sociologist of religion, leadership, and bureaucracy, traced the structure and action of the social group to a commitment to a particular belief system—a collective definition of the world and of the members themselves. It is the belief system that justifies the power of authorities, and this holds true for traditional, charismatic, and rational-legal systems. Both charisma and rational bureaucracy can bring about revolutionary social change—charisma by transforming the external environment. Tilly prefers the Marxian explanation, but he leaves open the possibility that Durkheim and Weber may also have been correct.[67]

Societal Breakdown: The Crucial Questions

The political scientist wants to know such things as (1) the degree to which various strata or groups within the population are being recruited into or are withdrawing from participation in the political system; (2) the ability of the political system to respond flexibly to the various demands made upon it and to produce outputs likely to inhibit the growth of pressures for revolutionary change; and (3) the extent and effectiveness of social and political control, as well as the acceptability of the methods whereby such control is maintained.

The comparative political scientist is interested, then, in securing data concerning the following:

- the extent to which people in various social groups feel themselves more loyal to than critical of the system;
- the extent to which they participate in elections, pay taxes, perform military service, and contribute other expressions of support for the military system;

- whether the intellectuals who are being educated within the system are also being satisfactorily absorbed by it, or whether they are being excluded and alienated from it;
- whether the system contains built-in "safety-valves" for the orderly release of social energies (e.g., economic competition, channels for criticism and the expression of new ideas, outlets for religious and humanitarian motivations, sports rivalry, etc.);
- what kind of relatively stable and cohesive social groups exist (churches, armed forces, trade unions, farmers' organizations, professional associations, political parties, etc.) and the direction they are taking within the system;
- the pattern in which symbolic honors, political power, and economic benefits are distributed among various groups within the system; and
- the proportionate allocation by various groups of fear-hostility attitudes inside and outside the nation.

The last factor bears upon the question of whether the conflict potential in a particular country is for international war or internal revolution. At this point we come back to the venerable hypothesis of political analysts, discussed earlier and never conclusively proved, that a government can head off impending domestic strife by fomenting a popular foreign war. Whether this can be accomplished may depend upon the presence of readily perceptible and historically significant group differences—ethnic-linguistic, religious, or tribal. If such differences are more pronounced across national borders than within the nation, the government will be in a better position to solidify the nation by going to war. However, if such differences are more pronounced intranationally, they may very well constitute an important factor in the potential for domestic conflict. In this case, going to war with a neighbor is likely to exacerbate the internal conflict if group affiliations extend across the boundaries of two warring nations. Whether or not there is international war, serious ethnic and religious differences within a country caught up in a revolutionary situation are likely to be exploited both by the incumbent government and by the revolutionary organization. The Iranian-Iraqi war was marked by nationalist tensions (Iranian versus Arab), religious conflict (Shi'ite versus Sunni), and the hostility of Islamic fundamentalism toward modernizing secularism.

The economic, psychological, sociological, and political conditions mentioned above provide the matrix out of which revolutionary conflict arises, but they cannot be set forth definitively as the cause of conflict. They are, as it were, the necessary but not the sufficient conditions. Within a society there may be fairly high levels of frustration, alienation, cognitive dissonance, sense of threat, and other attitudes of mind conducive to conflict. There may be asymmetrical rates of change. There may be in proximity highly visible groups that have a history of animosity toward each other. Communications between some groups may break down and reach a virtual vanishing point. Yet politically structured conflict will not occur until deliberate decisions to invoke political violence have been taken, and these decisions will normally not be taken until after there has developed a conflict organization capable of managing violence and of supplying political direction to existing resentments and aggressive impulses. The link between the social psychological state and the development of the conflict organization seems to be in the first instance the personalities of a small number of revolutionary leaders, combined with their life experiences in the environment that shaped them.

The Making of a Revolutionary

As Lawrence Stone has noted, we still do not know what makes a person become revolutionary.[68] What identifiable elements in one's personality (such as need for achievement, sense of moral indignation and social mission, propensity for risk-taking, and desire for power) and in one's personal background (childhood, relations with parents, socialization, education, religion, travel, reading, previous military training, and contacts with other conflict organizers) impel the revolutionary to undertake an attempt to overthrow the system by force instead of working from within to reform it? It would be surprising if the leaders of a revolution were motivated by the same psychic forces as are the masses—that is, that they are attracted to insurgency because they have suffered the deprivations of economic poverty. Revolutions are usually led by "elites," and it is an essential attribute of elites that they are moved by more subtle personality factors than those predicable of the masses. Elites and masses differ significantly in their reactions to frustration and in the sources of their frustration.[69] Revolutionary leaders seldom come from the poorest classes; more typically, they derive from middle-class families that have not known economic hardship. Their deprivations are more likely to be psychological rather than economic. What they want frequently are intangible rewards—prestige, a share in political power, fame as part of a charismatic movement struggling for justice, even the stimulation of excitement and danger. In the case of some revolutionary terrorists, the presence of psychopathological elements cannot be discounted.[70]

OBJECTIVES AND CHARACTERISTICS OF REVOLUTION

Modern revolutions have been fought to expel a colonial power and achieve national independence, to change the political system without radically altering the social systems, to terminate an intolerable minority status by achieving either local autonomy or territorial secession from the system, to determine the succession after the expected departure of a colonial regime, and to bring pressure to bear from one political system upon another. An insurgency ostensibly begun for one objective may undergo either a de facto or an avowed change of purpose during the course of the conflict. Avowed objectives while the revolution is in course are usually a matter of propaganda designed to gain political support. Some objectives of the revolutionary program, especially those related to the power drives of the leaders, are usually left unspoken. In contrast to the coup d'état, which brings a sudden personnel change in the top echelon of government but is not a genuine revolution, the total revolutionary process is of fairly long duration, usually a matter of several years. Mao Zedong insisted upon deliberate protraction and the avoidance of eschatological adventurism as essential elements in the strategy of revolutionary warfare.[71] The Vietnam War, which lasted nearly 30 years, was a notable exception to the pattern, ending in complete success for the revolutionary forces in the longest-lasting and most internationalized of all revolutionary wars.

The impression has long been common that revolutionary insurgency is a predominantly rural phenomenon, but this notion can be misleading. Social scientists question the stereotyped generalization of the "peasant revolution." Rural peasants are more tradition-bound and apathetic toward the political process than are urban dwellers. The dissatisfied peasant is more likely to migrate to the city than to revolt. Moreover, peasant insurrections, when they occur, are often led by revolutionaries from an urban background. In any event, as the sharp dichotomy between rural and urban cultures dissolves under the impact of modern communications, earlier ideas of the "peasant revolution" may lose some of their relevance.[72]

Revolutionary insurgency as an "inward" social-psychological process with important previolent stages seems likely to begin in urban centers where social mobility is high, where traditional norms are weakest and anomie is greatest, where ideas circulate more rapidly, and where certain psychological states such as frustration and dissonance may be more pronounced. But as an externalized strategic process, we often find that the violent stages of guerrilla insurgency begin in rural areas geographically remote from the political capital of the country.

Several considerations help to determine the location of revolutionary conflict. Insurgents are disposed to establish bases in regions with a record of previous revolutionary activity or sentiment.[73] They want access to major political targets, as well as economic self-sufficiency. They are anxious to secure a base in zones of weak political control, not easily accessible to and penetrable by government forces. Hence, they are attracted to provinces not served efficiently by road, rail, and air transport and to terrain that, although lending cover to small guerrilla bands, proves hostile to the movement of larger and more cumbersome conventional military forces—mountains, jungles, forests, river deltas, swamplands, and deserts. Not only physical geography but also political geography enters the picture. Whenever possible, insurgents usually find it advantageous to establish headquarters, training camps, and supply routes close to or across the borders of friendly or neutral countries. The guerrillas may then seek legal sanctuary or political haven when subjected to hot pursuit, thus compelling incumbent government forces to incur international censure if they carry their punitive action to the area of retreat. Moreover, border-lands are frequently zones of ethnic heterogeneity and diversity of politi-cal loyalties, factors revolutionists may find helpful. Quite naturally, logis-tical considerations always loom large. Sources and routes of foreign supply are extremely important factors in the political geography of guer-rilla revolution.

THE INTERNATIONALIZATION OF INTERNAL WAR AND LOW-INTENSITY CONFLICT

In nearly every historic age, the existence of revolutionary conditions within states has led to intervention by strong foreign powers.[74] Weaker revolutionary forces seek to augment their chances for success by inviting outside aid, usually from "revolutionary" or expansionist powers. During the period of United States nuclear superiority, the two principal powers committed to a reversal of the international status quo strongly supported "national liberation warfare" (as the Soviet Union called it) or "people's war" (as the Chinese called it). These modes of "indirect" conflict were relatively safe methods of carrying on the international revolutionary movement, compared with the more dangerous methods of direct con-frontation with what was then unquestionably a nuclear-superior West. If one superpower intervenes in a Third World internal war, the other usu-ally feels some temptation, pressure, or tendency to do likewise in support of the opposite side. In the 1960s, the United States, the Soviet Union, and China intervened at various times in Third World insurgencies, particu-larly in Asia. In the 1970s and subsequently, Asia and Africa were arenas of competition among the three major military powers. It was not at all uncommon to find, in such areas as Angola, Zimbabwe (formerly Rhodesia), and Eritrea, two or three competing revolutionary organiza-tions, each with a different ethnic or religious base, as well as incumbent regimes—all supported by different outside major powers, or pairs of them. In the 1980s, Afghanistan and Central America constituted princi-pal areas of competitive superpower intervention.

In the contemporary world, virtually every conflict that occurs within the purview of news-gathering agencies becomes an item in the environ-ment of international relations. A revolution may produce a spillover effect in a neighboring country. There may be spontaneous or organized demonstrations in distant foreign countries to support one side or to pro-test against the other. The world communications net plays a crucial role in the globalization of localized conflict. Revolutionaries must strive to acquire by slow degrees some semblance of an international personality as an object of potential foreign support in the forms of money, arms, diplomatic backing, organized political sympathy, and other kinds of assistance. Conflicts are drawn into the vortex of world politics when they become items in the decision-making processes of foreign governments, the United Nations, regional alliances (such as NATO, OAS, or OAU), political parties, churches, and ethnic and peace groups, not to mention intelligence agencies and terrorist bands.

It is extremely difficult to determine the relative weight to be assigned in a given revolutionary conflict to external and internal factors as determinants of the outcomes.[75] Obviously, certain internal factors may be of crucial significance, such as the morale, training, leadership, and strategic-tactical doctrines of revolutionary and governmental forces, their ability to utilize communications media and otherwise influence the attitudes of the people, and the ability of the existing system to respond to the revolutionary challenge with a variety of self-strengthening policies. In some cases, however, external factors may prove overriding. Without implying that any one form of external aid (such as military assistance) is necessarily decisive in ensuring the success or failure of a revolutionary insurgency, we can say that what appears at the start to be an indigenous conflict may become the focal point of international intervention, overt or clandestine, to such an extent that the conflict can no longer be regarded as an internal one. "If outside manpower, motives, money, and other resources appear to constitute the main capabilities committed to the struggle on both sides," writes Karl W. Deutsch, "then we are inclined to speak of 'war by proxy'—an international conflict between two foreign powers, fought out on the soil of a third country; disguised as conflict over an internal issue of that country; and using some or all of that country's manpower, resources, and territory as means for achieving preponderantly foreign goals and foreign strategies."[76] In this case, local parties to the conflict lose the power of initiative and control to a complex international process of strategic planning, diplomatic bargaining and negotiation, and political-military decision-making—a process in which the local parties within the conflict-ridden nation may play only a subordinate client role. Once the international political prestige of two great powers becomes engaged, their rivalry may very well overshadow in importance the social-psychological attitudes of the inhabitants of the country on whose soil the conflict is being waged.

In the 1970s, several scholars began to examine this nexus between the internal and external causes of revolutionary conflict in the Third World. This was an important and new direction in the research and analysis of internal war as well as recognition of the increasing significance of state-supported and, in some cases, state-sponsorship of insurgency, terrorism, and other forms of low-intensity conflict. Over the previous two decades, studies purporting to identify the causes of internal war had greatly emphasized the importance of indigenous factors, while giving only scant attention to the impact of forces and influences from outside the area of conflict. Although certain external causes were mentioned (including war, international political pressure, and regional economic crises), what tended to be overlooked was the degree to which foreign powers could contribute to the growth and expansion of revolutionary insurgent and terrorist movements through the provision of various kinds of military, political, and economic assistance.[77]

Bard O'Neill, Mark Hagopian, Thomas Greene, and Mostafa Rejai, among others, raised questions about this oversight in the scholarly analysis of internal war or low-intensity conflict.[78] They argued, to varying degrees, that while the initial causes or preconditions of internal war remain predominantly attributable to indigenous political, economic, and social developments, an important factor that could contribute to the growth of insurgent and terrorist movements to a more advanced stage is the presence of assistance from governments external to the conflict. In the late 1970s and 1980s, the examination of external factors proceeded in several directions. This included an assessment of the strategy and tactics of the Soviet Union and its allies and surrogates as they relate to this form of conflict. For example, Stephen Hosmer and Thomas Wolfe, Bruce Porter, and Joseph Whelan and Michael Dixon surveyed Soviet involvement in low-intensity conflicts throughout the Third World and documented the ways in which it had evolved and escalated. While noting that from the inception of the Soviet regime, the CPSU leadership has identified an almost symbiotic relationship between itself and national liberation movements in the Third World, they attributed the increase both in the level of support and number of movements receiving assistance to several factors, including:

1. military parity with the United States;
2. an enhanced Soviet capacity to project power and supply arms and other conflict technology well beyond its borders;
3. the sharpening of active measures, including propaganda, disinformation, agents of influence, international fronts, and related instruments of political and psychological warfare;
4. the declining willingness of the United States to maintain active security commitments in the Third World, as exemplified by its withdrawal from Vietnam,[79] and its subsequent hesitancy, perhaps due to neoisolationist tendencies, to become as directly involved in foreign conflicts (e.g., Angola, the Horn of Africa, Lebanon, the Gulf, and Central America) as it had been during the period when it played the role of "world policeman;" and
5. an increasing number of states and political organizations willing to cooperate with the Soviet Union for the purposes of fundamentally transforming the structure of the international system.

Some specialists have concentrated on the specific political and military instruments utilized by the USSR and its allies and surrogates to assist revolutionary insurgent and terrorist movements. For example, John Dziak and John Collins examine the paramilitary role played by the intelligence and security services of the Soviet bloc.[80] John Copper, Daniel Papp, and W. Scott Thompson focus on arms transfers, other kinds of military assistance, and force projection capabilities.[81] Yet other scholars have concentrated on the ways in which propaganda, psychological operations, and political warfare techniques have been employed by the Soviet bloc as part of its overall strategy for aiding revolutionary groups with tactics operationalized and integrated to advance the legitimacy of movements pursuing revolutionary warfare strategies.[82] Decades earlier, Paul Linebarger, William Daugherty and Morris Janowitz, Daniel Lerner, Harold Lasswell, and Jacques Ellul, to name the most prominent, had produced major studies on political and psychological warfare as instruments of statecraft.[83] However, the 1970s saw a marked decline in the attention paid by scholars to political, psychological, and paramilitary measures as tools of foreign policy. The 1980s have witnessed a rekindling of interest in the topic.[84]

Of special interest to Uri Ra'anan, Dennis Bark, and Richard Shultz has been the role of Soviet allies and surrogates in providing external support to internal war.[85] They argue that Soviet surrogates appear to be quite specialized in the tasks and missions they undertake, and that the degree of Moscow's control of influence seems to vary and depends on the ideological, political, geographical, and economic nature of the client state itself.

The role of Western countries, particularly the United States, in low-intensity conflicts in the Third World likewise received considerable scholarly and public policy attention during the 1980s.[86] However, the literature has been marked by considerable disagreement in defining the parameters of low-intensity conflict. At minimum, specialists such as Sam Sarkesian, Stephen Hosmer and George Tanham, and David Dean have argued that low-intensity conflict, as it relates to U.S. foreign and national security policy, includes counterinsurgency, insurgency (or resistance movements), counterterrorism, contingency operations (e.g., rescue, raids, and demonstration), and peacekeeping.[87] This subject, as it relates to policy studies, has generated a lively debate, which can be seen by contrasting the works of Sam Sarkesian, Frank Barnett et al., and Richard Shultz with those of Michael Klare and Peter Kornbluh, D. Michael Shafer, and John Prados.[88] Beyond these broader studies of policy and strategy there also is an extensive literature on each of the specific subcategories of low-intensity conflict, including several case studies.[89]

Recent new directions in the literature include, first, the comparative analysis of how open and closed systems have developed strategy and policy for low-intensity conflict; second, comparative analysis of Western perspectives; and third, an examination of how the countries of the Third World have approached different aspects of low-intensity conflict.[90] The study of internal war and low-intensity conflict within the theory and practice of international relations will continue to be of importance in the years ahead.

POLITICAL SCIENCE AND THE CAUSES OF WAR

We now turn to the principal problem of international relations in the contemporary world—war. Among political scientists, some can be found who are partial to their own single-factor explanations of war, but most are likely to be wary of theories that trace wars to one overriding cause, whether inner biological-psychological urges, the profit motives of capitalist imperialists, arms races, or alliances. Recalling the fate of earlier predictions that the replacement of monarchies by republics would lead to a more peaceful world, they are careful about postulating a precise connection between the form of government and the propensity to go to war. Nevertheless, Kenneth N. Waltz states a more broadly shared view when he asserts that democratic states are more peaceful than nondemocratic ones,[91] if only because pacifist sentiment can more readily be translated into an effective political force in democratic states than in authoritarian systems. Although democracies have occasionally been swept by war fever, it is also undeniable, as Paul Diehl has shown, that no two genuinely democratic states have ever engaged in war against each other. It is now axiomatic that no conflict between or among states escalates to war unless at least one is an authoritarian or totalitarian state.[92]

Political scientists are not for the most part easily impressed by the proposals of those who, diagnosing a single cause of war, prescribe a single panacea for it—universal socialism, free trade, universal brotherhood of good will, a radical new approach to education, world government, complete disarmament, or maximum military preparedness or standing firm at all times. Each is woven into a multidimensional framework, and some may be more important than others as a means of reducing the likelihood of specific wars.[93]

Quincy Wright, in his pioneering and comprehensive survey of the subject, stressed the multiple causality of war and warned against simplistic approaches to the problem: "A war, in reality, results from a total situation involving ultimately almost everything that has happened to the human race up to the time the war begins."[94] In his monumental study, which cannot adequately be summarized here, Wright put forth a four-factor model of the origins of war, corresponding to the levels of technology, law, social-political organization, and cultural values. Karl W. Deutsch, in his preface to a reissue of Wright's classic work, wrote of these levels:

> Whenever there is a major change at any level—culture and values, political and social institutions, laws, or technology—the old adjustment and control mechanisms become strained and may break down. Any major psychological and cultural, or major social and political, or legal, or technological change in the world thus increases the risk of war, unless it is balanced by compensatory political, legal, cultural, and psychological adjustments.[95]

According to yet another writer, Clyde Eagleton:

War is a means for achieving an end, a weapon which can be used for good or for bad purposes. Some of these purposes for which war has been used have been accepted by humanity as worthwhile ends; indeed, war performs functions which are essential in any human society. It has been used to settle disputes, to uphold rights, to remedy wrongs; and these are surely functions which must be served. . . . One may say, without exaggeration, that no more stupid, brutal, wasteful, or unfair method could ever have been imagined for such purposes, but this does not alter the situation.[96]

Nations resort to force to enhance their security by extending or preserving power, control, and influence over their environment—over the territory, populations, governments, and resources of societies with which they are in contact. In earlier times, nations were primarily concerned about disputes and contests of strength with neighbors who were geographically proximate or more remote yet reachable by maritime or overland transport. In modern times, developments in military and communications technology, as well as in international trade, investment, and monetary matters, have gradually forced a diplomacy until two centuries ago confined largely to Europe to become global in outlook. Along the way, governments have decided to go to war for many different reasons:

- to gain dominion over territory
- to enhance security
- to acquire wealth and/or prestige
- to preserve (by defending or extending) ethnic, cultural, and religious identity and values
- to preserve or extend dynastic interests
- to weaken a foreign foe
- to gain or hold a colonial empire
- to spread a political ideology
- to prevent secession and national dissolution or territorial loss
- to intervene in foreign conflicts (whether to honor a treaty obligation, support a friendly government, overthrow an unfriendly one, aid in a liberation struggle, etc.)
- to maintain alliance credibility
- to preserve or restore a balance of power and thwart the hegemonial aims of another power
- to protect a vital economic interest abroad
- to uphold the principle of freedom of the seas
- to fill a "power vacuum" (before someone else does)
- to fight a small war now rather than a larger one later, or a preventive war that can be won now against a growing power that would pose a greater threat later
- to carry out reprisals against governments for past injuries inflicted
- to protect endangered nationals
- to defend national honor and avenge a grave insult

Even this list is not exhaustive. There are many types of wars—personal, feudal, dynastic, national, civil, revolutionary, religious, ideological, imperialistic, and anticolonial, as well as alliance wars, local and general wars, proxy wars, limited wars, and total wars.

The motives for which political communities go to war change over time. Four hundred years ago, Europe was torn by a series of ferocious wars over religious issues. Most Europeans today would regard such a *casus belli* as unthinkable. (But the mixing of political and religious issues still occasionally appears, as in the Ulster conflict, the civil war in Lebanon, the Gulf War between Iran and Iraq, and the conflicts between Sikhs and Hindus, or between Buddhist Sinhalese and Hindu Tamils.)

Political scientists generally insist, therefore, that we cannot understand the causes of war exclusively in terms of biological, psychological, or other behavioral factors, but must always return to the level of political analysis to find out why a particular government regards certain foreign governments as allies and others as adversaries. It is out of a matrix of political communications—involving politicians and diplomats, the public, the press, the military, socioeconomic elites, special interest groups in the foreign policymaking process—that governments define their goals, interests, policies, and strategies, weighing the likely consequences of acting or not acting in specific situations, as well as the prospects of success or failure in invoking force. The findings of the behavioral scientists can serve as valuable illuminators to our understanding of the causes of war, provided that we place them in perspective as partial explanatory factors within the larger international political context in which those who wield the power of decision opt either to go to war or to refrain from it.[97]

Violent encounters between organized political communities may have myriad origins. The ground, sea, or air forces of two adversary societies might suddenly and spontaneously find themselves involved in hostile skirmishes without an authoritative political decision having been made by either government, or one government might order a unit of its armed forces to contrive a military confrontation with a unit of the adversary's forces merely to gauge the psychopolitical reaction without intending war. In an era of advanced military technology, many analysts have worried about the possibility of "accidental or unintentional war," as if nuclear war might be triggered automatically by an incident of technical malfunction.[98] Political scientists and other macrotheorists call attention to the fact that, so far as historical evidence goes, the initiation of war is a matter of conscious, deliberate choice, not of decisionless outbreak.[99]

A persistent cause of war has been the readiness of societies to resort to force in order to reduce a perceived threat to their security or to their political, religious, ideological, economic, or sociocultural value systems. Undoubtedly, there have been times when the threat perceived was real and proximate, just as there were occasions when the threat was so remote as to be virtually imaginary. When one or more societies act more "belligerently," "aggressively," or "imperialistically" than others, other societies become apprehensive and they seek to improve their security by engaging in some form of power balancing—especially by increasing their military preparations or by entering an alliance, or both.

The perception of threat, therefore, becomes a matter of importance to political scientists. For one state to perceive another as a threat, it must see the latter as having both the *capability* and the *intent* to block goal attainment or to jeopardize national security.[100] J. David Singer, for whom national security rather than abstract ideology constitutes *the* categorical imperative in United States and Soviet foreign policy, suggests that two powers that find themselves in a relationship of rivalry or hostility will each be inclined to "interpret each other's military capability as evidence of military intent," and he reduced threat-perception to the quasi-mathematical formula of Estimated Capability × Estimated Intent.[101] Singer hastens to assert that the Soviet Union is more concerned over the British or French nuclear capabilities than is the United States, indicating that the mere possession of nuclear weapons does not furnish, in the absence of political differences between parties, a basis for apprehension.

Raymond L. Garthoff has warned against possible fallacies in any effort to estimate and impute intentions. Among common examples of fallacious reasoning he cites the following:

1. Since overestimating the enemy's intentions merely costs dollars, whereas underestimating can cost lives, when in doubt it is best to assume the worst.
2. Because it is impossible to read intentions accurately, it is safer to estimate measurable military capabilities and assume an intention to maximize those capabilities.
3. Assume that the adversary's strategic perceptions and ways of thinking are either the same as your own or necessarily always different. (Garthoff advises that both pitfalls should be avoided.)
4. Assume that the leaders of the adversary nation either never mean what they say or always mean what they say. Both assumptions are unfounded.

Estimating intentions, he concludes, is difficult enough without allowing such fallacies as the foregoing to enter into the process.[102]

ARMAMENTS AND WAR

Do armaments themselves constitute a cause of war, or can they be a cause of peace through deterrence? Many analysts have been of the opinion that arms do not cause wars, but rather are symptoms and consequences of suspicions, hostility, and conflicts between societies. Frederick L. Schuman, noting that pacifists have long believed that arms lead to war and disarmament to peace, wrote: "In reality, the reverse is more nearly true: war machines are reduced only when peace seems probable, the expectation of conflict leads to competition in armaments, and armaments spring from war and from the anticipation of war."[103] Hans J. Morgenthau delivered this terse dictum: "Men do not fight because they have arms. They have arms because they deem it necessary to fight."[104] Michael Howard has suggested that weapons can be used for essentially four purposes: to deter an adversary from resorting to war, to defend oneself should deterrence fail, to wage aggressive warfare, or to engage in political intimidation. As such, weapons, the implements of conflict, are neutral instruments to be employed by the defender or the aggressor.[105]

RICHARDSON'S REACTION PROCESSES

One of the earliest efforts to mathematicize arms races was the reaction process model developed by the English pacifist physicist-mathematician Lewis Fry Richardson, whose ideas were posthumously given currency among American political scientists after 1957.[106] Using linear differential equations, Richardson sought to analyze the armaments acquisition policies of two rival parties within the framework of a mutual stimulus-response or action-reaction model.[107] He reduced the rate of change in the military budgets of rival states to the following equations:

$$\frac{dx}{dt} = ky - ax + g$$

$$\frac{dy}{dt} = lx - by + h$$

where
- x = the armaments of Country A
- t = time
- y = the armaments of Country B
- k = a positive constant standing for A's perception of the menace
- a = a positive constant representing "the fatigue and expenses of keeping up defenses"
- g = a constant standing for A's grievances against B
- $y, l, b,$ and h = corresponding values for Country B[108]

Dina A. Zinnes has pointed out that Richardson's focus was not, strictly speaking, a search for the cause of war, since he did not specifically consider wars in his models, but merely sought to describe processes that precede and may produce some—we would say few—modern wars.[109] Paul Diehl has presented convincing evidence to support his contention that in the nineteenth century none of the arms races led to war and none of the wars was preceded by an arms race.[110]

What Richardson put forth was a purely theoretical model of the way two rival states interact in the military expenditures dimension. Country A is stimulated by B's arms accumulation, and what A does by way of reaction serves as a further stimulus to B, but each country is constrained by its own total amount of arms and the effects of an increase of armaments upon its own economy. Like all purely theoretical models, it is a highly simplified one in which the only two variables are the unique geostrategic requirements of each party, the military preparedness or vulnerability of allied countries, and whether the rivals are pursuing initiative-aggressive or reactive-defensive policies. According to Richardson, the interactive process can be either stable or unstable. Nations, like individuals, usually behave toward others as others behave toward them. If both nations are xenophobic and mutually hostile, the reaction coefficient will be greater than one. Let us assume that each feels secure only with a 10 percent margin of superiority over the other. The accumulation of 100 units of arms on one side (A) will stimulate the other (B) to accumulate 110; this will provoke A to aim at 121, and in turn B will insist upon 133, and so on, in an indefinite escalation characteristic of an unstable system in which the acquisition lines move away from the equilibrium point. Conversely, as two parties attenuate their hostility and turn toward increased friendliness and cooperation, their reaction coefficient will be less than one, they will deescalate their rates of military expenditure, and their arms acquisition lines will converge toward a balance of power.[111]

Zinnes, who manifests considerable admiration for the pioneering research of Richardson, concedes that his basic model "is exceedingly naive in its assumptions, and perhaps also extremely narrow in its substantive concern."[112] She justifies devoting a great amount of attention to it on the grounds that it stimulated the efforts of many others to develop extensions, modifications, and refinements of mathematical arms race models and to apply Richardson's interaction processes to other fields.[113] (We shall look at several of these subsequent statistical studies when we take up the Correlates of War Project below.)

Richardson's basic model, it should be stressed, is more a purely theoretical construct than a hypothesis that can be empirically tested in the complex laboratory of history. The model has been criticized by Martin Patchen[114] on the grounds that it cannot explain more than a small portion of international behavior. Some of Richardson's modifications of his basic model fit the data for the military expenditures of France/Russia and Germany/Austria in the period of 1909 to 1914. His equations are less neatly applicable to the period prior to World War II, when the reluctance of the Western democratic states to modernize their military establishments encouraged the anti–status quo dictatorships to increase their armament rate and to become more aggressive in their foreign policies, rather than constraining them.

The Richardson model is no less "tautological" than conventional wisdom has often been thought to be, and it possesses no more predictive power. What it tells us is that if two rivals are engaged in an unbridled and constantly escalating arms race, then they are interacting in this one dimension in a tension-increasing manner, and this may indicate that they will end up at war sooner or later unless they alter their course, since arms acquisition policies usually reflect other basic disagreements. His equations cannot enable us to predict when the tensions become so great that the breaking point is reached.[115] Even the data from the period prior to World War I do not prove that the arms race caused that war, but only that it was one of the several factors that contributed to its onset.[116]

No simplified mathematical model can take into account the great variety of factors that affect the course of international relations and modify action-reaction processes,[117] perhaps leading one party to change more rapidly than the other, or one to misinterpret what the other is doing and to react in a manner not in accordance with the model. This, of course, is a shortcoming not only of the Richardson model, but of all single-factor explanations. Arms races are not easy to define. It is difficult to say how many there have been in this century. (Richardson was interested only in three—before 1914, before 1939, and after 1945. Other writers to be considered presently have examined larger numbers of arms races.) Nor can we always measure arms races merely by reference to levels of military spending, even after correcting for economic fluctuations to obtain "constant" currency units over a period of time. A technological breakthrough might enable a country to enhance its overall military capabilities at lower costs.[118] Conversely, it is quite conceivable, in a period of steady inflation and constantly rising personnel costs in comparison with weapons costs, that a nation's overall military capabilities would deteriorate despite modestly rising budgets.

It is reasonable to hold that the existence of armaments is a necessary condition of war, simply because in their total absence war could not be waged. They are not, however, a sufficient condition of war. Thus, to say that arms are a "cause" of war is, as David W. Ziegler has observed, about as helpful as the conclusion that "combustible materials cause fire" would be in a fire marshal's investigation.[119] It is virtually impossible to demonstrate scientifically that an "arms race" has been the primary cause of any specific international war in the modern era, rather than a consequence of other political causes, or one among several contributing factors. There is probably some theoretical validity to the action-reaction hypothesis concerning arms competition in the buildup of international tension that was a prelude to World War I (including the Anglo-German naval rivalry and the preoccupation of the Great Powers with the numbers of available combat-effective troops), and in the pattern of Arab and Israeli arms acquisition policies since 1948, but even in those cases the decisions for war were interwoven with other crucial factors.

It is appropriate to be skeptical about the applicability of the action-reaction model to the particular historical case to which many writers have attempted to apply it in recent decades—that is, the competition in advanced weapons technology between the United States and the Soviet Union. In an era of sophisticated and constantly changing military technology, not every addition of a new generation of missiles to a nation's deterrent forces is conducive to the eventual outbreak of war. The very fact that both superpowers have retired earlier generations of nuclear missiles without employing them in war is proof of that. Albert Wohlstetter argued that the action-reaction pattern does not provide a convincing explanation of the United States-Soviet arms competition. He found that over a nine-year period (1962–1971), instead of overreacting to the Soviet military buildup, the United States underreacted, reducing constant dollar expenditures on strategic weapons by two-thirds from the early 1960s to the early 1970s. Wohlstetter concluded that at least up to the mid-1970s there had not really been an "arms race" between the superpowers.[120] Many analysts, of course, would contend that over the whole period of superpower rivalry there has been an arms race, even though not an unrestrained one.

POWER AS DISTANCE: EQUALITY AND INEQUALITY

We turn next to relative levels of power (or power as *distance* between two actors) and to the dynamism of shifts in power relationships. From the standpoint of theory it is intriguing to ask which is more conducive to war—equality or inequality of power—and whether the probability of war increases or decreases as equality is approached. At first glance, one might deem it logical to assume that as two rival states move toward equality they should be able to deal with each other more fairly and even-handedly. Certainly one of the most commonly stated assumptions underlying United States-Soviet relations during the era of the strategic arms negotiations since 1969 has been that strategic parity is a prerequisite of stable mutual deterrence and of progress in arms limitation. The question, however, must be probed carefully.

A. F. K. Organski was among the first to call attention to the danger that the probability of war may increase during a period of power transition.[121] Perceptible inequality of power makes it foolish for the weaker side to initiate a war, while the stronger side need not be apprehensive. This is borne out by the experience of India and Pakistan following the Bangladesh War of 1971. Prior to that conflict, the two subcontinent neighbors lived in an almost constant fear of and readiness for war for a quarter-century. After Pakistan's population, territory, and resources were substantially reduced and India tested a nuclear explosive device, Pakistan's resentment ran high, but little could be done to alter the situation, and both the probability and fear of an Indo-Pakistani War in the proximate future declined markedly.[122]

One of Organski's principal objections to the classical "balance-of-power" theory (which he agrees had some validity in an earlier period) is that it presupposes a relatively stable distribution of power among units and an ability of prudent statesmen to act in time to compensate for disturbances in the balance—for example, by entering an alliance. In the twentieth century, industrial technology permits the occurrence of rapid shifts of power that perhaps cannot be prevented. Balances are unstable because they are not durable. As power parity is approached, two rivals may become increasingly nervous about the balance and sensitive to fluctuations within it, thereby increasing the danger of war. As the challenger overtakes the erstwhile leader, its more rapid growth rate may breed an excess of self-confidence and tempt it to seek complete victory.[123] The converse danger is that the dominant power, viewing apprehensively the expanding capabilities of its rival, may go to war to defeat the latter while it can.

Inis L. Claude has succinctly expressed the ambiguity of the situation: "If an equilibrium means that either side may lose, it also means that either side may win."[124] Michael P. Sullivan has suggested that the relationship between approaching equality may be curvilinear:

> The more equal two countries are, the greater the probability of conflict, *except* that at some point the opposite process, as suggested by Claude, begins to operate: high equality stifles aggressive tendencies because of the fifty-fifty chance of losing. . . . Gross inequality would have either low probability of conflict or low conflict; the greater the equality, however, the greater the chance of conflict and, if conflict does break out, the greater the chance of high levels of conflict. When two powers are exactly equal, however, the probability of conflict drops off and if conflict does occur, it will be low level.[125]

In our view, the process of taking a decision for war cannot be reduced to a probability based upon a mere quantitative comparison of power between rivals. Much may depend upon the attitude and outlook of the two states, the nature of their political systems, the hostility or friendship which marks their relationship, the extent to which their vital interests clash, the degree to which the dominant power accepts and accommodates its policies to the expanding power of the challenger, and so forth.[126] A timid preponderant power might lose its competitive spirit, whereas the challenger, though gaining, is still substantially weaker in terms of military power but stronger in ideology, morale, and self-confidence. Accommodation by the satisfied power may either appease the dissatisfied power, making it more patient and cooperative, or it may serve only to whet its appetite and make it more aggressive. We cannot therefore predict the point at which the opposite process begins to operate, nor can two powers know when they are exactly equal.

NATIONAL GROWTH AND INTERNATIONAL VIOLENCE

Nazli Choucri and Robert C. North have contended that the processes of national growth themselves are likely to lead to expansion, competition, rivalry, conflict, and violence.[127] Selecting World War I as a test case, they analyzed long-range trends over the period 1870 to 1914. They applied econometric techniques over time and across six major powers (Britain, France, Germany, Italy, Russia, and Austria-Hungary) to a variety of aggregate data—demographic, economic, political, and military—as well as interactions among those countries. Choucri and North focused their attention not upon such discrete events as the assassination of the Archduke or the Russian decision to mobilize, nor on the personality of key leaders, but rather on the dynamics of population and technological growth, changes in trade and military expenditures, the conflict of national interests, and patterns of colonial activity, alliance formation, and violence behavior. These are the variables, says Choucri and North, that produce changes in the international system conducive to crisis and war. In their view, the probability of war is not significantly lowered by good will alone, by deterrence strategy, or by détente and partial arms limitations.[128]

Choucri and North devote a great deal of effort to explaining their methodology, apologizing for the lack of statistical significance in many of the correlations, and pointing out the deficiencies of data in the book, which they call "a progress report on the initial phases of our research."[129] Here we are principally interested in the explanatory theory on the basis of which they proceed, which can be summarized as follows. As noted in Chapter 2, Choucri and North hypothesize that a growing population experiences an increasing demand for basic resources. As technology becomes more advanced, the greater will be the kinds and quantity of resources required by the society. If demands are not met, the development of new capabilities will be sought, and if these cannot be attained within the nation's boundaries, lateral pressures will be created to attain them beyond. Lateral pressure may be expressed through commercial activities, the building of navies and merchant fleets, the dispatch of troops into foreign territory, the acquisition of colonial territory or foreign markets, the establishment of military bases abroad, and in other ways. A country is not absolutely determined to obtain satisfaction of its needs beyond its territory. It might be content with less and mind its own business, but most modern industrialized countries manifest strong lateral pressures in some form.[130]

The expansion of one country's lateral pressure may be acquiesced in or resisted by other countries. All lateral pressure contains a potential for international conflict. As interests grow, it is usually assumed that they require protection. This means military expenditures and an increased sense of competition or rivalry. One colonial power is likely to feel threatened each time another acquires new territory. Alliances are formed both to enhance national capabilities and to moderate conflicts of interest among some parties, even though this may arouse the suspicion of others, prompt the formation of a countervailing coalition, and contribute to exacerbation of international conflict, as the "process of antagonizing" tends to become mutual.[131] The study partially validates the Richardson reaction-process hypothesis, but also modifies it in certain important respects because the data show that "arms increases are sometimes better explained by domestic growth factors than by international competition."[132]

The most important finding to emerge from the study is that domestic growth (measured by population density and per capita national income) is a strong determinant of national expansion, and that these are linked to military expenditures, alliances, and international violence. Such a finding, in the view of Choucri and North, has ominous implications for the conventional wisdom concerning the gap between the strong, rich nations and the poor, weak nations: "For a long time there was a widely shared assumption that by narrowing this gap through technological and economic growth, the probability of conflict and war would be lessened. This assumption now seems dubious."[133] In the end, they raise somber questions about the ability of populous societies, equipped with highly destructive military technology, to live together on a planet that now offers little room for further lateral expansion and increasingly limited opportunities for growth. If uninhibited growth and aggressive competition might lead to international violence on a massive scale, Choucri and North ask, might not the severe curtailment of growth lead just as surely to disaster?[134] Nearly a decade after publishing the book in which they set forth their lateral-pressure explanation of international conflict, North and Choucri reiterated the hypothesis in an assessment of the economic and political factors that enter into the bargaining and leverage of domestic and international actors. All forms of lateral pressure, they say, are ultimately traceable to individual needs, wants, desires, demands, and capabilities. The mix of leverages that states employ may lead to various outcomes—cooperation, competition, and conflict, producing peace or war.[135]

It should be obvious from the foregoing that it is not feasible to identify neatly *the* political causes of war. Historically, nations have expected wars to recur, and they have institutionalized their expectations in the form of military establishments. War in the contemporary world may be said to be a function of many factors, not all of which can be treated adequately within a few chapters of a single work.

THE CORRELATES OF WAR PROJECT AND STATISTICAL ANALYSES OF WAR

The age-old quest for an understanding of the "causes" of war has culminated in the collection of a vast amount of quantitative data on war and the myriad factors to which war may be related. Notable among the pioneering efforts in this field during the 1930s were the works of Pitirim A. Sorokin,[136] Quincy Wright,[137] and Lewis F. Richardson,[138] although the latter's research did not become well known until several years after the Second World War. Since the early 1960s, J. David Singer, Melvin Small, and others have built upon the earlier studies of those just mentioned by conducting continuous research based upon or flowing from the Correlates of War Project.[139] The two decades since the early 1970s have witnessed a considerable growth of interest in statistical studies of war, designed to relate the probability of war's occurrence with arms races, alliances, power transitions, and other relevant factors. Up to the present time, the statistical techniques have produced no startling surprises, and few conclusive or unambiguous results.

Initially and ultimately, Singer and Small were concerned with probing war's causes, but they realized that the raw data available to scholars on the phenomenon of war left much to be desired. They began, therefore, by compiling an inventory of information on the frequency, magnitude, severity, and intensity of international wars in the period from the end of the Napoleonic Wars (1816) onward. It was expected that other research efforts would be able to take their data as a point of departure.

Singer and Small gathered data for international conflicts (i.e., wars in which the total number of battle-connected deaths surpassed 1000). They also examined international conflicts between system members on the one hand and independent or colonial entities on the other hand that did not qualify for system membership at the time, and for which system-member battle deaths averaged 1000 per year. Civil wars were excluded. A total of 93 wars were identified—50 of them between system members and 44 between system members and extrasystemic entities, with 1 conflict cutting across both categories. They found that international war appears to be neither waxing nor waning, but that extrasystemic wars have naturally declined in frequency toward the zero point as colonial empires have been liquidated and nearly all political units have been incorporated into the state system.

Both Richardson in his analysis of deadly quarrels and Singer and Small found that as magnitude (measured in numbers of deaths) increases, frequency of war decreases. More recently, Jack S. Levy, who worked from a much longer time base than Singer and Small, collecting war data back to 1495, established empirically that during the last five centuries, wars between Great Powers have declined in frequency but have become more serious in extent, severity, and intensity, measured in numbers and rates of battle deaths.[140] (This is what a traditionalist relying on conventional wisdom would expect.) Not surprisingly, according to Singer and Small, most of the wars in the period after 1815 were fought by major powers, with England, France, Turkey, and Russia being the most war-prone in both the interstate and extrasystemic categories. This does not necessarily mean that those countries were basically more aggressive than others, but only that "the top-ranked nations were compelled to fight often and at length either to maintain their position or to achieve it."[141] As for won-lost records, most of the major powers (with the exception of Turkey) performed rather well. (Presumably that is why they are major powers; they are expected to win when pitted against lesser powers, as they are most of the time.) It has long been assumed that states initiate war when they expect to be victorious. Singer and Small found that the initiators did in fact prove victorious in about two-thirds of all the wars reviewed for major powers. John G. Stoessinger, however, after examining 11 major wars in the twentieth century, concluded that no nation that began the war emerged a winner, but not all would agree.[142]

Theorists of war have asked whether in the life of societies, war is inevitable in periodic cycles, such as a century (Arnold Toynbee) or the time needed for a new generation to forget the suffering and costs of the previous war (Lewis F. Richardson). In an early publication of partial project findings, Small and Singer wrote:

> Although cycles are not apparent when we examine the amount of war beginning in each year or time period, a discernible periodicity emerges when we focus on measures of the amount of war under way. That is, discrete wars do not necessarily come and go with regularity but with some level of interstate violence almost always present; there are distinct and periodic fluctuations in the amount of that violence.[143]

The notion that war occurs in every generation was usually thought to apply to a single society, where "forgetting the last war" might make some sense (even though policymakers and other elites are not very likely to forget). But the periodic occurrence of war levels throughout the entire international system would not seem to be explicable in terms of generational forgetting. Neither Lewis Richardson nor Pitirim Sorokin could discern a cyclical pattern.[144] If there is a real periodicity (and thus far the statistical evidence is not very convincing), theorists cannot yet offer any reasonable explanation. Perhaps it is related to worldwide economic cycles, of which a suggestion can be found in the thinking of Gaston Bouthoul and Jacques Ellul.[145] A. L. Macfie and Geoffrey Blainey hypothesized a link between the optimism that usually accompanies an expansive upswing in a nation's economy and the tendency to initiate war (the costs of which could more easily be borne), but William R. Thompson discovered no such correlation.[146] The authors of this text regard rigid cyclical theories of war and peace as deterministic, and hence are not inclined to take them seriously. In a sense, of course, all recurring phenomena can be called "cyclical"; the problem in the social universe is that virtually all cycles appear to be irregular.

The Correlates of War Project made available to scholars a much broader range of data than Richardson had employed, and it has led to a steadily growing number of statistical analyses concerning the relations between the outbreak of war and selected variables—arms races, alliances, power transitions, capabilities distribution, risk-taking propensity of leaders, and the assessment of war's expected utility in the minds of decisionmakers. Most prominent has been the work of Richard K. Ashley, Francis A. Beer, Michael Wallace, Bruce Bueno de Mesquita, John Vasquez, A. F. K. Organski, Paul Diehl, Jacek Kugler, and Jack S. Levy, although the writings of others should not be overlooked. Virtually all of them have built upon and elaborated the mathematical methods of Richardson and the data compiled by Singer and Small.

Richard K. Ashley assumes that human beings act according to a dialectical process to reduce the gap between what is and what ought to be. Human beings interact with their environment in an unending competition for scarce resources. Accepting as his point of departure the Choucri and North explanation of international conflict in lateral pressures, Ashley stresses demographic, technological, and economic factors both within nations and in their interactions. It seems that economic expansion is for Ashley the crucial factor generating international conflict. Population growth and technological progress produce ever-mounting demands for satisfaction. When the expanding demands of countries intersect, and cooperative solutions cannot be worked out, military conflict may result.[147]

Ashley's work, like that of several scholars who have analyzed war during the last decade or two, is useful in that it calls attention to the fact that state policies for peace and war are determined not only by what goes on within the domestic political systems but also as a result of interacting with other states. States can interact with other states, whether friendly or adversary, without necessarily becoming involved in the kinds of rigid action-reaction processes that Richardson and some of his most orthodox disciples have in mind when they speak of arms races. Arms competition is, in a real sense, a form of bargaining and leverage-building that need not end in war, and might lead to a more stable relationship marked by a relaxation of arms competition and a tendency to shift the competition to other (say, economic or diplomatic) foreign policy modes. The "decision" for war cannot be entirely isolated and attributed exclusively to one state—at least not in all cases. War is often the culmination of a dyadic rather than a purely unilateral process. It may be somewhat misleading, therefore, to investigate the attributes of single nation-states in an effort to discover which ones are more "inherently aggressive or war-prone" than others.[148]

Arms Races and the Escalation to War

Numerous studies have been addressed to the question of whether the competitive acquisition of arms is more frequently conducive to peace or war. The classical doctrine enunciated by the ancient Roman strategist Vegetius—*si vis pacem, para bellum* ("if you want peace, prepare for war")—has been quoted countless times as a justification for national military preparedness programs. In recent decades, several writers have expressed skepticism about the ancient maxim. Michael D. Wallace, for example, has called the evidence cited by the preparedness school "anecdotal and idiosyncratic," and argues that an arms race between two states is strongly associated with escalation to full-scale hostilities when they are involved in disputes.[149] As noted earlier, arms races are not easy to define. The fact that two rival powers spend additional sums on defense each year does not necessarily prove that they are in the kind of race implied in Richardson's reaction-process studies. Reference was made previously to

Wohlstetter's rejecting the concept of a U.S.-Soviet arms race. Francis A. Beer has pointed out that U.S. and Soviet arms expenditures kept pace with each other for about two decades, but that there was an independent drop in the relative U.S. defense effort with the winding down of the Vietnam War.[150] Miroslav Nincic has demonstrated that the continued growth of defense budgets and weapons arsenals is often the result of domestic economic or political pressure more than of the actual requirements of adequate military security, and other scholars have argued that the empirical data do not support Richardson's reaction-process model, while time series research indicates that expenditures in many alleged "arms races" were independent of each other.[151]

In the mid-1970s, John C. Lambelet could discover no causal link between arms races and the outbreak of wars.[152] Yet the view persisted that there was validity to the hypothesis propounded by Singer in 1958 that reciprocal or mutually reactive arms acquisition policies on the part of rival powers produced an "arms-tension spiral" that increased the probability of war.[153] Michael Wallace defined an arms race as a competition involving intense, bilateral, simultaneous growth in military expenditures (i.e., abnormal rates of increase about 10 percent annually) over a specified period (say, 3, 5, or 10 years) between either Great Powers or local comparable powers within a region, whose relations are mutually antagonistic. Wallace conceded that arms buildups alone usually do not provoke hostilities; other circumstances and events bring states into sufficiently severe confrontations that arms are seen as posing acute threats that contribute to the onset of war.[154] Using the Correlates of War Project Data on 99 serious major power disputes in the 1816–1965 period, he found a strong correlation, but not a causal link, between arms races and escalation to war. Later, Wallace found that crisis escalation was no more likely when the revisionist Great Power possessed a significant military advantage (on the order of 1.5 or greater) over its status quo adversary, or when it was both relatively stronger and increasing its lead. He concluded from this that a basic tenet of the preparedness school was disconfirmed—namely, that "keeping up" is necessary because military power shifts favoring the revisionist side increase the probability of war.[155] By the early 1980s, several analysts, including Michael Altfeld, Paul Diehl, and Erich Weede, had raised serious questions about the procedures on which Wallace's work was based.[156]

Power Transition and War

One of the most controversial aspects of the debate about arms races and escalation to war is the one attributing high danger to power transition. As we noted earlier, A. F. K. Organski has long been identified with the hypothesis that the probability of war increases as the "power gap" narrows, especially as a rival revisionist challenger comes closer to equalizing the capabilities of the once stronger guardian of the status quo. He has continued to adhere to this view in the book he coauthored with Jacek Kugler, *The War Ledger*. They write that "war is caused by differences in rates of growth among the great powers and, of particular importance, the differences in rates between the dominant nation and the challenger that permit the latter to overtake the former."[157] This would seem to conform to strategic logic, since Number One grows more edgy and may be tempted to strike preventively, while Number Two, aware of this, may initiate war to gain the advantage of a surprise first strike. The findings of Wallace do not very well support the conclusion reached by Organski and Kugler. Lest one be overwhelmed by much of the contemporary research on arms races and hastily interpret the statistics to mean that the concept of effective nuclear deterrence has little or no validity, it should be kept in mind that all the empirical data available pertain to the outbreak of conventional wars. The authors of *The War Ledger* observe correctly that nuclear weapons do not deter confrontation on all levels (for confrontation is not the same as war), but they follow it with the startling statement that "the tendency to go to war increases as the likelihood of great power involvement increases and as the possibility that nuclear weapons may be used becomes more real."[158]

Two Dutch scholars, Hank Houweling and Jan Siccama, agree with the Organski/Kugler hypothesis that war occurs when a powerful challenger overtakes a formerly powerful dominant nation, and they insist that this holds true for the nuclear as well as the prenuclear age.[159] According to this view, nuclear weapons and deterrence strategies do not fundamentally alter the normal behavior patterns of nations. Somewhat more optimistic than Wallace and much more so than Organski/Kugler and Houweling/Siccama, Michael D. Intriligator and Dagobert L. Brito contend, specifically in the context of a possible nuclear war model, that arms races can lead either to war or to the avoidance of war, depending on circumstances, just as disarmament could also lead either to the avoidance of war or to war itself.[160] Robert C. North and Matthew Willard concede that the proposition that nuclear weapons necessarily deter nations from war is a *post hoc ergo propter hoc* fallacy ("after that, therefore because of that"), but they fail to see any formal evidence for the Organski/Kugler finding quoted in the previous paragraph.[161] Urs Luterbacher points out in a similar vein that Organski and Kugler are unable to disprove empirically that mutual nuclear deterrence works, and that the concept is not so easily eliminated.[162] In this connection, it is worth noting that none of the seven U.S.-Soviet disputes cited by Wallace eventuated in war.[163]

Alliances and War

No less than in the case of military preparedness, political scientists have been divided over the question of whether alliances between states are more likely to contribute to peace or to bring on war. Some writers have argued that they increase security fears and tensions, thereby generating hostility and exacerbating conflicts; others view alliances as having a stabilizing and war-deterring effect. Certainly alliances are closely associated with wars, because they come fully into play in wartime, but whether they can be credited with preventing wars or blamed for causing them is harder to say.

Singer and Small attempted to correlate the "amount of war in the international system" with the number of alliances in the system. Thus they sought to determine whether alliance aggregation is a reliable predictor to the occurrence of war. They began with a theoretical model that might be characterized as the diplomatic equivalent of Adam Smith's "invisible hand"—a mechanism whereby the freedom of all nations to interact with each other as national interests dictate would redound to the stability and advantage of the whole international community. It would appear logical, then, that alliances, by reducing the interaction opportunities and freedom of choice of states, would increase polarization and the chances of war within the system. Under this line of reasoning, a highly polarized system should produce a high incidence of war. This is essentially the hypothesis tested by Singer and Small in a series of bivariate correlations between several alliance indicators and the magnitude, severity, and frequency of war, allowing time lags of 1, 3, and 5 years from the formation of the alliance to the onset of war. Over the whole period surveyed, from 1815 to 1945, they found no significant correlation. But when they divided the period into two parts—nineteenth and twentieth centuries—they found two contrary patterns. For the nineteenth century, the correlation between gross alliance aggregation and the frequency, magnitude, and severity of war was strongly negative. For the twentieth century, the same correlation was even more strongly positive—up to the end of World War II.[164]

Singer and Small, however, were unable on the basis of their data to explain why alliances appeared to be more successful in deterring war or limiting its magnitude in the nineteenth century than in the early decades of the twentieth century. Traditionalists had long realized, of course, that there was a considerable difference between international relations in the nineteenth-century "Concert of Total War." Singer and Small can only suggest that the structural variable they utilized—alliance aggregation—may be responsive to other properties of the international system, and that its predictive power may be a function of its interaction with these other variables. Undoubtedly, a study of the two principal alliance systems in the nuclear age (after that part of the twentieth century dealt with by Singer and Small) would show a reversion to a very strong negative correlation between alliance aggregation and war—much more significantly than in the nineteenth century if only the territorial area explicitly covered by the two major alliances is taken into account.[165]

Jack S. Levy studied not all international wars but Great Power wars over the period 1495–1975. He found that, apart from the nineteenth century, which was exceptional, the majority of alliances were followed within 5 years of their formation by wars involving at least one of the allies (but not necessarily all the members of the alliance). During the nineteenth century, there were no Great Power wars within the 5-year period of Great Power alliance-initiation.[166] Charles W. Ostrom and Francis W. Hoole have found in a somewhat similar vein that the formation of alliances correlates positively with an increased probability of war within a 3-year period, after which the danger of war's occurrence declines.[167] Even though alliances often eventuate in war, to say that they cause wars is a case of the well-known fallacious argument—*post hoc ergo propter hoc.* Throughout history, nation-states have often entered into alliances because they had an expectation of war within a few years.

John A. Vasquez has pointed out that "a major purpose of entering alliances is to increase relative military power; but this outcome often does not occur, because the making of an alliance usually leads to the creation of a counteralliance."[168] Vasquez cites studies by Randolph Severson and Joel King that demonstrate convincingly that alliances act as a Contagion Mechanism spreading war, and concludes that "alliances not only fail to prevent wars, but make it likely that wars that do occur will expand."[169] Vasquez suspects that alliances in general are not conducive to peace, but he is cautious about ascribing causality to them:

> Since there is often an interval between the alliance and the outbreak of war, it is a legitimate inference that alliances do not directly cause war, but help to aggravate a situation that makes war more likely. They may do this in two ways: by promoting an atmosphere that polarizes the system and by encouraging arms races.[170]

The issue of polarization seems quite relevant. Charles W. Kegley, Jr. and Gregory A. Raymond have contrasted Waltz's view that a rigid bipolar alliance helps prevent war by making superpower commitments clear (thereby *reducing* uncertainty) with the Deutsch/Singer view that flexible multipolarity enhances stability by *compounding* uncertainties and making it harder to predict the outcomes of adventurous policies. Kegley and Raymond seek a compromise between the two positions in Wallace's 1973 study, indicating that the relationship between alliances and wars is curvilinear: The magnitude and severity of war are at their peak when alliances are either extremely flexible or extremely rigid, while moderate polarization is associated with a moderate amount of war or no war. They suggest "alliance norms"—the degree to which alliance members have a known sense of obligation to honor treaty commitments—as a possible "missing piece" of the puzzle.[171]

Capability, Risk, and the Utility and Probability of War

Bruce Bueno de Mesquita has taken issue with a basic assumption of Realpolitik theorists—namely, that the probability of war involving specific key states depends on the distribution of power among those states.

The realists, as we have noted previously, are not entirely agreed among themselves concerning power distribution and war probability. Some think that peace is best assured when power is in equilibrium; others, when those states favoring a peaceful status quo possess a preponderance of power. Bueno de Mesquita casts doubt upon both the Kissinger view that an equal balance of power is a precondition of peace and lowers the probability of war between the two principal powers[172] and the hypothesis of Organski and Kugler that the probability of war among individual key states decreases as the inequality in the power distribution (or "power distance") increases.[173] Bueno de Mesquita similarly dismisses the comparable hypotheses of Zinnes et al. and Claude relating the low probability of war to equality or inequality in the distribution of power among coalitions of key states.[174]

Bueno de Mesquita concedes that the probability of achieving success in war is almost a certain function of relative power capabilities. If power is taken in its most comprehensive sense, this must be the case. The distribution of power, however, whether real or perceived, is not the only determinant of whether political decision-makers choose war or peace. In any conflict situation, individual decision-makers on both sides may assess differently the utility (or values) that attach to the possible outcomes of a given war (expanding, maintaining, or losing power for their state). Any given probability of success (expressed in rough percentages) may be sufficient for some leaders but not for others to undertake the risks of war.

Assuming that the probability of success in war does correlate highly with the power of one nation or coalition of nations relative to that of the adversary, and assuming further that whether leaders are risk-acceptant or risk-averse is independent of the actually prevailing power distribution, Bueno de Mesquita constructs nine hypothetical international systems with varying distributions of strong and weak states and varying risk-taking orientations among decision-makers. He analyzes each of the nine deductive models, covarying calculations of the probability of success, the actors' expected utility of war, and the actors' risk security levels. He also reviews Singer's Correlates of War Project, empirical studies flowing from it, and the theoretical debate (Deutsch and Singer versus Waltz).[175] He concludes that "no particular distribution of power has exclusive claim as a predictor of peace or war either in theory or in the empirical record of the period 1816–1965."[176] In his investigations, some systems marked by power predominance support Organski and Kugler; others, in which the probability of war decreases as the distribution of power approaches equality, lend weight to the Kissinger hypothesis. In short, the distribution of power alone, without reference to another crucial variable—the risk-taking propensity of individual decision-makers—"is not systematically associated with the incidence of war," and decision-makers who presume, perhaps too simplistically, that either a power equilibrium or a power predominance is essential to peace may be "acting on false, incomplete, and potentially lethal premises."[177] He laments the tendency of those who analyze war probability to focus almost exclusively on capability differentials and to neglect the factor of risk-taking orientation among governing leaders. The principal exception to this tendency, he adds significantly, is to be found in strategic analysts of deterrence, who pay a great deal of attention to the willingness of ruling elites to run great security risks of initiating war in the nuclear age. Unfortunately, he fails to elaborate on this extremely important exception. (Theories of deterrence will be examined in the next chapter.)

In three subsequent articles during the 1980s, Bueno de Mesquita (once in collaboration with David Lalman) continued to develop his "expected utility model" of international conflict. Assuming that the probability of escalation of a dispute increases monotonically with leaders' expectation of gain in comparison with the expected costs of conflict, he revised his earlier theory and discovered an improved statistical ability to discriminate between disputes that escalated to warfare and those that did not in Europe between 1816 and 1970. He showed that leaders, faced with a decisional problem of whether to challenge or not to challenge an adversary to alter his policies, estimate the relative utility of success and failure. Leaders who have adopted foreign policies that leave them near the extreme of their possible range of vulnerability are assumed to be more willing to accept risks than those who have diminished their vulnerability to external threats. "Differences in risk-taking propensities are viewed as the source of variations in actor perceptions."[178] De Mesquita and Lalman concluded that a continuous theory linking expected utility estimates to conflict escalation provides a powerful tool for the future analysis of international conflict both at the level of individual decision-makers and at the level of systemic action.[179]

John A. Vasquez has followed along the general lines of Bueno de Mesquita.[180] Both call attention to the "well-born" anomaly that appears in the findings of Singer and his colleagues—namely, that in the nineteenth century a low incidence of war was associated with the power-parity model, but in the twentieth with a predominant-power model. Vasquez rejects as unsatisfactory the explanation offered by the Singer group to explain the discrepancy—that diplomacy had been aristocratic in the earlier period and democratic in the later one. Aristocratic elites, who were agreed that modern war was becoming increasingly unprofitable for the state, found certainty in the balance of power known as the "Concert of Europe." In the democratic age, on the other hand, publics, interest groups, and influential decision-makers seem convinced that a preponderance of power is required to convince an adversary that war cannot be won. "Despite long-held realist beliefs to the contrary, the thrust of empirical analysis to date suggests that capability or differences of power are unrelated to the onset of war in any significant causal sense. Instead, it appears that capability and differences in power are related to the type of war that is fought and not to whether there will be peace or war."[181]

Vasquez constructs a typology in which he separates wars of rivalry from wars of opportunity. The former are waged between equals, and "are more oriented to the logic of the balance of power and prey to its deficiencies, such as mutual fear, suspicion and insecurity, arms races and preventive war."[182] Wars of opportunity are fought between unequals, when the stronger side perceives utility in starting a war. The contrasting logic of the two situations can become linked if a weak state manages to ally with one of two strong rival powers. Wars of rivalry are more likely than wars of opportunity to become total. Vasquez also distinguishes between dyadic wars and the general wars of the Great Powers "which grow out of wars that were initiated in the expectation that they would be limited" but which could not be confined to the initial parties. He finds expected utility theory less applicable to these complex wars than to dyadic wars. He concurs with Wallace and Bueno de Mesquita "that alliance-making that leads to polarization produces wars of the highest magnitude, severity and duration," although he is quick to add that the "reason for this is not fully explained in the literature."[183] In his very plausible explanation of the consequences of polarization, Vasquez shows convincingly that there are points where quantifying behaviorists and traditional scholars can find common ground in realistic deductive reasoning.[184]

Despite the proliferation of statistical studies of war (both inductive and deductive), none has been so definitive as to resolve the most significant problems. Most of them have been praised as efforts to cut new paths through the thicket, and some have been vested with a limited utility insofar as they have cast doubt upon or disconfirmed earlier assumptions or "pet" hypotheses concerning factors that make for war or peace. Although they deserve to be read and studied, if for no other reason than to illuminate the difficulty of the problem, within a few decades they are more likely to be relegated to footnotes rather than regarded as classics. All of them have been the target of criticism for their methodological deficiencies. Contradictions and anomalies appear in the findings of various scholars, and sometimes within the work of a single investigator. Even though many of them employ data on wars gathered and systemized by Pitirim Sorokin, Quincy Wright, and Singer and Small, they may interpret the data differently, use different classification (definitional) schemes, or select different universes of cases to test specific hypotheses. One persistent problem that plagues social scientists in statistical correlation and regression analysis was identified in the late nineteenth century by a pioneer in the field of statistical analysis—the English mathematician Sir Francis Galton, who worked in genetics, psychometrics, and anthropology. Galton warned that in any effort to correlate two variables, it is important to be sure that they are not both dependent upon a third factor, of which the investigator is unaware, in which case what may seem to be a significant correlation is spurious.[185] This is not to suggest that those who have attempted to build theory based on work such as the Correlates of War have not been aware of the fact that a given correlation may be spurious or that it does not automatically assume a causal relationship, for such an understanding is one of the first things taught in elementary statistics courses.

"If the scientific study of war is to be vindicated," says John A. Vasquez, "it will have to produce a set of empirical generalizations for which it has adduced new evidence and which, at least in some cases, reveal relationships previously not recognized."[186] Vasquez agrees up to a point with Kenneth Waltz's observation that knowledge is not produced simply by accumulating ever greater amounts of information.[187] (As early as the seventeenth century, Sir Francis Bacon realized that science is an instrument of inquiry, not a mere collection of data.[188]) Vasquez remarks that the expansion of the data base makes the need for an informing, guiding theory all the more necessary if we are to order and analyze the multitude of available information and to understand the causality of the war phenomenon. Robert C. North and Matthew Willard make sense when they call attention to the "convergence effect:"

> With varying degrees of directness and indirectness, remoteness and proximity, a great many diverse actors, interactive relationships, and associated factors *on different levels* of aggregation and organization may contribute to an outbreak of war or other event that needs explanation. Wars and other major international events may be seen, in short, as outcomes of "horizontal" or "vertical" phenomena converging from many different "directions."[189]

Quincy Wright, who devoted much of his life to studying and thinking about war, was carried to an extreme conclusion, mentioned earlier and worth repeating: "A war, in reality, results from a total situation involving ultimately almost everything that has happened to the human race up to the time the war begins."[190] Yet the purpose of theory, we are reminded, is to isolate those variables most able to explain as broad a range of phenomena as possible and thus to contribute to an understanding of war. Profundity does not lie in the compilation of ever-longer lists of possible causal factors, but instead in the creation of theories based upon parsimony, shortening the list of variables to emphasize those having broad explanatory power.

THE TERMINATION OF WAR

One of the most obvious explanations why wars come to an end is that one side clearly defeats the other. If the struggle is protracted, however, and there is no decisive victory for either party, governments find themselves under pressure to respond to the growing exhaustion of their people. The war fever that characterizes the period immediately prior to and following the outbreak of war begins to subside as the enemy proves stronger than anticipated and as battle casualties mount; war fever is replaced by war weariness and a growing desire for a negotiated peace.[191]

According to Lewis A. Coser, the final decision to end a conflict rests more with the loser than with the winner. Magnanimity on the part of the potential victor helps to make it easier for the vanquished to submit, but until the latter is willing to acknowledge defeat at least to itself, the struggle goes on. Sometimes the vanquished do not realize that they have been defeated, especially when unambiguous symbolic clues (such as the capture of a capital city) are not present and the contestants have no agreed norms for assessing their respective power positions in the struggle. In such cases, termination can be a very complex process. The leadership of the losing side may be willing to enter into peace negotiations but not acknowledge defeat, and it will try to manage the symbols in order to conceal the extent of the defeat.[192] Iran was long reluctant to agree to a truce in its war with Iraq and insisted that the blame for starting the war be levied against the latter.

William T. R. Fox once lamented that international relations theorists have focused on how to deter war while tending to ignore how to control, limit, deescalate, and terminate war once it has started.[193] Fox attributed this to the fear among scholars that they might appear to confer legitimacy upon "limited wars," thus increasing the probability of their reoccurring; to a lack of interest among military strategists in the problem of the rational political control of wartime violence; and to the traditional American approach to war, which under the presumed conditions of the nuclear age led to large-scale, protracted limited war in Korea and Vietnam. Fox described the internal and external structure of the Vietnam stalemate: Internally, American opinion was polarized between "peace with honor" and "peace at any price" with the result that the government was paralyzed:

> One need not summon up the image of an anthropomorphic, monster superpower on the edge of a nervous breakdown for the analogy of approach-avoidance to have relevance. In an atmosphere of polarized immoderation—with one group calling for early termination by victory, whatever the escalation necessary, however great the cost, and however evil the byproduct in domestic and world political consequences; and a second group calling for early termination, whatever the sacrifices of war aims necessary, however humiliating the frustration and failure, and however disastrous the events which follow abandonment of the struggle—resolute pursuit of some middle way may command wholly insufficient domestic political support; it matters not how rational the in-between, moderate policy may appear in cost-benefit terms. Paradoxically, the more urgent the demands for termination by groups with diametrically opposed programs for termination, the less may be the chance of a policy commanding sufficient domestic support which would in fact end the war.[194]

Externally, the meshing of strategies by the two parties made for stalemate. The superpower was anxious to wind down the fighting both for domestic and international political reasons, whereas the small-power belligerent was determined to outwait the opponent. It takes two to make peace, unless one side is willing to accept the ignominy of unconditional surrender or withdrawal. Since North Vietnam had the resources to continue the struggle, and believed that the longer the war dragged on, the better the peace terms it could extract, it adopted a policy of "no peace just yet." Fox concludes that it is not easy to combine the objectives of minimizing costs, optimizing gains, and achieving early termination:

> It thus appears in the case of limited war that for the turn toward negotiated peace to lead to peace, enough force must still be applied to keep the military situation stable. Political control over the use of that force must be carefully exercised, however, to insure that the force not be used in ways which destroy the credibility of the peace overture.[195]

Least-cost, highest-run, earliest-termination strategies call for a continuing calculus. On any reasonable estimate, sacrifices still to be endured must not appear disproportionate to gains still to be realized. This triple objective also calls for an open negotiating stance. Only the least possible may be required of the opponent if one is determined to attract an adversary to the bargaining table.[196]

THE DECISION TO ESCALATE

A special word is in order about the problem of escalation and the difficulty of controlling it. The term *escalation* did not appear in military literature much before 1960. The concept, however, was undoubtedly understood. Many of the wars of which we have historical knowledge were waged with some restraint. Even though World War II was a "total war," the contestants held back from using gas weapons on the battlefield, perhaps out of humanitarian considerations but, probably more importantly, because of the fear of retaliation.

Richard Smoke has written a definitive work in which he sums up and analyzes the earlier writing on escalation, and presents seven case studies of prenuclear-age wars in which efforts to control the action-reaction cycle succeeded or failed.[197] Smoke does not regard the escalation process as a very large number of small, graduated, almost imperceptible steps, which could be plotted as a homogeneous, continuous curve. Following Thomas C. Schelling, he treats escalation as a step, resulting from a calculated decision, that crosses a salient threshold objectively noticeable to all parties concerned, and that thus expands or contracts the general pattern of perceived limits of conflict. Not every increment of military force amounts to escalation. The concept of saliency is crucial (e.g., extending hostilities beyond a national boundary that had marked a limit in earlier stages of the conflict, or crossing the dividing line between conventional and nuclear weapons). The act of escalation represents an effort or a tacit proposal to set new ground rules. The decision-maker who escalates hopes that the new limits will stick, but an element of uncertainty is involved, since the escalation might spark an open-ended action-reaction cycle.[198]

Both the effort to establish stable limits to a conflict and the carrying out of controlled escalations are bargaining processes. Whether the escalation can be kept under control depends not only upon its immediate military consequences, but also upon the framework of the conflict. "One of the ways in which escalation gets out of control—one that is not always apparent—is a seemingly careful step that activates some nation's previously latent motive or interest."[199] Asymmetries in capabilities, motivations, and interests may produce a similar effect. The failure of decision-makers in one country to assess how the world looks to adversary decision-makers can lead to serious conceptual failures and the loss of escalation control. In his conclusions, Smoke deals at length with the interplay between objective political-military factors and the subjective perceptions of decision-makers—perceptions of present and future reality.

Smoke describes the complex problem of cognitive consistency that decision-makers encounter in trying to control escalation dynamics. Human beings in difficult and threatening situations try harder to preserve their own cognitive consistency when confronted with new information, and this makes them reluctant to modify their constructs of reality. In an environment of rising stakes and surprises, both of which may contribute to stress and anxiety, decision-makers feel pressures from three directions:

1. self-reinforcement—the need to prove that their earlier perceptions, assessments, and decisions were correct;
2. cross-reinforcement—resulting from the hostile action-reaction cycle; and
3. the tendency to simplify reality—which stems from deepening feelings of anxiety and threat, as well as from fatigue and the stress of information overload.

As escalation continues, decision-makers' subjective universes of perceptions and images become steadily narrower. The range of expectations tightens; fewer and fewer possibilities seem plausible. Policymakers begin to feel that the future is closing in on them. . . . The subjective future closes in faster than one anticipates it should because it is closing in for psychological, not just objective reasons.[200]

But in the final analysis, escalation can be controlled, and was in fact controlled in three of the seven cases Smoke studied. He deems it important, however, that an initial image of stable limits be established at the very beginning of the war, which is always a dramatic and dangerous event. If stability in the initial limits can lower the uncertainty, subsequent escalations, even major ones, are possible, and can be perceived as modifications of the basic pattern of a conflict under control.[201]

The Causes and Control of War

It is clear from the foregoing that there is no single explanation of what causes wars. Macrocosmic theorists have traced the origins of war in general or specific modern wars to a great variety of factors. These include

- nationalist rivalry, aggravated perhaps by ethnic-linguistic, religious, or ideological differences, combined with historical memories of hostility and conflict;
- capitalist imperialism;
- the existence or absence of alliances;
- the dynamics of military technology and of arms races driven by the interests of military-industrial complexes;
- the balance-of-power policy;
- conflict over territory deemed crucial to the security of two or more states;
- the domestic insecurity of ruling elites, leading to an effort to solidify their own position and restore internal unity by diverting domestic discontents to foreign targets;
- intervention in an internal conflict by rival foreign powers;
- ethnocentrism and the communications warp, with the mass media stirring chauvinistic and xenophobic attitudes inside countries while inadequate communication between countries leads to misunderstanding of goals, intentions, and policies, such that defensive moves appear to be aggressive threats;
- the absence of effective international peacekeeping machinery, resulting in the condition known as "international anarchy";
- the dialectic of international crisis; and
- the inability of people to devise what William James called the "moral equivalent of war" or to escape from the tendency, as Gordon Allport put it, to institutionalize the expectation of war.

The list could be extended, but it is already sufficiently impressive.

The pluralism of causes is reflected, as one would expect, in the plurality of remedies suggested for resolving international conflicts and eliminating war. Efforts have been put forth in every age, and have been greatly intensified in the nuclear age, to find nonviolent ways of conflict resolution. Our discussion of the problem of war would not be complete without reference to these efforts.

Historically, the members of the international system have not been involved in constant warfare. Even though states have usually retained a disposition to resort to force if necessary to protect their interests, and even though war could almost always be found being waged somewhere within the system, most states have lived at peace most of the time—many of them for prolonged periods. Conflicts of interest are forever arising, but states have traditionally had at their disposal, especially since the middle of the last century, a wide spectrum of instruments for settling disputes peaceably.

These means included diplomatic negotiation, resort to "good offices," mediation or conciliation by third parties, arbitration according to agreed rules, adjudication under recognized rules of international law, the application of diplomatic or economic sanctions (such as recall of an envoy, severance of diplomatic relations, or trade embargo), and the show or threat of force (e.g., a display of naval power) designed to make its actual use unnecessary. But war always remained the *ultima ratio* of foreign policy. As William D. Coplin has observed, all of the instruments of leverage available to governments for international bargaining purposes along the continuum from negotiation to war depended in the final analysis upon the relative distribution of war-waging capabilities among states.[202] Moreover, international law itself confirmed the acceptability and legality of war as a normal tool with which a state could vindicate a violation of its rights after peaceful remedies had been exhausted to no avail. This assumption concerning the legal permissibility of a state to initiate offensive warfare under certain circumstances began to be questioned only in this century, as efforts were made to prohibit the nondefensive use of force by states through adopting new legal norms or to deter such use of force through the collective action of states in international organizations.[203]

Both international law and international organization have played an integrating function within the global system, and have proven their utility in the peaceful settlement of disputes when the states involved, especially more powerful states, have favored such settlement. International law is generally regarded as "true law," but it is acknowledged to be weak law because it is often vague in content, because it lacks authoritative bodies for lawmaking and law enforcement, and because actors regard themselves as bound only by those rules to which they have given their consent and only in cases they have agreed to submit for adjudication. States normally prefer to conform to international legal norms because they find it in their interest to do so and to maintain their reputation as law-abiding members of international society; but when their vital interests are at stake, they are usually reluctant to accept a judicial judgment unless compelled to do so by political, economic, or military *force majeure.*[204]

Aside from the traditional reluctance of sovereign states to accept international law as binding upon them (except when they perceive it to be in their interest to do so), note should be taken of two additional and serious difficulties that continue to plague international law in the closing quarter of the century. Largely a product of Western culture and the Western state system, international law in both its form and content has been roundly criticized, and at least partially rejected, by Marxists who view it as the legal instrument of capitalist imperialism and by non-Western excolonial peoples who regard it as part of a culturally alien and economically oppressive system from which they seek liberation. Elites in both types of society place heavy emphasis upon such concepts as self-determination, nonintervention, resistance to all "infringements upon sovereignty," the invalidity of "unequal treaties" imposed during the period of colonial imperialism, and the right to expropriate foreign investments without satisfactory compensation under the traditional "international standard." Yet most communist and many non-Western states, while remaining opposed or extremely cool to the cultural, philosophical, and economic assumptions of traditional Western international law, manage to tolerate and accommodate themselves to selected aspects of that law that meet their needs, even though they may remain determined gradually to replace its "Western" and "capitalist" elements with "non-Western" and "socialist" values.[205]

As to the degree of international legal consensus that now exists, extremist views are to be avoided. Oscar J. Lissitzyn has given a fair assessment:

> The absolute dichotomy between the presence and absence of worldwide agreement on values is false. In the world community, as in national societies, there is a broad spectrum of values and of degrees of consensus on them. A large measure of agreement on values does, of course, strengthen the cohesiveness of a community and the efficacy of its legal order. But it is not a question of all or nothing.
>
> A black-and-white contrast between a world in which common ideological values prevail and in which peace rests securely on one hand, and a world in which lawlessness and naked force rule, on the other, is out of place here. These are but nonexistent extremes of a continuum in which, as history suggests, international law will play varying roles in different periods.[206]

It is too pessimistic to say that there can be no substantial development of international law before the world achieves a homogenization of cultural, ethical, and political values. If that is ever to be achieved, it may lie in the distant future. During the past few decades, some modest progress has been made in the development, by negotiated convention, of international law in specific areas—the law of diplomatic relations, of the seas, of outer space, of treaties, and so forth. Many of the issues over which cultural and ideological disagreement prevail pertain to the divergence of interests between industrialized and less developed countries, or between Marxist and market-economy systems. The inability of the global system to arrive at a consensus over questions of violent conflict (such as the definition of aggression or the best way to deal with terrorism) reflects the cultural and ideological divisions of the world, as well as sharply divergent attitudes over the utility of violence as a method of settling conflicts. But as technological developments make interstate military violence increasingly costly and dangerous, both economically and politically, it is possible that states might strive to rise above cultural and ideological differences for the purpose of controlling and limiting socially destructive violence at the interstate level.

The United Nations has made a significant contribution to international universalist integration in many functional dimensions—intellectual, economic, social, cultural, legal-diplomatic, and political. On occasion it has succeeded, through timely debate, education, conciliation, or coordinating international military intervention, in contributing toward the localization, containment, postponement, termination, or resolution of some international conflicts under conditions conducive to the successes of "preventive diplomacy."[207] United Nations peacekeeping forces consisting of units assembled from middle and smaller powers have played a useful role at times in a number of conflicts.[208] Throughout most of its history, however, the United Nations has not proved effective for handling international disputes involving the vital interests of one or more of the major powers.[209] As the decade of the 1980s neared its end, there were some indications—most notably in the termination of the Gulf War between Iran and Iraq and conflicts in southern Africa, Cyprus, Afghanistan, and elsewhere—that the five permanent members of the Security Council are capable on occasion of perceiving a mutual interest in controlling a conflict of high danger potential and, to that end, moving at least tacitly to revive the unanimity principle on which the charter was originally assumed to be founded.

The terms *conflict resolution* and *peace research* have come to encompass studies in functional integration, international economic development, the formation of national attitudes, cross-cultural understanding, the language of conflict, the social structure of conflict, distinctions between various forms of violence (physical and psychological, personal and structural, manifest and latent, etc.), the uses of game theory and simulation, theories of arms races and the causation of war, the psychology of leaders, the study of images and perceptions, the behavior of decision-makers under conditions of crisis, and so on.[210]

Conflict resolution theorists stress the importance of scientifically analyzing the structure, the parties, and the issues in conflict.[211] Accurate analysis itself, they believe, can contribute toward a resolution of conflict. Conflict can be conceptualized in terms of social organization and structure, patterns of interaction (e.g., escalation and deescalation), modes of violence employed, the values of the parties in conflict (both the values declared and the values actually pursued), changes in the hierarchy of values in the midst of conflict, the tendency for the range of threatened values to become more specific or more diffuse, the degree of incompatibility of goals, the genesis of conflict, the evaluation of symmetric and asymmetric perceptions among the conflict parties, symmetries as to power potential and loyalties, and the way in which the conflict is terminated.[212] Roger Fisher several years ago suggested that conflict might best be handled by "fractionating" it—that is, separating conflict issues into their smallest components and dealing with them one at a time to reduce the risks of war.[213] (See the discussion of Fisher's later work below.)

John W. Burton advanced the view in 1972 that conflict should be looked upon as essentially subjective, in contrast to the older view that it is objective—a view, he says, that is based on an assumption deeply ingrained in political thought, that there is a fixed amount of satisfaction to be shared in a given situation, and that what A gains B must lose.[214] The difference between the zero-sum game and the non-zero-sum game is a subject that has evoked a considerable literature in international relations, strategy, and bargaining. (See Chapter 12.) Burton argues that a conflict that at first sight appears to be waged over "objective" differences of interest can be transformed into one with a positive outcome for the combative parties once they "reperceive" each other and discover opportunities for peaceful functional cooperation from which they will both benefit. Those who would mediate in a conflict must help the parties to change their goals, as the risks and costs of trying to attain their original goals through conflict are seen to rise.[215] Since political conflicts usually have different parties at different levels of organization, agreements reached at government levels will not necessarily solve conflicts at localized levels of organization. Burton is convinced that mediators, instead of presenting their own plan to resolve the conflict, should draw the solution from the parties themselves. Moreover, he says, parties to a dispute should not be expected to compromise, because compromise settlements often leave the underlying conflict issues unresolved and both parties basically discontented. Conflict resolution, says Burton, should be a problem-solving rather than a bargaining exercise.[216]

More recently, Roger Fisher and William Ury have developed what they call a new method of *principled negotiation* that eschews the familiar haggling contest of wills that usually characterizes bargaining. They urge negotiators to abandon the customary pattern in which each side successively takes a sequence of positions, either "standing firm" or offering calculated concessions (often based on preplanned "fallback" decisions) to demonstrate how reasonable they are. Instead of "positional bargaining," they favor the resolution of conflict issues on their merits. This means evaluating the genuine interests of the parties according to objective criteria. Such an approach, they argue, is much more likely to avoid bitter recriminations and produce a "wise agreement," which they define as "one which meets the legitimate interest of each side to the extent possible, resolves conflicting interests fairly, is durable, and takes community interests into account."[217] This is much better than arguing stubbornly in defense of fixed positions, they say, because the latter process is inefficient, generates ill will, and normally leads to unsatisfactory, short-lived agreements.

If several parties are involved, write these two leaders of the Harvard Negotiation Project, positional bargaining may render agreement impossible to achieve. In two-sided negotiations, if one party is "soft"—reasonable, flexible, and obviously anxious to reach agreement—while the other is a "hard bargainer," who makes demands and threats, one can readily predict who would lose and who would gain from the process. Fisher and

Ury offer these points of advice: (1) In order to rise above emotionalism and deal with the merits, separate the people from the problem. (2) Focus on interests, not positions. (3) Instead of seeking "victory" and searching for the one right solution, invent a variety of options for the mutual gain of all. (4) Insist on the use of objective criteria to ensure a fair outcome. (5) Learn ways of coping with opponents who are more powerful, who refuse to play according to the rules of decent behavior, or who resort to "dirty tricks."[218] Many traditional negotiators, of course, would say that experienced practitioners have long been familiar with these maxims, implicitly if not explicitly, and that they are not totally incompatible with positional bargaining.

In conclusion, all theories that look to the entire elimination of war from human affairs presuppose profound changes in the behavior of large collectivities. All proposed changes are based, either implicitly or explicitly, on assumptions with regard to the causes of war. Inasmuch as social scientists cannot agree on the causes of war, it is not surprising that there is no consensus concerning the foundations on which humanity can build a genuine, durable peace.

NOTES

1. See Georg Simmel, *Conflict,* trans. Kurt H. Wolff, in *Conflict and the Web of Group-Affiliations* (New York: The Free Press, 1964), pp. 15–38; Jesse Bernard, "Parties and Issues in Conflict," *Journal of Conflict Resolution,* I (March 1957); and Ralf Dahrendorf, "Toward a Theory of Social Conflict," trans. Anatol Rapoport, ibid., II (June 1958). Dahrendorf, a German sociologist, argues that when certain social-structural arrangements are given, conflict is bound to arise. He traces the responsibility for the shift of emphasis within the field of sociology from social conflict to social stability to Talcott Parsons and his structural-functional approach to the study of society. (For a discussion of the work of Parsons and structural-functionalism, see Chapter 4.) This approach contains the following implicit postulates: (1) Every society is a relatively persisting configuration of elements. (2) Every society is a well-integrated configuration of elements. (3) Every element in a society contributes to its functioning. (4) Every society rests on the consensus of its members. Dahrendorf believes that this social equilibrium conception of society is not compatible with the serious study of conflict. The foregoing postulates not only fail to explain change and conflict, but they exclude these phenomena altogether. When confronted with instances of conflict, the "structural-functional" school treats them as abnormal, deviant, and pathological. In contrast to the "structural-functional" theory, Dahrendorf offers four different postulates: (1) Every society is subjected at every moment to change; change is ubiquitous. (2) Every society experiences at every moment social conflict; conflict is ubiquitous. (3) Every element in a society contributes to its change. (4) Every society rests on constraint of some of its members by others. Dahrendorf's postulates are not presented to replace the Parsonian view, but rather to complement it. The two organic models together, he suggests, would exhaust social reality, and a syn-

thesis of the two would supply us with a complete theory of society in both its enduring and its changing aspects. Dahrendorf, op. cit., esp. pp. 173–175.

2. Georg Simmel, op. cit., pp. 16–20.

3. Lewis A. Coser, *The Functions of Social Conflict* (Glencoe, Ill.: Free Press, 1964), p. 8. Western theorists as far apart in their fundamental premises as Saint Augustine and Karl Marx regarded conflict as the motor of social change. See Robert A. Nisbet, *Social Change and History: Aspects of the Western Theory of Development* (New York: Oxford University Press, 1969), pp. 76–90.

4. William Graham Sumner, *War and Other Essays* (New Haven: Yale University Press, 1911), excerpted in Leon Bramson and George W. Goethals, eds., *War: Studies from Psychology, Sociology, Anthropology,* rev. ed. (New York: Basic Books, 1968), pp. 210–212.

5. William James, "The Moral Equivalent of War," ibid., p. 23.

6. Richard N. Rosecrance, *Action and Reaction in World Politics* (Boston: Little, Brown, 1963), pp. 255, 304–305.

7. Clyde Kluckhohn, *Mirror for Man: A Survey of Human Behavior and Social Attitudes* (Greenwich, Conn.: Fawcett World Library, 1960), p. 173. See also Stephen Withey and Daniel Katz, "The Social Psychology of Human Conflict," in Elton B. McNeil, ed., *The Nature of Human Conflict* (Englewood Cliffs, N.J.: Prentice-Hall, 1965), p. 81; and Nicholas S. Timasheff, *War and Revolution* (New York: Sheed and Ward, 1965), ch. 5.

8. Robert F. Murphy, "Intergroup Hostility and Social Cohesion," reprinted from *American Anthropologist,* LIX, No. 6 (1957), 1018–1035, in J. K. Zawodny, ed., *Man and International Relations* (San Francisco: Chandler, 1966), pp. 602–603. R. F. Maher has reached a similar conclusion from his study of tribes in New Guinea. See Robert A. LeVine, "Socialization, Social Structure and Intersocietal Images," in H. C. Kelman, ed., *International Behavior: A Sociological Analysis* (New York: Holt, Rinehart and Winston, 1965), p. 47. For the case of the Teton Indians, supporting a comparable hypothesis in an obverse form, see Elton B. McNeil, "The Nature of Aggression," in McNeil, ed., op. cit., p. 37.

9. Georg Simmel, op. cit., p. 93. See also pp. 88–89. M. Mulder and A. Stemerding have shown that a group faced with a threat becomes cohesive and highly tolerant of strong leadership. "Threat, Attraction to Group, and Need for Strong Leadership," *Human Relations,* XVI (1963), 317–334.

10. Geoffrey Blainey, *The Causes of War* (New York: The Free Press, 1973), pp. 71–86. A third edition of this work was published in 1988.

11. Rudolph J. Rummel, "Dimensions of Conflict Behavior Within and Between Nations," *General Systems Yearbook,* VIII (1963), 24. See also by the same author, "Testing Some Possible Predictors of Conflict Behavior Within and Between Nations," *Peace Research Society, Papers 1, Chicago Conference,* (Philadelphia: University of Pennsylvania, 1963).

12. Raymond Tanter, "Dimensions of Conflict Behavior Within and Between Nations, 1958–1960," *Journal of Conflict Resolution,* X (March 1966), 65–73.

13. Raymond Tanter, "International War and Domestic Turmoil: Some Contemporary Evidence," in *Violence in America: Historical and Comparative Perspectives,* A Report to the National Commission on the Causes and Prevention of Violence, June 1969, prepared under the direction of Hugh Davis Graham and Ted Robert Gurr (New York: New American Library, 1969); Jonathan Wilkenfeld, "Domestic and Foreign Conflict Behavior of Nations," in William D. Coplin and Charles W. Kegley, Jr., eds., *Analyzing International Relations:*

A Multimethod Introduction (New York: Praeger, 1975), pp. 96–112, quoted on p. 96. Cf. also Philip M. Gregg and Arthur S. Banks, "Dimensions of Political System: Factor Analysis of a Cross-Polity Survey," *American Political Science Review,* LIX (September 1965), 602–614. See also Karen Rasler, "War, Accommodation and Violence in the United States, 1890–1970," *American Political Science Review,* 80 (September 1986); Ole R. Holsti and James N. Rosenau, *American Leadership in World Affairs: Vietnam and the Breakdown of Consensus* (Winchester, Mass.: George Allen & Unwin, 1984).

14. See Herbert S. Dinerstein, "The Transformation of Alliance Systems," *American Political Science Review,* LIX (September 1965), 589–601. Emile Benoit says that membership in a common defense alliance against an agreed potential aggressor is a powerful integrating factor, and "the reduced fear of such external aggression seems to have been a major factor in slowing down the European Economic Community . . . not only weakening the international alliance, but encouraging conflicts, internal dissidence, and secessionist movements within individual countries." "Kenneth Boulding as Socio-Political Theorist," *Journal of Conflict Resolution,* XXI (September 1977), 557.

15. Jacek Kugler and William Domke, "Comparing the Strength of Nations," *Comparative Political Studies,* 19 (April 1986), 66.

16. Clyde Kluckhohn, op. cit., p. 48. According to Alexander Lesser, the concept of war does not appear among Andaman Islanders, aboriginal Australians, Mission Indians, Arunta, Western Shishoni, Semang, and Todas. "War and the State," in Morton Fried et al., *War: The Anthropology of Armed Conflict and Aggression* (Garden City, N.Y.: Natural History Press, 1968), p. 94. In contrast, the Yanomamo who live along the Orinoco River in Venezuela and Brazil believe that humans are inherently fierce and warlike. Their entire culture is geared to the development of belligerence—threats, shouting, duels, wife-beating, a strong preference for male children, and encouraging the young to strike their elders. Napoleon A. Chagnon, "Yanomamo Social Organization and Warfare," ibid., pp. 109–159, esp. pp. 124–133.

17. Lewis F. Richardson showed that between 1820 and 1945, the number of foreign wars with more than 7000 war dead correlated with the number of bordering neighbors for 33 countries studied. *Statistics of Deadly Quarrels* (Pittsburgh, Pa.: Boxwood Press, 1960), p. 176. See also James Paul Wesley, "Frequency of Wars and Geographical Opportunity," *Journal of Conflict Resolution,* 6 (September 1962).

18. See Robert Redfield, "Primitive Law," in Paul Bohannan, ed., *Law and Warfare: Studies in the Anthropology of Conflict,* American Museum Sourcebooks in Anthropology (Garden City, N.Y.: Natural History Press, 1967), pp. 3–24.

19. Andrew P. Vayda, "Hypotheses About Functions of War," in Morton Fried et al., op. cit., pp. 85–89. According to J. P. Johansen, the Maoris of New Zealand sometimes resolved intragroup tensions by having a member of the tribe commit an act of violence against another tribe, thereby provoking a retaliation which would reestablish group unity. Cited by Andrew P. Vayda, "Maori Warfare," in Paul Bohannan, ed., op. cit., p. 380.

20. See, for example, Kaj Birket-Smith, *Primitive Man and His Ways* (New York: New American Library, 1963), pp. 67 and 195.

21. Anthony F. C. Wallace has observed that for the Iroquois the symbolically arousing stimulus that preceded mobilization for war was a report that a kinsman had been slain and a survivor was calling for revenge. "Psychological

Preparations for War," in Robert F. Murphy et al., eds., *Selected Papers from The American Anthropologist 1946–1970* (Washington, DC: American Anthropological Association, 1976), pp. 175–176.

22. Andrew P. Vayda, op. cit., pp. 89–91.

23. Andrew P. Vayda, "Primitive Warfare," in D. Sills, ed., *International Encyclopedia of the Social Sciences*, XVI, p. 468.

24. Bronislaw Malinowski, "An Anthropological Analysis of War," in Bramson and Goethals, eds., op. cit., p. 209.

25. Margaret Mead, "Warfare Is Only an Invention, Not a Biological Necessity," ibid., pp. 269–274.

26. William Graham Sumner, "War," reprinted from *War and Other Essays* (1911), ibid., p. 209.

27. Bronislaw Malinowski, op. cit., pp. 255 and 260.

28. Ibid., p. 260.

29. David Bidney, *Theoretical Anthropology* (New York: Schocken, 1967), pp. 231–232 and 361–362.

30. Margaret Mead and Rhoda Metraux, "The Anthropology of Human Conflict," in McNeil, ed., op. cit., p. 122.

31. Ibid., p. 128.

32. Clyde Kluckhohn, op. cit., p. 213.

33. Alex Inkeles, "National Character and Modern Political Systems," in Francis L. Hsu, ed., *Psychological Anthropology* (Homewood, Ill.: Dorsey, 1961), pp. 171–202.

34. See, for example, Margaret G. Hermann and Thomas W. Milburn, *A Psychological Examination of Political Leaders* (New York: The Free Press, 1977).

35. David E. Stannard denounced the psychoanalytic approach to history for overstressing childhood experience and failing to pass empirical tests. *Shrinking History: On Freud and the Failure of Psychohistory* (New York: Oxford University Press, 1980). Rudolph Binion, in a review of that work, defended psychohistory as "a discipline in its own right, independent of the Freudianism from which it is derived." *American Historical Review* (April 1981), 70.

36. Otto Klineberg, *The Human Dimension in International Relations* (New York: Holt, Rinehart and Winston, 1964) p. 95.

37. See Lewis Mumford, *Technics and Civilization* (New York: Harcourt Brace Jovanovich, 1934); J. F. C. Fuller, *Armament and History: A Study of the Influence of Armament on History From the Dawn of Classical Warfare to the Second World War* (London: Eyre & Spottiswoode, 1945); William F. Ogburn, ed., *Technology and International Relations* (Chicago: University of Chicago Press, 1949); John U. Nef, *War and Human Progress* (Cambridge, Mass.: Harvard University Press, 1950; New York: Norton, 1968); Bernard Brodie and Fawn Brodie, *From Cross-bow to H-bomb* (New York: Dell, 1962).

38. See, for example, Paul R. Brass, ed., *Ethnic Groups and the State* (Totowa, N.J.: Barnes and Noble, 1985). One should not overlook the fact that those multiethnic societies that are most violence-prone are usually characterized by perceived and objectively measurable political and economic inequality. See Christopher Hewitt, "Majorities and Minorities: A Comparative Survey of Ethnic Violence," *Annals of the American Academy of Political and Social Sciences*, No. 433 (September 1977), 150–160. For an explanation as to why Scottish, Quebecois, and Basque ethnonationalist movements have not enjoyed striking success, see Edward A. Tiryakian and Ronald Rogowski,

eds., *New Nationalisms of the Developed West* (Boston: Allen & Unwin, 1985).

39. Georg Simmel, op. cit., pp. 43–48; Lewis Coser, op. cit., pp. 67–72. See reference to Jesse Bernard in Note 1 supra.

40. Edward Luttwak, *Coup d'Etat: A Political Handbook* (Harmondsworth, England: Penguin, 1969); William G. Andrews and Uri Ra'anan, eds., *The Politics of the Coup d'Etat* (Princeton, N.J.: Van Nostrand, 1969); Morris, *Military Institutions and Coercion in the Developing Nations* (Chicago: University of Chicago Press, 1977); Amos Perlmutter and Gavin Kennedy, *The Military in the Third World* (New York: Charles Scribner's Sons, 1974); *The Military and Politics in Modern Times* (New Haven: Yale University Press, 1977); Robert W. Jackson et al., "Explaining African Coups d'Etat," *American Political Science Review,* 80 (March 1986).

41. Mark N. Hagopian, *The Phenomenon of Revolution* (New York: Dodd, Mead, 1974), p. 1, See ch. 1, "What Revolution Is Not." Other works worth consulting include Chalmers Johnson, *Revolutionary Change* (Boston: Little, Brown, 1966); Carl Leiden and Karl M. Schmitt, *The Politics of Violence: Revolution in the Modern World* (Englewood Cliffs: N.J.: Prentice-Hall, 1968); Peter Calvert, *Revolution* (New York: Praeger, 1970); Jacques Ellul, *Autopsy of Revolution* (New York: Knopf, 1971); James C. Davies, ed., *When Men Revolt and Why* (New York: The Free Press, 1971); John Dunn, *Modern Revolutions—An Introduction to the Analysis of a Political Phenomenon* (Cambridge: Cambridge University Press, 1972); Thomas H. Greene, *Comparative Revolutionary Movements* (Englewood Cliffs: N.J.: Prentice-Hall, 1974); A. S. Cohan, *Theories of Revolution* (London: Nelson, 1975); David Wilkinson, *Revolutionary Civil War* (Palo Alto, Calif.: Page-Ficklin, 1975); Mostafa Rejai, *The Comparative Study of Revolutionary Strategy* (New York: McKay, 1977); Anthony Burton, *Revolutionary Violence: The Theories* (New York: Crane, Russak, 1978); Peter Calvert, *Revolution and International Politics* (New York: St. Martin's Press, 1984).

42. Hannah Arendt, *On Revolution* (New York: Viking, 1965). See also Robert Blakey and Clifford Paynton, *Revolution and the Revolutionary Ideal* (Cambridge, Mass.: Schenkman, 1976); James Billington, *Fire in the Minds of Men: Origins of the Revolutionary Faith* (New York: Basic Books, 1980).

43. Frank E. Manuel, "Toward a Psychological History of Utopias," *Daedalus,* XCIV (Spring 1965), especially pp. 303–309; Karl Mannhein, *Ideology and Utopia: An Introduction to the Sociology of Knowledge* (New York: Harcourt Brace Jovanovich-Harvest Books, 1964); Melvin Lasky, *Utopia and Revolution* (Chicago: University of Chicago Press, 1976).

44. James H. Meisel, *Counterrevolution: How Revolutions Die* (New York: Atherton, 1966), pp. 3–16, 209–220. Peter A. R. Calvert warned against the assumption that there is an intrinsic correlation between revolution and significant social change. "Revolution: The Politics of Violence," *Political Studies,* V (February 1967), 3. Cf. also N. K. O'Sullivan, *Revolutionary Theory and Political Reality* (New York: St. Martin's Press, 1984); Seymour Martin Lipset, *Revolution and Counterrevolution: Change and Persistence in Social Structure,* rev. ed. (New Brunswick, N.J.: Transaction Books, 1987).

45. John Roberts, *Revolution and Improvement: The Western World, 1775–1847* (Berkeley: University of California Press, 1975), pp. 271–272.

46. See Crane Brinton, *Anatomy of Revolution* (New York: Norton, 1938). The praise came from James C. Davies, "The Circumstances and Causes of Revolution: A Review," *Journal of Conflict Resolution,* XI (June 1967), 248. For the other pre-World War II theories of revolution, see Lyford P. Edward, *The Natural History of Revolution* (Chicago: University of Chicago Press, 1927), and George Pettee, *The Process of Revolution* (New York: Harper & Row, 1938).

47. Ted Robert Gurr, "Psychological Factors in Civil Violence," *World Politics,* XX (January 1968), 252–253. He identified the frustration-aggression mechanism as "the primary source of the human capacity for violence," in *Why Men Rebel* (Princeton: Princeton University Press, 1970), p. 36, and noted that revolutions occur when discontents have been politicized. Ibid., p. 12.

48. James C. Davies, "Toward a Theory of Revolution," *American Sociological Review,* XXVII (February 1962), 7. The study to which Davies refers is B. Zawadzki and P. F. Lazarsfeld, "The Psychological Consequences of Unemployment," *Journal of Social Psychology,* VI (May 1935), 224–251. See also Ancel Keys et al., *The Biology of Human Starvation* (Minneapolis: University of Minnesota Press, 1950). Robert C. Stauffer, following Ancel Keys, James C. Davies, and others, notes that recurring and prolonged semistarvation produces attitudinal changes in the direction of irritability and apathy. Irritability often leads to increased individual aggressiveness and anomic violence, while apathy leads to modes of withdrawal and passivity that undermine the basis of political community but that preclude concerted revolutionary action against the political system because of the necessity of channeling human energy to the task of sheer survival. "The Biopolitics of Underdevelopment," *Comparative Political Studies,* 2 (October 1969), 364–365. Mark Hagopian has made a similar point in contrasting Marx's "misery theory" of revolution with de Tocqueville's "prosperity theory." *The Phenomenon of Revolution* (New York: Dodd, Mead, 1974), p. 171.

49. Manus Midlarsky, "Scarcity and Inequality: Prologue to the Onset of Mass Revolution," *Journal of Conflict Resolution,* 26 (March 1982), 3–8. Midlarsky notes that whereas industrial countries experience increasing equality with increasing abundance, agrarian LDCs experience increasing inequality as they develop.

50. James N. Rosenau, ed., *International Aspects of Civil Strife* (Princeton: Princeton University Press, 1964), p. 119.

51. Arnold Feldman, "Violence and Volatility: The Likelihood of Revolution," in Harry Eckstein, ed., *Internal War: Problems and Approaches* (New York: The Free Press, 1964), p. 119.

52. Alexis de Tocqueville, *The Old Regime and the French Revolution* (originally published in French in 1856), trans. Stuart Gilbert (Garden City, N.Y.: Doubleday-Anchor, 1955), pp. 174–177.

53. Manfred Halpern, *The Politics of Social Change in the Middle East and North Africa* (Princeton: Princeton University Press, 1963), p. 93. See also P. J. Vatikiotis, ed., *Revolution in the Middle East and Other Case Studies* (Totowa, N.J.: Rowman and Littlefield, 1972); and Gerard Chaliand, *Revolution in the Third World* (New York: Viking, 1977).

54. Crane Brinton, op. cit., p. 115. On this point see also Vernon Van Dyke, *International Politics,* 2nd ed. (New York: Appleton, 1966), p. 327.

55. Mancur Olson, Jr., has shown how rapid economic growth loosens the class and caste ties that bind people to the social order, and how a country's economic growth can significantly increase the number of people who perceive, often correctly, that their standard of living is declining, even though per capita income figures may be rising. "Rapid Growth as a Destabilizing Force," *The Journal of Economic History,* 23 (December 1963), 529–552. He concludes that "rapid economic growth, far from being the source of domestic tranquility it is sometimes supposed to be, is rather a disruptive and destabilizing force that leads to political instability." Ibid., p. 552. See also note 50 supra.

56. See, for example, Daniel Bell, *The Cultural Contradictions of Capitalism* (New York: Basic Books, 1976), pp. 223–227. Cf. also Eugene Linden, *Affluence and Discontent* (New York: Viking, 1979). Linden's basic theme is that traditional religious needs have been translated in modern secular culture into material appetites for new products and policies designed to promote economic well-being. These appetites cannot be satisfied because material answers to spiritual needs exacerbate the very discontents we are seeking desperately to abate. Wants have replaced needs, says Bell, and with the restraining effect of a religious ethic eliminated, wants become unlimited and insatiable.

57. James C. Davies, op. cit., p. 6.

58. Ted Robert Gurr and Mark Irving Lichbach note this in "Forecasting Internal Conflict: A Competitive Evaluation of Empirical Theories," *Comparative Political Studies,* 19 (April 1986), p. 4, where they cite earlier criticisms to this effect by A. S. Cohan and Harry Eckstein.

59. Ivo K. and Rosalind L. Feierabend, "Aggressive Behaviors Within Polities, 1948–1962: A Cross-National Study," *Journal of Conflict Resolution,* X (September 1966), 250–256. For a critical analysis of efforts to explain collective violence mainly by reference to "relative deprivation" (in the works of James Davies, Ted Robert Gurr, and I. K. and R. L. Feierabend), see David Snyder, "Collective Violence: A Research Agenda and Some Strategic Considerations," *Journal of Conflict Resolution,* Vol. 22 (September 1978), esp. pp. 501–504.

60. I. K. and R. L. Feierabend, op. cit., 257.

61. Ferdinand Tönnies, *Community and Society—Gemeinschaft und Gesellschaft,* Charles P. Loomis, trans. and ed. (East Lansing: Michigan State University Press, 1957).

62. Edward A. Shils, "The Intellectuals in the Political Development of the New States," *World Politics,* XII (April 1960), 329–368. See also Robert Waelder, "Protest and Revolution Against Western Societies," in Morton A. Kaplan, ed., *The Revolution in World Politics* (New York: Wiley, 1962).

63. Only the more important works can be cited here: Daniel Lerner, *The Passing of Traditional Society* (New York: The Free Press, 1958); Gabriel A. Almond and James S. Coleman, eds., *The Politics of Developing Areas* (Princeton: Princeton University Press, 1960); David E. Apter, *The Politics of Modernization* (Chicago: University of Chicago Press, 1965); Lucian W. Pye, *Aspects of Political Development* (Boston: Little, Brown, 1966); Samuel P. Huntington, *Political Order in Changing Societies* (New Haven: Yale University Press, 1968); Jason L. Finkle and Richard W. Gable, *Political Development and Social Change* (New York: Wiley, 1968); Robert Gamer, *The Developing Nations: A Comparative Perspective* (Boston: Allyn & Bacon, 1976); Edward L. Morse,

Modernization and the Transformation of International Relations (New York: The Free Press, 1976).

64. On mobilization and organization, see William H. Friedland et al., *Revolutionary Theory* (Totowa, N.J.: Allenheld, 1982).

65. Charles Tilly, *From Mobilization to Revolution* (Reading, Mass.: Addison-Wesley, 1978), ch. 2.

66. Tilly notes that most theories of collective behavior in this century have embodied the Durkheimian argument in one version or another. As examples, Tilly cites Chalmers Johnson, *Revolutionary Change,* and Samuel P. Huntington, *Political Order in Changing Societies* (see Notes 42 and 61 in this chapter).

67. Tilly, op. cit., p. 50. Tilly provides a comprehensive bibliography of American and European literature on social conflict, revolution, collective action, and related subjects, pp. 307–336.

68. Lawrence Stone, "Theories of Revolution," *World Politics,* XVII (January 1966), 168. See also Bruce Mazlish, *The Revolutionary Ascetic: Evolution of a Political Type* (New York: Basic Books, 1976).

69. Even individuals differ in their reaction. Frustration tolerance varies, and different people are frustrated by different things. Gardner Lindzey, "Frustration Tolerance, Frustration Susceptibility and Overt Disturbance," reprinted in Zawodny, ed., op. cit., vol. I, pp. 30–34. It is known, too, that a relationship exists between class background and modes of expressing aggressiveness: poorer, less educated classes are more prone to commit physical aggression; better educated middle classes, to psychological aggression. Martin Gold, "Suicide, Homicide and the Socialization of Aggression," in Bartlett H. Stoodley, ed., *Society and Self: A Reader in Social Psychology* (New York: The Free Press, 1962), pp. 278–293.

70. In André Malraux's great novel about the Chinese Revolution, published in 1933, we are given a picture of the revolutionary terrorist Ch'en who conceives of himself as a sacrificial priest before he kills his victims, who despises those who do not kill, who contemplates assassination with ecstasy, and who makes terror the whole meaning of life. *Man's Fate,* trans. Haakon M. Chevalier (New York: Random House [Vintage Books], 1967), pp. 10, 64, 163, and 233. "There was a world of murder, and it held him with a kind of warmth." Ibid., p. 10. For an analysis of Malraux's novel, consult Irving Howe, *Politics and the Novel* (New York: Fawcett, 1967), pp. 209–221. For an expansive discussion of *Man's Fate* as well as of Malraux's ideological posture as novelist, revolutionary, and minister, see Davis Wilkinson, "Malraux, Revolutionist and Minister," in Walter Laqueur and George L. Mosse, eds., *The Left-Wing Intellectuals Between the Wars, 1919–1939* (New York: Harper & Row [Torchbooks], 1967). For an analysis of violence as a search for significance and of the "secret love of violence" as something to be enjoyed ecstatically by the rebel, see Rollo May, *Power and Innocence: A Search for the Sources of Violence* (New York: Norton, 1972), chs. 8, 9, and 10.

71. Mao Tse-tung, "On Protracted War", in *Selected Works of Mao Tse-tung* (London: Lawrence and Wishart, 1954), vol. II, pp. 188, 201–202.

72. See A. F. K. Organski, *The Stages of Political Development* (New York: Knopf, 1965), especially pp. 132–133; Karl W. Deutsch, "Social Mobilization and Political Development," *American Political Science Review,* IV (September 1961); Gil Carl Alroy, *The Involvement of Peasants in Internal Wars* (Princeton: Center of International Studies, Princeton University, 1966); Theda Skocpol,

States and Social Revolutions (London: Cambridge University Press, 1979). Skocpol compares the roles of peasants in three revolutions.

73. Robert W. McColl, "A Political Geography of Revolution: China, Vietnam and Thailand," *Journal of Conflict Resolution*, I (June 1967), 153–167.

74. "That every internal war creates a demand for foreign intervention," writes George Modelski, is "implicit in the logic of the situation." "The International Relations of Internal War," in James N. Rosenau, ed., *International Aspects of Civil Strife* (Princeton: Princeton University Press, 1964), p. 20. See Richard Little, *Intervention: External Involvement in Civil Wars* (Totowa, N.J.: Rowman and Littlefield, 1975); Peter Calvert, *Revolution and International Politics* (New York: St. Martin's Press, 1984).

75. See Karl W. Deutsch, "External Involvement in Internal War," in Harry Eckstein, ed., *Internal War*, pp. 100–110.

76. Ibid., p. 102.

77. Ekkhart Zimmerman, *Political Violence, Crises, and Revolution* (Cambridge, Mass.: Schenkman, 1983); Jack A. Goldstone, "Theories of Revolution," *World Politics* (April 1980).

78. Bard O'Neill, William Heaton, and Donald Alberts, eds., *Insurgency in the Modern Age* (Boulder, Colo.: Westview Press, 1980); Mark Hagopian, *The Phenomenon of Revolution* (New York: Dodd, Mead, 1974); Thomas Greene, *Comparative Revolutionary Movements* (Englewood Cliffs, N.J.: Prentice-Hall, 1974); Mostafa Rejai, *The Comparative Study of Revolutionary Strategy* (New York: David McKay, 1977).

79. Stephen Hosmer and Thomas Wolfe, *Soviet Policy and Practice Toward Third World Conflicts* (Lexington, Mass.: Lexington Books, 1983); Bruce Porter, *The USSR In Third World Conflicts* (London: Cambridge University Press, 1984); Joseph Whelan and Michael Dixon, *The Soviet Union in the Third World: Threat to World Peace* (New York: Pergamon-Brassey's, 1986).

80. John Dziak, "Military Doctrine and Structure," in Uri Ra'anan, Robert L. Pfaltzgraff, Jr., Richard Shultz, Ernst Halperin, and Igor Lukes, eds., *Hydra of Carnage: International Linkages of Terrorism* (Lexington, Mass.: Lexington Books, 1985) and *Chekisty: A History of the KGB* (Lexington, Mass.: Lexington Books, 1987); John Collins, *Green Berets, SEALS, and Spetsnaz: U.S. and Soviet Special Military Operations* (New York: Pergamon-Brassey's, 1987).

81. John F. Copper and Daniel S. Papp, eds., *Communist Nations' Military Assistance* (Boulder, Colo.: Westview Press, 1983); W. Scott Thompson, *Power Projection* (New York: National Strategy Information Center, 1978).

82. Richard Shultz, *The Soviet Union and Revolutionary Warfare: Principles, Practices, and Regional Comparisons* (Stanford, Calif.: Hoover Institution Press, 1988); Uri Ra'anan et al., eds., op cit.; Dennis Bark, ed., *The Red Orchestra* (Stanford, Calif.: Hoover Institution Press, 1986); Walter Laqueur, ed., *The Patterns of Soviet Conduct in the Third World* (New York: Praeger Press, 1983). Shultz examines four specific instances in his thorough evaluation of Soviet successes and failures in the period from the late 1960s to the mid-1980s.

83. Paul Linebarger, *Psychological Warfare* (Washington, D.C.: Infantry Journal Press, 1948); William Daugherty and Morris Janowitz, eds., *A Psychological Warfare Casebook* (Baltimore, Md.: Johns Hopkins University Press, 1958); Daniel Lerner, ed., *Propaganda in War and Crisis* (New York: Stewart Publishers, 1950); Harold Lasswell et al., *Language of Politics* (New York: Stewart

Publishers, 1949); Jacques Ellul, *Propaganda: The Formation of Men's Attitudes* (New York: Alfred A. Knopf, 1965).

84. Richard Shultz and Roy Godson, *Dezinformatsia: Active Measures in Soviet Strategy* (New York: Pergamon-Brassey's, 1984); Paul A. Smith, Jr., *On Political Warfare* (Washington, D.C.: National Defense University Press, 1988); Carnes Lord, ed., *Psychological Warfare in U.S. Strategy* (Washington, D.C.: National Defense University Press, 1988); Donald Brown, *International Radio Broadcasting* (New York: Praeger, 1982); Ladislav Bittman, *The KGB and Soviet Disinformation* (New York: Pergamon-Brassey's, 1985) and *The New Image-Makers: Soviet Propaganda and Disinformation Today* (New York: Pergamon-Brassey's, 1988).

85. Ra'anan et al., eds., op. cit.; Bark, ed., op. cit.; Shultz, *The Soviet Union and Revolutionary Warfare* and "Soviet Use of Surrogates to Project Power into the Third World," *Parameters* (Autumn, 1986).

86. The term *low-intensity conflict* began to be used by U.S. national security specialists in the latter half of the 1970s. See George Tanham et al., "United States Preparation for Future Low-Level Conflict," *Conflict,* No. 1–2 (1978); Sam Sarkesian and William Scully, eds., *U.S. Policy and Low Intensity Conflict* (New Brunswick, N.J.: Transaction Books, 1981). The terminology may have been borrowed from the British specialist, Frank Kitson. See Kitson, *Low Intensity Operations* (Harrisburg, Pa.: Stackpole, 1971).

87. Sam C. Sarkesian, *The New Battlefield* (Westport, Conn.: Greenwood Press, 1986); Stephen Hosmer and George Tanham, *Countering Covert Aggression* (Santa Monica, Calif.: The Rand Corporation, 1986); David Dean, ed., *Low Intensity Conflict and Modern Technology* (Maxwell Air Force Base, Ala.: Air University Press, 1986). See also U.S. Army Training and Doctrine Command Pamphlet 525–44, *U.S. Army Operational Concept for Low Intensity Conflict* (Fort Monroe, Va.: Army Training and Doctrine Command, 1986).

88. Sarkesian, op. cit.; Frank Barnett, Hugh Tovar, and Richard Shultz, eds., *Special Operations in U.S. Strategy* (Washington, D.C.: National Defense University Press, 1984); Richard Shultz, "Discriminate Deterrence and Low Intensity Conflict: The Unintentional Legacy of the Reagan Administration," *Conflict* (forthcoming, 1989); Michael Klare and Peter Kornbluh, *Low Intensity Warfare* (New York: Pantheon, 1988); D. Michael Shafer, *Deadly Paradigms* (Princeton: Princeton University Press, 1988); John Prados, *President's Secret Wars* (New York: William Morrow, 1986).

89. See, for example, A. J. Bacevich, James D. Hallums, Richard H. White, and Thomas Young, *American Military Policy in Small Wars: The Case of El Salvador* (New York: Pergamon-Brassey's, 1988).

90. Collins, *Green Berets, SEALS, and Spetsnaz: U.S. and Soviet Special Military Operations;* Richard Shultz, Robert L. Pfaltzgraff, Uri Ra'anan, William Olsen, and Igor Lukes, eds., *Guerrilla Warfare and Counterinsurgency: U.S. Soviet Policy and the Third World* (Lexington, Mass.: Lexington Books, 1988); David Charters and Maurice Tugwell, eds., *Armies in Low Intensity Conflict* (Ottawa: Department of National Defense, 1985); Ian F. W. Beckett and John Pimlott, eds., *Armed Forces & Modern Counterinsurgency* (New York: St. Martin's Press, 1985); William Burgess, "Iranian Special Operations in the Iran-Iraq War," *Conflict* (Nov. 1, 1986).

91. Kenneth N. Waltz, *Man, the State and War* (New York: Columbia University Press, 1958), p. 101.

92. See the following articles by Paul Diehl: "Arms Races and Escalation: A Closer Look," *Journal of Peace Research* 20, 3 (1983), pp. 205–212; "Arms Races to War: Testing Some Empirical Linkages," *Sociological Quarterly* 26, 3 (1985), pp. 331–349; "Armaments Without War: An Analysis of Some Underlying Effects," *Journal of Peace Research,* 22, 3 (1985), pp. 249–259.

93. Dean G. Pruitt and Richard C. Snyder, eds., *Theory and Research on the Causes of War* (Englewood Cliffs, N.J.: Prentice-Hall, 1969), pp. 4–5.

94. Quincy Wright, *A Study of War,* vol. I (Chicago: University of Chicago Press, 1942), p. 17. See also vol. II, p. 739, where he asserts that war "has politico-technological, juroideological, socioreligious and psychoeconomic causes." Wright's classic was reprinted in 1983.

95. Karl W. Deutsch, "Quincy Wright's Contribution to the Study of War: A Preface to the Second Edition," *Journal of Conflict Resolution,* XIV (December 1970), 474–475.

96. Clyde Eagleton, *International Government,* rev. ed. (New York: Ronald, 1948), p. 393. See Quincy Wright on "The Political Utility of War," in *A Study of War,* vol. II, pp. 853–860.

97. For a thoughtful and critical analysis of the contributions behavioral scientists had made prior to 1959 toward the control of interstate violence, see Kenneth N. Waltz, op. cit., pp. 42–79. Waltz anticipated the conclusion reached here—namely, that the behaviorists must take into greater account the political framework of war-peace issues. See also L. L. Farrar, Jr., ed., *War: A Historical, Political and Social Study* (Santa Barbara, Calif.: ABC-Clio, 1978); Geoffrey Blainey, op. cit.; and Manus I. Midlarsky, *On War: Political Violence in the International System* (New York: The Free Press, 1975).

98. See Franklyn Griffiths and John C. Polanyi, eds., *The Dangers of Nuclear War* (Toronto: University of Toronto Press, 1979); Richard Ned Lebow, *Between Peace and War: The Nature of International Crisis* (Baltimore, Md.: Johns Hopkins University Press, 1981); Daniel Frei, with the collaboration of Christian Catrina, *Risks of Unintentional Nuclear War,* United Nations Institute for Disarmament Research (Totowa, N.J.: Allenheld, Osmun, 1983).

99. See Theodore Abel, "The Elements of Decision in the Pattern of War," *American Sociological Review,* VI (December 1941), 853–859.

100. "Motives and Perceptions Underlying Entry into War," Introduction to part 2 in Pruitt and Snyder, eds., op. cit., pp. 22–26.

101. J. David Singer, "Threat Perception and National Decision-Makers," in Pruitt and Snyder, eds., op. cit., pp. 39–42.

102. Raymond L. Garthoff, "On Estimating and Imputing Intentions," *International Security,* 2 (Winter 1978), 22–32. See Richard Pipes, "Why the Soviet Union Thinks It Could Fight and Win a Nuclear War," *Commentary,* 64 (July 1977), 21–34; Paul H. Nitze, "Deterring Our Deterrent," *Foreign Policy,* No. 25 (Winter 1976–1977), 195–210; "Soviet Strength and Fears," Report by the Center for the Study of Democratic Institutions in *World Issues* (October-November 1977), 22–30; Bernard Brodie, "The Development of Nuclear Strategy," *International Security,* 2 (Spring 1978), 65–83; and Stanley Sienkiewicz, "SALT and Soviet Nuclear Doctrine," 84–100.

103. Frederick L. Schuman, *International Politics,* 5th ed. (New York: McGraw-Hill, 1953), p. 230.

104. Hans J. Morgenthau, *Politics Among Nations: The Struggle for Power and Peace,* 4th ed. (New York: Knopf, 1967), p. 392.

105. Michael Howard, *The Causes of Wars* (Cambridge, Mass.: Harvard University Press, 1983), ch. 3, "The Strategic Approach to International Relations."

106. In 1957, Anatol Rapoport wrote a special monograph issue of *The Journal of Conflict Resolution* devoted exclusively to the work of Richardson. Richardson was first noted for his scientific work in the field of meteorology, for which he was selected as a fellow in the Royal Society in 1926. His experience in meteorology influenced his method of research on arms races and war. Recognizing the difficulty of predicting even the next day's weather by using as many as 60,000 computers of that era, he was nevertheless convinced that events that seem to be governed by chance (such as weather) are subject to natural laws and therefore predictable provided that sufficient data can be processed. See Anatol Rapoport, "Lewis Fry Richardson," *International Encyclopedia of the Social Sciences*, op. cit., vol. 13, p. 514.

107. Lewis F. Richardson's principal work on the mathematics of arms races is *Arms and Insecurity: A Mathematical Study of the Causes and Origins of War* (Pittsburgh, Pa.: Boxwood Press, 1960). In another work, *Statistics of Deadly Quarrels*, he classified deadly quarrels between states on the basis of the number of persons killed, and examined the frequency of war between dyads of states, the length of wars and peace intervals the pattern of war repetitions, the probability that allies and enemies group themselves similarly in subsequent wars, and the correlation between the incidence of wars and such factors as geographical proximity, population, religion and language.

108. Lewis F. Richardson, *Arms and Insecurity*, op. cit., pp. 13–15.

109. Dina A. Zinnes, *Contemporary Research in International Relations* (New York: The Free Press, 1976), p. 332. She adds that "while it is probably fair to say that an underlying assumption of the arms race models is that they provide a possible explanation for processes that appear to result in some wars, it must be admitted that Richardson does not formally link defense expenditure and the outbreak of war in any of the arms race models which he constructs." Ibid., p. 332. This is an extremely important point to keep in mind, inasmuch as so many writers who have not studied Richardson as carefully as Zinnes has or perhaps have not even read him invariably cite his research as demonstrating scientifically and conclusively that arms races lead to wars. The student trained in mathematics will find a complete exposition and analysis of Richardson's basic model in Zinnes, op. cit., pp. 333–369.

110. Paul Diehl, "Arms Races and Escalation: A Closer Look," *Journal of Peace Research*, 20(3), (1983), 205–212; "Arms Raises to War: Testing Some Empirical Linkages," *Sociological Quarterly* 26(3), (1985), 331–349.

111. See Dina A. Zinnes, op. cit., pp. 339–354; Kenneth Boulding, *Conflict and Defense* (New York: Harper & Row, 1962), pp. 19–40; and Robert C. North, Richard A. Brodie, and Ole R. Holsti, "Some Empirical Data on the Conflict Spiral," *International Peace Research Society Papers*, 1 (1964), 1–14.

112. Dina A. Zinnes, op. cit., p. 369.

113. Dina A. Zinnes devotes ch. 15 to the work of Quincy Wright, Kenneth Boulding, Dean Pruitt, and several others. For the description of an effort to apply the Richardson model to arms negotiations, see P. Terrence Hopmann and Theresa C. Smith, "An Application of a Richardson Process Model: Soviet-American Interactions in the Test Ban Negotiations, 1962–1963," *Journal of Conflict Resolution*, XXI (December 1977), 701–726.

114. Martin Patchen, "Models of Cooperation and Conflict: A Critical Review," *Journal of Conflict Resolution*, XIV (September 1970), 389–408. Charles W. Ostrom, Jr., after empirically testing two models of the U.S. defense expenditure decision-making process, could not distinguish the arms race model from the organizational process model (see Chapter 11, "Decision-Making Theories") so far as accuracy of forecasts was concerned. "Evaluating Alternative Foreign Policy Decision-Making Models," ibid., XXI (June 1977), 235–266.

115. John V. Gillespie, Dina A. Zinnes, and others have noted that Richardson's model contains no decision calculus. "The equations are merely a description of what people would do if they did not stop to think." "An Optimal Control Model of Arms Race," *American Political Science Review*, LXXI (March 1977), 226–244, quoted on p. 226. Later, Zinnes and Robert G. Muncaster concluded from a model of hostility dynamics that it is possible to predict the time war will occur and the level of hostility necessary to provoke its onset. "The Dynamics of Hostile Activity and the Prediction of War," *Journal of Conflict Resolution*, 28 (June 1984), 187–229. See also J. David Singer, "Confrontational Behavior and Escalation to War, 1816–1980: A Research Plan," *Journal of Peace Research*, 19, No. 1 (1982).

116. See Note 45 in Chapter 6. Michael D. Wallace has adduced evidence to indicate that disputes preceded by arms races usually do in fact escalate to war (23 out of 28 times) while disputes not preceded by arms races hardly ever escalate to war (3 out of 71 times). "Arms Races and Escalation," *Journal of Conflict Resolution*, 23 (March 1979), 3–16.

117. When an effort is made to introduce additional variables, such as minimum acceptable arms levels and acceptable ratios of arms levels of rival states, the mathematics becomes much more complex. See William R. Caspary, "Richardson's Model of Arms Races: Description, Critique and an Alternative Model," *International Studies Quarterly*, XI (March 1967), 63–88.

118. David W. Ziegler, citing Samuel P. Huntington, writes: "In the 1860s the British replaced their wooden ships with ironclad ships in response to French innovation, yet they spent less on their navy in these years than they had in preceding ones." *War, Peace and International Politics*, 4th ed. (Boston: Little, Brown, 1987), p. 206.

119. Ibid.

120. Albert Wohlstetter, "Is There a Strategic Arms Race?" *Foreign Policy*, 15 (Summer 1974), 3–20; and "Rivals, But No 'Race'," ibid., 16 (Fall 1974), 48–81. Another analyst, after studying U.S. and Soviet arms expenditures over the period 1948–1970, suggested that U.S. military budget increases could be explained in substantial measure by *changes* in U.S. military technology, while the expansion of productive capabilities at a more stable level of military technology was salient in the case of the Soviet Union. W. Ladd Hollist, "An Analysis of Arms Processes in the United States and the Soviet Union," *International Studies Quarterly*, 21 (September 1977), 503–528. Earl R. Brubaker has shown that decisions to accumulate weapons depend partly on anticipations about the military-technological character of future war and the problem of residual stocks after the initial expenditure of weapons and subsequent strikes. "Economic Models of Arms Races," *Journal of Conflict Resolution*, XVII (June 1973), 187–205.

121. A. F. K. Organski, *World Politics* (New York: Knopf, 1958), ch. 12; (2nd ed., 1968), ch. 14.

122. See G. S. Barghava, *India's Security in the 1980s* (London: International Institute of Strategic Studies; Adelphi Paper No. 125, Summer 1976), pp. 5–6. Erich Weede has found that overwhelming or ten-to-one preponderance is favorable to the prevention of war. "Overwhelming Preponderance as a Pacifying Condition Among Contiguous Asian Dyads, 1950–1969," *Journal of Conflict Resolution,* XX (September 1976), 395–411.

123. A. F. K. Organski, op. cit., 1958, pp. 319–320; 1968, pp. 357–359. The hypothesis that lethal international violence between pairs of contiguous states is more probable if the two states are equally powerful was substantiated in an empirical study of a recent five-year period. See David Garnham, "Power Parity and Lethal International Violence, 1969–1973," *Journal of Conflict Resolution,* XX (September 1976), 379–391.

124. Inis L. Claude, *Power and International Relations* (New York: Random House, 1962), p. 56.

125. Michael P. Sullivan, *International Relations: Theories and Evidence* (Englewood Cliffs, N.J.: Prentice-Hall, 1976), pp. 166–167.

126. John. W. Burton has argued that Japan resorted to a policy of force in the 1930s because other powers "were not prepared to make the adjustments necessary to allow Japan to develop" through access to international markets. *Peace Theory: Preconditions of Disarmament* (New York: Knopf, 1962), p. 9.

127. Nazli Choucri and Robert C. North, *Nations in Conflict: National Growth and International Violence* (San Francisco, Calif.: Freeman, 1975).

128. Ibid., p. 2.

129. Ibid., p. 278.

130. Ibid., pp. 15–17.

131. Ibid., pp. 17–22.

132. Ibid. The authors also found that increases in the military budget of one country might be due to a rival expansion in a nonmilitary area. See ch. 13, "Military Expenditures."

133. Ibid., p. 284.

134. Ibid, pp. 285–286. The authors point out that actions taken in one part of a system to relieve distress may produce unexpected consequences in another part, and that policies aiming at desirable short-term outcomes may often involve a high long-term price.

135. Robert C. North and Nazli Choucri, "Economic and Political Factors in International Conflict and Integration," *International Studies Quarterly,* 27 (December 1983), 451–453, 459.

136. Pitirim A. Sorokin, *Social and Cultural Dynamics* (New York: American Book, 1937), vol. 3, *Fluctuation of Social Relationships, War, and Revolution.* Sorokin counted 862 European wars in the period 1100–1925. Ibid., p. 283. Sorokin's classic study was published in four volumes (Englewood Cliffs, N.J.: Bedminster Press, 1962).

137. Quincy Wright, op. cit. Wright estimated that there were about 200 major wars between 1480 and 1941. Ibid., p. 651.

138. Lewis F. Richardson, *Statistics of Deadly Quarrels,* ch. 2. Richardson lumped together major international and domestic violence, identifying a total of 317 incidents between 1820 and 1949. His totals are comparable to those of Singer and Small (see Note 164) for both categories. Singer and Small discovered 367 such incidents between 1816 and 1942.

139. The primary data base for the Correlates of War Project is to be found in J. David Singer and Melvin Small, *The Wages of War, 1816–1965: A Statistical Handbook* (New York: Wiley, 1972). Their original research was updated and refined in J. David Singer, ed., *The Correlates of War*, Vol. I, *Research Origins and Rationale* (New York: The Free Press, 1979); Vol. II, *Testing Some Realpolitik Models* (New York: Free Press, 1980); Melvin Small and J. David Singer, *Resort to Arms: International and Civil Wars, 1816–1980* (New York: The Free Press, 1980); and Melvin Small and J. David Singer, eds., *International War: An Anthology and Study Guide* (Homewood, Ill.: Dorsey Press, 1985). See also J. David Singer, "Accounting for International War: The State of the Discipline," *Journal of Peace Research*, 18, no. 1 (1981), For an account of the development of the Correlates of War Project and the follow-on research it stimulated, see the excellent review article by John A. Vasquez, "The Steps to War: Toward a Scientific Explanation of Correlates of War Findings, *World Politics*, (Vol. 40 No. 1, 1988), 108–145.

140. Jack S. Levy, "Historical Trends in Great Power War, 1495–1975," *International Studies Quarterly*, 26 (June 1982), 298; Jack S. Levy and T. Clifton Morgan, "The Frequency and Seriousness of War: An Inverse Relationship?" *Journal of Conflict Resolution*, 28 (December 1984), 731–749.

141. Singer and Small, *The Wages of War*, p. 287.

142. John G. Stoessinger, *Why Nations Go To War* (New York: St. Martin's, 1974), p. 219. Stoessinger agrees that initiators were usually winners in the nineteenth century. For an account of the misguided faith of many initiators of wars who believed that quick victory would be theirs, see Geoffrey Blainey, op. cit., ch. 3, "Dreams and Delusions of a Coming War."

143. Melvin Small and J. David Singer, "Patterns in International Warfare," in *The Annals (Collective Violence)*, No. 391 (September 1970), 147–149. In this article, the authors mentioned tentatively the possibility of a 20-year cycle. They also cited the work of Frank H. Denton and Warren Phillips, who have derived from the data of Wright, Sorokin, and Richardson a cycle of war every 30 years since 1680. "Some Patterns in the History of Violence," *Journal of Conflict Resolution*, XII (June 1968), 182–195. Singer and Small finally fixed the cycle at between 20 and 40 years, which would seem to be a somewhat irregular cycle. The century cycles of Arnold Toynbee and the generational cycles of Lewis F. Richardson are discussed in Geoffrey Blainey, op. cit., pp. 5–9.

144. Francis A. Beer, *Peace Against War: The Ecology of International Violence* (San Francisco, Calif.: W. H. Freeman, 1981), p. 50. Beer provides useful summaries of a vast amount of literature, by both traditional and behavioral-quantitative researchers, on the causes, characteristics, and consequences of war.

145. Gaston Bouthoul said that war breaks out when there is a "plethora of young men surpassing the indispensable tasks of the economy." Jacques Ellul, citing this statement, writes: "It is the multiplication of men who are excluded from working which provokes war." *The Technological Society* (New York: Random House [Vintage Books], 1964), p. 137.

146. William R. Thompson, "Phases of the Business Cycle and the Outbreak of War," *International Studies Quarterly*, 26 (June 1982). See also his "Uneven Economic Growth, Systemic Challenges, and Global Wars," ibid., 27 (Decem-

ber 1983), and Raimo Vayrynen, "Economic Cycles, Power Transitions, Power Management and Wars between Major Powers," ibid. Thompson's later article addresses the broader question of whether changes in the economic power structure in the capitalist world economy constitute the roots of war among the major powers during the past 500 years, as Christopher Chase-Dunn has argued. Thompson raises critical questions about the Chase-Dunn model.

147. Richard K. Ashley, *The Political Economy of War and Peace* (London: Francis Pinter; New York: Nichols, 1980).

148. Benjamin A. Most and Harvey Starr, "Conceptualizing 'War': Consequences for Theory and Research," *Journal of Conflict Resolution,* 27 (March 1983), 154–157.

149. Michael D. Wallace, "Arms Races and Escalation: Some New Evidence," *Journal of Conflict Resolution,* 23 (March 1977), 3–16; and "Armaments and Escalation," *International Studies Quarterly,* 26 (March 1982), 37–56.

150. Francis A. Beer, op. cit., 234. With reference to the point about the decreased U.S. defense effort, Beer cites W. Laddis Hollist, op. cit. (Note 120 supra).

151. Miroslav Nincic, *The Arms Race* (New York: Praeger, 1982); Stephen J. Majeski and David L. Jones, "Arms Race Modeling: Causality Analysis and Model Specification," *Journal of Conflict Resolution,* 25 (June 1981), 259–288.

152. John C. Lambelet, "Do Arms Races Lead to War?" *Journal of Peace Research,* 12, no. 2 (1975), 123–128.

153. J. David Singer, "Threat Perceptions and the Armament-Tension Dilemma," *Journal of Conflict Resolution,* 2 (March 1958), 90–105.

154. Michael D. Wallace, "Arms Races and Escalation," 4–6.

155. Michael D. Wallace, "Armaments and Escalation," 40–48.

156. Michael F. Altfeld, "Arms Races?—and Escalation? A Comment on Wallace," *International Studies Quarterly,* 27 (June 1983), 225–231; Erich Weede, "Arms Races and Escalation: Some Persisting Doubts," *Journal of Conflict Reduction,* 24 (June 1980), 285–287. See also note 110 above.

157. A. F. K. Organski and Jacek Kugler, *The War Ledger* (Chicago: University of Chicago Press, 1980), p. 61.

158. Ibid., p. 161. Organski and Kugler also show, not too surprisingly, that following wars, losers usually catch up with winners and within 15 to 18 years are usually back up to the levels they would have achieved had there been no war. Ibid., p. 212.

159. Hank Houweling and Jan Siccama, "Power Transitions as a Cause of War," *Journal of Conflict Resolution,* 32 (March 1988).

160. Michael D. Intriligator and Dagobert L. Brito, "Can Arms Races Lead to the Outbreak of War?" ibid., 28 (March 1984), 63–84. For a critique, see Thomas F. Mayer, "Arms Races and War Initiation: Some Alternatives to the Intriligator-Brito Model," ibid., 30 (March 1986), 3–28.

161. Robert C. North and Matthew Willard, "The Convergence Effect: Challenge to Parsimony," *International Organization,* 37 (Spring 1983), 352. Jacek Kugler rejoined with the argument that there is no empirical evidence to support the proposition that the absence of massive war during the previous 35 years was accounted for by the threat of nuclear weapons. "Terror Without Deterrence: Reassessing the Role of Nuclear Weapons," *Journal of Con-*

flict Resolution, 28 (September 1984), 470–506. There is, fortunately, no empirical evidence on the correlation between nuclear weapons and the outbreak of massive war—except its prolonged absence. One cannot prove a negative—that is, why something did *not* happen. Persuasive arguments combining deductive logic and historical experience (which is "empirical") can be made (and will be made in Chapter 9) concerning the validity of deterrence theory.

162. Urs Luterbacher, "Last Words About War?" *Journal of Conflict Resolution,* 28 (March 1984), 174.

163. Michael D. Wallace, "Arms and Escalation," 55.

164. J. David Singer and Melvin Small, "Alliance Aggregation and the Onset of War, 1815–1945," in J. David Singer, ed., *Quantitative International Politics,* (New York: Free Press, 1968), pp. 247–286. Reprinted in J. David Singer, ed., *The Correlates of War: I. Research Origins and Rationale* (New York: The Free Press, 1979), pp. 225–264.

165. Most of the 16 member states of NATO and 7 member states of the Warsaw Pact (or the predecessor states of the latter) had been participants in both world wars in this century. (The Netherlands and the Scandinavian states remained neutral in World War I, and would have preferred to follow that course in World War II but the Netherlands, Denmark, and Norway were quickly overrun by German forces. Only Spain remained neutral throughout both wars. Turkey was neutral until February 1945, when she joined the Allies.) For the last four decades, no member of the two European alliance systems has been involved in a military conflict with a member of the opposite alliance.

166. Jack S. Levy, "Alliance Formation and War Behavior: An Analysis of the Great Powers, 1495–1975," *Journal of Conflict Resolution,* 25 (December 1981), 581–613.

167. Charles W. Ostrom, Jr. and Francis W. Hoole, "Alliances and War Revisited: A Research Note," *International Studies Quarterly,* 22 (June 1978), 215–236. See also Michael F. Altfeld, "Arms Races? And Escalation?: A Comment on Wallace," *International Studies Quarterly,* 27 (June 1983), 225–231.

168. John A. Vasquez, "The Steps to War: Toward a Scientific Explanation of Correlates of War Findings," *World Politics,* XL (October 1987), 121. Vasquez observes that it is difficult to determine whether alliances cause wars, for the simple reason that states often join them because they anticipate war. Ibid., p. 120.

169. Ibid., p. 121. See Randolph Siverson and Joel King, "Alliances and the Expansion of War," in J. David Singer and Michael D. Wallace, eds., *To Auger Well: Early Warning Indicators in World Politics* (Beverly Hills, Calif.: Sage Publications, 1982), pp. 37–49.

170. Vasquez, op. cit., p. 123.

171. Charles W. Kegley, Jr. and Gregory A. Raymond, "Alliance Norms and War," *International Studies Quarterly,* 26 (December 1982), 572–595.

172. Bruce Bueno de Mesquita, "Risk, Power Distributions, and the Likelihood of War," *International Studies Quarterly,* 25 (December 1981). The author's major book-length work is *The War Trap* (New Haven: Yale University Press, 1980). The article cited and other articles written since 1980 contain refinements of his major work. See also his "Systemic Polarization and the Occur-

rence and Duration of War," *Journal of Conflict Resolution,* 22 (June 1978), 241–267; "The Costs of War: A Rational Expectation Approach," *American Political Science Review,* 77 (June 1983), 347–357; and "The War Trap Revisited: A Revised Expected Utility Model," ibid., 79 (March 1985), 157–177. With additional refinements, he says, "the revised version . . . is a powerful tool for integrating many extant hypotheses about conflict" and he expresses confidence that his approach may yield "significant, lawlike generalizations about the initiation, escalation and termination of international conflict." Ibid., pp. 156, 172.

173. Ibid. See note 142 supra.

174. Ibid. Cf. Dina A. Zinnes et al., "Capability, Threat and the Outbreak of War," in James A. Rosenau, ed., *International Politics and Foreign Policy: A Reader in Research and Theory* (New York: Free Press, 1961). See note 109 supra.

175. See the discussion on Waltz and Deutsch/Singer in Chapter 4; also J. David Singer et al., "Capability Distribution, Uncertainty and Major Power War, 1820–1965," in Bruce Russett, ed., *Peace, War and Numbers* (Beverly Hills, Calif.: Sage Publications, 1972).

176. Ibid., p. 541.

177. Ibid., p. 567.

178. Ibid., p. 564. For a fuller elaboration of his views on the risk orientation of leaders, see *The War Trap,* op. cit. and his *Strategy, Risk, and Personality in Coalition Politics* (Cambridge: Cambridge University Press, 1976). In a penetrating and moderately critical review of *The War Trap,* R. Harrison Wagner observed that the author provides only limited evidence concerning the tendency of leaders to maximize expected utility, and no evidence, one way or the other, on the question of how theories of individual rational choice can explain the foreign policy decisions of states. "War and Expected Utility Theory," *World Politics,* XXXVI (April 1984), 423.

179. Bruce Bueno de Mesquita and David Lalman, "Reason and War," *American Political Science Review,* 80 (December 1986), 1119. Their analysis was an outgrowth of ideas in Bruce Bueno de Mesquita, "The Costs of War: A Rational Expectations Approach" and "The War Trap Revisited" (note 172 supra).

180. John A. Vasquez, "Capability, Types of War, Peace," *Western Political Quarterly,* 39 (June 1986).

181. Ibid., p. 313.

182. Ibid., p. 322.

183. Ibid., p. 315.

184. Ibid., p. 324.

185. Urs Luterbacher, op. cit., pp. 167–168. For other works on war correlations, see Jack S. Levy, "Misperceptions and the Causes of War," *World Politics,* XXXVI (October 1983), and "Theories of General War," ibid., XXXVI (April 1985); Randolph M. Siverson and Michael P. Sullivan, "The Distribution of Power and the Onset of War," *Journal of Conflict Resolution,* 27 (June 1983); Randolph M. Siverson and Michael R. Tennefoss, "Power, Alliance and the Escalation of International Conflict, 1815–1965," *American Political Science Review,* 78 (December 1984); George Modelski and Patrick Morgan, "Understanding Global War," *Journal of Conflict Resolution,* 29 (September 1985); Paul A. Anderson and Timothy J. McKeown, "Changing Aspirations, Limited Attention, and War," *World Politics,* XL, no. 1 (October 1987).

186. John A. Vasquez, "The Steps to War," pp. 113–114.

187. Ibid., 112. Cf. Kenneth N. Waltz, *Theory of International Politics* (Reading, Mass.: Addison-Wesley, 1979), p. 4.

188. Sanford A. Lakoff, "The Third Culture: Science in Social Thought," in the book he edited, *Knowledge and Power: Science and Government* (New York: The Free Press, 1966), pp. 5–6.

189. Robert C. North and Matthew Willard, op. cit., 342.

190. Quincy Wright, op. cit., p. 14.

191. Lewis F. Richardson had called attention to the "pacifism, war-fever, war-weariness, pacifism" cycle. He used a model similar to that employed to explain the spread and decline of epidemic diseases. "War Moods," part I, *Psychometrika*, 13 (September 1948), 147–174; part II, ibid. (December 1948), 197–232. See also Joel T. Campbell and Leila S. Cain, "Public Opinion and the Outbreak of War," *Journal of Conflict Resolution*, IX (September 1965), 318–329; Geoffrey Blainey, op. cit., ch. 1.

192. Lewis A. Coser, "The Termination of Conflict," *The Journal of Conflict Resolution*, V (December 1961), 347–353.

193. William T. R. Fox, "The Causes of Peace and the Conditions of War," in *The Annals (How Wars End)*, 392 (November 1970), 2–3.

194. Ibid., p. 8.

195. Ibid., p. 9.

196. Ibid., p. 11.

197. Richard Smoke, *War: Controlling Escalation* (Cambridge: Harvard University Press, 1977).

198. Ibid., pp. 30–35, 241–245. Smoke concedes that saliency may be blurred by breaking up the escalatory step into many small increments, but he points out that we usually know when a saliency is being blurred.

199. Ibid., p. 235.

200. Ibid., pp. 294–295. See also Fred C. Iklé, "When the Fighting Has to Stop," *World Politics*, XIX (July 1967), 692–707.

201. Richard Smoke, op. cit., pp. 296–297.

202. William D. Coplin, *The Functions of International Law* (Chicago: Rand-McNally, 1966), ch. 1.

203. For treatment of the changing status of the concept of war under international law in the twentieth century, see Hans Kelsen, *Principles of International Law*, 2nd ed., revised and edited by Robert W. Tucker (New York: Holt, Rinehart and Winston, 1966), pp. 22–101. See also Julius Stone, *Legal Control of International Conflict* (New York: Holt, Rinehart and Winston, 1959); Louis Henkin, *How Nations Behave: Law and Foreign Policy* (London: Pall Mall, 1968); Richard A. Falk, *Legal Order in a Violent World* (Princeton: Princeton University Press, 1968); Karl W. Deutsch and Stanley Hoffmann, eds., *The Relevance of International Law* (Garden City, N.Y.: Doubleday, 1971). More recently, Bruce Bueno de Mesquita has taken issue with those who base the relationship between polarity and war upon decision-maker response to uncertainty. He has found that the occurrence and duration of wars in this century are closely linked to increases in the tightness of the international system. "Systemic Polarization and the Occurrence and Duration of War," *Journal of Conflict Resolution*, 22 (June 1978), 241–267.

204. See Morton A. Kaplan and Nicholas de B. Katzenbach, *The Political Foundations of International Law* (New York: Wiley, 1961), especially pp. 341–342;

Stanley Hoffmann, "International Systems and International Law," in Klaus Knorr and Sidney Verba, eds., *The International System* (Princeton: Princeton University Press, 1961), pp. 205–327; Georg Schwarzenberger, *International Law and Order* (London: Stevens, 1971); James P. Piscatori, "The Contribution of International Law to International Relations," *International Affairs*, 53, No. 2 (April 1977), 217–231.

205. For fuller discussion of Marxist and non-Western views see Edward McWhinney, "Soviet and Western International Law and the Cold War in the Era of Bipolarity," reprinted from *The Canadian Yearbook of International Law*, vol. 1 (1963), in Richard A. Falk and Saul H. Mendlovitz, eds., *The Strategy of World Order*; vol. 2, *International Law* (New York: World Law Fund, 1966); and Richard A. Falk, "Revolutionary Nations and the Quality of International Legal Order," in Morton A. Kaplan, ed., *The Revolution in World Politics* (New York: Wiley, 1962).

206. Oscar J. Lissitzyn, "International Law in a Divided World," *International Conciliation*, 542 (March 1963), 68.

207. See Joel Laurus, ed., *From Collective Security to Collective Diplomacy* (New York: Wiley, 1965).

208. These included the Congo, West New Guinea, Jordan, Cyprus, Kashmir, the Lebanese-Syrian border, and some phases of the Arab-Israeli conflict, especially in the Sinai.

209. These included Berlin, Czechoslovakia, Hungary, Algeria, the Cuban Missile Crisis, Nigeria, Vietnam, Tibet, Bangladesh, the Middle East Wars of 1967 and 1973, and the U.K.-Argentina War over the Falkland (Malvinas) Islands.

210. Kenneth E. Boulding, "Accomplishments and Prospects of the Peace Research Movement," *Arms Control and Disarmament, 1986*, vol. I (London: Pergamon, 1968), pp. 43–58; Johan Galtung, "Violence, Peace and Peace Research," *Journal of Peace Research*, VI, no. 3 (1969), 167–191; Joan Bondurant, *Conquest of Violence: The Gandhian Philosophy of Conflict* (Berkeley: University of California Press, 1967); Erik Erikson, *Gandhi's Truth: On the Origins of Militant Nonviolence* (New York: Norton, 1969); Elise Boulding, "Peace Research in Transition: A Symposium," in Clinton F. Fink and Elise Boulding, eds., *Journal of Conflict Resolution*, XVI (December 1972); Morton Deutsch, *The Resolution of Conflict: Constructive and Destructive Processes* (New Haven: Yale University Press, 1973); Lewis Lipsitz and Herbert M. Kritzer, "Unconventional Approaches to Conflict Resolution," *Journal of Conflict Resolution*, 19 (December 1975), 713–733.

211. Cf. Jesse Bernard, "Parties and Issues in Conflict," *Journal of Conflict Resolution*, I (June 1957), 111–121.

212. "Peace Research and the Concepts of Conflict: Summary and Criticism: Introduction by the Editors," in Bengt Hoglund and Jorgen William Ulrich, eds., *Conflict Control and Conflict Resolution*, Interdisciplinary Studies from the Scandinavian Summer University, Vol. I (Copenhagen: Munksgaard; New York: Humanities Press, 1975), pp. 13–35.

213. Roger Fisher, "Fractionating Conflict," ch. 5 of the work he edited, *International Conflict and Behavioral Science* (New York: Basic Books, 1964), p. 103. Fisher was aware that, if there is not much risk of war, a country may be interested not only in peaceful settlement but also in winning a dispute, in which case it may find the coupling of issues more advantageous. Ibid., pp. 103–104.

214. John W. Burton, "Resolution and Conflict," *International Studies Quarterly,* 16 (March 1972), 9–10.
215. Ibid., pp. 10–11.
216. Ibid., p. 20.
217. Roger Fisher and William Ury, *Getting to Yes: Negotiating Agreement Without Giving In* (Middlesex, England: Penguin Books, 1983), p. 4.
218. The first four points are treated in pp. 6–14 and elaborated in chs. 6, 7 and 8, ibid.

Chapter
9

Macrocosmic Theories of Conflict: Nuclear Deterrence and Arms Control

THE NATURE OF DETERRENCE

No single concept has dominated international strategic theory during the past two decades so much as that of nuclear deterrence. According to Robert Jervis, deterrence theory is "probably the most influential school of thought in the American study of international relations," perhaps because most American scholars accepted realism and found the theory congenial.[1] Two analysts of the subject have furnished this definition: "In its most general form, deterrence is simply the persuasion of one's opponent that the costs and/or risks of a given course of action he might take outweigh its benefits."[2] Thus broadly understood, the concept of deterrence is a very old one. One can find examples in the writings of Thucydides and Machiavelli, even though they never used the term. The balance-of-power system that prevailed in Europe for a century after the Napoleonic Wars was essentially a technique for the management of power in which statesmen usually sought to make war unprofitable. Deterrence was implicit in such "signaling" or warning communications as the dispatch of naval forces, the exchange of military observers, or the conclusion of alliances, but it came to mean more in the nuclear age, when it took on the character of an explicit threat of heavily damaging retaliation.[3]

The term *deterrence* did not appear in the literature of international relations or strategic theory prior to World War II, although it had been common since the latter part of the nineteenth century for legal theorists to justify punishment as a means of deterring others from criminal behavior. Since the development of nuclear weapons, wrote Bernard Brodie, "the term has acquired not only special emphasis but also a distinctive connotation."[4] Whereas in the past, a nation's military forces were expected to prepare for whatever kind of war current technology made possible, and to wage such a war for the purpose of winning it, in the nuclear age the outbreak of a war fought with nuclear weapons came to be viewed as the greatest of all catastrophes, and henceforth the adequacy of a Great Power's military establishment was measured by its ability to deter a general nuclear war.[5] This was to be accomplished by discouraging any potential aggressors (assuming their decision-making rationality) from thinking that the gains to be achieved by deliberately resorting to nuclear war could ever outweigh the costs of embarking upon such a course. Thus the concept of nuclear deterrence rests ultimately upon the assumption that governmental policymaking bureaucracies tend toward rational rather than irrational behavior, and normally perform the kind of cost-to-gains ratio analysis of which economic theorists have long been fond. Besides rationality, however, fear is also involved, and fear may be regarded as rational under some circumstances and irrational under others.

The theory of deterrence did not emerge suddenly, but evolved gradually and was developed in stages (or what Jervis calls "waves").[6] During the period when the United States enjoyed a monopoly on atomic weapons (1945–1949), there was no systematic strategic theory of deterrence. It was preceded by the policy of *containment,* based on a concept recommended by George F. Kennan.[7] The policy of containment as a response to the threat of Soviet expansion did not involve any specific military doctrine for supporting the policy. In fact, Kennan neither emphasized nor ruled out military means of containment, but assumed that they were part of the panoply of diplomatic instruments, along with political and economic leverages available.[8] True, the idea was gradually taking shape in many quarters that the very existence of atomic weapons had radically altered the character of warfare and would hopefully preclude henceforth the waging of all-out war. The Soviets, however, did not yet possess such weapons. Among American military planners in the Truman years, it was taken for granted that if general war should break out between the United States and the Soviet Union, the former would achieve victory, as in World War II, by relying on its long-range bomber force, the principal difference being that the planes would carry the new "absolute" weapons rather than conventional bombs.[9] Still recuperating from heavy losses in World War II, the Soviet Union hardly appeared ready to become embroiled in all-out war with the world's only nuclear power, the United States. It was under the impact of certain developments and perceptions in the early 1950s that Western analysts began to sharpen and refine their theories of nuclear deterrence. These developments and perceptions included the Korean War; the growing awareness that two powers would soon possess substantial arsenals of nuclear weapons (both atomic and thermonuclear); and an apprehension that the Western countries, having carried out rapid military demobilization after World War II, were inferior to the Communist bloc in conventional forces and probably would find it politically and economically difficult to match the Communist states at that level for a global application of the containment policy over the long haul.

The Korean War produced a strategic literature devoted to the concept of "limited war." The costly, prolonged, and ambiguous conflict in East Asia had proved highly frustrating to the American people, who had become accustomed in this century to fighting all-out war to total victory and unconditional surrender of the enemy. Even though the Soviet Union was not prepared for general war at the time (and the People's Republic of China less so), the United States, under strong political pressure from its European allies to contain the conflict, and unwilling to become involved in a large-scale ground war on the Asian mainland, imposed severe limits upon its military operations. It refrained from employing atomic weapons (despite its near monopoly) and from bombing beyond the Yalu River, and prevented the forces of Chiang Kai-shek's Nationalist government on Formosa (as Taiwan was then still known) from joining the United Nations' "police action." Against General Douglas MacArthur's declaration that "in war there is no substitute for victory," the advocates of limited war argued that in the emerging nuclear era, wars must be kept nonnuclear, and war aims strictly limited. In their view, it was essential to devise ground rules for preventing war from escalating, even if this meant an agonizingly bitter struggle that resulted only in stalemate.[10]

The debate over nuclear deterrence began in earnest after the Eisenhower Administration enunciated the doctrine known as "massive retaliation." The United States would no longer feel constrained to fight an indefinite number of costly and protracted limited wars of the Korean variety without resort to nuclear weapons. According to Secretary of State John Foster Dulles, "Local defenses must be reinforced by the further deterrent of massive retaliatory power. . . . The way to deter aggression is for the free community to be willing and able to respond vigorously at places and with means of its own choosing."[11] It is important to keep in mind that the doctrine proclaimed by Dulles was not at all identical with the policy of deterrence that emerged gradually throughout the 1950s, but was only an early, crude, and controversial application of the concept of deterrence, and soon came in for much criticism. The Air Force had been arguing for strategic nuclear forces vastly superior to those of the USSR, such that the United States could "prevail" in a strategic exchange. President Eisenhower, however, as a fiscal conservative concerned about the economics of deterrence and defense over the "long haul," was convinced that superiority and a counterforce capability (to destroy enemy forces before they could inflict heavy damage on the United States and its allies) would be too expensive. This would undermine the notion that nuclear weapons provided an economically efficient substitute for large conventional forces. Eisenhower settled for the concept of strategic "sufficiency," which presupposed the maintenance of large, yet not unlimited, nuclear forces—a posture midway between strategic superiority and minimum deterrence. "This strategy," wrote Jerome H. Kahan, "did not merely reflect a doctrinal choice but represented a bureaucratic compromise between those who argued that America had too much strategic power and those who argued that it had too little."[12] Even with such a policy, the United States enjoyed de facto strategic superiority over the USSR for many years, but the U.S. government never seriously considered the option of preventive war during the period when it could have achieved a decisive victory. Richard Smoke has stated that it will always be to the "nation's credit" that it "possessed the one opportunity in history to be master of the globe and was not even seriously tempted."[13]

Within a relatively short time, the credibility of the Dulles doctrine as an effective bulwark against Communist expansion—except in the case of large-scale attack against Western Europe—was being questioned by several critics. The doctrine of "massive retaliation" implied that the United States would reply to a future Communist attack on such in-between areas as Asia, as well as on NATO territory, with nuclear strikes by the Strategic Air Command against the Soviet Union and/or China. William W. Kaufmann raised objections against such an operational policy. Although conceding that the United States possessed the capacity for carrying out long-range strikes, he questioned whether the policy met the fundamental requirements of effective deterrence when considering the problem of making intentions *credible*. Kaufmann gave his reasons:

> They [the Communist leaders] would see that we have the capability to implement our threat, but they would also observe that, with their own nuclear capability on the rise, our decision to use the weapons of mass destruction would necessarily come only after an agonizing appraisal of costs and risks, as well as of advantages. . . . Korea and Indochina are important symbols of our reluctance, not only to intervene in the peripheral areas, but also to expand the conflicts in which we have become engaged. . . . Finally, the state of domestic and allied opinion provides them with ample reason to believe that the doctrine would be, if not a case of outright bluff, at the very most a proposal that would still have to undergo searching and prolonged debate before becoming accepted policy.[14]

Paul Nitze, who had served earlier as Director of the Policy Planning Staff in the Department of State, criticized the Dulles pronouncement by distinguishing between a purely "declaratory policy" designed for a psychological or a political purpose and an "active policy" that lends itself realistically to implementation. Nitze contended that the Dulles doctrine contained too wide a gap between what was declared and what could be done.[15] In the mid-1950s, Western strategic analysts sought to tone down the doctrine of "massive retaliation" and reduce the gap between rhetoric and reality by speaking of "graduated deterrence." The term was not a particularly apt one, insofar as it implied that deterrence itself can be graduated. One can argue that aggression either is or is not deterred, but that the application of military force can be graduated once aggression has occurred. The exponents of graduated deterrence suggested that the

Western deterrent would be more credible if the West's inferior conventional posture were to be compensated for by a doctrine calling not for "massive retaliation" but for the minimum amount of nuclear force needed to discourage, repel, or defeat aggression—entailing the use of "tactical nuclear weapons" against the Communist Heartland.[16]

Bernard Brodie

The earliest and foremost theorist of deterrence in the post–World War II era was Bernard Brodie of Yale University and subsequently of the RAND Corporation. Convinced that total nuclear war would destroy all political and social values, he rejected those approaches to strategic planning that in his view would increase the probability of nuclear war—preventive war, striking preemptively when war seemed imminent, and massive retaliation.[17]

Brodie clearly understood the strategy of deterring general war, but he linked it firmly to the complementary principle of limiting those military conflicts that might break out from time to time.[18] There was no doubt in his mind that total nuclear war must be avoided "at almost any cost." He was sure that the U.S. government would not deliberately start a nuclear war in order to gain the substantial advantage that accompanies a first strike. Thus, it is essential to convince enemies that they could never gain any significant advantage by striking first.[19] The only way to do this is to ensure the survivability of U.S. retaliatory forces capable of wreaking devastating damage upon an aggressor. No pioneer strategist of the nuclear deterrence era came closer to the heart of the matter than he did:

> For one thing, it [the policy of deterrence] uses a kind of threat which we feel must be absolutely effective, allowing for no breakdowns ever. The sanction is, to say the least, not designed for repeating action. . . . Deterrence now means something as a strategic policy only when we are fairly confident that the retaliatory instrument on which it relies will not be called upon to function at all. Nevertheless, that instrument has to be maintained at a high pitch of efficiency and readiness and constantly improved . . . at high cost.[20]

Brodie perceived that there would be little or no problem of credibility of U.S. deterrent policy with regard to a direct, strategic nuclear attack upon the United States, since no adversary, plotting a first strike, could count upon the inability, much less the unwillingness, of U.S. leadership to retaliate. The crucial problem, in his view, arose from the likelihood that the adversary would find it hard to believe that the United States would ever retaliate massively in cases of less than massive aggression, since no government would risk resorting to nuclear weapons unless vital national interests were gravely threatened. Yet he hastened to caution that it would be a tactical mistake to give the enemy an advance assurance that nuclear war is so "unthinkable" as to be impossible, for this might tempt the foe to make the wrong prediction and inadvertently precipitate total nuclear war by taking an ill-conceived gamble.[21] Although he did not admire "massive retaliation" as an operative doctrine, he did not object to allowing the enemy to think that this was the American policy when the United States enjoyed nuclear superiority. He was more worried about those who would place "less reliance upon deterrence of vast retaliatory power" and to resort to the use of tactical nuclear weapons in local wars. Dulles himself, stung by criticisms of his "massive retaliation" stance, appeared willing to move in this direction in 1957, and Brodie had misgivings about a shift that might increase the risk of nuclear war's occurrence.[22] Even in the early days of deterrence theory, there were subtleties in the debate as to whether it was possible to distinguish clearly between "strategic" and "tactical" nuclear weapons, whether such a theoretical distinction could be maintained under actual combat conditions, and whether a war involving nuclear weapons of any sort—"tactical" or "strategic"—could be kept limited. Questions like these have come up repeatedly in the theoretical debate about deterrence during the last three decades since Bernard Brodie and his colleagues at the RAND Corporation, notably Albert Wohlstetter and Herman Kahn, were laying the foundations for a new strategic literature.

Brodie was not in complete agreement with his cotheorists of deterrence at RAND. In his view, Wohlstetter's analysis concerning the requirements of deterrence was too technological and failed to take into account relevant political and psychological factors.[23] (See the next section.) Although he respected Herman Kahn's competence and originality, he deemed Kahn's optimism regarding the ability of the United States to survive thermonuclear war as unwarranted.[24] For more than a quarter-century, Brodie was a consistent advocate of credible deterrence through the maintenance of a survivable "second-strike" retaliatory capability. He was skeptical of most proposals for policies, weapons systems, conventional buildups (or counterinsurgency buildups), and strategic and tactical options that might tempt policymakers to plunge incautiously into conflict situations with a potential for escalation to nuclear war. "One effective way of keeping out of trouble is to lack the means of getting into it."[25] By no means did he regard nuclear weapons as "useless." Their most important use is to inhibit large-scale military hostilities with potentially catastrophic consequences.[26]

The Utility of Military Force

The advent of nuclear weapons did not by any means prompt either governments or military advisers to conclude that military power had lost its utility, as Walter Millis[27] and other writers suggested. Klaus Knorr, Barry Blechman and Stephen Kaplan, Laurence Martin, and Robert Gilpin, as well as others, noted that military forces, both nuclear and conventional, would continue to cast a shadow of power capable of influencing the political behavior of states, even though they might not be used in combat; that conventional wars might still be waged with significant international consequences while remaining below the level of the nuclear threshold, and that the implicit threat of escalation to the nuclear level could serve as a powerful deterrent to conventional aggression in some areas.[28] Martin argued trenchantly that the strategic nuclear balance between the two superpowers had produced a widespread but unwarranted belief that nuclear weapons can have no function beyond neutralizing each other in the framework of nuclear deterrence, and that the inaccurate assumption concerning the "uselessness" of nuclear weapons for positive purposes had helped to shape both elite and popular attitudes toward the utility of military force in general.[29] In his view, nuclear weapons could be said to possess considerable utility, since they provide "the only firm assurance of immunity from attack and the only reliable guarantee against extreme pressure from other, blackmailing, nuclear powers."[30] He also made a convincing case that nuclear weapons, combined with adequate conventional defenses, can deter a Soviet attack by superior conventional forces on U.S. allies in Europe, even if such an attack did not threaten the survival of the United States.[31] To call military power a "political instrument" is to pay it a supreme compliment.

TECHNOLOGICAL INNOVATION AND DETERRENCE

The *credibility* of deterrence constituted one problem—a continuing one, largely of a political and psychological nature. A second problem, related to but theoretically and practically distinct from the first, arose out of the fact that modern weapons technology undergoes constant dynamic change. This is the technical problem of the degree of *vulnerability* or *invulnerability* of nuclear weapons. The concept of deterrence refers primarily to the holding of nuclear weapons capabilities for the purpose of confronting a potential nuclear aggressor with the threat of having to absorb an "unacceptable level of damage" in a retaliatory blow even after having carried out a surprise first strike against the deterrer. In the late 1950s, especially after the USSR launched its first earth-orbiting satellite *Sputnik* in 1957, voices were raised in warning against assuming the survivability of nuclear forces, strategic stability, and the automaticity of deterrence. In 1959, Albert Wohlstetter pointed out publicly that impending technological development would render strategic weapons more vulnerable to surprise attack and that deterrence could be maintained only as a result of difficult defense choices pertaining to the dispersal, mobility, and protection of missile systems.[32]

Analysts argued that if a nation maintained a force of strategic bombers and missiles that were unprotected, these would be "provocative" and would invite attack because it could not be argued that they were intended to serve a purely defensive second-strike role. Since they would not survive to carry out a second strike, they would appear to have a first-strike mission and would give rise to apprehensiveness on the part of an adversary. If both sides retained unprotected (or "unhardened") strategic forces, the international situation would be characterized by a condition of "trigger-happy" nervousness that would make mutual deterrence unstable. Deterrence would become more stable if both sides moved toward secure, invulnerable, second-strike capabilities. By the mid-1960s, there was a widespread assumption among strategic analysts that the superpowers either had achieved or were moving toward such stable mutual deterrence as a result of dispersing and protecting land-based ICBMs and sea-based SLBMs, although Soviet strategists appeared much less interested than their American counterparts in a "second-strike" strategy, and the USSR did not achieve a significant degree of invulnerability of missile forces until the early 1970s.[33]

However, stable mutual deterrence is not something to be achieved once and for all. Weapons technology continues to advance, and governments remain anxiously preoccupied with the fine points of the military balance at the strategic level. New developments in the fields of ballistic missile defense, multiple independently targeted reentry vehicles (MIRVs), and several other significant areas of advanced military technology prompted writers throughout the 1960s to express concern over the possibility that the international strategic situation, viewed in objective mathematical terms, would again become unstable. It was suggested that a ballistic missile defense, if deployed to protect a nation's population centers, might arouse an adversary's fears that the nation was enhancing its first-strike option by preparing to blunt the retaliatory blow; MIRVs were looked upon by some as means of increasing the number, penetrability, and accuracy of warheads, and thus of threatening to eliminate a large part of a land-based ICBM force on which the ability to carry out assured destruction in retaliation depended heavily. Some analysts discerned an action-reaction relationship in superpower armaments competition: If one side insisted on deploying a ballistic missile defense to protect its strategic missiles, the other allegedly would probably develop MIRVs in order to compensate with augmented offensive power, and might actually overcompensate, thus prompting the first party both to speed up its strategic defense efforts and also eventually to develop MIRVs.[34] Essentially similar arguments, appropriately updated, were revived in the 1980s by the critics of proposals for strategic space-based defense. Yet it is equally plausible to suggest that deterrence could be defensively based. Under such circumstances conflict would be deterred by the ability of one side, or both parties, to protect against the destructive consequences of an attack by the other. It is such an interest in altering fundamentally the deterrence paradigm—from offense to defense—that motivated proponents of the Strategic Defense Initiative and contributed to a debate about the basis for deterrence in the 1980s, to be discussed later in this chapter.

The arguments of strategic theorists did not always reflect the complexity of the international environment and the superpowers' domestic environments. The United States enjoyed a wide margin of economic-technological superiority over the Soviet Union, but operated under a much more complex set of political-economic constraints and pressures in defense programming than did the Soviet Union.[35] Nor were the strategic theorists always consistent. Some of them opposed ballistic missile defense on the grounds that it was technically and militarily of low effectiveness against incoming missiles, and at the same time criticized it because it would allegedly be highly destabilizing. Some argued that if the Soviets insisted on deploying their own antimissile missiles, it would be much cheaper and more effective for the United States to upgrade its offensive capabilities by deploying MIRVs; they later argued against MIRVs because they were destabilizing, would set the arms race into an upward spiral, and would not substantially improve the security of the United States or the effectiveness of the deterrent, since they would supposedly provoke the Soviet Union into a compensatory effort.

The strategic literature of the past two decades has abounded with esoteric technical and military terms and acronyms. Writers have distinguished between *preventive war* (premeditated to be carried out at a time of the attacker's own choosing) and *preemptive war* (resorted to by a government under the pressure of a conviction that the outbreak of nuclear war is imminent and that it must strike first rather than forfeit to the adversary the undoubted advantages of executing a disarming blow). They have also distinguished between a *countervalue* strategy (under which the adversary's population centers are targeted) and a *counterforce* strategy (which aims at destroying the adversary's strategic weapons sites and other military capabilities). A distinction, too, has often been drawn between the strategy of deterrence, which may implicitly involve the threat of all-out use of nuclear weapons (or "spasm response"), and the damage-limiting strategy of actually using nuclear weapons with restraint in military operations once deterrence has failed and war has broken out.[36] Whereas earlier deterrence theory was focused on assured retaliatory destruction, deterrence theorists subsequently showed heightened interest in such concepts as selective targeting and limited nuclear options, thereby provoking a debate over whether a shift to the latter type of strategic doctrine increases or decreases the possibility that nuclear weapons might actually be used someday. We shall return to this subject later in the chapter.

The student of international relations theory should be familiar with these basic concepts of nuclear strategy, and also with the various factors that enter into the calculus of deterrence and defense capabilities—multiple warheads, hardening, dispersal and mobility, warning times, effectiveness of surveillance, C^3 systems (command, control, and communication), reliability and guidance-system accuracy of missiles, the performance characteristics of different offensive and defensive types of weapons, and so forth—on which the data can be expected to change along with the technology.

DETERRENCE AND THE BALANCE OF POWER

The concept of mutual deterrence is, in a sense, the classical notion of "balance of power" in modern guise. Many writers, including Bernard Brodie, Hedley Bull, Henry A. Kissinger, Robert Bowie, Robert Osgood, Donald G. Brennan, Thomas C. Schelling, and Herman Kahn have treated "mutual deterrence," "stable deterrence," "balanced deterrence," and "stable arms balance" in terms remarkably reminiscent of earlier treatises on the balance of power, and these writers reflect a keen awareness of the same difficulties which plagued the older theory. It has often been said that the balance of power does not provide a good theoretical basis for foreign policy decision-making because it is uncertain (since there are no reliable criteria for measuring comparative power) and because it is unreal (since nations, feeling uncertain, are not content to aim at achieving a balance, but seek instead a margin of superiority or a unilaterally "favorable balance of power"). Thus, contemporary statesmen and their advisors have difficulty in determining whether "stable mutual deterrence" describes a condition that exists or prescribes a course that should be pursued, whether it is an objective situation best achieved automatically by the continued efforts of both sides to attain superiority in military technology or whether it is a policy requiring a cooperative conscious quest for parity by rival governments.

PSYCHOLOGICAL AND POLITICAL FACTORS IN DETERRENCE

It has long been recognized that deterrence is as much a psychological-political concept as a military concept. It depends not only upon the objective military-technological situation, but also upon the perception and the evaluation that go on in the mind of the potential aggressor. Henry Kissinger wrote:

> From the point of view of deterrence a seeming weakness will have the same consequences as an actual one. A gesture intended as a bluff but taken seriously is more useful as a deterrent than a bona fide threat interpreted as bluff. Deterrence requires a combination of power, the will to use it, and the assessment of these by the potential aggressor. Moreover, deterrence is a product of those factors and not a sum. If any one of them is zero, deterrence fails.[37]

A deterrent capability to be effective cannot be kept secret. A certain amount of knowledge about it must be communicated to the adversary. If one side deploys additional weapons or modernizes its weapons arsenal in total secrecy, then it has not really upgraded the effectiveness of its deterrent force. (For a discussion of strategic communication, see the section on Thomas C. Schelling in Chapter 11.) At any given time, of course, governmental policymakers may feel comfortable with their estimates of the existing military situation. All governments carry on intelligence-gathering activities and expect others to do likewise. Different departments and agencies of a government may disagree among themselves concerning intelligence estimates. Individuals may fear inadequate data, contradictions in the data, deliberate deception or distortion of data, and interpretations of the data that are deemed unduly optimistic or pessimistic. Although deterrence requires that some knowledge be communicated to the other side, transmitting too much intelligence might weaken the deterrent if it were to facilitate planning an attack.[38] Uncertainties increase as military technology becomes more complex. The question arises as to whether an increase in uncertainty in the calculus of possible nuclear exchange effects, resulting from the deployment of new weapons systems, is more likely to strengthen or to weaken the condition of mutual deterrence.

Robert E. Osgood has aptly described the part played by uncertainty in the delicate and fragile calculus of deterrence—a calculus that involves a process of "mutual mind reading" in an effort to second-guess an opponent with respect to intentions, values assigned to an objective, estimated costs and effectiveness of certain actions, and the probability of specific interactive responses. He notes that up to a point the element of uncertainty in nuclear deterrence, taken together with the frightful implications of miscalculation, may contribute to caution and restraint, and thus to international stability. But he warns against an excessive reliance upon uncertainty:

> It leads to a kind of strategic monism that relies too heavily upon the undeviating self-restraint and low risk-taking propensities of statesmen. It ignores the provocative effect of the fearful uncertainties and risks, to breed unwarranted confidence in the regularity and predictability of that balance, which in turn diminishes the restraints upon military action.[39]

More recently, Stanley Sienkiewicz has named uncertainty as the central problem in contemporary strategic analysis. A nuclear aggressor planning an attack does not know whether the potential victim will launch vulnerable retaliatory forces as soon as it is clear that an attack is underway, nor can the aggressor predict how the enemy's command and control system will function, and how well the retaliatory forces will operate. Sienkiewicz concludes that "the greater the operational uncertainty associated with the forces of both sides—particularly with those that have first-strike capabilities—the greater the crisis stability of the strategic nuclear balance."[40]

Raymond Aron has argued that "there is no deterrent in a general or abstract sense; it is a case of knowing *who* can deter *whom, from what, in what circumstances, by what means.*"[41] Thus, according to the late political sociologist of the University of Sorbonne, deterrence must always be analyzed in specific, concrete terms. What deters one government might not deter another. What succeeds in one geographical-cultural context might fail in another. For this reason Aron questioned the value of a certain type of "strategic fiction" that describes dozens of conflict situations or scenarios reduced to simplified schemes that lack historical reality. Such writing, in Aron's view, might make statesmen "overestimate the technical aspect of the diplomatic or military problems, and underestimate the importance of the psychological, moral, and political data" that are unique in each situation.[42] Ole R. Holsti, in a similar vein, points out that although the assumptions of deterrence are valid in most times and circumstances, nevertheless deterrence does presuppose rational and predictable decision processes, and therefore he warns that no system of deterrence

> is likely to prove effective against a nation led by a trigger-happy paranoid, or by someone seeking personal or national self-destruction or martyrdom, or by decision makers willing to play a form of international Russian roulette, or by leaders whose information about and communication with an adversary are so incomplete that their decision-making processes are dominated by guesswork, or by those who regard the loss of most of their nation's population and resources as a reasonable cost for the achievement of foreign-policy goals.[43]

Successful deterrence involves a nonevent. It is difficult enough in the realm of human affairs to demonstrate why something did happen; it is impossible to prove conclusively why something did not happen. Can we be certain, for example, that the Cuban Missile Crisis did not lead to war because nuclear deterrence was successful in that case? Or is this all that is meant by deterrence—namely, that the thing feared (nuclear war) did not occur under circumstances where it appeared to be a distinct possibility? Was either superpower strongly motivated to go to war at the time, only to be held back by an assessment of the consequences, or were both superpowers determined throughout the series of events comprising that crisis to do their utmost to achieve their objectives without resorting to actual warfare? (The Cuban Missile Crisis is treated in Chapter 11, "Decision-Making Theories.") Such questions can probably never be answered with finality. The strategic theory of deterrence is not quite the same as mathematics, which proceeds by an intrinsic logical necessity of its own. The analysis of deterrence always involves debatable factors of human judgment, such as political common sense based on experience (which some might call "intuition" or a "hunch"), the interplay of individual and bureaucratic rationality, and "second-guessing" as well as risk-taking. Some scholars, however, have warned that intuitive evaluations of deterrence credibility are unreliable.[44]

Patrick M. Morgan has drawn a useful distinction between *general* deterrence and *immediate* deterrence. General deterrence implies a policy stance of regulating an adversary relationship and balancing power over what may be a long period of time, through maintenance of a satisfactory level of forces. Most of the time adversaries do not regard war as imminent or proximate. Immediate (or pure) deterrence, in contrast, implies a specific situation in which one side is seriously considering mounting an attack, whereas the other side is preparing a threat of retaliation in order to prevent it, and both sides realize what is going on.[45]

THE LEVELS OF DETERRENCE

George and Smoke called attention to the fact that deterrence theory and practice developed at three different levels: strategic war, limited war, and "sublimited"* conflict at the lower end of the spectrum of violence. Since the mid-1950s, the deterrence of strategic war has received the greatest amount of attention in the literature and has become a separate and fairly precise discipline in itself, replete with its own specialized concepts, technical vocabulary, and methodologies—game and economic utility theories, systems analysis, and computerized war-gaming. The core concept, of course, on the basis of which the requirements of strategic deterrence are calculated, is the maintenance of an Assured Destruction capability for retaliation after a surprise attack.[46] Virtually all analysts agree that what the policy of strategic nuclear deterrence is designed primarily to deter is strategic, all-out, or large-scale nuclear war, and *perhaps* all nuclear war, however limited (although this latter point is controversial) or even, as in the case of NATO-Europe, the outbreak of a conventional war that might escalate to limited or all-out nuclear conflict.

What other types of undesirable actions or behaviors can be deterred? Does the existence of a strategic deterrent force sufficient to discourage a surprise nuclear attack automatically deter a limited conventional attack? It probably cannot do this by itself, but it is generally assumed that one nuclear superpower cannot realistically expect to inflict upon another nuclear superpower a defeat in a conventional limited war without running the grave risk that the conflict would escalate to the nuclear level. Thus, strategic deterrence combined with the normal behavioral characteristics of Great Powers and the fear of uncontrollable escalation produces a definite inhibiting effect against the outbreak of conventional war directly embroiling any of the military forces of nuclear great powers. Laurence Martin holds that strategic nuclear deterrence can, in combination with other nuclear and conventional defense capabilities, be extended for the purpose of protecting formal allies or other friendly client states against the danger of either nuclear or conventional attack.[47] A decade earlier, John H. Herz had argued that the very same nuclear developments that have rendered modern industrial states so vulnerable to the threat of physical annihilation have also made the use of conven-

---

*The term *sublimited conflict* was introduced in the 1960s to refer to a broad spectrum of conflict below the level of conventional war. It included insurgency, infiltration, demonstration of force, naval blockades, and similar modes of applying pressure. In recent years, it has been replaced by the term *low-intensity conflict.*

tional military force "unavailable" in the direct relations between major nuclear powers and their allies.[48]

As George and Smoke have pointed out, deterrence at the level of limited war and "sublimited" conflict is much more complex than at the strategic level. Whether we consider the objectives of the players or the means at their disposal, the number of variables involved is greater. Each side is likely to be unsure of its own motivation and that of the other side to achieve various objectives. Deterrence of lower-level conflict is not as readily modeled as "assured destruction." The selection of the means to be employed must be subordinated to the imperatives of escalation control and the political objectives of the respective actors in the conflict, as well as the placation of allies, neutrals, and domestic opinion. At lower conflict levels, deterrence is a context-dependent problem, George and Smoke conclude. "It is dependent not upon comparatively few technical variables, known with high confidence on both sides, but upon a multiple of variables, many of them partially subjective, that fluctuate over time and are highly dependent upon the context of the situation."[49]

Bruce M. Russett made an empirical study of 17 cases over the 1935 to 1961 period in an effort to determine under what circumstances "extended deterrence" has been successful in preventing attack upon third parties. His cases therefore stretched over both the prenuclear and the nuclear era. He examined instances in which a major power attacker had overtly threatened a "pawn" with military force and a defender had given some commitment in time to prevent the threatened attack. Admittedly, his study excluded what may be regarded as the most successful instances of deterrence—those in which the potential attackers are dissuaded even from making an overt threat against the pawn. Russett found that the enjoyment of strategic and local military superiority by the defender did not guarantee successful deterrence. More important for the credibility of deterrence was a demonstration of the economic, political, and military interdependence of defender and pawn.[50] Later, Russett and other international scholars came to the conclusion that there are serious limitations in using statistical-correlative methods in the analysis of decision-making variables in deterrence cases, because these variables are often subtle and complex, and may not be perceived by decision-makers at the time of the choice in the same way as they are seen by scholars who review them later.[51]

A policy of nuclear deterrence is not relevant to conventional wars between states that lack nuclear weapons themselves or are not firmly allied to a nuclear-weapon power with a binding commitment. Moreover, nuclear weapons will be unlikely under most conceivable circumstances to deter revolution, civil war, and guerrilla insurgencies (which Communists call "wars of liberation") and other forms of low-intensity conflict. Prior to the Gorbachev era, the Soviet leadership often publicly declared its willingness to support this last category of warfare. The threat of nuclear retaliation cannot possibly be brought to bear against organized international terrorism, and cannot even be realistically hurled against the government of a small nonnuclear-weapon state that carries out an act of physical provocation against an aircraft or naval vessel belonging to a nuclear-weapon power. In other words, in the nuclear age, weakness can become a source of bargaining strength and strength can lead to paralysis.

Finally, since deterrence presupposes rational decision-making, even though it proves perfectly successful in discouraging a deliberate choice for nuclear war, it has no direct relevance to the possibility of unintended acts of destructiveness, whether nuclear or conventional, resulting from technical accident, human psychic failure, misinterpretation of warning signals, the seizure and use of nuclear weapons by unauthorized persons or terrorist groups, and similar causes not flowing from the choice of governmental decision-makers. The dangers of cataclysmic destruction that are inherent in the possession of strategic deterrent forces, however, motivate responsible governments to take precautions against the occurrence of unintentional events that might escalate beyond the bounds of control.[52]

Robert Jervis's Critique of Deterrence

The concept of deterrence has had numerous critics, including some who perceived its deficiencies yet felt constrained to give it grudging support in the absence of politically feasible and available alternatives. One of the earlier and more viscerally emotional critics was Philip Green, who expressed his fundamental thesis in the title of his book, *The Deadly Logic: The Theory of Nuclear Deterrence.*[53] Many thoughtful analysts have raised serious questions about deterrence and the assumption of policymakers' rationality on which it is founded. Robert Jervis is perhaps most representative of this group. Jervis highlights the paradoxical nature of deterrence, "in which each side hopes to gain security, not by being able to protect itself, but by threatening to inflict unacceptable damage on the other."[54] Such a definition is important, for it expresses the strategic philosophy that underlay the SALT I Antiballistic Missile (ABM) Treaty, and provides a hint as to why certain arms control analysts became apprehensive about the Strategic Defense Initiative (SDI) of President Reagan, since they feared that strategic defense might undermine before it could replace deterrence. More will be said about SDI later.

Jervis called deterrence a theory "about the ways in which an actor manipulates threats to harm others in order to coerce them into doing what he desires."[55] One must be careful not to confuse *deterrence* with *compellence.* There is a considerable difference between trying to dissuade an adversary from undertaking an action you want to prevent and trying to compel the other party to take some positive action that you want done. The threat of nuclear punishment can be used to deter, but hardly to compel, except perhaps to *reverse* a dangerous process already set in motion that might conceivably lead to nuclear war (e.g., removing Soviet missiles from Cuba).[56] A threat to employ U.S. strategic nuclear superiority in the 1950s to force the Soviet Union to withdraw from Eastern Europe would have lacked any semblance of credibility or political-strategic prudence. Jervis himself admits that deterrence theorists "present reasonable arguments about why compellence is usually more difficult than deterrence,"[57] but he expresses doubt that it is easier to deter than to compel in all circumstances, especially if the aggressor decides to risk taking the initiative:

> It has been said that the state trying to change the status quo is in a weaker bargaining position because it can drop its demand without raising the danger that the status-quo power will raise new demands. But it is hard for the latter to retreat without damaging its ability to stand firm against demands for further changes; therefore, it should be able to prevail. There is a difficulty with this argument, however. One must look at what each side will gain if it prevails. Here the very advantage just ascribed to the status-quo power turns out to be a disadvantage. What the aggressor can gain is not limited to the specific issue, but includes an increased chance of prevailing in future attempts to alter the status quo. The status-quo power, by contrast, gains only a temporary respite.[58]

Jervis criticized deterrence theory on the grounds that "it says little about how to change . . . an adversary or to determine whether changes have taken place."[59] As a guide for statesmen, it tells them how to maintain a hostile, mutually dangerous relationship, but not how to alter the situation. Thus, "it provides a greater help in understanding crises than in understanding long-run disputes," but it offers no advice on how to avoid crises or how to decide whether the national interests at stake are sufficient to warrant the resort to military force; and it is inadequate because it fails to take into account that "successful accommodation usually requires at least some change in the values and goals of both sides."[60] The classical theorists of deterrence had never suggested that it was intended to serve such purposes, but only that, somewhat like the policy of containment with which it was related, it would fend off undesirable developments—war or Soviet expansion—until the situation could change and the dangers be removed.

Jervis charges further that deterrence theory neglects the role of rewards and compromises in the resolution of confrontational crises because "it is simpler to ignore outcomes that are not clear-cut" and because realist scholars who dominate the field assume that promises of rewards are less potent than threats of punishment in influencing the behavior of states.[61] He also finds the theory wanting because it is derived from the experience, culture, and values of the West—in short, it is ethnocentric. It rests on the assumption that while nations may pursue contrary goals, they all share the same basic behavioral patterns.

> It does not consider that people from other cultures might develop quite different analyses. For example, both interest and tradition may lead the USSR

to view nuclear strategy more in terms of defense than deterrence; to seek the capacity to fight and win wars; and to reject the axiom that neither side should try to endanger the other's second-strike capability. . . . Deterrence theory may then explain American but not Soviet policy, and American actions would not have the impact expected by American leaders or predicted by the theory.[62]

Jervis subtly observes that the theory does not demand *total* rationality to be valid. He does not agree with Morgan when the latter cites a basic paradox—namely, that the classic deterrence theory may be counterproductive if it always seeks to enhance the confidence of governments in their ability to remain perfectly cool and deliberate in times of crisis. Jervis moves closer to one of the most sophisticated theorists of deterrence, Thomas C. Schelling, in the following passage:

The paradox is not as great as Morgan thinks. There is an irreducible minimum of unpredictability that operates, especially in situations which engage a state's highest values. Thus, even though there is no rational argument for a countercity response to a Soviet attack on the United States or Western Europe, the mere possibility may be an effective deterrent. . . . [I]t is bizarre for a state to maintain its security by making its adversaries believe that it is prepared to bring about the end of its civilization. This policy makes more sense when we consider threats that leave something to chance: it can be rational to threaten, and carry out, a move that increases slightly the danger of an all-out war, while it would be completely irrational to launch an attack. Indeed, much of deterrence rests on the fact that both sides know that events are not entirely under their control.[63]

The "threat that leaves something to chance" was a Schelling invention. The fear of "things getting out of hand" was Schelling's favorite method of solving the credibility problem. "A response that carries some risk of war can be plausible, even reasonable at a time when a final, ultimate decision to have a general war would be implausible or unreasonable."[64] While the fear of irrational action can strengthen deterrence, an excess of "rationality" might lead to an unwanted war, according to Jervis, if one rational party initiates a crisis or decides to stand firm in the conviction that the other is bound to retreat, while the latter calculates that it can make one more "last safe move" because the former is thought rational enough to back down. The status-quo or defending power may fear the "domino effects" of retreating in a crisis, including the impact of such behavior upon third party allies and upon the self-confidence of the aggressive party in future confrontations. Beyond the dangers of misunderstanding, misperception, and misjudgment, there also lurks the danger of the accidental and the irrational, either of which can cause things to go wrong or to get out of hand, thus interfering with the neat, calculable operation of deterrence prescribed by the intellectual theory of deterrence. In the final analysis, Jervis, following Brodie and Schelling, is more interested in achieving deterrence through manipulating the level of risk than through acquiring a military capability for the "escalation dominance" favored by Paul Nitze. He sees deterrence through the acceptance of a spectrum of risks as preferable to deterrence through a spectrum of planned violence:

> The first problem with the escalation dominance logic is that a state confident of winning at a given level of violence may be deterred because it judges the cost of fighting at that level to be excessive. On the other hand, even if defense cannot succeed, the threat to defend can deter if the other side thinks that the status quo power is sufficiently strongly motivated to fight for a losing cause. Nuclear weapons have not changed the fact that defeating an enemy is not worthwhile if the costs entailed are greater than the gains.
>
> . . . It is not correct to claim that the threat to escalate will be credible only if it is believed the action will bring a military victory; one must consider the price that both sides would have to pay. Thus, the U.S. might deter a Soviet invasion of Western Europe by threatening to use tactical nuclear weapons even if the Soviets believed that they could win such a war.[65]

This line of reasoning leads Jervis to the conclusion that strategic superiority does not matter.[66] Other strategic analysts (see the next section, "Strategic Doctrines") would not agree unless both sides subscribe equally to that position.

The theory of nuclear deterrence, it bears repeating, usually presupposes a high degree of rationality on the part of national decision-makers. Rationality is a transcendental notion that cannot be precisely defined. Some may think of "rational" policy choices in moral or ethical terms, others in terms of prudent rather than reckless behavior, still others in contrast to "irrational" options that would employ any use of military force. The authors of this book conceive of "rationality" as a normal human trait that tends to relate ends and means in a proportionate manner. In political-strategic assessments, it implies a mode of analysis that weighs gains versus costs. Both advocates and critics of deterrence accept this notion, however much they may disagree over the possibility, difficulty, or impossibility of estimating the values that policymakers assign to particular goals or objectives, and estimating their willingness to bear the potential risks and costs of adopting specific courses of action that might lead to the initiation of nuclear war.[67] The question raised by Jervis and others—whether rationality prescribes the same mode of strategic thinking for the United States and the Soviet Union, and whether the two superpowers adopt essentially similar approaches to deterrence—deserves a careful answer. First, however, it is necessary to say something about strategic doctrines.

Strategic Doctrines

Theories of deterrence are influenced not only by military-technological developments but also by strategic doctrines, which are in turn products of national character, experience, ideology, and historic military thinking.

The debate over different approaches to strategic deterrence within the United States has been in no small degree a function of different perspectives of Soviet objectives and intentions. Those who believe that the Soviet Union is an inherently expansionist power bent on the eventual achievement of global hegemony will take one approach to the Soviet threat; those who consider the Soviet Union a traditional nation-state given to revolutionary rhetoric but increasingly defensive in outlook will take quite another. Even the former group divides between those who think that the leadership in Moscow strongly prefers a psychopolitical strategy that prescribes the avoidance of a decisive, frontal military encounter at all costs and those who are convinced that Moscow seeks military superiority for a strategic first strike.

Fritz Ermarth defined strategic doctrine as "a set of operative beliefs, values and assertions that in a significant way guide official behavior with respect to strategic research and development (R&D), weapons choice, forces, operational plans, arms control, etc."[68] Do the two superpowers subscribe to the same doctrine of strategic deterrence? Up to the mid-1970s many American strategic analysts (for the most part civilians influenced by economic bargaining theory) were inclined to answer in the affirmative. Soviet strategic writers (military officers, for the most part) had often given answers that the more optimistic American strategists preferred to ignore, while hoping that Soviet planners could gradually be persuaded to adopt American theories of deterrence and arms control.

Perhaps the most crucial issue in the strategic debate (prior to the emergence of the controversy over strategic defense) was the relationship between deterrence and a war-fighting capability. Those who followed along the path marked out by Bernard Brodie (including, in a sense, the U.S. Catholic Bishops in their 1983 Pastoral Letter, discussed in Chapter 5) held that the only purpose of possessing stockpiles of nuclear weapons is to deter nuclear war or any war with a potential for escalating to the nuclear level. For this school of thought, nuclear war must remain "unthinkable" and nuclear weapons must never be used. The mere existence of nuclear weapons should be sufficient to dissuade the opponent from carrying out a strategic-nuclear first strike against the United States or large-scale conventional aggression against Western Europe.

Others, following more along the lines suggested by Herman Kahn and Albert Wohlstetter, have argued that deterrence, to be most credible and effective, requires an operational doctrine and a perceived capability for fighting, winning, surviving, and recovering from a nuclear war. This type of strategy presupposes the achievement of strategic military superiority, involving invulnerable (hardened, dispersed, and/or mobile forces), a damage-limiting capability (to destroy the adversary's nuclear weapons before they could be used), active antimissile and passive civil defenses, a highly efficient and survivable C^3I system (command, control, communications, and intelligence) for early warning and battle management, an arsenal of reliable missiles and warheads accurate enough to "kill" hardened targets, all combined with the political will and psychological readiness to strike first or to "launch on warning."

The two alternative policies described above are not, and cannot be, completely dichotomous. The essential factor of credibility imperatively demands a certain overlap. It is a matter of which alternative is to be given greater emphasis in the strategic thinking, military doctrine, and force posture planning of each superpower. All through the first quarter-century of the nuclear age, from the later 1940s to the early 1970s, official U.S. deterrent policy was based on the concept of threatening a retaliatory second strike. Gradually it became clear that the United States must maintain an invulnerable retaliatory force capable of carrying out a second strike that would inflict an "unacceptable level of damage" upon the foe, usually defined by the McNamara defense establishment as the destruction of a quarter or more of the population and two-thirds or more of the economic-industrial structure of the USSR.[69] Defense Secretary McNamara called it deterrence by the threat of Assured Destruction. As Soviet strategic forces grew, it became known as Mutual Assured Destruction (MAD), which was presumed to be the basis of mutual deterrence and mutual restraint.

Prior to the mid-1980s, Soviet strategic writings did not reflect a commitment to the concept of deterrence as it was understood in the West. Comparison was never an easy matter because whereas the United States was sometimes too explicit in promulgating its official policy and doctrine, the Soviet government placed a much higher premium on secrecy. A United Nations publication in 1980 carried the following statement:

> The concept of military doctrine is used in somewhat different ways by the major military powers. . . . Soviet nuclear doctrines are generally not as openly expressed as is the case in the United States. Soviet thinking on the subject to a large extent has to be deduced from very general statements, from military force dispositions, and from Soviet military writing.[70]

The problem of comparing was compounded by the fact that governments themselves must distinguish between public declaratory policies (variously aimed at domestic audiences, allies, world public opinion, and the adversary) and actual operational plans for the development, acquisition, deployment, and use of nuclear weapons.[71] Such requirements to explain policies and doctrines place a heavy burden on democratic governments, and often lead to apparent ambiguities and contradictions that generate doubts, anxieties, fears, and confusion in one quarter or another. One Soviet spokesman complained that American strategic thinking follows a "zig-zag" course.[72] It cannot be denied that, as the international strategic-technological environment has changed, and new generations of nuclear weapons have emerged, the terminology in which U.S. strategic doctrine has been couched has also undergone generational changes.

Most American students of Soviet strategic writings were long skeptical as to whether the Soviet Union accepted the concept of mutual deterrence as understood in the West. Robert Legvold contended that while the United States had a doctrine of deterrence based on bargaining theory, the Soviet Union had no theory of deterrence, only a science of war, and regarded the sophisticated subtleties of the American theorists as rationales for using nuclear weapons.[73] Benjamin Lambeth, Michael Salomon, Donald G. Brennan, Fritz Ermarth, and others doubted that the Soviet Union attached much importance to such goals as strategic parity in the SALT I negotiations.[74] There was no evidence that Soviet strategists would be content with a doctrine that calls for retaliation after absorbing a first strike. Indeed, in their view, such a doctrine was not a rational one, and they may not have believed that the United States would abide by its own professed doctrine in a crisis. All the writers mentioned above, as well as Richard Pipes, John Erickson, Paul Nitze, and Dimitri K. Simes, were inclined to think that the Soviet political and military leaders, even though they might wish to avoid general nuclear war at all costs, preferred active to passive deterrence.[75] This involved an effort to achieve a war-fighting, war-winning, and war-recovery capability, and a readiness to strike preemptively if nuclear war should ever appear to be unavoidable and imminent. Raymond Garthoff agreed that a war-fighting and war-winning capability constituted the most credible deterrent in the eyes of Soviet strategists, but he was also willing to give them the benefit of the doubt on whether or not they accepted deterrence in the Western sense. In contrast to the other writers cited above, who tended to think that the Soviet leadership regarded "strategic parity" only as a step along the way to "strategic superiority," Garthoff argued that the aim of Soviet nuclear policy was parity, not superiority, and that Moscow considered "negotiated strategic arms limitation as a desirable means to contribute to this maintenance of parity and balance."[76]

The debate over mutual deterrence through the threat of mutual assured destruction reached a climax during the 1970s, especially after the SALT I agreements had ostensibly codified strategic parity. American strategists became concerned over the threat that Soviet heavy missiles (numbering more than 300) would pose to U.S. land-based intercontinental ballistic missiles (ICBMs) once they had been fitted with multiple independently targetable reentry vehicles (MIRVs). Secretary of Defense James R. Schlesinger and his successor, Harold Brown, began to worry lest the continuing buildup of Soviet strategic capabilities (even within the permitted SALT I ceilings) would create a situation in which the United States might no longer feel confident that it possessed sufficient survivable retaliatory force to deter a Soviet first strike. (The sea-based deterrent, of course, would survive an attack on land-based forces, but at the time submarine-launched ballistic missiles, or SLBMs, were considered both less reliable than ICBMs because of communications problems and less accurate than ICBMs, and therefore less suitable to a counterforce than a countercity role.) The policy of deterrence based on MAD became less attractive. (Mounting criticism of the MAD doctrine on religious and ethical grounds was treated in Chapter 5.) Schlesinger identified a need for the United States to back away from the idea of a massive retaliatory strike and to consider "limited nuclear options" and "selective targeting,"[77] thereby implying that the United States would not necessarily wait for a direct strategic attack before using strategic weapons of its own in a future conflict. The latter part of the decade was marked by observations in the annual publications of the International Institute for Strategic Studies (IISS) in London that the global military balance was tilting steadily in favor of the East.[78] Soviet ideologues were boasting that the "world correlation of forces" was shifting in the direction of the socialist camp. Richard L. Garwin cautioned those strategists who were preoccupied with the "window of vulnerability" (the theoretical possibility that 90 percent of the U.S. ICBM force might be destroyed in a surprise first strike) not to advocate a policy of "launch on warning."[79] The Carter Administration undertook a study to determine whether the U.S. strategic deterrent remained effective in the face of the Soviet buildup, and this led to the adoption in 1980 of the "countervailing strategy," which was widely interpreted as a sign that the United States was regearing from deterrence to war-fighting plans.[80] Colin Gray was foremost among those calling clearly for a war-fighting strategy, including ballistic missile defense, designed to produce victory.[81] The central issues in this phase of the debate were (1) whether the adoption of a war-fighting strategy by the United States would strengthen the deterrent against war or make war more likely to occur, besides the obviously controversial issue of whether nuclear war could be "won" in any politically meaningful sense; and (2) whether nuclear war, should it ever begin, could be limited and controlled below the level of mutual extinction of the superpowers and the destruction of a large part of the human race and its civilizations.[82] The answer to the first question is highly subjective, for it depends on the psychology and politics (or psychopolitical characteristics) of each individual making the judgment. Some would argue, with McGeorge Bundy, that no rational American or Soviet leader would be willing to contemplate the loss of even one or two cities for the sake of "winning" a foreign policy crisis.[83] At the opposite side of the psychopolitical spectrum, some would insist that the Soviet Union, having recovered from the highly destructive World War II (in which military and civilian deaths in excess of twenty million were a hundred times greater than American losses) might be willing to place a higher price upon a nuclear war that it thought, in a critical confrontation, it might win and from which it could recover.

The second question—Can nuclear war, once begun, be limited and controlled?—is more technical. The limitation of nuclear war would require on both sides a great deal of political self-restraint as well as a highly developed system of command, control, communications, and intelligence (C^3I). Even if we assume a very strong mutual determination to prevent uncontrollable escalation, and a desire to avoid damaging the adversary's C^3I structure (despite powerful military incentives in some cases to destroy it), so that the adversary can know the intention to limit and can respond in kind, nevertheless the performance of that structure may not prove adequate to the heavy demands placed upon it during a nuclear exchange because of many factors—jamming, deception, infiltration, and sabotage by *spetznaz* ("special forces"), or defense-suppression attacks by NATO-Warsaw Pact or U.S.-Soviet strategic forces; staffing by incompetent or poorly trained personnel who undergo psychological shock once nuclear hostilities have been initiated; improper netting and coordination of communicating units; technical equipment failures; time-lags; human operating errors under conditions of extreme stress; misinterpretation of information and/or orders; atmospheric and ionospheric disturbances; communications blackout effects (lasting several hours) of electromagnetic pulse (EMP) from the detonation of large thermonuclear weapons in and above the atmosphere; and other causes.[84]

Desmond Ball has analyzed these vulnerabilities of C^3I systems and their implications for the control of nuclear war. He points out that the National Command Authority is vulnerable to attack by submarine-launched ballistic missiles (SLBMs), for which the warning time would be minimal. Ball describes technologically more complex difficulties and failures that could arise in the operation of airborne C^3 systems of the Strategic Air Command or the Navy, affecting the communications links between command centers and ICBMs or SLBMs, or both; of satellite warning, reconnaissance, and communication systems (thereby degrading intelligence concerning what is actually happening worldwide); of the Washington-Moscow Hot Line on which superpower emergency communications depend; and of the submarine command and control system, not because of the submarine survivability factor but rather because of the special problems associated with maintaining reliable communications with submerged submarines, properly functioning navigation systems, and the ability to use SLBMs selectively. Ball and other analysts, including Michael Howard, Andrei Sakharov, Spurgeon M. Keeny, Wolfgang K. H. Panovsky, Ian Clark, and Robert McNamara, have concluded that nuclear war cannot be controlled, except perhaps for a relatively small portion of strategic nuclear forces, only for a brief period, and only in situations where the Soviet Union practices restraint, but not in a high-level nuclear exchange in which strategically important military, political, and administrative power and C^3 centers are being destroyed at a rapid rate.[85] Soviet analysts throughout most of the nuclear age, while insisting that the use of nuclear weapons must always be subject to political control, have not thought about controlled or limited war as have earlier Western advocates of the concept. For Soviet theoreticians, selectivity is to be understood in the context of simultaneous and massive blows against any and all targets capable of causing damage to the Soviet Union, not sequential, restrained, discriminating "surgical" strikes.

The world will be better off if the principal decision-makers in all nuclear-weapon states remain firmly convinced in advance of the outbreak of war that a nuclear exchange cannot be limited. Such a shared conviction would tend to strengthen deterrence against a deliberate choice for initiating any war that contains a built-in potential for escalation to the nuclear level. The logic of deterrence itself demands this type of rationality. Uncertainty should compel responsible leaders to conduct themselves with consummate prudence in time of crisis. Responsible governments, however, cannot be content with this. They must also be prepared for the possibility—however low the probability may be—that deterrence might fail. They must be ready to do whatever they can to compensate with rational decision-making *after* the fact of the outbreak of war for the collapse of rational decision-making *before* the fact. If deterrence should fail, it will then be of the utmost urgency for political and military leaders on both sides to become convinced quickly that it can and must be limited, that city destruction must be avoided, that the C^3 networks of the adversary must be left intact for the sake of controllability, and that if nuclear weapons are introduced their use against strictly military targets must be as discriminating as possible, with minimal collateral damage to innocent populations and civilizational structures, until the conflict can be terminated as quickly as possible on terms less disadvantageous to each side than a continuation of nuclear war would be for both and for the international community.

EXTENDED NUCLEAR DETERRENCE: EUROPE

Deterrence of a Soviet attack upon the United States is called *direct,* and of a Soviet attack upon Western Europe *indirect* or *extended.* The latter has usually been regarded as a more difficult problem than the former, because it is much harder for a nation to maintain the credibility of a threat that it will run the risk of nuclear war for allies just as it would for its own vital national interest or even survival. The U.S. pledge to defend Western Europe was quite believable all through the 1950s, when the United States enjoyed unquestioned strategic nuclear superiority by virtue of its long-range bomber force. The members of the Atlantic Alliance and its integrated military organization, NATO, had no choice from the beginning but to rely upon U.S. nuclear power because of the Soviet-Western conventional force imbalance and the prohibitive cost of trying to match Warsaw Pact conventional strength over the "long haul." Prime Minister Winston Churchill and President Dwight Eisenhower were convinced in the early 1950s that nuclear deterrence would be much less costly and militarily much more effective than conventional deterrence.[86]

Ideally, it is desirable to have both a high deterrent posture and a high degree of defense readiness in case deterrence fails. Such a combination of nuclear threat and war-fighting capability enhances the credibility of deterrence, for it eliminates the danger of self-paralysis in time of crisis that inheres in the possession of a capability to make only an "all-or-nothing" response. In contrast to the last years of the Eisenhower Administration, when the air was filled with talk about a "conventional pause," "dual-capability forces," and "tactical" or "limited" nuclear war, the Kennedy Administration tried to separate nuclear from conventional forces and responses by time, geography, and command and control systems.

There was something to be said for each of the diverging positions taken by the Americans and the Europeans. The Kennedy Administration pursued what it regarded as the prudent and responsible way of reducing the probability of nuclear war and increasing the options available between holocaust and surrender. American policymakers believed that, in order to minimize the risk of escalation to all-out nuclear war, NATO had to reduce its reliance on tactical nuclear weapons and maintain a clear "firebreak" between conventional and nuclear hostilities because the distinction between "tactical nuclear war" and "strategic" or "central nuclear war" would be highly ambiguous and extremely difficult to maintain under actual combat conditions.[87]

West European strategists and policymakers, analyzing the situation from a very different geostrategic space and geopolitical perspective, were quite understandably of two minds on the subject. At times they feared that in a crisis the United States would not be willing to defend them with nuclear weapons; at other times their fear was that it *would* be willing to do so. Most European policymakers, remembering the terrible carnage of the two world wars—"conventional" wars—preferred maximum reliance upon nuclear deterrence to preclude any war at all. They certainly did not want tactical, limited nuclear war, nor did they want a purely conventional response by NATO, involving a NATO fallback and a subsequent "liberation counteroffensive." (They had had a taste in World War II of what that would mean.) Some American policymakers and strategic analysts undoubtedly regarded the European attitude as illogical, unrealistic, or perhaps ostrich-like in its characteristic avoidance of thinking through the potential consequences of relying too heavily upon a nuclear strategy. In the minds of many Europeans, the Americans were being too logical and too mathematical, but not sufficiently intelligent in terms of European psychology and politics. The strategy of deterrence works, the Europeans argued. By taking a remote hypothesis of how deterrence might break down, and making that the basis of a new strategic doctrine for NATO, the United States in European eyes might increase the probability of military conflict that could eventually become nuclear. From one European perspective, "flexible response" involved a weakening rather than a strengthening of deterrence.

National Deterrent Forces in Europe

For years, West European strategic analysts expressed mounting concern over changes in the U.S.-Soviet global strategic balance and also in the theater balance between NATO and the Warsaw Pact. It was long assumed that, against a backdrop of U.S. strategic superiority, American tactical nuclear weapons in NATO compensated for the Pact's three-to-one margin in armor. In the mid-1970s, however, having achieved the formal codification of strategic parity in the Strategic Arms Limitation Talks, the Soviet Union began to acquire a formidable array of theater nuclear capabilities, including land-based missile delivery systems of considerably longer range than those at the disposal of NATO. Worries grew that European defense might gradually be "decoupled" from the strategic deterrent capabilities of the United States. There was fear that the Soviet Union, by projecting a shadow of unmatchable military power, would be able to "Finlandize" Western Europe, bringing about its eventual political and economic orientation toward Moscow.[88]

Some French theorists, emphasizing the enormous destructive potential of a single thermonuclear weapon, have argued that a nation need not possess a nuclear force as powerful as that of the United States in order to pursue successfully a policy of deterrence (or "dissuasion") even against the Soviet Union. Pierre Gallois, a retired French Air Force General, in the early 1960s advanced the thesis that deterrence is a matter of proportion. Unlike the United States, smaller countries such as Great Britain and France do not constitute decisive obstacles to the world hegemonial ambitions of an aggressive power. In order to seize those countries, an aggressive Soviet Union would not run the risks that it might be willing to contemplate for the purpose of removing the threat of its principal rival, the United States. The latter is obliged to maintain an absolute deterrent. A lesser power should be able to deter attack with proportionately smaller nuclear forces. Gallois advocated a countercity *force de dissuasion.* If France could be certain of an ability to penetrate Soviet defenses and strike, let us say, 50 targets in the USSR, the Soviet leaders would conclude that the value of overrunning France would not be worth the risk. A national deterrent in the hands of a threatened European nation, Gallois argued, would be more credible than a promise by the United States or a deterrent force controlled by a group of European governments (each of which would almost certainly retain a veto power). If a smaller power decides to use nuclear weapons against a superpower, it must be prepared to commit suicide, but if it commits itself to an automatic response, the strategy of dissuasion will work.[89] Despite the morbid and risky elements in Gallois's theory, it suited the purposes of President Charles de Gaulle, Europe's leading advocate of national deterrence. Britain also possessed national strategic nuclear forces, but these were integrated into the NATO military command as "an independent contribution to the deterrent."[90] At a time when neither French nor British nuclear forces had achieved anything approaching strategic "respectability," most defense officials in Europe could perceive no practical alternative to relying on the American deterrent.

Throughout the 1970s, misgivings over the shifting balance in strategic and theater nuclear forces became more pronounced. The post-Vietnam, post-Watergate syndrome weakened the president of the United

States in the conduct of foreign policy. This was reflected in the apparent inability of the United States to deal with developments in Angola, the Horn of Africa, Iran, and Afghanistan. When the Soviet Union began targeting Western Europe with newly deployed mobile SS-20s, West German Chancellor Helmut Schmidt called attention to NATO Europe's growing vulnerability, sparking a reassessment that led to the Alliance's "two-track decision" in Brussels in December 1979 on intermediate-range nuclear forces: to try to negotiate with Moscow a more equitable nuclear balance in Europe while simultaneously preparing to deploy Pershing II and Tomahawk ground-launched cruise missiles in five European countries.[91] This development led to an intensification of interest in East-West arms control negotiations. Disarmament and arms control had been a persistent theme in superpower diplomacy ever since the early postwar years. To these subjects we now turn our attention.

DISARMAMENT AND ARMS CONTROL

Arms control and disarmament are related but distinct concepts. They overlap occasionally yet reflect divergent approaches to the arms problem. Whereas disarmament in the strict sense involves the destruction of armaments and the prohibition against their future production, arms control presupposes that nations will continue to possess arms and aims at managing them to enhance security and promote desirable political and strategic objectives, rather than allowing weapons technology to dictate policies in ways that reduce the safety and controllability of the international environment. Thus, arms control policies typically seek to impose some kind of restraint or regulation on the qualitative design, quantitative production, method of deployment, protection, control, transfer, and planned, threatened, or actual use of military forces and weapons. Such policies may imply collaboration between adversaries—formal agreements, tacit understandings, or informal cooperation. They may also embrace unilateral decisions taken with the hope or expectation of reciprocal action, or unilateral decisions deemed worth taking even if the adversary does not respond, simply because they enhance the stability of the deterrent, controllability, security against unintended war, and damage limitation if war should occur. Central to the thinking of most arms control proponents is the reduction of tensions, risks, and dangers without weakening deterrence. Specific arms control proposals, however, may have other purposes in the minds of their supporters—for example, to promote détente, to effect budget cuts, to permit a shift of resources to nondefense programs, to preserve "arms control momentum," to satisfy public opinion, and so on.[92]

Some arms control measures have been carried out unilaterally. These included the acquisition by the United States of an invulnerable second-strike capability for the sake of effective deterrence; the introduction of two-key systems and electronic permissive action links in NATO Europe to create a clear "firebreak" between conventional and nuclear operations in case of war; and President Reagan's Strategic Defense Initiative (SDI), which will be discussed below. Some arms control measures have either led to no significant results (e.g., the "no-cities strategy")[93] or limited results in areas outside the crucially sensitive region of Europe (e.g., in the agreements to create nuclear-free zones in Latin America and the South Pacific).[94]

It is not the function of a text on international relations theories to detail the provisions of those diplomatically negotiated instruments. We shall limit our attention here to selected arms control subjects. Some have lent themselves to theorizing only to a limited degree. Take the nuclear test ban, for example. Originally, the Western powers refused to accept a cessation of nuclear testing except as an integral part of a comprehensive nuclear disarmament program, on the plausible grounds that so long as nuclear weapons were necessary for deterrence, nuclear testing would also be essential for keeping the deterrent technologically up to date. Later, when radioactive fallout from testing became a serious problem, the superpowers agreed to eliminate all except underground testing. Two nuclear powers, France and China, have never signed the Partial Test Ban Treaty. The nonaligned bloc has long urged a comprehensive test ban as a means of curbing the arms race and nuclear proliferation. The superpowers, however, have continued underground detonations to proof-test the reliability of their stockpiles and to modernize their nuclear weapons systems (offensive or defensive), while citing either the nonuniversality of adherence or differences over verification means as reasons for their inability to reach agreement.[95]

TOWARD DEFENSIVELY BASED DETERRENCE?

In the 1980s, the international arms control scene was fundamentally transformed—gradually at first but at a quickening pace—as a result of several factors: (1) President Reagan's Strategic Defense Initiative, announced on March 23, 1983; (2) NATO's deployment of INF; (3) the rise of Gorbachev, who was anxious to avoid an outright arms race in outer space and willing to reach an INF agreement rejected by his predecessors, and who withdrew Soviet troops from Afghanistan, manifested an interest in attenuating conflict in other regions, and adopted a more practical approach in other arms limitation areas. Whether his new stance, less intransigent and far more flexible than that of Brezhnev, Andropov, and Chernenko, was due primarily to the demands of internal *perestroika* cannot be known for certain, but there can be no doubt that Gorbachev's diplomacy proved remarkably successful in both Western Europe and in the United States at a time when significant elements on both sides of the Atlantic were, for a variety of political and economic reasons, reassessing the Atlantic Alliance, as well as the need and cost of alternative strategies.

In his SDI speech, President Reagan challenged the scientific community to determine the possibility of building a stable system of defense that would rest no longer on the threat of retaliatory annihilation to deter war, but could intercept and destroy nuclear missiles before they could reach their targets—in short, to render nuclear weapons "impotent and obsolete" even if this might not be accomplished until after the turn of the century. He admitted that defensive systems pose problems and ambiguities, especially if paired with offensive systems, which would make them appear to be a preparation for aggression. He insisted, however, that the United States was not seeking military superiority, but rather a less morally monstrous method of preventing nuclear war than the strategy of assured destruction. He added that if a workable strategic defense should be found technically feasible, the United States ought in some way to share it with the Soviet Union.[96]

For about four years, newspapers, weekly and monthly periodicals, and scholarly journals were filled with sensational or serious articles about "Star Wars" (a term the President never used), to be fought with kinetic energy weapons, electromagnetic rail guns, neutral particle beams, a variety of lasers (e.g., chemical and X-ray), mirrors for bouncing off beams from ground-based free-electron or excimer lasers, and other exotic systems. Much of the writing pro and contra was based on pure speculation. If heavy power sources could not be lifted into space, could mirrors in space redirect the beams from ground-based lasers? Could atmospheric distortion of laser beams be overcome? Would it be possible to destroy enemy missiles in the boost phase? Could a strategic defense system be nullified by countermeasures—increasing the number of offensive warheads, launching dummy rockets along with real missiles, developing faster-burning fuels to shorten the boost phase to a minute or two, deploying "space mines," or reducing the vulnerability of missiles to laser beams by rotating them in flight or by coating them with deflecting substances? Could midcourse defenses be saturated with balloons and decoys, or could particle-beam weapons discriminate between real missiles and decoys? Even with supercomputers capable of performing tens of millions of computations per second, could information systems experts produce the hundred-million lines of software code that might be needed to program the operation efficiently? Would the system be "politically do-able" and cost-effective at the margin, meaning essentially that an added unit of defense would eventually be cheaper than added units of Soviet offensive capability or countermeasures or defense suppression?[97]

Administration spokespersons and other advocates of SDI argued that with several layers of defense (as many as seven), each based on a different technology, the leakage rate could be reduced almost to zero; that it is easier to conjure up countermeasures in the mind than to engineer them; that obviously it would make no sense to deploy a system that was not survivable; that eventually the NATO allies would come round to see the value of a research effort into futuristic technology with a potential "spin-off" for Europe's conventional as well as nuclear defense; and that critics' estimates that strategic defense would cost \$1–2 trillion were irrelevant to the debate since no one knew, or could know, what specific technologies would be chosen, or whether the whole idea would prove to be possible. That, after all, was the purpose of the research effort known as SDI. Britain, West Germany, and Italy signed Memoranda of Understanding with the United States allowing governmental or private sector participation in SDI. The allies, however, wanted to make sure that Western Europe would benefit from the research and obtain some leverage over a future decision to deploy strategic defense.

SDI had a significant impact on Soviet thinking about arms control in the Gorbachev era. Prior to the Reagan-Gorbachev Summit Meeting in Geneva in November 1985, the Soviet Union made an unprecedented announcement: It was ready to negotiate reductions of strategic nuclear weapons on the order of 50 percent if the United States would renounce SDI. (Back in 1977, it had summarily rejected President Carter's call for 25 percent cuts.) In his January 1986 plan for a world without nuclear weapons by the year 2000, Gorbachev proposed an early liquidation of Soviet and U.S. intermediate-range missiles in Europe. On February 28, 1987, Gorbachev agreed to "unlink" the INF issue from those of strategic missiles and space defense, which were more complicated, and he accepted Reagan's "zero-zero" option of November 1981.

In the new dialectic of offense versus defense set in motion by SDI, the two superpowers did not regard an indefinitely prolonged and acrimonious polarization as an attractive alternative. Probably neither expected a total triumph, seeing a synthesis of their positions as a natural outcome. From 1986 onward, there were some signs of convergence toward a mutual willingness to observe the ABM Treaty for several years while continuing strategic research, development, and testing within its terms. Whether this will be embodied in a formal agreement linked to the Strategic Arms Reduction Talks (START) or carried on informally and tacitly, with each side carefully monitoring the other, remains to be seen.

DETERRENCE AND ARMS CONTROL IN THE 1990s

The West European political-strategic environment has undergone changes since the INF Treaty. Once it became clear that intermediate-range missiles were to be removed from Europe, leaving only "tactical" or "battlefield" weapons—most of which would be likely in a future nuclear war to fall only on German territory (East or West), it was perhaps inevitable that many in Germany would look with favor on the "third zero solution"—to eliminate all nuclear weapons in Central Europe. West Germany was cool toward carrying out NATO's 1983 Montebello decision to modernize some of the Alliance's short-range nuclear weapons. Other allies, concerned lest a denuclearized Central Europe would foreshadow a drift by the Federal Republic toward neutralism as a prelude to national reunification, insisted on going forward as planned. Whereas the Soviet Union called for denuclearization, NATO gave higher priority to the reduction of conventional forces with the aim of achieving greater stability in Europe at the conventional level.

There had been a running debate throughout the 1980s over the relationship between nuclear and conventional deterrence in Europe and the possibility of shifting emphasis from the former to the latter. Some analysts, as well as the American Catholic Bishops, urged NATO to adopt a policy of "no first use" of nuclear weapons; others contended that such a shift would seriously undermine deterrence.[98]

While committed to the strengthening of conventional capabilities as part of NATO's Flexible Response strategy calculated to deter the adversary, repel aggression at any level, and defend against Soviet attack as far forward as possible without early use and, if possible, without any use of nuclear weapons, the political and military leaders of NATO nevertheless have refused to renounce nuclear deterrence by adopting a "no first use" policy. In contrast to such theorists as John J. Mearsheimer and Samuel P. Huntington, who have sought to demonstrate that NATO might be able to rely upon conventional deterrence,[99] others have argued that conventional deterrence alone is less effective than a mixed conventional-nuclear strategy. Richard K. Betts, for example, has reiterated the position of the "classical" nuclear strategists—namely, that conventional deterrence has frequently failed in modern history and nuclear deterrence has not up to this time because of the difference between *denial* and *punishment.* In a conventional war, the worst that aggressors need expect is to be frustrated in their design—to be denied all or part of their objectives. In that situation it is easier for the aggressor to calculate the maximum potential cost of attacking. If, on the other hand, an aggressor has reason to think that a conventional attack may provoke a nuclear response that contains a danger of uncontrollable escalation, it becomes impossible to estimate in advance the cost of the devastation that might follow. According to Betts, a NATO doctrine of Flexible Response that poses uncertain risks is preferable to any alternative of purely conventional deterrence.

> Confidence in conventional deterrence by defense is unwarranted because denial is inherently a weaker deterrent than punishment—the costs of failure are much smaller. . . . It is more tempting to gamble against a moderately high probability of denial than against a moderately low probability of devastation.
> . . .
> Any scheme for pure conventional deterrence fails because, in optimizing hedges against one challenge, it weakens deterrence against another. . . . The only policy choices that hedges suboptimally against all contingencies is one that combines enhanced denial capabilities and continued threats of nuclear punishment should denial fail.[100]

In January 1988 the Commission on Integrated Long-Term Strategy delivered to the Secretary of Defense and the Assistant to the President for National Security Affairs a report entitled *Discriminate Deterrence.* [101] The report noted that the next few decades will probably bring significant changes in the number of major military powers, the acquisition of advanced weapons technology by lesser powers, the impact of arms agreements on superpower forces both nuclear and conventional, and the uncertain behavior of allies and friends. All of these will modify the international environment to which policies and strategies of deterrence must be addressed:

> We should emphasize a wider range of contingencies than the two extreme threats that have long dominated our alliance policy and force planning: the massive Warsaw Pact attack on Central Europe and an all-out Soviet nuclear attack. By concentrating on these extreme cases, our planners tend to neglect attacks that call for discriminating military responses and the risk that in these situations some allies might opt out.[102]

The report advised the U.S. government that in defending allies and interests abroad, it should not rely on threats that would provoke national annihilation if carried out; that it should diversify and strengthen its ability to bring discriminating, nonnuclear force to bear where needed in time to defeat aggression; that its forces, both conventional and nuclear, should be based on a mix of offensive and defensive systems, including a capability for conventional counteroffensive operations deep into enemy territory and for discriminate nuclear strikes to deter a limited nuclear attack or an overwhelming conventional invasion; and that the control of space in wartime will become increasingly important. The authors were careful not to appear favorable to removing the threat of a nuclear response to an attack in Europe, but in the reordering of defense priorities in an era of budgetary constructs, they seemed to stress the need for conventional forces and precise, "smart" weapons of pinpoint accuracy.

To sum up, some theorists of international relations believe that nuclear deterrence should be totally abandoned, and preparations for conventional defense substituted for it. At the opposite extreme are those strategists who believe that complete reliance ought to be placed upon nuclear deterrence, while all actual war-fighting defense strategies are to be shunned because they will make the occurrence of war, and therefore nuclear war, more likely. Yet, three decades ago, Glenn H. Snyder observed that "considerations of reducing the probability of war and of mitigating its consequences must be evaluated simultaneously," and that planning for the consequences of deterrence failure is a matter of political judgment that must be weighed against the likelihood that deterrence will succeed.[103] Preparations for the failure of deterrence are essential, but such preparations should not increase its likelihood. This problem is closely related to, and compounded by, the new directions of Soviet policy in the Gorbachev era. If, as Richard Ned Lebow has dichotomized, the Soviet Union has merely muted its long-range goal of global domination, then it is essential for the West to emphasize a policy of deterrence against the threat of a Soviet attack; but if the Soviet motives are becoming more traditionally defensive, then a policy of reassurance may be more appropriate for the West. Most analysts find neither interpretation satisfactory. "To the extent that Soviet policy is in fact motivated by a mix of offensive and defensive goals, then some combination of deterrence and reassurance is required to cope with it."[104]

Deterrence and arms control are both closely related to changing weapons technology. Since effective deterrence requires constant modernization, arms control agreements between the superpowers must permit modernization. At the same time, all the major nuclear powers perceive a coincident interest in pursuing policies to reduce the likelihood that other states would be able to destabilize the international strategic situation to such a degree that the nuclear-weapon states could not remain in ultimate control of their own security. Thus they cooperate, formally or tacitly, in discouraging the "horizontal proliferation" of nuclear weapons and delivery systems to other states. In recent years, moreover, they have shown some interest in reinvigorating the diplomatic effort, just about as old as the century, to outlaw at least the *use* of lethal chemical weapons (sometimes called the "poor country's nuclear weapons") even if verification problems compound the difficulty of enforcing a total international ban on the production and possession of such weapons, which some nations may wish to hold for deterrent purposes.[105]

While the arms control scene has begun to undergo apparently important changes in recent years, the condition of deterrence at the superpower level is likely to remain solid. Despite charges by each side in earlier years that the other was trying to achieve a first-strike capability, both may have reached the conclusion long ago that neither can achieve such a margin of superiority as to invest the notion of strategic war with a semblance of political or moral justifiability. It is necessary for both sides to believe that, and to have confidence in the fundamental "rationality" of the other side's decision-making processes on that score. If they do not, enduring arms control agreements cannot be achieved. If they do, and if they pursue intelligent policies of "do's" and "don't's,"[106] they may assume that the deterrence of all-out nuclear war can last for an indefinitely long time[107]—long enough to allow the historic security dilemmas of states to be fundamentally transformed.

NOTES

1. Robert Jervis, "Deterrence Theory Revisited," *World Politics,* XXXI (April 1979), 289. Jervis attributes the popularity of the theory to its "formidable intellectual virtues" and to the fact that it is parsimonious—that is, logical, simple, neat, and clear. Ibid., p. 290. The views of Jervis, a leading theorist of deterrence during the last decade, will be treated more fully later in this chapter.

2. Alexander L. George and Richard Smoke, *Deterrence in American Foreign Policy: Theory and Practice* (New York: Columbia University Press, 1974), p. 11. See also Frank C. Zagare, *The Dynamics of Deterrence* (Chicago and London: University of Chicago Press, 1987), p. 7.

3. Ibid., pp. 14–16. See also Patrick M. Morgan, *Deterrence: A Conceptual Analysis* (Beverly Hills, Calif.: Sage, 1977), ch. 1; and George H. Quester, *Deterrence Before Hiroshima* (New York: Wiley, 1966).

4. Bernard Brodie, "The Anatomy of Deterrence," *World Politics*, XI (January 1974), 174.

5. Within months of Hiroshima and Nagasaki, Bernard Brodie, the pioneer theorist of strategic deterrence, had written: "Thus far the chief purpose of our military establishment has been to win wars. From now on its chief purpose must be to avert them. It can have almost no other useful purpose." *The Absolute Weapon* (New York: Harcourt, Brace, 1946), p. 76. Even though in that last sentence Brodie overstated his case, subsequent history substantiated the main point he was trying to make at the dawn of the nuclear age—so far as strategic, all-out war is concerned. See also Henry A. Kissinger, *The Necessity for Choice* (Garden City, N.Y.: Doubleday, 1962), pp. 11–12. Thomas C. Schelling insisted that in the nuclear era what a nation wants from its military forces is not so much "victory" as bargaining power. *Arms and Influence* (New Haven: Yale University Press, 1966), p. 31.

6. Robert Jervis, op. cit., p. 291.

7. Kennan's famous "long telegram" of February 22, 1946, from Moscow to the State Department in Washington is to be found in the U.S. Department of State Series, *Foreign Relations of the United States, 1946* (Washington, D.C.: U.S. Government Printing Office), Vol. VI, pp. 696–709. Kennan's policy views were published in modified form in the article signed by "X," "The Sources of Soviet Conduct," *Foreign Affairs*, XXV (July 1947). Concerning George F. Kennan's background, especially his "outpost" service as a young diplomat in Riga, where his attitudes toward the Soviet Union were formed, see Daniel Yergin, *Shattered Peace: The Origins of the Cold War and the National Security State* (Boston, Mass.: Houghton Mifflin, 1978), ch. 2. One of the most influential, although not uncontroverted, interpretations of Kennan's concept of containment and the meanings attached to it by various administrations is to be found in John Lewis Gaddis, *Strategies of Containment: A Critical Appraisal of Postwar American National Security Policy* (New York: Oxford University Press, 1982). See also Walter Isaacson and Evan Thomas, *The Wise Men: Six Friends and the World They Made* (New York: Simon & Schuster, 1986), pp. 238–239, 353–355, and 484–485.

8. John Lewis Gaddis, op. cit., pp. 39–40.

9. Donald M. Snow, *Nuclear Strategy in a Dynamic Age* (University: University of Alabama Press, 1981), p. 50; Richard Smoke, *National Security and the Security Dilemma*, 2nd ed. (New York: Random House, 1987), p. 53. See also Samuel P. Huntington, *The Common Defense: Strategic Programs in National Politics* (New York: Columbia University Press, 1961), pp. 33–47.

10. Alexander L. George and Richard Smoke, op. cit., pp. 23–27; Richard Smoke, op. cit., pp. 77–82. For a thorough examination of the theory of limited war, see Henry A. Kissinger, *Nuclear Weapons and Foreign Policy* (New York: Harper, 1957); Robert E. Osgood, *Limited War* (Chicago, Ill.: University of

Chicago Press, 1957); Klaus Knorr and Thornton Read, eds., *Limited Strategic War* (New York: Frederick A. Praeger, 1962); Robert E. Osgood, *Limited War Revisited* (Boulder, Colo.: Westview Press 1979).

11. Excerpts from Address to the Council on Foreign Relations, New York, January 12, 1954, in *The New York Times*, January 13, 1954. Dulles published a clarification of his views in "Policy for Security and Peace," *Foreign Affairs*, XXXII (April 1954). For an account of the alarm raised by some of Dulles's statements, see Louis J. Halle, *The Cold War as History* (New York: Harper & Row, 1967), pp. 276–282. For a later retrospective account, cf. Samuel F. Wells, "The Origins of Massive Retaliation," *Political Science Quarterly*, 96 (Spring 1981).

12. Jerome H. Kahan, *Security in the Nuclear Age: Developing U.S. Strategic Arms Policy* (Washington, D.C.: The Brookings Institution, 1975), p. 34.

13. Richard Smoke, op. cit., p. 54.

14. William W. Kaufmann, "The Requirements of Deterrence," in W. W. Kaufmann, ed., *Military Policy and National Security* (Princeton: Princeton University Press, 1956), pp. 23–24.

15. Paul Nitze, "Atoms, Strategy and Policy," *Foreign Affairs*, XXXIV (January 1956), 188–198.

16. See Sir Anthony Buzzard et al., "The H-Bomb: Massive Retaliation or Graduated Deterrence?" *International Affairs* (London), XXXII (April 1956), and Arnold Wolfers, "Could A War In Europe Be Limited?" *Yale Review*, XLV (Winter 1956).

17. Bernard Brodie, *Strategy in the Missile Age* (Princeton, N.J.: Princeton University Press, 1959), ch. 7.

18. Ibid., pp. 268–269.

19. Ibid., p. 271.

20. Ibid., pp. 272–273. As early as 1945, Brodie had observed that in the atomic age, American security made it essential "to take measures to guarantee to ourselves in case of attack the possibility of retaliation in kind." *The Absolute Weapon*, p. 76.

21. *Strategy in the Missile Age*, p. 274.

22. Ibid., pp. 261–263.

23. Bernard Brodie, *War and Politics* (New York: Macmillan, 1973), p. 380.

24. Ibid., pp. 419–420.

25. Ibid., p. 126.

26. Ibid., ch. 9, "Nuclear Weapons: Utility in Nonuse."

27. Walter Millis, *A World Without War* (Santa Barbara, Calif.: Center for Democratic Institutions, 1961).

28. Klaus Knorr, *On the Uses of Military Power in the Nuclear Age* (Princeton: Princeton University Press, 1966), and "On the International Uses of Military Force in the Contemporary World," *Orbis*, 21 (Spring 1977); Barry M. Blechman and Stephen S. Kaplan, *Force Without War: U.S. Armed Forces as a Political Instrument* (Washington, D.C.: The Brookings Institution, 1978); Laurence Martin, *Strategic Thought in the Nuclear Age* (Baltimore, Md.: The Johns Hopkins University Press, 1981); Robert Gilpin, *War and Change in World Politics* (Cambridge: Cambridge University Press, 1981).

29. Laurence Martin, op. cit., p. 5.

30. Ibid.

31. Ibid., p. 9.

32. Albert Wohlstetter, "The Delicate Balance of Terror," *Foreign Affairs*, XXXVIII (January 1959). Brodie, however, did not agree that the balance of terror was as *delicate* as Wohlstetter implied. "Many things are technologically feasible that we have quite good reason to believe will not happen." *War and Politics*, p. 380. Brodie's observation is correct. Nevertheless, military planners and strategic policymakers within the governments of the superpowers have shown keen concern over the need for constantly modernizing nuclear weapons technology. See Laurence Martin, op. cit., pp. 6–7. The Harvard Nuclear Study Group placed the modernization of the strategic triad at the very top of its agenda for avoiding nuclear war. Graham T. Allison, Albert Carnesale, and Joseph S. Nye, Jr., eds., *Hawks, Doves and Owls: An Agenda for Avoiding Nuclear War* (New York: W. W. Norton), p. 21.

33. Thomas C. Schelling and Morton H. Halperin, *Strategy and Arms Control* (New York: Twentieth Century Fund, 1961), pp. 50–54; Morton H. Halperin, *Contemporary Military Strategy* (Boston, Mass.: Little, Brown, 1967), pp. 19–20; Jerome H. Kahan, op. cit., p. 271. The 1961 work by Schelling and Halperin, long considered a classic in its field, was published in a second revised edition by Pergamon Press in 1985.

34. For a representative sampling of the literature, see Carl Kaysen, "Keeping the Strategic Balance," *Foreign Affairs*, XLVI (July 1968), 665–675; Harold Brown, "Security Through Limitations," and Donald G. Brennan, "The Case for Missile Defense," *Foreign Affairs*, XLVII (April 1969); 422–432 and 443–448, respectively; and J. W. Fulbright, et al. "Missiles and Anti-Missiles: Six Views," *Bulletin of the Atomic Scientists*, XXV (June 1969), 20–28; William R. Kintner, ed., *Safeguard: Why the ABM Makes Sense* (New York: Hawthorne, 1969); Abram Chayes and Jerome B. Weisner, eds., *ABM: An Evaluation of the Decision to Deploy an Anti-Ballistic Missile System* (New York: Harper & Row, 1969); Morton H. Halperin, "The Decision to Deploy the ABM: Bureaucratic and Domestic Politics in the Johnson Administration;" *World Politics*, XXV (October 1972).

35. See Charles J. Hitch and Roland N. McKean, *The Economics of Defense in the Nuclear Age* (Cambridge, Mass.: Harvard University Press, 1960); Samuel P. Huntington, *The Common Defense*, chs. 6–12, 14, 16, and 18.

36. On this last distinction between the deterrent threat *before* and the actual defense *after* war begins, see Raymond Aron, *The Great Debate: Theories of Nuclear Strategy*, trans. Ernest Pawel (Garden City, N.Y.: Doubleday, 1965), pp. 32–33, and Glenn H. Snyder, *Deterrence and Defense: Toward a Theory of National Security* (Princeton: Princeton University Press, 1961), pp. 3–16, 33–40. Richard Rosecrance also draws a distinction between the threat of devastating damage posed before aggression occurs and the response actually made after hostilities break out. *International Relations: Peace or War?* (New York: McGraw-Hill, 1973), p. 284.

37. Henry A. Kissinger, *Nuclear Weapons and Foreign Policy*, p. 12.

38. For an excellent account concerning the efforts of the American intelligence community to monitor and predict the development of Soviet nuclear forces, as well as the debates over the reliability of various estimates, see Lawrence Freedman, *U.S. Intelligence and the Soviet Strategic Threat*, 2nd ed. (New York: Macmillan, 1986). See also Robert L. Pfaltzgraff, Jr., Uri Ra'anan, and Warren H. Milberg, eds., *Intelligence Policy and National Security* (London:

Macmillan, 1981); Christopher Andrew and David Dilks, eds., *The Missing Dimension: Governments and Intelligence Communities* (London: Macmillan, 1984); and Jeffrey Richelson, *The U.S. Intelligence Community* (Cambridge, Mass.: Ballinger, 1985). Noteworthy earlier works include Sherman Kent, *Strategic Intelligence for American World Policy* (Princeton: Princeton University Press, 1966), and Lyman B. Kirkpatrick, *The Intelligence Community* (New York: Hill and Wang, 1973).

39. Robert Osgood, "Stabilizing the Military Environment," in Dale J. Hekhuis et al., eds., *International Stability* (New York: Wiley, 1964), p. 87; A. R. Hibbs, "ABM and the Algebra of Uncertainty," *Bulletin of the Atomic Scientists*, XXIV (March 1968), 31–33; D. G. Brennan, "Uncertainty Is Not the Issue," ibid., 33–34.

40. Stanley Sinkiewicz, "Observations on the Impact of Uncertainty in Strategic Analysis," *World Politics*, XXXII (October 1979), 98–99. See also the references in the text, p. 417 and note 100 below to the views of Richard K. Betts on the role of uncertainty in NATO's nuclear deterrent.

41. Raymond Aron, "The Evolution of Modern Strategic Thought," in *Problems of Modern Strategy: Part One, Adelphi Papers No. 54* (London: Institute for Strategic Studies, February 1969), p. 9.

42. Ibid.

43. Ole R. Holsti, *Crisis, Escalation, War* (Montreal: McGill-Queens University Press, 1972), pp. 8–9.

44. Claudio Cioffi-Revilla, "A Probability Model of Credibility: Analyzing Strategic Nuclear Deterrent Systems," *Journal of Conflict Resolution*, 27 (March 1983).

45. Patrick M. Morgan, op. cit., pp. 28–43.

46. Alexander L. George and Richard Smoke, op. cit., pp. 38–41.

47. See pp. 410–413 in the text and note 87 below.

48. John H. Herz, "The Territorial State Revisited: Reflections on the Future of the Nation-States," in James N. Rosenau, ed., *International Politics and Foreign Policy* (New York: Free Press, 1969) pp. 80–81.

49. Alexander L. George and Richard Smoke, op. cit., p. 54.

50. Bruce M. Russett, "The Calculus of Deterrence," *Journal of Conflict Resolution*, VII (March 1963), 97–109. See also Franklin B. Weinstein, "The Concept of a Commitment in International Relations," *Journal of Conflict Resolutions*, XIII (March 1969), 39–56.

51. See Bruce M. Russett, "Pearl Harbor: Deterrence Theory and Decision Theory," *Journal of Peace Research*, 4, No. 2 (1967), 80–106.

52. See Daniel Frei with Christian Catrina, *Risks of Unintentional Nuclear War* (Geneva: United Nations Institute for Disarmament Research, 1982), especially ch. VI; Milton Leitenberg, "Accidents of Nuclear Weapons Systems," in Stockholm International Peace Research Institute, *World Armaments and Disarmament, SIPRI Yearbook* (Cambridge: MIT Press, 1977), pp. 52–82.

53. Philip Green, *The Deadly Logic: The Theory of Nuclear Deterrence* (Columbus: Ohio State University Press, 1966).

54. Robert Jervis, op. cit., p. 292.

55. Ibid.

56. Kennedy's ability to persuade Khrushchev to withdraw Soviet missiles from Cuba in 1962 was due not only to U.S. strategic superiority prevailing at the time, but also to U.S. local conventional military superiority in the region of critical confrontation. On the difference between deterrence and compel-

lence, see Patrick M. Morgan, op. cit., p. 31; Thomas C. Schelling, *Arms and Influence* (New Haven, Conn.: Yale University Press, 1966), pp. 69–91; and the concluding chapter of Alexander George et al., *The Limits of Coercive Diplomacy* (Boston, Mass.: Little, Brown, 1971).

57. Robert L. Jervis, op. cit., p. 297.
58. Ibid., p. 298.
59. Ibid., p. 292.
60. Ibid., p. 293.
61. Ibid., pp. 295–296, 304.
62. Ibid., pp. 296–297.
63. Ibid., pp. 299–300.
64. Thomas C. Schelling, op. cit., pp. 37–38.
65. Robert Jervis, op. cit., p. 302.
66. Robert L. Jervis, "Why Nuclear Superiority Doesn't Matter," *Political Science Quarterly*, 94 (Winter, 1979–80), 626–633. R. Harrison Wagner criticized the Jervis article on the grounds that Jervis based his analysis too much on the game of Chicken, which Wagner deemed irrelevant to the problem of deterrence. "Deterrence Bargaining," *Journal of Conflict Resolution*, 26 (June 1982). Wagner argued that a strategy of limited nuclear exchange is a more potent deterrent than the threat of all-out retaliation. Ibid., p. 356. Barry M. Blechman and Robert Powell have pointed out that the possession of nuclear superiority in the early 1950s probably helped President Eisenhower in his efforts to bring the Korean War to an end in 1953, but that the threats and decisions of that era have little if any relevance in the present period, when both superpowers possess nuclear capabilities ample and secure enough to withstand a first strike and still inflict devastating retaliatory destruction upon the opposing society. "What in the Name of God Is Strategic Superiority?" *Political Science Quarterly*, 97 (Winter 1982–83), 601–602. See also Hans Bethe, "Meaningless Superiority," *Bulletin of the Atomic Scientists*, 37 (October 1981).
67. To say that this or that course of action is "rational" or "irrational" presupposes a prior judgment or assumptions concerning objectives or goals, which are based on values that lie beyond "rational" assessment. See Stanley Hoffmann, *The State of War*, (New York: Praeger, 1965), pp. 12–13; William A. Scott, "Rationality and Nonrationality of International Attitudes," *Journal of Conflict Resolution*, 2 (March 1958), 8–16. Robert Jervis, citing Milton Friedman and Kenneth N. Waltz, notes that "theorizing based upon assumptions that people are rational is not defeated by empirical studies showing that they engage in mental operations that violate this assumption." Robert Jervis et al., *Psychology and Deterrence* (Baltimore, Md.: The Johns Hopkins University Press, 1985), p. 5.
68. Fritz Ermarth, "Contrasts in American and Soviet Strategic Thought," *International Security*, 3 (Fall 1978), 138. Cf. also Stanley Sinkiewicz, "SALT and Soviet Nuclear Doctrine," ibid., 2 (Spring 1978).
69. The precise percentages apparently varied over time and according to sources. See Richard Smoke, op. cit., p. 116; Alain C. Enthoven and K. Wayne Smith, *How Much Is Enough: Shaping the Defense Program, 1961–1969* (New York: Harper and Row, 1971), p. 174; Lawrence Freedman, *The Evolution of Nuclear Strategy* (London: Macmillan, 1981), p. 246.

70. United Nations General Assembly, *Comprehensive Study on Nuclear Weapons* (A/35/392) (New York: United Nations, 1980), pp. 94, 103.
71. Milton Leitenberg, cited in Daniel Frei, op. cit., p. 62.
72. Gennadi Gerasimov, *War and Peace in the Nuclear Age* (Moscow: Novosti Press, 1982), p. 56.
73. Robert Legvold, "Strategic 'Doctrine' and SALT: Soviet and American Views," *Survival*, 21 (January/February, 1979), 9.
74. Benjamin Lambeth, "The Political Potential of Soviet Equivalence," *International Security*, 4 (Summer 1979); Donald G. Brennan, "Commentary," ibid., 3 (Winter 1978–79); Michael D. Salomon, "New Concepts for Strategic Parity," *Survival*, 19 (November/December 1977). Benjamin Lambeth later noted that "a great deal of uncertainty remains about Soviet strategic uncertainty. There is much we do not know (and cannot know) about how Soviet leaders would act in the face of a major test. Uncertainty can cut two ways, depending on how the Soviet leadership perceives the risks and stakes of a situation. It could either make them hesitant or provide a powerful incentive for the leaders to seize the initiative and try to dominate the outcome before it is too late." "Uncertainties for the Soviet War Planner," *International Security*, 7 (Winter 1982–83), 164–165.
75. Richard Pipes, "Why the Soviet Union Thinks It Could Fight and Win a Nuclear War," *Commentary*, 64 (July 1977); John Erickson, "The Chimera of Nuclear Deterrence," *Strategic Review*, VI (Spring 1978); Paul Nitze, "Assuring Strategic Stability in an Era of Détente," *Foreign Affairs*, 54, 2 (January 1976); Dimitri K. Simes, "Deterrence and Coercion in Soviet Policy," *International Security*, 5 (Winter 1980–81). According to Leon Gouré, the Soviet strategy of deterring war by preparing to wage it requires a much greater interest on the part of military planners in problems of civil defense and post-attack recovery than has been shown since the early 1960s by their American counterparts. *War Survival in Soviet Strategy: USSR Civil Defense* (Miami: Center for Advanced International Studies, University of Miami, 1976). Cf. also David Holloway, *The Soviet Union and the Arms Race* (New Haven: Yale University Press, 1983), pp. 176–77.
76. Raymond L. Garthoff, "On Mutual Deterrence: A Reply to Donald Brennan," *International Security* 3 (Spring 1979), 198. See also his "Mutual Deterrence and Strategic Arms Limitation in Soviet Policy," ibid., 2 (Summer 1978).
77. *Report of the Secretary of Defense to the Congress on the FY 1975 Defense Budget* (Washington, D.C.: U.S. Government Printing Office, March 4, 1974), pp. 35–41.
78. See the following publications of the International Institute for Strategic Studies (London): *The Military Balance* for 1974–75, p. 4; for 1978–79, pp. 3–4; for 1979–80, pp. 3–4; and *Strategic Survey* for the following years: 1977, pp. 10–11; 1978, p. 6; 1979, pp. 2, 4; and 1980–81, pp. 3–6.
79. Richard L. Garwin, "Launch Under Attack to Redress Minuteman Vulnerability?" *International Security*, 4 (Winter 1979–80). Albert Carnesale, Paul Doty, and others in the Harvard Nuclear Study Group also doubted that the Soviet Union would ever attack the U.S. land-based ICBM force alone (which carry fewer than a quarter of all American strategic nuclear warheads), on the expectation that the President of the United States would choose neither to launch the ICBMs on warning nor to retaliate with submarine-launched mis-

siles after a Soviet attack on the Minuteman force. In short, the Harvard Group considered a Soviet attack on Minuteman alone unlikely. *Living With Nuclear Weapons* (New York: Bantam Books, 1983), p. 52. See also Albert Carnesale and Charles Glaser, "ICBM Vulnerability: The Cures Are Worse Than the Disease," *International Security,* 7 (Summer 1982).

80. Excerpts from Address by Defense Secretary Harold Brown, Naval War College, Newport, Rhode Island, August 20, 1980, in *The New York Times,* August 21, 1980. According to Walter Slocombe, this country's doctrine had never been "based simply and solely on reflexive massive attacks on Soviet cities and population," despite widespread misconceptions to that effect in the past. He asserted that "previous administrations, going back almost two decades, recognized the inadequacy of a strategic targeting doctrine—a plan for use of weapons if deterrence failed—that would give us too narrow a range of employment options." He added that the "unquestioned attainment of strategic parity by the Soviet Union has underscored what was clear long before—that a policy based only on massive retaliation against Soviet cities is an inadequate deterrent for the full spectrum of potential Soviet aggressions." "The Countervailing Strategy," *International Security,* 5 (Spring 1981), p. 19. During the debate that accompanied the writing of the Catholic Bishops' Pastoral Letter on War and Peace discussed in Chapter 5 (see note 18 in that chapter), National Security Adviser William P. Clark issued a statement that said in part: "For moral, political and military reasons, the United States does not target Soviet civilian population as such. . . . We do not threaten the existence of Soviet civilization by threatening Soviet cities." Defense Secretary Caspar Weinberger submitted a parallel statement. Quoted in note 81 of the Pastoral Letter.

81. See Colin Gray, "Nuclear Strategy: The Case for a Theory of Victory," *International Security,* 4 (Summer 1979); Colin S. Gray and Keith Payne, "Victory Is Possible," *Foreign Policy,* 39 (Summer 1980). Defense Secretary Weinberger spoke of "protracted war" and "horizontal escalation," but he did not use the term *protracted nuclear war,* although critics assumed that it was implicit in his thinking. He officially expressed the conviction that neither superpower could win a nuclear war. *Annual Report to the Congress FY 1984* (Washington, D.C.: U.S. Government Printing Office, February 1, 1983), p. 51. Donald W. Hanson, criticizing Colin Gray's thesis, wrote: "It is one thing to insist that deterrence can fail, as it surely could, and to argue that nuclear weapons may have to be used: that is, to posit the need for a viable employment doctrine. But it is quite another thing to claim that, because the need is there, it must be the case that a strategy for victory and survival also exists." "Is Soviet Strategic Doctrine Superior?" *International Security,* 7 (Winter 1982–83), 83. One might plausibly argue that military theoreticians and planners have a certain psychological need to propound a goal of victory for the sake of strategic logic and the morale of military forces, simply to avoid a sense of utter futility of a prolonged period of deterrence, and this need not be dangerous so long as the military remains under the control of rational political leaders who can calculate the political consequences of nuclear war. In any event, Hanson makes a point in positing the need for a viable employment doctrine. Michael Howard, a leading British theorist, has made the case that the West does not need a "war-fighting" capability, not for the purpose of trying to gain an impossible mutually annihilative "victory," but one that will "set on victory

for our opponent a price he cannot possibly afford to pay." "On Fighting a Nuclear War," ibid., 5 (Spring 1981), 16. In sum, for all sensible advocates of deterrence the only victory lies in preventing nuclear war.

82. McGeorge Bundy, "To Cap the Volcano," *Foreign Affairs,* 48 (October 1969), 9.

83. Desmond Ball, *Can Nuclear War Be Controlled?,* Adelphi Papers No. 169 (London: IISS, Autumn 1981), pp. 9–14. See also Desmond Ball, "U.S. Strategic Forces: How Would They Be Used?" *International Security,* 7 (Winter 1982–83).

84. Michael Howard, op. cit.; Andrei Sakharov, "The Danger of Nuclear War," *Foreign Affairs,* 61 (Summer 1983), esp. 1009–1011; Spurgeon M. Keeny and Wolfgang K. H. Panovsky, "MAD vs NUTS: The Mutual Hostage Relationship of the Superpowers," *Foreign Affairs,* 60 (Winter 1981–82); Ian Clark, *Limited Nuclear War* (Princeton: Princeton University Press, 1982); and Robert S. McNamara, "The Military Role of Nuclear Weapons," *Foreign Affairs,* 62 (Fall 1983).

85. Desmond Ball, *Can Nuclear War Be Controlled?,* pp. 30–35; Raymond L. Garthoff, "Mutual Deterrence and Strategic Arms Limitation in Soviet Policy," *Strategic Review,* 10 (Fall 1982); Richard Pipes, *Soviet Strategic Doctrine: Another View,* ibid.; Gerhard Wettig, "The Garthoff-Pipes Debate on Soviet Strategic Doctrine: A European Perspective," ibid., 11 (Spring 1983); and Jonathan S. Lockwood, *The Soviet View of U.S. Strategic Doctrine* (New Brunswick, N.J.: Transaction Books, 1983), esp. chs. 8 and 9.

86. For an account of how the views of Churchill and Eisenhower influenced the development of NATO's nuclear deterrent strategy, see James E. Dougherty and Robert L. Pfaltzgraff, Jr., *American Foreign Policy: FDR to Reagan* (New York: Harper & Row, 1985), pp. 101–102.

87. See the references to Thomas C. Schelling in Note 33; Bernard Brodie, *War and Politics* (New York: Macmillan, 1973), pp. 396–412; Laurence M. Martin, "Changes in American Strategic Doctrine—an Initial Interpretation," *Survival,* XVI (July/August 1974); Michael J. Brenner, "Tactical Nuclear Strategy and European Defense: A Critical Reappraisal," *International Affairs* (London), LI (January 1975); *Tactical Nuclear Weapons: European Perspectives,* Stockholm International Peace Research Institute (London: Taylor and Francis, 1978).

88. The term "Finlandization" was apparently first used by Professor Richard Löwenthal of the Free University of Berlin in "After Cuba, Berlin?" *Encounter* (December 1962). Prior to the signing of the 1975 Helsinki Accords at the Conference on Security and Cooperation in Europe, the Soviet Union went out of its way to pay tribute to Finland and the Soviet-Finnish relationship "as a model for the development of relations between states with different social systems." *Pravda,* April 5, 1975. See James E. Dougherty, "The Soviet Strategy of Finlandization of Western Europe," in Walter F. Hahn and Robert L. Pfaltzgraff, Jr., *Atlantic Community in Crisis: A Redefinition of the Transatlantic Relationship* (New York: Pergamon Press, 1979), ch. 9.

89. Pierre Gallois, *The Balance of Terror: Strategy for the Nuclear Age* (Boston, Mass.: Houghton Mifflin, 1961), pp. 119–122, 136–142, 195–210.

90. See Peter Nailor and Jonathan Alford, *The Future of Britain's Deterrent Force,* Adelphi Papers No. 156 (London: IISS, Spring 1980); *Future United Kingdom Strategic Nuclear Deterrent Force* (London: Her Majesty's Stationery Office,

July 1980). During the 1980s, plans to modernize the British and French strategic nuclear forces enhanced their deterrent credibility. See David S. Yost, *France's Deterrent Posture and Security in Europe: Parts I and II,* Adelphi Papers No. 194 and 195 (London: IISS, Winter 1984/85); John Prados, Joel S. Wit, and Michael J. Zagurek, Jr., "The Strategic Nuclear Forces of Britain and France," *Scientific American,* 255 (August 1986).

91. See text of the Foreign and Defense Ministers Final Communique of December 12, 1979 in *NATO Review* (February 1980), 25–26; and *The Modernization of NATO's Long-Range Theater Nuclear Forces,* House Committee on Foreign Affairs, 96th Congress, 2nd Session, December 31, 1980 (Washington, D.C.: U.S. Government Printing Office, 1981). The cruise missiles were to be deployed in Britain, Italy, the Federal Republic of Germany, Belgium, and the Netherlands. All of the Pershing IIs were to be deployed in the Federal Republic.

92. For the variety of meanings of the term "arms control," see Donald G. Brennan, ed., *Arms Control, Disarmament, and National Security* (New York: Braziller, 1961); Hedley Bull, *The Control of the Arms Race,* (New York: Praeger, 1961), pp. 168–169; Thomas C. Schelling and Morton H. Halperin, op. cit.; J. David Singer, *Deterrence, Arms Control and Disarmament* (Columbus: Ohio State University Press, 1962); Richard N. Rosecrance, ed., *Dispersion of Nuclear Weapons* (New York: Columbia University Press, 1964); David V. Edwards, *Arms Control in International Politics* (New York: Holt, Rinehart and Winston, 1969); Franklin A. Long and George Rathjens, eds., *Arms, Defense Policy and Arms Control* (New York: W. W. Norton, 1975); Bernard Brodie, "On the Objectives of Arms Control," *International Security,* 1 (Summer 1976), 17–36.

    Philip Towle, *Arms Control and East West Relations* (New York: St. Martin's Press, 1983); Coit D. Blacker and Gloria Duffy, eds., *International Arms Control,* 2nd ed. (Stanford, Calif.: Stanford University Press, 1984); Wolfram F. Hanreider, ed., *Technology, Strategy and Arms Control* (Boulder, Colo.: Westview Press, 1986).

93. Robert McNamara had enunciated a "no-cities" strategic doctrine in his Ann Arbor speech of June 1962. See "National Security and NATO," *Department of State Bulletin,* 47 (July 9, 1962), 67. He soon abandoned it, however, in favor of the doctrine of Mutual Assured Destruction. For a discussion of the incongruity between the idea of a strategic counterforce strike and the public U.S. policy of launching strategic weapons only in a retaliatory second strike, see Russell F. Weigley, *The American Way of War: A History of United States Military Strategy and Policy* (Bloomington: Indiana University Press, 1973), p. 444.

94. In February 1967, the Latin American states (except for Cuba) signed the Treaty of Tlatelolco, Mexico City, prohibiting nuclear weapons in their region. In August 1985, 8 of the 13 members comprising the South Pacific Forum signed the Treaty of Rarotonga, establishing a Nuclear Free Zone in which the manufacture, testing, and storage of nuclear weapons, but not their passage in international waterways, would be prohibited.

95. For background narrative and text of the Treaty Banning Nuclear Weapons Tests in the Atmosphere, in Outer Space and Under Water, see *Arms Control and Disarmament Agreements: Texts and Histories of Negotiations,* 1982 Edition (Washington, D.C.: U.S. Government Printing Office, 1982), pp. 34–

47. See also *The Nuclear Test Ban Treaty, Report of the Committee on Foreign Relations,* U.S. Senate, September 3, 1963; Harold K. Jacobson and Eric Stein, *Diplomats, Scientists and Politicians: The United States and the Nuclear Test Ban Negotiations* (Ann Arbor: University of Michigan Press, 1966); Donald G. Brennan, "A Comprehensive Test Ban: Everybody or Nobody," *International Security,* 1 (Summer 1976); Donald R. Westervelt, "Candor, Compromise and the Comprehensive Test Ban," *Strategic Review,* V (Fall 1977); Paul Doty, "A Nuclear Test Ban," *Foreign Affairs,* 65 (Spring 1987); Frank von Hippel et al., "A Low Threshold Nuclear Test Ban," *International Security,* 12 (Fall 1987).

96. "President's Speech on Military Spending and New Defense," *The New York Times,* March 24, 1983. The address has been reprinted in several anthologies of nuclear age issues.

97. Extensive series of articles on SDI and space defense appeared in *The New York Times,* March 3–8, 1985; *The Baltimore Sun,* March 16–19, 1985; and *The Christian Science Monitor,* November 5–12, 1985. For criticisms of space-based defense, see Richard L. Garwin et al. *The Fallacy of Star Wars* (New York: Random House, 1984); Hans Bethe et al., "Space-Based Ballistic Missile Defense," *Scientific American,* 251 (October 1984); McGeorge Bundy et al., "The President's Choice: Star Wars or Arms Control," *Foreign Affairs,* 63 (Winter 1984/85); Charles L. Glaser, "Do We Want the Missile Defenses We Can Build?" *International Security,* 10 (Summer 1985). A well-balanced treatment of the technical issues may be found in Harold Brown, "Is SDI Technically Feasible?", *Foreign Affairs—America and the World 1985,* 64, No. 3 (1986). The most thorough technical study in the public domain is *Ballistic Missile Defense Technologies* (Washington, D.C.: Congress of the United States, Office of Technology Assessment, September 1985).

98. For the debate about a NATO "no-first-use" policy, see McGeorge Bundy et al., "Nuclear Weapons and the Atlantic Alliance," *Foreign Affairs,* 60 (Spring 1982); Karl Kaiser et al., "Nuclear Weapons and the Preservation of Peace," ibid. (Summer 1982); John D. Steinbruner and Leon V. Sigal, eds., *Alliance Security and the No-First-Use Question* (Washington, D.C.: Brookings Institution, 1983); and Marc Trachtenberg, "The Question of No-First Use," *Orbis,* 29 (Winter 1986).

99. See the following writings of John J. Mearsheimer, "Maneuver, Mobile Defense and the NATO Central Front," *International Security,* 6 (Winter 1981/82); "Why the Soviets Can't Win Quickly in Central Europe," ibid., 7 (Summer 1982); "Nuclear Weapons and Deterrence in Europe," ibid., 9 (Winter 1984/85). See also Richard K. Betts, "Conventional Strategy: New Critics, Old Choices," ibid., 7 (Spring 1983); Samuel P. Huntington, "Conventional Deterrence and Conventional Retaliation in Europe," ibid., 8 (Winter 1983/84); and the Symposium on the European Conventional Balance, ibid., 12 (Spring 1988).

100. Richard K. Betts, "Conventional Deterrence: Predictive Uncertainty and Policy Confidence," *World Politics,* XXXVII (January 1985), 177–179.

101. Fred C. Iklé, Albert C. Wohlstetter, Henry Kissinger, et al., *Discriminate Deterrence, Report of the Commission on Integrated Long-Term Strategy* (Washington, D.C.: U.S. Government Printing Office, January 1988).

102. From the *Commission's Summary of Findings and Recommendations,* ibid., i.

103. Glenn H. Snyder, *Deterrence and Defense: Toward a Theory of National Security* (Princeton: Princeton University Press, 1961), pp. 4–5.

104. Richard Ned Lebow, "The Deterrence Deadlock: Is There a Way Out?" in Robert Jervis et al., *Psychology and Deterrence* (Baltimore, Md.: The Johns Hopkins University Press, 1985), p. 194. In Jervis's Introduction to that same volume and in Lebow's Conclusions, both writers concede that the theory of deterrence, which assumes the rationality of decision-makers, represents a powerful piece of abstract logic. Both, however, harbor doubts that leaders can always, under all circumstances, be expected to act as rationally as the theory prescribes.

105. "Chemical Weapons and Arms Control," in *Strategic Survey 1987–1988* (London: IISS, 1988), pp. 56–63.

106. "An Agenda for Action," ch. 9 in Graham T. Allison, Albert Carnesale, and Joseph S. Nye, Jr., eds., op. cit. They urge that a credible nuclear deterrent be maintained; that a credible conventional deterrent be obtained; that efforts to enhance crisis stability continue, along with efforts to reduce the probability of accidents; that procedures for war termination be developed; that nonproliferation policies be strengthened; that the dangers of misperceptions be reduced; and that alternatives be sought that will permit governments to decrease reliance on nuclear deterrence.

107. Joseph S. Nye, Jr., "Ethics and the Nuclear Future," *The World Today* (August/September 1986), pp. 151–154.

Chapter
10

Theories of International Integration, Regionalism, and Alliance Cohesion

CONSENSUS, FORCE, AND POLITICAL COMMUNITY

Central to the study of politics is the identification and analysis of forces that contribute to the formation and integration of political communities. Two questions are fundamental both to the study of integration and of politics itself: (1) why subjects or citizens give deference and devotion to the political unit within which they live (or why they do not); and (2) how procedural and substantive consensus is achieved and sustained within political systems. It is possible to outline essentially two theories of political integration. First, political systems gain and retain cohesiveness because of widely shared values among their members and general agreement about the framework of the system. Such systems are based on procedural consensus, or general agreement about the political framework and the legal processes by which issues are resolved, and substantive consensus, or general agreement about the solutions to problems the political system is called upon to solve. The greater the procedural and substantive consensus, the greater the integration of the political system. As used here, the term *consensus* is similar to legitimacy, as discussed in Chapter 3 with respect to Europe's classical balance of power and, specifically, Henry A. Kissinger's theory of international relations.

Second, as an alternative theory, it has been argued that political systems become or remain cohesive because of the presence, or threat, of force. Writers such as Hobbes and, in contemporary sociology, Dahrendorf have argued for a recognition of the importance of coercive power in the integration of political communities.[1] In the study of international relations, proponents of world government have often seen in the monopolization of power at the international level the key to the reduction of violence, and so-called political realists such as Niebuhr and Morgenthau, as noted in Chapter 3, have argued that world government is not possible without the development of far greater consensus at the global level about the scope, purpose, and control of such an international order than has existed in this or preceding centuries.[2]

FUNCTIONALISM AND THE INTEGRATIVE PROCESS

Contemporary students of political integration owe a considerable intellectual debt to the concept of functionalism that, as Johan K. De Vree has suggested, has provided an alternative to the more traditional legal conceptions of the state and of sovereignty.[3] Central to functionalism is the work of David Mitrany, whose writings greatly influenced subsequent integration theorists. Mitrany wrote during the years between the two world wars, as well as in the generation following World War II. He suggested that the growing complexity of governmental systems had increased greatly the essentially technical, nonpolitical tasks facing governments. Such tasks not only created a demand for highly trained specialists at the national level, but also contributed to the emergence of essentially technical problems at the international level, whose solution lies in collaboration among technicians, rather than political elites. The growth in importance of technical issues in the twentieth century is said to have made necessary the creation of frameworks for international cooperation. Such functional organizations could be expected to expand both in their numbers and in scope as the technical problems confronting humankind grew in both immensity and magnitude. As a result, organizations for functional collaboration might eventually supersede, or make superfluous, the political institutions of the past.

In Mitrany's theory there is a doctrine of "ramification," whereby the development of collaboration in one technical field leads to comparable behavior in other technical fields. Functional collaboration in one sector generates a felt need for functional collaboration in another sector. The effort to create a common market, for example, gives rise to pressure for further collaboration on pricing, investment, transport, insurance, tax, wage, social security, banking, and monetary policies. Mitrany assumed that functional activity could reorient international activity and contribute to world peace. Eventually such collaboration would encroach upon, and even absorb, the political sector. Hence, functionalism contrasts sharply with realist theory, which places emphasis upon competition and conflict as a principal, if not the dominant, feature of international politics (see Chapter 3). In contrast, functionalism, as Paul Taylor and A. J. R. Groom suggest, "begins by questioning the assumption that the state is irreducible and that the interests of governments prevail, and proceeds to the active consideration of schemes for cooperation; it is peace-oriented and seeks to avoid a win-lose stalemate framework."[4]

Integration as a Process and Condition

Thus Mitrany, like others considered in this chapter, was concerned with the process by which political communities become integrated. Although more recent students of integration have drawn upon Mitrany's work, they have developed their own definitions of integration. Ernst Haas defines integration as a process "whereby political actors in several distinct national settings are persuaded to shift their loyalties, expectations, and political activities toward a new center, whose institutions possess or demand jurisdiction over the preexisting national states."[5] In a later work, Haas conceives of integration as "referring *exclusively* to a process that links a given concrete international system with a dimly discernible future concrete system. If the present international scene is conceived of as a series of interacting and mingling national environments, and in terms of their participation in international organizations, then integration would describe the process of increasing the interaction and the mingling so as to obscure the boundaries between the system of international organizations and the environment provided by their national-state members."[6]

Referring to integration as a condition, Amitai Etzioni asserts that the possession by a political community of effective control over the use of the means of violence represents one criterion by which its level of integration is measured. Such a community has a center of decision-making that allocates resources and rewards and forms the dominant focus of political identification for the large majority of politically aware citizens.[7] In Etzioni's scheme, political unification is the process whereby political integration as a condition is achieved. Unification increases or strengthens the bonds among the units that form a system.[8] Making use of Haas's definition, Leon N. Lindberg, in his work on the European Community, defines integration as "(1) the processes whereby nations forego the desire and ability to conduct foreign and key domestic policies independently of each other, seeking instead to make *joint decisions* or to *delegate* the decision-making process to new central organs; and (2) the process whereby political actors in several distinct settings are persuaded to shift their expectations and political activities to a new center."[9] Subsequently, Lindberg viewed political integration as part of a broader process of international integration in which "larger groupings emerge or are created among nations without the use of violence," and in which there is "joint participation in regularized, ongoing decision-making," as a result, or as part of "the evolution over time of a collective decision-making system among nations."[10]

According to Charles Pentland, "International political integration is frequently identified with the circumvention, reduction, or abolition of the sovereign power of modern nation-states."[11] Donald J. Puchala proposes a definition of integration as a "set of processes that produce and sustain a Concordance System at the international level"—that is, "an international system wherein actors find it possible consistently to harmonize their interests, compromise their differences, and reap mutual rewards from their interactions."[12] Karl W. Deutsch refers to political integration as a process that may lead to a condition in which a group of people has "attained within a territory a sense of community and of institutions and practices strong enough to assure, for a long time, dependable expectations of peaceful change among its population."[13] Deutsch suggests that "integration is a matter of fact, not of time."[14] He also maintains that political integration can be compared to power, for we recall that power can be thought of as a relationship in which at least one actor is made to act differently from the way that actor would act otherwise (i.e., if this power were absent).[15] In another analysis, Philip E. Jacob suggested that political integration has "generally implied a relationship of *community* among people within the same political entity. That is, they are held together by mutual ties of one kind or another which give the group a feeling of identity and self-awareness."[16]

According to other writers, especially those since the early 1970s, it is essential to focus upon the structural and institutional dimensions of integration. Thus, Johan K. De Vree suggests that integration can be defined as the "process of the formation and development of institutions through which certain values are authoritatively allocated for a certain group of political actors or units."[17] In short, integration at the international level is conceptualized as the institutionalization of the political process among two or more states. According to James A. Caporaso and Alan L. Pelowski, integration consists of the development of "new structures and functions at a new system level which is more comprehensive (either geographically or functionally) than previously."[18] Integration consists of the emergence of new structures that may overlay, but not necessarily replace, older ones. These reflect a growing sense of interrelatedness between, or among, political or economic structures. The process by which integration occurs can be measured by using indicators of the growth of decisional capabilities within a specific unit such as the European Community.

Writers on integration have several features in common. All are concerned with the process by which loyalty is shifted from one center to another. They share an interest in communications within units to be integrated. According to Deutsch and Etzioni, people learn to consider themselves members of a community as a result of human communications patterns. In general, integration theorists hold that persons adopt integrative behavior because of expectations of joint rewards or penalties. Initially, such expectations are developed among elite groups both in the governmental and private sectors. Successful integration depends upon a people's ability to "internalize" the integrative process—that is, for member elites, rather than external elites, to assume direction of an integrative process. Moreover, Deutsch, Etzioni, and Haas have utilized systems theory in developing integration models. Each emphasizes the effect of integration in one sector upon the ability of participating units to achieve integration in other sectors. Finally, it is broadly assumed that integration is a multidimensional phenomenon.

TRANSACTIONS AND COMMUNICATIONS: IMPLICATIONS FOR SECURITY COMMUNITIES

To a greater extent than other writers on integration, Karl Deutsch uses both communications and systems theory, drawing upon the mathematician Norbert Wiener's writings on cybernetics and on Talcott Parsons's work on general systems discussed in Chapter 4. Deutsch quotes with approval the following passage from Wiener:

> The existence of social science is based on the ability to treat a social group as an organization and not as an agglomeration. Communication is the cement that makes organizations. Communication alone enables a group to think together, to see together and to act together. All sociology requires the understanding of communication.[19]

Communications among people can produce either friendship or hostility depending upon the extent to which the memories of communications are associated with more or less favorable emotions. Nevertheless, in Deutsch's scheme political systems endure as a result of their ability to abstract and code incoming information into appropriate symbols, to store coded symbols, to disassociate certain important information from the rest, to recall stored information when needed, and to recombine stored information entered as an input into the system. The building of political units depends upon the flow of communications within the unit as well as between the unit and the outside world.

Deutsch is concerned with the relationship between communications and the integration of political communities.[20] Countries are "clusters of population, united by grids of communication flows and transport systems, and separated by thinly settled or nearly empty territories."[21] Peoples are groups of persons joined together by an ability to communicate on many kinds of topics; they have complementary habits of communication. Generally, boundaries are areas in which the density of population and communications decline sharply. Peoples become integrated as they become interdependent. "Wherever there is immediate interdependence, not for just one or two specialized goods or services but for a very wide range of different goods and services, you may suspect that you are dealing with a country."[22] Interdependence among nations is far lower than interdependence within nations. In fact, measured by foreign trade, most countries are less interdependent today than they were in the nineteenth century. Trade, as a percentage of GNP, has declined.[23]

Deutsch's major substantive contribution to integration theory is found in his work on the conditions for political community in the North

Atlantic area. Drawing upon historical data, Deutsch and his collaborators examined 10 cases of integration and disintegration at the national level.[24] Since Deutsch's cases, in contrast to Etzioni's, are examples of building political communities at the national level—the implicit assumption of his work is that generalizations derived from these comparative studies are relevant to understanding integration at the international level—that there are similarities, or isomorphisms, between the process of community-building both at the national level and beyond the nation-state. Research and analysis undertaken in this work yielded several important conclusions about conditions for forming of security communities. Deutsch and his associates set forth two kinds of security communities: *amalgamated*, in which previously independent political units have formed a single unit with a common government; and *pluralistic*, in which separate governments retain legal independence. The United States is an example of an amalgamated security community, and the United States-Canada or France-Germany since World War II are pluralistic security communities.[25]

For the creation of an amalgamated security community, several conditions were found to be necessary:

1. mutual compatibility of major values;
2. a distinctive way of life;
3. expectations of joint rewards timed so as to come before the imposition of burdens from amalgamation;
4. a marked increase in political and administrative capabilities of at least some participating units;
5. superior economic growth on the part of some participating units and the development of so-called core areas around which are grouped comparatively weaker areas;
6. unbroken links of social communication, both geographically between territories and between different social strata;
7. a broadening of the political elite;
8. mobility of persons, at least among the politically relevant strata; and
9. a multiplicity of communications and transactions.[26]

Pluralistic Security Communities

For the formation of pluralistic security communities three conditions were found essential: (1) compatibility of values among decision-makers, (2) mutual predictability of behavior among decision-makers of units to be integrated,[27] and (3) mutual responsiveness. Governments must be able to respond quickly, without resort to violence, to the actions and communications of other governments. In a pluralistic security community, the member units forego war as a means toward settling disputes.

In their study of political community and the North Atlantic area, Deutsch and his collaborators examined cases such as the Austro-Hungarian Empire, the Anglo-Irish Union, and the union between Norway and Sweden, in which political communities disintegrated. Several tentative conclusions emerged about conditions conducive to disintegration: (1) extended military commitments; (2) an increase in political participation on the part of a previously passive group; (3) the growth of ethnic or linguistic differentiation; (4) prolonged economic decline or stagnation; (5) relative closure of political elites; (6) excessive delay in social, economic, or political reforms; and (7) failure of a formerly privileged group to adjust to its loss of dominance.

In Deutsch's conception the integrative process is not unilinear in nature. The essential background conditions do not come into existence simultaneously, nor are they established in any special sequence. "Rather it appears to us from our cases that they may be assembled in almost any sequence, so long as all of them come into being and take effect."[28]

On the basis of findings concerning the building and disintegration of national units, Deutsch and his associates suggested that the North Atlantic area, "although it is far from integrated, seems already to have moved a long way toward becoming so."[29] Several countries have achieved "pluralistic interaction": the United States and Canada, and the United Kingdom and Ireland. An essential condition for integration in the North Atlantic area is the development among countries of a greater volume of transactions and communications, especially those associated with rewards and expectations of gain. Deutsch and his collaborators suggested the need to develop new functional organizations within the North Atlantic area and to "make NATO more than a military alliance" by developing the "economic and social potentialities of this unique organization."[30] The Organization for Economic Cooperation and Development (OECD) at the Atlantic level, but also including Japan, together with the European Community represent functional organizations that are illustrative of, and said to be crucially important to, community-building beyond the nation-state.

NEOFUNCTIONALISM

Neofunctionalism represents the intellectual descendant of functionalism. Its principal contribution lies in the elaboration, modification, and testing of hypotheses about integration. Neofunctionalist writings include works by Ernst Haas, Philippe Schmitter, Leon Lindberg, Joseph Nye, Robert Keohane, and Lawrence Scheineman. Many, but by no means all, of the writings of neofunctionalists focus on the formation and evolution of the European Community. As Charles Pentland has suggested, referring to the neofunctionalist literature of the 1960s, "neofunctionalism embodied a desire toward middle range theory, which enabled it to come forth rather early with a convincing and useful—if not always verified—analysis of the European situations."[31]

In contrast to the more comparative focus of Deutsch and Etzioni, the work of Haas deals with specific cases, which Haas analyzes with the use of an elaborate theoretical framework. In his work on the European Coal and Steel Community, Haas postulates that the decision to proceed with integration, or to oppose it, depends upon the expectations of gain or loss held by major groups within the unit to be integrated. "Rather than relying upon a scheme of integration which posits 'altruistic' motives as the conditioners of conduct, it seems more reasonable to focus on the interests and values defended by them as far too complex to be described in such simple terms as 'the desire for Franco-German peace' or the 'will to a United Europe.' "[32] Haas assumes that integration proceeds as a result of the work of relevant elites in the governmental and private sectors, who support integration for essentially pragmatic rather than altruistic reasons. Elites having expectations of gain from activity within a supranational organizational framework are likely to seek out similarly minded elites across national frontiers.

Haas attempts to refine functionalist theory about integration. Criticizing Mitrany for having taken insufficient account of the "power" element, Haas postulates that power is not separable from welfare. Since few people make the pursuit of power an objective, power may be defined as "merely a convenient term for describing violence-laden means used for the realization of welfare aims." But Haas advances the proposition that "functionally specific international programs, or organizationally separated from diffuse orientations, maximize both welfare and integration." Such programs give rise to organizations whose "powers and competences gradually grow in line with the expansion of the conscious task, or in proportion to the development of unintended consequences arising from earlier task conceptions."[33]

Moreover, as a result of a learning process, power-oriented governmental activities can evolve toward welfare-oriented action. As actors realize that their interests are best served by a commitment to a larger organization, learning contributes to integration. Conceptions of self-interest and welfare are redefined. Haas advances the corollary: "Integrative lessons learned in one functional context will be applied in others, thus eventually supplanting international politics."[34] Crucial to integration is the "gradual politicization of the actors' purposes which were initially considered 'technical' or 'noncontroversial.' "[35] The actors become politicized, Haas asserts, because, in response to initial technical purposes, they "agree to consider the spectrum of means considered appropriate to attain them."

To the functionalist proposition that a welfare-orientation is achieved most readily by leaving the work of international integration to expert or technical groups, Haas offers two qualifications: (1) that such groups from a regional setting, such as Western Europe, are more likely to achieve integration than an organization with representatives from all over the world; and (2) that experts responsible to no one at the national level may find that their recommendations are ignored. Therefore, he suggests that expert managers of functionally specific national bureaucracies joined together to meet a specific need are likely to be the most effective carriers of integration. Haas rephrases the functionalist proposition to read: "International integration is advanced most rapidly by a dedication to welfare, through measures elaborated by experts aware of the political implications of their task and representative of homogeneous and symmetrical social aggregates, public or private."[36]

Again with qualifications, Haas accepts the functionalist proposition that political loyalties are the result of satisfaction with the performance of important functions by a governmental agency. Since it is possible for peoples to be loyal to several agencies simultaneously, there may be a gradual transfer of loyalty to international organizations performing important tasks. Haas accepts this proposition with the caveat that it is not likely to hold if the integrative process is influenced by nations with ascriptive status patterns, or traditional or charismatic leadership.[37]

"Spill-over" and the Integrative Process

Central to Haas's work is the concept of *spill-over*,[38] or what Mitrany called the doctrine of ramification. In his examination of the European Coal and Steel Community (ECSC), Haas found that among European elites directly concerned with coal and steel, relatively few persons were initially strong supporters of the ECSC. Only after the ECSC had been in operation for several years did the bulk of leaders in trade unions and political parties become proponents of the Community. Moreover such groups, as a result of gains that they experienced from the ECSC, placed themselves in the vanguard of other efforts for European integration, including the Common Market. Thus there was a marked tendency for persons who had experienced gains from supranational institutions in one sector to favor integration in other sectors. "Earlier decisions spill-over into new functional contexts, involve more and more people, call for more and more interbureaucratic contact and consultations, meeting the new problems which grow out of the earlier compromises."[39] Thus there was an "expansive logic" that contributed to "spill-over" from one sector to another. The process is one whereby the nations "upgrade" their national interests in a larger integrative setting.

In a study of the International Labor Organization, Haas developed a model that brought together the functional analysts of general systems theory and refined the "spill-over" concept found both in his earlier work and in Mitrany's writings in the form of the doctrine of ramification. Haas is concerned with the extent to which an international organization can transcend national boundaries and thus transform the international system. Governmental policies, the product of the interaction of national actors and their environment, constitute inputs into the international system. The organizations and accepted body of law form the structure of the international system. The structures receive inputs and convert them from tasks into actions. Collective decisions are the outputs of the international system. Such outputs may change the international environment in such a way as to produce either integrative or disintegrative tendencies within the international system. If the weak structures of the international system are inadequate to the tasks given them, their outputs enter an international environment in which national actors are predisposed either to strengthen or to weaken institutions for collaborative action at the international level. In either eventuality, the purposes (defined as consciously willed action patterns) of the actors are likely to produce new functions (defined as the results of actions that may bring unintended consequences). Purposes and functions may transform the international system by (1) producing a form of learning that enhances the original purposes of the actors and thus leads to integration; and (2) resulting in a learning experience that contributes to a reevaluation of purposes and thus leads to disintegration.[40]

The integration experience of Western Europe in the 1960s led Haas to modify further the spill-over concept. Similarly, Philippe Schmitter has suggested that the spill-over concept must be modified, refined, and qualified in a typology of strategic options available to actors. These include besides spill-over, *spill-around*, that is, an increase in the scope of functions performed by an integrative organization but not a corresponding growth in authority; a *build-up*, or increase in decisional autonomy and authority of an integrative organization, without entry into new issue areas; *retrenchment*, or increases in the level of joint arbitration while reducing the authority of an integrative organization; and *spill-back*, a retreat both in scope of functions and authority of an integrative organization to a previous situation. Schmitter hypothesizes that "successive spill-overs or package deals" encompassing new issues, as well as less conspicuous forms of "spill-around" may provide the basis for major strides toward political integration.[41]

Political Leadership: Implications for Sector Integration

Examining the European integration movement in the 1960s, Haas concluded that there was some "spill-over." The progress of the Common Market, in achieving such objectives as a common external tariff, uniform rules of competition, a freer market for foreign labor, and a Community agricultural policy, had "come close to voiding the power of the national state in all realms other than defense, education, and foreign policy." Although major decisions are made by the EEC Council of Ministers, which represents the member governments, the agreements reached have usually resulted in "increased powers for the Commission to make possible the implementation of what was decided."[42]

Despite these developments, Haas concluded that the "phenomenon of de Gaulle" was missing from his earlier integration framework. Events of the 1960s showed that "pragmatic interest politics concerned with economic welfare has its own built-in limits." This earlier work, it will be recalled, emphasized the development of expectations of gain among elites in the units to be integrated. The integrative experience of Western Europe after 1957 led Haas to conclude that interest based upon pragmatic considerations—for example, expectations of economic gain—is "ephemeral," because it is not "reinforced with deep ideological or philosophical commitment." A political process that is "built and projected from pragmatic interests, therefore, is bound to be a frail process, susceptible to reversal." If it proves possible to satisfy pragmatically based expectations with modest advances in integration, support for dramatic integrative steps will be lacking. Herein, Haas admits, lies one of the important limitations of pragmatically based expectations of gain.[43]

By the mid-1970s, Haas had developed even greater reservations about the logic of incrementalism and "spill-over," especially in the European Community context. For example, he saw no imminent prospect for a common monetary policy as the logical next step after the formation of a customs union and European Community agricultural policy. Although the issues confronting national governments have grown more complex and numerous, the likelihood that political elites will choose supranational solutions has not grown apace. Instead, Haas proposed a concept termed *fragmented issue linkage* that is said to occur "when older objectives are questioned, when new objectives clamor for satisfaction, and when the rationality accepted as adequate in the past ceases to be a legitimate guide to future action."[44]

Central to the integrative logic of functionalism, as we have seen, is the development of issues in which scientists and technicians play vitally important roles. It is appropriate, therefore, to examine the attitudes of scientific personnel in international organizations in order to ascertain their belief patterns with respect to the relationship between specialized knowledge and collective action for attaining economic, political, and social objectives, and to assess the extent to which international science and technology programs have increased in scope in relating specialized knowledge to growing economic, political, and social objectives. As Haas puts it, "If we could say that a given idea, a certain discovery, or an identifiable network of specialists triggered the development of a political consensus, which in turn legitimated a new international program, we could make a definite observation about the impact of science on collective problem solving."[45]

The evidence currently available fails to yield findings of a positive nature. Haas and his associates interviewed 146 scientists in a large number of international organizations concerned with such fields as environmental protection, industrial development, and agriculture. They included the European Communities, the Organization for Economic Cooperation and Development, the World Bank, the World Health Organization, the Food and Agriculture Organization, the United Nations Environment Program, and the Global Environmental Monitoring System, to mention just a few. But there was little evidence of any widespread faith among those interviewed in the development of strengthened international institutions or the efficacy of comprehensive global, or regional, scientific-technical planning for the application of rational policies. Haas concluded that despite the growth of multilateral institutions and forums for deliberating scientific issues—and the ever-increasing importance of scientific knowledge in the late twentieth century—the power of international organizations to bring about change, or to compel members to alter their policies, remains as weak as ever.[46] International conferences have typically ended by recognizing the complexity of the problems discussed and calling blandly for regional initiatives and national policies suitable to particular circumstances.

In summary, although Haas has developed an integration framework that embodies features of systems theory and functionalism, he has sought to point up some of the major limitations as well as the potential utility of functionalism in explaining integration at the international level. Therefore, in addition to his own work on international organizations and integration, Haas has provided a critique and elaboration of functionalism.

Other scholars have viewed integration as a multidimensional phenomenon. Hence the first task is to develop a concept, or concepts, of integration that encompasses its major dimensions or to deal conceptually with each of the various components of integration in such fashion as to explicate the linkages among them. According to Philippe Schmitter, "Understanding and explanation in this field of inquiry are, as in other fields such as political development, best served not by the dominance of a single accepted grand model, or paradigm, but by the simultaneous presence of antithetic and conflictive ones, which, while they may converge in certain aspects, diverge in many others."[47] As Barry B. Hughes and John E. Schwarz have written: "If, as appears to be the case, integration consists of several dimensions or components, another set of questions is raised. Is there a relationship among the different dimensions of integration, and, if there is, what is it?"[48]

JOSEPH NYE AND NEOFUNCTIONALISM

Building upon the work of Haas, and of Mitrany before him, several scholars have made an effort to refine neofunctionalist theories of integration. Among such scholars is Joseph Nye, whose contribution lies in developing a neofunctionalist model based upon "process mechanisms" and "integrative potential." Nye sets forth a theoretical framework based upon a neofunctionalist approach that, to a greater extent than that of Haas or Mitrany, is not "Eurocentric." Thus Nye bases his conceptualization upon an analysis of the conditions for integration drawn specifically from European *and* non-Western experiences and modifies greatly the notions of "automatic politicization" and "spill-over."[49]

Nye suggests that neofunctionalist literature contains seven "process mechanisms," around which he reconceptualizes and reformulates neofunctionalist theory.

1. Functionalist linkage of tasks, or the concept of spill-over. Nye holds that this mechanism has been applied, wrongly in his opinion, to include "any sign of increased cooperation," arising, for example, from linkages, or relationships, among problems because of their inherent technical characteristics, or because of actual efforts by integrationist elites to cultivate spill-over. Nye hypothesizes that "imbalances created by the functional interdependence or inherent linkages of tasks can be a force pressing political actors to redefine their common tasks."[50] However, such redefinition of tasks does not necessarily lead to an "upgrading of common tasks. The experience can also be negative."[51] Thus, if the linkage of tasks can cause spill-over, it can also produce spill-back. (Nye's observation on this point may be applicable to the European Economic Community, where elites and interest groups benefited in the earlier stages of integration, but with economic growth they later became reluctant to take additional integrative steps when growth rates dropped off. When growth rates declined as a result of the energy crisis, national protectionist sentiment flared up and governments hesitated to upgrade common interests if they feared adverse effects upon employment, inflation, payments, and monetary problems.)

2. Rising transactions. As noted elsewhere in this chapter, integration is hypothesized to be accompanied by an increase in transactions, including trade, capital movement, communications, and exchange of people and ideas. Political actors in a scheme for regional integration, faced with heavy demands upon common institutions resulting from an increasing volume of transactions, may choose to deal with them on a strictly national basis, or they may decide to strengthen the common institutions. According to Nye, "Rising transactions need not lead to a significant widening of the scope (range of tasks) of integration, but to intensifying of the central institutional capacity to handle a particular task."[52]

3. Deliberate linkages and coalition formation. Here, Nye focuses once again upon spill-over, or what he terms *accentuated spill-over,* in which "problems are deliberately linked together into package deals, not because of technological necessity, but because of political and ideological projections and political feasibilities."[53] Drawing heavily upon the experience of the European Community, Nye points to the efforts of politicians, international bureaucrats, and interest groups to create coalitions based upon linked issues. Although such efforts may promote integration, they may have a negative effect if, for example, the political fortunes of a group supporting integration, or an issue identified with integration, decline. The extent to which integration can be broadened in appeal is a function of the extent to which a coalition in favor of integration enjoys widespread public support.

4. Elite socialization. Nye cites numerous examples of the growth of support for integration arising from elites who have participated actively in an integrative scheme. The extent to which national bureaucrats become participants in regional integration will determine the level of their socialization—deemed important because national bureaucrats are said to be wary of integration because of the possible loss of national control. However, if other "process mechanisms" considered by Nye are negative, the socialization elites, especially bureaucratic groups, in favor of regional integration may serve to isolate them from the mainstream of attitudes and of policy in their home countries.

5. *Regional group formation.* Regional integration is said to stimulate the creation, both formally and informally, of nongovernmental groups or transnational associations. Viewed in the context of both the European Community and other settings, such as Central America and Africa, Nye asserts, such associations remain weak. Only the more general interests are aggregated by such groups at the regional level, whereas the more specific interests remain within the purview of national-level interest groups.[54]

6. *Ideological-identitive appeal.* The establishment of a sense of identity represents a powerful force in support of regional integration. According to Nye, "The stronger the sense of permanence and the greater the identitive appeal, the less willing are opposition groups to attack an integration scheme frontally."[55] Under such conditions, members are more likely than otherwise to tolerate short-term losses, and businesses are more likely to invest in the expectation that they will benefit, on a continuing basis, from the presence of a large market. However, the existence of rational integrative institutions may satisfy a "weak popular sense of regional identity."[56] The growth of ideological-identitive appeal within some groups may serve only to increase the opposition of insecure nationalist leaders and private sector groups, especially if the perceived gains from integration at the regional level are uncertain.

7. *Involvement of external actors in the process.* To a greater extent than earlier neofunctionalist theory, Nye posits the importance of external actors and their active involvement in his neofunctionalist model as a part of the process mechanism. He notes the importance of outside governments and international organizations, as well as nongovernmental actors, as catalysts in regional integration schemes.

Central to Nye's neofunctionalist model is what he terms *integrative potential*—that is, the integrative conditions stimulated by the "process mechanism." Here, he sets forth four conditions that are said to influence both the nature of the original commitment and the subsequent evolution of an integrative scheme.

1. *Symmetry or economic equality of units.* It matters not so much whether there exist "core areas" for integration or whether the prospective participants are relatively equal in size. Instead, a relationship is said to exist among trade, integration, and level of development, measured by per capita income. Such compatibility appears to be important for regional integration. The size of potential participants, measured in total GNP, seems to be of relatively greater importance in integrative schemes among less developed states than in the case of highly industrialized countries. Nye hypothesizes: "It almost looks as if the lower the per capita

income of the area, the greater the homogeneity in size of economy must be.[57]

2. Elite value complementarity. Nye acknowledges that the extent to which elite groups within integrating entities think alike is of considerable importance. In fact, he suggests that the higher the level of elite complementarity, the more likely the prospects for sustained impetus toward regional integration. However, he holds also that elites that have worked together effectively on a transnational basis may subsequently embrace divergent policies that are not conducive to integration.

3. Existence of pluralism. Functionally, specific groups are said to enhance the likelihood of integration. Here, Nye points to a major difference between the West European experience and that of the Third World, where such groups are relatively absent. According to Nye, "The greater the pluralism in all member states, the better the conditions for an integrative response to the feedback from the process mechanisms."[58]

4. Capacity of member states to adapt and respond. This factor is said to depend vitally upon the level of mutual responsiveness within the political units to be integrated into a larger regional entity. The higher the level of domestic stability and the greater the capacity of key decision-makers to respond to demands within their respective political units, the more likely they are to be able to participate effectively in a larger integrative unit.

Next, Nye sets forth three perceptual conditions that are affected by the integrative process. They include: (1) the perceived equity of distribution of benefits—with the hypothesis that "the higher the perceived equitable distribution in all countries, the better the conditions for further integration";[59] (2) perceived external cogency—that is, the perceptions of decision-makers concerning their external problems, including dependence upon exports, threats from larger powers, and the loss of status in a changing international system; and (3) low (or exportable) visible costs, or the extent to which integration can be made to be perceived as relatively cost-free, especially in its initial phases—a concept, as Nye points out, that is central to neofunctionalist theory and strategy.

Finally, four conditions are likely to characterize the integration process over time: (1) politicization, or the means by which problems are resolved and competing interests are reconciled or the extent to which the resultant benefits are sufficiently widespread to ensure broadening and deepening support; (2) redistribution, with the crucial issue being the phasing of the changes in status, power, and economic benefits among groups within the integrating unit. Central to the integrative process is the extent to which redistribution, benefiting some regions more than others, is compensated by growth to the benefit of the unit as a whole; (3) redistribution of alternatives or the extent to which, as the integrative process proceeds, decision-makers face pressures to increase the level and the scope of integration and conclude that the alternatives to integration are less satisfactory; and (4) externalization, or the extent to which members of an integrating unit find it necessary to develop a common position on issues in order to deal with nonmembers, as has happened with the European Community in its various sets of negotiations with outside parties, including the United States. Nye hypothesizes that "the further integration proceeds, the more likely third parties will be to react to it, either in support or with hostility."[60]

A neofunctionalist model such as that developed by Nye provides a framework for comparing integrative processes in more developed and less developed regions of the world, and for assessing the extent to which microregional, or functionally specific, economic organizations hold potential for further development toward federations. More likely, neofunctionalist model-building can provide, and has provided, more explicit theoretical propositions essential to understanding the limits, as well as the potential, of this segment of theory both in explaining integration and providing a strategy for advancing an integrative process.

Analyzing the roles, respectively, of macroregional political organizations [such as the Organization of American States (OAS), the Organization of African Unity (OAU), and the Arab League] and the microlevel economic organizations [including the European Economic Community (EEC), the Central American Common Market (CACM), and the East African Community (EAC)], Nye drew several tentative conclusions with respect to neofunctionalism. Microregional economic organizations are unlikely to develop into new units that encroach greatly upon, or supersede, the existing nation-states. However, microregional economic and macroregional political organizations have contributed to the development of "islands of peace" in the world and "their costs for world peace in terms of conflict creation have been less than their modest benefit to the world in conflict diversion."[61] Given the limited results of the regional organizations studied, the growth of multinational enterprises may be a more important trend in international organizations.

Although the impact of technology upon existing political units is such as to reduce the autonomy of the nation-state, only a portion of its national powers are redistributed at the regional level. In summary, microregional economic organizations have strengthened functional links that in turn have improved relationships among members. Macroregional political organizations have played a constructive role in controlling interstate conflict among members, although such organizations were unsuccessful in cases of primarily internal conflict—a serious limitation, Nye admits, in light of the importance of such conflict in the late twentieth century.[62] Indeed, the point can be made, and has been, that in many countries of the world the more immediate challenge to nationalist sentiment in recent decades comes not from universal or regional integration, but from centrifugal subnational forces in favor of local autonomy, secession, expulsion of an unwanted group from the national domain, and the substitution of the domination of one ethnic, linguistic, or religious group for that of another.

LEON LINDBERG AND NEOFUNCTIONALISM

Elsewhere in this chapter we have noted the importance attached by many, if not most, students of integration to the need for theory based upon a recognition of integration as a multidimensional phenomenon. The neofunctionalist theorist of recent decades has drawn upon systems theory and decision theory for the study of integration—for the analysis of what Leon Lindberg identifies as the "multiple properties of collective decision-making systems."[63] Thus, Lindberg views integration as an "interactive multidimensional process" that must be identified, compared, measured, and analyzed. The integrative process contains properties that "bear a systematic relationship to each other at any given point in time and . . . over time as well."[64] The level of collective decision-making—of integration—at any specific time is the product of the past decisions of the system, a system within which decisions are made.

Lindberg sets forth what he terms the variable properties that are said to describe the extent to which a group of nations engages in collective decision-making:

- functional scope of collective decision-making, or the extent to which it embraces a large number or just a few issue areas;
- the stage in decision-making at which collective processes are involved—at only the beginning or at a whole range of decisional stages, including the choice of options and their implementation;
- the importance of collective decision-making in determining public allocations on important or only marginal issue areas;
- the extent to which demands, large or few in number, are articulated into the collective arena for action;
- the degree to which collective decision-makers have available resources that are adequate to their needs;
- the continuity and strength of leadership at the level of the collectivity;
- the extent to which the bargaining modalities of the system help maximize the individual interests of nations or enhance those of the collectivity;
- the effect of collective decisions on the behavior of individuals, whether large or only small numbers of people are affected;
- the degree to which collective decisions meet with compliance, apathy, or outright opposition; and
- the distributive consequences of collective decisions, whether they are important or very marginal for constituent systems and for actors within them.

Certain concepts set forth in Lindberg's paradigm were studied in an analysis of the European Community by Leon N. Lindberg and Stuart A. Scheingold. For example, a tabulation of the number of issue areas subject to joint decision-making within the EEC in selected periods between 1950 and 1970 yielded evidence of a substantial increase—from no issue areas in 1950 to 7 in 1957, to 17 in 1968.[65] Ordinal rankings were assigned to issue areas depending upon the "locus of decision-making" in the European Community at different times in the 1950–1970 period. Indicators of institutional capacity and structural growth were developed: the size of administrative staff, the quantity of organizational subunits, the numbers of meetings held, and proposals made by the collective unit and acted upon. Trade data were utilized to assess economic interest perceptions, and attitudinal data were analyzed to determine levels of expectations of future gains, belief in legitimacy of collective decision-making, conceptions of a common interest, and a sense of mutual political identification. In the European Community, Lindberg and Scheingold concluded, there existed " 'a permissive consensus' among the general public and elite groups as far as the legitimacy of the Community and its institutions was concerned. This extended to a very wide range of economic and social functions and to a strong, independent role for the supranational Commission."[66]

DELINEATING INTERNATIONAL REGIONS: A QUANTITATIVE ANALYSIS

In an effort to develop empirical evidence about factors that aid or hinder the process of integration, Bruce M. Russett has posed the following questions:

> (1) How many groups [regions] are necessary for an adequate summary description of the similarities and differences among types of national political and social systems? (2) What countries are to be found in each group? (3) How do these groups compare with the groupings we call regions, now in use by social scientists? (4) What are the discriminating variables for distinguishing groups in general, and in distinguishing between specific groups? (5) What is the relevance of our groupings to theories of comparative and international politics?[67]

In a quest for tentative answers to such questions, Russett focused attention on regions of social and cultural homogeneity, on regions of states that share similar political attitudes or external behavior as identified by the voting patterns of governments in the United Nations, on regions of political interdependence where countries are joined together by a network of supranational or intergovernmental political institutions, on regions of economic interdependence as identified by intraregional trade as a proportion of a state's national income, and on regions of geographical proximity. Such analysis may contribute to the identification of those areas of the world where the potential for further integration is great, as well as areas with little prospect for further integration.

Russett used factor analysis to delineate regional groupings. He factor-analyzed 54 social and cultural variables on 82 countries. Included were such variables as GNP per capita, primary and secondary school pupils as a percentage of population, percentage of adult literacy, foreign mail per capita, infant mortality rate, different religious groups as a percentage of population, and rates of population increase. Using factor analysis, Russett reduced the 54 separate variables to four dimensions or factors. In other words, he produced four clusters from the 54 separate variables: (1) economic development, (2) communism, (3) Catholic culture, and (4) intensive agriculture. For example, the first factor, economic development, was so labeled because many variables loaded heavily on it—that is, were highly correlated with it. These included per capita GNP, newspapers and radios per capita, life expectancy, pupils in primary and secondary schools, and hospital beds and physicians per capita. After following a similar procedure to derive the other three factors, countries were grouped according to the extent to which they resembled each other among a variety of variables. Those countries that loaded most heavily on each factor were grouped and were given regional names. Thus a grouping called "Afro-Asia" loaded heavily on the first factor, *economic development*. Countries in this region resembled each other in relatively low levels of economic development.

A grouping called "Western Community" was clustered around a factor that included such variables as governmental expenditure and revenue, total voting turnout, and rate in increase of GNP per capita. A grouping called "Latin America" that also included the Philippines, as well as another grouping termed "semideveloped Latins" loaded heavily on the factor called *Catholic culture*. In this factor were such variables as Christians as a percentage of population, votes for socialist parties, language, and land inequality. A grouping designated "Eastern Europe" emerged from a factor termed *intensive agriculture*. This factor included such variables as overall population density and population density as related to farming land.

ALLIANCE COHESION

At both the international and domestic levels, groups are formed to enable their members to achieve a shared objective. Since such groups are disbanded when the objective for which they were created has been attained, they are far less enduring than the political communities whose formation and structure are of concern to writers whose work has been discussed earlier in this chapter. Alliances are designed to facilitate the attainment of goals by, as Robert L. Rothstein has suggested,

> introducing into the situation a specific commitment to pursue them; to a certain extent, it legitimizes that pursuit by inscribing it in a treaty; and it increases the probability that the goals will be pursued because the alliance

creates a new status which makes it more difficult for the parties to renege on each other, not only because they would be dishonoring their commitment, and earning a reputation for perfidy, but also because their new status usually creates a response in the external world, such as a countervailing alliance, which would tend to strengthen the bonds in the original alliance. It may also stabilize a situation by forcing enemy decision-makers to throw another weight into the opposing scales.[68]

According to Robert E. Osgood, an alliance is a "latent war community, based on general cooperation that goes beyond formal provisions and that the signatories must continually estimate in order to preserve mutual confidence in each other's fidelity to specified obligations."[69] Thus, alliances have usually been formed in international contexts in which conflict, or the threat of conflict, is present.[70] Because of the historic importance of alliances in the international system, and the widespread use of coalitions by political groups intent upon attaining elective office, such collaborative efforts have been the object of scholarly investigation especially by the political realists examined in Chapter 3,[71] but also by writers concerned more specifically with the dynamics and the operation of alliances.

Two scholars in particular, George F. Liska and William R. Riker, have developed theories of alliance behavior. In their theoretical frameworks, Liska and Riker are similar in several respects. First, they agree that alliances or coalitions disband once they have achieved their objective, because they are formed essentially "against, and only derivatively for, someone or something."[72] Although a "sense of community" may reinforce alliances or coalitions, it seldom brings them into existence. In forming alliances to achieve some desired objective, decision-makers weigh the costs and rewards of alignment. A decision to join an alliance is based upon perception of rewards in excess of costs. Each country considers the marginal utility from alliance membership, as contrasted with unilateral action. Ultimately, the cohesiveness of an alliance "rests on the relationship between internal and external pressures, bearing on the ratio of gains to liabilities for individual allies."[73] Once costs exceed rewards, the decision to realign is taken. According to Liska, nations join alliances for security, stability, and status. In Liska's theory a primary prerequisite for alliance cohesion is the development of an "alliance ideology." The function of alliance ideology is to provide a rationalization for alliance. In performing this function, ideology "feeds on selective memory of the past and outlines a program for the future."[74] Periodic consultation, especially between a leading member and its allies, both on procedural and substantive issues, contributes to the development and preservation of alliance ideology and thus alliance cohesion.

After victory, first, the size of the alliance or coalition must be reduced if additional gains are to accrue to the remaining participants. Second, alliances or coalitions are crucial to attaining a balance of power. In Riker's framework, the formation of one coalition contributes to the formation of an opposing coalition. When one coalition is on the verge of victory, neutral actors often join the weaker of the coalitions to prevent the stronger from attaining hegemony. If neutral members do not align themselves with the weaker side, some members of the leading coalition must shift to the weaker of the two coalitions if the system is to regain equilibrium. Equilibrium is the likely result of the existence of two "quasipermanent blocking coalitions," or the presence of such coalitions that "play the role of balancer if a temporary winning coalition sets the stakes too high."[75] In establishing his own rules for equilibrium Riker draws upon those set by Kaplan in his balance-of-power system.[76] Moreover, in relating alliances or coalitions to balance of power, Liska and Riker incorporate into their theories ideas found in realist international relations theory.

The Optimum Size of Alliances

Liska and Riker suggest that alliance builders, if they act "economically," do not form alliances haphazardly with all available allies. Instead, Liska considers the "marginal utility of the last unit of commitment to a particular ally and the last unit of cost in implementing commitments."[77] Riker stresses the "size principle," according to which participants create coalitions adequate to union and no larger than necessary to achieve their commonly shared objective. If actors have perfect information, they will form a coalition of exactly the minimum size needed to win. Without complete information, members of a winning coalition build a larger coalition than necessary to achieve their objectives; the less complete the information, the larger the coalition. This fact, which Riker observes at both the national and international levels, contributes to the short lifespan of alliances or coalitions.

Liska and Riker address themselves to the question of rewards from joining an alliance or coalition. According to Liska, the gains and liabilities associated with alignment can be grouped into pairs. For example, the pair peculiar to security is protection and provocation—"the first to be derived from a particular alliance and the second producing counteraction and counteralliance." Burdens and gains, as well as potential for status enhancement and possible losses in capacity for independent action, must be balanced. Liska contends that "in order to assess a particular alignment all these factors must be compared with hypothetical gains and liabilities of other alignments, with nonalignment, or at least with a different implementation of an unavoidable alliance."[78] By contrast, in Riker's theory, actors join alliances or coalitions for several reasons: the threat of reprisal if they refuse to align themselves, to receive payments of one kind or another, to obtain promises about policy or subsequent decisions, or to gain emotional satisfaction.

As noted elsewhere (see Chapter 3), there has been increased interest in the past generation in studying the behavior of small powers in the international system. Alliances usually encompass small powers as well as great powers. Such states join alliances because they must rely fundamentally—and to an extent greater than large states—upon other states. Great powers seek alignment with small states both for the political and military gains afforded, and also in order to restrain the latter from certain actions.[79] But smaller powers, Robert Rothstein notes, may prefer to align themselves with a less powerful state or with a combination of lesser states, rather than with a great power. Small power alliances, however, are said to provide ineffective instruments if a state's goal is to increase its military strength. Their principal potential value lies in maintaining a local or regional status quo, or resolving grievances among small powers without outside great power intervention. Provided small powers can maintain agreement among themselves, they can make it difficult for a great power to intervene in their region.[80]

Alliance Cohesion and Disintegration

Despite the existence of many important differences, one or the other theories of alliance behavior have certain features in common with theories of integration. Riker emphasizes the importance of communications among actors in the formation of coalitions of optimal size. The absence of adequate communications contributes to the formation of coalitions larger than are needed to achieve their initial objective. Riker's size principle has its counterpart in the proposition advanced by Mancur Olson that the likelihood of achieving an optimum number of partners diminishes as the size of the coalition grows.[81] The larger the coalition, the smaller the percentage of group benefits that will be available to any single partner, and hence the less attractive will be the reward for collective action. But it could be plausibly argued that the group benefits increase as the membership of the coalition grows. Stated differently, the collective good is maximized as the size of the coalition is expanded. As in Haas's earlier formulations, pragmatic interests play a major role in leading nations to align or to dealign themselves. The fact that such interests do not endure contributes to the disintegration of alliances, as well as the ephemeral nature of some of the support for integration noted elsewhere in this chapter.

Central to an understanding of international politics is the question of how states respond to threats and the role of alliances in their calculus of security needs. Do they attempt to find allies in an effort to achieve a balance against the party threatening them? Alternatively, do threatened states seek an accommodation with the power that poses the threat? According to Stephen M. Walt, the quest for a balance in order to achieve security from a threatening state is far more likely than a movement toward accommodation. The former he terms "balancing," while he refers to the latter as "bandwagoning."[82] A state that engages in a balancing policy allies itself with others against the prevailing threat; a state that embraces a bandwagoning policy aligns itself with the source of danger.[83] According to Walt, such a distinction is crucial because of the uncertainty that has often existed in the minds of scholars and policymakers alike concerning the response of states to the threats facing them. In this respect, Walt, in discussing the raison d'être for the formation of alliances, places himself in fundamental agreement with traditional balance-of-power theory. For a state to align itself with the hegemonic power would be tantamount to placing its trust in the benevolence of the dominant state. Instead, states are likely to form alliances or alignments with other threatened states in order to assure their survival. Walt contends that not only is balancing more common than bandwagoning, but also that the stronger the state, the greater is likely to be its tendency to balance, or to ally itself with other states in order to cope with the threat posed by the politically dominant power. Conversely, according to Walt, the weaker the state, the more likely it is to bandwagon instead of balancing. Such a condition is attributed to the fact that weak states can contribute little to the strength of a defensive coalition. Because they cannot affect the outcome in any event, such states are likely to choose the dominant side. A decision to join the weaker group in a quest for balance, contrasted with bandwagoning, will be taken if a state perceives that such action will turn a losing coalition into one that has the prospect of winning. To the extent that a state, by such a decision, actually contributes to the victory of an otherwise losing coalition, its influence is commensurately enhanced.

In Walt's formulation, the focus is what is termed a balance of threat rather than a balance of power as the basis for the formation of alliances at the international level. States join together in alliances in response to threats, not all of which may be based on the power of the opposing state. Thus, Walt places emphasis more on intention or ambition rather than simply power itself as the basis for threat and thus for the response taken by balancing or bandwagoning states. Hence arises his preference for what is termed the balance of threat in place of the balance of power as the basic reason for alliance or alignment. Because threat perception strongly influences a decision to align as a basis for balancing, such a policy is likely to characterize behavior in peacetime, when the focus is deterrence, or in the early stages of a conflict, when the object is defeat of the power posing the greatest threat. As the outcome becomes more certain, lesser states are likely to defect from the losing side and thus to move toward a policy of bandwagoning with the victorious alliance. With the achievement of victory, the grouping that has defeated the would-be hegemonic power is itself likely to disintegrate.

To what extent, Walt also asks, is ideology likely to constitute a basis for alliance formation? States with similar political systems have often aligned with each other. According to Walt, the significance of ideology as a unifying factor in alliances diminishes as threat increases. Confronted with a serious challenge to their survival, states are likely to align with each other with little regard for ideological differences. In such circumstances, pragmatic interests prevail over considerations of ideology. Thus, the more secure a state perceives itself to be in the international setting in which it finds itself, the greater will be its quest for ideologically similar or compatible postures in alliance choices. By the same token, states that are domestically unstable have a tendency to align themselves with ideologically similar states in order to bolster their internal legitimacy.

In their continuing quest for security, states are said to make choices between alliances and armaments. According to Michael F. Altfeld, such decisions are based on a calculus of cost—namely, what the decision-makers must sacrifice in making the necessary choices.[84] To the extent that alliances permit a broader sharing of the cost of security among several parties, the burden to any one state is likely to be lower than what it would pay for security in the absence of an alliance. Because the means available to states are finite, the purchase of armaments, to the extent that it reduces total resources in the civilian economy, represents a cost factor to be calculated in the decision to establish or to join an alliance. Moreover, alliance membership can be expected to carry with it a reduction in the autonomy of a state as a result of the promise by each side contained in the alliance to take specific actions in the event of specific contingencies. Thus there are several variables that enter into the calculation with respect to alliance membership: the extent to which security can be achieved by a mix between greater or lesser levels of alignment or armaments. Altfeld postulates conditions under which a government will be in equilibrium with respect to security, wealth, and autonomy. Of central importance is the marginal utility of alliance membership to the marginal utility of autonomy. Clearly related is the marginal utility of armaments to the marginal utility of domestic wealth. Stated simply, decision-makers are likely to weigh the value of alliance against that of additional armaments, and to relate both alliance membership and armaments to the cost with reference to the lost autonomy, or independence of action, at the international level, and the price of additional armaments to the domestic economy. Similarly, in Altfeld's analysis, the dissolution of alliances can "be expected to occur in any of five circumstances: an increase in the marginal product of armaments; an increase in the marginal utility autonomy; a decline in the marginal utility of civilian wealth; a decline in the marginal productivity of alliances; or a decrease in the marginal utility of security."[85]

INTEGRATION THEORY: PROBLEMS OF CONCEPTUALIZATION AND DEFINITION

Although the theorists examined in this chapter have suggested a series of indicators for assessing the level of integration, the theory is not sufficiently advanced that there exists either a commonly accepted definition

of integration or general agreement on the relevant indicators of integration.[86] Some writers, as we have seen, emphasize transaction flows such
as trade, travel, mail, telephone, radio, and other forms of technical communication as indicators of integration. In examining transaction flows, or
communications, Ernst Haas has suggested that the question remains
whether a rise in transactions precedes, reinforces, results from, or causes
integration. According to Haas, the question of *when* these conditions are
expected is vital when we try to devise a rigorous theoretical framework
to explain the causes of integration. Especially in the case of indicators
based on social communication we must know whether the transactions
measured among the elites to be integrated preceded the integrative
process or whether they are present as a result of events that characterized the region after integration has occurred for several years. In the
latter case, we have merely defined an existing community in terms of
communications theory, but we have not explored the necessary steps for
arriving there.[87]

Indicators of Integration

In the mid-1960s Deutsch, using transaction flows as one of his indicators
to assess the level of European integration, concluded that "European
integration has slowed since the mid-1950s and it has stopped or reached
a plateau since 1957–1958." In part, he based this conclusion on the fact
that since then there had been no increases in transaction flows "beyond
what one would expect from mere random probability and increase in
prosperity in the countries concerned."[88] In support of his conclusion
Deutsch marshaled other evidence, including elite interviews and content
analysis of selected key newspapers in France and Germany. Thus, in
addition to transaction flows, statistical analysis of opinions expressed by
elites and attention accorded in the press are said to form indicators of
integration.

Other scholars, employing in some cases different indicators and in
other instances similar ones, have reached conclusions about the status of
European integration diametrically opposed to those of Deutsch. For example, if integration is defined as Leon Lindberg conceives it—namely,
as "the process whereby nations forego the desire and ability to conduct
foreign and key domestic policies independently of each other, seeking
instead to make joint decisions or to delegate the decision-making process
to a new central organ"—it is possible to conclude, as Lindberg does, that
Western Europe, during the five-year period after the formation of the
EEC in 1958, experienced substantial progress toward integration.[89]

Another study, using different attitudinal data, concluded that European integration, far from having halted in the late 1950s, may have
moved in some respects into full gear only since then.[90] Although the full
implications of the single European act calling for the dismantling of
remaining barriers to the movement of persons, goods, and services within

the European Community by 1992 remain to be seen, this is hardly the description of an integrative organization in stagnation, stalemate, or disintegration. In a self-administered questionnaire in 1964 to 1965, incorporating questions from previous adult surveys, Ronald Inglehart found that a majority of youths in a sample drawn from schools considered to be representative of important social and economic groups in Britain, France, the Netherlands, and Germany were overwhelmingly favorable to European unification. Although there was substantial opposition among adults, especially in France, the younger generation strongly supported further steps toward European integration.[91] Inglehart's assumption attributed the differing attitudes among age groups to the fact that the adults in the sample received their basic political orientation during nationalist periods and that these attitudes were not easily changed. The youths in the sample received their political orientation when nationalism was less in favor. Postulating the stability of attitudes acquired during their formative years, it is possible to project that the generation from which the sample data were drawn will manifest a relatively "European" outlook as adults. Conceivably this generation will make its impact on the further evolution of the European Community in the 1990s.

Using other indicators, Carl J. Friedrich concluded that Western Europe had become more integrated since 1957, the year of the signing of the Rome Treaty, creating the Common Market.[92] Criticizing Deutsch's contention, and his indicators, that integration had slowed, Friedrich examined the development of sentiment and contacts at the European level in business, agriculture, the trade union movement, and the academic community. In each of these areas he found a marked increase in contacts across frontiers and support among such groups for European integration. Moreover, Friedrich criticized Deutsch and his associates both for their choice of indicators and for their use of statistical data in supporting their conclusions[93]—in short, for giving excessive emphasis to *quantitative* means based on aggregate data and for allegedly having overlooked *qualitative* indicators of integration.

In their examination of economic and political integration in Europe, James A. Caporaso and Alan Pelowski found that the EEC was rapidly integrating in the 1960s even though there was "as yet limited responsiveness" among its various subsystems.[94] Exports from the Federal Republic of Germany to other European Community members, one of the indicators chosen for examination, had tripled since 1958, and there had been an even greater increase in the number of political decisions and regulations at the Community level, another indicator of integration in this study. Moreover, there was a growth in predictability of behavior among members of the EEC, an indicator utilized not only by Caporaso and Pelowski, but also in Deutsch's work of the late 1950s on integration in the North Atlantic area.

Other writers have suggested additional indicators of integration. Claude Ake, for example, proposed quantitative measures, including:

1. the legitimacy score, or the extent to which citizens give loyalty to the state and see it as the embodiment of their interest;
2. the extraconstitutional behavioral score, or the frequency distribution of the preference of political actors between constitutional and extraconstitutional behavior;
3. the political violence score, or the extent to which actors resort to violence to attain objectives;
4. the secessionist demand score;
5. the alignment pattern score, or the extent to which major groups competing for power draw their support from more than one geographical area and ethnic, religious, social, and economic group;
6. the bureaucratic ethos score, or the extent to which the members of a political system are prepared to give loyalty to their political unit and its office holders in spite of personal feelings about them;
7. the authority score, or the degree to which the people accept their political unit as legitimate and are prepared to accept its rule without coercion.[95]

International Systemic Factors and Integration

Integration theorists have been criticized for having given insufficient emphasis to factors in the international environment that affect the integration process. Hoffmann, for example, argues that the apparent failure of spill-over in Western Europe may be attributed at least in part to two variables—namely, the diversity of the national units and the allegedly bipolar international system of the post–World War II period. While the Benelux countries were prepared to rely almost exclusively upon the United States for defense, France sought to accelerate tendencies in the international system toward multipolarity. France's ambivalence toward European integration reflected the attitude that "integration is good if it leads to an entity that will emancipate Europe from any bipolar system, bad if it does not and merely chains France to German national desiderata,"[96] or subordinates France to the United States. In European integration Germany, in the aftermath of World War II, found a framework to regain a place of respectability in the family of Western nations as well as an outlet for national energies. Britain's outlook toward European integration was strongly influenced by British global perspectives on foreign policy. In short, Hoffmann contends, relations among Western European nations have been "subordinated to their divergences about the outside world"; the "regional subsystem becomes a stake in the rivalry of its members about the system as a whole."[97] Beyond Hoffmann's analysis, it is possible to adduce additional examples of variables from the international environment that appear to influence the level of integration in a region such as Western Europe, as well as the decision to join an alliance.

In fact, it has been postulated that the lower the regional autonomy of a regional subsystem such as the European Community, the greater the importance of "exogenous factors." The integrative experiences of Western Europe, and especially those of Latin America and East Africa, "reflect a dynamic interaction between an internal regional dialectic, analyzed by present theory, and changing international environmental pressures relatively unexplored in current neofunctionalist literature."[98]

Research on integration has been criticized not only on the basis of the variables and indicators chosen for examination, but also for the lack of an appropriate theoretical framework. In particular, such criticism has been directed toward research, such as that undertaken by Russett, which relies heavily upon factor analysis in the development of inductive theory.[99] In the absence of a deductive theoretical framework, Young argues, empirical investigation is not likely to provide an adequate basis for predictive theory to take account of intervening variables or offer an adequate explanation of relationships among variables. Such a discussion reflects the disagreement among scholars about the nature of theory noted in Chapter 1. Moreover, the lack of a shared definition of integration inhibits research. According to Donald J. Puchala, who himself proposed a definition, as noted earlier in this chapter: "More than fifteen years of defining, redefining, modeling, and theorizing have failed to generate satisfactory conceptualizations of exactly what it is we are talking about when we refer to 'international integration' and exactly what it is we are trying to learn when we study this phenomenon."[100] Puchala's observation, written in the early 1970s, remains valid a generation later.

In a concluding chapter to a volume containing essays by several scholars on regional integration, representative of the literature of the early 1970s, Stuart Scheingold pointed to the paucity of information based upon a form of cost-benefit analysis—the losses and gains to groups within societies—although several authors have attached great importance to expectations of joint reward as a catalyst to integration. According to Scheingold, additional research should be conducted to assess the ways in which integrative processes impinge upon national policies in such areas as agriculture, antitrust, medium-term planning, and general commercial policy, as well as upon world politics. Such questions, it is suggested, are more broadly relevant to comparative politics and to international politics. Therefore, they would attract interest, as well as potential intellectual contributions, from a larger segment of the academic community. In short, Scheingold saw the need for approaches that were essentially inductive and for the collection of data on a more extensive basis as necessary prerequisites for further theorizing about integration.[101]

Limitations of Functionalism and Neofunctionalism

Functionalism itself has been the object of several kinds of criticisms and modifications, especially in the latter case by neofunctionalists surveyed in this chapter. Among the alleged deficiencies of functionalism are the following: (1) that it is difficult, if not impossible, to separate the economic and social tasks from the political; (2) that governments have shown them-selves unwilling to hand over to international authority tasks that en-croach upon the political; (3) that certain economic and social tasks do not "ramify" or "spill-over" into the political sector; and (4) that the road to political integration lies through political "acts of will," rather than func-tional integration in economic and social sectors. Research conducted thus far has not produced agreement among students of integration about spill-over or about the catalysts that initiate and sustain the integrative process. There is no widely accepted deductive model about integration in which definitions and conditions for integration as well as processual steps and transformation rules are set forth. To a considerable extent, the disagreement about functionalism may be reduced to a debate between the proponents and opponents, respectively, of the coercion and consen-sus theories of community discussed earlier in this chapter. But the cri-tique of neofunctionalism by Haas himself is based upon the notion that they are obsolete because they do not address "the most pressing and important problems on the global agenda of policy and research." Haas states that neofunctionalism was inspired by a "sense of orderly process and by the assumption that states manage to cope collectively according to the rationality of disjointed incrementalism."[102] Neofunctionalism is not considered to be wrong, but instead to be inadequate in light of the "turbulent field" of international relations, with its numerous global issues in the late twentieth century.

In another critique of functionalism, Charles Pentland concluded that, at least in light of the Western European experience since World War II, there is little evidence to suggest that technology and economic growth, in a shrinking world, by themselves will produce integration through functional cooperation. "The relation between functional need and struc-tural adaptation, central to the theory, is 'necessary' only in the sense of being an ideal or norm, not in the sense of predetermining the direction of change."[103] Moreover, political influences and pressures have proven to be of major importance in effecting the integrative process in Western Europe. There has been little or nothing that is "nonpolitical" in nature in the integration experience of Western Europe since World War II, although the institutions of the European Community, adequate for the formation of a customs union, may not be relevant to the fundamental problem of Western European integration—forming a political federation.

Nor is a neofunctionalist integration model necessarily adequate for the study of Third World integrative systems. In contrast to industrialized actors, Third World states are likely to have fewer goals that can be satisfied by integration. For example, expectations of economic gains from rising levels of trade, facilitated by the lowering or removal of tariff barri-ers, have furnished a major motivation for the formation of customs un-ions, especially in Western Europe. However, the structure of trade and production in much of the Third World, based historically upon the supply of agricultural products and raw materials to advanced industrialized states, has hindered the prospects, at least in the short run, for economic complementarity of a level sufficient to promote integration within the Third World by the formation of customs unions or Common Markets comparable to the European Community.[104] Even in areas such as Latin America and the Arab world, where the existence of a common language and common cultural values would appear to be conducive to integration, the fact that national economies are oriented outward toward the industrialized areas of the world rather than toward each other poses a serious obstacle to regional integration. Therefore, integration modes adequate to Third World conditions differ substantially from those having relevance for industrialized states, and models examined in this chapter contribute to an explanation for the lack of integration in the Third World.

THE DEVELOPMENT OF INTEGRATION THEORY

What is needed is a model that incorporates propositions from neofunctionalist literature as well as writings that give greater importance to the role of coercion and the impact of the international environment upon integration. Current integration models may be faulted for their relative neglect of the role of conflict as an integrating force. Students of postwar Europe agree, in general, that the experience of World War II was important, if not crucial, as a catalyst in the subsequent European integration movement. Yet the phenomenon of conflict—perhaps like the "phenomenon of de Gaulle" in Haas's critique of *his* own earlier works—is missing from models of integration, even when they are applied to the post–World War II European experience. Except perhaps as a result of normative biases of students of integration, it is difficult to understand the reason for this oversight, since both traditional and contemporary writers in the field of conflict have examined in considerable depth the integrative role of conflict, as discussed in Chapter 8. Moreover, the integrative impetus of post–World War II Europe was based largely upon disillusionment with the nation-state as a result of the Second World War. Thus, even in the European context, conflict may have played an integrative role that is given less prominent consideration than it deserves in the integration literature on Europe.

Several writers have suggested that integration is a multidimensional concept. According to Joseph Nye, conceptual distinctions should be made among categories of catalysts, the external environment in which integration takes place, and the types of discontinuities in the integrative process.[105] There is need for integration to be broken down into economic, political, and legal components, which in turn might be divided into subtypes, each of which could be measured. "Rather than allowing us to talk about integration in general and confusing terms, this disaggregation will tend to force us to make more qualified, and more readily falsified, generalizations with the *ceteris paribus* clauses filled in, so to speak, and thus pave the way for more meaningful comparative analysis than that provided by the general schemes used so far."[106] Especially in the 1970s, there were efforts, as we have noted, to study integration as a multidimensional phenomenon. Integration theory has been subjected to extensive quantitative analysis. Nevertheless, major conceptual problems, as well as disagreement about definitions, variables, and indicators, remain, despite the contributions of scholars, especially during the past generation, to theoretical knowledge about integration at the international level.

In the 1980s the literature of international integration did not experience a growth in any way comparable to that of the three decades following World War II. At that time, as we have noted, the regional integrative experience, focused on but not confined to Western Europe, furnished both a laboratory and a rich source of data for the development and testing of theories of integration based on a variety of approaches, definitions, criteria, and indicators. Yet the process of integration continued in the 1980s within regional organizations in various parts of the world. By the end of the 1980s there was increasing discussion and speculation about the prospects for the European Community in the years leading beyond 1992, when remaining barriers to the free movement of goods, resources, people, and capital are scheduled to be eliminated. If there was a consensus, it was to the effect that Western Europe would experience at least modest momentum toward further integration in the years ahead. The European Community would play a growing role both in Europe and in the world as a whole, as a major economic actor and potentially even as a political force of enhanced importance. Although the integration theories examined in this chapter afford insights, hypotheses, findings, and indicators useful to the student of the European experience, they do not furnish an agreed basis on which fully to evaluate or to forecast the likely evolution of the European Community in the 1990s.

Just as the post–World War II integrative process provided both an incentive and a basis for the development of integration theory, and just as that of previous years had for the earlier generation represented by David Mitrany, conceivably the years ahead will lead to a renaissance of integration theory based on the evolving European Community experience, together with that of other regions and analytic levels in the international system.

NOTES

1. Thomas Hobbes, *Leviathan* (Oxford: Basil H. Blackwell, 1967), pp. 109, 174. Ralf Dahrendorf, *Class and Class Conflict in Industrial Society* (Stanford: Stanford University Press, 1959), p. 157, and *Essays in the Theory of Society* (Stanford: Stanford University Press, 1968), pp. 147–150. See Chapter 5 for an examination of other writers, traditional and contemporary, who have posited the existence of relationships between conflict and the integration of political and social units.

2. Reinhold Niebuhr, "The Illusion of World Government," *Bulletin of the Atomic Scientists*, V (October 1949), 289–292; Hans J. Morgenthau, *Politics Among Nations* (New York: Knopf, 1978), pp. 499–507. For an examination of literature on world government, see Inis L. Claude, Jr., *Power and International Relations* (New York: Random House, 1962), pp. 205–285.

3. Johan K. De Vree, *Political Integration: The Formation of Theory and Its Problems* (The Hague-Paris: Mouton, 1972), p. 45.

4. A. J. R. Groom and Paul Taylor, "Functionalism and International Relations," in Groom and Taylor, eds., *Theory and Practice in International Relations: Functionalism* (New York: Crane, Russak), p. 2.

5. Ernst B. Haas, *The Uniting of Europe* (Stanford: Stanford University Press, 1958), p. 16.

6. Ernst B. Haas, *Beyond the Nation-State* (Stanford: Stanford University Press, 1964), p. 29. (Italics in original.)

7. Amitai Etzioni, *Political Unification* (New York: Holt, Rinehart and Winston, 1965), p. 4. "A political community is a community that possesses three kinds of integration: (a) it has an effective control over the use of the means of violence (though it may 'delegate' some of this monopoly to member-units); (b) it has a center of decision-making that is able to affect significantly the allocation of resources and rewards throughout the community; and (c) it is the dominant focus of political identification for the large majority of politically aware citizens." Ibid., p. 329.

8. Ibid., p. 332.

9. Leon N. Lindberg, *The Political Dynamics of European Economic Integration* (Stanford: Stanford University Press, 1963), p. 6.

10. Leon N. Lindberg, "Political Integration as a Multidimensional Phenomenon Requiring Multivariate Measurement," in Leon N. Lindberg and Stuart A. Scheingold, eds., *Regional Integration: Theory and Research* (Cambridge, Mass.: Harvard University Press, 1971), pp. 45–46.

11. Charles Pentland, *International Theory and European Integration* (London: Faber and Faber, 1973), p. 29.

12. Donald J. Puchala, "Of Blind Men, Elephants and International Integration," *Journal of Common Market Studies*, X, No. 3 (March 1972), 277.

13. Karl W. Deutsch et al., *Political Community and the North Atlantic Area* (Princeton: Princeton University Press, 1957), p. 5.

14. Ibid., p. 6.

15. Karl W. Deutsch, *The Analysis of International Relations*, 2nd ed. (Englewood Cliffs, N.J.: Prentice-Hall, 1978), pp. 198–199.

16. Philip E. Jacob and Henry Teune, "The Integrative Process: Guidelines for Analysis of the Bases of Political Community," in Philip E. Jacob and James V. Toscano, eds., *The Integration of Political Communities* (Philadelphia: Lippincott, 1964), p. 4.

17. Johan K. De Vree, op. cit., p. 11.

18. James A. Caporaso and Alan L. Pelowski, "Economic and Political Integration in Europe: A Time-Series Quasi-Experimental Analysis," *American Political Science Review*, 65, No. 2 (June 1975), 421–422.

19. Quoted in Karl W. Deutsch, *The Nerves of Government* (New York: The Free Press, 1964), p. 77. See Norbert Wiener, *Cybernetics* (Cambridge, Mass.: M.I.T. Press, 1965).

20. In his work on nationalism, Deutsch wrote: "The community which permits a common history to be experienced as common is a community of comple-

mentary habits and facilities of communication. It requires, so to speak, equipment for a job. This job consists in the storage, recall, transmission, recombination, and reapplication of relatively wide ranges of information, and the 'equipment' consists in such learned memories, symbols, habits, operating preferences, and facilities as will in fact be sufficiently complementary to permit the performance of these functions. *A larger group of persons linked by such complementary habits and facilities of communication* we may call a people." *Nationalism and Social Communication* (Cambridge, Mass.: M.I.T. Press, 1953), p. 96. (Italics in original.)

21. Karl W. Deutsch, "The Impact of Communications Upon International Relations Theory," in Abdul Said, ed., *Theory of International Relations: The Crisis of Relevance* (Englewood Cliffs, N.J.: Prentice-Hall, 1968), p. 75.

22. Ibid., p. 76.

23. Ibid., pp. 84–90.

24. Deutsch et al., *Political Community and the North Atlantic Area,* p. 58. They included the formation of the United States, its breakup in the Civil War, and the reunion that followed—the union of Scotland and England, the disintegration of the Anglo-Irish Union, German unification, Italian unification, the Hapsburg Empire, the union of Norway and Sweden, and the Swiss Confederation. Two other cases, the union of Wales and England and the formation of England itself in the Middle Ages, were studied "less intensively."

25. Ibid. The reader may wish to refer to Chapter 1, where the point is made concerning John H. Herz's theory to the effect that in the nuclear age the ability of the territorial state to provide its citizens with a sense of security has been put in doubt. However, Deutsch's idea of a security community is that members of such a community do not hold an expectation of war with each other, not that they are necessarily more secure against external attack inside than outside such a community.

26. Ibid.

27. This idea is similar to Parsons's social system, in which persons develop expectations about each other's behavior. See Chapter 4, 143–145.

28. Deutsch et al., *Political Community and the North Atlantic Area,* p. 70.

29. Ibid., p. 199.

30. Ibid., p. 203.

31. Charles Pentland, "Functionalism and Theories of International Political Integration," in A. J. R. Groom and Paul Taylor, eds., op. cit., p. 18.

32. Ernst B. Haas, *The Uniting of Europe,* p. 13. For an analysis of expectations of British official and nonofficial elite groups from European integration, see Robert L. Pfaltzgraff, Jr. *Britain Faces Europe, 1957–1967* (Philadelphia: University of Pennsylvania Press, 1969).

33. Ernst B. Haas, *Beyond the Nation-State,* p. 47.

34. Ibid., p. 48.

35. Ernst B. Haas and Philippe C. Schmitter, "Economics and Differential Patterns of Political Integration: Projections about Unity in Latin America," *International Organization,* XVIII (Autumn 1964), 707. Reprinted in *International Political Communities* (New York: Doubleday, 1966), p. 262.

36. Ernst B. Haas, *The Uniting of Europe,* p. 49.

37. Ibid., p. 50.

38. Haas refers to "spill-over" as "the expansive logic of sector integration," and suggests: "If actors, on the basis of their interest-inspired perceptions, desire to adapt integrative lessons learned in one context to a new situation, the

lesson will be generalized." *Beyond the Nation-State* (Stanford: Stanford University Press, 1964), p. 48.

39. Ernst B. Haas, "International Integration: The European and the Universal Process," *International Organization,* XV (Autumn 1961), 372.
40. Ernst B. Haas, *Beyond the Nation-State,* p. 81. According to Haas, "The major and perhaps the sole justification for using systems theory in the discussion of international politics is its ability to link the will of governments with the shape of the world to come. It is policy that produces the 'system,' though the system then goes on to constrain future policy or dictate its limits." Ernst B. Haas, *The Web of Interdependence: The United States and International Organizations* (Englewood Cliffs, N.J.: Prentice-Hall, 1970), p. 106, and *Tangle of Hopes: American Commitments and World Order* (Englewood Cliffs, N.J.: Prentice-Hall, 1969), pp. 10–12.
41. Philippe C. Schmitter, "A Revised Theory of Regional Integration," *International Organization,* 24, No. 4 (1970), 846.
42. Ernst B. Haas, "The 'Uniting of Europe' and the Uniting of Latin America," *Journal of Common Market Studies,* V (June 1967), 324.
43. Ibid., pp. 323–325.
44. Ernst B. Haas, "Turbulent Fields and the Theory of Regional Integration," *International Organization,* 30, No. 2 (1976), 184.
45. Ernst B. Haas, Mary Pat Williams, and Don Babai, *Scientists and World Order: The Uses of Technical Knowledge in International Organizations* (Berkeley: University of California Press, 1977), p. 9.
46. Ibid., pp. 7, 352–355.
47. Philippe C. Schmitter, "A Revised Theory of Regional Integration," *International Organization,* 24, No. 4 (1970), 868.
48. Barry B. Hughes and John E. Schwarz, "Dimensions of Political Integration and the Experience of the European Community," *International Studies Quarterly,* 16, No. 3 (September 1972). See also Leon N. Lindberg, "Political Integration as a Multidimensional Phenomenon Requiring Multivariate Measurement," *International Organization,* 24 (Autumn 1970), 649–732; Donald S. Puchala, "Integration and Disintegration in Franco-German Relations, 1954–1965," ibid. (Spring 1970), 183–208; Joseph S. Nye, "Comparative Regional Integration: Concept and Measurement," ibid., 22 (Autumn 1968), 855–880.
49. J. S. Nye, *Peace in Parts: Integration and Conflict in Regional Organization* (Boston: Little, Brown, 1971) pp. 56–58.
50. Ibid., p. 65.
51. Ibid., p. 66.
52. Ibid., p. 67.
53. Ibid., p. 68.
54. Ibid., pp. 71–72.
55. Ibid., p. 73.
56. Ibid.
57. Ibid., p. 80.
58. Ibid., p. 82.
59. Ibid., p. 74.
60. Ibid., p. 93.
61. Ibid., p. 182.
62. Ibid., pp. 172, 198–199; and Donald Rothchild, "Ethnicity and Conflict Resolution," *World Politics,* XXII (July 1970), 597–616.

63. Leon N. Lindberg, "Political Integration as a Multidimensional Phenomenon Requiring Multivariate Measurement," in Leon N. Lindberg and Stuart A. Scheingold, eds., "Regional Integration: Theory and Research," Special Issue *International Organization,* CCIV, No. 4 (Autumn 1970), 651.

64. Ibid., p. 652.

65. Leon N. Lindberg and Stuart A. Scheingold, *Europe's Would-Be Polity: Patterns of Change in the European Community* (Englewood Cliffs, N.J.: Prentice-Hall, 1970), p. 74.

66. Ibid., p. 121.

67. Bruce M. Russett, *International Regions and the International System: A Study in Political Ecology* (Chicago: Rand McNally, 1967), pp. 7–8.

68. Robert L. Rothstein, *Alliances and Small Powers* (New York: Columbia University Press, 1968), p. 55.

69. Robert E. Osgood, *Alliances and American Foreign Policy* (Baltimore: Johns Hopkins Press, 1968), p. 19.

70. See "Introduction" and J. David Singer and Melvin Small, "Alliance Aggregation and the Onset of War, 1815–1945," in Francis A. Beer, ed., *Alliances: Latent War Communities in the Contemporary World* (New York: Holt, Rinehart and Winston, 1970).

71. See, for example, Hans J. Morgenthau, "Alliances in Theory and Practice," in Arnold Wolfers, ed., *Alliance Policy in the Cold War* (Baltimore: Johns Hopkins Press, 1959).

72. George F. Liska, *Nations in Alliance: The Limits of Interdependence* (Baltimore: Johns Hopkins Press, 1962), p. 12; William H. Riker, *The Theory of Political Coalitions* (New Haven: Yale University Press, 1962), pp. 32–76. See also Bruce M. Russett, "Components of an Operational Theory of International Alliance Formation," *Journal of Conflict Resolution,* XII (September 1968), 285–301. For a selection of essays from the literature on alliances, see Julian R. Friedman, Christopher Bladen, and Steven Rosen, eds., *Alliance in International Politics* (Boston: Allyn & Bacon, 1970); Francis A. Beer, ed., op. cit. For a dyadic study (the United States and Italy), see Valentine J. Belfiglio, *Alliances* (Lexington, Mass.: Ginn Press, 1986).

73. Liska, op. cit., p. 175.

74. Ibid., p. 61.

75. William Riker, op. cit., p. 188. For another application of Riker's framework, see Martin Southwold, "Riker's Theory and the Analysis of Coalitions in Precolonial Africa," in Sven Groennings, E. W. Kelley, and Michael Leiserson, eds., *The Study of Coalition Behavior: Theoretical Perspectives and Cases from Four Continents* (New York: Holt, Rinehart and Winston, 1970), pp. 336–350. For an effort to relate Riker's framework to balance-of-power literature, see Dina A. Zinnes, "Coalition Theories and the Balance of Power," ibid., pp. 351–368.

76. For an examination of Kaplan's rules for the balance-of-power systems, see Chapter 4.

77. George F. Liska, *Nations in Alliance,* p. 27. See also George F. Liska, *Quest for Equilibrium: America and the Balance of Power on Land and Sea* (Baltimore: Johns Hopkins Press, 1977), p. 6.

78. Ibid., p. 30.

79. Robert L. Rothstein, op. cit., p. 50.

80. Ibid., pp. 173–176.

81. Mancur Olson, Jr., *The Logic of Collective Action* (Cambridge, Mass.: Harvard University Press, 1965), p. 48.

82. Stephen M. Walt, *The Origins of Alliances* (Ithaca, N.Y., and London: Cornell University Press, 1987), p. 5.

83. Ibid., p. 17.

84. Michael F. Altfeld, "The Decision to Ally: A Theory and Test," *The Western Political Quarterly*, 37, No. 4 (December 1984), 523–543.

85. Ibid., p. 528.

86. See, for example, Joseph S. Nye, Jr., "Comparative Regional Integration: Concept and Measurement," *International Organization*, XXII (Autumn 1968), 857. For a collection of contemporary writings on integration at the international level, see, by the same author, *International Regionalism: Readings* (Boston: Little, Brown, 1968).

87. Ernst B. Haas, "The Challenge of Regionalism," *International Organization*, XII (Autumn 1958), 445.

88. Karl W. Deutsch, *France, Germany and the Western Alliance* (New York: Scribner's, 1967), pp. 218–220. Deutsch bases his findings on the Relative Acceptance Index, which purports to separate "the actual results of preferential behavior and structural integration from the mere effects of the size and prosperity of the country."

89. According to Lindberg, "Significant national powers have been thrust into a new institutional setting in which powerful pressures are exerted for Community solutions, that is, solutions which approximate the up-grading-of-common interests type. Our case studies have revealed that important and divergent national interests have been consistently accommodated in order to achieve a decision." Moreover, since the founding of the EEC, there has been a shift in political activities and expectations—another part of Lindberg's definition of integration: "This has been most striking at the level of high policy-makers and civil servants, for the EEC policy-making process, by its very nature, engages an ever-expanding circle of national officials." Leon N. Lindberg, *The Political Dynamics of European Economic Integration* (Stanford: Stanford University Press, 1963), pp. 6, 286–288. See also Leon N. Lindberg and Stuart A. Scheingold, *Europe's Would-Be Polity: Patterns of Change in the European Community*, pp. 24–100.

90. Ronald Inglehart, "An End to European Integration," *American Political Science Review*, LXI (March 1967), 91. For a study of continuity and change in foreign policy attitudes, see Neal E. Cutler, "Generational Succession as a Source of Foreign Policy Attitudes: A Cohort Analysis of American Opinion, 1946–1966," *Journal of Peace Research*, VII (1970), 33–47; by the same author, but not related specifically to foreign policy, "Generation, Maturation, and Party Affiliation: A Cohort Analysis," *Public Opinion Quarterly*, XXXIII (Winter 1969–1970), 583–588.

91. Ronald Inglehart, op. cit., p. 92.

92. Carl J. Friedrich, *Europe: An Emergent Nation?* (New York: Harper & Row, 1969), esp. pp. 196–215.

93. Ibid., pp. 35–46.

94. James A. Caporaso and Alan L. Pelowski, op. cit., 432–433.

95. Claude Ake, *A Theory of Political Integration* (Homewood, Ill.: Dorsey Press, 1967), pp. 8–11.

96. Stanley Hoffmann, *Gulliver's Troubles, or the Setting of American Foreign Policy* (New York: McGraw-Hill, 1968), p. 401. At various times European and American analysts have speculated on the feasibility of a European nuclear

deterrent. See, for example, Henry A. Kissinger, *The Necessity for Choice* (Garden City, N.Y.: Doubleday, 1962), pp. 129–131; Robert Strausz-Hupé, James E. Dougherty, and William R. Kintner, *Building the Atlantic World* (New York: Harper & Row, 1962), ch. 5. For analysis of European elite attitudes toward a European nuclear force, see Karl W. Deutsch, *Arms Control and the Atlantic Alliance* (Melbourne, Fla.: Krieger, 1967), pp. 34, 99, and 136.

97. Stanley Hoffmann, "The Fate of the Nation-State," *Daedalus,* VC (Summer 1966), 865.

98. Roger D. Hansen, "Regional Integration: Reflections on a Decade of Theoretical Efforts," *World Politics,* XXI (January 1969), 270. For another review and critique of the Haas-Schmitter work, see J. S. Nye, Jr., "Patterns and Catalysts in Regional Integration," *International Organization,* XIX (Autumn 1965), 870–884.

99. Oran R. Young, "Professor Russett, Industrious Tailor to a Naked Emperor," *World Politics,* XXI (April 1969), 486–511. For Russett's reply, see "The Young Science of International Politics," *World Politics,* XXII (October 1969), 87–94.

100. Donald J. Puchala, op. cit., p. 267.

101. Stuart A. Scheingold. "Consequences of Regional Integration" in Leon N. Lindberg and Stuart A. Scheingold, eds., *Regional Integration: Theory and Research,* pp. 395–398.

102. Ernst B. Haas, *The Obsolescence of Regional Integration Theory,* Research Series, No. 25, Institute of International Studies, University of California, Berkeley, 1975, p. 17.

103. Charles Pentland, *International Theory and European Integration* (London: Faber and Faber, 1973), p. 98.

104. Lynn Krieger Mytelka, "The Salience of Gains in Third-World Integrative Systems," *World Politics,* 25, No. 2 (January 1973), 237–243. See also David Morawetz, "Harmonization of Economic Policies in Customs Unions: The Andean Group," *Journal of Common Market Studies,* XI, No. 4 (Fall 1970). "It is extremely unlikely that the Andean Group is an optimum, or even close to an optimum currency area." This stems from labor immobility within and between countries, artificially low foreign trade percentages because of import-substitution policies, heavy vulnerability of the balance of payments to external forces, and significant differences in inflation rates among member states.

105. J. S. Nye, "Patterns and Catalysts in Regional Integration" reprinted in Joseph S. Nye, *International Regionalism: Readings,* pp. 333–349.

106. Joseph S. Nye, Jr., "Comparative Regional Integration: Concept and Measurement," p. 858.

Chapter
11

Decision-Making Theories

DECISION-MAKING ANALYSIS: ITS NATURE AND ORIGINS

Decisions are, in David Easton's terminology, the "outputs" of the political system, by which values are authoritatively allocated within a society. The concept of decision-making had long been implicit in some of the older approaches to diplomatic history and the study of political institutions. The study of how decisions are made first became the subject of systematic investigation in other fields outside of political science. Psychologists were interested in the motives underlying an individual's decisions and why some persons had greater difficulty than others in making decisions. Economists focused on the decisions of producers, consumers, investors, and others whose choices affected the economy. Business administration theorists sought to analyze and increase the efficiency of executive decision-making. In government and especially in defense planning in the 1960s, techniques known generally as "cost effectiveness" were utilized in the decision-making process, including the acquisition of new weapons systems. Decision-making was a focal point for political scientists interested in analyzing the decisional behavior of voters, legislators, executive officials, politicians, leaders of interest groups, and other actors in the political arena.[1] Thus, the study of foreign policy decision-making concentrated on one segment of a more general phenomenon of interest to the social sciences and to policymakers. Because many analysts have concerned themselves with decision-making in crisis situations, the latter part of the chapter will deal with that subject.

Decision-making is simply the act of choosing among available alternatives about which uncertainty exists. In foreign policy perhaps even more than in national politics—because the terrain of the former is usually less familiar—policy alternatives are seldom "given." They must often be gropingly formulated in the context of a total situation in which disagreements will arise over which estimate of the situation is most valid, what alternatives exist, the consequences likely to flow from various choices, and the values that should serve as criteria for ranking the various alternatives from most to least preferred. There are controversies both over the nature of the decision-making process and over the appropriate paradigms for its study. Within the last generation, attention has shifted from decision-making as mere abstract choice among possible maximum-utility alternatives to decision-making as an incremental process containing partial choices and compromises among competing organizational interests and bureaucratic pressures.

APPROACHES TO DECISION-MAKING THEORY

The decision-making approach to an understanding of international politics is not novel. Twenty-four centuries ago the Greek historian Thucydides, in his *Peloponnesian War,* examined the factors that led the leaders of city-states to decide the issues of war and peace, as well as alliance and empire, with as great precision as they did under the circumstances confronting them. He focused not only on the conscious reasons for statesmen's choices and their perceptions of the systemic environment—both of which are reflected in the speeches he attributes to them—but also on the deeper psychological forces of fear, honor, and interest that in varying combinations motivated them as individuals and set the prevailing tone of their particular societies. Thus, Thucydides was indeed an early student of decision-making.

Decision-making theory, the focus of this chapter, identifies a large number of relevant variables, and it suggests possible interrelationships among these variables. DM theory (as we refer to it here) marks a significant shift from traditional political analysis in which writers sometimes have been prone to reify or personify nation-states as the basic actors within the international system. DM theory directs attention not to states as metaphysical abstractions, or to governments, or even to such broadly labeled institutions as "the Executive," but instead seeks to highlight the behavior of the specific human decision-makers who actually shape governmental policy. As Richard Snyder, H. W. Bruck, and Burton Sapin put it: "It is one of our basic methodological choices to define the state as its official decision-makers—those whose authoritative acts are, to all intents and purposes, the acts of the state. State action is the action taken by those acting in the name of the state."[2] By narrowing the subject of investigation from a larger collectivity to a smaller unit of persons responsible for decisions, DM theorists hope to make the locus of political analysis more concrete and more precise, and thus more amenable to systematic analysis. Nevertheless, it is assumed that decision-makers act within a total perceived environment that includes their national political system as well as the international system as a whole—an internal environment as well as an external environment.

Perception is assigned a central place in DM theory. When dealing with the "definition of the situation," most DM theorists regard the world as viewed by decision-makers to be more important than objective reality.[3] They thereby accept the distinction drawn by Harold and Margaret Sprout between the "psychomilieu" and the "operational environment" (discussed in Chapter 2). Joseph Frankel, however, argues that DM theory must take the objective environment into account, for even though factors not present in the minds of policymakers cannot influence their choices, such factors may be important insofar as they set limits to the outcome of their decisions.[4] Similarly, Michael Brecher insists that "the operational environment affects the results or outcomes of decisions directly but influences the choice among policy options, that is, the decisions themselves, only as it is filtered through the images of decision-makers."[5]

THE DECISION SITUATION (OR OCCASION)[6]

Braybrooke and Lindblom suggest that decision-making, although it cannot be fully identified with rational problem solving, nevertheless may be generally equated with it.[7] The question now arises as to how decision-makers define the situation in relation to the problem confronting them. How do they see objects, conditions, other actors, and their intentions? How do they define the goals of their own government? What values strike them as most important, not in the abstract but insofar as they appear to be at stake in this particular situation?

Snyder observes that some situations are more highly structured than others. Some are readily grasped in their meaning, whereas others may be more fluctuating and ambiguous. The urgency of situations, or the pressure to take action, will also vary widely. Whether a problem is considered primarily political, economic, military, social, or cultural will normally have implications for how it is to be handled and by whom. It is difficult, out of the welter of opinions from professional diplomats, scholars, journalists, and others, to arrive at a relatively accurate assessment of the various trends and forces active in a foreign situation (and here foreign policy decision-making is probably more complex than domestic). Analyzing another state's intentions can be even more treacherous. Decision-makers in one state, anticipating a policy initiative by their counterparts in another, may regard their own move to deter or preclude as a purely defensive response, but these measures might seem offensive to their foreign counterparts, as we noted in Chapter 8.

BUREAUCRATIC POLITICS

We have referred to the hypothesized tendency of decision-makers to allow their conceptions of national interest to be colored by their perceptions of what is good for their own bureaucratic unit. The importance of bureaucracies has long been recognized by students of politics. Max Weber, for example, wrote: "In a modern state the actual ruler is necessarily and unavoidably the bureaucracy, since power is exercised neither through parliamentary speeches nor monarchical enunciations but through the routines of administration."[8] Although Weber wrote about the era before the 1920s, his work contains antecedents for understanding bureaucratic structures and decision-making in the late twentieth century. As Weber points out, in all advanced political systems and economies, there arise bureaucratic structures that themselves shape both the decision-making process and its outputs in the form of decisions. Yet bureaucracies, like governments themselves, especially in democratic political systems, face budgetary constraints. Therefore, advocates of various types of foreign policy and defense programs find themselves in competition for the allocation of scarce resources. Foreign policy and defense programs compete not only with domestic programs (education, health, social security, agriculture, transportation, welfare, energy, construction, conservation, crime control, and urban renewal), but with each other—various types of military-technological programs and arms transfers, force deployments, alliance diplomacy, foreign development assistance, information and cultural exchange programs, intelligence activities, support for international organizations, and the strengthening of peaceful change processes. Differing interests within and among the departments and agencies that have a role in foreign policy and national security, as well as differences among the military services, are illustrative of the bureaucratic politics dimension of decision-making.

Morton H. Halperin, in a study of several foreign policy decisions, has shown how "politics within a government influence decisions and actions ostensibly directed outward"[9] and how the way in which officials focus on issues often depends on their bureaucratic position and perspective. Halperin concludes that actions or proposals by one government to influence the behavior of another government are usually based on the simple model of two individuals communicating accurately with each other, when in fact they have probably emerged from a complex bureaucratic process of "pulling and hauling" that is not fully understood by those who must carry out the decision. Furthermore, he asserts, the response of the foreign government is likely to be the result of a similar bureaucratic process of pulling and hauling.[10] (See the subsequent section, "Allison's Three Models.")

Francis E. Rourke has cited the law of bureaucratic inertia: "Bureaucracies at rest tend to stay at rest, and bureaucracies in motion tend to stay in motion."[11] Recent presidents have been exasperated on occasion at the slowness with which bureaucracies at rest respond to their orders, but Rourke observes that this might save a political leader from the consequences of a rash decision. Conversely, executive agencies that have been stimulated to develop certain capabilities, whether for waging combat, exploring space, negotiating arms control agreements, or selling arms or grain abroad, may feel compelled to prove their usefulness through activity that justifies expanded budgets. Once bureaucracies gain momentum, they are difficult to slow down. Rourke points out that the "irreversibility" of certain types of activity by large organizations contradicts the hypothesis that policymaking in the United States "moves incrementally in one sequential step after another from initial decision to final outcome, thus permitting a discontinuance of effort or the reversal of direction at any point."[12] He concludes that, while they can shape the views of political leaders and the public on foreign policy issues, and often possess technical capabilities that enable them to influence the flow of events, nevertheless bureaucratic agencies compose only one part of a democratic political system. Their power ultimately depends upon the willingness of others— for example, Congress and the president—to support them, accept their advice, or legitimize their activities by going along with them.[13]

Alexander L. George has called attention to the fact that the Executive, instead of using centralized management practices to neutralize intrabureaucratic disagreements over policy, can use a "multiple advocacy model"—a mixed system combining elements of centralized management with certain features of pluralistic participatory models to harness diversity of views and interests for the sake of enhancing rational policymaking.[14] One of the dangers of bureaucratic politics against which the Executive wishes to guard is the possibility that organizational subunits might restrict competition with each other and work out compromises among themselves before the policy issues are aired at the highest level, so that the final decision is likely to be based on the preferred option that results from the internal bargaining process. Under these conditions, of course, policy options that might be viable but are unpopular with the bureaucracy are rendered unavailable as a result of unfavorable presentation or inadequate information. But George warns the Executive against overcentralizing and overbureaucratizing the early "search" and "evaluation" phases of policy analysis prior to "choice." In an overcentralized system, the Executive might receive too narrow a range of "orthodox" options based upon cues transmitted, whether intentional or not, from the top down.

According to George, conflict and bargaining within the bureaucracy might contribute to a better policymaking process if it can be managed and resolved properly. He therefore espouses a multiple advocacy model as "an integral part of a *mixed system* in which centralized coordination and Executive initiative would be required."[15] The Chief Executive encourages competition among bureaucratic units while reserving the power to evaluate, judge, and choose among the various policy options articulated by the advocates. Since the advocates compete with each other only for the Executive's attention, this is a system of perfect competition, highly preferable to the imperfect competition that prevails in the bureaucratic bargaining-and-compromise model.

MOTIVATIONS AND CHARACTERISTICS OF DECISION-MAKERS

Snyder has drawn a useful distinction between two types of motivation—"in order to" motives and "because of" motives.[16] The former are conscious and articulable: The decision-makers are taking this particular decision in order to accomplish such and such an objective of the state which they serve. For example, the administration of President Johnson sought the Nonproliferation Treaty "in order to" promote international stability by restricting the number of states that might independently opt for the initiation of nuclear hostilities. Similarly, President Reagan chose his Strategic Defense Initiative as a means of eventually rendering nuclear weapons "impotent and obsolete." "Because of" motives, on the other hand, are unconscious or semiconscious motives, those arising out of the previous life experience, and previous organizational conditioning of the treaty's most ardent proponents. As we have seen in Chapters 7 and 8, however, most macrotheorists are wary of "psychohistory" as a means of explaining the decisions and actions of political leaders.

Most decision-making theorists, like most political historians, would agree that biographical knowledge about policymakers—including their education, religion, critical life experiences, professional training, foreign travel, mental and physical health, and previous political activities—might help to cast light upon the deepest motives and values of those who make specific decisions. However, little is known about the relationship between the total inner psychic experience of individuals and their overt policy choices in an organizational context.

It is one thing to acknowledge that an individual's background is significant, especially in cases where there are unusual behavioral aberrations from what would "normally" be expected on the basis of the analysis of known social roles and processes. But it is quite another thing to draw a definite causal link between the previous psychic event (perhaps years earlier) and the present deviant action. One of the difficulties with psychohistorical explanation is that it can lend itself too easily to the workings of an overactive dramatic imagination as a substitute for rigorous analysis of real evidence.

THE DECISION-MAKING PROCESS

David Easton has defined politics as "the authoritative allocation of values for a society."[17] This, in essence, is what political decision-making is all about. But DM theorists are not in general agreement as to whether the process of political decision-making is fundamentally the same as the process of nonpublic or private decision-making. As political scientists, the authors of this book are strongly inclined to agree with those who postulate important differences among decisions in a family, in a university, in a business corporation, and in a government department.[18] Even though private and public decision-making are both characterized by various mixes of individual and collective processes, nevertheless the frames of reference and the "rules of the game" exhibit rather specific properties.

Since economists and students of business administration have made significant early inputs to DM theory, the theory as originally developed reflected many of the assumptions of the Enlightenment and Benthamite Utilitarians, with their emphasis upon reason and education in the making of human social choices. It assumed a rational person who is clearly aware of all the available alternatives and who is capable of both calculating their respective outcomes and then freely choosing according to the order of value preferences. Such assumptions have been seriously questioned in this century.

According to the classic model of decision-making, policymakers make a calculation in two basic dimensions—utility and probability—and, assuming that they are "rational," they will attempt to maximize expected utility. In other words, after all the available alternatives have been surveyed and the product of weighted values and assessed probabilities has been obtained, decision-makers can choose their optimal course.[19] Snyder points out that "decision-makers may be assumed to act in terms of clear-cut preferences," but that these preferences, instead of being entirely individual, derive from the rules of the organizational system, shared organizational experience over a period of time, and the information available to the decisional unit, as well as from the biographies of individuals.[20] Snyder, however, refrained from subscribing fully to the classic explanatory formula of "maximization of expected utility," which had already been subject to question before he wrote his principal essay on the subject.[21]

Next we must raise the question of whether the theories with which we are dealing in this chapter presuppose the rationality of the DM process, and whether they confine themselves to the rational components of that process. For many decades, the Western intellectual's faith in the essential rationality of human behavior (inherited from the Enlightenment) has steadily disintegrated. Freud virtually completed the erosion process with his discoveries concerning the powerful role played in life by the unconscious. Nevertheless, political science and international relations students tend to assume that there are some rational elements in the political process insofar as individuals set forth in explicit fashion their goal priorities and devise categories of means for attaining them. Moreover, if our knowledge of the individual prompts us to postulate irrationality, the demands of social organization require us to grope in the direction of rationality, and to employ the criteria of "rationality" in order to identify and understand "the irrational." The assumption of rational behavior has been deemed to be central to much of international relations theory. Rationality is socially defined.

However, decision-making theory—for example, that developed by the Snyder group—does not necessarily assume the rationality of decision-makers. Rationality is an element to be validated by empirical analysis rather than to be assumed. But Snyder and his associates do not differ substantially from those modern theorists of governmental decision-making who have been influenced by Max Weber's concept of bureaucracy, which develops according to a rational plan. There is in the theory an assumption of purposeful behavior and explicit motivation; behavior is seen not as merely random activity. The DM process is said to combine rational elements; value considerations in which the rational may be synthesized with the nonrational, the irrational, or the supranational; and such irrational or nonrational factors as the psychic complexes of the policymakers. J. David Singer, among others, has pointed out that under conditions of stress and anxiety decision-makers may not act according to standards of utility that could be called rational,[22] and Martin Patchen has suggested the need for greater attention to the presence of nonrational and partly conscious factors in the personalities of those who make decisions.[23] After examining both nonrational and rational models of decision-making, Sidney Verba concludes that it may be useful under certain circumstances to assume that governments "make decisions as if they were following the rules of means-end rationality" and choose the alternative that enables them best to attain the ends or promote the values of the decision-makers.[24]

Braybrooke and Lindblom reject as unsatisfactory for most important decisions (i.e., those that affect significant changes in the external social world) the "synoptic conception" of decision-making by which policymakers are presumed to spread out before them all their available alternatives and to measure, against their scale of preferred values, all the probable consequences of the social changes implicit in the various courses of action under consideration. This synoptic schema in their view simply does not conform to reality. It presupposes omniscience and a kind of comprehensive analysis that is prohibitively costly and that time pressures normally do not permit. Every solution, they assert, must be limited by several factors, including the individual's problem-solving capacities, the amount of information available, the cost of analysis (in personnel, resources, and time), and the practical inseparability of fact and value.[25]

No one has challenged the classic model of rational decision-making more fundamentally, while yet remaining within a rational framework, than the eminent economist and theorist of administration Herbert Simon, who postulates a world of "bounded rationality." For the classic concept of *maximizing* or *optimizing* behavior, he substituted the notion of "satisficing" behavior. This presupposes that the policymakers do not really design for themselves a matrix that shows all available alternatives, the value "pros" and "cons" of each, and the probability assessments of expected consequences. Instead, Simon suggests, decision-making units examine alternatives sequentially until they come upon one that meets their minimum standards of acceptability.[26] In other words, people keep rejecting unsatisfactory solutions until they find one which they can agree is sufficiently satisfactory to enable them to act. (It was for this theory that Simon won the 1978 Nobel Prize for Economics.) Braybrooke and Lindblom, who are partial both to Simon's "satisficing" model and to Karl Popper's idea of "piecemeal engineering," suggest that pragmatic experimentalism embodies a strategy of "disjointed incrementalism." Put in its simplest form, this means that policymakers, especially in democratic states, prefer to separate their decision-making problems into small segments that enable them to make "incremental" or "marginal" rather than far-reaching or profound choices.[27]

Decision-making is not only an intellectual process involving the insight, perception, and creative intuition of policymakers, but it is also a matter of social and quasi-mechanical processes.[28] Among political scientists, Arthur F. Bentley and David B. Truman have done much to stress the importance of interest groups in the decisional process, and William F. Riker, in his study of coalitions, suggests that decision-making may depend at least partially upon quasi-mechanical processes in which the actors are unconscious of their decision-making roles.[29] A striking example of group conflict in United States policy in the Middle East is the divergent interests of pro-Israeli elements and the oil industry. Quasi-mechanical processes may be illustrated in the case of individuals who, for motives of personal economic advantage, engage in international economic transactions such as importing, foreign investment, travel, or capital flight to overseas banks, which virtually compel governmental policymakers to adopt regulatory decisions (e.g., in a balance-of-payments crisis). Robinson and Majak conclude that decisions can normally be understood best in the light of three types of processes (intellectual, social, and quasi-mechanical), even though all three may not be equally relevant in a given instance.[30]

ALLISON'S THREE MODELS

According to Graham T. Allison, most foreign policy analysts think about and explain governmental behavior in terms of the Rational Actor Model or "Classical" Model, in which policy choices are seen as the more or less purposive acts of unified governments based on logical means of achieving given objectives. The model represents an effort to relate an action to a plausible calculation.[31] Morgenthau's statesman contemplating what the national interest calls for in a certain situation, Schelling's game theorist calculating the requirements of stable mutual deterrence or the points of saliency at which limited wars can be kept limited, Herman Kahn's strategic analyst playing out scenarios of nuclear war by a mathematical process of gain-to-cost reckoning—all use a form of Rational Actor Model.[32] Rational people discern clearly their objectives, the options available, and the likely consequences of each alternative choice before making their decision.[33]

"Although the Rational Actor Model has proved useful for many purposes," says Allison, "there is powerful evidence that it must be supplemented, if not supplanted, by frames of reference that focus on the governmental machine."[34] Allison offers two such frames of reference: an Organizational Process Model and a Bureaucratic Politics Model. In the latter he owes a considerable intellectual debt to the writings of Max Weber. The Organizational Process Model envisages governmental behavior less as a matter of deliberate choice and more as independent outputs of several large organizations, only partly coordinated by government leaders. "Government leaders can substantially disturb, but not substantially control, the behavior of these organizations,"[35] which is determined primarily by standard routine operating procedures, with seldom more than gradual, incremental deviations except when a major disaster occurs.[36] The Organizational Process Model that Allison prefers is that of Herbert Simon, based on the concept of bounded rather than comprehensive rationality, and characterized by factoring or splitting up problems, the parceling out of problem parts to various organizational units, the type of "satisficing behavior" described previously, limiting the search to the first acceptable alternative, and avoidance of uncertainty or risk through developing short-run feedback and corrective procedures.[37] Organizations operate to solve problems of immediate urgency rather than to develop strategies for coping with longer-range issues.[38]

Allison's third model, the Bureaucratic Politics Model, builds on the Organizational Process Model, but instead of assuming control by leaders at the top, the Bureaucratic Politics Model hypothesizes intensive competition among the decision-making units, and foreign policies are the result of bargaining among the components of a bureaucracy. The players are guided by no consistent strategic master plan, but rather by conflicting conceptions of national, bureaucratic, and personal goals. Sometimes one group may triumph over other groups committed to different alternatives. Often, however, different groups pulling in different directions produce a resultant or decisional mix that is distinct from that intended by an individual or group. The outcome depends not on the rational justification for the policy or on routine organizational procedures, but on the relative power and skill of the bargainers.[39]

All theories of the decision-making process encounter conceptual difficulties. Miriam Steiner, after analyzing comparatively the works of Snyder and Allison, concluded that each contains contradictions. Snyder claims to put human plans and purposes at the center of his conceptual framework, but does not follow through consistently. "When in the interests of 'objectivity,' he attempts to outfit himself with a 'hard methodology,' he inadvertently reduces his responsible decision-makers to organizationally programmed automatons."[40] Allison, on the other hand, insists for the sake of accuracy that events be explained not teleologically in terms of goals and purposes, but scientifically in terms of causal determinants that are subject to investigation. But into his integrated explanation, "he unwittingly introduces goals and purposes as 'the essence of decision.'"[41] Thus, neither Snyder nor Allison, in Steiner's view, succeeds in providing an approach that achieves objectives consonant with its own distinctive methodology. Instead, each begins at an opposite pole and moves in the direction of the other. Perhaps this is inevitable.

THE REFINEMENTS OF SNYDER AND DIESING

Glenn H. Snyder and Paul Diesing have tested empirically three theories of decision-making in about 50 cases of crisis:[42] (1) utility maximization (the classical rational theory); (2) bounded rationality (borrowed from Simon's "satisficing" model); and (3) bureaucratic politics. Their Rational Actor Model, like Allison's, is based on the choice of one alternative out of all those available that maximizes expected utility. In the bounded rationality tradition, one assumes that if a choice must be made between two different values (e.g., peace and national security), there is no rational way of calculating how much of one should be sacrificed to obtain a given amount of the other. Decision-makers cannot maximize; they operate under constraints and search for an acceptable course. Snyder and Diesing argue plausibly that maximizing and bounded rationality are not irreconcilable explanations, but may be combined by taking either theory as basic and the other as supplementary. They also make the sensible suggestion that the bureaucratic politics theory supplements rather than competes with the other two theories. "It focuses on the internal political imperatives of maintaining and increasing influence and power rather than on the purely intellectual problems of choosing a strategy to deal with an external opportunity or threat."[43] The problem-solving theories apply best to some cases; the bureaucratic politics theory, to others. The former are most applicable when only one or two people are involved in the decision. When three or more people are involved, as in a committee or a cabinet, the Bureaucratic Politics Model—which Snyder and Diesing see as a process of forming a dominant coalition—applies best.[44]

Snyder and Diesing draw an interesting distinction between "rational" and irrational" bargainers in a crisis. Rational bargainers do not pretend to know at the very beginning of a crisis what the precise situation is, or what the relative interests, power relations, and main alternatives are. They recognize that their initial judgment may be mistaken, but they are able to correct initial misjudgment and perceive the outlines of the developing bargaining situation in time to deal with it effectively.[45] They make tentative guesses as they go along, and constantly modify their assessments as new information is received.

"Irrational" bargainers, on the other hand, proceed from a rigid belief system. They are certain about the adversary's ultimate aims, bargaining style, preferences, and internal problems. They receive advice (which they seek especially from those whose opinions they value) but make their own decisions. They see themselves as the architects of the one strategy that has a chance of succeeding, and they firmly adhere to that strategy in spite of all difficulties, regardless of new incoming information. If their initial strategy was correct, irrational bargainers can be highly successful; if not, they are unlikely to realize their mistake in time to avert defeat or disaster.[46] Deception is always a problem in bargaining. Rational bargainers are open to being deceived by the opponent; Irrational bargainers, by themselves. In solving the information-processing problem, a rigid image of the adversary as totally untrustworthy may be as much a hindrance as a rigid image of the adversary as totally trustworthy.[47]

THE CYBERNETIC THEORY OF DECISION

We have seen that the classical utilitarian theory of decision-making, based upon the assumption of a rational weighing of value-costs and value-outcomes, has come under increasing criticism in recent decades. As an alternative to the traditional "analytic paradigm," John D. Steinbruner has set forth the "cybernetic paradigm" as a foundation for theories and models of decision-making, because the former does not explain all the observed phenomena of decision-making. He doubts that human beings normally try to analyze complex problems by breaking them down into all their logical components (which rational theory requires them to do), or that they have access to all of the information and perform all of the calculations, especially with regard to value trade-offs (which the classical theory presupposes). Steinbruner, moreover, expresses dissatisfaction with most of the efforts the analytic school has made thus far to apply to collective decisions concepts originally developed to explain decisions by individuals.[48] For example, Steinbruner notes that some glaring failures of deterrence might be attributable to the fact that governments have acted against what would appear to have been compelling analytic logic. He cites as cases in point Japan's attack on the U.S. fleet at Pearl Harbor and the mobilization of the Egyptian Army before the outbreak of the Six Day War in June 1967.[49]

Steinbruner offers as potentially more fruitful than the analytic paradigm a cybernetic one, by which highly successful or adaptive behavior might be explained without resort to elaborate decision-making mechanisms. He begins by describing a few more or less familiar instances of simple cybernetic decisions. When worker bees locate pollen-bearing flowers at a place remote from the hive, they inform other workers of its location by engaging in a dance that contains instruction for navigating according to the angle and direction of the sun in reference to the field. In another example, practiced tennis players are cybernetic decision-makers. Each time they move to meet the ball with their rackets, they select one pattern of psychomotor responses out of thousands of possible patterns, and they do it without making mathematical calculations of the speed and trajectory of the oncoming ball, their precise point of interception, the stroke they will use to hit it, and their target point in the opposite court. Steinbruner draws additional analogies pertaining to cybernetic servomechanisms from the thermostat that keeps temperature within desired bounds, the Watt governor that regulates the speed of an engine, radar homing devices, the cat who changes position near the hearth as the fire grows hotter or dimmer, the retail store manager who adjusts item prices according to volume of sales, and the cook who follows a recipe and keeps tasting when performing a sequence of culinary operations without having a clear, rational concept of the final product.

The cybernetic decision-maker, in other words, deals with situations that we call "simple," but that nevertheless have a complexity of their own, by eliminating variety, ignoring elaborate calculations concerning the environment, and tracking a few simple feedback variables that trigger a behavioral adjustment. Cybernetic decision-makers, believing the decision process to be a simple one, strive to minimize the calculations they must perform, whether they be mathematical or value-related. They monitor a small set of critical variables, and their principal value is to reduce uncertainty by keeping these variables within tolerable ranges. They see no need for a careful calculation of probable outcomes, which they are not likely to make in any case. The sequence of decisional behaviors is related less to an intellectual analysis of the problem at hand than to past experience, from which there emerges an almost intuitional approach to problem-solving.[50]

It is relatively easy, of course, to accept the cybernetic paradigm as applied to the tennis player, the cook, or the retail store manager, each of whom faces a small number of simple choices on each sequence. The question is whether the validity of the cybernetic paradigm is affected by the much greater complexity of decisions in the foreign policy and the defense fields. Steinbruner is convinced that the cybernetic model is applicable to highly complex decisions, which he defines as decisions affecting two or more values, in which there is a trade-off relationship between the values, in which there is uncertainty, and in which the decision-making power is dispersed over a number of individual actors and/or organizational units. He concedes that greater complexity entails greater variety, and that "under conditions of complexity the decision-maker must have a more elaborate response repertory if he is to retain adaptive capacity."[51]

The problem is solved by increasing the number of decision-makers within a collectivity. Complex problems are not analyzed comprehensively by all the members of the decision-making group. Instead, they are broken down into a large number of limited-dimension problems, each confronted by a separate decision-maker or unit. "This is the natural cybernetic explanation for the rise of mass bureaucracy."[52]

To sum up, Steinbruner relies upon theories of organizational behavior to extend the cybernetic paradigm from individual decision-making in relatively simple situations to collective decision-making designed to cope with a highly complex environment. The higher levels of organizational hierarchy do not perform the integrating calculations called for by the analytic paradigm. Drawing upon the work of Cyert and March, Steinbruner summarizes as follows:

> Top management, in their view, focuses in sequential order on the decision issues raised by separate subunits and does not integrate across subunits in its deliberations. Decisions are made solely within the context of the subunit raising the issue. Complex problems are thus fragmented by organizations into separate components having to do with subunit organization, and the decision process at the highest levels preserves the fragmentation.[53]

Organizational theory alone is not enough, however. Steinbruner combines it with highly intricate modern theories of cognitive processes, including those developed by Noam Chomsky, Ulric Neisser, Leon Festinger, Robert P. Abelson, and others. He calls attention to the consensus among cognitive theorists that "a great deal of information processing is conducted apparently prior to and certainly independently of conscious direction and that in this activity the mind routinely performs logical operations of considerable power."[54] Steinbruner surveys the findings of many studies relating to perception, learning, memory, inference, consistency, belief, and the ways in which the human mind either controls or copes with uncertainty, and concludes that cognitive theory provides an analysis of the effects of uncertainty on the decision process that is fundamentally different from that of the analytic and cybernetic paradigms. Thus, he uses cognitive theory to modify the cybernetic paradigm, especially with regard to the subjective resolution of uncertainty, and to introduce into his treatment of political and organizational phenomena the concepts of *grooved thinking,* in which the decision-maker rather simplistically categorizes the problems into a small number of basic types; *uncommitted thinking,* in which the decision-maker who does not know what to think about the problem oscillates between groups of advisers, and may adopt different belief patterns at different times on the same decision problem; and *theoretical thinking,* in which the decision-maker is committed to abstract beliefs, usually organized around a single value in patterns that are internally consistent and stable over time, even under conditions of uncertainty.[55]

Steinbruner devotes the major part of his work to applying his modified cybernetic-cognitive paradigm to studying a single complex policy decision issue—that of sharing control of nuclear weapons among members of the Atlantic Alliance in the early 1960s. The United States was caught in a value trade-off between its general political purposes in Europe (including the credibility of the United States defense guarantee) and the requirements of stable deterrence, to which the proliferation of national nuclear weapons capabilities was seen as a threat. It is not possible to do justice to the ample treatment accorded to the strains in the alliance caused by the two-value problem—the development of nuclear sharing proposals and the rise and demise of the NATO Multilateral Force (MLF).[56] Steinbruner concludes that the ability of the State Department to produce momentum for the deployment of an MLF, to which the Secretary of Defense and most United States military leaders and Europeans generally were opposed, was a "political anomaly" that might best be understood in terms of the cognitive and cybernetic processes of bureaucratic decision-makers rather than in terms of the analytic paradigm.

Clearly, Steinbruner does not regard the cybernetic-cognitive paradigm as intrinsically superior to the analytic one. Rather he suggests that the two paradigms operate as substitutes for one another in processing complex problems, and produce different types of decisions. In our effort to understand governmental decision-making under conditions of complexity and uncertainty, the cybernetic-cognitive approach may provide a coherent explanation of behavior that, in an analytic framework, appears to be stupid, absurd, incompetent, or incomprehensible, without in any way implying approval of such an outcome.[57] Interestingly enough, Steinbruner suggests that President Johnson's decision in December 1964 to reverse his advisers and to kill the MLF "can readily be understood by analytic logic."[58] In the end we are left with two competing paradigms, each partially confirmed. Fitting them together in a satisfactory synthesis remains a task for future analysis.

DECISION-MAKING IN CRISIS

Since the mid-1950s, a considerable amount of literature has appeared on specific foreign policy decisions. Until the 1970s much of it was in the form of case studies of decisions telescoped in time and circumscribed as to the number of decision-makers. Since that time there has been an increasing effort, as discussed later in this chapter, to study crises on a comparative basis in order to develop a data base across time and crises, and to build a theory, or theories, drawn from such analysis. In the generation before the 1970s, the focus of crisis literature was the creation of conceptual frameworks and hypotheses that were applied to the study of one and, in some instances, more than one case study. Such frameworks could have been utilized on a broader basis had scholars chosen to do so. In the 1960s, moreover, there was the beginning of an effort both to set forth alternative models to delineate propositions for the analysis of international crisis behavior. Most notable was the work of Charles F. Hermann and Linda P. Brady, who abstracted 311 propositions concerning crisis from research completed in the 1960s.[59] As they suggested, such hypotheses were advanced by the authors from which they were catalogued "as discrete relationships rather than as components of some larger theoretical framework."

The work of this earlier period includes the decisions that led to the outbreak of World War I, the United States intervention in Korea, British intervention in the Suez crisis, and United States responses to crises in or over Berlin, Quemoy, the Bay of Pigs, and the emplacement of Soviet missiles in Cuba.[60] The study of international crisis has included examination of the role played by third parties such as the United Nations and other mediating organizations or groups.[61] There have been studies of decisions characterized by longer time frames and complex groups of actors, including legislative bodies, political parties, and governments. Such decisions, which may be of historic significance and yet not "crisis decisions" in the sense used here, might pertain to such events as the French scuttling of the European Defense Community in 1954, Britain's quest over more than a decade for entry into the European Economic Community, and the United States decision-making concerning arms control agreements with the Soviet Union, a negotiated peace settlement in the Middle East, or, as in Steinbruner's study, a policy analysis of the nuclear-sharing issue in NATO. This type of study is often more difficult than the "crisis" type to cast in the mold of precise decision-making analysis because it involves a harder-to-research cumulative process that takes place in a sprawling bureaucratic labyrinth and a more comprehensive political arena over a longer time period. Such studies may encompass decision-making under more or less routine circumstances. In this respect they are likely to differ substantially from crisis decision-making in such factors as the level of the policy structure at which decisions are taken and the time available to do so. The case studies of crisis decision-making include, for example, the U.S. intervention in Korea in 1950, the outbreak of World War I in 1914, and the Cuban Missile Crisis of 1962, to which we turn before examining more recent efforts to develop a comparative basis for the analysis of crisis behavior in historic and contemporary contexts.

The United States Decision to Intervene in Korea

Among the case studies mentioned earlier, one that was consciously designed for the purpose of applying a theoretical DM model was Glenn D. Paige's account of seven days of United States national decision-making in response to the Korean crisis. Paige reflects an awareness of the problem of applying to a single case the Snyder-Bruck-Sapin model, and of trying to verify any hypotheses merely on the basis of the Korean decision. He acknowledges that the single case produces lessons that can lead only to "a relatively low level of abstraction."[62] Paige is essentially faithful to the Snyder-Bruck-Sapin model, with its emphasis upon such concepts as "spheres of competence," "motivation," "communication and information," "feedback," and the "path of action."

The Korean decision, Paige contends, can be viewed either as a unified phenomenon or as a developmental sequence of choices (of which most decision-makers were aware) that contributed "to a stagelike progression toward an analytically defined outcome"—a sequence in which policymakers were apparently affected by "positive reinforcement" in the form of supporting UN military action, favorable editorial opinion, and Congressional and international expressions of approval, as well as evidence of a temperate Soviet response.[63] Many of Paige's conclusions are stated as hypotheses that postulate relationships among the nature of the decision-making group, the perceived threat to values, the role of leadership, the quest for information, the framework of past responses, the shared willingness to make a positive response, the effort to secure international support, and so forth. Some of the propositions are novel and interesting, and some might strike the reader as slightly tedious confirmations of what might otherwise be deduced logically; but it should be remembered that the validation of "obvious" truths, based on data, is essential to the scientific method and thus to the development of social science theories.

Perception and Decision-Making: The Outbreak of World War I

The use of content analysis with a stimulus-response model represents a quite different methodological approach to the study of decision-making. In studies of the outbreak of World War I and the Cuban Missile Crisis, Ole R. Holsti, Robert C. North, and Richard A. Brody have attempted to measure the messages exchanged during crisis situations.[64] Such an approach focuses not upon interaction *within,* but rather upon interaction *between* the decisional units.

The model used in these studies relates perceptions to behavior (S-r: s-R). The symbol S is the stimulus or input behavior: It is a physical event or a verbal act. The symbol R represents the response action. Both S and R are nonevaluative and nonaffective; r is the decision-maker's perception of the stimulus (S), and s is the expression of intentions or attitude. Both r and s include factors such as personality, role, organization, and system that affect perceptual variables.

The authors of the study undertook correlational analyses between the perception data and various types of "hard" or action data, because they recognized that the value of content analysis depends upon the relationship between the statements and the actual decisions made by statesmen. Thus, the authors attempted to find correlations between the results of the content analysis and such actions as mobilization, troop movements, and the breaking of diplomatic relations. Other actions, such as the financial indicators—gold movements and the price of securities, which are sensitive to international tension levels—were examined. Correlating the 1914 perception data with the spiral of military mobilizations, the authors concluded that a rise in hostility preceded acts of mobilization. Stated differently, decision-makers responded "to verbal threats and diplomatic moves, rather than troop movements."[65]

Among the hypotheses tested was the notion that "in a situation of low involvement, policy response (R) will tend to be at a lower level of violence than the input action (S), whereas in a high involvement situation, the policy response (R) will tend to be at a higher level of violence than the input action (S)."[66] It was found that the highly involved Dual Alliance was indeed consistently overreacting to the threats, whereas the less involved Triple Entente underreacted. Since the action variables, S and R, alone failed to account for the escalation of war, the intervening perceptual variables, r and s, were analyzed. No significant difference was found between the two coalitions in the s-R step. In both low- and high-involvement cases, the response action (R) was at a higher level of violence than was suggested by their leaders' statements of intent (s). Moreover, in the r-s link, there was again little difference between the Triple Entente and Dual Alliance: In both groupings of nations the level of hostility was perceived to be consistently greater in the other's policy (r) than in their own statements of intent (s).

However, a significant difference appeared in the S-r step which could account for the escalation. In the low-involvement situation, r tended to be at a lower level than S, whereas in the high-involvement situation, r tended to be higher than S. Decision-makers in the highly involved Dual Alliance consistently overperceived the level of violence of the Triple Entente. The leaders of the less deeply involved Triple Entente underperceived the actions of the Dual Alliance. Moreover, in the latter stages of the crisis, after both alliances had become highly involved, there was less difference between the two coalitions in the way actions (S) were perceived (r) than before. The authors concluded, therefore, that intervening perception may perform an accelerating or decelerating function. In this case, the S-r link served a "magnifying" function. "This difference in perceiving the environment (the S-r link) is consistent with the pronounced tendency of the Dual Alliance to respond at a higher level of violence than the Triple Entente."[67]

L. L. Farrar, Jr., adopts a different interpretation of the 1914 crisis. Following Theodore Abel and Bruce M. Russett, he suggests that one should not seek causes but analyze processes, beginning with the background from which the decisions of governments emerge. The final decision for war is not reached on the spur of the moment and is not triggered by the irrational motivations and emotional elements often associated with decision-making under conditions of stress. Rather it is based on a series of rational calculations that may antedate the crisis by several years. The crisis itself may be the result of precrisis decisions involving an assessment over a long period of time concerning several alternative ways acting under a variety of circumstances. Although leaders may experience stress during the crisis, the crisis is due not to psychological tensions but to decisions previously taken, which are more important than personality characteristics. Farrar presents the 1914 crisis as the logical result of rational policy considerations, given the assumptions underlying the state system.

The Cuban Missile Crisis

Using their same interaction model described earlier, Holsti, Brody, and North also investigated the Cuban Missile Crisis of 1962. An example of escalation conflict, like the 1914 case, the Cuban Missile Crisis provides an opportunity, therefore, both for comparison and contrast with the earlier study. An effort was made to find "patterns of behavior that distinguish the situation which escalated into general war (as in the 1914 crisis) from those in which the process of escalation is reversed"[68] (as in the Cuban Missile Crisis).

In the Cuban Missile Crisis, unlike the 1914 crisis, there was found to be "close correspondence between the actions of the other party (S) and perceptions of the adversary's action (r)." Here both sides accurately perceived the nature of the adversary's actions and acted at an appropriate level. Efforts made by either party "to delay or reverse the escalation were generally perceived as such and responded to in a like manner."[69] Such behavior differed from that of the 1914 crisis in which, at the beginning, the Dual Alliance consistently reacted at a higher level than the Triple Entente and also consistently overperceived the level of violence in actions taken by the Triple Entente. Subsequently, this difference in the S-r link between the two coalitions lessened as both were drawn into escalation and war. From the analysis of the 1914 crisis and the 1962 crisis, Holsti, Brody, and North found indications that "the more intense the interaction between parties, the more important it is to incorporate perceptual data into the analysis."[70]

Graham T. Allison applied each of his decision-making models (discussed previously) to the Cuban Missile Crisis. He concludes that his three case studies "do not settle the matter of what happened and why," but "do offer evidence about the nature of explanations produced by different analysts."[71] The Rational Actor Model analyst explained the crisis in terms of strategic choices by the two superpowers. The USSR placed missiles in Cuba not merely as a bargaining counter for the withdrawal of U.S. missiles in Turkey, nor to attract a U.S. move against Cuba to cover a Soviet move against Berlin, nor to deter a U.S. attack against Cuba to demonstrate to the world that the USSR could make with impunity a bold Cold War move against an indecisive United States, but rather to bring about quickly and at low cost a rectification of the adverse nuclear missile balance by converting Cuba into an "unsinkable carrier" and doubling the

Soviet capability for a first strike against the United States.[72] The United States decision to respond with a naval blockade was an apt, limited, yet effective, way of exploiting U.S. superiority at both strategic nuclear and local conventional levels to carry out a value-maximizing escalation while minimizing Moscow's humiliation.[73] Most American strategic analysts agreed that Khrushchev, recognizing Soviet military inferiority in the vicinity of Cuba in the face of implicit threats of further action (e.g., an air strike against or invasion of Cuba), had no choice but to withdraw the missiles from the island.[74]

In his Organizational Process Model approach to the Cuban Missile Crisis, Allison stresses the amount of organizational activity and degree of coordination required to move more than 100 shiploads of medium- and intermediate-range missiles, Beagle Bombers, MiG-21 interceptor aircraft, surface-to-air missiles, cruise missiles and patrol boats, and 22,000 Soviet soldiers and technical personnel to Cuba.[75] But American experts were puzzled that the Soviets, who could not have expected their missile sites in Cuba to escape detection by U-2s, failed to complete their radar system and SAM network prior to installing the MRBMs, and made no attempt to camouflage the missiles until after the United States publicly disclosed what the Soviets were doing.[76] Some analysts of the "rational model school" sought motives to explain the apparent inconsistencies of Soviet behavior. Allison suggests that the anomalies might best be explained simply by assuming that large organizations "do what they know how to do." SAM sites and missile sites were constructed in Cuba just as they had been in the Soviet Union, without either camouflage or hardening.[77] Other construction and phasing anomalies can be similarly explained by the characteristic problem that typically besets large organizations—lack of a strategic overview, poor coordination, delays in communication and implementation of directives, and cumbersome operating procedures. Allison also speculates plausibly that the actual Soviet decision to place missiles in Cuba may have been pressed upon the Praesidium by the relatively new Strategic Rocket Forces. These Forces, locked into a budgetary rivalry with the Soviet Ground Forces, had been compelled to defer acquisition of ICBMs and they worried about the strategic nuclear balance after the Kennedy Administration announced in November 1961 that not only was there no "missile gap" but that the United States actually enjoyed strategic nuclear superiority.[78]

On the American side, writes Allison, the precise timing of the Cuban Missile Crisis was a function of the organizational routines and standard operating procedures of the U.S. intelligence community, for these factors determined when the crucial information came to the President. Many reports and isolated items of information had to be pieced together and analyzed before U-2 surveillance flights over Cuba were ordered, and then several more days passed while the State Department urged a less risky alternative and the Air Force and CIA carried on a jurisdictional dispute over who should fly the U-2. When a "surgical air strike" was being considered as a possible course of action, there was a vast discrepancy between what that term meant to President Kennedy and his White House advisers (who would have restricted it to the missile sites) and what it meant to the military (who added the missile sites to the existing contingency plan for an air strike against all Cuban storage depots, airports, and artillery batteries opposite the U.S. naval base at Guantanamo). A hastily formulated and probably erroneous military estimate that an air strike could be only 90 percent but not 100 percent effective against the missiles, of which a small number might be launched first, prompted the political leaders to eliminate the air strike option and to concentrate on the naval blockade.[79]

Allison concedes that it is difficult to analyze Soviet decision-making in the Cuban Missile Crisis in terms of the Bureaucratic Politics Model, but the documentation for applying this model to the United States action is abundant. After the Bay of Pigs fiasco, Kennedy was under heavy pressure from public opinion and from critics in Congress to prevent the Soviet Union from converting Cuba into an offensive base. In September 1962, when reports of the Soviet military buildup began reaching the United States, the President distinguished between defensive and offensive preparations, and gave public assurance that the latter would not be tolerated. Administration figures denied the presence of Soviet offensive missiles, discounted the suspicions of CIA Director John McCone, and elicited from the United States Intelligence Board on September 19 an estimate to the effect that the emplacement of Soviet offensive missiles in Cuba was "highly unlikely." Early in September a U-2 had been shot down over Mainland China. Fear that another U-2 might be lost contributed to a 10-day delay after a decision was taken on October 4 to carry out photograph reconnaissance flights. Confronted with the evidence, the President was angered by Khrushchev's duplicity: "He can't do that to *me!*" Given the political environment, with congressional elections only three weeks away, Kennedy knew that signs of weakness had to be avoided and firm action taken. Recommendations from his advisers varied from "doing nothing" or "taking a diplomatic approach" to "air strike" or "invasion" before the Soviet missiles became operational. Attorney General Robert Kennedy was responsible for working out a near consensus on a compromise between inaction and potentially unlimited action—the limited response of a naval blockade.[80] Allison calls the blockade decision "part choice and part result—a melange of misconception, miscommunication, misinformation, bargaining, pulling, hauling, and sparring, as well as a mixture of national security interests, objectives, and governmental calculations."[81]

In the final analysis, however, the blockade alone did not lead to the withdrawal of Soviet missiles from Cuba. That was accomplished only after a conciliatory offer to give a United States assurance against an invasion of Cuba combined with a threat of "overwhelming retaliatory action" unless the President received immediate notice that the missiles would be withdrawn.[82] But whether the ultimatum "caused" the withdrawal, as the

Rational Actor Model would argue, or whether the language of threat was a public posturing designed to screen a private deal offered by President Kennedy to Premier Khrushchev—withdrawal of Soviet missiles in Cuba for withdrawal of United States missiles in Turkey (something that Kennedy had ordered before the Cuban Missile Crisis developed and that was actually carried out a few months afterward)—Allison leaves in the realm of unanswered questions.[83] His study "demonstrates each model's tendency to produce different answers to the same question," as well as "differences in the ways the analysts conceive of the problem, shape the puzzle, unpack the summary questions, and pick up pieces of the world in search of an answer."[84]

TOWARD A THEORY OF CRISIS BEHAVIOR

James A. Robinson has asserted that "there is no theory of crisis."[85] Nevertheless, several international relations analysts have devoted many years of effort to acquire a better understanding of crisis behavior and to gain deeper insights into why some crises lead to war while others lend themselves to nonviolent resolution, and to ascertain why certain crises are short and others protracted in duration.[86] Others, as noted in this chapter, have attempted to develop a theory of crisis behavior that might yield systematic knowledge for the study of crisis and for crisis management and resolution. According to Michael P. Sullivan, crisis is now the most widely researched situational variable of all occasions for decision.[87]

Charles A. McClelland has noted that analysts of international crisis behavior have focused on five "approaches": (1) definition of crisis; (2) classifications of types of crisis; (3) the study of ends, goals, and objectives in crises; (4) decision-making under conditions of crisis stress; and (5) crisis management.[88] An earlier, widely accepted definition of crisis developed by Robinson and Hermann had postulated three elements: (1) threat to high-priority goals of the DM unit, (2) restricted amount of time available for response, and (3) surprise.[89] According to Gilbert R. Winham, a crisis can arise "in situations ranging from a fundamental military challenge to the balance of power to an insignificant border dispute that escalates into a major confrontation."[90] Later studies did not deem surprise essential.

Glenn H. Snyder and Paul Diesing define international crisis as "a sequence of interactions between the governments of two or more sovereign states in severe conflict, short of actual war, but involving the perception of a dangerously high probability of war."[91] Glenn Snyder suggests that crisis is a characteristic feature of international politics. The crisis has always been central to international politics—a moment of truth in which several latent elements "such as power configurations, interests, images, and alignments tend to be more sharply clarified, to be activated and focused on a single well-defined issue."[92] In the nuclear age, crises are looked upon as surrogates for war, rather than merely dangerous episodes that are the prelude to war. "Their systemic function is to resolve without violence, or with only minimal violence, those conflicts that are too severe to be settled by ordinary diplomacy and that in earlier times would have been settled by war."[93] According to Oran R. Young, an international crisis consists of a "set of rapidly unfolding events which raises the impact of destabilizing forces in the general international system or any of its subsystems substantially above normal (average) levels, and increases the likelihood of violence occurring in the system,"[94] which in turn produce responses which have the effect of leading the originators of demands to additional activities; hence there is feedback. Richard Ned Lebow maintains that an international crisis is defined according to three operational criteria: (1) the presence of a perceived threat to concrete national interests, the country's bargaining reputation, and the ability of its leaders to remain in power; (2) the perception on the part of policymakers that actions taken to counter the threat increase the possibility of war; and (3) the existence of perceived time constraints in responding to the crisis situation.[95] Glenn H. Snyder suggests that an international crisis is "international politics in microcosm."[96] By this statement Snyder means that elements that lie at the core of the international politics come fully into focus in crises. They include, in addition to conflict itself, bargaining, negotiations, force and the threat to use force, escalation and deescalation, deterrence, alternative power configurations, interests, values, perceptions, the use (or nonuse) of international law and organization, and decision-making. As Snyder suggests, international crises originate, unfold, and are resolved within different system structures and usually encompass relations within and between alliances or coalitions of states. To the extent that international politics is seen as the study of interacting units having between or among them a clash of vital interests, the building of theory about crisis behavior represents a contribution of central importance to international relations theory.

In the crisis management literature, an effort is made to relate crisis behavior to such variables as the structure of the international system. Thus, there are numerous points of linkage between theoretical constraints related to polarity and structural realism and international crisis as described subsequently in this chapter. The behavior of states in a crisis is said to be affected by the structure of the system (bipolar or multipolar) and by the nature of military technology. In this perspective, the rivalry of the United States and the Soviet Union was ordained more by structure (their power preponderance over all others) than by ideology. Snyder and Diesing agree with Kenneth N. Waltz's hypothesis that a bipolar system is more likely than a multipolar one to be stable. Such analysis accords with findings from the work of Michael Brecher, Jonathan Wilkenfeld, and Sheila Moser, discussed below. In the bipolar system, alignments are clear and realignments do not alter the balance of power significantly. In the multipolar system, alignments may be unclear and shifts may be important. Because of their greater ambiguity, multipolar systems are more prone to changes in the perception of interests, to gambling or risk-taking, and to miscalculations that make crises more dangerous. The tension between bargaining among allies and bargaining between adversaries (or between restraining the ally and deterring the opponent) is more difficult to manage in a multipolar system crisis.[97] By the same token, however, crises that break out between two actors, or between two blocs of actors, in a bipolar system are likely to hold the potential for escalation to general war, or to be system dominant, rather than confined to one of the regional subsystems. A crisis can break out, however, in which superpowers are drawn into a confrontation by client states, as they were in the 1973 Yom Kippur War.

Nuclear weapons technology has had a considerable effect on international crises by widening enormously the gap between the value of the interests in conflict and the possible cost of war for the holders of such weapons. Nuclear powers strive to protect, and indeed to advance, their interests, but they are said to be motivated by the "disaster-avoidance" constraint to be more cautious and prudent in crisis management and to raise, as if by tacit consent, the "provocation threshold" of war, thereby increasing the range for maneuvering in crises.[98] The nuclear powers have substituted for war itself psychological force in the form of carefully managed risks of war.[99] In this respect crisis management, including the use of a variety of instruments of statecraft and the threat, real or perceived, to use force, has become a surrogate for the actual use of military capabilities, including nuclear weapons. Herein lies a linkage between crisis decision-making and deterrence theory, which, as noted in Chapter 9, encompasses both the threat of escalation, and escalation itself. The power able to demonstrate to its opponent the capacity to punish at a higher level of conflict—or a higher rung on the escalatory ladder—holds the potential for deterring in a crisis situation or for escalation dominance.

Crisis management, it may be inferred, is the ability of one of the parties, by credibly threatening escalation, to deter its adversary from escalation and to produce a crisis deescalation outcome in accord with its interests. This does not mean, however, that a crisis ends only when one adversary party capitulates or backs away. A crisis may also be resolved through a process in which both contestants exercise restraint and seek a face-saving path of mutual retreat or a compromise that transforms the situation without being incompatible with the irreducible interests of either. Nor does it mean that there is universal agreement among theorists concerned with crisis behavior about the dual relationship between military power and escalation dominance, or between deterrence capabilities and crisis management. According to Lebow, motivation is a key element in crisis behavior. His analysis of 20 crises since 1898 led him to conclude: "To the extent that leaders perceive the need to act, they become insensitive to the interests and commitments of others that stand in the way of the success of their policy." By the same token, Lebow suggests that leaders may be unwilling to commit resources at their disposal to policies that do not serve what they regard as important interests. In short, increased capabilities may not inevitably translate into policies of confrontation. As a result, leaders may discard or discount information that runs counter to the course of action on which they have embarked in support of their established goals. "In the absence of compelling domestic and strategic needs most leaders may be reluctant or unwilling to pursue confrontatory foreign policies even when they seem to hold out an excellent prospect of success."[100] In short, perceived will to use capabilities in support of vital interests appears to be central to crisis management.

THE SYSTEMATIC STUDY OF INTERNATIONAL CRISIS BEHAVIOR

In an effort to contribute to the development of a comprehensive theory of crisis behavior, Michael Brecher, Jonathan Wilkenfeld, and Sheila Moser assembled data about 278 international crises for the 50-year period between 1929 and 1979. Their objective, in the International Crisis Behavior Project, was to examine on a comparative basis with the use of quantitative research a large number of crises displaying various and differing characteristics. They sought to generate systematic knowledge about crises on a global basis. The Project had as its focus crises between major powers, as well as those between major powers and smaller powers, and smaller powers themselves. They sought to illuminate such dimensions of international crisis as the images and behavior of major powers, the behavioral patterns of weak actors, the role of deterrence, bargaining between adversaries, the role of alliance partners in crisis management, the catalysts or triggering factors producing crises, how and why crises are resolved in alternative types of outcomes; and, finally, to identify the consequences of crises for the power and status, as well as subsequent perceptions, of participant states.[101] The authors examine crisis behavior at both the macro- and microlevels. At the macrolevel they address crisis behavior between or among actors. An international crisis has as its defining characteristic "disruptive interactions between two or more adversaries" accompanied by the probability of military hostilities or, if war has already broken out, the potential for an adverse change in the military balance. Furthermore, an international crisis is said to pose a challenge to the existing structure of the international system or the subsystem within which it takes place. According to Brecher, Wilkenfeld, and Moser, moreover, it is necessary to address crisis behavior at the microlevel from the perspective of the individual actors and their foreign policies. Therefore, they define a foreign policy crisis as having two necessary and sufficient conditions that are derived from a change in the state's internal or external environment. These are perceptions held by the highest decision-makers that there is (1) a threat to basic values, together with an awareness of finite time for response to the threat; and (2) a high probability that military hostilities will ensue. In short, at the level of the international system stand the interactive patterns between or among the crisis participants. For each of the states that are parties there is a foreign policy crisis. In the study of crisis management, it is possible to focus upon the macrolevel—interaction between and among crisis participants—or to address the foreign policy behavior of individual states at the microlevel. The International Crisis Behavior Project was designed to encompass both levels of analysis. In this conceptualization there is an inextricable link between the macro- and microlevels. A decision or action taken by one state elicits a response from another state, generating an interactive process that in itself makes the crisis international.

Within the 50-year period addressed it was found that crises occur in diverse geographical and strategic environments with varying levels of participation by major powers.[102] Crises may occur without leading to actual military hostilities, or they may be the prelude to war. In other cases, crises were found to take place as part of an ongoing conflict or war. The authors found that crises were more frequent in Asia in the period between 1929 and 1979 than in any other part of the world. Such crises were longer, proportionately, than crises that took place in other regions. In contrast to the 69 crises that erupted in Asia, the Americas were the locus of 33 crises, the smallest number of any region. Europe ranked just behind Asia, with 57 crises between 1929 and 1979. The crises that took place in Europe tended to be multiactor crises; those that actually led to war occurred before 1945. Ranking just behind Europe was the Middle East, with 55 crises during the 50-year period of the study. More than half of the Middle East crises had at least six actors. Most of the crises in the region erupted after World War II, and had varying levels of U.S. and Soviet involvement. Africa, the region containing the youngest states, most of which gained independence in the 1960s, provided the setting for 64 crises. More than half of these crises formed part of protracted conflicts. In Africa, nonstate entities accounted for the largest number of triggering factors. The United States played an active role, principally political and economic, in nearly half of the post–World War II African crises. The Soviet Union took part in slightly fewer crises than the United States in Africa, although its military-related activity was greater than the United States.

In the International Crisis Behavior Project, the global system was divided into four polarity periods: multipolar (1929–1939); World War II (1939–1945); bipolar (1945–1962); and polycentric (1963–1969). According to their findings, which may be read in the context of our discussion of the impact of international systemic structure upon conflict (see Chapters 3–4), the polycentric system of the period after 1963 was said to be less stable than the preceding bipolar system. Polycentrism, with its diffusion of decisional centers reflecting the emergence of a large number of additional actors, resulted in a sharp increase in crises having violent breakpoints. In the earlier multipolar decade before World War II, nearly all of the crises had the major powers as direct participants. This period ranked highest in the use of pacific techniques to achieve crisis termination—a preoccupation with appeasement as a means of war avoidance. In the subsequent period, World War II, in nearly all cases the crisis management techniques utilized were for the most part violent in nature. In the bipolar period that followed, there was a decline in the overt use of violence, and especially full-scale war, as a crisis management technique.

In keeping with their effort to discuss crisis at the macro- and microlevels, Brecher, Wilkenfeld, and Moser suggest a further delineation within the international system itself. Their conceptualization provides for a categorization of crises within the dominant system, such as Europe before 1945 or between East-West blocs since that time, contrasted with the several regional subsystems. Crises that break out in a subsystem such as the Middle East or Africa, with the direct participants being in the subsystem, can escalate into the dominant system. Similarly, as the authors found, crises that begin on a dominant system can spill over into a subsystem. Among their findings they conclude that all but 64 crises had a subsystem, rather than a dominant system, as their context. Dominant-system crises tended to be longer in duration than crisis at other system levels. Dominant-system crises were more threatening, dangerous, and destabilizing than subsystemic crises because of the greater capacity of major powers for violence. The occurrence of violence in dominant-system crises was more likely to be marked by full-scale war, while serious or minor clashes were more frequent in subsystem crises. Furthermore, crises at the dominant-system level had a greater propensity than those at other levels to provide definitive outcomes, such as victory or defeat, rather than stalemate or compromise. The effectiveness of international organizations, especially the United Nations, was greater at the subsystem level than within the dominant system.

Among the phenomena studied were the types of crisis conflict environment. Brecher, Wilkenfeld, and Moser differentiated among settings that included (1) long-term hostility between adversaries over multiple issues, leading to periodic violence resulting in protracted conflict; (2) extended wars that form part of a protracted conflict; and (3) crises that are not set within the context of any protracted conflict. They found that crises were more likely than not to occur within one or the other protracted conflict setting. The most threatening and destabilizing crises occurred within a prolonged violent conflict. In such situations, as might be expected, crisis actors were more prone to resort to violence than were their counterparts in other conflict situations. Moreover, the authors concluded that, where power discrepancies between adversaries were low, there was a greater likelihood of violent breakpoints or triggers in the outbreak and escalation of the crisis. It is suggested that strong states facing weak adversaries find resort to violence to be less necessary than states with few or no major power disparities with their enemies. Stated differently, the most frequent type of breakpoint or triggering factor in crises characterized by substantial gaps in capabilities between protagonists was nonviolent in nature.

In their discussion of actor attributes or characteristics, Brecher, Wilkenfeld, and Moser concluded that in all crises actors opted for smaller rather than larger decision-making units. The higher the level of superpower involvement, the greater is the frequency of the head of government to be the principal communicator. Furthermore, the longer a state had existed, the greater was the likelihood that its crisis decision-making unit would contain more than 10 persons. However, the basic decisional unit consisted of four persons or less in 51 percent of all actor cases, and in only 22 percent was the unit larger than 10 persons. It was also found that negotiation and other nonviolent techniques were most frequently employed by older states in crisis management. The more authoritarian the regime, it was found, the greater was the possibility that it would resort to violent crisis triggers. According to the data analyzed, the democratic political systems had an almost equal tendency to utilize small, medium, or large decisional units in a crisis. In contrast, authoritarian political systems, as might be expected, opted for a small decisional unit, composed of one to four persons.

PSYCHOLOGICAL COMPONENTS OF DECISION-MAKING IN CRISIS

One of the most interesting aspects of crisis decision-making pertains to the element of choice under pressure of time. We have already reviewed the Holsti-North-Brody study, in which perceptions of hostility in both verbal communications and action signals were shown to be important, the more so as the decision-makers became more deeply engaged and involved in the crisis. Holsti has asked whether decision-makers, under the stress of crisis that may require a round-the-clock watch, can be expected to be efficient in identifying major alternative courses of action, estimating the probable costs and gains of each option, discriminating between relevant and irrelevant information, and resisting premature cognitive closure and action.[103] Analysts are not in agreement on whether moderate stress improves human performance[104] or interferes with problem solving.[105]

Richard Ned Lebow suggests the importance of cognitive and motivational processes as a necessary basis for analyzing decision-making behavior under crisis conditions. Yet the relative explanatory power of cognitive and motivational models in the study of crisis decisions is not easily determined. Lebow's examination of international crises led to the conclusion that they provide competing explanations for many of the same phenomena, and notably for information distortion. For example, according to cognitive theory, decision-makers seek to achieve cognitive consistency—that is to say, they are likely to interpret, incorporate, or discard information that is received as a crisis proceeds, in accordance with their existing assumptions, predispositions, and perceptions. Especially under conditions of extreme time constraints, the reluctance to reopen a decision already taken is likely to be proportionate to the difficulty experienced in making it in the first place. Such was the problem, according to Lebow, confronting Austria and other major powers in the weeks leading to the outbreak of World War I after the crisis had begun. Aside from the pressure of time, there is likely to be a reluctance, under crisis conditions, to seek alternative sources of information. In the case of the United States, which in 1950 downplayed the likelihood of Chinese military intervention in the Korean War, political-military leaders "had no desire to challenge advisors who told them what they wished to hear."[106] Intelligence estimates and official policy analyses may be distorted as a result of cognitive closure. Once committed to a policy of confrontation, or brinksmanship, in a crisis, leaders tended to disregard information that challenged their assumptions and expectations about success. By the same token: "When initiators recognized and corrected for initial misjudgments, they usually succeeded in averting war, although this often required a major cooperative effort, as in the Fasboda and Cuban missiles crises."[107] Similarly, motivational theory, which explains misperception by reference to the emotional needs of the actors, is said to offer insights that, according to Lebow, serve to reinforce and complement findings from the cognitive model. Lebow suggests that the need on the part of decision-makers to believe that the policy on which they have embarked will succeed helps to account for reluctance or unwillingness to make changes in spite of evidence to the contrary. This motivational need may itself play an important role in shaping cognitive choices. The quest for cognitive consistency is said to be related to motivational need. Thus Lebow, in his discussion of the U.S. decision to discount the prospect of Chinese military intervention into the Korean War, asks: "Did American military intelligence in Tokyo, for example, underestimate the number of Chinese in Korea because this conformed to their expectations or because it satisfied their needs? A good case can be made for either explanation."[108] It can be said that all crisis decisions give rise to situations of threat and counterthreat that produce tension within the participants whether in the form of excitement, fear, anxiety, frustration, dissonance, or some other psychic state. A knowledge of how conditions of stress affect the solidarity and problem-solving ability of small groups may cast light on the way leaders behave at crucial decision-making junctures.

Psychologists have designed experiments to test the effects of stress upon group integration and the problem-solving efficiency of groups. It has been found, as one might expect, that individuals in groups react differently to stress. Herman Kahn has noted that in a crisis a decision-maker "may be able to invent or work out quickly and easily what seems in normal time to be . . . complex or otherwise difficult."[109] We know that for both individuals and groups, increased stress may lead to aggression, withdrawal or escape behavior, regression, or various neurotic symptoms.

John T. Lanzetta has furnished the following description of his experiments with groups:

> It was found that as stress increased there was a decrease in behaviors associated with friction in the group; a decrease in the number of disagreements, arguments, aggressions, deflations, and other negative social-emotional behaviors, as well as a decrease in self-oriented behaviors. Concomitant with this decrease was an increase in behaviors which would tend to result in decreased friction and better integration of the group; an increase in collaborating, mediating, cooperating behaviors.[110]

Lanzetta suggests that the reason for this phenomenon is to be found in the tendency of group members, faced with conditions that produce stress and anxiety, to seek psychological security in the group through cooperative behavior. But the hypothesis of group integration under stress seems to be valid only up to a point. It may be that group members provide mutual reinforcement for each other only while they expect to be able to find a solution to their common problem. Robert L. Hamblin designed an experiment that led him to suggest that group integration during a crisis will begin to decrease if no likely solution appears to be available. Cooperation is likely while it is potentially profitable, but when the members of the group meet one failure after another no matter what they do, they experience a frustration that leads to the displacement of antagonism against one another. In some cases, individuals attempt to resolve the crisis problem for themselves by withdrawing and leaving the other members to work out their own solution if they can—a process tantamount to group disintegration.[111]

Hamblin's findings may prove relevant for understanding the behavior of leadership groups in international conflict when they perceive that the tide is beginning to turn against them, regardless of which strategy or tactics they pursue. But here a caveat is in order: The behavior of national or other political leadership groups is a more complex phenomenon than the behavior of a small ad hoc group playing an experimental game. The stress conditions encountered during the course of a struggle that lasts for weeks, months, or even years are much more intricate psychologically than those experienced in a 2-hour game. The internal and external settings are infinitely richer in variety, as are the values, perceptions, cross-pressures, information, and political-cultural guidelines that impinge upon the decision-makers. In a larger-scale and more prolonged crisis, the time factor may permit various subtle adjustment mechanisms to come into play that can never operate in a brief experiment.

One cannot deny, however, that there is some relationship between stress and problem-solving efficiency. Dean G. Pruitt, synthesizing the findings of several writers in the field, concludes that the relationship is probably curvilinear, with some stress being necessary to motivate activity, but too much stress causing a reduction in efficiency.[112] Crisis inevitably brings in its wake a foreshortened perspective, a difficulty in thinking ahead and calculating consequences, and a tendency to select for consideration only a narrow range of alternatives—those that occur most readily to the decision-makers.[113] Naturally, if more time were available, a wider spectrum of choices could be evaluated, but the preciousness of time is built into the definition of crisis. Contingency planning can help, but the crisis that comes is invariably somewhat different, at least in its details, from the crisis that was abstractly anticipated in contingency plans.

Holsti lists other effects of stress uncovered as a result of empirical research: increased random behavior, increased rate of error, regression to simpler and more primitive modes of response, problem-solving rigidity, diminished focus of attention, and a reduction in tolerance for ambiguity.[114] He notes that "the common use during crisis of such techniques as ultimatums and threats with built-in deadlines is likely to increase the stress under which the recipient must operate" because they heighten the salience of the time element and increase the danger of fixation upon the single, familiar approach regardless of its effectiveness in the present situation.[115] Other analysts have found that diplomatic communications transmitted during international crises that were settled peacefully (Morocco, 1911; Berlin, 1948; Cuba, 1962) were characterized by greater flexibility and subtlety of distinctions, as well as by more extensive information search and usage, than were communications during crises that led to war in 1914 and 1950.[116] Finally, in connection with the time variable it should be noted that if in the past international crises were often marked by insufficient information, in recent decades technological conditions, combined with the desire of bureaucrats to generate and transmit vast amounts of information during crises, create the opposite danger of "overloading" the circuits of the decision-making system.

Other scholars in recent years have attempted to develop, as a measure of crisis decision-making behavior, what is called voice stress analysis.[117] Such work represents an analysis of stress levels derived from public statements of U.S. presidents, from Kennedy to Nixon, during international crisis of their respective administrations. The authors suggest that much of crisis behavior consists of communications between opposing decision-makers at the highest level. Statements from such leaders, even those addressed primarily to their own publics or the outside world, contain symbols and nuances that convey messages to their opposite number and furnish data for scholarly analysis. Psycholinguistics provides the basis for research into the cognitive basis for language behavior and thus for efforts to develop a measure of stress in decision-makers under crisis conditions by reference to changes in speech patterns. Stress is defined as the "negative affect, anxiety, fear and/or biophysiological change which develops as the internal response of an individual to an external load placed on him/her by an international crisis (pathogenic agent/stressor) which is perceived to pose a severe threat to one or more values of the political decision-maker."[118] By examining multiple documents such as speeches and press conferences from the 1961 Berlin, 1965 Dominican Republic, and 1970 Cambodia crises, it was possible, the authors suggest, to chart levels of stress on the part of the president as each crisis unfolded. Although they call for additional research development to advance voice stress analysis, they conclude that prepared statements manifested the highest stress levels. Conceivably, this indicates that, at times of greatest crisis intensity and stress, decision-makers are more prone than otherwise to resort to prepared, rather than extemporaneous, materials.

Last but not least, the study of crisis or other decision-making behavior by the utilization of political psychophysiology is regarded as a subarea of biopolitics, itself the use of biological indicators in the analysis of political behavior. To what extent, it is asked, do the physical-psychological conditions of decision-makers contribute to, or detract from, their ability to manage crises or otherwise shape their behavioral characteristics? According to Thomas Wiegele, a "truly profound understanding of human nature must ultimately include both biological and nonbiological considerations."[119] The extent to which advances in social science research, and in particular, the study of decision-making, will be advanced by research focused on biopolitics remains to be seen.

Groups that make the most crucial decisions in national security cases are usually limited in size—perhaps 12 to 20 persons. Irving Janis has analyzed what he calls "groupthink" and has described its characteristics. The members of a small group of decision-makers often share an illusion of invulnerability that may encourage them to take extreme risks. Their self-confidence is mutually reinforcing, such that they may discount warnings or information that runs counter to their own assumptions. They often have a stereotyped and simplified view of the enemy, and an unquestioned belief in their own inherent morality. They are quick to censure and drive out of circulation viewpoints that do not conform to the dominant assessments and judgments of the group, and they take the silence of dissenting or doubtful members to mean that there exists virtual unanimity in the thinking of the group.[120] It should not be taken for granted that "groupthink" is necessarily bad. The dominant element within the group may well be correct in its assessment of the situation and in its views on the proper course to be pursued. Furthermore, the tendency of a group to impose a dominant view upon all its members—a natural social phenomenon—may produce more adverse consequences in an ideologically monolithic society than in a democratic one, and also more adverse consequences at lower bureaucratic echelons, where individuals are less independent and outspoken, than at top levels, where more powerful personalities are usually present to speak their minds.

CONCLUSIONS

The field of decision-making is a broad one, and we do not pretend to be able to cover it all. The decision-making process is a function of many different factors relating to the behavior of individuals and of large organizational structures. The DM role is shaped by both the system and the individual's interpretation of it, and the influence of personality in comparison with social ideology will vary markedly from one system to another. Democratic and totalitarian states make foreign policy in very diverse ways. Most decision-making theories developed in the United States have, quite understandably, focused upon the American political experience—upon the role of public opinion, the state of Executive-Congressional relations, the nature of the bureaucratic competition in the annual battle of the budget in Washington, and so on. There is an inevitable tendency on the part of social scientists, unless they guard against it, to universalize from particulars, and to assume that at least certain aspects of a phenomenon studied in one cultural-political context can be *mutatis mutandis* given a more generalized application. Thus, there is a danger that when Americans think about such basic concepts as rationality in decision-making, or bureaucratic competition for scarce resources, or action-reaction processes in prolonged arms "races," or in acute crisis, lessons drawn from an observation of the behavior of American decision-makers can be readily carried over to the behavior of the decision-makers in vastly different environments—Moscow, Peking, Tokyo, New Delhi, or Cairo.

We must admit that we do not know a great deal about foreign policy decision-making in non-Western capitals, particularly those far removed from any constitutional democratic experience. Even among the Western democratic states with which American political scientists are generally most familiar—Britain, France, Italy, and the Federal Republic of Germany—considerable differences exist in the organization of governments for the conduct of foreign affairs, as well as in the ways elites typically conceive of their national interests. The difficulties of extrapolating from American experience to foreign decision-making processes become even more pronounced when we are dealing with governments and countries that are politically, ideologically, socioeconomically, and culturally very different from those of the West. Within the past two decades, significant strides have been made in the comparative study of leadership, bureaucracy, value orientations of elites, and decision-making in Communist or Socialist countries.[121] More specifically, the student should become acquainted with the comparative study of foreign policy decision-making in Western societies, Communist societies, and the developing societies of the Third World.[122] The field of comparative foreign policies is distinct from that of international relations theory, and specifically from theories of decision-making in the international system, but the former has much to contribute to the latter by way of concrete data and perhaps of insights leading to useful new theoretical approaches.

NOTES

1. See Paul Wasserman and Fred S. Silander, *Decision-Making: An Annotated Bibliography* (Ithaca, N.Y.: Graduate School of Business and Public Administration, Cornell University, 1958).

2. "Decision-Making as an Approach to the Study of International Politics," in Richard C. Snyder, H. W. Bruck, and Burton Sapin, eds., *Foreign Policy Decision-Making* (New York: The Free Press, 1963), p. 65; see also pp. 85–86.

3. Ibid., p. 65. See also Robert Jervis, *Perception and Misperception in International Politics* (Princeton: Princeton University Press, 1976).

4. Joseph Frankel, *The Making of Foreign Policy: An Analysis of Decision-Making* (New York: Oxford University Press, 1963), p. 4.

5. Michael Brecher, *The Foreign Policy System of Israel: Setting, Images, Process* (New Haven: Yale University Press, 1972), p. 4. For a thorough discussion of objective environment and decision-makers' perception, see Hyam Gold, "Foreign Policy Decision-Making and the Environment: The Claims of Snyder, Brecher and the Sprouts," *International Studies Quarterly*, 22 (December 1978), 569–586.

6. Students of decision-making have suggested several different ways of analyzing the phenomenon. Harold Lasswell, for example, presents seven functional stages: information, recommendation, prescription, invocation, application, appraisal, and termination. *The Decision Process: Seven Categories of Functional Analysis* (College Park: University of Maryland Press, 1956). See also James A. Robinson and R. Roger Majak, "The Theory of Decision-Making," in James C. Charlesworth, ed., *Contemporary Political Analysis* (New York: The Free Press, 1967), pp. 178–181, including bibliographical references; John P. Lovell, *Foreign Policy in Perspective: Strategy, Adaptation, Decision-Making* (New York: Holt, Rinehart and Winston, 1970), especially pp. 205–261. Michael Brecher makes elite image the decisive input of a foreign policy system. Op. cit., p. 11.

7. David Braybrooke and Charles E. Lindblom, *A Strategy of Decision* (New York: The Free Press, 1963), p. 40.

8. Max Weber, *Economy and Society: An Outcome of Interpretative Analogy.* Edited by Guenther Roth and Claus Wittich. Vol. 2. (Berkeley: University of California Press, 1978), p. 1393.

9. Morton H. Halperin with the assistance of Priscilla Clapp and Arnold Kanter, *Bureaucratic Politics and Foreign Policy* (Washington D.C.: The Brookings Institution, 1974).

10. Ibid., p. 312.

11. Francis Rourke, *Bureaucracy and Foreign Policy* (Baltimore, Md.: Johns Hopkins University Press, 1972), pp. 49–50.

12. Ibid., p. 54.

13. Ibid., pp. 62–65.

14. Alexander L. George, "The Case for Multiple Advocacy in Making Foreign Policy," *American Political Science Review*, LXVI (September 1972), 751–785.

15. Ibid., p. 758. See also chs. 7 and 8 on advocacy of interest groups and competing elites in Brecher, op. cit.

16. Richard C. Snyder et al., op. cit., p. 144.

17. David Easton, *The Political System* (New York: Knopf, 1953), p. 129.

18. Paul Diesing attributes a distinctive rationality to economic, social, technical, legal, and political decisions. *Reason in Society: Five Types of Decisions and Their Social Conditions* (Urbana: University of Illinois Press, 1962). Others, too, including R. C. Wood and William L. C. Wheaton, have cautioned against extrapolating from private to public decision behavior. Cf. Robinson and Majak in Charlesworth, ed., op. cit., pp. 177–178. Anthony Downs, on the other hand, is thought to equate private with public decision-making. Ibid., p.

178. But even he differentiates sharply between individual and organizational decision-making. See *Inside Bureaucracy*, A RAND Corporation Research Study (Boston: Little, Brown, 1967), pp. 178–179.

19. See for example Marshall Dimock. *A Philosophy of Administration* (New York: Harper & Row, 1958), p. 140; J. David Singer, "Inter-Nation Influence: A Formal Model," *American Political Science Review*, LXII (June 1963), 424; Bruce M. Russett, "The Calculus of Deterrence," *Journal of Conflict Resolution*, VII (June 1963), 97–109.

20. Richard Snyder et al., op. cit., p. 176. Snyder emphasizes that the explanation of DM motivation implies a concept of multiple membership of the individual in a culture and society, in such social groupings as the profession and class, in the total political institutional structure, and in the decisional unit. Ibid., p. 172.

21. Snyder had accepted earlier the notion of "maximization of expected utility." See his "Game Theory and the Analysis of Political Behavior," in *Research Frontiers and Government* (Washington, D.C.: The Brookings Institution, 1955), pp. 73–74.

22. J. David Singer, op. cit., pp. 428–430.

23. Martin Patchen, "Decision Theory in the Study of National Action," *Journal of Conflict Resolution*, LVII (June 1963), pp. 165–169.

24. Sidney Verba, "Assumptions of Rationality and Nonrationality in Models of the International System," in James N. Rosenau, ed., *International Politics and Foreign Policy*, rev. ed. (New York: The Free Press, 1969), p. 231.

25. David Braybrooke and Charles Lindblom, op. cit., ch. 4.

26. See Herbert A. Simon, *Administration Behavior* (New York: Macmillan, 1958); "A Behavioral Model of Rational Choice," *Quarterly Journal of Economics*, LXIX (February 1955), 99–118; and "A Behavioral Model of Rational Choice," in Simon, ed., *Models of Man: Social and Rational* (New York: Wiley, 1957), pp. 241–260. See also William D. Coplin, *Introduction to International Politics: A Theoretical Overview* (Chicago: Markham, 1971), pp. 32–37.

27. David Braybrooke and Charles Lindblom, op. cit., pp. 71–79 and ch. 5.

28. James Robinson and Roger Majak, op. cit., pp. 180–183.

29. Ibid., p. 182. The references are to Arthur F. Bentley, *The Process of Government* (Chicago: University of Chicago Press, 1908); David B. Truman, *The Governmental Process* (Chicago: University of Chicago Press, 1951); and William H. Riker, *The Theory of Political Coalitions* (New Haven: Yale University Press, 1962).

30. James Robinson and Roger Majak, op. cit., pp. 182–184.

31. Graham T. Allison, *Essence of Decision: Explaining the Cuban Missile Crisis* (Boston: Little, Brown, 1971), pp. 4–5, 10–11.

32. Ibid., pp. 13–18.

33. Ibid., pp. 29–30.

34. Ibid., p. 5.

35. Ibid., p. 67.

36. Ibid., p. 68. For more on this, see section, "The Cybernetic Theory of Decision."

37. Ibid., pp. 71–72.

38. Ibid., p. 77.

39. Ibid, pp. 144–145. See also Graham T. Allison and Morton H. Halperin, "Bureaucratic Politics: A Paradigm and Some Policy Implications," *World Politics*, XXIV (Spring Supplement 1972), 40–79.

40. Miriam Steiner, "The Elusive Essence of Decision," *International Studies Quarterly,* 21 (June 1977), 419.
41. Ibid.
42. Glenn H. Snyder and Paul Diesing, *Conflict Among Nations: Bargaining, Decision-Making and System Structure in International Crises* (Princeton: Princeton University Press, 1977).
43. Ibid., p. 355.
44. Ibid., pp. 355–356. The authors did not find that attitudes of leading decision-makers are significantly determined by bureaucratic role. "Thus the most distinctive point of the Allison-Halperin 'bureaucratic politics' theory does not survive our analysis" (note on p. 408).
45. Ibid., pp. 333–335.
46. Ibid., pp. 337–338.
47. Ibid., pp. 338–339.
48. John D. Steinbruner, *The Cybernetic Theory of Decision: New Dimensions of Political Analysis* (Princeton: Princeton University Press, 1974), chap. 1.
49. Ibid., p. 47.
50. Ibid., pp. 48–67. Steinbruner acknowledges that some of his own criticisms of the analytic paradigm had been anticipated in Herbert Simon's "satisficing" model, but in his view Simon had not gone far enough. Ibid., p. 63.
51. Ibid., p. 68.
52. Ibid., p. 69.
53. Ibid., p. 72. The reference is to Richard M. Cyert and James G. March, *A Behavioral Theory of the Firm* (Englewood Cliffs, N.J.: Prentice-Hall, 1963), ch. 6. It should be noted that Steinbruner incorporates into the cybernetic paradigm the work of Charles Lindblom (especially his "incrementalism") and the *Organization Process Model of Graham Allison* (see pp. 77 and 80). He fully agrees with those who hold that organizational routines, once established, are very difficult to alter.
54. John Steinbruner, op. cit., p. 92. Cf. also Robert Jervis, *Perception and Misperception and International Politics,* ch. 4.
55. Ibid., ch. 4. According to Snyder and Diesing, Steinbruner's "theoretical thinker" is equivalent to their "irrational bargainer." *Conflict Among Nations,* p. 337.
56. These matters are thoroughly covered in Steinbruner, op. cit., chs. 6 to 9.
57. Ibid., p. 70. See also ch. 10, especially p. 329.
58. Ibid., pp. 320–321.
59. Charles F. Hermann and Linda P. Brady, "Alternative Models of International Crisis Behavior," in Charles F. Hermann, ed., *International Crises: Insights from Behavioral Research* (New York: The Free Press, 1972), p. 281; pp. 304–320
60. See, for example, Ole R. Holsti, "The 1914 Case," *American Political Science Review,* LIX (June 1965), 365–378; Ole R. Holsti, Robert C. North, and Richard A. Brody, "Perception and Action in the 1914 Crisis," in J. David Singer, ed., *Quantitative International Politics* (New York: Free Press, 1968); Glenn D. Paige, *The Korean Decision, June 24–30, 1950* (New York: The Free Press, 1958); Erskine B. Childer, *The Road to Suez* (London: MacGibbon and Kee, 1962); Charles A. McClelland, "Access to Berlin: The Quantity and Variety of Events, 1948–1963," in Singer, ed., op. cit., pp. 159–186, and "Decisional Opportunity and Political Controversy: The Quemoy Case," *Journal of Conflict Resolution,* VI (September 1962), 201–213; Graham T. Allison, *Essence of*

Decision: Explaining the Cuban Missile Crisis (Boston: Little, Brown, 1971); and Herbert S. Dinerstein, *The Making of a Missile Crisis* (Baltimore, Md.: Johns Hopkins Press, 1976); Michael Brecher with Benjamin Geist, *Decisions in Crisis: Israel 1967 and 1973* (Berkeley and Los Angeles: University of California Press, 1980); Alan Dowty, *Middle East Crisis: U.S. Decision-Making in 1958, 1970, and 1973* (Berkeley and Los Angeles: University of California Press, 1984); Richard G. Head, Frisco W. Short, and Robert C. McFarlane, *Crisis Resolution: Presidential Decision-Making in the Mayaguez and Korean Confrontations* (Boulder, Colo.: Westview Press, 1978); Thomas M. Cynkin, *Soviet and American Signaling in the Polish Crisis* (London: Macmillan, 1988).

61. See, for example, Oran R. Young, *The Intermediaries: Third Parties in International Crisis* (Princeton: Princeton University Press, 1967); Oran R. Young, *The Politics of Force: Bargaining During International Crises* (Princeton: Princeton University Press, 1968); Mark W. Zacker, *International Conflicts and Collective Security, 1946–77* (New York: Praeger, 1979).

62. Glenn D. Paige, op. cit., p. 10.

63. Glenn D. Paige, op. cit., pp. 276–279.

64. Ole R. Holsti et al., op. cit., pp. 123–158. Ole R. Holsti later discussed the limits of validity of relying on financial data as indicators of international tensions and concluded that such data constitute only a partial and indirect check on the validity of content data from other sources such as diplomatic documents. See the section, "Perceptions of Hostility and Financial Indices in a Crisis," in ch. 3 of *Crisis, Escalation, War* (Montreal: McGill-Queens University Press, 1972), pp. 51–70.

65. Ibid., p. 46. The phenomenon described here is similar to the hostility-friendliness continuum and the unstable reaction coefficients studied by Lewis F. Richardson in his research on the arms races of 1908–1914 and 1929–1939. See *Arms and Insecurity* (Pittsburgh, Pa: Boxwood, 1960), and *Statistics of Deadly Quarrels* (Chicago: Quadrangle Books, 1960), discussed in chapter 8.

66. Ole Holsti et al., op. cit., p. 152.

67. Ibid., p. 157.

68. Ole R. Holsti, Richard A. Brody, and Robert C. North, "Measuring Effect and Action in the International Reaction Models: Empirical Materials from the 1962 Cuban Crisis," *Journal of Peace Research,* I (1964), 174. See also Eliot A. Cohen, "Why We Should Stop Studying the Cuban Missile Crisis," *National Interest,* 2 (1986), 3–13; Richard Ned Lebow, "The Cuban Missile Crisis: Reading the Lessons Correctly," *Political Science Quarterly,* 98 (1983), 431–458.

69. Ibid.

70. Ibid., p. 158. See also Ole R. Holsti, "Time, Alternatives and Communications: The 1914 and Cuban Missile Crises," in Hermann, ed., op. cit., pp. 58–80.

71. Graham T. Allison, op. cit., p. 245.

72. Ibid., pp. 40–56. Albert and Roberta Wohlstetter provided the military argument for the "rectifying the nuclear balance" hypothesis in *Controlling the Risks in Cuba,* Adelphi Papers No. 17 (London: Institute for Strategic Studies, April 1965).

73. Graham T. Allison, op. cit., pp. 58–62.

74. Ibid., pp. 62–66.

75. Ibid., pp. 102–106.

76. Ibid., pp. 106–108.

77. Ibid., pp. 109–113.

78. Ibid., pp. 113–117.

79. Ibid., pp. 117–126.
80. Ibid., pp. 187–210.
81. Ibid., p. 210.
82. Ibid., p. 228.
83. See ibid., pp. 220–330, 248–249.
84. Ibid., p. 249.
85. James A. Robinson, "An Appraisal of Concepts and Theories," in Charles F. Hermann, ed., op. cit., p. 27.
86. In addition to the book by Graham T. Allison on the Cuban Missile Crisis, other important contributions to the subject include Charles F. Hermann, ed., op. cit.; Ole R. Holsti, *Crisis, Escalation, War;* and the March 1977 issue of *International Studies Quarterly.* See also Thomas J. Price, "Constraints on Foreign Policy Decision-Making, ibid., 22 (September 1978), 357–376; and Michael Brecher, "State Behavior in International Crisis," *Journal of Conflict Resolution,* 23 (September 1979), 446–480.
87. Michael P. Sullivan, *International Relations: Theories and Evidence* (Englewood Cliffs, N.J.: Prentice-Hall, 1976), p. 82.
88. Charles A. McClelland, "Crisis and Threat in the International Setting: Some Relational Concepts," unpublished memo cited in Michael Brecher, "Toward a Theory of International Crisis Behavior," *International Studies Quarterly,* 21 (March 1977), 39–40.
89. Charles F. Hermann, "International Crisis as a Situational Variable," in James N. Rosenau, ed., op. cit., p. 414.
90. Gilbert R. Winham, ed., *New Issues in International Crisis Management* (Boulder, Colo., and London: Westview Press, 1988), p. 5.
91. Glenn H. Snyder and Paul Diesing, op. cit., p. 7.
92. Ibid., p. 4.
93. Ibid., p. 455. Although crises are dangerous, they are seen to be more functional than dysfunctional.
94. Oran R. Young, *The Intermediaries: Third Parties in International Crises,* p.10.
95. Richard Ned Lebow, *Between Peace and War: The Nature of International Crisis* (Baltimore and London: Johns Hopkins Press, 1981), pp. 9–12.
96. Glenn H. Snyder, "Crisis Bargaining," in Charles F. Hermann, ed., op. cit., p. 217.
97. Ibid.
98. Ibid., pp. 419–445.
99. Ibid., pp. 450–453.
100. Richard Ned Lebow, *Between Peace and War: The Nature of International Crisis* (New York: The Free Press, 1981), p. 275.
101. Michael Brecher, Jonathan Wilkenfeld, and Sheila Moser, *Crises in the Twentieth Century: Handbook of International Crises,* vol. I (Oxford: Pergamon Press, 1988), p. 1.
102. Ibid., vol. 2, 171–201.
103. Ole R. Holsti, *Crisis, Escalation, War,* p. 10. See also the reference in ch. 7 to Thomas C. Wiegele's work on biological factors in crisis decision-making. Ibid., p. 266. See also Wiegele's "The Psychophysiology of Elite Stress in Five International Crises," *International Studies Quarterly,* 22 (December 1978), 467–512.
104. See Kurt Back, "Decisions under Uncertainty," *American Behavioral Scientist,* IV (February 1961), 14–19.

105. See Wilbert S. Ray, "Mild Stress and Problem Solving," *American Journal of Psychology*, LXXVIII (1965), 227–234.
106. Lebow, op. cit., p. 335.
107. Ibid., p. 223.
108. Ibid., p. 225.
109. Herman Kahn, *On Escalation: Metaphors and Scenarios* (New York: Praeger, 1965), p. 38.
110. John T. Lanzetta, "Group Behavior Under Stress," *Human Relations*, VIII (1955); reprinted in J. David Singer, ed., *Human Behavior and International Politics: Contributions from the Social-Psychological Sciences* (Chicago: Rand McNally, 1965), pp. 216–217.
111. Robert L. Hamblin, "Group Integration During a Crisis," *Human Relations*, XI (1958), in J. David Singer, ed., op. cit., pp. 226–228.
112. Dean G. Pruitt, "Definition of the Situation as a Determinant of International Action," in Herbert C. Kelman, ed., *International Behavior: A Social-Psychological Analysis* (New York: Holt, Rinehart and Winston, 1965), p. 395.
113. See ibid., p. 396, where Pruitt refers to the work of M. J. Driver and Charles E. Osgood.
114. Ole R. Holsti, *Crisis, Escalation, War*, p. 13.
115. Ibid., pp. 14–15.
116. Peter Suedfeld and Philip Tetlock, "Integrative Complexity of Communications in International Crises," *Journal of Conflict Resolution*, XXI (March 1977), 169–184.
117. Thomas C. Wiegele, Gordon Hilton, Kent Layne Oots, and Susan S. Kiesell, *Leaders Under Stress: A Psychophysiological Analysis of International Crisis* (Durham, N.C.: Duke University Press, 1985).
118. Ibid., pp. 26–27.
119. Thomas C. Wiegele, "Is A Revolution Brewing in the Social Sciences?" in Thomas C. Wiegele, ed., *Biology and The Social Sciences: An Emerging Revolution* (Boulder, Colo.: Westview Press, 1982), p. 6. See also Thomas C. Wiegele, *Biopolitics: Search for a More Human Political Science* (Boulder, Colo.: Westview Press, 1979); Thomas C. Wiegele, "Behavioral Medicine and Bureaucratic Processes: Research Foci and Issue Areas," in Elliott White and Joseph Losco, *Biology and Bureaucracy: Public Administration and Public Policy from the Perspective of Genetic and Neurobiological Theory* (Lanham, Md.: University Press of America, 1986), pp. 503–525.
120. Irving Janis, *Victims of Groupthink* (Boston: Houghton Mifflin, 1972), pp. 197–198.
121. See R. Barry Farrell, ed., *Political Leadership in Eastern Europe and the Soviet Union* (Chicago: Aldine, 1970); Alvin Z. Rubinstein, Carl Beck, et al., *Comparative Communist Political Leadership* (New York: McKay, 1973); Vernon V. Aspaturian, "Moscow's Options in a Changing World," in Gary K. Bertsch and Thomas W. Ganschow, eds., *Comparative Communism* (San Francisco: Freeman, 1976), pp. 369–393.
122. See David Wilkinson, *Comparative Foreign Relations* (Encino, Calif.: Dickenson, 1969); James N. Rosenau, "Foreign Policy as Adaptive Behavior," *Comparative Politics*, II (April 1970), 365–387; Roy C. Macridis, ed., *Foreign Policy in World Politics*, 7th ed. (Englewood Cliffs, N.J.: Prentice-Hall, 1974); James N. Rosenau et al., *World Politics* (New York: The Free Press, 1975).

Chapter
12

Game Theory, Gaming, Simulation, and Bargaining

GAME THEORY AND THE STUDY OF POLITICAL PHENOMENA

Game theory is based upon an abstract form of reasoning, arising from a combination of mathematics and logic. Nearly all game theorists would agree that the theory with which they deal is addressed to what is "rationally correct" behavior in conflict situations in which the participants are trying to "win," rather than to the way individuals actually do behave in conflict situations. Individuals can and often do conduct themselves irrationally and emotionally in conflict situations, but for the sake of theoretical analysis, games theorists assume rational behavior, simply because they find this assumption more profitable for theory-building than the obverse of it. If we were to assume that all human behavior is fundamentally absurd, neurotic, or psychotic, then there could be no theory, either of games or of any other social phenomena. Games theorists, then, subscribe to some such notion as the following: If people in a certain situation wish to "win,"—that is, to accomplish an objective that the other party seeks to deny them—we can sort out the intellectual processes by which they calculate what kind of action is most likely to be advantageous to them, assuming that they believe their opponents also to be rational calculators like themselves, equally interested in "second-guessing" and trying to outwit the opponent.[1]

A few rudimentary concepts should be considered. Every game is characterized by the following elements: players who presumably are trying to "win" or optimize outcomes; payoffs that may mean various things to different players depending upon their value systems; a set of ground rules appropriate to the game; information conditions that determine the quantity and quality of knowledge each player has of the environment and of the choices made by the other player(s), either immediate or delayed; the total environment in which the game is played, whether fully perceived by the players or not; and the interaction of competing moves, in which each successive choice by a player may prompt the other player(s) to modify subsequent choices.

Zero-Sum Games

The most commonly drawn preliminary distinction in game theory is that between a zero-sum game and a non-zero-sum game, with variations of each. In a zero-sum game between A and B, what A wins, B loses. (Non-zero-sum games are those in which the sum of players' gains need not add up to zero. These will be treated later.) Chess, checkers, two-person poker, or blackjack—all of these are zero-sum games. Each game ends with one player having a score of plus one and the other minus one, and the value of "one" for the game depends upon the "stakes" or the size of the "pot." Examples of real-life situations that contain aspects of zero-sum games would include an electoral race between two candidates for a Congressional seat; most military tactical situations in which the objective that one side seizes is lost to the other, at least temporarily, such as an "air duel" or a battle over a hill; and the rivalry of two men for a woman's hand in marriage. It should be noted that a three-man race for an elective office is not really a zero-sum game unless we break it down into two different contests between the winner and each loser. We might also observe that in a tactical military situation the ground gained by one side equals the ground lost by the other, but there might have been a considerable discrepancy in the cost to each side when measured in casualties. The same notion holds true for the election campaign and for courting a fair lady: There is a single payoff, but the contending parties may spend widely varying sums in the effort to win. Writers on game theory distinguish the *outcome* of a game (win, lose, or draw) from the *payoff* (the value attached by a player to an outcome). The relationship between payoff and motivation is critically important, but it is difficult to establish.[2]

Two-Person Zero-Sum Games

In most of the literature on the subject, games are schematically represented in a "normalized" form in which no details of the game are given, but in which the strategies for each player and the accompanying payoffs are depicted in a matrix. Moreover, the payoff values are often assigned in a purely arbitrary manner, merely to facilitate the illustration of a point. (The student therefore need not worry too much about how the payoff values were arrived at—at least not yet.) Moreover, the strategies may consist of fairly complex plans and yet be designated simply as Strategy 1 or Strategy 2, or Strategy N for each player. Thus, in mathematical theory, both strategies and payoffs are treated abstractly. In the most helpful form of notation, each matrix contains the payoff that each player receives when he or she chooses one of the two strategies that converge at that point. The student may, however, come across a matrix that shows only the payoffs to one player. The following three simplified 2-by-2 matrices, borrowed or adapted from Shubik, will be sufficient to illustrate our discussion of two-person zero-sum games:

MATRIX I   Strategy for Player 2

		A	B
Strategy for	A	+4, −4	−3, +3
Player 1	B	−3, +3	+4, −4

MATRIX II   Strategy for Player 2

		A	B
Strategy for	A	−5, +5	−7, +7
Player 1	B	+8, −8	+1, −1

MATRIX III   Strategy for Player 2

		A	B
Strategy for	A	−20, −20	+5, −5
Player 1	B	−5, +5	−2, −2

Matrix I refers to a game in which there is no saddlepoint. First it will be noticed that in each matrix the sum of the payoffs is zero.[3] But there is no point at which the strategies of the competing players logically converge. If both players opt for the A strategy, No. 1 wins 4 and the other loses 4. If No. 1 plays the B strategy and No. 2 chooses the A strategy, the former loses 3 and the latter gains 3. If students analyze this payoff matrix for a minute, they will see that the best strategy for each player in a long series of runs is a random strategy, determined by the toss of a coin, for this will eventually produce a balancing-out of the wins and losses of 4s and 3s. In other words, the game schematized in Matrix I reduces to a game of chance with which game theory is not directly concerned.

Matrix II refers to a zero-sum game in which there is a saddlepoint. This is the point at which the minimum values in the rows (across) and the maximum values in the columns (up and down) converge at equality, or where the maximum values in the rows and the minimum values in the columns converge. The point of convergence is known as the *minimax value.* It is an axiom of game theory that in a two-person zero-sum game, a rational strategy is based on the minimax principle: Each player should seek to maximize the minimum gain of which he or she can be assured, or to minimize the maximum loss that needs to be sustained. If both parties do this, their strategies may converge at a *saddlepoint* and they will tend to balance wins or losses in the long run. If one observes this principle and the other merely plays hunches, the former should win over a large number of plays. Strategic theorists, military commanders, insurgency leaders, stock market speculators (who play alone, as it were, against all others in the market), labor-management negotiators, employees seeking a raise or a promotion, diplomats bargaining their way to a bilateral treaty, and high school students cajoling their parents over the use of the family car all seem to have an intuitive understanding of this minimax principle, with its upper and lower boundaries. Put most simply: When you hold the right cards, press your advantage as far as possible; when luck turns against you, cut your losses. Strictly speaking, the utility of the minimax strategy can be validated only in an extended series of plays, not in a one-shot game. In certain types of simple games it can be a rather dull, no-fun strategy, but it may be unavoidable under the circumstances of a prolonged context with a series of plays.

Let us suppose, again following Shubik, that Player 1 is a police force in a country torn by guerrilla insurgency and Player 2 is the guerrilla force. The police in this particular game can choose either to go into the jungle in pursuit of the insurgents (Strategy A) or to avoid the jungle and to protect key areas (Strategy B). The choice of open battle or attritional skirmishes is up to the guerrilla force. The police do better out of the jungle than in it, where they stand to lose in both battles and skirmishes (-5 and -7, respectively). The guerrillas' preferred strategy, whether in or out of the jungle, is to skirmish, for in this way they can maximize their gains ($+8$) or hold their losses to a minimum (-1). In the simplified game described, two rational players would tend to converge at the saddlepoint of $+1$, -1; that is, the police would probably choose key areas outside the jungle, whereas the guerrillas would skirmish and eschew open battle, thus holding their losses to -1 instead of -8.[4] This, of course, only describes the tactical encounter between guerrillas and police. For an insight into the strategic outcome of a guerrilla insurgency, something much more complex than a simple 2-by-2 matrix would be required. (In real life, the guerrillas might lose most tactical exchanges and yet win strategically because of psychopolitical factors.)

The minimax strategy is a cautious strategy. Five points are to be remembered in connection with the minimax strategy: (1) It applies only to zero-sum games. (2) It is proof against information leakage. (3) It is useful and normative only against an opponent who is presumed to be playing a rational game. If the adversary is stupid, prone to make blunders, or usually motivated by emotional factors (which might, e.g., incline the person to play his or her "hunches"), then the minimax strategy is not necessarily the optimum one to pursue. (4) The utility of the minimax strategy is validated in a series of plays, not in a one-shot game. (5) It is a rather unexciting, no-fun strategy, but it may be advisable. Shubik offers the following caveat:

> Apart from appreciating the two-person zero-sum game as the definition of a strictly competitive situation, the general political scientist will not gain too much insight from an intense study of this topic. . . . There is also a considerable amount of misinterpretation concerning the role in general game theory of the famous result concerning two-person zero-sum games known as the minimax or saddlepoint theorem. Zero-sum games are of extremely limited interest in the behavioral sciences in general.[5]

Non-Zero-Sum Games

The type of game referred to in Matrix III above leads us partially out of two-person zero-sum games (ZSG) toward the non-zero-sum (NZSG) in that it is not exclusively competitive in the sense that what one gains another must lose. The sum of gains and losses need not add up to zero. NZSGs may involve only two or a larger number of players. There is room in this type of game for elements of both conflict and cooperation; on some plays, both or some parties might win, and at the end of the game both or some parties might be ahead by varying amounts. In a non-zero-sum game there are often several different payoffs, some of which may be very good or very bad, some marginally good or bad. The payoffs depend upon whether the players cooperate with each other, cut each other's throats, or mix their strategies of conflict and cooperation in varying combinations.

What is interesting about Matrix III is the fact that it refers to a game that might be a ZSG under some circumstances and a NZSG under others, depending upon the outcome. Actually, this matrix depicts the possible payoffs in a game of Chicken, similar to that popularized many years ago in a Hollywood film, in which two youths drive toward each other in their fathers' automobiles at 80 miles an hours, each with his left set of wheels on the highway dividing line. If neither one swerves to the right, they will both be killed in the crash—an outcome that is arbitrarily assigned a numerical value of -20 for each. It could just as easily have been -200 or another figure, but in any event this becomes a minus-sum game in which both players lose as heavily as possible. If one stays on the course and the other veers, one gains esteem and the other loses in the eyes of the peer group. The latter is "chicken." This condition is indicated in the two matrices containing a $+5$ and -5. Thus if either driver swerves and the other holds longer to the course, the game turns out to be zero-sum. If both veer to the right simultaneously, each suffers dishonor in the eyes of the peer group, but since the reputation for being "chicken" is shared between them, so that no invidious comparisons can be drawn, each suffers only a -2. We should hasten to point out that the payoff matrix as shown is partly a function of the distorted value system of the youthful peer group, as perceived by the two drivers. Actually, the peer group chiefly craves the excitement of the game, and regrets the tragic outcome later. Certainly the parents and fiancées of the two youths would assign a larger negative valuation to their deaths and a high positive valuation to an outcome in which both have enough sense to veer off course before it is too late.[6] It ought to be made clear that the game of Chicken, played with human life at stake, is a game that is entered into only by irrational players, one or both of whom may become rational enough during the course of the game to save their lives. The analogy between the game of Chicken and the collision course of two nuclear superpowers in a crisis has been drawn many times, but the latter is vastly more complex than the former. There is ample reason to believe that the governmental decision-making structures of the two superpowers are of a higher order of rational caution from that of two adolescents who may have had too much to drink. More will be said about this later.

Two-person non-zero-sum games can be played either "cooperatively" or "noncooperatively." In a "cooperative" game, the players are permitted to communicate with each other directly and to exchange information in advance concerning their intended choices. In a "noncooperative" game, overt communication is not permitted, but the choice of each becomes obvious to the other after the play. There is, however, a slight ambiguity in this terminology. Even if a game is "noncooperative" insofar as the rules prohibit overt or direct communication, it is possible for the players to cooperate tacitly through inferred communication, by which one player interprets the other's intentions from the kinds of choices made in a long series of plays.

The "Prisoner's Dilemma" Game (PDG)

The best-known example of a two-person NZSG is "Prisoner's Dilemma." Two individuals are taken into police custody and accused of a crime. Since they are interrogated separately, neither knows what the other will tell the district attorney. Each is aware that if both remain silent or deny all allegations, the worst they can expect is a sentence of 60 days in the county jail for vagrancy. If one turns state's evidence and the other remains silent, the former will receive a 1-year commuted sentence and the other will be sent to the state penitentiary for 10 years. If both confess, both will receive from 5 to 8 years in prison, with a parole possible at the end of 5. Their optimum strategy is a tacit agreement to remain silent, but in the absence of communication, neither can trust the other. Each makes the following assessment of the situation: If I remain silent, I will get either 60 days or 10 years, depending upon whether my partner confesses. If I confess, I will receive a commuted sentence of either 8 or 5 years, depending upon whether he confesses. In either case I can assure myself of a lighter sentence by confessing. Since he is undoubtedly making the same sort of calculation, the chances are that he will confess, and hence I would be foolish to remain silent and count upon the slim chance that he would do likewise. Thus each, by choosing what seems to be the safer course, contributes to an outcome highly disadvantageous to both—a sentence of 5 years instead of 60 days.[7]

Games theorists have devised several variations of Prisoner's Dilemma, but at this juncture two general points must be reiterated. First, there is an important difference between game theory, which is based on mathematical-logical analysis and which purports to show what kind of strategy a rational player *should* play (when he or she presumes the opponent to be rational), and experimental gaming, which is designed to furnish empirical evidence of how individuals *actually do behave* in game situations. Second, there is an important difference between "one-shot" games and games that are played over a series of runs by the same players who, as a result of experience, acquire insight into the strategic thought processes of each other.

Games (both Prisoner's Dilemma and Chicken) have also been devised to determine whether sex differences influence the choice for cooperative or competitive behavior. The results have been somewhat inconclusive, whether subjects play against programmed opponents (who have been instructed as to their choice) or play against each other (in mixed-sex and same-sex pairs).[8] The results have been less ambiguous for Prisoner's Dilemma than for Chicken. Three PDG experimenters all found that males opposing males tend to be more cooperative than females opposing females.[9] Another concluded that females are more "rational" (i.e., capable of earning more money) in a "one-shot" game, whereas males earn more in a series, when optimal strategy requires a longer time horizon.[10] Conrath, after research on games of Chicken, finds the explanations of sex role behavior in games thus far inadequate. If differences do exist, the "why" is important. "It is not likely that the biological aspect . . . is the determining factor, but rather the social and educational roles which distinguish the sexes."[11]

Prisoner's Dilemma has become a staple item in the literature of games, a full bibliography of which now runs into scores of articles, book chapters, and other studies. *The Journal of Conflict Resolution, The Journal of Social Psychology, The Journal of Personality and Social Psychology,* and other periodicals have consistently carried articles on the subject for many years. One authority on games has noted that "research in bargaining utilizing the Prisoner's Dilemma paradigm has become less concerned with questions of cooperation, competition, and the bargaining process, and more concerned with studying the Prisoner's Dilemma paradigm itself."[12] But Schlenker and Bonoma defend the preoccupation with the paradigm as being "necessary to understand the limits and dimensions of the laboratory world before useful experiments can be conducted."[13]

N-Person Games

This brings us to N-person non-zero-sum games, involving three or more players, all of whom are assumed to be independent decision-making units and to possess some method for evaluating the worth of outcomes.[14] As might be expected, much less is known about these than about two-person games, because the number of permutations or interacting strategies increases at an exponential rate with the number of players. Physicists have never found a mathematical solution to the "three body" problem. Hence it is not surprising that no single theory has yet been developed for N-person games. Probably the most fruitful avenue of inquiry to date has been in the area of coalition formation. (For an examination of literature on alliances and coalitions, see Chapter 10.) When several players are in a game, it becomes quite natural for two or more to form a coalition against the others, in which case the others are induced to do likewise in order to ensure their survival and maximize their gains. Sometimes the rules of the game may encourage the alignment of coalitions before starting to play; sometimes coalitions are formed, either tacitly or overtly, after the game is in progress. If two coalitions emerge, forcing all players to choose one or the other, the game in effect is reduced to a two-person zero-sum game.[15] It is conceivable, however, that at a particular stage of the game there might be three coalitions, one of which would eventually find itself under pressure to coalesce with one of the other two. The crucial question, it would appear, is to work out to the satisfaction of all the allies "a rational division of the spoils."[16]

If coalitions are formed before the start of the game, all the partners should be considered equal and entitled to an equal share of the payoff. What is much more interesting, of course, is a situation in which the payoff is divided according to the contribution each partner makes to the victory of the coalition, and in which the contribution is in some sense a function of "power" and "weakness." Sometimes there may be "founding members" of the coalitions, with others permitted to join later after bargaining for terms that reflect both the power of the coalition leaders and the more desperate straits of the applicants for entry. In addition to the division of the payoff and to the circumstances under which coalitions are formed, other questions worthy of games theorists' attention pertain to the motives that might drive a member of one coalition to defect to another and whether it is possible for a coalition to enforce against its own members any sanction that is stronger and more efficacious than the bond of mutual interest.[17]

INTERNATIONAL RELATIONS AS A "GAME"

One is entitled to ask what all this has to do with international relations or, more narrowly, with international politics. First, it should be made clear that international relations—or the operation of the international system—cannot be fully comprehended merely within the analytical framework of a "game." But the patterns and processes of international relations often manifest certain gamelike characteristics. Since game theory and gaming are closely related to decision-making and bargaining, they are bound to have some relevance to the study of international relations—a field in which we commonly speak of making moves on the diplomatic chessboard, bluffing, upping the ante, using bargaining chips, and trying to second-guess or outwit the opponent. The application of analytical techniques derived from game theory can therefore aid in improving our understanding of the subject, provided that this approach is employed with the balanced intellectual perspective of those who regard it as one among several useful tools.

Virtually all international theorists who perceive some utility in game theory agree that international relations can be best conceptualized as an N-person non-zero-sum game, in which gains by some parties are not necessarily at the expense of other parties. The more advanced industrialized countries need not suffer a loss in their absolute or relative economic position as the national economies of Asia, Latin America, and Africa undergo development. Indeed, economic expansion in less developed countries often leads to an intensification of trade, aid, and investment relations with the wealthier countries of the Western system. Several writers who have pioneered in the effort to apply game theory to the social sciences (e.g., Oskar Morgenstern, Thomas C. Schelling, Martin Shubik, and J. C. Harsanyi) have had economic training or have done extensive research into problems of economic competition. Competition between economic firms can be either a zero-sum or a non-zero-sum game. Economic analysts see the latter as the preferable, more rational alternative because both firms stand to gain, at least in the shorter run, if the mutual wounds of excessive competition can be avoided. Perhaps it is not too much to say that within the American economy the desirable has gradually become, or is becoming, the actual: The rivalry among the largest corporations in a field is looked upon as a non-zero-sum game. "Most social phenomena," writes Martin Shubik, " . . . are best represented by nonconstant sum games. In other words, the fates and fortunes of the parties involved may easily rise or fall together. There is no pure division into total opposition."[18]

International Relations as a Game of Conflict and Cooperation

But whether international politics can be as readily reduced as international economics to a non-zero-sum game will probably be for a long time a subject of debate between political scientists and economists. To be sure, there are some political scientists who do not distinguish sharply between politics on the one hand and economics or psychology on the other. But the authors of this book are convinced that "the political" is not perfectly interchangeable with "the economic" or the "psychological." As we pointed out in a previous chapter, there are important differences between political decisions and decisions made by business firms or by individuals.[19] William D. Coplin has also persuasively argued that there is a considerable difference between the bargaining process in domestic society from the process that goes on in the international setting.[20] Hence, we caution against efforts to make a hasty and uncritical transfer of the NZSG concept to international politics. In our view, international politics can be best understood within the game theoretical framework as involving a complex and fluctuating mixture of tendencies toward zero-sumness and non-zero-sumness.

Joseph Frankel suggests that French relations with Germany, for example, "developed from a zero-sum game in the early postwar period, when the French wished—and hoped to be able—to keep the Germans down, into a variable-sum game within the [European] Communities in which cooperation changed the competitive character of the game and rapidly increased the payoff for both sides."[21] John W. Burton has proposed a method of resolving such conflicts as that between Greeks and Turks over Cyprus by inducing the parties to view the situation as one not with a fixed-sum outcome that requires a compromise "cutting of the cake," but with outcomes from which both sides can gain through functional cooperation that will produce a larger cake.[22] There may be a circularity in the reasoning that prescribes resolving a political conflict of passionate nationalism by transforming it into a process of mutually beneficial economic cooperation. Yet that is what was accomplished in the Franco-German rapprochement and that is what many hope to see accomplished in relations between other countries.

The shift from the ZSG to the NZSG perspective does not, of course, solve all problems of conflict in international relations or in other dimensions of life. Both Prisoner's Dilemma and Chicken games are mixed-motive non-zero-sum games that human beings do not always play according to the strategies prescribed by rationality. In the former, the player is tempted to choose a noncooperative strategy by suspicion that the other player will not cooperate; in the latter, the players must make a last-moment choice between prestige and survival. Glenn H. Snyder has drawn the following contrast:

> The spirit or leading theme of the prisoner's dilemma is that of the frustration of the mutual desire to cooperate. The spirit of a chicken game is that of a contest in which each party is trying to prevail over the other. In both games, perceptions of the other party's intentions are crucial, and the actors face a problem of establishing the credibility of their stated intentions. But in the prisoner's dilemma, establishing credibility means instilling *trust*, whereas in chicken it involves creating *fear*.[23]

Neither game, when applied to international relations, is likely to lead to optimistic conclusions. Anatol Rapoport has applied the Prisoner's Dilemma model to the problem of international disarmament and found that, although ideally both parties might prefer to benefit economically from disarmament, neither one can be sure of the long-range intentions of the other, and thus both pursue the more prudent course of maintaining a costly balance of armaments.[24] Critical confrontations between the nuclear superpowers, such as the Cuban Missile Crisis, have often been likened to the game of Chicken.[25] Schelling distinguishes between a game of Chicken, in which one has been deliberately challenged in a test of nerves, and a game into which two parties have been drawn by the course of events. He admits that in the real international world it is hard to know which kind of crisis one is confronted with.[26] In a dangerous international crisis requiring careful management the rules of procedure are well defined.[27] Those who treat critical confrontations between superpowers as instances of Chicken usually do not want to press the analogy too far. In the Cuban Missile Crisis, Brams observes, "Neither side was eager to take any irreversible steps, such as the teenage driver in a game of Chicken might do by defiantly ripping off his steering wheel in full view of his adversary, thus foreclosing his alternative of swerving."[28]

R. Harrison Wagner has analyzed the balance of power within the framework of games theory, beginning with William Riker's contention that international systems are inherently unstable.

> Several scholars have tried to dispute Riker's conclusion in two major ways. One is to maintain that it rests on the false assumption that the international system has the properties of a zero-sum game. The other is to maintain that it rests on the false assumption that the international system has the properties of a game that is played only once. No one, however, has provided rigorous proof that either of these two changes in Riker's assumptions is necessary or sufficient to lead to a different conclusion.[29]

Wagner examined a simple model of an international system as an N-person noncooperative game, and investigated the stability of systems with two, three, four, and five major actors.

> I found not only that constant-sum systems are stable, but also—contrary to most people's intuition—that stability is actually fostered by conflict of interest among states. I also found that . . . a nonconstant-sum system will have most of the properties of a constant-sum system. Thus, paradoxically, uncertainty about the future, by fostering conflict, promotes stability.
>
> Systems with any number of actors from two through five can be stable but, contrary to some unsupported assertions in the literature, there is a well-defined sense in which the most stable system is one with three actors. Moreover, for any number of actors from two through five, there is at least one distribution of power that leads not only to system stability but also to peace. Some of these peaceful distributions are more stable than others. . . . These more stable distributions are characterized by inequality among states. If one wants to say that power is "balanced" when it is distributed in one of these ways, then one can say that there is no connection whatever between a balance of power and an equal distribution of power.[30]

The anarchical character of the international system invests that system with the essential trait of a multiperson non-zero-sum game—namely, the absence of a central authority capable of defining common goals and regulating the players' choices. Each player-state determines for itself the requirements of survival, vital self-interest, and policies conducive to the enhancement of its own well-being. Sometimes the calculus of national interest demands a promise among player-states—whether two, several, many, or nearly all—to cooperate with a view toward advancing mutual benefits. This fact goes a long way to explain, although not fully, why there are such things as international customary law, treaties, and conventions that prescribe certain types of decent reciprocal behavior and create legally obligating regimes in specific functional areas—communications, transport, maritime law, narcotics control, trade, arms limitation, environmental protection, and so on. State promises, however, cannot be considered absolutely binding in an anarchical system where there is no mechanism to enforce the "rules." The observance of promises and rules is contingent upon each player-state's continuing assessment of the degree to which other actors seem to be observing *their* promises.

There can be no doubt that it is highly desirable in the nuclear age to stress the elements of mutual interest and tacit cooperation in the avoidance of general war, in the hope that these will outweigh the elements of divergent interests and conflict. But the understandable desire to attenuate the dangerous excesses of international ideological conflict has perhaps led some analysts to overlook the fundamental difference between the *ought* and the *is*. The conduct of international politics would probably be more restrained if the political leaders of all the major powers were convinced that international politics is a non-zero-sum game in the nuclear age. However, to assert that it always has been so, and always will be necessarily so, is to propound conclusions that a serious study of history does not substantiate.

It might be more accurate to say that international politics is usually a non-zero-sum game for most "players," because most governments normally tend to observe rational limits in their decision-making processes. But in every age there may be some political-strategic adversaries who view their confrontation with each other as having certain characteristics analogous to those encountered in a two-person zero-sum game. Undoubtedly, much of the zero-sum quality that marks certain bilateral interstate relations in this century is a function of ideological attitudes combined with the dialectics of communications systems and mass politics. In some cases, leaders may feel compelled to pay lip service to the ideological objective of "the annihilation of the enemy" even if they have no serious intention of embarking upon an Armageddon during their tenure of rule. But if individuals and groups in one country speak frequently as if the bilateral relationship is a zero-sum game, their counterpart in the second country will sooner or later do likewise. It will always be important to distinguish the way in which a bilateral conflict is viewed by the governmental policymakers, by various politically conscious social groups, and by individuals. If an ideologically oriented group that perceives the conflict as a zero-sum game should seize control of the government, the conflict may indeed become a zero-sum game.

International Relations: Limitations of Game Theory

Those who would apply the game theoretical framework to the analysis of international politics require a greater precision of language than they have sometimes employed in the past. It is not enough to say merely that we are dealing with a non-zero-sum game. We must carefully define the structure of the game we are discussing: the players, the rules and objectives of the game; the payoffs and the values the players attach to them; the whole context in which the game is played; and the interaction of the various strategies pursued. A specific game might appear to be a zero-sum game in the eyes of the country's leaders but not in the eyes of the whole people. Take, for example, World War II as it was waged between Germany and the Allied Powers. The strategic objective of "unconditional surrender" enunciated by Roosevelt and Churchill certainly made the war look like a zero-sum game to Hitler's Nazi regime because the latter could not possibly accept such terms and still survive politically, even though the German people could survive "unconditional surrender" and endure as a nation, albeit a divided one. In short, when two parties are striving toward mutually exclusive objectives and one succeeds and the other fails, this is a zero-sum game. If the contest ends in a complex compromise that leaves neither party entirely satisfied, but in which both parties are willing to settle for less than their original objectives rather than bear the cost of prolonging the struggle, then this is a non-zero-sum game. Thus the zero-sumness or non-zero-sumness of a subgame in international politics must be defined in terms of the various alternative outcomes and payoffs as these are perceived by the players.

The difference between a ZSG and NZSG does not, contrary to popular opinion, depend on whether the game is conceptualized in such a way that one side must survive while the other perishes. Extreme Communist ideologues might perceive their conflict with "capitalism" in this way, and so might extreme Arab nationalists describe the solution of the problem of "Israeli-occupied Palestine." But zero-sumness pertains to the exclusive winning or losing of a payoff, not necessarily to the players' survival except in a weird game of tic-tac-toe in which the loser forfeits his or her life, or in a game of Russian Roulette, which goes on until one player dies. Fortunately, most zero-sum games are not so absurd, either in the parlor or in the international arena. Take, for example, the conflict between India and Pakistan over Kashmir. Control over this region is the payoff in a zero-sum game; as long as India retains control, Pakistan is deprived of it. But the Pakistanis may continue to hope that someday the situation may be reversed, just as a person who has lost a chess game to the opponent may aspire to win the next round. This raises the interesting question as to when both parties in a specific international conflict recognize that the zero-sum game is over and is not to be replayed. This might require an uncommonly high degree of political rationality. The frequent historic replay of zero-sum games between two states over the control of a disputed territory might eventually arouse political passions to such a point that the stakes are escalated far beyond the original objective of the game, to include the physical integrity of the players.

Kenneth A. Oye has probed the question as to what strategies states can adopt to foster cooperation. He begins by discussing how payoffs affect the prospects for cooperation. He found that the structure of payoffs in a given round of play—the benefits of mutual cooperation relative to mutual defection, and the benefits of unilateral defection compared to unreciprocated cooperation—is fundamental to analyzing international cooperation in both the security and economic fields. He illustrates his analysis with examples drawn from the games of Prisoner's Dilemma, Stag Hunt,[31] and Chicken. He remarks that "these games have attracted a disproportionate share of scholarly attention precisely because cooperation is desirable but not automatic."[32] He warns that conscious cooperation is not always required for parties to advance their mutual interests:

> Where harmony prevails, cooperation is unnecessary to the realization of mutual interests. Where deadlocks exist, . . . conflict is inevitable. . . . When you observe conflict, think Deadlock—the absence of conflict—before puzzling over why a mutual interest was not realized. When you observe cooperation, think Harmony—the absence of gains from defection—before puzzling over how states were able to transcend the temptations of defection.[33]

Payoff structures, then, are of critical significance. Oye agrees with Robert Jervis's finding[34] that the long-term likelihood of cooperation can be increased by willful modification of the payoff structure through unilateral, bilateral, and multilateral strategies. Examples include a government's decisions to procure weapons that are defensive rather than offensive, thereby reducing both the adversary's fear of being attacked and the gains that would accrue to itself by launching an attack; to deploy troops along the vulnerable border of an ally to make defection by either ally more costly and less likely; and to publicize agreements for a similar purpose. In situations resembling single-play Prisoner's Dilemma, Stag Hunt, and Chicken, states may be tempted to defect. States, however, must consider the long "shadow of the future" in which they expect to continue dealing with each other. Every defection for the sake of immediate one-time gain decreases the prospects for cooperation; concern for repeated interactions in the future increases it.[35]

In the final analysis, it is difficult in the extreme—perhaps impossible—for either the human mind or the world's largest computer to grasp the "game" of international politics in its utter complexity. A three-person parlor game in which a very limited number of simple moves and countermoves can be made may be reducible to mathematical analysis. However, the triangular relationship of the United States, the Soviet Union, and the People's Republic of China is comparable not to such a parlor game but to the "three body" problem in Newtonian physics, which, as we noted previously, is still insoluble in a precise mathematical formula.[36] Moreover, it is impossible to conceive of a purely triangular relationship in which the interactions of those three powers are insulated from interactions with Western Europe, Eastern Europe, Japan, and other actors on the world scene. Nevertheless, although recognizing the limitations of game theory, we can still find it a useful means for suggesting hypotheses that may illuminate the study of strategic choices faced by foreign policy decision-makers.[37]

SCHELLING'S BARGAINING THEORY

Thomas C. Schelling of Harvard University, although widely regarded as a leading game theorist, is not primarily concerned with the mathematics of games. Like Morgenstern, he began as an economist and soon began to focus his attention upon bargaining.[38] In Schelling's work we find a combination of the social-psychological and the logical-strategic approaches to the subject of human conflict—conflict viewed not exclusively as the opposition of hostile forces, but rather as a more complex and delicate phenomenon in which antagonism and cooperation often subtly interact in the adversary relationship. His theory seeks to make use of game theory, organization and communication theory, and theory of evidence, choice, and collective decision. This strategic theory, according to Schelling, "takes conflict for granted, but also assumes common interest between the adversaries; it assumes a 'rational' value-maximizing mode of behavior; and it focuses on the fact that each participant's 'best' choice of action depends on what he expects the other to do, and that 'strategic behavior' is concerned with influencing another's choice by working on his expectation of how one's own behavior is related to his."[39]

Schelling, then, is mainly interested in such problems as conducting negotiations, maintaining credible deterrence, making threats and promises, bluffing, double-crossing, waging limited conflict, and formulating formal or tacit arms control policies. His writing reflects a conviction that in most international strategic situations the notion of the zero-sum game is simply irrelevant. In his view, the two superpowers cannot rationally suppose themselves engaged in a zero-sum rivalry that could be played out to the bitter end of a full-scale nuclear exchange. The resultant score of such a game would in all probability be not zero but minus two. (If one asks "minus two what?" the answer is, at the very least, "minus two superpowers.") Schelling therefore does not devote much attention to the rational analysis of this ultimate irrationality. Indeed, his "theory of interdependent decisions," as he prefers to call it, is addressed less to the *application* than to the threat of violence as a means of influencing another party's behavior. Going to war might be the height of folly under certain circumstances, but posing a controlled threat or risk of war might prove to be a strategically shrewd move.[40]

Although Schelling is very much interested in what constitutes rational behavior between parties in a conflict situation, he shies away from the notion that rationality can be neatly measured along a quantitative utility scale. This may be possible in respect to human action in the economic order, in which a precise monetary standard is available. But he deems the concept of utility as applied to international political and strategic decision-making much more ambiguous and fluid, and hence less relevant. Thus, instead of looking for the "minimax solution" to conflict situations, Schelling is more interested in what we might not inaptly call "motivational dialectics." He goes so far as to suggest that even though rationality is a desirable commodity, it is not always and under all circumstances desirable to *appear* rational.

> It is not a universal advantage in situations of conflict to be inalienably and manifestly rational in decision and motivation. . . . It is not true, as illustrated in the example of extortion, that in the face of a threat it is invariably an advantage to be rational, particularly if the fact of being rational or irrational cannot be concealed. It is not invariably an advantage, in the face of a threat, to have a communication system in good order, to have complete information, or to be in full command of one's own actions or of one's own assets. . . . The very notion that it may be a strategic advantage to relinquish certain options deliberately, or even to give up all control over one's future actions and make his responses automatic, seems to be a hard one to swallow.[41]

Schelling focuses particularly upon what is sometimes called the "limited adversary" relationship, or what he himself refers to as "the theory of precarious partnership or . . . incomplete antagonism."[42] This implies a situation in which parties to a conflict, despite their strategic opposition to each other, perceive some minimum mutual interest, even if this amounts to no more than the avoidance of reciprocal annihilation. Even when, for one reason or another, parties cannot carry on direct or overt communication with each other, they can nevertheless tacitly coordinate their moves by fixing upon certain salient points of common interest and converging expectation. He illustrates the possibility of tacit communication by citing several examples from nonhostile relationships in which two parties share an interest in finally arriving at the same meeting place.

If a husband and wife become separated in a department store, each might try to figure out where the other is most likely to go with a view to rendezvous. In another situation, two parachutists drop into the same vicinity at some distance from each other. In order to be rescued, they must get together quickly, but they cannot communicate directly concerning their exact location. Each one knows, however, that the other carries a copy of the same map of the area, showing a central salient feature (such as a bridge) that furnishes a focal point for coordinated behavior. In a third example, a number of people in New Haven, Connecticut, were told that they were to meet someone in New York City on a specified date, but they received no instructions as to the exact place or time. Since they could not communicate with the other party, they had to make an intelligent guess. A majority of those queried chose the information booth in Grand Central Station at high noon on the date given.[43]

It might be objected in reference to this last illustration that people taking the train from New Haven to New York always pass through Grand Central. But this need not vitiate the validity of Schelling's theory. Perhaps it only serves to demonstrate that choices based upon mutual expectation of convergent decisions reflect not merely abstract logic but also concrete historical experience—an input that might help to render prediction more reliable. There is no guarantee, of course, that this method of tacit bargaining will work in any particular two-party situation. Schelling modestly claims no more than that a shrewd selection of those convergence points that seem likely in the mind of one party to be relatively unique and unambiguous is superior to a system of purely random guesses as to a focal point of agreement.

Bargaining parties are not motivated solely by a desire to agree. Divergent interests skew the quest for convergence. But if agreement is finally reached, it means that forces for agreement proved stronger than forces for severance of negotiations. Moreover, although tacit coordination does not at first glance seem applicable to explicit bargaining in which formal communication is normal, nevertheless it is probably present even under explicit bargaining conditions. As examples, Schelling cites the tendency to "split the difference" in price haggling, and the recurring willingness to follow a conspicuous precedent embodied in an earlier compromise. Although the power to communicate alters a bargaining situation, it does not repeal the relevance of convergent expectations and the role of objective coordinating signals. Granted that in bargaining contests one side often manifests either greater power or a stronger determination to press for a unilaterally favorable settlement, still Schelling notes that the outcome can often be predicted "on some basis of some 'obvious' focus for agreement, some strong suggestion contained in the situation itself, without much regard to the merits of the case."[44]

Schelling contends that the limitation of conflict is not only theoretically possible but also historically actual. Recent cases in point include the mutual abstention from using gas weaponry in World War II and the various restrictions imposed upon the conduct of the Korean War with respect to geographical boundaries, the political identification of parties involved, the kinds of weapons employed, and the types of military operations permitted. Tacit agreements, he argues, require terms of reference that can be distinguished qualitatively, not just quantitatively. Thus, Schelling would wish to preserve a clear firebreak between conventional and nuclear weapons on the battlefield, and would not recommend the deployment of such low-yield tactical nuclear weapons in Europe as to provide a continuum that would blur the distinction and render escalation inevitable. In short, the step levels of conflict limitation must be unambiguous so that they can be clearly perceived under the pressures of time and emotional confusion that crisis generates in any decision-making system.[45]

Schelling also suggests that it may be possible to make arrangements prior to the outbreak of conflict that increase the likelihood that limits could be observed once hostilities are under way. This involves keeping channels of communication open, clarifying in advance the authority and authenticity of messages calculated to reduce the pressures for uncontrollable escalation, and identifying parties who might plausibly act as intermediaries. But he concedes that there are certain exigencies in the strategy of threats, bluffs, and deterrents that may render one or both superpowers in the nuclear age reluctant to enter into such contingency plans as might reduce the fear of unrestrained war. In other words, the strategic condition of mutual nuclear deterrence might be gradually undermined by a growing assumption that one or both adversaries would seek desperately to keep war limited once it had been initiated and to terminate it as soon as possible. But the fact that advance preparations by one side are not reciprocated by the other at the time does not necessarily mean that they are useless. Unilateral prior signaling might later prove advantageous if the message is remembered by the adversary after the onset of the crisis.[46]

Perhaps Schelling's principal contribution to this sector of international relations theory is his stress upon the necessity of avoiding extreme formulations. At one extreme of the spectrum he sees the zero-sum game as the limiting case of pure conflict, not as a point of departure for realistic strategic analysis. At the opposite extreme he places the "pure collaboration" game in which there is no divergent interest because the players always win or lose together. Schelling is primarily interested in the situations that lie in between—that is, in those bargaining or "mixed-motive" games that contain elements of both conflict and mutual dependence, of divergence and convergence of interest, of secrecy and revelation—all in what he calls the "spiral of reciprocal expectations,"[47] which is usually a matter more of psychological than of mathematical calculus.

The major objective in bargaining, Schelling constantly reiterates, is for each party to make commitments, threats, and promises credible to the other party, so that the latter cannot conclude that the former is bluffing. If your adversary thinks that you are leaving yourself an avenue of retreat, he or she will take seriously neither your commitment nor your threat. Hence, there may be a strategic advantage in making an overt commitment from which there can be no retreat and in communicating this clearly to the adversary. This can be achieved by staking your reputation on the adherence to the commitment or the execution of the threat, or by making it clear that if the other party commits an act you wish to deter, you will have no flexibility in respect to punishing the party, simply because you have already set up an automatic response that is irreversible. This makes the threat of punishment not merely probable but certain, and the adversary must take this into account before deciding to make a move.[48] It is the rich variety of subtle signaling problems associated with this type of political game that makes Schelling's *The Strategy of Conflict* one of the most interesting and readable works in international relations theory.

SIMULATION IN INTERNATIONAL RELATIONS

Simulation is different from game theory and gaming, although related to them. Whereas game theory seeks the optimum mathematically rational strategy for playing a game (purely as a game, with no reference to the "real world"), simulation theory deals with a "let's pretend" situation. A simulation experiment is a game that has been designed not merely for the sake of "playing the game," but rather for the purpose of demonstrating a valid truth about actual social processes through the unfolding of an artificially constructed yet dynamic model. Thus, simulation techniques are essentially laboratory techniques or nonlaboratory contrivances that permit the study of replicated human behavior. Through the use of these techniques, researchers attempt to learn something significant about a complex phenomenon "out there," which they cannot control, by creating "in here" a more simplified version of a specific phenomenon that they can control and that is in some way analogous or isomorphic. Social scientists have long complained that it is virtually impossible to obtain from the real world certain kinds of data needed to verify their hypotheses. The experimental method of simulation represents an effort to compensate for these data deficiencies.[49]

The Uses and Limitations of Simulation

Many proponents of simulation techniques are convinced that their greatest utility is in teaching. In one rather well-known version, Inter-Nation Simulation, which was developed as an educational device by Harold Guetzkow, participants role-play the key domestic and foreign policy decision-makers of five or six fictitious states. (Fictitious rather than real states are used so that subjects can make their decisions in response to the interactive process of the game, uncomplicated by presuppositions and theories as to how the leaders of actual countries ought to act in various situations.)[50] Players learn about their roles and their country situations by reading background papers. They learn the game both by orienting themselves to its rules and even more by playing it. This, like the great majority of all political games, is characterized by the compression of real time; for example, a few hours of play might be made to represent a month or a year of historical time. National goals may be either given at the outset or defined by the participants as play proceeds. Periodically, each nation is assigned basic resources that can be allocated by the leaders' choices to internal or external purposes. Aside from national goals, action is guided by the presumed desire of the decision-makers to remain in office. They can be replaced if either domestic consumer satisfaction or national security falls below a minimum standard that fluctuates somewhat arbitrarily according to rules that permit differentiating democratic from totalitarian regimes. The game permits both bilateral and multilateral communications—the former through "restricted messages" and the latter through a "world newspaper."[51] Simulation experiments may involve the periodic feeding of game results to a computer for the purpose of speeding up the evaluation of decision-consequences according to a preprogrammed formula, but computerization is not a necessary part of simulation.

SIMULATION AS A TEACHING DEVICE

Advocates of simulation for teaching purposes argue that participation in a game enables a student to become actively involved in an interactive process that emulates selected basic features of international reality. Those educators who evaluate gaming most highly are likely to be those who believe that "doing something" is a superior learning experience to "hearing something." They point out that games stimulate interest and motivation essentially because they are "fun"; they provide an opportunity for students to test their theoretical knowledge gained from reading, lectures, and other sources; they introduce students to the concrete pressures that impinge upon the policymakers, the dilemmas that face them, and the constrictions that limited resources place upon them; they enable students to experience decision-making in a group context; and they furnish a glimpse into a model world that students can grasp more easily than they can the real international system.[52]

Simulation as a heuristic device, however, is not without its critics. It has been pointed out that a substantial proportion of students can be expected to be uninterested or skeptical; that gaming may arouse interest in the fun of the game without producing a serious attitude toward the study of international relations; that students seldom know enough about either the real political world or the roles they are supposed to play to act "even remotely as real-world politicians do in making their institutions and their political machinery work."[53] In other simulation exercises, used within and outside government, scenarios are developed for situations such as international crises. The participants are students or even policymakers, who play the roles of decision-makers in real states such as the United States or the Soviet Union.

GAMING AND THE POLICY SCIENCES

In games designed to serve the policy sciences, an effort is usually made to achieve as much "realism" as possible. Professional policymakers generally derive greater profit by representing officials not of fictitious countries but of actual states engaged in the subtleties and complexities of the international interactive process that professionals understand best. Players might be instructed to play either "predicted strategies" (based upon the way specific governments would be expected to behave from historical experience) or "optimal strategies" (based upon what the individual deems best under the circumstances, regardless of existing domestic and other constraints), or a combination of the two approaches. Frequently the element of "nature" or "fate" is introduced into the game by allowing the control group to provide for such unexpected events as technological breakthroughs, the death of key leaders, and the outbreak of civil turbulence. Occasionally the "scenario" will be used to project the opening of the game sufficiently far into the future to prevent the simulation from being overtaken by daily news developments. Participants have found that by participating in a gaming experiment of a critical international problem they have acquired fresh insights into the complexities of situations, into the unexpected turns that events might take, and into the psychological-moral-intellectual pressures and uncertainties that accompany making foreign policy decisions.[54] It is impossible, however, from the outcome of a "crisis game" to predict the actual outcome of a real-world political encounter, no matter how many times the game is played with similar results.

GAMING AND THEORY-BUILDING

The third principal use of political gaming is in the area of research and theory-building. Here the primary objective is not to provide a worthwhile personal experience via the gaming process either to student or to policymakers, but rather to test social science hypotheses. The utility of simulation as a tool for confirming or disconfirming theoretical propositions about the international system is a matter of considerable controversy within the field of international relations theorists and among the "simulators" themselves. One might admit that from carefully observing the behavior of a group of experienced policymakers in a realistically simulated crisis (e.g., a future Berlin crisis), one might be able to make some interesting inferences concerning the political values, strategic preconceptions, psychological attitudes, and preferred methods of conflict management that would be likely to characterize those particular policymakers if a real crisis were soon to arise in a closely similar form. But this, after all, would be a highly particularized and concretized kind of prediction, more appropriate to diplomatic intelligence than to social science. The social scientist is much more interested in universally applicable generalizations than in those subtle nuances of unique historical situations that compose the special intellectual competence of the country or area expert. Policymakers wish to know as much as possible about "this" particular crisis or policy situation so that they can favorably influence its outcome. Social scientists, on the other hand, are not primarily oriented to "this" situation. Their principal concern is with universal generalizations and probabilities. Of what use can simulation be to them in this more comprehensive quest?

The crucial question is: What is the relation between a game and reality? What can we learn about the real political world from empirically observing the results of political gaming? A game, after all, is only an analogical model, which may or may not be partially parallel to the real world in respect to both elements and interactive processes, depending upon the intelligence that has gone into the construction of the model combined with the maturity and seriousness with which the game is played out. Eugene J. Meehan of Brandeis University lays down the following useful guidelines:

> If a model is used as an aid to explanation, then the interaction of elements in the system is prime; if the model is used for prediction, the outcome of dynamic processes in model and empirical world must be similar. . . . Models are always partial and approximate, as are analogies. It follows that there will be properties of observed reality not duplicated in the model, at least potentially, and it is always possible that models have properties that are not duplicated in the empirical world. Furthermore, models and analogies may be useful in creating some expectations with regard to reality (supposing them to have congruence with reality) but may be quite useless and even misleading in other respects.[55]

THE GAME WORLD AND THE REAL WORLD

The first question to be asked is whether the game is "isomorphic" or congruent with reality. Richard E. Dawson has implicitly recognized the need for traditional political knowledge in simulation experiments when he noted that before researchers can validly model a real political system, they have to know a great deal about the workings of that system.[56] It is not enough that a game be "realistic" in flavor: In its substantive details, a game might bear a superficial resemblance to a real-world political situation and yet be quite unlike reality in the playing—that is, in its basic dynamic processual features.

Richard C. Snyder asks whether participants can ever escape the realization that what they are involved in is only a game and not "the real thing." He then cites evidence to the effect that people can become totally absorbed in the simulation exercise.[57] But the fact remains that total absorption in a game does not necessarily bridge the gap between simulation and reality. We are faced here with such problems as the compression of time and the concomitant pressure of hurried decisions from a sketchy information base; the selection of a small number of nations out of the whole complex international system; the cultural provincialism of nearly all gaming experiments to date—virtually all decision-makers have been Americans; the fact that national decisions are made by a small number of decision-makers, completely abstracted from an institutionalized context; and the realization that the reward-punishment matrix and indeed the whole sociopsychological environment of decision-making in a game are quite different from those in real life.

For guidance in constructing models and evaluating the results of simulated international interaction, students of simulation have turned to the writings of scholars in other fields, both traditional and contemporary, who have theorized about international relations. Similarly, models of international simulation have provided for the observation of the behavior of actor participants in differing environments and in a multiplicity of relationships over time. Although simulation models have necessarily been more parsimonious than the literature of international relationships, students of simulation have attempted to compare simulation models with models explicit or implicit in international relations literature to compare the *results* of simulation runs with empirically derived descriptions of international behavior—for example, in crisis simulations.[58]

GAMING AND SIMULATION: THE DEVELOPMENT OF INTERNATIONAL RELATIONS

To summarize, it can be said that simulation experiments are regarded as potentially useful heuristic devices by many teachers of international relations, provided that suitable facilities are available and the students are properly motivated to learn from them. But games are time-consuming and they require very careful planning and administration. The teacher should not take it for granted that simulation is in all circumstances worthwhile merely because it gets the students "actively involved." Policy-oriented games played by experienced decision-makers can also prove valuable tools for the improved understanding of specific foreign policy problems, insofar as they may cast light upon factors and suggest alternatives that might otherwise be overlooked. But here, too, it must be recognized that the best games take several days or even a few weeks to run, and the time that government officials can devote to such exercises is strictly limited. As for the use of simulation in research and theory-building, some writers are more optimistic than others about the possibility of using political games to validate hypotheses about the real political world. But nearly all the authorities in this area cautiously refrain from asserting that simulation techniques can produce any predictive capability. Most would probably agree that much more needs to be known before simulation can be accepted as a reliable tool for the verification of theory.

NOTES

1. As Anatol Rapoport has asserted quite cogently, a theory is a collection of theorems, and a theorem "is a proposition which is a strict logical consequence of certain definitions and other propositions." "Various Meanings of 'Theory,' "

American Political Science Review, LII (December 1958), 973. He notes that Freudian "depth psychology" is "singularly poor in predictive capacity, either deterministic or statistical" (ibid., p. 982), but he does not suggest that the reason for this perhaps resides in the basic irrationality of the subject matter. If one really assumes the irrationality of behavior, a person must at the same time accept its unpredictability, at least for the time being, until the behavior becomes rationally penetrable. In the social universe, observers can ascribe no greater rationality to their own theoretical explanation of a phenomenon than they are willing to attribute to the "decision-makers" who collectively constitute the action-situation or process they are trying to describe and explain. Rapoport does concede, however, that the special merits of game theory derive from its assumption of "perfectly rational players" (ibid., p. 984). This may, of course, also constitute a major weakness if, in contrast to Freudian psychoanalytic theory, which emphasizes irrationality, game theory runs to the opposite extreme and places excessive stress upon the mathematically rational factors that enter into human decisional behavior. The notion of "second-guessing" may be more psychological than logical-mathematical. Which strategic philosophy do good strategists adopt? Do they play the board, or do they play the opponent? Do they formulate their strategy on the basis of a mathematical computation of available moves, or do they formulate it much as psychological warfare experts would try to size up their adversary? Rapoport, who is a mathematician-psychologist-game theorist at the University of Michigan, concedes that pure game theory is essentially mathematical and hence contains no uncertainties. "Although the drama of games of strategy is strongly linked with the psychological aspects of the conflict, game theory is not concerned with these aspects. Game theory, so to speak, plays the board. It is concerned only with the logical aspects of strategy. It prescribes the same line of play against a master as it does against a beginner." "The Use and Misuse of Game Theory," *Scientific American,* CCVII (December 1962), 110.

2. Martin Shubik, *Games for Society, Business and War: Towards a Theory of Gaming* (New York: Wiley, 1964), pp. 50 and 56.

3. Details of a simple game may help the student to envisage the game. Let us call it Defenders and Attackers. The latter can strike at either of two towns. The Defenders can fully protect only one. If the Defenders select the right town and meet the Attackers, the latter will be destroyed. If Defenders select one town and Attackers select the other, the town is destroyed. Martin Shubik, "The Uses of Game Theory," in James C. Charlesworth, ed., *Contemporary Political Analysis* (New York: The Free Press, 1967), p. 247.

4. Martin Shubik, "Game Theory and the Study of Social Behavior: An Introductory Exposition," in Martin Shubik, ed., *Game Theory and Related Approaches to Social Behavior* (New York, Wiley, 1964), pp. 15–17.

5. Martin Shubik, "The Uses of Game Theory," in Charlesworth, ed., op. cit., p. 248. See also his *Games for Society, Business and War,* pp. 93–97. "Social, political, and economic problems," Shubik notes, "almost always call for a non-zero-sum formulation." Ibid., pp. 97–98.

6. The mathematicization of utilities or value preferences is always a tenuous business. Even in respect to zero-sum games, Thomas C. Schelling notes that the value systems of two individuals are incommensurate. "If two feudal noblemen play a game of cards, one to lose his thumb if he loses and the other to lose his eyesight, the game is 'zero-sum' (as long as neither cares

about the other's gain) and there may be no way of comparing what they risk losing. It is precisely *because* their value systems are incommensurable that, if their interests are strictly opposed, we can arbitrarily represent them by scales of value that make the scores of payoffs add up in every cell to zero." "What is Game Theory?" in Charlesworth, ed., op. cit., p. 216. An approach that contrasts with that of Schelling is presented by Morton A. Kaplan in his discussion of the work of Duncan Luce and Howard Raiffa. In an analysis of some variant games, Kaplan agrees with Luce and Raiffa that in certain games the outcome will be determined by the *psychologies* of the players. "A Note on Game Theory and Bargaining," in Morton A. Kaplan, ed., *New Approaches to International Relations* (New York: St. Martin's Press, 1968), pp. 507–509.

7. Many descriptions of Prisoner's Dilemma can be found. See A. W. Tucker and P. Wolfe, eds., *Contributions to the Theory of Games*, vol. III, *Annals of Mathematic Studies*, No. 30 (Princeton: Princeton University Press, 1957); R. Duncan Luce and Howard Raiffa, *Games and Decisions* (New York: Wiley, 1957), pp. 94ff; Anatol Rapoport and A. M. Chammah, *Prisoner's Dilemma* (Ann Arbor: University of Michigan Press, 1965); and Martin Shubik, "The Uses of Game Theory," in Charlesworth, ed., op. cit., pp. 264–268. The problem of "trust" and "suspicion" between players in mixed-motive games has been dealt with by Morton Deutsch, "Trust and Suspicion," *Journal of Conflict Resolution*, VII (September 1963), 570–579. Two psychologists at Kent State University conducted gaming experiments on a variation of Prisoner's Dilemma in which they separated "temptation" (i.e., the desire to obtain the largest payoff by being the only defector) from "mistrust" (i.e., the fear that the other would like to be the lone defector), and found that "temptation" is a more likely source of noncooperative behavior than is "mistrust." V. Edwin Bixenstine and Hazel Blundell, "Control of Choices Exerted by Structural Factors in Two-Person, Non-Zero-Sum Games," *Journal of Conflict Resolution*, X (December 1966), especially p. 482.

8. Daniel R. Lutzker, "Sex Role, Cooperation and Competition in a Two-Person, Non-Zero-Sum Game," *Journal of Conflict Resolution*, V (December 1961), 366–368. See also Philip S. Gallo, Jr., and Charles G. McClintock, "Cooperative and Competitive Behavior in Mixed-Motive Games," *Journal of Conflict Resolution*," IX (March 1965), 68–78; and J. T. Tedeschi et al., "Start Effect and Response Bias in the Prisoner's Dilemma Game," *Psychonomic Science*, 11 (1968).

9. David W. Conrath, "Sex Role and 'Cooperation' in the Game of Chicken," *Journal of Conflict Resolution*, XVI (September 1972), 433–443. For additional subtle sex-related differences see William B. Lacy, "Assumptions of Human Nature, and Initial Expectations and Behavior as Mediators of Sex Effects in Prisoner's Dilemma Research," *Journal of Conflict Resolution*, 22 (June 1978), 269–281.

10. Conrath, op. cit., p. 434.

11. Ibid., p. 442.

12. C. Nemeth, "A Critical Analysis of Research Utilizing the Prisoner's Dilemma Paradigm for the Study of Bargaining," in Leonard Berkowitz, ed., *Advances in Experimental Social Psychology*, vol. 6 (New York: Academic Press, 1972), p. 204. See also Jeffrey Pincus and V. Edwin Pixenstine, "Cooperation in the Decomposed Prisoner's Dilemma Game: A Question of Revealing or Conceal-

ing Information," *Journal of Conflict Resolution,* XXI (September 1977), 510–530.

13. Barry Schlenker and Thomas Bonoma, "Fun and Games: The Validity of Games for the Study of Conflict." *The Journal of Conflict Resolution,* 22 (March 1978), pp. 14–15. The December 1975 issue of the *Journal of Conflict Resolution* carried seven articles on the subject.

14. Martin Shubik, *Games for Society, Business and War,* p. 32.

15. Anatol Rapoport and C. Orwant, "Experimental Games: A Review," *Behavioral Science,* VII (January 1962), 1–37.

16. Abraham Kaplan, "Mathematics and Social Analysis," *Commentary,* VII (September 1952), 284. The mathematical and psychostrategic intricacies of the three-person game can be appreciated by reading William H. Riker, "Bargaining in a Three-Person Game," *American Political Science Review,* LXI (September 1967), 642–656.

17. For theoretical insights into the formation and dissolution of coalitions, see Chapter 10 and the following works: George F. Liska, *Nations in Alliance: The Limits of Interdependence* (Baltimore, Md.: The Johns Hopkins Press, 1962); William H. Riker, *The Theory of Political Coalitions* (New Haven: Yale University Press, 1962); Julian R. Friedman, Christopher Bladen, and Steven Rosen, *Alliance in International Studies* (Boston: Allyn & Bacon, 1970); Swen Groennings, E. W. Kelley, and Michael Leiserson, eds., *The Study of Coalition Behavior: Theoretical Perspectives and Cases from Four Continents* (New York: Holt, Rinehart and Winston, 1970); and Martin Shubik, *Games for Society, Business and War,* pp. 49–51, 149–151, 170, and 259–260.

18. Martin Shubik, *Games for Society, Business and War,* p. ix.

19. See Chapter 11, p. 468.

20. William D. Coplin, *Introduction to International Politics: A Theoretical Overview* (Chicago: Markham, 1971), pp. 258–269.

21. Joseph Frankel, *Contemporary International Theory and the Behavior of States* (New York: Oxford University Press, 1973), p. 96.

22. John W. Burton, "Resolution of Conflict," *International Studies Quarterly,* 16 (March 1972), 5–30.

23. Glenn H. Snyder, " 'Prisoner's Dilemma' and 'Chicken' Models in International Politics," *International Studies Quarterly,* 15 (March 1971), 84. For an analysis of the qualitative differences between prisoner's dilemma and public good conceptions of international trade (or, put differently, "beggar my neighbor" tariff policies versus policies that benefit the larger international common good), see John A. C. Conybeare, "Public Good, Prisoner's Dilemma and the International Political Economy," *International Studies Quarterly,* 28 (March 1984), pp. 5–22.

24. Anatol Rapoport, *Strategy and Conscience* (New York: Harper & Row, 1964), pp. 48–52.

25. See Steven J. Brams, *Game Theory and Politics* (New York: The Free Press, 1975), pp. 39–47; Thomas C. Schelling, *Arms and Influence* (New Haven: Yale University Press, 1966), pp. 120–123.

26. Ibid., p. 121.

27. Martin Shubik, *Games for Society, Business and War,* p. 37.

28. Steven J. Brams, op. cit., p. 42.

29. R. Harrison Wagner, "The Theory of Games and the Balance of Power," *World Politics,* 38 (October 1986), 547.

30. Ibid., 574–575.

31. Jean-Jacques Rousseau devised the analogy of the Stag Hunt to demonstrate the difficulty of cooperation under international anarchy. If all members of a hunting team work together to trap the stag, all will eat well. But one or more may chase a passing rabbit, with the result that all eat less well, and some perhaps not at all. *The First and Second Discourses* (New York: St. Martin's, 1964), pp. 165–167.

32. Kenneth A. Oye, "Explaining Cooperation Under Anarchy: Hypotheses and Strategies," *World Politics*, XXXVIII (October 1985), 6.

33. Ibid., p. 7.

34. Robert Jervis, "Cooperation Under the Security Dilemma," ibid., 30 (January 1978).

35. Kenneth A. Oye, op. cit., pp. 9–13.

36. Pierre Maillard, "The Effect of China on Soviet-American Relations," in *Soviet-American Relations and World Order: The Two and the Many*, Adelphi Papers, No. 66 (London: Institute for Strategic Studies, 1970).

37. Steven J. Brams, op. cit., p. 50.

38. Thomas C. Schelling, *National Income Behavior: An Introduction to Algebraic Analysis* (New York: McGraw-Hill, 1951), and "An Essay on Bargaining," *American Economic Review*, XLVI (June 1956), 281–306.

39. Thomas C. Schelling, *The Strategy of Conflict* (New York: Oxford University Press, 1963), p. 15.

40. Ibid., p. 15. Schelling notes that "inmates of mental hospitals often seem to cultivate, deliberately or instinctively, value systems that make them less susceptible to disciplinary threats and more capable of exercising coercion themselves." A self-destructive attitude expressed as a threat ("I'll cut a vein in my arm if you don't let me . . . ") can put an "irrational" person in an advantageous position vis-à-vis a "rational" one. Ibid., p. 17.

41. Ibid., pp. 18–19.

42. Ibid., p. 15.

43. For these and analogous examples, see ibid., pp. 53–58.

44. Ibid., p. 68. See also pp. 71–74, where he speaks of the "mutually identifiable resting place," the search for which characterizes both tacit and explicit bargaining. "If one is to make a finite concession that is not to be interpreted as capitulation, he needs an obvious place to stop." Ibid., p. 71.

45. Ibid., pp. 74–77.

46. Ibid., pp. 77–80. For other discussions by Schelling of the problems of limiting conflict, see his "Reciprocal Measures for Arms Stabilization," in Donald G. Brennan, ed., *Arms Control, Disarmament and National Security* (New York: Braziller, 1961); see also Thomas C. Schelling and Morton H. Halperin, *Strategy and Arms Control* (New York: The Twentieth Century Fund, 1961), especially chs. 2 and 8.

47. Thomas C. Schelling, *The Strategy of Conflict*, p. 87.

48. Ibid., pp. 22–46, 119–139. "Hardly anything epitomizes strategic behavior in the mixed motive game so much as the advantage of being able to adopt a mode of behavior that the other party will take for granted." Ibid., p. 160.

49. Richard C. Snyder, "Some Perspectives on the Use of Experimental Techniques in the Study of International Relations," in Harold Guetzkow et al., *Simulation in International Relations: Developments for Research and Teaching* (Englewood Cliffs, N.J.: Prentice-Hall, 1963), pp. 2–5.

50. The notion of relating game decisions to personality factors was given an interesting reverse application in a study designed to investigate the use of an actual historical situation to validate simulation. An effort was made (with somewhat inconclusive results) to select participants for the roles of such figures as Edward Grey, Ràymond Poincaré, the Kaiser, and the Tsar by matching personality characteristics as much as possible. See Charles F. Hermann and Margaret G. Hermann, "An Attempt to Simulate the Outbreak of World War I," *American Political Science Review*, LXI (June 1967), especially pp. 404–405.

51. Harold Guetzkow, "A Use of Simulation in the Study of Inter-Nation Relations," in Guetzkow et al., op. cit., pp. 24–38. This is a reprint of his article that appeared in *Behavioral Science*, V (July 1959). For a description of student games that involved a specific international crisis, see Lincoln P. Bloomfield and Norman J. Padelford, "Three Experiments in Political Gaming," *American Political Science Review*, LIII (December 1959), pp. 1107ff.

52. Chadwick F. Alger, "Use of the Inter-Nation Simulation in Undergraduate Teaching," in Guetzkow et al., op. cit., pp. 152–154.

53. Bernard C. Cohen, "Political Gaming in the Classroom," *Journal of Politics*, XXIV (May 1962), 374. Cohen is quite skeptical in regard to what it is that the students find interesting about the game, as well as their level of political knowledge, their serious desire to emulate real decision-makers, and their willingness even to observe the basic rules of the game, compared with their determination to make sport of their personal acquaintances who are supposed to represent "foreign countries." For evidence that simulation is not superior to the case study as a teaching device, see James A. Robinson et al., "Teaching with Inter-Nation Simulation and Case Studies," *American Political Science Review*, LX (March 1966), 53–65.

54. Herbert Goldhamer and Hans Speier, in Rosenau, ed., *International Politics: Foreign Policy: A Reader in Research and Theory* (New York: Free Press, 1961), pp. 499–502. Richard E. Barringer and Barton Whaley report that "the political-military game is a most intense and vivid experience, seemingly for even the most sophisticated individuals," that the insights gained depend largely upon the knowledge and experience of the participant and that the game suggests *unanticipated* policy alternatives. "The M.I.T. Political-Military Gaming Experience," *Orbis*, IX (Summer 1965), 444–448.

55. Eugene J. Meehan, *Contemporary Political Thought: A Critical Study* (Homewood, Ill.: Dorsey, 1967), pp. 31–32.

56. Richard E. Dawson, "Simulation in the Social Sciences," in Harold Guetzkow, ed., *Simulation in Social Sciences* (Englewood Cliffs, N.J.: Prentice-Hall, 1962), pp. 13ff.

57. Richard C. Snyder, "Some Perspectives on the Use of Experimental Techniques in the Study of International Relations," pp. 12–14.

58. See, for example, William D. Coplin, "Inter-Nation Simulation and Contemporary Theories of International Relations," *American Political Science Review*, IX (September 1966), 562–578; Richard W. Chadwick, "An Empirical Test of Five Assumptions in an Inter-Nation Simulation about National Political Systems," *General Systems*, XII (1967), 177–192; Walter C. Clemens, Jr., "A Propositional Analysis of the International Relations Theory in Temper—A Computer Simulation of Cold War Conflict," in William D. Coplin, ed., *Simulation in the Study of Politics* (Chicago: Markham, 1968), pp. 59–101.

Chapter
13

International Studies: Toward the Third Millennium

E. H. Carr has suggested that "when the human mind begins to exercise itself in some field an initial stage occurs in which the element of wish or purpose is overwhelmingly strong, and the inclination to analyze facts and means weak or nonexistent."[1] Whatever the validity of this statement in the development of other disciplines, it describes the growth of international relations, especially in its formative years between the two world wars.[2] Since the early twentieth century, the study of international relations has passed through three stages, which may be characterized as utopian, realist, and behavioral—or, stated differently, normative, empirical-normative, and behavioral-quantitative.[3] By the end of the 1960s the study of international relations had entered a fourth phase.[4]

In this fourth, or postbehavioral, phase the quest continues for concepts and methodologies from other disciplines, but with less certainty or optimism about the outcome of such efforts than in the preceding phase. Although the emphasis remains on comparative studies at many levels and units of analysis, there has been a renewed interest in efforts to bridge the gap between normative and behavioral-quantitative theories, and between theory and policy. Far from having reached a consensus on a paradigm for the building of theory in the 1990s and beyond, international relations appeared to have become even more fragmented in the 1980s. Rather than having yielded a widely accepted framework for analysis based on methodological consensus, the phases through which international relations had passed have led instead to questioning whether the "new" theories of recent decades are not for the most part simply restatements of old ideas, or "old wine in new bottles."[5]

THE BEHAVIORAL CRITIQUE

That the present critique of the state of international relations theory should contain such fundamental debates about the prospects for theoretical advances is of major consequence, for only a generation ago the hope was widely held in the behavioral phase that paradigmatic and methodological advances might produce major theoretical breakthroughs. If by the 1950s political realism had largely replaced the earlier utopian-normative orientation in the study of international relations and thus the field had moved from its first to its second stage of development, a rising generation of scholars was no more satisfied than its predecessors with prevailing modes of analysis. Then as now, much of the literature of international relations reflected a dissatisfaction with the state of the field that subsequent theoretical efforts have not significantly diminished.[6] It should be recalled that in the behavioral-quantitative stage of the development of international relations, essentially the following critical themes were present:

1. Earlier approaches had only limited utility in the identification and analysis of important problems, because the research tools available to the practitioner of traditional research were considered to be crude. Even when traditionally oriented scholars had identified the most important problems, they had not stated them in such a way as to enhance the prospects for their systematic and scientific investigation.

2. Traditional theory has been based upon models of international systems that differed fundamentally from the contemporary world. Therefore, it provides inadequate concepts for the building of theory addressed to the existing, or the emerging, international system.

3. Because the explanatory and predictive capacity of international relations theories is limited, these theories cannot be utilized with great confidence, by the scholar or the policy-maker, in evaluating the present or predicting the future. Scholars and, to an even greater extent, policy-makers therefore revert to pragmatic solutions for specific and immediate problems.

4. The literature of international relations is replete with untested and implicit assumptions about human behavior and international conduct.

5. Many of the most widely used terms of international relations, such as *balance of power* and *collective security,* as well as *conflict, integration,* and *power,* are employed in virtually incompatible ways by different scholars, and even by the same scholar. Such usage contributes not only to theoretical fuzziness, but also to difficulty in communicating within the discipline.[7]

6. The absence of widely accepted agreement on usage of terminology hinders the development of cumulative literature of international relations. We have noted this problem in several chapters, especially in our discussion of power, decision-making, conflict, and integration. Be-

cause even those behaviorally-quantitatively oriented scholars have often not addressed themselves to similar concepts, theories, paradigms, and hypotheses and more traditionally oriented scholars have assumed the uniqueness of events, the building of a body of generalizations about international phenomena has progressed only haltingly—to some, all too slowly and to others, hardly at all.

7. The availability of quantitative methodologies and conceptual frameworks borrowed or adapted from other disciplines supposedly provides the tools for major breakthroughs in the building of theory. The advent of the computer and advanced technologies of information storage, retrieval, and analysis are said to enhance the prospects for testing theory and allegedly furnish unprecedented opportunities for developing international relations theory. Since the conduct of research in international relations, as in other disciplines, has usually been strongly influenced by younger scholars impatient with the conventional wisdom of their elders, "credibility gaps" and "generation gaps" emerge periodically, as they have since the 1950s. Such a gap, by the late 1970s, was based in part upon a division between those who assigned primacy to empirical-analytic theory and the proponents of normative theory, and between those who attached greater or lesser importance to qualitative or quantitative techniques of research and analysis. At the end of the decade of the 1980s, the gap appeared even more fundamental, for it extended to the discussion of whether paradigmatic agreement itself was possible.

Although the assumptions of traditional writers were sometimes not explicitly stated, the "conventional wisdom" of international relations has contained a series of assumptions that scholars, especially since the 1950s, have questioned and sought to subject to more systematic examination:

1. It was once assumed that nations were sovereign in their domestic affairs and that foreign powers could not exert major internal influence upon them. Clearly, such a model does not fit the contemporary international system and perhaps it never provided an adequate conceptualization, because states, however legally sovereign, have always confronted domestic problems resulting from the impact of events originating outside their frontiers. Since the late 1960s, in fact, a burgeoning literature has emerged whose authors have sought to examine "linkages" between national and international systems, and to study "penetrated" political systems whose domestic policies are influenced by developments beyond their boundaries.[8] In the 1980s, the adequacy of such concepts themselves was questioned in a world said to be characterized by "cascading interdependence."[9]

2. As noted at the beginning of this chapter, the critique of our understanding of the contemporary international system, related in turn to the inadequacy of models or theories inherited from the past, is based largely on alleged changes—structural, procedural, and substantive—especially of the past generation in the international system.[10] The international system of the late twentieth century, for the first time in history, is global

in nature. It is said to include as a central feature latter-day variants of traditional military and security issues, together with new conflict-laden issues, as noted subsequently. But it also contains a broadening range of problems, some of them associated with economics—the politics of economics and the economic dimensions of political relationships—in a North-South context and in relations between industrialized states. Some issues are transnational in nature, as noted later in this chapter and elsewhere in this text.

The international system of the late twentieth century is said to contain a large number of diverse, divergent, and incompatible forces—nationalism-internationalism, cosmopolitanism-parochialism, power-welfare, economic growth-redistribution, interdependence-dependence, integration-disintegration—all of which increase the complexity of the task confronting both the scholar and the policymaker.

3. Decision-making units, it was assumed in models positing the centrality of a national actor decision-making approach, were not subject to major internal strains and conflicts concerning objectives, policies, and the nature of the national interest, and little effort was made to study the decision-making process as such, especially with the use of models such as bureaucratic and incremental decision-making, both of which gained increasing prominence in and beyond the 1970s. Particularly since World War II, however, literature on foreign policy has accorded a prominent position both to the domestic factors that impinge upon foreign relations and, especially since the 1960s, to a variety of decision-making models,[11] including those encompassing bureaucratic factors noted in Chapter 11.

4. The traditional assumption was that only nation-states were the actors of international politics. The rise of international organizations at the global and regional level, the increasing importance of the multinational corporation and other nonstate actors, including—especially since the 1970s—terrorist and revolutionary movements and the expansion of transnational contacts and notions of interdependence, have given a new set of dimensions to international relations, reflected in the literature, as noted in our earlier chapters.

5. Political behavior in an international context, it was assumed, differs fundamentally from political behavior within the national unit. Therefore, studies of international political behavior could be separated from the analysis of political activity within the national unit. The distinction between domestic and international behavior stemmed principally from a model in which decision-making was centralized in the former case and decentralized in the latter instance. Governments within the national units held a monopoly of the coercive capabilities of the units, in contrast to the decentralization of decision-making and coercive capabilities in the international system. Increasingly, scholars have stressed similarities rather than differences between the political process at the national and international levels, although the centralization-decentralization distinctions still appear relevant, in an abstract sense, in delineating international

relations and studies of other political phenomena. Since the 1950s, scholarly interest in the political systems of less developed areas, in which tribal
loyalties often compete with modernizing forces and effective political
power remains decentralized, has contributed to a reassessment of older
notions about the uniqueness of international political processes as contrasted to those at other levels.

Central to the present paradigmatic debate remains the perceived
need to identify nonstate actors and to analyze their respective roles in the
international system of the late twentieth century. Richard W. Mansbach
and John A. Vasquez call for the replacement of the state-centric paradigm by one that is based on issues, with politics being defined as the
"authoritative allocation of values through the resolution of issues; i.e.,
through the acceptance and implementation of a proposal(s) to dispose of
the stakes that compose the issue under contention."[12] It is suggested that
the actors of international politics encompass entities from individuals
operating on their own behalf to large collectivities having common
strategies and goals, and working in collaborative fashion within themselves. Of direct interest is the process by which issues are defined, addressed, and resolved within and among the manifold entities, state and
nonstate, that compose the paradigm of the international system. In this
respect, Mansbach and Vasquez cite and echo the call of John W. Burton
for a new paradigm in which the study of international relations would be
superseded by the study of world society. In Burton's perspective the
concept of world society can best be seen "if we were to map it, without
reference to political boundaries, and indeed without reference to any
physical boundaries."[13] Richard K. Ashley goes so far as to ask, in critique
of the state-centric paradigm, how "are actions coordinated, energies concerted, resistance tamed, and boundaries of conduct imposed such that it
becomes possible and sensible simply to represent a multiplicity of domestic societies, each understood as a coherent identity subordinate to the
gaze of a single interpretative centre, the sovereign state?"[14] In this perspective, such a paradigm is clearly inadequate at a time of vast transnational interaction on the part of a variety of nonstate actors.

International relations research, as has been noted throughout this
book, has been guided by a variety of concepts, theories, models, and
paradigms. One student of the history of science, Thomas S. Kuhn, has
suggested that in the natural sciences, periods of "scientific revolution"
have alternated with eras of "normal science." One set of concepts has
furnished the basis for cumulative knowledge only eventually to be discarded and superseded by yet another paradigm. He defines scientific
revolutions as "noncumulative developmental episodes in which an older
paradigm is replaced in whole or in part by an incompatible new one."[15]
According to Arend Lijphart, international relations has followed such a
pattern of development.[16] The traditional paradigm, based upon conceptions of state sovereignty and international anarchy, was challenged, as
noted previously, even though a large body of theory about international

relations had evolved, dating from antiquity and providing a "basis for a coherent tradition of research."[17] The scientific revolution embodied in the quantitative-behavioral phase was based on a large number of new approaches and methodologies. It was assumed that Kuhn's characterization of paradigmatic change in the natural sciences was similarly applicable in the social sciences. In turn, the paradigm that eventually emerged in the study of international relations would form the basis for broad theoretical advances based on the widespread application of agreed methodologies to important research questions.

In the 1980s and into the present decade, the search for an adequate paradigm continued deeply to divide international relations as a field or discipline. The paradigmatic fragmentation that has occurred in the late twentieth century results in part from a rejection, necessary as it may be, of an international system with the state as its core unit. As long as a state-centric paradigm was dominant, there was broad agreement that the proper focus of international relations was the study of the issues causing, contributing to, or associated with war and peace in a horizontally organized, anarchic system of states, some of which were major powers and others lesser actors. Since the 1970s, as K. J. Holsti and others have pointed out, the state-centric paradigm has faced challenges beyond those resulting from the emergence of nonstate actors and its extension of the system for the first time to a global system. The state-centric paradigm has as its focal point a concern with "peace, war, and order," while one of its principal competitors, dependency theory (discussed in Chapter 6), is preoccupied with issues of "inequality, exploitation, and equality. The empirical connection between war and inequality remains problematic."[18] The present paradigmatic debate brings to the fore disagreement about the priority problems to be addressed, as well as "fundamentally different ideas about the appropriate units of analysis, the important processes, and the kind of context in which actions and processes take place."[19] According to Philippe Braillard, the study of international relations is fragmented to such an extent that it is "characterized by the absence of a paradigm and by the fact that there are several general explanatory models pitted against one another, several conceptions of its object," a situation that is said to be "characteristic of the whole field of investigation covered by the social sciences."[20]

Other critics in the 1980s went so far as to question whether the scientific progression set forth by Thomas Kuhn and widely accepted during the quantitative-behavioral phase accurately describes the process of theory-building in the social sciences contrasted with natural science. In Kuhn's perspective, it has been suggested earlier in this chapter, science advances in such a fashion that one dominant paradigm is replaced by another, with each in turn furnishing a framework for intellectual inquiry, setting a research agenda, and as a result providing a basis for the growth of scientific knowledge and theory. The replacement of one paradigm by another occurs as a result of the inability of the then-existing dominant paradigm to account for important phenomena. However, the evolution of theory, following the rejection of an existing paradigm, depends in Kuhn's frame of reference on the ability of the community of scholars to reach agreement on a new paradigm as the basis for future inquiry. Conceivably, the present period of fragmentation in international relations represents a necessary prelude to the emergence of an eventual paradigmatic consensus upon which the research agenda of the early twenty-first century can be built. From the vantage point of the present, however, it may be equally plausible to suggest that the fragmentation of international relations theory simply mirrors the heterogeneous global system of the late twentieth century, including the growth of a scholarly community that is politically, ideologically, and geographically more diverse and diffuse than in any previous era. In such case, the prospects for the formation of an agreed paradigm upon which scholarly inquiry can be based appear to have receded in the final generation of this century.

For all of the discussion of the inadequacies of the traditional paradigm during the qualitative-behavioral phase, its demise did not give rise to an alternative paradigm that could conceivably have formed the necessary basis for theoretical advances. In fact, according to Yale H. Ferguson and Richard Mansbach: "Although packaged as a paradigm, behavioral scholarship was preoccupied by questions of methodology rather than theory, and its practitioners have had little impact on the ways in which international phenomena are conceived."[21] Behavioralists focused on research methods designed to test hypotheses but without reference to an agreed paradigm upon which cumulative theory in the sense described by Kuhn could have been based. Meanwhile, the quantitative-behavioral revolution coincided with the emergence of an international system containing far more numerous actors and characterized by greater diversity and complexity than at any previous time.

The heterogeneity of the international system of the late twentieth century is reflected not only in the difficulty of developing an adequate paradigm but also in the diverse approaches to the study of international relations. If international relations constitutes an interdiscipline, its scope is global. The rise of new actors in many parts of the world will heighten the globalization of the study of international relations—its transformation from a literature that has been heavily influenced by the scholarship of Western Europe and the United States to a much broader global focus. As a result of such change, the prospect for any one comprehensive, agreed paradigm or unifying theory is likely to diminish rather than to be strengthened in the years ahead. For example, Hayward R. Alker, Jr. and Thomas J. Biersteker suggest the need to encompass such diversity by considering international relations as the "intersection and union of behavioral-scientific, dialectical Marxist and traditional approaches."[22] Partly because of the deeply political divisions of the world, "no single research approach has managed to gain worldwide acceptance in, or impose a globally shared intellectual interpretation on, this century of disorder."[23] Hence they propose that the study of international relations be conceptualized as constituting a dialectical triad among the traditional, the radical/Marxist, and behavioral approach, with each generating its own paradigm-like research programs and evaluating the results according to its own criteria.

We need not agree that the approaches they enumerate will form the dominant forces shaping the future study of international relations to accept the notion of diversity as the likely characterization of international relations theory-building efforts into the next century. However, the globalization of the study of international relations, with a diversity of approach to paradigms, raises the question of the extent to which, even more so in the social sciences than in the physical sciences, objective scholarship can advance on a universal level if commensurate freedom of inquiry does not exist. If scholars are unable to examine critically their own political systems, they are hardly likely to be able to make seminal contributions to international relations theory. Stated differently, "Western" international relations theory has arisen in societies that furnish the necessary basis for academic freedom of inquiry. In any event, given global diversity, such a problem is likely to shape the study of international relations within political units enjoying greater or lesser amounts of freedom of intellectual inquiry.

THE NATURE OF QUANTITATIVE-BEHAVIORAL
RESEARCH AND ITS POSTBEHAVIORAL LEGACY

The basic trends that characterized international relations in its behavioral-quantitative stage may be summarized as follows:

1. the adaptation of theories, propositions, conceptual frameworks, methodologies, and ideas from other disciplines, including in particular sociology, social psychology, management-administrative science, psychology, anthropology, economics, and mathematics;
2. an attempt to relate phenomena from other disciplines to allegedly similar phenomena at the international level, which takes the essentially two mutually reinforcing forms of the examination of international phenomena by (a) the use of conceptual frameworks, theories, and propositions by which similar phenomena in other disciplines have been examined and (b) the comparative analysis of phenomena such as conflict, integration, bargaining, negotiation, and deterrence in international and other contexts and other fields;
3. a focus upon problems of units of analysis, including attempts to distinguish conceptually and methodologically among the individual decision-maker, the state, international subsystems, and the international system itself;

4. an effort to draw clear-cut distinctions between macrotheory, or grand theory, and the so-called middle ranges of theorizing, and a tendency for scholars to focus explicitly upon one or the other levels of theory;

5. a greater effort to become comparative within the study of international relations that has had essentially two dimensions: (a) a comparative analysis of phenomena in a contemporary context and (b) a systematic attempt to compare various aspects of international relations in a historic context and to draw comparisons between contemporary and historic international phenomena;

6. a focus upon problems of data collection, an attempt to exploit more skillfully existing data, to develop new resources, and to build archives or data banks equipped with facilities for the storage and retrieval of materials for scholarly use;

7. an increase in the range of methodologies, but a lack of consensus as to those most appropriate for the study of international phenomena; and

8. a more conscious effort to link research to theory-building, including the development of criteria of relevance for research, and the statement of problems and their investigation in such a fashion as to make it possible for other scholars to replicate, or duplicate, such research and to attempt to develop knowledge that is cumulative.

A major contribution of quantitative research, it has been suggested, has been the production of findings that separate "useful conceptions of international relations from those that are inadequate."[24] These are said to include inventories, albeit preliminary, of the "causes and effects of national power, the political characteristics of the international system, national support of supranationalism and integration, and the dynamics of conflict-cooperation."[25] From this view quantitative research has resulted in the reformulation and testing of propositions from earlier literature.

The problems of scope, methodology, the nature of theory, and the relevance of other disciplines to the study of international relations remain unresolved, even though the postbehavioral phase has been characterized by a recognition of the need for diverse approaches, both qualitative and quantitative, to building international relations theory. Among the criticisms of quantitative-behavioral research is its alleged propensity to study issue areas for which data are either already available or easily generated. The result is to focus on state actors and to neglect other phenomena for which data are not readily obtainable.[26] Critics of certain of the trends outlined above have doubted the extent to which events or other political phenomena can be treated as similar. Moreover, skepticism remains as to whether the most important problems of international relations can be made operational so that meaningful and adequate indicators of a quantitative nature[27] can be developed. The authors of this book conclude that dogmatism about such issues, either "traditional" or "behavioral," does little to enhance the development of international relations. Such dogmatism, as well as the focus upon questions of method and scope, indicates the uncertainty that students of international relations have about the appropriate techniques and focal points for analysis as well as the paradigms themselves. The issue is not whether one methodology or another, one form of theorizing or another, or one analytical focal point or another is appropriate. Far from being mutually exclusive, alternative methodologies and research interests—qualitative and quantitative—are potentially mutually reinforcing.[28] It seems obvious that the only appropriate criterion for judging the alternative approaches is the extent to which they fulfill the specific research task set for them.[29]

MAJOR FOCAL POINTS OF CONTEMPORARY RESEARCH

Several major focal points of research over the past generation are indicative of the interests of scholars in the behavioral-quantitative and post-behavioral phases of international relations. In other chapters, we have examined systems theory, as well as conflict, integration, and decision-making theories, all of which have drawn upon other disciplines in their conceptualization and in methodologies.[30] Especially in the 1960s, general systems theory, for example, had a major impact upon theorizing efforts of a macrolevel as well as the middle-range theories of decision-making, conflict, and integration, although by the late 1970s, as noted in Chapter 4, there was considerable skepticism about the future utility of systems theory for international studies, even though an alternative macrolevel theoretical framework had not replaced it.

Writings in conflict and integration illustrate the growth of both a comparative and quantitative focus based upon systems theory. The literature of the 1960s and the succeeding generation manifested an interest in comparing such phenomena in an international context with supposedly similar phenomena in other settings. Writings in these fields, as well as those using systems theory, indicated the growth of interest in broadening both the data base and the focus of concern not only to comparative materials, but also to points of time in the recent and distant past. Studies employing general systems theory and decision-making theory, in particular, reflect the concern with developing more explicitly defined units of analysis. Central even to global society models and dependency theories—a vital point for theory development since the early 1970s—is the notion of interaction among the entities that are the objects of inquiry. If, according to the proponents of world society models, state-centric behavior does not provide an adequate or appropriate basis for inquiry, then the proper units for study—actors and processes allegedly contributing to hunger, poverty, economic dependence, social stratification, political oppression, and ultimately human conflict—are themselves said to be the crucially important interactive elements.

Theory-building efforts of the past two generations have produced several macrotheories, or grand theories. In political science, Almond's and Easton's formulations of the 1960s illustrate conceptualization at the macrolevel—the political system. In international relations, realist theory and general systems theory represent approximations to macrotheory. Realism has been a theorizing effort at the macrolevel because its proponents generally sought to isolate one variable—namely, power—in order to explain and predict a broad range of international behavior. In addition to its focus on power as a crucially important variable, realism provided frameworks for the analysis both of international politics and of foreign policy or, stated differently, furnished conceptualization both at the level of the international system (macrotheory) and of the national actor. At the level of the international system, realist writers often used a classical balance-of-power framework similar to the balance-of-power model subsequently developed more formally by Morton A. Kaplan and discussed in Chapter 4. The neorealist literature since the late 1970s has emphasized both the enduring importance of power and the impact of systemic structure—what Hedley Bull and Kenneth Waltz, among others, termed an anarchic system—on the latitude available to actors in shaping their policies and actions. In its broadest dimension, the neorealism of the 1980s represented an attempt to come to grips with the paradigmatic and methodological controversies that have swept across the landscape of international relations theory and thereby to derive from the realist tradition a theoretical approach capable of explaining as fully as possible the global system of the late twentieth century and beyond.

Realists in the traditional mode concerned themselves with the elements of national power, and for comparative purposes developed a classificatory scheme for analyzing the respective capabilities of nations, although in the case of at least one preeminent theorist-practitioner, Henry A. Kissinger, an effort was made to relate foreign policy behavior to alternative models of status quo and revolutionary political systems, respectively. Thus, the proponents of realism took account of what J. David Singer has termed the "level of analysis problem" in international relations;[31] they concerned themselves with analysis both at the international systemic level and at the level of individual states and their foreign policies. Indeed, the most extensive elaboration of levels of analysis is to be found in the work of Kenneth Waltz[32] and, in particular, his structural realism discussed in Chapter 3 of this text. Building upon conceptualization delineating various levels of analysis, the proponents of neorealist theory since the late 1970s have sought to delineate propositions about the impact of international systemic structures themselves as an independent variable upon the foreign policy behavior of interacting units.

Many of the theorizing efforts of the past generation and before represent "islands" of theory that may (or may not) be linked one day into a grand theory of international relations although, as we have seen, there is no consensus among theorists about the appropriate paradigm, or the methodologies, for a macrolevel or grand theory of international relations. Such accord, if it eventually comes about, is likely to be the result of a conceptual breakthrough that itself forms the basis for such agreement by pointing the way toward the theoretical integration of existing "islands" of theory and of setting agreed priorities for future research and data analysis. How such linking might take place, whether by enlarging extant "islands" or by creating new "islands" of theory, or by a major advance toward macrotheory within which middle-range theories could be linked, has been an object of debate among social scientists. The emphasis of the 1970s upon the narrow theory-building efforts in the so-called islands of theory produced in turn a concern that the larger dimensions of theory at the macrolevel—the linking of the islands in a grand theory—would be neglected. Whatever the apprehension, it quickly was overshadowed in the 1980s by debates at the broader level about the adequacy of existing paradigms of the global system. Such issues are likely to remain unresolved for some time to come. However fundamental to the development of theory at the macrolevel, the very diversity and complexity of international relations in the late twentieth century both renders such paradigmatic agreement less than likely and simultaneously makes abundantly important the need for theoretical breakthroughs wherever possible at a microlevel. It is possible, if by no means certain, that the development of more adequate theories will result from the efforts of scholars at both the macrolevel and microlevel.

Expectations of major breakthroughs have proven premature. Judged by such a criterion, the results of the theory-building efforts of the behavioral-quantitative phase and subsequently have been slim indeed. The research under way in the present phase shows no assurance of registering more than modest increments in building a cumulative theory of international relations. Perhaps for this reason, a broader conception of the nature of the growth of knowledge and cumulative theory gained adherents in the 1970s, especially among those committed to the scientific study of international relations. According to this conception, the reconceptualization of existing theories—the development of a variety of comparative methodologies and data bases, and the constant quest for knowledge by research at more than one level of analysis—represents in itself a contribution to cumulative theory. As a proponent of this broader conception, Bruce Russett contends that a greater effort should be made to link and expand various "islands" of theory through detailed incremental research on specific problems. At the same time, however, it is doubtful, as Russett suggests, that a "narrow and exclusive application of the cumulative model would produce marginal returns comparable to those to be expected from maintaining, along with it, a more broad-based attack on international relations theory and substance."[33]

THE POSTBEHAVIORAL STUDY OF INTERNATIONAL RELATIONS

The prevailing trends in international relations theory in the "postbehavioral" stage reflect the interests of the large and diverse group of scholars of the late twentieth century, including:

1. not only the continuing effort to delineate the nature and scope of international relations, but also an attempt to establish international relations more firmly as an "autonomous" field of study. Even though problems of scope, definition, and conceptualization remain largely unresolved, such issues have been superseded by a renewed emphasis upon substantive, in contrast to methodological, debates of the preceding phase.
2. the kinds of theorizing appropriate to building theories with greater explanatory and predictive capacity with perhaps by the 1970s a realization that quantitative *and* qualitative analyses were indispensable to the development of theory.
3. the division of labor between "basic" and "applied" research and the question of the "relevance" of international relations research to the crucial international problems of the late twentieth century.
4. efforts to develop more precise linkages among various levels of analysis (or "actors") along the continuum from the microcosmic (the individual person) to the macrocosmic (the international system).
5. a debate of growing proportions and intensity about the appropriate paradigm for the conduct of research as discussed earlier in this chapter.

In summary, the development of a broad range of methodologies, together with the research and substantive interests of the past generation, may have given somewhat greater stature to international relations as a field of study or discipline, although it has not resulted in agreement about an appropriate research agenda or framework on which inquiry could broadly proceed. In any event, given the nature of international relations, the need remained at least as great as it had been to continue to draw upon other, older disciplines that have focused upon problems of central interest to international relations. In particular, they include anthropology, economics, history, political science, psychology, public administration, social psychology, and sociology.[34] International relations is becoming, if it has not already become, a discipline—or an interdiscipline—that incorporates, builds upon, and synthesizes insights from most, if not all, of the social sciences and, where appropriate, from the natural and physical sciences.[35] Such a condition is likely to remain a central characteristic of international relations theory-building efforts in the years leading into the next century.

EMERGING SUBSTANTIVE INTERESTS

Several specific substantive interests are likely to continue to be dominant in the theory-building efforts of international relations for at least the next decade. In light of the raison d'être of international relations from its early years, together with the large number of conflict-laden issues and the availability of weapons of unprecedented lethality to a growing number of state and nonstate actors, the problems of war and peace will not cease to attract principal attention both among scholars and policymakers, although such studies will form a part of a discipline whose global focus encompasses other issues and priorities unprecedented in their number and diversity. In the years ahead, the study of conflict theory will differ from earlier approaches largely by the focal points, techniques, methodologies, conceptual frameworks, and data bases employed in theory-building. Sociology, psychology, and perhaps even psychiatry may afford important insights into the motivations for the terrorism and hijacking so prevalent in the late twentieth century, and thus provide knowledge about social and political behavior with potentially important policy implications. The utilization of findings from psychology about personality theory and the effects of organizational variables upon social and political behavior could conceivably contribute to a greater understanding of several important problems of international relations, including conflict, integration (or community-building), and decision-making. Some of the promising subject areas worthy of further research for theory-building purposes are elaborated upon briefly below.[36]

Conflict

There is a relative dearth of knowledge concerning the relationship between international and intrasocietal aggression, and those studies, especially quantitative in nature, completed since the early 1970s, have failed to yield definitive insights. The causes of conflict are said to lie within each of the levels of analysis—the structure of the international system, the states and the domestic structures, nonstate actors, and the individuals who ultimately form the larger political entities. The questions that remain to be adequately answered are those that have long been of central importance. To what extent, for example, do the causes of conflict lie in the structural, institutional, and other environing circumstances? In what sense, by contrast, is conflict a manifestation of political differences that, once resolved, lead to a diminution in tensions and the end of conflict? Can we study conflict more productively by making it the independent variable or by giving primacy to political differences? Over the past generation, intrasocietal conflict has risen in many states, including, as noted elsewhere in this text, some of those most politically and industrially advanced. The emergence of large numbers of new entities and other groups into the political process, together with the increased availability and lethality of weaponry as a result of advances in technology, will undoubt-edly accelerate and exacerbate conflict at differing levels of intensity. What are the implications of various modes and levels of socioeconomic development for the incidence of tensions, conflict, and violence, as well as for stability or instability, within the units that compose the interna-tional system? This latter question is of long-standing interest to those scholars who have studied conflict, and especially revolution, as noted in Chapter 8. Intrasocietal conflict is relevant to international relations re-search not only because it gives rise to a large number of the nonstate actors in the late twentieth century—groups seeking revolutionary change within existing states and, in some instances, the formation of new political entities—but also because it often leads to interaction by outside intervening powers. Finally, what part do the electronic media play in molding attitudes with respect to issues of international cooperation and conflict, détente, and crisis and in establishing and accelerating interna-tional-domestic linkages, especially in societies such as the United States and those other countries having pluralistic political systems and high levels of technological development?

Such questions have been the object of research in the past decade, although the analysis, in particular, of the implications of television news for shaping public opinion or foreign policy remains in its infancy. But there has been renewed interest of substantial proportions in geopolitical, or geostrategic, analysis and in studies of the relationship among re-sources, population, growth, technology, food, and the environment, as noted in Chapters 2 and 8. Such interest was the result of the major importance attached to energy and other resource issues in the 1970s, as well as the revival of neo-Malthusian analyses of the impact of resource constraints upon population and conflict at that time and subsequently.

Integration

The study of integration—of long-standing concern to students of interna-tional relations, especially since the work of David Mitrany in the period between the two world wars—continues to attract the attention of schol-ars. The creation of international organizations at the global and regional levels in the generation after World War II not only contributed to rising interest in the study of integration, but also provided an important source of data for scholarly investigation. In the 1970s, the growing importance of the multinational corporation, together with an interest among scholars in nonstate actors, added yet another object of study of international relations.[37] The emergence of this entity coincided with the publication of numerous books and article-length studies based in particular on neo-functionalist propositions and analyzing transnational relationships be-tween and among nongovernmental entities in a world hypothesized to be increasingly interdependent, with increasing numbers of relationships across state boundaries between official and nongovernmental units. The conceptualization of interdependence, and its relationship to concepts of integration and of power, attracted the interest of scholars in the 1970s, just as in the 1980s attention came to be focused on the role of hegemonical states in shaping regimes at the international level within which cooperative relationships are developed and sustained. (See Chapters 3 and 10.) More recently, regime analysis has been a focal point of academic attention not as a major contribution to integration theory—which it is not—but instead as a basis for studying and understanding the frameworks, norms, decisional procedures, and processes in such issue areas as diplomacy, defense, economics, and law within which collaborative patterns evolve in response to international needs. The patterned relationships characterized as regimes undoubtedly form the basis for more integrated structures and processes. In this sense, regime analysis focuses on the study of relationships that are the result of mutual need and interest in an international system, leading to higher levels of integration. It also furnishes a basis for analyzing and evaluating the behavior or performance of international organizations and their various institutional frameworks. As a result, it has been suggested, such study "has become more theoretical, more rigorous in a social science sense and has generated a better understanding of the general phenomenon of international cooperation."[38]

Existing theories of political integration owe a considerable intellectual debt to earlier studies of nationalism as well as cybernetics and systems theory. The study of the normative conditions for political community, especially characteristic of international relations in its first stage, gave way to specific case studies and comparative analyses of integration, at both the global and regional levels, although scholars concerned with the development of empirically based theory have usually had a strong interest in, if not philosophical commitment to, the normative implications of integration. The earlier work, especially of Karl Deutsch, on transactions as indicators of integration led to further such efforts, especially in the 1970s. Such studies, discussed in Chapter 10, examined and in some cases refined relationships among transactions such as exchanges of people and trade flows, communication patterns, and memberships and voting behavior in international organizations.

Efforts were made, moreover, to conceptualize more fully the linkage among institutional growth, intergovernmental cooperation, and elite and mass attitudes—that is, to consider integration as a phenomenon having institutional and attitudinal dimensions. A need remains for greater definitional and conceptual clarity in the integration literature. This is a task to which students of international relations have turned in the past generation. The neofunctionalist refinement of propositions with respect to spill-over, for example, is illustrative. The achievement of greater agreement among writers about the nature of integration, its necessary components, and the stages and transformation rules by which it is achieved might contribute to major breakthroughs in knowledge about the building and disintegration of political communities. The need exists to develop a theory, or theories, of integration encompassing interaction between and among official elites (governmental decision-makers), nonofficial elites (important nongovernmental groups and actors), and the mass level. To what extent, if at all, can integration take place, or at least be pressed forward decisively, by nongovernmental elites? At what level, and at what stage in an integrative process, is support at each of these levels indispensable to success? Moreover, a theory of integration adequate to the needs of the future should probably be based upon conceptualization including a process model—how and when does the integrative process lead from a condition of separateness to a condition defined as political community, and what are the stages and relevant indicators that are present during the integrative process?

Subnational Forces

If a major thrust of scholarly literature and thought in international relations theory has been building political units beyond the nation-state, there is evidence that scholars and policymakers have neglected an especially salient phenomenon of the past generation—the emergence of centrifugal forces within the existing national units. Neither developed nations nor developing states have been immune from the rise of linguistic-ethnic nationalism. Even units such as the United Kingdom, France, and the United States, where the literature of political science, in its conventional wisdom, long ago dismissed forces making for separateness in favor of assumptions about the homogeneity of population and in the case of the United States, the "melting pot," have faced disintegrative forces. Other states, including, for example, Canada, Cyprus, Belgium, Nigeria, India, Pakistan, Sri Lanka, and Zaire, have been beset with separatist movements that sometimes have resulted in communal strife and, in some cases, even secession and civil war, which have raised questions about their political future. If the decade following World War II was characterized by a movement toward regional organization as reflected in the literature of international relations, it was followed by a period of dissatisfaction by peoples in many parts of the world with the political units in which they live. The rise to political consciousness of larger numbers of previously quiescent groups in the years ahead is likely to heighten the problems confronting political entities in many parts of the world. Indeed, as noted elsewhere in this chapter, one of the principal forces shaping the global system of the late twentieth century is the quest of large numbers of groups in all parts of the world for greater status, power, and recognition.

Although the causes of this ferment are complex, those who have expressed dissatisfaction with the status quo aspire to such goals in order to (1) gain a greater voice in the decision-making process of existing units, (2) achieve in some cases greater decentralization of power, or (3) replace existing units with wholly new structures. The late twentieth century is an era of opposition to the bigness of units that reflect the impersonal forces of bureaucracy and technology—an era that has spawned literature on technology and society and, in particular, the effects of technology on political, social, and economic structures.[39] We face several conflicting forces, some of which, such as technology, give impetus to larger political units; others contribute to the perpetuation of existing political units; and still others enhance the prospects for the fragmentation of present units. The study of such forces, together with devising political forms that reconcile the need for bigness with the desire of peoples for freedom from centralized controls, is a task that will confront scholars of international relations and policymakers alike over the remaining years of this century and beyond. At the very least, however, an understanding of the nature of integration as a result of more adequate conceptualization as noted above could yield insights into the process by which existing units are fragmented, as well as the necessary conditions for integration.

Comparative International Studies and Decision-Making

The effort to examine linkages between foreign policy and domestic politics, as well as to understand the domestic and international determinants of foreign policy, reflects the growth of interest in comparative international studies. In the 1970s increased emphasis was placed on the comparative study of foreign policy, although such interest was by no means new to international relations. The quest for theoretical frameworks for decision-making and notably the conceptualization and research nearly two generations ago of Richard C. Snyder[40] and his associates, as well as such efforts as those of Wolfram F. Hanrieder and James N. Rosenau,[41] are indicative of such interest. Events data analysis, together with the study of decision-making, especially under crisis conditions, is illustrative of the interest manifested since the early 1970s in the comparative study of foreign policy. As in other areas, such as conflict and integration, numerous propositions about decision-making behavior (see Chapter 11) have been generated and tested with uncertain results. The potential linkage between theory and policy in crisis decision-making studies, especially since the early 1970s, contributed to a growing interest in crisis indicators that could be made available to official policymakers. A capability for the analysis of intelligence and other relevant data with the use of crisis indicators would have obvious implications both for crisis management and decision-making and for the development of more adequate theories of crisis management, escalation, deescalation, communications, and other phenomena related to patterns of interaction within, between, and among decision-making units.

Especially since the late 1960s decision-making research has focused on the development of models, together with the conduct of research designed to test hypotheses. As noted in Chapter 11, decision-making under conditions of crisis has continued to attract attention. Large numbers of hypotheses have been tested, some of them with the use of events data based on the analysis of patterns of interaction between opposing decisional units at the international level during periods of crisis. An effort has been made, moreover, to draw conclusions about crisis behavior and crisis management from the comparative study drawn from the recent and distant past. Undoubtedly, such analysis furnishes a basis for enhancing our knowledge of crisis in its international dimension.

In a collection of essays reporting on research on international crisis conducted in the late 1960s, including decision-making, Charles Herman listed 311 hypotheses. They include the effects of stress, fatigue, and constraints on the time available for the search for alternative courses of action; the nature of the decisional unit and the level of participation of decision-makers; the volume and quality of messages between and within decisional units, perceptions, and expressions of hostility; crisis escalation and bargaining; and the credibility of threats between adversaries.[42] In turn, such work was followed in the subsequent generation by efforts systematically to collect and analyze data about twentieth-century crises widely separated geographically and in time in order to develop a basis for cumulative theory. This work is surveyed in Chapter 11. It represents a contribution, however limited, to a theoretical understanding of crisis behavior.

Theory and Security Studies

Closely related is the need for more adequate conceptualization in the field of security studies. The study of security as a central component of international relations theory is itself interdisciplinary, for it encompasses the historic, economic, cultural, and psychological dimensions, together with the military and political components.[43] The study of military strategy and the development of theories of security have concerned both the scholarly community and the military to an unprecedented level since World War II, although the causes of conflict, the role of power, and the conditions under which alliances are formed and dissolved have long been the focal point of much of international relations theorizing.

It was the development of nuclear weapons, together with the emergence of the United States as a world power in the aftermath of World War II, that to an unprecedented extent attracted scholars to the study of security. The result was seminal theoretical analyses whose purpose was to create a strategic framework within which nuclear weapons could be integrated into the other means of statecraft and national security policy. This work produced an abundant literature on the nature of, and conditions for, the deterrence of war between the possessors of nuclear weapons. Its focus, as noted elsewhere in this text, was escalation, force survivability, first-strike retaliation, risk-taking, and assured destruction as a basis for preventing the outbreak of atomic warfare. Yet, existing theories remain inadequate in several respects. First, the deterrence theory of the nuclear age has been based for the most part upon strategic-nuclear bipolarity. To what extent, it should be asked, in a world in which the economic and military instruments of power are spreading, is such theory relevant to a world of several nuclear powers? Stated in practical and specific terms, what are the conditions, including the force levels, necessary for the deterrence of more than one potential adversary? Alternatively, it has been hypothesized that nuclear multipolarity reduces the risks of nuclear confrontation by making it impossible for any single nuclear power to destroy the retaliatory capability of all or perhaps even several other nuclear powers. Among the questions that should be addressed is whether and to what extent, if at all, nuclear multipolarity will enhance the prospects for stable deterrence,[44] or whether and under what circumstances nuclear proliferation, ipso facto, is undesirable, as is generally assumed.

A second problem inherent in deterrence theory is ambiguity in the meaning of rationality—the assumption of a calculus between potential risk and potential gain. American strategic theory has contained such a calculus derived largely from a projection to adversaries of what for the United States would constitute "unacceptable damage" in a nuclear exchange. Are calculations made in America, or in any other state in fact, accurate in a world in which peoples have widely differing value systems, cultures, conceptions of national security, and international objectives? Do such calculations as the bases for rationality err in merely "mirror-imaging" Soviet values and goals from American values and goals, and do they thus represent little more than an exercise based upon ethnocentrism? Closely related are basic differences between states, notably the superpowers, as suggested in Chapter 9, in strategic-military doctrines and conceptions of the adequacy of force levels for attaining their respective objectives.

Until the 1980s, the focal point of nuclear deterrence was offense dominance—the ability of a state to inflict unacceptable levels of devastation on its adversary as a basis for deterring the use of force by either side under conditions in which both would be destroyed. President Reagan's March 23, 1983, address, which posed the question of whether nuclear weapons could be made "impotent and obsolete" by the creation of the means of strategic defense, has formed the basis not only for research on such technologies, but also for the development of a deterrence paradigm based on defense. To the extent that technologies for strategic defense emerge in the years ahead, as in the decades of deterrence based on offense dominance, there is likely to be a burgeoning literature designed to build and analyze a paradigm based, to use President Reagan's phrase, upon the means to save rather than to avenge lives. The creation of defensively based theoretical constructs would in themselves represent an important contribution to strategic theory.

Among the other focal points of security studies that, in the 1980s, attracted interest that can be expected to endure is the ethical basis for conflict, spurred of course by the dilemmas of nuclear deterrence. Such inquiry built upon the "just war" tradition. Its purpose was to effect a reconciliation, if possible, between the requirements for deterrence and the ethics of Western societies under conditions of unprecedented weapons destructiveness. The result was an effort to make explicit the assumptions on which alternative schools of deterrence were based and to assess the means-ends relationships—or what could be termed the "ethic of intention" and the "ethic of consequence" inherent in the threat to use nuclear weapons contrasted to their actual use. The growth in lethality of nuclear weapons, as well as the other means of destruction, together with whatever potential emerges for defensively based deterrence in the years ahead, can be expected to give increased importance to the study of ethical issues associated with deterrence and security.

The sharp contrasts between United States and Soviet strategic-military thought, noted in Chapter 9, point up the need for comparative strategic-military analysis. As Fritz Ermarth has suggested, "Systematic comparative studies of strategic doctrine could serve to clarify what we think and how we ourselves differ on these matters, as well as to organize what we know about Soviet strategic thinking."[45] Comparative research, focused not only on the superpowers but also on other states, might yield insights into such issues as the purposes of strategy and its relationship to force levels, political goals, and the nonmilitary dimensions of security; the decision-making process with respect to strategic-military capabilities and other elements of statecraft; the propensity of states to invoke various forms of military power to achieve political objectives; and the historic, doctrinal, and psychological factors that shape the propensities of diverse groups to resort to violence, or to threaten to do so on behalf of their respective interests.

To a large extent, the academic study of security, as reflected in its literature, has been an American preoccupation. The danger inherent in such a condition, as Colin Gray has suggested, is that "the United States is only one culture, and for a field of inquiry as critical to the human future as strategic studies to be rooted in so narrow and unique a set of predispositions can only impoverish its capacity to accommodate the true diversity of strategic styles that exists worldwide."[46] To the extent that the armed conflicts of the future have their locus in the Third World and encompass as direct participants a host of actors other than the United States or other Western nations, the need will be apparent for an understanding of diverse cultures, historic factors, differing value systems, and geostrategic relationships. In short, security studies can be separated from area and country studies only at grave peril, because the strategic culture within which conflict unfolds represents a necessary point of departure for understanding the causes of war, the conditions for deterrence, the ways in which force will be used, and the basis for conflict resolution. The growth of interest in the 1980s in the study of low-intensity conflict points up the need for such an understanding of the various states and regions as the setting for such wars.

In recent years the focus of security studies, to a certain extent reflecting the multidimensional nature of conflict in a heterogeneous global international system, has broadened to take greater account of the pervasive impact of technology on strategy and to give increased place to the emergence of new types of conflict and actors. This includes interest in the domestic and psychological variables associated with deterrence; the examination of deterrence in nonnuclear situations; the greater utilization of history to assess its lessons for contemporary and future armed conflict; and the relationship between economic factors, military power, and conflict. Yet, there is a need for continued theory-building efforts focused on the enduring question of the causes of war; the deterrence paradigm with respect to offense- and defense-dominance; the impact of new technologies in deterrence, conflict, and war; the cultural dimensions of conflict; national security decision-making in crisis and noncrisis situations, especially in complex organizational contexts; the nexus, to the extent that it exists, between deterrence stability, offensively or defensively based, and arms control; the impact of domestic politics, especially in pluralistic societies, on national security policy; concepts of security in their military, economic, and political dimensions under conditions of regional and global interdependence; the basis for conventional deterrence if nuclear-based deterrent relationships diminish; and the causes, varieties, strategies, and effects of terrorism. Thus, there is an abundant agenda for security studies both in the building of theory and inevitably the generation of policy options having relevance in a conflict-laden international environment.

Power

Power has always been difficult to conceptualize in international relations, as we have noted especially in Chapter 3. The problems of conceptualization have grown as a result of the advent of nuclear weapons and the emergence of issues, such as resource scarcity, that may afford new forms of power—to withhold or not to withhold scarce resources—from those in need of them. Within the past generation we have seen numerous efforts both to conceptualize and to measure power more precisely as a multifaceted phenomenon and, in the neorealist literature, to refine its meaning and to establish it within a structural context. The concept of power, of course, is inextricably linked to alternative structures of the international system—for example, bipolar and multipolar structures. Polarity as a defining characteristic of the international system connotes a hypothesized distribution of power. Hence, a necessary prerequisite to understanding such international systems lies in the study of power itself. For this reason, the increased emphasis in the last generation on international systems characterized by the diffusion of capabilities to new actors coincided with an effort to understand more fully the nature of power itself. If we may foresee the growth in number of international actors—state and non-state—in and beyond the late twentieth century, together with weapons of unprecedented destructiveness and new conflict issues, it follows that the conceptualization of power in its many dimensions—military, economic, psychological, and ideological—will continue to hold central interest for scholars and policymakers alike.

There has been uncertainty about the political utility of military power in an era when the potential for devastation is unprecedented as a result of the revolutionary changes in weapons technology of the twentieth century. The question of the meaning of disparities between and among states in the conception of power and its political utility arises, especially at the level of strategic-nuclear weapons and the debate over the nature and the meaning of strategic-nuclear superiority. If one state concludes that vast military power is in fact usable either to threaten or actually to coerce an adversary, does that state not gain a considerable, and perhaps even decisive, political-diplomatic advantage over its adversary? More reliable knowledge about the relationship between military force and other national capabilities, the development of strategic doctrine, and the propensity of nations to use specific types of power unilaterally or in collaboration with other nations would represent in itself a significant contribution to international relations theory. This problem, of course, is closely related to the question raised above with respect to the implications of differences in values, culture, and national objectives for a state's propensity to use force, and at what level, to attain its objectives.

Equally notable has been a lack of concern for the analysis of the techniques of statecraft—how power has been actually used to achieve specified objectives. Instead, as numerous commentators have pointed out, emphasis within international relations literature, especially since World War II, has been placed on the study of the policy process—how policy is formulated, instead of the instruments by which policy is made and the actual outputs of the process.[47] To the extent that studies of power have been comparative in scope, according to David Baldwin, their emphasis has been the comparison of actors rather than of techniques. In Baldwin's perspective, the need exists to find answers to such questions as what types of influence are likely to succeed in achieving their stated objectives? What techniques, including violent and nonviolent means, together or in isolation from one another, can be expected to succeed or to fail? For example, under what conditions are economic embargoes likely to be more useful than military invasions? How and to what effect have the regulations of foreign trade and the granting of foreign aid been used as techniques of statecraft? Of fundamental importance in this context is a precise understanding not only of statecraft itself but, in Baldwin's view, of the relationship between the economic instruments and the other elements of power and influence that are available to and are actually employed by nations in pursuit of their national security goals. To judge from work of the 1980s such a focus can be expected to grow in importance in the literature of international relations theory. It not only represents a logical extension of studies of power but, in addition, is integral to work that seeks more fully to link economic elements as necessary components of international politics. Such an integral relationship is symbolized by the older term *political economy* and embodied in contemporary writings, as noted elsewhere in this text, or, for example, regime analysis and hegemony.

Comparative and Cross-National Research

Since the mid-1960s the tendency toward a more comparative focus in international relations research has been manifested in a growth of interest in cross-national analyses at the subnational level.[48] Such problems include ecological change and its implications for the social and political order, urban studies and violence, and the political values of elites. The growth of issue areas of common concern to postindustrial, industrial, or industrializing societies is likely to accelerate the tendency toward the comparative study of problems that until recently have not been considered central to the field of international relations—or what as a result of such interests is now called "international studies"—or a greater interest in transnational studies, the comparative analysis of phenomena other than governmental entities themselves.

As in the past, students of international relations will be faced with both too much and too little data for testing theories. On the one hand, vast amounts of data have always been available to the student of international relations; on the other hand, the development of quantitative research techniques, together with elaborate theoretical frameworks, increases the need for large amounts of new data. Many of the most important kinds of data relevant, for example, to the study of foreign policy decision-making (including health records and psychological profiles of decision-making)[49] are not easily gathered, and, in fact, may never be available to the scholar. Much of decision-making analysis has emphasized international crises, which are, as Thomas C. Wiegele has suggested, "stress-inducing" situations whose effect is to "put pressures upon the foreign policy decision-maker."[50] It follows that, as the author concludes, biological factors such as physical and mental health, fatigue, age, biological rhythms, and the use of various forms of medication should be stressed. Since the 1970s there has been increasing scholarly interest in the development of conceptual models of stress for political analysis.[51] This in turn points up the need for research on the "intersection between psychological variables" and "decision-making variables."

Advanced storage and retrieval systems now make it possible to desensitize data from governmental sources for the use of the scholarly community. The diffusion of computer technology to office and home desk-top use and the acquisition of computer skills on a massive scale can be expected to influence both the study and analysis of international relations in ways that are unprecedented. This includes access to and the instantaneous transmission of data from storage systems, including bibliographic and literature surveys, quantitative materials, and other information. The cumulative effect is already to enhance greatly the human capacity for scholarly research and analysis. Clearly, we are entering an era in which the ability to utilize computers will be vastly enhanced to the extent that complex problems can be solved at the speed of light—two hundred times faster than the conventional computer of the 1980s. The creation of a national archive storage and retrieval system consisting of data from governmental and other sources would contribute greatly to the conduct of research in international relations and other social sciences. It has been estimated that in the Department of State alone, "original" items and distributed copies of "communications" were on the order of 64 million in one year.[52] Such archives, to the extent that they could be based on declassified information that lessened the need for the collection of new data for certain types of projects, would bring an unprecedented range of research problems within the capabilities of the individual scholar. They would be especially useful in the quantitative analysis of foreign policy by means of events data, as discussed especially in Chapter 4, and in the testing of propositions about communications between, and among, decision-making units—for example, in crisis situations considered in Chapter 11. Data sources are already as close to the researcher as the nearest computer, thus conferring unparalleled means for ascertaining rapidly the availability of relevant source materials both in the form of bibliography and actual data. With the passage of time, the diffusion of computerized data acquisition and processing capabilities, and the expansion of computer literacy, our ability to conduct research and present findings in a range of qualitative and quantitative formats will be unprecedented.

A QUALITATIVE-QUANTITATIVE SYNTHESIS?

In light of the expanding research capabilities conferred by unfolding technology, it is not difficult to anticipate greater efforts to develop more refined operational concepts and indicators and, at the same time, to introduce a greater qualitative element into quantitative studies. The quest for a reconciliation between quantitative and qualitative theory-building efforts may have important implications both for teaching and research. One example will suffice. In the post–World War II period, the so-called area program and studies of specific countries, especially the Soviet Union, took hold in political science and international relations programs in American universities at a time of increasing interest in international affairs both in the official and private sectors in the United States. Because of their emphasis on governmental systems as well as on the intellectual and political history, literature, language, and economic problems of specified regions, such programs attracted not only students preparing themselves for academic careers, but also persons in training for governmental and business careers abroad.

The rise of specific country and area studies programs in universities closely followed the growth of interest in a country or an area as the United States became more actively engaged as a global power in the generation after World War II. Hence, those scholars interested in specific countries and regions—almost by definition concerned with the uniqueness of political phenomena—parted intellectual company with the behavioral-quantitatively oriented scholar whose interest was the development of techniques and methods for examining political phenomena, such as conflict and integration—on a comparative basis cutting across older delineations both geographically and academically.[53] The growth in recognition of the need to minimize ethnocentrism in international studies itself furnishes a powerful catalyst for regional, area, and even country-specific studies. The construction of a paradigm for the global study of international relations highlights the immense historic, cultural, religious, ideological, linguistic, and ethnic diversity of a world in which unprecedented numbers of groups demand greater political participation. Such phenomena can be expected to accentuate the need for academic focus on such national entities, nations, and regions if we are better to understand the basis for conflict and integration, war and peace.

Data about problems under examination can sometimes be found only in one region. For example, the study of historical political development, integration at the international level, and the behavior of nations in alliance of necessity must be based largely upon the experience of the North Atlantic area, although there have been numerous examples, as noted in Chapter 10, of efforts to study integration in Third World settings. Moreover, much of the study of integration, especially the neofunctionalist research of the early 1970s discussed in Chapter 10, as well as conceptualization of regional subsystems examined in Chapter 4, focused on the regional level corresponding to traditionally defined areas—for example, Latin America, Africa, and the Middle East, in addition to Europe.

Studies of areas, regions, states, or even smaller entities have potentially valuable qualitative contributions to make to the quantitative study of political phenomena—for example, both in proposing hypotheses and interpreting the findings of persons engaged in bivariate or multivariate analysis. The area specialist or the scholar specializing in any other aspect of international relations, depending on the focal point of research, may be able both to give meaning to the correlations presented by quantitatively oriented students of politics and to provide a qualitative dimension to the quantitative flows of information and transactions contained in literature, such as that related to integration, conflict, or alignment.[54] Area and country specialists can contribute to knowledge of national processes and the uniqueness of certain kinds of phenomena and make us properly wary of sweeping generalizations, just as the theorist can provide an understanding of the broader meaning of seemingly discrete phenomena.

THE QUEST FOR RELEVANCE

As Richard Smoke has suggested, policymakers have little interest per se in how often a particular combination of variables has been present in historic context, unless, of course, that combination is present in a current situation of immediate interest.[55] Therefore, it is by no means accidental that the scholar interested in basic research and theory and the policymaker concerned with the immediate have often had interests seemingly irrelevant to each other. Much of international relations research may seem not only unintelligible, but also irrelevant to the immediate concern of the policymaker, as perhaps indeed it is. Although it is difficult to assess with precision the impact of international relations research upon policymakers, nevertheless the policy community has made extensive use of academic writings. In particular, the development in international relations of a subfield in strategic affairs or national or international security studies, especially deterrence and defense, has furnished a body of literature upon which policymakers have drawn not only insights, but also the theoretical framework and the explicit assumptions upon which United States strategic-nuclear forces have been based. To an unprecedented extent, the development and study of strategy, and more broadly, military affairs, have passed from the professional military to the civilian policy analysts and theorists. Much of the literature of this field of international relations theory is examined in Chapter 9. Gaming exercises designed to sensitize policymakers, including those at the highest level, to the opportunities and constraints confronting them, especially in hypothetical international crises, are widely utilized in the official policy community. Such gaming models both draw upon and contribute to the academic literature in the field of simulation.

The longer-range outcome of basic research, including theory-building and testing, if the proponents of such research have their way, would be to produce a body of knowledge that would explain and perhaps even predict patterns of interaction among political variables. For example, it might eventually be possible to specify with a higher degree of certainty than now exists the conditions essential to political integration within a national or international context, or to state with a greater degree of precision within carefully specified parameters the conditions that give rise to particular forms of international conflict. If the study of international relations theory were to reach this stage of development, we would have achieved an understanding of those international phenomena deemed most important to scholars and we would have developed a body of theories of importance to the policymaker. Although the quest for such an understanding of international phenomena will continue to be pressed, the research conducted thus far holds promise, at best, of only limited success in reaching such a goal.

Among the ultimate benefits of our ability to develop and test theories about, for example, such phenomena as political integration or international conflict would be a series of "if-then" propositions relevant to the needs of scholars and policymakers. For example, a greater knowledge of the essential conditions for integration or conflict would make possible an understanding of alternative outcomes of various policy choices, since certain kinds of policy choices could be expected to produce certain kinds of outcomes. A new linkage between international relations theory and policy formulation would have been forged, unless, of course, an understanding of the implications of alternative policy outcomes permitted policymakers to alter the basic variables upon which the theory was based and thus to invalidate the theory itself. Herein may lie one of the fundamental differences between theory-building in the physical and natural sciences and in the social sciences—the capacity in the latter case for the objects of study—human beings—to effect changes in their behavior as a result of knowledge gained from a particular theory of behavior. In this respect political and social phenomena differ fundamentally from elements in a test tube.

POLICYMAKING AND INTERNATIONAL RELATIONS THEORY

The literature of international relations—traditional and contemporary, qualitative and quantitative—contains assumptions and conclusions which may have relevance to the policymaker. Policy decisions are frequently dictated by the underlying assumptions of the policymaker even though these assumptions may be only implicitly stated, or perhaps not even recognized as such. One objective of the study of international relations, we note parenthetically, should be to sensitize the student to the assumptions, or the propositions, contained in his or her theory of international relations, or in those of decision-makers whose policy choices we must study as scholars or evaluate as citizens. Such an understanding is indispensable to one's own analysis of international relations whether we are policymakers or observers of the political process. As Trevor Taylor has suggested, one of the functions of international relations is the development of explicitly stated assumptions and propositions on which to base research and policy, since all analyses of a problem of international relations or foreign policy rest on hypotheses of some kind.[56] For this reason the need exists to engage in a systematic examination of the assumptions that guide policymakers in the formulation of major policies. The statements of policymakers and the memoirs of statesmen can, and should, be analyzed to understand the assumptions that guide policy choices. An attempt should be made to match, compare, and contrast such assumptions, as well as policies, with assumptions and policies contained in theoretically oriented literature of international relations.

An inventory and matching of major assumptions, theories, and findings about international phenomena from policy statements and the literature of international relations would enhance the relevance of academic research to the needs of the policymaker. Such a matching exercise could provide insights into the theories, explicit or implicit, that guide policymakers, and would contribute to a better understanding of those theories of international relations that have had the greatest impact upon thought in the policy community.

THEORIZING ABOUT THE FUTURE

Although for centuries efforts have been made to set forth conceptions of the future, the need for more systematic forecasts (the development of statements about the future to which is attached a higher or lower probability, as in a weather forecast based on, say, a 30 or 60 percent probability of rain or snow) has grown with an increase in the lead-time for policy planning. The complexity of issues and urgent problems facing policymakers has also increased the need to influence to the extent possible the impact of technology upon the political order and transform technology from the "independent" to the "dependent" variable, if such an analogy to international relations theory is appropriate here. The result has been the emergence of the "futurologist," who seeks to "invent the future" by technological forecasting.[57] If technological forecasting could clarify the choices available to nations by reducing uncertainty about the future, it could contribute to innovative efficiency by making it possible to calculate more accurately the lead-time and the resources needed for alternative policy choices. Forecasts about future patterns of interaction among variables, especially resources, have existed at least since the writings of Thomas Malthus in the late eighteenth century. In the 1970s, as noted in Chapters 1, 2, and 8, there was renewed interest in forecasting, especially the development of a series of neo-Malthusian projections into a future allegedly characterized by population pressure, resource scarcity, and technological change. Whatever else can be said about the world of the early twenty-first century, it will contain burgeoning populations with likely heightened competition for resources and at the same time an unprecedented diffusion of economic and technological capabilities to new actors on a global scale.

The urgency of problems facing political systems—postindustrial, industrial, and less developed—together with the quest for as "relevant" a field of inquiry as possible is likely to give increasing impetus and importance to the development within international relations of a subfield called "futurology." But straight-line projections will be no more adequate in the future than they were in the past. The question of course is which, if any, of the trends that can be discerned in a present context will be operative in a future timeframe. What new forces will intervene to shape the future? If projections based largely upon extrapolating the future from the present are inadequate in themselves, can alternative hypothetical future international systems, or their subsystems, be developed? Such an exercise places a high premium upon creative imagination about the future and upon the generation of hypotheses about variables, and interaction among variables, that may have no place in today's scheme of things. Technologies that cannot be foreseen today may transform the future, just as technologies that were not imaginable a century, or even 50 years ago, have profoundly altered the world of the late twentieth century. Such hypothetical models of international systems have their analogy in deductive theory, as discussed in Chapter 1. The projection of existing trends from the present to the future, in turn, is analogous to inductive theory, considered in the same chapter. Hence, understanding the forces shaping the emerging world lies in the creative intermingling of inductive and deductive approaches to futurology.

This is not to suggest that theories of international relations will achieve a level of predictability even about existing phenomena sufficient to make possible a high degree of specificity of alternative policy choices. To expect such levels of predictability from international relations theory on a broad range of issue areas, given the many variables that must be considered until and unless more parsimonious and reliable theories are developed, would be to anticipate a level of performance that lies even beyond theories in the physical sciences. As Morton Kaplan has suggested:

> Modern theoretical physical science has reared its present lofty edifice by setting itself problems that it has the tools or techniques to solve. When necessary, it has limited ruthlessly the scope of its inquiry. It has not attempted to predict the path a flipped chair will take, the paths of the individual particles of an exploded grenade, or the paths of the individual molecules of gas in a chamber. In the last case, there are laws dealing with the behavior of gases under given conditions of temperature and pressure, but these deal with the aggregate behavior of gases and not the behaviors of individual particles. The physicist does not make predictions with respect to matter in general but only with respect to the aspects of matter that physics deals with; and these, by definition, are the physical aspects of matter.[58]

Nevertheless, theories examined in preceding chapters, to varying degrees, have contained predictive statements that have enhanced, to a greater or lesser extent, our understanding of a period after they were formulated. For example, Mackinder's analysis of the impact of the technology of land mobility upon power relationships in Eurasia, as well as Nicholas Spykman's view of the shape of the post–World War II international system, noted in Chapters 2 and 3, are illustrative of a capacity to make use of certain variables in combination to examine the future with a considerable degree of accuracy. Such variables—implications of geography, resources, and technology for national capabilities—can be utilized in an analysis of the forces shaping the world of the late twentieth century. Perhaps it is less than coincidental that there has been a revival of interest in geopolitical analysis that has coincided with a growth in salience of resource issues and of forecasting the future.

THE ROLE OF NORMATIVE THEORY

In the current stage of its development, international relations has been marked by efforts to establish linkages between normative theory on the one hand and empirical-analytic theory on the other. The question of a value-free study of politics is of long-standing interest to students of politics, although it is a matter of debate among scholars as to whether such an objective is either desirable or attainable. Given the nature of the objects with which international relations deals and the enormously important questions associated with war and peace, normative theory can be expected to remain central to this field. One of the leading proponents of quantitatively based scientific theory of the 1960s, Rudolph Rummel, writing in the mid-1970s, concluded that human behavior cannot be understood by reference to cause-effect processes comparable to those of physical objects. Because man is "teleologically guided by his future goals," Rummel maintains, "the future lies in his hands and not in some causative features of his environment such as distance, power, geography, poverty, deprivation, and underdevelopment."[59] Thus Rummel raised fundamentally important questions for the conduct of scientific research about international behavior. Can the human being be studied scientifically, for example, as one would study the interaction of elements in a test tube? If people are guided in their political behavior by some objective, is there an inherent and logical contradiction in the idea of a value-free study of politics? Does the very selection of the object or topic to be studied represent a value choice on the part of the student or researcher?

By the end of the decade of the 1960s, there was a growing belief that if social scientists and other scholars chose to emphasize empirical-analytic theory to the relative neglect of normative theory, they would have removed themselves from a problem area that historically had been of great concern. They would have opted to ignore the task of defining the meaning of good and evil, the designing of political structures, and the establishment of normative standards for humankind in a future fraught with growing problems and dangers of unprecedented dimensions. The urgent issues created by the impact of technology upon institutions, the changes in the political environment resulting from ideology and technology, and the implications of increasing popular pressures and demands upon existing political structures will continue to lead students of international relations, and politics more generally, toward a greater interest in normative theory. Empirical-analytic theories have not provided adequate answers to the question of the kinds of political institutions, practices, and values appropriate to the world of the future, although from the findings of such studies the student of policy and the policymaker alike may gain vitally important insights.

In almost dialectical reaction against the so-called behavioral revolution of the 1960s, the "new revolution" of postbehavioralism of the 1970s, according to David Easton, contained the following arguments: "(1) it is more important to be relevant to contemporary needs than to be methodologically sophisticated; (2) behavioral science conceals an ideology based upon empirical conservatism; (3) behavioral research, by its focus upon abstraction, loses touch with reality; (4) the political scientist has the obligation to make knowledge available for the general benefit of society."[60] The emphasis in this critique was upon questions of values, goals, or preferences and upon the development of policy choices for immediate problems and the generation of objectives, and norms of behavior, for future international systems. As Rosenau has suggested, in the early 1970s there emerged in international relations studies a "crisis of confidence," together with a loss of faith in the "slow, painstaking methods of science," as scholars sought to make themselves "relevant in ways that but a few years ago we would have found irresponsible and illusory."[61]

That crisis remained unresolved in the 1980s in part because the international system was itself in the midst of change so profound and pervasive that theoretical efforts, it appeared, could not keep pace. Theory itself faced the prospect of diminishing relevance and correspondence to a real world that was in the process of rapid transformation. Nevertheless, in keeping with a renewed emphasis on normative theory, Charles W. Kegley, Jr. has suggested the need for a "neo-idealist conception of world politics" that would assure that "moral ideals can play a constructive role in the creation of a more stable world order."[62] Such a formulation would draw on a synthesis of "the moral idealism of the liberal creed with the sober conservatism of the realist approach." It would derive its validation from empirically verified theories.

By the end of the decade of the 1980s, the paradigmatic uncertainty discussed earlier in this chapter extended to a discussion of the normative basis for theory. According to Ferguson and Mansbach, the history of theory from the ancient world to the present follows the value or normative preferences of the age. The theoretical controversies at any time represent debates about normative commitments and political preferences. In this perspective, schools of thought based on realism and idealism form competing sets of norms more than they represent coherent theories of international relations. In the history of political thought, it is possible to delineate central concepts—notably, anarchy and interdependence—that successively come to the fore attired in different theoretical and linguistic garb. Normative arguments and commitments lie at the core of discussions about which actors, variables, or levels of analysis should be studied. The objects chosen for investigation are said to be derived from value-based interests and concerns on the part of the student and scholar. Research agendas based on the issues of war and peace, conflict and cooperation change as human needs are altered; that is to say, international relations research is contextually specific, just as the raison d'être for the emergence of international relations in the early decades of the twentieth century lay in the quest for an understanding of the means necessary to eliminate war.

To assert, as Ferguson and Mansbach do, that theoretical preoccupations derive from the normative theories of the age "fully as much as do ideas in art and literature" is to suggest yet another limitation to the emergence of an agreed paradigm and, of course, to indicate the inherent inability completely to separate research from values. To be sure, the research preferences of those who work in the physical sciences are shaped by the normative issues of the day, such as environmental pollution or finding a cure for dreaded diseases. However, what is said to distinguish the physical sciences from international relations is the high number of variables likely to be relevant in the latter case. Of even greater importance, moreover, is the fact that, unlike the physical sciences, where we seek purposely to isolate the elements from their environment in, for example, a test tube, the study of international phenomena outside their social context or milieu is self-defeating and counterproductive. That such a separation has often been consciously attempted, especially in quantitative analyses devoid of historical or societal context, further diminishes the value of such research. To quote Ferguson and Mansbach again: "There is a more important set of complexity that becomes apparent in efforts to isolate and study specific variables; such reductionism isolates selected factors from their milieu when it is the milieu itself in which we are interested."[63] In sum, the environing circumstances constitute the normative context that gives meaning to the data that are analyzed. By the same token, in this perspective, from the milieu are derived the normative issues of the age and the theoretical interests are evolved that become the focus of intellectual inquiry in international relations.

Last but not least, in the field of international relations there have always been groups of scholars whose principal interest was the development and analysis of public policy. In the second half of the twentieth century, this preoccupation has been evident in the literature of international relations and security studies. In its utopian and realist phases, moreover, international relations study was strongly focused upon policy. Over the past generation, the efforts of scholars to give the field a more theoretical orientation and to emphasize the methodological basis of inquiry have represented more a supplement to, rather than a replacement of, a concern for policy problems.[64] Indeed, considerable emphasis has been placed on the creation of more rigorous techniques for the analysis of public policy, especially in the form of systems analysis.[65] The goal has been to devise criteria to aid in choosing and evaluating alternative policies or strategies, or mixes of policies or strategies, for the attainment of specified objectives. The effort has been to find "optimal" or preferable solutions among a series of alternatives based upon relative costs and benefits by using such techniques as mathematical models, gaming, and the canvassing of expert opinion. Such cost-benefit studies represented a reaction against policy recommendations based upon unstated assumptions, untested hypotheses, and uncertainty as to the implications of alternative choices and outcomes. The deficiencies of systems analysis in dealing with such irrational forces as charisma and ideology, or the propensity of actors to adopt high-risk or low-risk strategies, and its inadequacies in explicating the value assumptions of analysis all serve to point up the need for additional work toward a policy science field either within international relations or as a separate discipline, or "interdiscipline."[66]

Given the likely increase in pressing political problems, it is necessary to strike an acceptable balance, if possible, between empirical-analytic theory and normative theory, and between basic and applied research. Normative theory can continue to suggest alternative goals and preferences for political institutions and can also provide propositions for testing; empirical-analytic theory can furnish guidance as to the kinds of political behavior that are essential for attaining desired goals.

In summary, just as the study of international relations moved from the extreme preoccupation with the normative theory of the 1920s to the empirical-analytic theory of the 1960s, a more recent generation of scholars has sought to achieve theories of international relations relevant to the manifold problems facing international society, while at the same time attempting to find broadly based explanations and to develop a predictive capacity, but perhaps with a greater realization than in the 1960s of the difficulties inherent in achieving such a goal. There is a continuing pursuit of objectives that have been sought by preceding generations of students of international relations theory, based upon a greater synthesis among those concerns that have been of principal importance in each of the stages through which the field has passed since the early years of this century, and noted in and derived from antecedents dating from the ancient world of Plato and Aristotle to our own day and age. Thus, the search for a theory, or theories, adequate to the needs of an ever-changing international system continues as we move toward the threshold of a new century and into the third millennium.

NOTES

1. E. H. Carr, *The Twenty Years' Crisis, 1919–1939* (New York: Harper & Row [Torchbooks], 1964), p. 4. See also Richard Little, "The Evolution of International Relations as a Social Science," in R. C. Kent and G. P. Nielsson, eds., *The Study and Teaching of International Relations: A Perspective on Mid-Career Education* (New York: Nichols Publishing Co., 1980), pp. 5–7.

2. See Kenneth W. Thompson, *Political Realism and The Crisis of World Politics* (Princeton: Princeton University Press, 1960); William T. R. Fox, *The American Study of International Relations* (Columbia: University of South Carolina Press, 1968), pp. 1–35.
3. This is not to suggest that the concerns of students of international relations during each of these stages have been mutually exclusive. Examples of each can be found at every stage of the development of international relations.
4. For an examination of such trends in political science, see David Easton, "The New Revolution in Political Science," *American Political Science Review,* LXIII, No. 4 (December 1969), 1051–1061. Because the study of international relations has been linked closely to political science, the methodological, conceptual, and substantive trends of political science have been expected to influence the development of international relations.
5. See Yale H. Ferguson and Richard W. Mansbach, *The Elusive Quest: Theory and International Politics* (Columbia: University of South Carolina Press, 1988), pp. 3–9.
6. See Andrew M. Scott, *The Functioning of the International System* (New York: Macmillan, 1967), pp. 2–6.
7. See Inis L. Claude, Jr., *Power and International Relations* (New York: Random House, 1962), pp. 11–39; Ernst B. Haas, "Balance of Power: Prescription or Propaganda," *World Politics,* V, No. 2 (1953), 442–447.
8. See, for example, James N. Rosenau, ed., *Linkage Politics: Essays on the Convergence of National and International Systems* (New York: The Free Press, 1969); "Compatibility, Consensus, and an Emerging Political Science of Adaptation," *American Political Science Review,* LXI, No. 3 (December 1967), 983–988; and Wolfram F. Hanrieder, "Compatibility and Consensus: A Proposal for the Conceptual Linkage of External and Internal Dimensions of Foreign Policy," *American Political Science Review,* LXI, No. 3 (December 1967), 971–982.
9. See James N. Rosenau, "A Pre-Theory Revisited: World Politics in an Era of Cascading Interdependence," *International Studies Quarterly,* 28, No. 2 (1984), 245–305.
10. See Donald J. Puchala and Stuart I. Fagan, "International Politics in the 1970s: The Search for a Perspective," *International Organization,* 28, No. 2 (Spring 1974), 247.
11. See, for example, Gabriel Almond, *The American People and Foreign Policy* (New York: Harcourt Brace Jovanovich, 1950). For a more recent example of such literature, see James N. Rosenau, ed., *Domestic Sources of Foreign Policy* (New York: The Free Press, 1967).
12. Richard W. Mansbach and John A. Vasquez, *In Search of Theory: A New Paradigm for Global Politics* (New York: Columbia University Press, 1981), pp. 68–69.
13. John W. Burton, *World Society* (Cambridge: Cambridge University Press, 1972), p. 42.
14. Richard K. Ashley, "Untying the Sovereign State: A Double Reading of the Anarchy Problematique," *Millennium: Journal of International Studies,* 17, No. 2 (Summer 1988), 229.
15. T. S. Kuhn, *The Structure of Scientific Revolutions* (Chicago: University of Chicago Press, 1970), p. 92.

16. Arend Lijphart, "The Structure of the Theoretical Revolution in International Relations," *International Studies Quarterly,* 18, No. 1 (March 1974), 41–73.

17. Ibid., p. 207.

18. K. J. Holsti, *The Dividing Discipline: Hegemony and Diversity in International Theory* (Boston: Allen & Unwin, 1987), p. 74.

19. Ibid., p. 11. See also M. Banks, "Inter-Paradigm Debate," in M. Light and A. J. R. Groun, eds., *International Relations: A Handbook of Current Theory* (London: Francis Pinter, 1985), pp. 7–26; Mark Hoffman, "Critical Theory and the Inter-Paradigm Debate," *Millennium: Journal of International Studies,* 16, No. 2, (Summer 1987), 231–249; Fred Halliday, "State and Society in International Relations: A Second Agenda," ibid., pp. 215–230; Steve Smith, "Paradigm Dominance in International Relations: The Development of International Relations as Social Science," ibid., pp. 189–206; Ekkehart Krippendorf, "The Dominance of American Approaches in International Relations," ibid., pp. 207–214.

20. Philippe Braillard, "The Social Sciences and the Study of International Relations," *International Social Science Journal,* 36, No. 4 (1984), 631.

21. Ferguson and Mansbach, op. cit., p. 28.

22. Hayward R. Alker, Jr. and Thomas J. Biersteker, "The Dialectics of World Order: Notes for a Future Archeologist of International Savoir Faire," *International Studies Quarterly,* 28, No. 1 (1984), 121.

23. Ibid., p. 122.

24. John A. Vasquez, "Statistical Findings in International Politics," *International Studies Quarterly,* 20, No. 2 (June 1976), 171–218.

25. Ibid., p. 207.

26. Ferguson and Mansbach, op. cit., p. 30.

27. For an examination of this debate, see the following: Klaus Knorr and James N. Rosenau, "Tradition and Science in the Study of International Politics"; Hedley Bull, "International Theory: The Case for a Classical Approach"; Morton A. Kaplan, "The New Great Debate: Traditionalism vs. Science in International Relations"; J. David Singer, "The Incompleat Theorist: Insight without Evidence"; Marion J. Levy, Jr., " 'Does It Matter if He's Naked?' Bawled the Child," in Klaus Knorr and James N. Rosenau, eds., *Contending Approaches to International Politics* (Princeton: Princeton University Press, 1969), pp. 3–110.

28. See Johan Galtung, "The Social Sciences: An Essay on Polarization and Integration," in Knorr and Rosenau, eds., op. cit, pp. 243–285.

29. There is, of course, a need for criteria both for the establishment of research agendas and for the conduct of research itself. Given the differing conceptions of the nature of theory and the disparate research and methodological interests of students of international relations, prospects for reaching agreement upon such criteria are not great.

30. The word *theory* itself has been used in several ways in the field of international relations, and there is disagreement among scholars about the nature of theory. See Chapter 1 for a discussion of the various uses of the term *theory.*

31. See J. David Singer, "The Level-of-Analysis Problem in International Relations," in Klaus Knorr and Sidney Verba, eds., *The International System: Theoretical Essays* (Princeton: Princeton University Press, 1961), pp. 77–92. See also the treatment by the authors of this text in Chapter 1, pp. 22–26.

32. See, in particular, Kenneth N. Waltz, *Man, The State and War: A Theoretical Analysis* (New York: Columbia University Press, 1959), and, by the same author, *Theory of International Politics* (Reading, Mass.: Addison-Wesley Publishing Company, 1979), esp. ch. 4.

33. Bruce M. Russett, "Apologia pro Vita Sua," in James N. Rosenau, ed., *In Search of Global Patterns* (New York: The Free Press, 1976), p. 36.

34. For a useful effort to delineate the boundaries of international relations, see E. Raymond Platig, *International Relations Research: Problems of Evaluation and Advancement* (Santa Barbara, Calif.: Clio Press, for the Carnegie Endowment for International Peace, 1967), especially pp. 26–44.

35. One contemporary student of international relations, Johan Galtung, has suggested: "One may say that the relationship between international relations and political science is the same as the relationship between sociology and psychology: It is the transition from the meticulous study of one unit at the time to the study of the interaction structure between the units that characterize the relations between these pairs of sciences." Johan Galtung, "Small Group Theory and the Theory of International Relations," in Morton A. Kaplan, ed., *New Approaches to International Relations* (New York: St. Martin's Press, 1968), p. 271.

36. See Walter Isard, in association with Tony E. Smith, Peter Isard, Tze Hsiung Tung, and Michael Dacey, *General Theory: Social, Political, Economic, and Regional* (Cambridge, Mass.: M.I.T. Press, 1969).

37. See, for example, Richard W. Mansbach, Yale H. Ferguson, and Donald E. Lampert, *The Web of World Politics: Nonstate Actors in the Global System* (Englewood Cliffs, N.J.: Prentice-Hall, 1976).

38. Philip Alston and Raul Pangalangan, *Revitalizing the Study of International Organizations* (Report of a Conference on "Teaching About International Organizations from a Legal and Policy Perspective"), Medford, October 28–31, 1987. (Medford, MA: The Fletcher School of Law & Diplomacy, Tufts University), p. 25.

39. See, for example, Zbigniew Brzezinski, *Between Two Ages: America's Role in a Technetronic Era* (New York: Viking, 1970); Victor Basiuk, *Technology, World Politics, and American Policy* (New York: Columbia University Press, 1977); Hans J. Morgenthau, *Science: Servant or Master?* (New York: American Library, 1972); Eugene B. Skolnikoff, *International Imperatives of Technology: Technological Development and the International Political System* (University of California International Studies, 1972); Hilary Rose and Steven Rose, *Science and Society* (Baltimore, Md.: Penguin, 1970); Ira Spiegel-Rosing and Derek de Solla Price, eds., *Science, Technology and Society* (Beverly Hills, Calif.: Sage, 1977).

40. See Richard C. Snyder, H. W. Bruck, and Burton Sapin, eds., *Foreign Policy Decision Making* (New York: The Free Press, 1963).

41. See Wolfram Hanrieder, op. cit.; James N. Rosenau, "External Influences on the Internal Behavior of States," in R. Barry Farrell, ed., *Approaches to Comparative and International Politics* (Evanston, Ill.: Northwestern University Press, 1966), pp. 27–92; James N. Rosenau, "Comparative Foreign Policy— Fad, Fantasy, or Field." Paper prepared for presentation at the Conference Seminar of the Committee on Comparative Politics, University of Michigan, 1967; Randolph C. Kent, "Foreign Policy Analysis: Search for Coherence in a Multifaceted Field," in R. C. Kent and G. P. Nielsson, eds., op. cit., pp. 90–110.

42. Charles F. Hermann, ed., *International Crises: Insights from Behavioral Research* (New York: The Free Press, 1972), pp. 304–320.

43. For recent analyses of international security studies as a field, see, for example, Colin Gray, *Strategic Studies: A Critical Assessment* (Westport, Conn.: Greenwood Press, 1982); Robert Jervis, Joshua Lederberg, Robert North, Stephen Rosen, John Steinbrunner, and Dina Zinnes, *The Field of National Security Studies: Report to the National Research Council* (Washington, D.C.: 1986); Richard Smoke, "National Security Affairs," in Fred I. Greenstein and Nelson W. Polsby, eds., *Handbook of Political Science*, vol. 8, *International Politics* (Reading, Mass.: Addison-Wesley, 1975); Colin S. Gray, *Strategic Studies and Public Policy* (Lexington: University Press of Kentucky, 1982); Joseph S. Nye, Jr. and Sean M. Lynn-Jones, "International Security Studies: A Report of a Conference on the State of the Field," *International Security* (Spring 1988), 5–27; and A. J. R. Groom, "Strategy: The Evolution of the Field," in R. C. Kent and G. P. Nielsson, eds., op. cit., pp. 47–59.

44. See Geoffrey Kemp, Robert L. Pfaltzgraff, Jr., and Uri Ra'anan, *The Superpowers in a Multinuclear World* (Lexington, Mass.: D. C. Heath, 1974). See also Robert L. Pfaltzgraff, Jr., "The Evolution of American Nuclear Thought," in B. Mitchell Simpson, III, ed., *War, Strategy and Maritime Power* (New Brunswick, N.J.: Rutgers University Press, 1977), pp. 280–282.

45. Fritz W. Ermarth, "Contrasts in American and Soviet Strategic Thought," *International Security*, 3, No. 2 (Fall 1978), 139.

46. Colin S. Gray, *Strategic Studies and Public Policy*, p. 194.

47. For an extended survey of such literature, together with an important effort to define, categorize, and analyze economic policies as instruments of statecraft, see David A. Baldwin, *Economic Statecraft* (Princeton: Princeton University Press, 1985), esp. ch. 2. See also Roger Tooze, "The Unwritten Preface: International Political Economy and Epistemology," *Millennium: Journal of International Studies*, 17, No. 2 (Summer 1988), 288–293.

48. See, for example, Robert T. Holt and John E. Turner, *The Methodology of Comparative Research* (New York: The Free Press, 1970).

49. However, there are two volumes of potential use in a study of decision-making that take account of the medical histories of key participants. They include Hugh L'Etang, *The Pathology of Leadership* (London: William Heinemann Medical Books, 1969); Lord Moran, *Churchill: Taken from the Diaries of Lord Moran, The Struggle for Survival, 1940–1965* (Boston: Houghton Mifflin, 1966).

50. Thomas C. Wiegele, "Decision-Making in an International Crisis: Some Biological Factors," *International Studies Quarterly*, 17, No. 2 (June 1973), 305. See also Thomas C. Wiegele, ed., *Biology and the Social Sciences* (Boulder, Colo.: Westview Press, 1982); Thomas C. Wiegele, *Biopolitics: Search for a More Human Political Science* (Boulder, Colo.: Westview Press, 1979); Thomas C. Wiegele, Gordon Hilton, Kent Layne Oots, and Susan V. Kisiel, *Leaders Under Stress: A Psychophysiological Analysis of International Crises* (Durham, N.C.: Duke University Press, 1985); Thomas C. Wiegele, "Models of Stress and Disturbances in Elite Political Behaviors: Psychological Variables and Political Decision-Making," in Robert S. Robins, ed., *Psychopathology and Political Leadership* (New Orleans: Tulane University, 1977), pp. 79–111; Kent Layne Oots and Thomas C. Wiegele, "Terrorist and Victim: Psychiatric and Physiological Approaches from a Social Science Perspective," *Terrorism: An Interna-*

tional Journal, 8, No. 11 (1985), 1–32; James M. Schubert, Thomas C. Wiegele, and Samuel M. Hines, "Age and Political Behavior in Collective Decision-Making," *International Political Science Review,* 8, No. 2 (1987), 131–146; Samuel Long, ed., *Political Behavior Annual,* vol. 1 (Boulder, Colo.: Westview Press, 1986); Thomas C. Wiegele, "Signal Leakage and the Remote Psychological Assessment of Foreign Policy Elites," in Lawrence S. Falkowski, ed., *Psychological Models in International Politics* (Boulder, Colo.: Westview Press, 1979); Thomas C. Wiegele, "The Psychophysiology of Elite Stress in Five International Crises: A Preliminary Test of a Voice Measurement Technique," *International Studies Quarterly,* 22, No. 4 (December 1978), 467–511; Thomas C. Wiegele, "The Life Sciences and International Relations: A Bibliographic Essay," *International Studies Notes of the International Studies Association,* 11, No. 2 (Winter 1984–1985), 1–7.

51. Thomas C. Wiegele, "Models of Stress and Disturbances in Elite Political Behaviors: Psychological Variables and Political Decision-Making," in *Psychological and Political Leadership* (New Orleans: Tulane University Studies in Political Science); see also, by the same author, "Physiologically Based Content Analysis: An Application in Political Communication," in Brent D. Rupin, ed., *Communication Yearbook* 2 (New Brunswick, N.J.: Transaction Books, 1978), pp. 423–436; "Health and Stress During International Crisis: Neglected Input Variables in the Foreign Policy Decision-Making Process," *Journal of Political Science,* III, No. 2 (Spring 1976), 139–144.

52. Willard Fazan, "Federal Information Communities: The Systems Approach." Paper prepared for the annual meeting of the American Political Science Association (September 1966). Quoted in Davis B. Bobrow and Judah L. Schwartz, "Computers and International Relations," in Bobrow and Schwartz, eds., *Computer and the Policy-Making Community: Applications to International Relations* (Englewood Cliffs, N.J.: Prentice-Hall, 1968), p. 9.

53. In addition, area programs have been affected by reduced government funding.

54. For a critique of such literature and an attempt to engage in qualitative analysis of transnational interaction and integration in Europe, see Carl J. Friedrich, *Europe: An Emergent Nation?* (Boston: Little, Brown, 1969), pp. 24–25. See also Oran R. Young, *Systems of Political Science* (Englewood Cliffs, N.J.: Prentice-Hall, 1967), pp. 60–62.

55. Richard Smoke, "Theory for and About Policy," in James N. Rosenau, ed., *In Search of Global Patterns,* p. 191.

56. Trevor Taylor, "Introduction: The Nature of International Relations," in Trevor Taylor, ed., *Approaches and Theory in International Relations* (New York: Longmans, 1978), p. 3.

57. There are three general types of technological forecasts: the exploratory, opportunity, and normative. The exploratory forecast suggests future technology likely if the current level of support continues. The opportunity forecast depicts probable effects of increased effort in one technological "problem area" or another. The normative forecast combines desired goals and technological possibilities, using the goals as a guide for the allocation of resources.

Numerous techniques have been used to obtain such forecasts. The most frequently used is still the trend correlation and its variations: trend correlation in several fields and growth analogy. A new technique for obtaining "intuitive" rather than statistical forecasts is the Delphi method, an elaborate polling device for obtaining an expert consensus without a conference or panel discussion. Systems analysis, such as Program Evaluation and Research Technique (PERT), originally developed by the U.S. Navy, has been especially helpful for opportunity forecasting as well as R & D administration. Finally, mathematical modeling and the "feedback" concept are intended to aid normative forecasting in correlating the goals of government and industry with technological capabilities.

The most comprehensive general treatment of technological forecasting is Eric Jantsch, *Technological Forecasting in Perspective* (Paris: OECD Publication, 1967). An explanation of forecasting techniques may be found in Robert V. Ayres, *Technological Forecasting and Long-Range Planning* (New York: McGraw-Hill, 1969). See also James R. Bright, *Technological Forecasting for Industry and Government: Methods and Applications* (Englewood Cliffs, N.J.: Prentice-Hall, 1968). For the more literary and speculative side of the movement, see Bertrand de Jouvenel, *The Art of Conjecture,* trans. N. Lary (New York: Basic Books, 1967); Herman Kahn and A. J. Wiener, *The Year 2000: A Framework for Speculation* (New York: Macmillan, 1967); Dennis Gabor, *Inventing the Future* (New York: Knopf, 1964); Daniel Bell, ed., *Toward the Year 2000: Work in Progress* (Boston: Houghton Mifflin and the American Academy of Arts and Sciences, 1968); and Neville Brown, *The Future Global Challenge: A Predictive Study of World Security,* 1977–1990 (New York: Crane, Russak, 1977).

58. Morton A. Kaplan, "Problems of Theory Building and Theory Confirmation in International Politics," in Klaus Knorr and Sidney Verba, eds., *The International System: Theoretical Essays* (Princeton, N.J.: Princeton University Press, 1961), p. 7.

59. Rudolph J. Rummel, "The Roots of Faith," in James N. Rosenau, ed., *In Search of Global Patterns,* p. 30.

60. David Easton, "The New Revolution in Political Science," *American Political Science Review,* LXIII, No. 4 (December 1969), 1052. Similarly, Easton was among the first to discern the behavioral revolution in political science. See David Easton, *The Political System: An Inquiry into the State of Political Science* (New York: Knopf, 1954), especially pp. 37–125; by the same author, *A Framework for Political Analysis* (Englewood Cliffs, N.J.: Prentice-Hall, 1965), pp. 6–9.

61. James N. Rosenau, "Assessment in International Studies: Ego Trip or Feedback?" p. 346.

62. Charles W. Kegley, Jr., "Neo-Idealism: A Practical Matter," *Ethics and International Affairs,* vol. 2 (1988), pp. 195–196; and Charles W. Kegley, Jr. and Gregory A. Raymond, "Normative Constraints on the Use of Force Short of War," *Journal of Peace Research,* 23, No. 3 (1986), 213–227. For other recent normative analyses, see Mervyn Frost, *Toward a Normative Theory of International Relations* (Cambridge: Cambridge University Press, 1986); Hidemi Suganami, "A Normative Enquiry in International Relations: The Case of 'Parta Sunt Servanda,'" *Review of International Studies,* 9, No. 1 (1983); Robert Cordis, "Religion and International Responsibility," in Kenneth W. Thompson, ed., *Moral Dimensions of American Foreign Policy* (New Brunswick, N.J.: Transaction Books, 1984); Ray Maghroori and Bennett Ramberg, eds., *Globalism Versus Realism: International Relations Third Debate* (Boulder, Colo.: Westview Press, 1982); Louis René, *Reason and Realpolitik* (Lex-

ington, Mass.: Lexington Books, 1984); J. E. Hare and Carney B. Joynt, *Ethics and International Affairs* (New York: St. Martin's, 1982); John A. Vasquez, *The Power Politics: A Critique* (London: Francis Pinter, 1983); Stanley Hoffmann, "The Political Ethics of International Relations," Seventh Morgenthau Memorial Lecture on Ethics and Foreign Policy, Carnegie Council on Ethics and International Affairs, New York, 1988; Kenneth Kipnis and Diana T. Meyers, eds., *Political Realism and International Morality: Ethics in the Nuclear Age* (Boulder, Colo., and London: Westview Press, 1987); Terry Nardin, *Law, Morality and the Relations of States* (Princeton: Princeton University Press, 1983); Charles R. Beitz, Marshall Cohen, Thomas Scanlon, and A. John Simmons, eds., *International Ethics* (Princeton: Princeton University Press, 1985); Chris Brown, "The Modern Requirement? Reflections on Normative International Theory in a Post-Western World," *Millennium: Journal of International Studies,* 17, No. 2 (Summer 1988), 339–348; Bruce M. Russett, "Ethical Dilemmas of Nuclear Deterrence," *International Security,* 8, No. 4 (Spring 1984), 36–54; Charles R. Beitz, *Political Theory and International Relations* (Princeton: Princeton University Press, 1979); James W. Child, *Nuclear War, the Moral Dimension* (New Brunswick, N.J.: Transaction Books, 1986); Michael Novak, *Moral Clarity in the Nuclear Age* (New York: Thomas Nelson Publishers, 1983); Joseph S. Nye, Jr., ed., *Nuclear Ethics* (New York: The Free Press, 1986); William V. O'Brien and John Langan, eds., *The Nuclear Dilemma and the Just War Tradition* (Lexington, Mass.: Lexington Books, 1986); Robert L. Pfaltzgraff, Jr., *National Security: Ethics, Strategy, and Politics, A Layman's Primer* (Washington, D.C.: Pergamon-Brassey's, 1986); and James E. Dougherty, *The Bishops and Nuclear Weapons* (Camden, Conn.: Archon, 1984).

63. Ferguson and Mansbach, op. cit., p. 216. For a discussion of continuity in the major premises and issues of international relations theory, see N. J. Rengger, "Serpents and Doves in Classical International Theory," *Millennium: Journal of International Studies,* 17, No. 2 (Summer 1988), 215–225.

64. For a collection of essays by scholars concerned with the relationship between social science and public policy in the post–World War II period, see Daniel Lerner and Harold D. Lasswell, eds., *The Policy Sciences* (Stanford: Stanford University Press, 1951). For a more recent discussion, see Norman D. Palmer, ed., *A Design for International Relations Research: Scope, Theory, Methods, and Relevance.* Monograph 10, The American Academy of Political and Social Science (October 1970), especially pp. 154–274.

65. Charles J. Hitch and Roland N. McKean, *The Economics of Defense in the Nuclear Age* (Cambridge: Harvard University Press, 1963); Roland McKean, *Efficiency in Government Through Systems Analysis* (New York: Wiley, 1958); Raymond A. Bauer and Kenneth J. Gergen, eds., *The Study of Policy Formation* (New York: The Free Press, 1968); Harold Lasswell, "Policy Sciences," in *International Encyclopedia of the Social Sciences* (New York: Macmillan and The Free Press, 1968), pp. xii, 181–189.

66. See Yehezkel Dror, *Analytical Approaches and Applied Social Sciences* (Santa Monica, Calif.: The RAND Corporation, 1969); monograph.

Name Index

Abel, Theodore, 376n, 485
Abelson, Robert P., 481
Adorno, T. W, 310n
Ake, Claude, 66n
Alberts, Donald, 374n
Alcock, Norman Z., 128n
Alexander the Great, 234
Alford, Jonathan, 427n
Alker, Hayward R., Jr., 139, 176n, 541, 570n
Allende, Salvador, 255
Allison, Graham T., 422n, 430n, 472, 476, 478, 486–489, 502n, 503n, 505n
Allport, Gordon W., 295, 299n, 309n, 361
Almond, Gabriel A., 146, 147, 148, 178n, 268n, 372n, 545, 569n
Alroy, Gil Carl, 373n
Alston, Philip, 571n
Altfeld, Michael F., 350, 381n, 382n, 454, 466n
Ambrose, Saint, 194
Amery, Leopold, 72, 79n
Anderson, Paul A., 383n
Andrew, Christopher, 423n
Andrews, William G., 370n
Andriole, Stephen J., 180n
Andropov, Yuri, 233, 414
Angell, Norman, 4, 6, 43n, 200, 218n, 236

Antoninus of Florence, 195
Apter, David E., 48n, 268n, 372n
Aquinas, Saint Thomas, 195
Archimedes, 319
Ardrey, Robert, 279, 302n
Arendt, Hannah, 262n, 321, 370n
Aristotle, 2, 7, 18, 21, 47n, 53, 76n
Aron, Raymond, 10, 27, 46n, 49n, 55, 76n, 114–119, 134n, 235, 237, 262, 265n, 266n, 307n, 397, 398, 422n, 423n
Art, Robert J., 212n,
Ashby, W. Ross, 156, 181n
Ashley, Richard K., 135n, 348, 349, 381n, 539, 569n
Aspaturian, Vernon V., 506n
Attlee, Clement, 262n
Augustine, Saint, 194, 234, 367n
Ayala, Balthazar, 196, 217n
Ayres, Robert V., 574n
Azar, Edward, 180n

Babai, Don, 464n
Bacevich, A. J., 375n
Back, Kurt, 506n
Bacon, Sir Francis, 357
Bainton, Roland H., 216n, 220n
Bakunin, Mikhail, 206
Baldwin, David A., 45n, 85, 87, 128n, 557, 572n
Ball, Desmond, 409, 427n

Subject Index